DUE DATE

201-6503			Printed in USA

THE HAJJ

THE
HAJJ

THE MUSLIM PILGRIMAGE TO

MECCA AND THE HOLY PLACES

F. E. Peters

PRINCETON UNIVERSITY PRESS

· PRINCETON, NEW JERSEY ·

Library of Congress Cataloging-in-Publication Data
Peters, F. E. (Francis E.)
The hajj : the Muslim pilgrimage to Mecca and the
holy places / F. E. Peters.
p.   cm.
Includes bibliographical references (p.) and index
ISBN 0-691-02120-1
ISBN 0-691-02619-X (PBK.)
1. Muslim pilgrims and pilgrimages—Saudi Arabia—
Mecca—History I. Title.
BP187.3.P475 1994
297'.55—dc20   93-47292 CIP

This book has been composed in Adobe Garamond

Princeton University Press books are printed on
acid-free paper and meet the guidelines for permanence and
durability of the Committee on Production Guidelines for
Book Longevity of the Council on Library Resources

Printed in the United States of America
by Princeton Academic Press

Second printing, and first paperback printing, 1996

2   4   6   8   10   9   7   5   3

For Kassem Toueir and his Family

WHO TOOK ME INTO THEIR HOME AND

THEIR COUNTRY AND ALLOWED

ME TO LOVE BOTH

Contents

List of Illustrations

FOR INFORMATION on photographers and collections, see "The Hajj in Early Photo Documents," which follows this list. The designations L/OI (for Leiden: Oriental Institute) and NINO (for Netherlands Institute for the Near East) refer to clusters of photographs found in those collections under Dr. E. van Donzel's direction, which the King Fahd Archive began cataloguing in 1983.

Following page 190

10. The Northwestern Arch of the Kaʿba and the Praying Places of the Four Caliphs in the Mosque. The Pilgrims Praying in their Afternoon Worship. [Rifʿat Pasha #262]

11. A Copy of a Letter in the Same Size as That Written on the Band of the Kaʿba. Rifʿat Pasha meticulously recorded gold embroideries such as this detail from the *tob* or *kiswa*, the black cloth covering woven each year in Egypt and brought inside the Mahmal. [Rifʿat Pasha #115]

12. A View of Zamzam with Pilgrims Drinking from It. [Rifʿat Pasha #99]

13. Pilgrims round the Kaʿba Kissing the Black Stone. [Rifʿat Pasha #59]

14. Al-Sayyid Abd al-Ghaffar, Physician of Mecca (1885–1889): The Sanctuary at Mecca. First re-identified by F. Allen and C. Gavin in 1981 (by reconstructing the signatures found erased on the plates that Snouck Hurgronje had published in 1889 in *Bilder aus Mekka*), this princely physician seems quite certainly to have been the first Meccan photographer. [L/OI:F.5]

15. Al-Sayyid Abd al-Ghaffar, Physician of Mecca (1885–1889): Prayers Around the Kaʿba. [L/OI:F.4]

16. The Kaʿba. [H. Mirza of Delhi (probably pre-1904)]

17. Keeper of the Zamzam Well. (This label was found on the back of an original albumen photograph discovered in Leiden in 1983 with a group of almost 100 Meccan portraits. Stylistically, the compositions resemble much more the signed work of Abd al-Ghaffar, rather than the sullen expressions in the portraiture characteristic of pilgrim groups recorded by Snouck Hurgronje.) A photogravure of this same image was reproduced by Snouck Hurgronje (as Plate IX of his 1889 *Bilderatlas*) with a very different caption: Gatekeeper of the Kaʿba (from the Shaybi family which has held this office from the pre-Islamic period). [NINO 2.22: photographer uncertain, possibly C. Snouck Hurgronje or Al-Sayyid Abd al-Ghaffar]

Following page 300

18. A View of the Mahmal Passing through Aqaba on the Caravan Route of al-Wigh before the Station al-Khatala in 1326/1908. [Rifʿat Pasha #302]

19. A View of the Palanquins of Camels at Arafat. [Rifʿat Pasha #198]

20. A View of the Mahmal at Arafat in 1321/1909. [Rifʿat Pasha #199]

The Hajj in Early Photo Documents

C.E.S. GAVIN

Illustrations for this book were chosen by the author from among thousands of photographic records assembed over the past two decades to form a comprehensive visual encyclopedia for *al-Haramayan*, which is being prepared in close consultation with historians, architects, and elders of the Holy Cities. All illustrations have been prepared by Elizabeth Carella from copy negatives made by herself and William Corsetti, often from originals that were discovered and photographed in the course of inventories undertaken between 1983 and 1985 by the King Fahd Archive (KFA). Initiated with funds graciously provided by the Custodian of the Two Holy Mosques, the KFA grew out of the International F.O.C.U.S. Conferences convened in 1978 and 1981 in Cambridge, Massachusetts. It was established on 2 September 1982 "to find and preserve previously inaccessible or endangered photo-collections important for the history and cultural heritage of the peoples and places of the Middle East." Preliminary reports of KFA results have been issued in *Museum* (UNESCO) 37, no. 1/no. 145 (1986), 4–12, and in "Photography and Social Sciences—In Light from Ancient Lands," in *The Invention of Photography and Its Impact upon Learning*, edited by L. T. Amber and M. Banta (Cambridge, Mass.: Harvard University Library, 1989), 48–61. The first formal publication of KFA inventories appeared as *Imperial Self-Portrait: The Ottoman Empire as Revealed in the Sultan ʿAbdul-Hamid II's Photographic Albums Presented as Gifts to the Library of Congress (1893) and to the British Museum (1894)*, edited by C.E.S. Gavin as a special volume (XII) of the *Journal of Turkish Studies* in 1989 (for a brief review of pre-photographic visual records for the pilgrimage to Mecca, see especially pp. 13–16).

From Islamic sources, we have highly diverse yet quite informative diagrams for pilgrim encampments and other aspects of the Hajj, such as those preserved in the library at Topkapi (as reported in *Journal of Turkish Studies* 7 [1983], 407–413). From Occidental travelers come careful pictures made on the spot: in 1762 on the Red Sea by Georg Bauernfeind, who accompanied Carsten Niebuhr; in 1778 in both Mecca and Medina by an anonymous Stambouli painter who accompanied the Ottoman general chosen to serve as *Amir al-Hajj*; and in Mecca in 1806 by the highly trained Ali Bey al-Abbassi.

The Begum of Bhopal seems to have been the first pilgrim to have published an account of her Hajj (1868?) illustrated with photographs, although none of them were made in Arabia. In 1873 the painter and scholar Osman Hamdi Bey published the first photo records of traditional Hijazi dress (worn by photographic models posing in Istanbul). Photographic reports from the Holy Cities themselves began in 1880 with the glass plates exposed by the Egyptian colonel M. Sadic Bey after he obtained permission from the Sharif Awn al-Rafiq.

In presenting these early photo documents, we wish most specially to express our gratitude to Dr. E. van Donzel, the editor-in-chief of the *Encyclopedia of Islam*, who, as president of Het Oosters Instituut in Leiden, has graciously permitted us to reproduce precious documents assembled by his late predecessor Professor C. Snouck Hurgronje.

EARLY PHOTOGRAPHERS OF THE HAJJ

M. Sadic Bey (1880). An eminent cartographer who had researched the tribes and roads of the Hijaz for decades, Mohammed Sadic (he seems to have preferred this form for the Roman alphabet but also spelled his name Sadik and Sadiq) made the photographs published here while a colonel in the Egyptian army (with the honorific "Bey"). In 1881 he published his views in portfolio format on the occasion of the Third International Congress of Geographers in Venice, where his work was awarded a medal. Subsequently, Sadic Bey was elected president of the Khedival Geographic Society, and he eventually retired from the military as *Liwa* (Lieutenant General) M. Sadic Pasha.

Bilderatlas (pre-1889, mostly 1884) and *Bilder aus Mekka* (pre-1889, but after 1884/5). Both of these books were published in 1889 by C. Snouck Hurgronje to accompany his *Mekka*. *Bilderatlas*, which contains lithographic reproductions of Sadic Bey's photographs and color plates of Meccan objects, primarily features pilgrim groups photographed by Snouck himself, often at the Netherlands Consulate in Jidda. *Bilder aus Mekka* consists entirely of photographic plates that were sent to Snouk after he had left Mecca and that reached Leiden too late for inclusion within the *Bilderatlas* portfolio. The creator of those valuble pictorial documents, whose name Snouck never mentions, was Al-Sayyid Abd al-Ghaffar.

Al-Sayyid Abd al-Ghaffar (from 1884 on). In 1981 F.H.S. Allen and C. Gavin first identified the earliest Arabian photographer by deciphering his elaborately calligraphed signatures, which without exception had been erased from the plates reproduced by Snouck Hurgronje: *"Futugrafiyat al-Sayyid ʿAbd al-Ghaffar, tabib Makka"* (The Photography of the Sayyid

Abd al-Ghaffar, physician of Mecca). This princely eye surgeon had been host to the young Snouck in Mecca immediately after the Dutchman's conversion to Islam. Snouck claimed to have taught his host how to use a camera and attributes to him (without ever mentioning his name) the pictures reproduced in *Bilder aus Mekka*. KFA teams have recovered scores of informal portraits made by the physician in Mecca subsequent to 1889 and sent on to Leiden by Dutch consuls.

H. Mirza of Delhi (pre-1904). This Indian photographer/publisher produced a series of twelve albumen prints, each surrounded by Urdu poetry elegantly calligraphed in red ink. They have survived in the collection of Fouad C. Debbas of Beirut, with whose gracious permission selected exemplars have been here reproduced. The date for Mirza's work has been suggested by Professor Ali al-Asani, who has prepared translations of the Urdu. Al-Asani noted that the texts do not contain any reference whatsoever to the Hijaz Railway, as one would have expected after 1904, since monetary contributions for that project had been extensively solicited among Indian Muslims from that date onward.

Rif ʿat Pasha (pre-1925). In 1925 *Liwa* Ibrahim Rifʿat Pasha published his two-volume work *Mirat al-Haramayn* (Mirror of the Two Sanctuaries) at Cairo's National Library Press. Frustrated at his inability to describe adequately the inspiring sites he saw on his 1901 Hajj, the general decided to learn to take photographs himself. He could then make a pictorial record of his subsequent pilgrimages, because "however precise my verbal descriptions I could never have been able to depict the whole truth nor fascinate you in any way [as effectively] as looking and beholding can."

Preface

BOOKS ARE COMPLEX THINGS and draw nourishment from many sources, and so authors are sometimes at a loss on whom to acknowledge and thank and in what order: Not so here. This book would surely have been written, but it would equally certainly not have been what it is now, without the assistance of Jack Hayes and the officers at the Mobil Oil Corporation in New York and Mobil Saudia in Jidda who made it possible for me to travel over the same lands and enter some of the same places as the Hajjis themselves.

I did not go to those places as a pilgrim, nor in the meaner role of the skeptic to scoff or despise, but simply, and I hope honorably, as a historian, and I gratefully thank those Americans and Saudis who graciously assisted me there. They did not know what I would write, of course, and so bear no responsibility whatsoever for what I have in fact written.

There are debts closer to home as well. Early on I was helped by Reuven Firestone and Elisabeth Koehldorfer-Cain, and in the later stages of this work I had the invaluable assistance of Imad Khachchan, another of my graduate students at New York University. I must thank too Patricia Jorquera and Marlana Opitz for watching the company store with great energy and *esprit* when I was otherwise occupied; Carol Brennan for her unflagging encouragement of the pursuit of things Arab, and Eamon for putting up with it; and as always Professor E. P. Fitzsimmons, who unselfishly interrupted his own studies in Eastern Europe to allow me to profit from his acuity in matters of language and style, and Edward Oakes, who postponed his Tertianship on my behalf; and Mary Peters, of course.

Stockport, New York
July 31, 1993

Acknowledgments

TRANSLATIONS done by others are noted either in the text itself or in the final section of this volume, Works Cited, where all particulars regarding authors, publishers, and dates and places of publication are provided.

Nevertheless, the author wishes to make special acknowledgment to the following for their kind cooperation in the use of previously published and copyrighted material: E. J. Brill, Cambridge University Press, Jonathan Cape, Constable and Company, Darwin Press, Faber and Faber, The Hakluyt Society, Robert Hale, Her Majesty's Stationery Office, Oleander Press, Oxford University Press, The Persian Heritage Foundation, Princeton University Press, State University Press of New York, University of Texas Press, Wayne State University Press.

Introduction

EVERY MUSLIM, anywhere in the world, is obliged to perform, at least once in a lifetime, the *Hajj*, or ritual pilgrimage to Mecca. Although the obligation is a conditioned one—the Muslim is not expected to perform the act if it exceeds his or her physical or economic means—it issues from God Himself, in His Holy Quran.

The Muslim's Hajj is not simply a visit to a holy place or shrine, as pilgrimage is understood in Christianity, and indeed as other forms of pious sojourning are understood in Islam; nor is it even presence at, or participation in, a ritual, as it was in Temple Judaism. The Hajj's timing is absolutely fixed, as are the sequence and nature of its ritual acts: at no other time save the eighth, ninth, and tenth days of the last month of the Muslim year and by no other actions than those prescribed is the obligation fulfilled. And the *Hajji*, as the Muslim pilgrim is called at the completion of the ritual, though surrounded by tens or hundreds of thousands of others performing the same act, is the only actor, the only celebrant, in this unique Islamic rite.

In 1900, in the midst of a fierce debate on the merits of building a railway from Damascus to Medina, the Ottoman publicist Muhammad Arif al-Munir wrote *The Book of the Increasing and Eternal Happiness* in support of the project. Most of his arguments were directed toward the benefits that would follow from the construction of the railway. But he also cast his net somewhat wider and undertook to explain to his readers the "secular" as well as the spiritual advantages accruing to Islam from the institution of the pilgrimage itself.

> The advantages of the pilgrimage, as mentioned in the Quran, are obscure, indefinite, and stated in a general way—not clear, definite and detailed enough to convey classification and amplification. This is why their wording is mostly in the plural. They are not limited to one area but relate to matters of both this world and the next.

There are, in the first place, the spiritual benefits, including this Muslim version of the Christians' "indulgence":

> Some of the advantages of the pilgrimage which relate to the next world may be found in what al-Bazzar and others have handed down about the Prophet . . . who said, "The pilgrim intercedes for four hundred of his relatives and is as sinless as on the day his mother gave birth to him." . . . Between one Umra and another, all sins are redeemed, while the reward for the blessed Hajj is nothing short of Paradise.

Munir was, however, a modern Muslim and so had no hesitation in also adducing the worldly profits connected with the Hajj:

> Among the benefits of the pilgrimage for this world are the following: Muslims get in touch with each other and get better acquainted with conditions, news and affairs from near and far; they conclude agreements and assist one another in their worldly and religious matters; they cooperate reciprocally until they become as one. . . . Yet another benefit is the establishment of commerce. When pilgrims meet, they are accustomed to ask after commercial matters. They make deals and form companies. Sometimes, they exchange wares with one another, they get acquainted with the ways of sending merchandise and enlarging their business from land to land, as well as with the manner of engaging in business. Men ask around about persons with whom they would like to trade or enter into a partnership. (Arif al-Munir 1971: 113–114)

This present book, like Munir's own secular endeavor, has more to do with the place of the pilgrimage in the affairs of this world rather than in those of the next, more spiritual realm. Thus it is not so much concerned with the rituals at Mecca in the manner of the classic 1923 study by Maurice Gaudefroy-Demombynes—although they are here described, and at some length, by eyewitnesses—as with the actors upon the Hijaz stage; and not so much with the lives of the Hajjis as with their impressions of the extraordinary activities in which they were engaged or which they witnessed.[1]

Within a short interval after Muhammad's death, the "Abode of Islam," as the Muslims called the lands under their sovereignty, stretched from Spain to the borders of China. Thus pilgrims were drawn to Mecca from across an immense terrain, which has grown even more extensive in modern times. The Hajj was not simply a few days of ritual in Mecca and vicinity. It was not so much an act as an experience, and so for many that experience began thousands of miles from the Holy City. It is not my intention, however, to trace the progress of pilgrims from the moment they crossed their thresholds in Cordova or Bukhara to that moment—sometimes many years later, if at all—when they returned to their homes. In these pages the would-be Hajjis will come into focus much closer to their goal, when they join the great caravans marshaled at Cairo or Damascus or Baghdad, for example, or disembark at Jidda, or enter Mecca. Likewise, what impulse turned a particular Muslim to the Hajj or how the experience transformed him or her also remains unexplored. Psychological and spiritual wellsprings are left untapped, except in those few cases where they bubble, unsummoned, to the surface.[2]

If the spiritual dimensions of the pilgrimage are generally passed over, its political aspects are not. The Hajj had implicated, from its remote pre-Islamic origins down to the present day, the question of sovereignty, sovereignty over Mecca and then over all the lands through which the pilgrims had to pass thither and hence. The Hajjis' economic and physical well-being, indeed, their very lives, depended on who exercised that sovereignty—caliph or sultan, governor or sharif, gendarme or bedouin—and in what manner and at what price. The actual Hajj, in its narrow sense of a ritual act, we know was a profoundly elevating experience for many, but the total pilgrimage experience was often an arduous and frightening and painful one, sometimes enormously profitable and sometimes financially ruinous, and filled with extraordinary sights and sounds and sentiments. All of them are reflected here, as well as the political and economic circumstances that made them such. Put another way, I have attempted to compose not an anthology but what is, in its shambling and somewhat discontinuous way, a history.

I begin, generally, where the Muslim Hajj begins, with the Quran. The Holy Book, however, directs our attention backward to an even earlier day, when Abraham instituted the Meccan Haram and pilgrimage ritual at God's behest. We need not take the Quran's word: Muslim and non-Muslim alike are agreed that both the Ka'ba and the Hajj antedated Islam. We do always know what to do with that conviction, and so the pre-Islamic history of both the building and the institution is reduced to an essay in reconstruction, assembling the various pieces of the Muslim tradition and modern scholarship into some kind of coherent portrait of what might have been. The same is true with regard to events in Muhammad's own lifetime: the testimonial ground under foot is often slippery with uncertainty and mined with the retrojections of a later age. Essay, not evidence, is likely the appropriate word here as well.

As we progress into the Islamic era the procession of eyewitnesses begins, a thin trickle at first, but eventually swelling into an ever broader stream. Between Muhammad and Sharif Husayn, a great many Muslims have undertaken the extraordinary voyage called the Hajj. Most of them were silent on the experiences or shared them only with family and friends; but a great many Hajjis, and some who were simply visiting, recorded their impressions of the event and the place for the instruction or edification of other Muslims, some of them in quite extraordinary detail, like the eleventh-century traveler Ibn Jubayr and the early twentieth-century scholar-bureaucrat Batanuni. The former incorporated his immediate Hajj experience into a more broadly framed travel book, a *rihla*, while Batanuni's more qualified title, *A Hijaz Journey* (*al-rihla al-hijaziyya*) betrays his narrower focus on the Hajj itself.[3]

Such witnesses are not beyond fictions and exaggerations, of course, but they were undoubtedly there; and their numbers and the variety of their accounts serve as a more than adequate control for the careful reader.

There are many more: only a very partial number of accounts of the Hajj or the Holy Cities available in Arabic, Persian, Turkish, and the other languages used by Muslims has seen the light of print. I have tried to select the most interesting and revealing and varied among the available texts, as well as from the medieval chroniclers and geographers.

There is archival material as well. From the sixteenth century onward, the Ottoman rulers of western Arabia kept ever more systematic and complete records of taxes, disbursements, and judicial procedures in the Hijaz, and required an equally detailed accounting of the finances of the Hajj for which they were then responsible. From about the same time, various pieces of political and financial *Ottomanica* show up in the archives of Western foreign ministries; and in the nineteenth century, when the Muslim Holy Cities were identified as major transmission centers for cholera, the European powers began to count heads as well as customs dues and tax receipts. I have attempted to make some use of such material in the later chapters of this work, but there is much more to be investigated, some of it lying close to the surface in the works of Batanuni and Rifʿat Pasha toward the end of the Ottoman era,[4] much more buried deeper in the Ottoman archival records in Cairo, Damascus, and Istanbul.[5]

If the sources seem overwhemingly literary, it could hardly be otherwise. Due to the presence of both chronic flooding and constant rebuilding, and the absence of scientific archeology in and around Islam's most sacred shrines, there is little or no material evidence for the past of the Holy Cities. The historian is reduced, then, principally to texts.

I end not in the immediate present but in 1926, at the end of the Hashimite Kingdom of the Hijaz. I do so not for any political motive but out of my own conviction that from that date forward the circumstances of the Hajj underwent so radical a change that thereafter Mecca, Medina, and the ways thither were socially, politically, and economically other than they had been almost from the beginning. After 1926 begins the era of the "modern" Hajj, whose modalities were revolutionized by oil and the airplane and so would require a quite different and equally elaborate study. Thus, it is petroleum and propellers and not the mere displacement of the House of Hashim by the House of Saʿud that writes *finis* to the narrative.

Maps

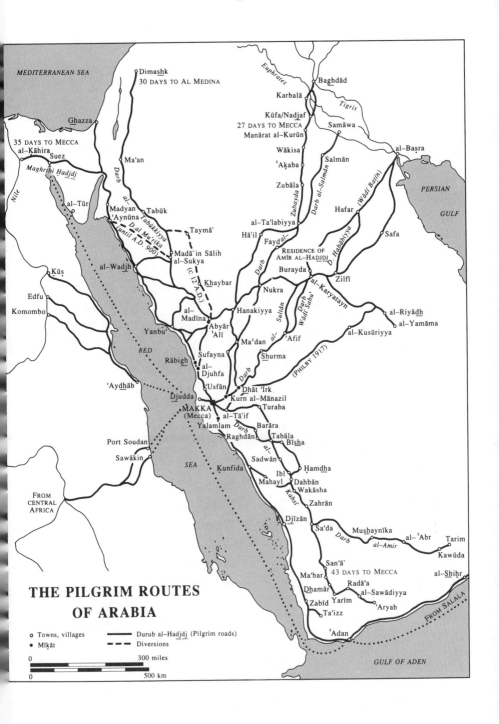

MEDITERRANEAN SEA

Dimashk
30 DAYS TO AL MEDINA

Euphrates

Baghdād

Karbalā

Tigris

Kūfa/Nadjaf
27 DAYS TO MECCA
Manārat al-Kurūn

Samāwa

Ghazza

35 DAYS TO MECCA
al-Kāhira
Suez

Maghribi Ḥadjdj

Nile

al-Ṭūr

Ma'an

Wākisa

'Akaba   Salmān

al-Baṣra

PERSIAN
GULF

Zubāla

Madyan
'Aynūna
D. al-Mu'rika
(until A.D. 900)

Tabūk

Taymā'

al-Ta'labiyya

Ḥā'il

Hafar

Safa

Madā'in Sālih
al-Sukya
(c 12 A.D.)

Faydal

RESIDENCE OF
AMĪR AL-ḤADJDJ

Kūṣ

al-Wadjh

Khaybar

Burayda

Zilfī

al-Karyatayn

al-Riyādh

al-Yamāma

Edfu
Komombo

al-Madīna

Nukra

Hanakiyya

Ma'dan   'Afif

Shurma

al-Kusūriyya

Yanbu'

Abyār
'Alī

(PHILBY 1917)

RED

Rābigh

Sufayna
al-Djuhfa

'Aydhāb

Usfān

Dhāt 'Irk

Djudda

MAKKA
(Mecca)   al-Tā'if

Kurn al-Mānazil

Turaba

Port Soudan

Yalamlam

Raghdān

Barāra

Tabāla

Bīsha

Sawākin

SEA

Kunfida

Sadwān

Hamdha

FROM
CENTRAL
AFRICA

Ibl
Mahayl

Dahbān
Wakāsha

Zahrān

Djīzān

Sa'da

Mushaynīka

al-'Abr   Tarim

Kawūda

San'ā'
43 DAYS TO MECCA

al-Shihr

FROM SALALA

Ma'bar

Dhamār

Radā'a
al-Sawādiyya

Zabīd   Yarīm

Aryab

Ta'izz

THE PILGRIM ROUTES
OF ARABIA

'Adan

○ Towns, villages   ──── Durub al-Hadjdj (Pilgrim roads)
● Mīkāt   ─ ─ ─ Diversions

GULF OF ADEN

0 _____ 300 miles

0 _____ 500 km

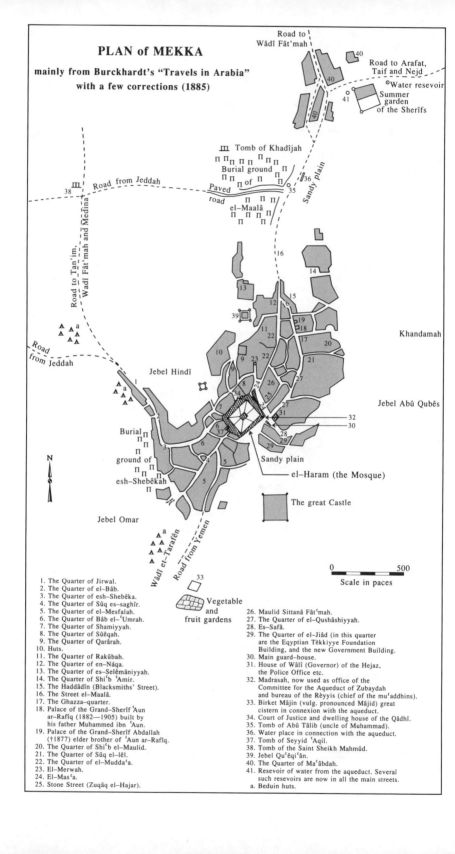

PLAN of MEKKA

**mainly from Burckhardt's "Travels in Arabia"
with a few corrections (1885)**

Road to
Wâdî Fât'mah

40

Road to Arafat,
Taif and Nejd

40

Water resevoir

41

Summer
garden
of the Sherîfs

Ⅲ Tomb of Khadîjah

Burial ground

of

Paved

road

el-Maalâ

36

Sandy plain

35

Ⅲ

38

Road from Jeddah

Road to Tan'im,
Wadi Fât'mah and Medina

16

14

13

15

12

6

39

19

18

Khandamah

11

22

17

20

Road
from Jeddah

10

9

23

22

21

Jebel Hindî

8

22

27

1

34

26

Jebel Abû Qubês

7

24

25

27

31

32

Burial

6

28

30

ground of

6

37

28

29

esh-Shebêkah

3

4

5

29

Sandy plain

el-Haram (the Mosque)

N

5

Jebel Omar

The great Castle

33

Vegetable
and
fruit gardens

Wâdi et-Tarafên

Road from Yemen

0   500

Scale in paces

1. The Quarter of Jirwal.
2. The Quarter of el-Bâb.
3. The Quarter of esh-Shebêka.
4. The Quarter of Sûq es-saghîr.
5. The Quarter of el-Mesfalah.
6. The Quarter of Bâb el-ʿUmrah.
7. The Quarter of Shamiyyah.
8. The Quarter of Sûêqah.
9. The Quarter of Qarârah.
10. Huts.
11. The Quarter of Rakûbah.
12. The Quarter of en-Náqa.
13. The Quarter of es-Selêmâniyyah.
14. The Quarter of Shiʿb ʿAmir.
15. The Haddâdîn (Blacksmiths' Street).
16. The Street el-Maalâ.
17. The Ghazza-quarter.
18. Palace of the Grand-Sherîf ʿAun
    ar-Rafîq (1882—1905) built by
    his father Muhammed ibn ʿAun.
19. Palace of the Grand-Sherîf Abdallah
    (†1877) elder brother of ʿAun ar-Rafîq.
20. The Quarter of Shiʿb el-Maulid.
21. The Quarter of Sûq el-lêl.
22. The Quarter of el-Mudda'a.
23. El-Merwah.
24. El-Mas'a.
25. Stone Street (Zuqâq el-Hajar).

26. Maulid Sittanâ Fât'mah.
27. The Quarter of el-Qushâshiyyah.
28. Es-Safâ.
29. The Quarter of el-Jiâd (in this quarter
    are the Eqyptian Têkkiyye Foundation
    Building, and the new Government Building.
30. Main guard-house.
31. House of Wâlî (Governor) of the Hejaz,
    the Police Office etc.
32. Madrasah, now used as office of the
    Committee for the Aqueduct of Zubaydah
    and bureau of the Rèyyis (chief of the muʿaddhins).
33. Birket Mâjin (vulg. pronounced Mâjid) great
    cistern in connexion with the aqueduct.
34. Court of Justice and dwelling house of the Qâdhî.
35. Tomb of Abû Tâlib (uncle of Muhammad).
36. Water place in connection with the aqueduct.
37. Tomb of Seyyid ʿAqil.
38. Tomb of the Saint Sheikh Mahmûd.
39. Jebel Quʿêqiʿân.
40. The Quarter of Maʿâbdah.
41. Resevoir of water from the aqueduct. Several
    such resevoirs are now in all the main streets.
a. Beduin huts.

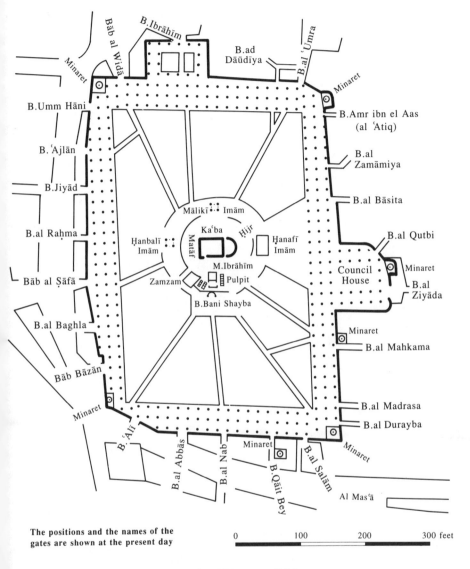

B.Umm Hāni

B. ʿAjlān

B.Jiyād

B.al Raḥma

Bāb al Ṣafā

B.al Baghla

Bāb Bāzān

Minaret

Bāb al Widāʿ

Minaret

B.Ibrāhīm

B.ad Dāūdīya

B.al ʿUmra

Minaret

B.Amr ibn el Aas (al ʿAtiq)

B.al Zamāmiya

B.al Bāsita

Mālikī Imām

Kaʿba Ḥijr

Ḥanbalī Imām

Maṭāf

Ḥanafī Imām

B.al Qutbi

Minaret

Council House

B.al Ziyāda

M.Ibrāhīm

Zamzam

Pulpit

B.Bani Shayba

B.al Mahkama

Minaret

B.al Madrasa

B.al Durayba

Minaret

B. ʿAlī

B.al Abbās

B.al Nab

Minaret

B.Qāit Bey

B.al Salām

Minaret

Al Masʿā

The positions and the names of the
gates are shown at the present day

0   100   200   300 feet

Plan of the Mosque of Mecca

(after Rutter)

THE HAJJ

CHAPTER I

Origins

THE RELIGION OF ABRAHAM

THE QURAN does not explain or accept pagan ritual as such, of course, but it does offer clues. What was done at Mecca in the name of religion in the days before Islam was in part the work of a debased paganism, but it also bore some trace of what Islam's holy book calls "the religion of Abraham" (2:130), the practices that God had earlier commanded should be instituted in connection with His House in that city. The Quran says nothing, however, about the remote origins of a holy place at Mecca; it speaks only of the era of Abraham and of Ishmael there, and of the providential construction of the Ka'ba, this "sacred House" (5:100), this "ancient House" (22:29), that sat in the midst of the town. But Islamic tradition did not rest on that scriptural testimony alone. Later generations of Muslims who had access, through Jewish and Christian converts to Islam, to a vast body of stories and legends about the earliest times of God's dispensation, were able to trace the history of the Ka'ba and its sanctuary back to the very beginning of Creation, and even before.

Abraham and Ishmael in Mecca

The Quran traces the progression of God's will through the history of mankind from Adam to Abraham, with special emphasis on Noah. But Noah has no link with Mecca, and it is not until the thread of Sacred History reaches Abraham that biblical history converges with the Quran. The Quran's Abraham is called both a *muslim* and a *hanif*, terms that, in this context at least, appear to mean the opposite of an "associator," a pagan polytheist. Abraham's father and other relatives were such; and although the Quran is neither a history nor a treatise in systematic theology, we are given a fairly clear idea of the paganism from which the Patriarch had liberated himself: like the Meccans of Muhammad's day, the family of Abraham worshiped idols (Quran 21:56–65).

The Quran passes directly from Abraham's "conversion" from the paganism of his father to God's command to construct the Ka'ba. There is no mention in the sacred text of Hagar or Sarah, or of the Bible's elaborate story of the births of Ishmael and Isaac. It was left for the later tradition, which possessed more detailed and sophisticated information, to spell out the events that brought Abraham and Ishmael from the land of Palestine to distant Mecca in the Hijaz. More than one Muslim version recounts how that occurred, and the historian Tabari presents a conflation of a number of them.[1]

> *According to ... al-Suddi: Sarah said to Abraham, "You may take pleasure in Hagar, for I have permitted it." So he had intercourse with Hagar and she gave birth to Ishmael. Then he had intercourse with Sarah and she gave birth to Isaac. When Isaac grew up, he and Ishmael fought. Sarah became angry and jealous of Ishmael's mother. . . . She swore to cut something off her, and said to herself, "I shall cut off her nose, I shall cut off her ear—but no, that would deform her. I will circumcise her instead." So she did that, and Hagar took a piece of cloth to wipe the blood away. For that reason women have been circumcised and have taken pieces of cloth (as sanitary napkins) down to today.*
>
> *Sarah said, "She will not live in the same town with me." God told Abraham to go to Mecca, where there was no House at that time. He took Hagar and her son to Mecca and put them there. . . .*
>
> *According to ... Mujahid and other scholars: When God pointed out to Abraham the place of the House and told him how to build the sanctuary, he set out to do the job and Gabriel went with him. It was said that whenever he passed a town he would ask, "Is this the town which God's command meant, O Gabriel?" And Gabriel would say: "Pass it by." At last they reached Mecca, which at that time was nothing but acacia trees, mimosa, and thorn trees, and there was a people called Amalekites outside Mecca and its surroundings. The House at that time was but a hill of red clay. Abraham said to Gabriel, "Was it here that I was ordered to leave them?" Gabriel said, "Yes." Abraham directed Hagar and Ishmael to go to al-Hijr,[2] and settled them down there. He commanded Hagar, the mother of Ishmael, to find shelter there. Then he said, "My Lord, I have settled some of my posterity in an uncultivable valley near Your Holy House . . . that they may be thankful" (Quran 14:37). Then he journeyed back to his family in Syria, leaving the two of them at the House.*

At his expulsion from Abraham's household, Ishmael must have been about sixteen years old, certainly old enough to assist his father in the construction of the Kaʿba, as is described in the Quran and is implicit from the last line of the Tabari's narrative from Mujahid and others. Tabari's version of what next occurred is derived from Genesis 21:15–16, transferred from a Palestinian setting to a Meccan one. The object is now clearly to provide an "Abrahamic" explanation for some of the landmarks of the Meccan sanctuary and the features of the pilgrimage to it. The helpless Ishmael sounds much younger than sixteen in the tale, and some

Muslim versions of the story in fact make him a nursing infant,[3] which means, of course, that Abraham will have to return on a later occasion to build the Ka'ba with him.[4]

> Then Ishmael became very thirsty. His mother looked for water for him, but could not find any. She listened for sounds to help her find water for him. She heard a sound at al-Safa and went there to look around and found nothing. Then she heard a sound from the direction of al-Marwa. She went there and looked around and saw nothing. Some also say that she stood on al-Safa praying to God for water for Ishmael, and then went to al-Marwa to do the same.

Thus the origin of the pilgrimage ritual of "running" back and forth between the two hills of Safa and Marwa on the eastern side of the Meccan sanctuary. Tabari continues:

> Then she heard the sounds of beasts in the valley where she had left Ishmael. She ran to him and found him scraping the water from a spring which had burst forth from beneath his hand, and drinking from it. Ishmael's mother came to it and made it swampy. Then she drew water from it into her waterskin to keep it for Ishmael. Had she not done that, the waters of Zamzam would have gone on flowing to the surface forever. (Tabari, Annals 1.278–279 = Tabari 11: 72–74)

Abraham the Builder

Though the Quran knows nothing of Adam's connection with Mecca or the Ka'ba there, it is explicit on the subject of Abraham as the builder of God's House.

> Remember We made the House a place of assembly for the people and a secure place; and take the station of Abraham (maqam Ibrahim) as a prayer-place (musalla); and We have a made a pact with Abraham and Ishmael that they should sanctify My House for those who circumambulate it, those using it as a retreat, who bow or prostrate themselves there.
> And remember Abraham said: My Lord, make this land a secure one, and feed its people with fruits, those of them who believe in God and the Last Day. . . .
> And remember Abraham raised the foundations of the House, yes and Ishmael too, (saying) accept (this) from us, for indeed You are All-hearing and All-knowing. (Quran 2:125–127)

And again:

> Behold, We gave to Abraham the site of the House; do not associate anything with Me (in worship)! And sanctify My House for those who

circumambulate, or those who take their stand there (qaʾimun), who bow
or prostrate themselves there. (Quran 22:26)

What the Muslims were told on divine authority about the ancient cult
center at Mecca is summed up in those verses. It was left to later generations of Muslims to seek out additional information. And many of them
did. The authority here is Zamakhshari (d. 1144 C.E.), commenting on
Quran 2:127:

> Then, God commanded Abraham to build it, and Gabriel showed him
> its location. It is said that God sent a cloud to shade him, and he was told
> to build on its shadow, not to exceed or diminish (its dimensions). It is
> said that he built it from five mountains: Mount Sinai, the Mount of
> Olives, Lebanon, al-Judi, and its foundation is from Hira. Gabriel
> brought him the Black Stone from Heaven.
> It is said that Abu Qubays brought it forth,[5] and it was taken out of the
> place where it had been hidden during the days of the Flood. It was a
> white sapphire from the Garden, but when menstruating women touched
> it during the pre-Islamic period, it turned black.
> It is said that Abraham would build it as Ishmael would hand him the
> stones.
> "Our Lord" (2:127) means that they both said "Our Lord" [that is, not
> Abraham alone], and this activity took place in the location where they
> erected (the House) in (its) position. Abdullah demonstrated that in his
> reading, the meaning of which is: "The two of them raised it up, both of
> them saying, 'Our Lord.'" (Zamakhshari, Tafsir, 311)

Zamakhshari does not pretend to add historical detail; he simply fleshes
out the story at one or another point, as does the commentator Tabarsi
(d. 1153 C.E.) on Quran 2:125. Tabarsi was by then convinced, as were all of
his contemporaries, that the Quran's not entirely self-evident reference to
a "station of Abraham" referred to a stone venerated in the Mecca Haram.

> God made the stone underneath Abraham's feet into something like
> clay so that his foot sunk into it. That was a miracle. It was transmitted on
> the authority of Abu Jaʿfar al-Baqir (may peace be upon him) that he said:
> Three stones were sent down from the Garden: the Station of Abraham,
> the rock of the children of Israel, and the Black Stone, which God en-
> trusted Abraham with as a white stone. It was whiter than paper, but
> became black from the sins of the children of Adam.
> "Abraham raised the foundations of the House" (2:127). That is, the
> base of the House that was [already there] before that, from Ibn Abbas
> and Ata, who said: Adam was the one who built it. Then its traces were
> wiped out. Abraham ploughed it (in the original place to establish the
> foundations). That is the tradition from our Imams. But Mujahid said:

Abraham raised it up (originally) by the command of God. Al-Hasan used to say: The first to make the pilgrimage to the House was Abraham. But according to the traditions of our comrades, the first to make the pilgrimage to the House was Adam. That shows that he was [the one who built it] before Abraham. It was related on the authority of al-Baqir that he said: God placed four columns beneath the Throne. . . . He said: the angels circumambulate it. Then, He sent angels who said, "Build a House like it and with its measurements on the earth." He commanded that whoever is on the earth must circumambulate the House. (Tabarsi, Tafsir 1.460, 468)

This, then, is how most later Muslims understood the proximate origin of the Ka'ba, as alluded to in the Quran: to wit, the patriarch Abraham, on a visit to his son Ishmael in Mecca, put down, on God's command, the foundation of the House on a site already hallowed by Adam.[6]

The Beginning of the Hajj

Once the building of the Ka'ba was completed, God ordered Abraham to make public proclamation of the pilgrimage to be performed there.

Announce to the people the pilgrimage. They will come to you on foot and on every lean camel, coming from every deep and distant highway that they may witness the benefits and recollect the name of God in the well-known days (ayyam ma'lumat) over the sacrificial animals He has provided for them. Eat thereof and feed the poor in want. Then let them complete their rituals[7] and perform their vows and circumambulate the Ancient House.

Such is it [that is, the pilgrimage]. Whoever honors the sacred rites of God, for him is it good in the sight of his Lord. (Quran 22:27–30)

It is clear from these and similar Quranic texts that the original pilgrimage rituals were not so much being described to Abraham as alluded to for the benefit of a Meccan audience that was already quite familiar with them.[8] It was once again left for later commentators to fill in the details, not of the Hajj, to be sure, which was well known to all, but of Abraham and Ishmael's connection with it. The authority here is al-Azraqi (d. 834 C.E.), who, though not a Quranic commentator, was one of the earliest historians of Mecca and so an expert whose interests were somewhat different from those of Zamakhshari or Tabarsi. In this passage he describes how Abraham, at God's urging, performed that original pilgrimage ritual.

Abu al-Walid related to us . . . (from) Uthman ibn Saj: Muhammad ibn Ishaq reported to me: When Abraham the Friend of the Merciful finished building the sacred House, Gabriel came and said: "Circle it seven times!" and he circumambulated it seven times with Ishmael, touching all the corners during each circumambulation. When they had completed seven, he and Ishmael prayed two prostrations behind the stone [maqam].

He said: Gabriel got up with them and showed him all the ritual stations: al-Safa, al-Marwa, Mina, Muzdalifa, and Arafat.

He said: When he left Mina and was brought down to (the defile called) al-Aqaba, the Devil appeared to him at Stone-Heap of the Defile (jamrat al-Aqaba). Gabriel said to him: "Pelt him!" so Abraham threw seven stones at him so that he disappeared from him. Then he appeared to him at the Middle Stone-heap (al-jamra al-wusta). Gabriel said to him: "Pelt him!" so he pelted him with seven stones so that he disappeared from him. Then he appeared to him at the "Little Stone-heap" (al-jamra al-sughra). Gabriel said to him: "Pelt him!" so he pelted him with seven stones like the little stones for throwing in a sling. So the Devil withdrew from him.

Then, Abraham finished the pilgrimage and Gabriel waited for him at the ritual stops and taught him the ritual stations up through Arafat. When they arrived there, Gabriel said to him: "Do you know your ritual stations?" Abraham answered: "Yes." He said: It is called "Arafat" because of that statement: "Do you know your ritual stations?"[9]

He said: Then Abraham was commanded to call the people to the pilgrimage. He said: Abraham said: "O Lord, my voice will not reach (them)." God answered: "You call! The reaching is My responsibility."

He said: So Abraham climbed onto the stone [maqam] and looked out from it. He became (as high as) the highest mountain. The entire earth was gathered for him on that day: the mountains and plains, the land and the sea, the humans and the jinn so that everything heard him.

He said: He stuck a finger in each ear and turned to face the south, the north, the east, and the west, and he began with the southern side. He said: "O you people! The pilgrimage to the ancient House is written as an obligation for you, so answer your Lord!" So they answered from the seven regions, and from the east and the west to the broken soil: "At Your service, O God, at Your service!"

He said: The stones were as they are today except that God desired to make the stone [maqam] a sign, so his footprint remains on the stone [maqam] to this day. . . .

He said: Everyone who has made the pilgrimage to this day was one of those who answered Abraham. Their pilgrimage (today) is a result of their response on that day. Whoever makes the pilgrimage twice has answered positively twice, three pilgrimages, answered thrice.

He said: Abraham's footprint on the stone [maqam] *is a sign, which is demonstrated by the verse: "In it are clear signs [such as] the* maqam Ibrahim. *Whoever enters it is secure" (Quran 3:97). (Azraqi 1858: 33–34)*[10]

As these accounts attempt to demonstrate, the complex ritual the Muslims call the Hajj or Pilgrimage can be traced back, in general and in each specific detail, to Adam and, more proximately, to Abraham, whose intent and practices Muhammad was to restore so many centuries later. For the non-Muslim, however, the Meccan rituals are striking remnants of a pagan, albeit Semitic, past in Arabia, which the Prophet of Islam permitted to survive by incorporating them into his own prescriptions. For the Muslim, it is Abraham who transforms those same rites into an authentic Muslim cultus. Abraham, the first of the submitters (*muslimum*: Quran 2:131, and elsewhere), was also the first of the generation after the Flood to perform the rites, and Muslims are simply commemorating what the Patriarch himself had done under God's guidance.[11]

THE PRIMITIVE SANCTUARY

Midway in the Arabian peninsula, between the Jordanian border on the north and that of Yemen on the south, forty-five miles inland from the Red Sea port of Jidda, stands the city of Mecca and, in its midst, an unusual building called simply *al-Ka'ba* or "the Cube." The flat-roofed building rises from a narrow marble base on mortared courses of a local blue-gray stone, and its dimensions are not exactly cubical: it is fifty feet high, and while its northeast wall and its southwestern mate are forty feet long, the two "side" walls are five feet shorter. It is the corners rather than the walls that are oriented toward the compass points. The northeastern face is the facade in the sense that in it is the only door of the building, about seven feet above ground level. Inside is an empty room with a marble floor and three wooden pillars supporting the roof. There are some inscriptions on the walls, hanging votive lamps, and a ladder leading up to the roof. Built into the eastern corner of the Ka'ba, about four feet above the ground, is a blackish stone of either lava or basalt, which is fractured and now held together by a silver band. The building is draped with a black brocade cloth embroidered in gold with Quranic texts; the bottom edge can be raised or lowered by a series of cords and rings.

The Ka'ba stands in the midst of an open space enclosed by porticoes. This is the Haram, the "sanctuary," and there are some other constructions in it. Facing the northeastern facade wall of the Ka'ba is a small domed building called the Station of Abraham (*maqam Ibrahim*), a title that applies equally to the stone that it enshrines and in which human footprints are impressed. Behind this building is a colonnaded wellhead called Zamzam, and next to that a pulpit.

For hundreds of millions of Muslims the Ka'ba is the holiest building in the world, and its holiness, like that of the Zamzam and the Station of Abraham and, indeed, of the entire sequence of pilgrimage rituals that surround them and the environs of Mecca, derives, as we have already seen, from their connection with Abraham, the biblical patriarch. It is to this shrine complex that we now turn.

The Haram

Mecca the *haram*, the holy place, appears to antedate Mecca the city. The later Muslim authorities credit establishment of the latter to Qusayy, who, if he is a historical personage, must be dated in the late fourth or early fifth century C.E.[12] That there was a shrine before a settlement in that inhospitable valley we assume simply from the circumstances of the place: Mecca possessed none of the normal inducements to settlement, none, certainly, that would give the place a history or even a long tradition of contested possession. A holy place, on the other hand, requires little beyond the sanctity of the site, a sanctity connected with a spring, a tree, or a mountain. Only its sanctity, however obscure the origins of that holiness, explains the existence of Mecca, and only a shrine linked to other considerations—social, economic, or political—explains the eventual presence of a city there.

It was the Zamzam, then, or perhaps the two high places called Safa and Marwa,[13] that established the sanctity of the site of Mecca, though how long before Qusayy we cannot say. Our sources, as we have seen, trace the sanctity of the Meccan Haram exclusively to the Ka'ba, the edifice built at God's express command by Abraham and Ishmael. In the face of this unyielding unanimity in the literary sources, there are two ways to approach the shrine at Mecca: to compare the evidence of ancient Semitic cult centers that seem similar to the arrangement in Mecca; and to examine more contemporary evidence in the expectation that some of the older practices survived the advent of Islam. What we know of early practice comes chiefly from literary sources like Ibn al-Kalbi (d. 821 C.E.), and such information will be noted in due course. As for archeological evidence, it is sparse indeed, particularly from Arabia, where excavation is still in its very early stage and the sparse results are speculative in the extreme.[14]

At least for the time being, then, we are left with the Muslim literary authorities. More promising than archaeological tidbits are other examples of the shrine phenomenon, some from ancient sources and some reflecting more contemporary practice in Arabia, which can be used to understand and interpret the often random information supplied by the early Muslim authors.

Before Islam, Arab law was what it continued to be in many places even after Islam, namely, customary law, a set of procedures that governed the behavior of one member of a tribe toward all other members of the same tribe. This "internal" law was neither divinely prescribed nor supernaturally guaranteed but was rather constituted by a type of *mos majorum*, defined by constant usage within the tribe and reinforced by the tribe's willingness to impose sanctions on its own members.

No such system prevailed among the tribes, however, and the Arab version of international law had to appeal to other, more universal grounds. We are less certain of how this larger order operated, under what aegis tribe met tribe and conducted social and economic business or resolved differences in an atmosphere of security. We can find no divinely revealed or guaranteed law and order prevailing among tribes, yet the religious component seems more apparent on this international scale than it does within tribes. The tribes came together in sacred months, on sacred terrain, and often under the (temporary) tutelage of what are clearly religious figures.

There was and is more than one holy domain at Mecca. At the heart of the present city, and of the settlement for as long as we have records, there is a holy building, the Ka'ba, which is venerated by a series of ritual acts but which is apparently no more taboo than the space that surrounds it: entry is not restricted, for example, as it was in the Holy of Holies in Jerusalem.[15] The Ka'ba is in turn surrounded by two larger areas, both defined in the manner of a *temenos* and both marked by prohibited and privileged behavior within them. The one immediately surrounding the Ka'ba is called the "sacred shrine" (*al-masjid al-haram*) and was regarded in Muslim times as a mosque. A third and far larger area, the true *haram* and called simply by that name, extends well beyond the settled area of Mecca city and is defined by stone boundary markers (*ansab al-haram*).[16] This is the sacred territory prohibited to non-Muslims throughout its history.

The Ka'ba

The Quran's interest in the history of the Ka'ba, "the House," as the sacred book often calls it, extends no further than Abraham and Ishmael's role in its construction. But God's Book gave it a central place in the new Islamic cult, both as the continuing center of certain rituals, such as the circumambulation long practiced in Mecca, and as the *qibla*, or focal point, to which every Muslim would turn in the new liturgical prayers prescribed by Islam. With that incentive, Muslims turned to reconstructing out of their own memories, and out of the stuff of legend, a history of "the House." The task was neither simple nor direct: between Abraham's original construction and the building remembered by the earliest Muslims were a series of possessions at the hands of various pagans who had occupied Mecca. Consequently, there was a strong likelihood that the building had been modified to one degree or another.[17]

In a chapter entitled "The Building of the Ka'ba by the Quraysh in the Age of Barbarism," the Meccan historian al-Azraqi (d. 834 C.E.) collected some of the traditions still extent on the early appearance of the House before its substantial reconstruction during the early manhood of Muhammad.

> Some men from Quraysh sat in the sanctuary . . . and were remembering the building of the Ka'ba and they described how it was before that time. It was built of dried [unmortared] stones and not with clay or mud. Its door was on ground level and it had no roof or ceiling. The curtain (kiswa) was hung on its wall on one side and was tied to the top of the center of the wall. On the right as one entered the Ka'ba there was a pit where gifts of money and goods for the Ka'ba were deposited. In this pit sat a snake to guard it, which God had sent at the time of the (tribe of) Jurhum. . . . The horns of the ram that Abraham had slaughtered (in place of Isaac or Ishmael) were hanging on the wall facing the entrance. The were ornaments hanging in it which had been given as gifts. (Azraqi 1858: 106)

Tabari tells a story from Ibn Ishaq that casts a little more light on the earlier building:

> The reason for their [the Quraysh's] demolition of the Ka'ba (early in the seventh century C.E.) was that at this time it consisted of loose stones rising to somewhat above a man's height, and they wished to make it higher and roof it over since some men, Quraysh and others, had stolen the treasure of the Ka'ba, which was kept in a well in its interior. (Tabari, Annals 1.1130 = Tabari VI: 51)

By this account the Ka'ba does not appear to be a house at all but rather some kind of enclosure built around a pit or dry well, an enclosure that was, however, draped with a cloth curtain (kiswa) in a manner to give it the appearance of a tent. Some Arab authors in fact called the early Ka'ba by the same name used to describe the Israelites' tent or tabernacle in the desert.[18] It is unlikely, however, that such a rude enclosure would be called, as the Meccan edifice was for as long as we have a historical tradition, "the cube," for that is indeed what ka'ba means. A tentlike structure makes more sense, and it has been plausibly suggested that the later cubiform stone building, the ancestor of the one that stands in Mecca today, succeeded a square or quadrangular tent and so was distinguished from the round tents of the inhabitants of the settlement.[19] The sequence would not be very different, then, from the Israelite one: the Ark of the desert wanderings continued to be housed in a tent even after its transfer to urban Jerusalem (2 Samuel 6:17); and when it was finally housed in a stone building, that "holy of holies" was likewise a *ka'ba*, twenty cubits in length and width and height (1 Kings 6:20).

Nor was Mecca's the only such building in Arabia. An early Muslim historian of the antiquities, Hisham ibn al-Kalbi, reported the presence of other *ka'bas* in and around the peninsula:

> The Banu al-Harith ibn Ka'b had in Najran a ka'ba which they venerated. It is the one mentioned by al-A'sha in one of his poems. It has been claimed that it was not a ka'ba for worship, but merely a hall for people mentioned by a poet. In my opinion this is very likely the case since I have not heard of the Banu al-Harith ever mentioning it in their poetry.
>
> The Iyad had another ka'ba in Sindad, (which is located) in a region between Kufa and Basra (in Iraq). It is mentioned by al-Aswad ibn Ya'fur in one of his poems. I have, however, heard that this house was not a place of worship. Rather it was just a famous building and it was for that reason that al-Aswad mentioned it.
>
> A certain man of the Junayna named Abd al-Dar ibn Hudayb once said to his people, "Come, let us build a house, to be located in a spot in their territory called al-Hawra, with which we might rival the Ka'ba (at Mecca), and so attract to ourselves many of the bedouin." They deemed his suggestion very grave and refused his request. (Ibn al-Kalbi 1952: 38–39)

As Ibn al-Kalbi somewhat reluctantly testifies, in Mecca we are in the presence of a not unusual type of Arabian, or perhaps even Semitic, temple building. The Meccan exemplar is unusual only in that it housed no deity. Unhappily, all the evidence is literary: we have no preserved examples save the Meccan one of what might reasonably be called a *ka'ba*. We cannot say, then, how typical the obviously crude Meccan structure was. But whether typical or not, its primitive and makeshift architecture comes as no surprise: not only was it situated in a wadi, and so vulnerable to the normal destructive consequences; but the Meccan Ka'ba was also built to serve people who were originally nomads and who had, even by the late sixth century, so little skill at construction that they required the assistance of a foreign carpenter to put a timber roof on the edifice. But for all that, it was a temple and had all the primary characteristics of such: a quadrangular cella oriented to the cardinal compass points,[20] a sacred rock and sacred spring, a characteristic *haram* with the usual privileges of the right of asylum, and so on.[21]

In most ancient temples, in obvious contrast to later synagogues, churches, and mosques, whatever ritual was required was practiced outside the building, generally in the form of sacrifice upon an altar. The inner parts of the building might be entered; but because they were regarded as the domicile of the god, entry was denied to the profane, those who stood "before the shrine." Indeed, at that other Semitic temple in Jerusalem, access to the *ka'ba*, the cube-shaped Holy of Holies, was severely limited to the high priest, and then under strictly controlled circumstances. Although it is true that the primary liturgy connected with the Mecca building, the ritual circumambulation, was performed outside, there is almost no trace, either before or under Islam, of the notion that the interior of the Ka'ba was in any way more sacred than the surrounding Haram. Access to it was controlled, as we shall have many occasions to see, but exclusively, it would appear, on the grounds of political privilege. People, including Muhammad himself, prayed both inside and outside the Ka'ba[22] and visited it whenever the privilege was granted to them. The Ka'ba was not, then, a more sacred *haram* within the larger Haram that surrounded it. The truly profane non-Muslims were kept out of Mecca, or even Arabia at times, and no Muslim might approach the *precincts* of Mecca as a pilgrim without having previously entered, like a Jerusalem high priest, a state of ritual purity.

The Black Stone

Built into the southeast corner of the Ka'ba, about four feet from the ground, is the Black Stone. According to Muslim tradition, this had been a part, though not a structural part, of the building from the beginning, that is to say, from Adam's original construction of the House of God. But the tradition also remembered that the stone had come from Abu Qubays, a mountain overlooking Mecca.[23] The two strands of tradition were harmonized in an account whereby the stone was concealed on Abu Qubays during the era of the Flood, when Adam's original Ka'ba was destroyed, and then restored to Abraham for inclusion in his version of the Ka'ba.[24]

But the harmonization was not perfect. Other traditions recollected that the Black Stone, or at least its inclusion in the Ka'ba, was of much more recent origin. Ibn Sa'd says that the Quraysh brought it down from Abu Qubays only four years before Muhammad's first revelation.[25] In another account, from al-Fakihi, it is traced back to the Quraysh's first reconstruction of the building, possibly at the time of Qusayy.[26]

Was the Black Stone part of the construction of the Kaʿba from the beginning? The sources are obviously uncertain on the question, and so too are we, though the probability seems high that it was. On one account, the gathering of local idols into the Meccan sanctuary goes back to the time of the pre-Quraysh ruler Amr ibn Luhayy;[27] and as a sacred stone from Abu Qubays, the Black Stone too would have been part of Amr's religious *synoikism*.[28] But if, as seems equally likely, the stone was originally one of the portable betyls of the early settlers at Mecca, its incorporation into the structure of the Kaʿba, like the depiction of similar stones on the walls of temples at Madaʾin Salih and elsewhere, would signal the decision of nomads to make a fixed settlement.[29]

The *Hijr*

Opposite the northwestern face of the Kaʿba is an area of special sanctity defined by a low semicircular wall (*hatim*). The area is called the *hijr*, and Muslim tradition identifies it as the burial place of Ishmael and Hagar.[30] Not much is said of it in pre-Islamic times. The area first becomes prominent when Ibn al-Zubayr, a seventh-century Muslim ruler of Mecca, incorporated it into the Kaʿba by connecting the *hatim* to the building. His work was shortly undone, and the *hatim* was left a free-standing wall, as it is today. There are few plausible explanations of why there should be a wall there in the first place. It has been suggested, for example, that a low wall, and so the *hijr* enclosure, once surrounded the Kaʿba on all sides and marked the area within which the idols were worshiped through sacrifice,[31] or, more enticingly but less convincingly, that the *hatim* represents the remains of the apse of a Christian church oriented toward Jerusalem, which, it will be seen, was the direction in which once Muhammad prayed while he was still at Mecca.[32]

The word *hijr* itself means "inviolable" or "taboo," and it occurs once in that sense in the Quran (6:137–139), in reference not to the area near the Kaʿba but to animals and crops earmarked as belonging to the gods, a sense that supports the contention that the *hijr*, whatever its original extent, may have served as a pen for the animals destined for sacrifice to the idols around the Kaʿba.[33] Whether it was so used in Muhammad's own lifetime seems doubtful, however, at least on the evidence of the Muslim authorities. As the *hijr* is portrayed in Muhammad's day, it was a place of common assembly where political matters were discussed, or people prayed, or, as it appears, slept.[34]

We may be misreading the evidence, however. The sleepers in the *hijr* are generally dreamers, and their dreams have a divine purport: Abd al-Muttalib was inspired to discover the Zamzam while sleeping there, the mother of the Prophet had a vision of her son's greatness, and Muhammad was visited by Gabriel there before beginning his celebrated Night Journey—all commonplace examples of inspiration in the course of an incubation, that is, sleeping in a sacred place.[35] The latter example is particularly striking in light of the fact that Jacob's dream of the ladder reaching to heaven (Genesis 28:11–19) took place at the "House of God" and the "gate of heaven," a spot that the Jewish tradition identified as the place where Abraham was about to sacrifice Isaac—or Ishmael, as the Muslims sometimes had it—and where the Temple was later located. Ishmael too, the Muslims claimed, had been promised by God that a gate into heaven would be opened for him in the *hijr*.[36]

Another Stone: The *Maqam Ibrahim*

The Black Stone was not the only venerated stone in the Meccan sanctuary. In Islamic times visitors were shown one bearing the footprint of Abraham himself and called the "station" or "standing place" of Abraham (*maqam Ibrahim*). The latter expression occurs twice in the Quran. The mention at 3:97 is connected with a place called Bakka, apparently the site of the House[37] and the place in which are God's manifest signs, including the Station of Abraham, an allusion that suggests a place within the Haram. In 2:125 the believers are urged to "take the *maqam Ibrahim* as a place of prayer (*musalla*)," or, more literally, "take some place from the *maqam Ibrahim* as a place of prayer," a mode of expression that suggested to some commentators that the "station of Abraham" might refer to the entire sanctuary or even the entire area of the pilgrimage.[38] In the end, however, the consensus settled upon the free-standing stone also located within the sanctuary.

As with much else connected with the sanctuary, there was no great assurance on why this particular stone was called the Station of Abraham.[39] Although it made easy sense to suggest that Abraham stood upon it while building the Ka'ba, a far more likely explanation traces it back to Abraham's place of prayer. Indeed, there is an explicit reference in Genesis 19:17 to just such a place: "Abraham rose early and went to the place where he had stood (*maqom*) in the presence of the Lord." The Talmud cites this passage (BT Berakhot 6b) when it recommends that each believer should have a personal *maqom* for prayer.[40]

Whatever was being referred to in the Quranic verse, there was a stone in the Haram at Mecca, measuring roughly two feet by three feet; and as we shall see, it had a history in the Islamic era. Part of that history was the discovery (or rediscovery) in 870 C.E. that there was writing on the stone. The occasion was a refurbishing of the stone—it had earlier become cracked and the parts pinioned together—and there was a very good witness present, the subsequent historian of the city, al-Fakihi, who recorded the events of that occasion in his *Chronicle of Mecca.*

When the stone was brought on the 1st of I Rabi*ʿ* to the government house . . . people examined it closely. And I looked on with them.

Fakihi noted a variety of lines and geometric shapes on the stone and an inscription:

There is an inscription on the stone in Hebrew, but some say it is in Himyari script. It is the inscription which the Quraysh found in the Age of Barbarism. I copied the inscription from the maqam on the order of (the governor) Ali ibn al-Hasan with my own hand. I copied it (exactly) as I saw it inscribed on the stone and I spared no effort. And this is what I copied.

The Fakihi manuscript reproduces three lines of the inscription. The rest was unclear to him, and he did not copy it. He inquired among other scholars as to the meaning of the lines, and Abu Zakariyya al-Maghribi, an expert in Egyptian hieroglyphics, translated it for him: "I am God, there is no deity except Me" ⟨first line⟩ "a king who is unattainable" ⟨second line⟩ "Isbaut" ⟨third line⟩. Abu-l-Hasan al-Faridi quoted from the *Tafsir* of Sunayd a passage for the elucidation of the meaning of the trans-literated but untranslated *Isbaut* as corresponding to *al-Samad*, "the Eternal," in Arabic.[41] Al-Fakihi then records a tradition traced back to Ibn Abbas stating that there is an inscription on the *maqam* saying: "This is the House of God, He put it on the quadrangles of His throne, its sustenance will come from this and that, its people will be the first to suspend its sanctity."[42]

The Zamzam

Close by the Kaʿba is a well from whose depths water can be drawn for the benefit of the pilgrims who cherish the well-attested blessings that come to those who drink it. If pilgrims are drawn to it, so too are historians, who see in the source called Zamzam a plausible explanation of why there was a sanctuary in the wadi of Mecca in the first place. In the nineteenth century Julius Wellhausen pronounced the Zamzam "the only spring of Mecca and so likely the origin of the holy place as well as the city," and other authorities have generally been inclined to agree.[43] There are problems, however. Other wells quenched Mecca,[44] as Ibn Ishaq reveals when speaking of the Zamzam.

Zamzam utterly eclipsed the other wells from which the pilgrims used to get their water, and the people went to it because it was in the sacred

enclosure and because its water was superior to any other; and also be-
cause it was the well of Ishmael, son of Abraham. Because of it the Banu
Abd Manaf behaved boastfully towards the Quraysh and the other Arabs.
(Ibn Ishaq 1955: 65)

The Zamzam was not, then, unique; it was simply superior, and the basis
of that superiority—leaving aside the debated question of the quality of
its water—was that its origin went back to Abrahamic days, when, as we
have seen, it was miraculously discovered and saved the life of Ishmael.
Zamzam, it was argued, was thus mentioned in the Bible, particularly if
one accepted its identification with the miraculous life-saving spring
mentioned in Genesis 21:19.[45]

The Zamzam was said to have been hidden by the pagan Jurhum who
succeeded Ishmael, and it remained unknown and unused down to the
days of Abd al-Muttalib, Muhammad's grandfather. Abd al-Muttalib was
a descendent of Abd Manaf, the son to whom Qusayy, that founder of
Quraysh—and Meccan—fortunes, handed on as a hereditary trust the
office of *siqaya*, the privilege of supplying water to the Meccan pilgrims.
On the face of it, this possibly lucrative honor could have had nothing to
do with the Zamzam, because the well was unknown to Qusayy and every
member of Abd Manaf down to Abd al-Muttalib. Did the Zamzam replace the other wells of Mecca at some point, perhaps at some very late
date in the history of the city, when the Abrahamic story began to circulate? There are grounds for thinking so, not the least of which is the lack
of any essential connection between the Zamzam and its water and the
pre- or post-Islamic Hajj.[46]

Safa and Marwa

Somewhat to the east of the Ka'ba were two low hills, which have since
disappeared under the leveling topography of modern Mecca. The one on
the south was called Safa and that on the north Marwa, and there occurred between them one of the ritual acts connected with the religious
life of Mecca. It was, in fact, another form of circumambulation, a cir-
cling back and forth between the two places, part of which had to be
conducted at a run, whence its later name, "the running" (*sa'y*). The practice was later incorporated into the Umra and the Hajj, though obviously
not without some objection, as is manifest from the Quran's reference
to it:

Indeed, Safa and Marwa are among the indications of God. So for
those who make the Hajj to the House or the Umra, there is no sin in
circumambulating them. (Quran 2:158)

This is as much as the Quran says. But the Muslim tradition offers two explanations for the practice, one "pagan" and one "Abrahamic." As we have already seen, the latter simply identifies Hagar's frantic search for water for the infant Ishmael with the ritual running between the hills before her providential discovery of the Zamzam. What is obviously an older and more primitive explanation has to do with two humans named Asaf and Na'ila, members of the Jurhum:

(The Quraysh) adopted Asaf (or Isaf) and Na'ila by the place of Zam-zam, sacrificing beside them. They were (originally) a man and a woman of Jurhum . . . who copulated in the Ka'ba so God transformed them into two stones. . . . But God alone knows whether this is the truth. (Ibn Ishaq 1955: 37)

Despite Ibn Ishaq's explicit misgivings, the colorful story became current in the Muslim authors and has been the point of departure for a wide variety of attempts to explain the reality, if any, behind the story and its connection with the "running" ritual.[47] The names, which have to do with stones, appear to be Aramaic rather than Arabic and so have suggested foreign origins. What were transparently sacred stones, or perhaps stone idols—the Jurhum story may reflect an etiological myth or be a distant echo of some form of ritual prostitution at the Ka'ba or nearby[48]—were originally worshiped atop the "high places" of Safa and Marwa and then brought down somewhere in the vicinity of the Ka'ba by Qusayy himself. The circumambulation ritual continued to be performed at the two hills, but thereafter sacrifices were offered at the new sites of the idols.[49]

ARABIAN PAGANISM

The Muslim Arab authorities were not at all certain who of the early Arab intruders, the Jurhum or the Khuza'a, was first or chiefly responsible for turning Ishmael's holy place into a pagan city. More, their version of the degradation of the Meccan cultus has to do principally with the cult of idols, though we are assured by somewhat wider evidence that who was being worshiped in Arabia, and how and why, were much broader questions than our eighth- and ninth-century sources were willing to allow. The inhabitants of Arabia assuredly had a religious tradition before Islam, and although we are not particularly well informed about it, that tradition appears to have been quite complex. And this is what we would expect to discover in societies that were splintered into tribes and clans of widely varying sizes, some of them sedentary and some of them nomadic, with a number of the latter ranging seasonally over enormously broad terrains.

The inhabitants of the Hijaz worshiped the way they lived: the small settled population at fixed shrines in oases; the bedouin in transit, carrying their gods with them.[50] The objects worshiped were principally stones and trees and heavenly bodies,[51] or rather, the gods thought to reside in them, or possibly—and here we begin to enter a world we do not fully understand—the gods represented by them.[52] What is reasonably clear is that in the more recent Arabian past sacred stones were more often being shaped into human likenesses rough or fine,[53] perhaps, it has been surmised, because of the extension of Hellenistic styles into the peninsula.[54] Ibn al-Kalbi describes what one of them might have looked like, on the authority of his scholar-father, who poses the question in this passage.

I requested Malik ibn Haritha, "Describe to me (the god) Wadd in such a way which would make it appear vividly before me." Malik replied: "It was the statue of a huge man, as big as the largest of human beings, covered with two robes, clothed with the one and cloaked with the other, carrying a sword at his waist and a bow on his shoulder, and holding in one hand a spear to which had been attached a standard, and in the other a quiver full of arrows." (Ibn al-Kalbi, Book of Idols, 56 = Ibn al-Kalbi 1952: 49)

However the devotees thought of it, Arabian cultus was highly volatile. The deities often shared characteristics, or were harmonized into families, or passed into the possession now of this tribe and now of that. There is a distinctly tribal notion to the Arabs' worship of the gods. On the basis of the South Arabian evidence, with which the more meager Arab tradition concurs, each tribe or tribal confederation had a divine patron whose cult gave the group a focus for its solidarity. And in a practice that points directly to what was occurring at Mecca, each of these "federal deities" was the "lord" of a shrine that served as the cult center of the federation.

What seems to be clear is that the bedouin came into the towns to worship at the fixed shrines of the gods there. The incentive may have been principally commercial—fairs are a consistent feature of such urban shrines—and there was undoubtedly conscious policy at work: the movement of the effigy of a popular god into a town shrine meant that its worshipers would eventually follow, if certain conditions could be guaranteed. The chief of those was security. Bedouin were ill at ease in very close quarters: a vividly remembered network of tribal vendettas and blood feuds incurred from earlier collisions on the steppe made any tribal encounter potentially dangerous. The solution was the usual one of the "truce of God," sacred months when hands and weapons were restrained by divine injunction. Under such security, tribes came together, worshiped, and traded, and then returned to their more normal ways.

Sacred shrine, sacred truce, worship, and trade is a combination with a venerable history. Small wonder, since it worked to everyone's advantage, and not least to that of the guardians of the shrine—the Quraysh at Mecca, for example.

How Paganism and Idol Worship Came to Mecca

One aspect of the worship of the pre-Islamic Arabs that attracted the attention not only of Greek and Latin authors who came in contact with Arab society but also of later Muslim authorities on the Age of Barbarism was a widespread cult of stones. For both sets of observers it seemed odd to venerate stones, whether they were totally unshaped or fashioned into some kind of very rudimentary idol. It was not, of course, the stones that were being worshiped but an animated spirit within them.[55] The practice is testified to among sedentarized Arabs like the Nabateans of Petra and the priestly Arabs of Emessa in Syria, who had enshrined one such stone within their temple—which their high priest Elagabalus carried off to Rome with him when he became emperor—as well as among the nomads who carried stones enclosed in portable shrines into battle with them.[56]

Later Muslims had some idea of these practices, and they traced them back to the earliest history of Mecca, when the sons of Ishmael lapsed into paganism. Ibn al-Kalbi, who made a special study of the pre-Islamic past of Arabia in his *Book of Idols*, connected idol worship directly to the degeneracy of the Banu Ishmael:

The reason that led them [the descendents of Ishmael] to the worship of images and stones was the following. No one left Mecca without carrying away with him a stone from the stones of the Sacred House as a token of reverence to it, and as a sign of deep affection to Mecca. Wherever he settled he would erect that stone and circumambulate it in the same manner he used to circumambulate the Ka'ba (before his departure from Mecca), seeking thereby its blessing and affirming his deep affection for the Holy House. In fact, the Arabs still venerate the Ka'ba and Mecca and journey to them in order to perform the pilgrimage and the visitation, conforming thereby to the time-honored custom which they inherited from Abraham and Ishmael.

In time this led them to the worship of whatever took their fancy, and caused them to forget their former worship. They exchanged the religion of Abraham and Ishmael for another. Consequently they took to the worship of images, becoming like nations before them.

At this point, Ibn al-Kalbi ties his story to an explanation of Quran 71: 20–24:

Noah said: "O Lord, they rebel against me, and they follow those whose riches and children only aggravate their ruin." And they plotted a great plot, and they said, "Forsake not your gods; forsake not Wadd and Suwaʿ, nor Yaghuth and Yaʿuq and Nasr." And they caused many to err.

Ibn al-Kalbi's text continues:

They sought and determined what the people of Noah had worshiped of those images and adopted the worship of those which were still remembered among them.

It was important, however, in the light of Muhammad's own adoption of certain of the cult practices in the Mecca of his day, to maintain some kind of continuous link with the authentic Abrahamic past.

Among these devotional practices were some which had come down from the time of Abraham and Ishmael, such as the veneration of the House and its circumambulation, the Hajj, the Umra [or lesser pilgrimage], the "standing" on Arafat and Muzdalifa, sacrificing she-camels, and raising the voice (tahlil) (in acclamation of God) at the Hajj and Umra, but they introduced into the latter things that did not belong to it.

Ibn al-Kalbi then supplies an example of just such an "unorthodox" pre-Islamic "acclamation" (*talbiyya*):

Here we are, O Lord! Here we are! Here we are! You have no partner save the one who is Yours; You have dominion over him and whatever he possesses.

Ibn al-Kalbi continues his own remarks:

Thus they declared His unity through the talbiyya and at the same time associated their gods with Him, placing their [that is, their gods'] affairs in His hands. (Ibn al-Kalbi, Book of Idols, 6–7 = Ibn al-Kalbi 1952: 4–5)

Stone worship is not quite the same thing as idol worship, as even Ibn al-Kalbi understood. According to most authorities, including Ibn al-Kalbi, the pagan practices in Mecca took a new turn when Khuzaʿi intruders under their leader Amr ibn Luhayy—who had married the daughter of Amr ibn al-Harith, the Jurhum chief—replaced the Jurhum as the paramount tribe in the settlement.

When Amr ibn Luhayy came (to Mecca) he disputed Amr ibn al-Harith's right to its custody, and with the aid of the Banu Ishmael he fought the Jurhumites, defeated them and cleared them out of the Kaʿba; he then drove them out of Mecca and took over the custody of the House after them.

Amr ibn Luhayy then became very sick and was told: There is a hot spring in Balqa in Syria.[57] If you go there, you will be cured. So he went to the hot spring, bathed therein and was cured. During his stay there he noticed that the inhabitants of the place worshiped idols. So he questioned them: "What are these things?" To which they replied, "To them we pray for rain, and from them we seek victory over the enemy." Thereupon he asked them to give him (some) and they did. He took them back with him to Mecca and erected them around the Kaʿba. (Ibn al-Kalbi, Book of Idols 8 = Ibn al-Kalbi 1952: 7)

Later Ibn al-Kalbi turns his attention to the cult of the idols:

Every family in Mecca had at home an idol which they worshiped. Whenever one of them purposed to set out on a journey, his last act before leaving the house would be to touch the idol in hope of an auspicious journey; on his return, the first thing he would do was to touch it again in gratitude for a propitious return. . . .

The Arabs were passionately fond of worshiping idols. Some of them had a temple around which they centered their worship, while others adopted an idol to which they offered their adoration. The person who was unable to build himself a temple or adopt an idol would erect a stone in front of the Sacred House [the Kaʿba at Mecca] or in front of any other temple he might prefer, and then circumambulate it in the same manner in which he would circumambulate the Sacred House. The Arabs called these stones "betyls" (ansab), but whenever these stones resembled a living form they called them "idols" (asnam) and "images" (awthan). The act of circumambulating them they called "circumrotation" (dawar).

Whenever a traveler stopped at a place or station (to spend the night), he would select for himself four stones, pick out the finest of them and adopt it as his god, and then use the remaining three as supports for his cooking pot. On his departure he would leave them behind, and would do the same at the other stops.

And, like many other Muslims, Ibn al-Kalbi was convinced that Arab paganism was simply a degenerate form of the rituals of the Kaʿba:

The Arabs were accustomed to offer sacrifices before all these idols, betyls and stones. Nevertheless, they were aware of the excellence and superiority of the Kaʿba, to which they went on pilgrimage and visitation. What they did on their travels was merely a perpetuation of what they did at the Kaʿba, because of their devotion to it. (Ibn al-Kalbi, Book of Idols, 32–33 = Ibn al-Kalbi 1952: 28–290)

The Meccan Pantheon

Ibn Ishaq provides a kind of catalog of which tribes worshiped which idols and where:

> Quraysh had an idol by a well in the middle of the Kaʿba called Hubal. And they adopted Asaf and Naʾila by the place of Zamzam, sacrificing beside them. They were a man and woman of Jurhum—Asaf ibn Baghy and Naʾila bint Dik—who copulated in the Kaʿba and so God transformed them into two stones.[58] Abdullah ibn Abu Bakr . . . on the authority of Amra bint Abd al-Rahman . . . that she said, I heard Aisha [one of the wives of Muhammad] say, "We always heard that Asaf and Naʾila were a man and a woman of Jurhum who copulated in the Kaʿba so God transformed them into two stones." But God alone knows the truth.
>
> Al-Lat belonged to the Thaqif in Taʾif, her overseers and guardians being the Banu Muʿattib of the Thaqif. Manat was worshiped by the Aws and the Khazraj, and such of the people of Yathrib who followed their religion, by the sea-shore in the direction of al-Mushallal in Qudayd. (Ibn Ishaq 1955: 38–39)

HUBAL

Among the gods worshiped by the Quraysh, the greatest was Hubal, this on the expert testimony of Ibn al-Kalbi:

> The Quraysh had several idols in and around the Kaʿba. The greatest of these was Hubal. It was made, as I was told, of red agate, in the form of a man with the right hand broken off. It came into the possession of the Quraysh in this condition, and they therefore made for it a hand of gold. . . . It stood inside the Kaʿba, and in front of it were seven divinatory arrows. On one of these was written the word "pure," and on another "associated alien." Whenever the lineage of a new-born was doubted, they would offer a sacrifice to Hubal and then shuffle the arrows and throw them. If the arrows showed the word "pure," the child would be declared legitimate and the tribe would accept him. If, however, the arrows showed "associated alien," the child would be declared illegitimate and the tribe would reject him. The third arrow had to do with divination concerning the dead, while the fourth was for divination about marriage. The purpose of the three remaining arrows has not been explained. Whenever they disagreed concerning something, or proposed to embark upon a journey, or undertake some other project, they would proceed to Hubal and shuffle the divinatory arrows before it. Whatever result they obtained they would follow and do accordingly. (Ibn al-Kalbi, Book of Idols 28–29 = Ibn al-Kalbi 1952: 23–24)

Some additional details on this cleromantic deity, the most powerful of the pagan idols of Mecca, is supplied by the Meccan historian Azraqi. Abraham, as we have seen, had dug a pit inside the Ka'ba, and it was here that the Khuza'i Amr ibn Luhayy set up the idol of Hubal:

> Amr ibn Luhayy brought with him (to Mecca) an idol called Hubal from the land of Hit in Mesopotamia.[59] Hubal was one the Quraysh's greatest idols. So he set it up at the well inside the Ka'ba and ordered the people to worship it. Thus a man coming back from a journey would visit it and circumambulate the House before going to his family, and he would shave his hair before it.
>
> Muhammad ibn Ishaq said that Hubal was (made of) cornelian pearl in the shape of a human. His right hand was broken off and the Quraysh made a gold hand for it. It had a vault for the sacrifice, and there were seven arrows cast (on issues relating to) a dead person, virginity and marriage. Its offering was a hundred camels. It had a custodian (hajib). (Azraqi 1858: 73–74)

Finally, among the pictures that decorated the interior of the Ka'ba in pre-Islamic days, there was one, as Azraqi says, "of Abraham as an old man." But because the figure was shown performing divination by arrows, it seems likely that it was Hubal. The suspicion is strengthened by the fact that when Muhammad finally took over the sanctuary, he permitted the picture of Jesus to remain but had that of "Abraham" removed with the dry comment, "What has Abraham to do with arrows?"[60]

Has Hubal depicted as "Abraham the Ancient" anything to do with the "Ancient House," as the Ka'ba is often called? Or, to put the question more directly: Was it Hubal rather than Allah who was "Lord of the Ka'ba"?[61] Probably not. The Quran, which makes no mention of Hubal, would certainly have raised the contention. Hubal was, by the Arabs' own tradition, a newcomer to both Mecca and the Ka'ba, an outsider introduced by the ambitious Amr ibn Luhayy, and the tribal token around which the Quraysh later attempted to construct a federation with the surrounding Kinana, whose chief deity Hubal was. Hubal was introduced into the Ka'ba, but he never supplanted the god Allah, whose House it continued to be.

THE DAUGHTERS OF ALLAH

If the Quran is silent on Hubal, it often adverts to three other deities of the many worshiped at Mecca in pre-Islamic days: Manat, al-Uzza, and al-Lat, called collectively by the Quraysh the "daughters of Allah." "What," the Quran complains, "has Allah taken daughters out of His creation and allowed you the choice of sons?" (43:16), an odd arrangement indeed in a society in which female infants were often left to die. One of the characteristics of Arab paganism as it has come down to us is the absence of a mythology, stories that might serve to explain the origin or history of the gods. Rather, the gods are cult objects, and we have only the cult, and an occasional nominal qualifier, to instruct us about them. Thus we have no idea why the Quraysh should have assigned them their filial roles, save perhaps simply to introduce some order into the large and somewhat chaotic Meccan pantheon. Nothing we know suggests that Allah was otherwise thought to have had daughters or that the three goddesses possessed any family relationship. They often swapped characteristics and shared shrines, but Manat, Uzza, and Lat were quite discrete divinities, and the best examples, by all accounts, of the personified worship of heavenly bodies.[62]

Even though their principal shrines lay north and east of Mecca, al-Lat, al-Uzza, and Manat were all worshiped by the Quraysh of Mecca, and at least al-Uzza numbered no less than Muhammad himself among her worshipers.[63] The same three goddesses appear—and then disappear—in an extremely curious and much-discussed place in Sura 53 of the Quran. The exact context is unknown, but Muhammad was still at Mecca and was apparently feeling the pressures of the Quraysh resistance to his message:

When the Messenger of God saw how his tribe turned their backs on him and was grieved to see them shunning the message he had brought to them from God, he longed in his soul that something would come to him from God that would reconcile him with his tribe. With his love for his tribe and his eagerness for their welfare, it would have delighted him if some of the difficulties which they made for him could have been smoothed, and he debated with himself and fervently desired such an outcome. Then God revealed (Sura 53) . . . and when he came to the words "Have you thought al-Lat and al-Uzza and Manat, the third, the other?" (vv. 19–20) Satan cast on his tongue, because of his inner debates and what he desired to bring to his people, the words: "These are the high-flying cranes; verily their intercession is to be hoped for."

When the Quraysh heard this, they rejoiced and were happy and delighted at the way in which he had spoken of their gods, and they listened to him, while the Muslims, having complete trust in their Prophet with respect of the message which he brought from God, did not suspect him of error, illusion or mistake. When he came to the prostration, having completed the Sura, he prostrated himself and the Muslims did likewise. . . . The polytheists of the Quraysh and others who were in the mosque [that is, the Meccan Haram] likewise prostrated themselves because of the reference to their gods which they heard, so that there was no

one in the mosque, believer or unbeliever, who did not prostrate him-
self. . . . Then they all dispersed from the mosque. The Quraysh left de-
lighted at the mention of their gods. (Tabari, Annals 1.1192–1193 = Tabari
VI: 108–109)

This is the indubitably authentic story—it is difficult to imagine a Muslim inventing such a tale—of the notorious "Satanic verses." It has profound implications for Islamic scriptural theology and jurisprudence, but
what is important here is what it reveals of the contemporary regard for
the three goddesses. What was first granted and then rescinded was permission to use the three goddesses as intercessors with Allah. It was, as has
been suggested, a critical moment in Muhammad's understanding of the
distinction between Allah as simply a "high god," the head of the Meccan
or Arabian pantheon within which the lesser gods and goddesses might be
invoked as go-betweens,[64] and the notion that eventually prevailed: Allah
is uniquely God, without associates, companions, or "daughters." The
goddesses were, as the revision (Quran 53:23) put it, "nothing but names,"
invented by the Quraysh and their ancestors.

And what precisely are we to understand by "exalted cranes"? The
Muslim authorities were uncertain about the meaning of *gharaniq*, as are
we.[65] But what they did know was that this was the refrain that the
Quraysh used to chant as they circumambulated the Ka'ba: "Al-Lat, and
al-Uzza and Manat, the third, the other; indeed these are exalted (or lofty,
'ula) *gharaniq*; let us hope for their intercession."[66] It is as close as we shall
come, perhaps, to a Qurashite prayer formula offered up to Allah—clearly
not the goddesses in question—as the devotees moved in a processional
liturgy around His Holy House.

THE HIGH GOD ALLAH

Muhammad no more invented Allah than he did al-Lat, al-Uzza, and
Manat. The cult of the deity termed simply "the god" (*al-ilah*) was
known throughout southern Syria and northern Arabia,[67] and it was obviously of central importance in Mecca, where the building called the
Ka'ba was indisputably his house. Indeed, the Muslim profession of faith,
"there is no *ilah* except *al-ilah*," attests to precisely that point: the
Quraysh are being called upon to repudiate the very existence of all the
other gods save this one. It seems equally certain that Allah was not
merely a god in Mecca but was widely regarded as the "high god," the
chief and head of the Meccan pantheon, perhaps the result, as has been
argued, of a natural progression toward henotheism or of the growing
influence of Jews and Christians in the peninsula.[68] The most convincing
piece of evidence that the latter was at work is the fact that of all the gods
of Mecca, Allah alone was not represented by an idol.

How did the pagan Meccans view their god Allah? The Quran provides direct and primary evidence.

If you ask them [the pagan Quraysh] who created the heavens and the earth and made subject the sun and the moon, they will certainly reply "Allah." . . . And indeed if you ask them who sends down the rain from the sky and so restores life to the earth after its death, they will certainly reply, "Allah." (Quran 29:61, 63)

And if you ask them who created them, they will certainly reply, "Allah." (Quran 43:87)

Say: Who is it who sustains you from the sky and from the earth? Or who is it who has power over hearing and sight? And who is it who brings out the living from the dead and the dead from the living? And who is it who rules and regulates all affairs? They will soon answer, "Allah."

If you ask them who created the heavens and the earth, they will certainly say "Allah." Say: Those (female) things you call upon apart from Allah, do you think that if God wills evil to me, they can remove this evil, or, if He wills mercy to me, they can hold back this mercy? (Quran 39:38)

In this latter verse the "high god" relationship is quite marked. On the one hand, there is Allah, the creator, sustainer, and ruler of the universe, and on the other, a host of minor deities—the "daughters of Allah" among them—who intercede with the lord of the gods, precisely the view that is attacked in the Quran:

They serve apart from Allah that which neither harms nor benefits them, and they say, "These are our intercessors with Allah." Say: Are you informing God of something He knows not in the heavens or on earth? Glory be to Him! He is far above any partners. (Quran 10:18)

When they embark upon ships, they call upon Allah, putting their faith in Him (alone); but once He has delivered them safely back to land, they associate (others with Him). (Quran 29:65)

The Quran is our most certain testimony to the religious life in Mecca before the appearance of Islam. At least at the beginning of his career, Muhammad was concerned not with regulating the life of a community of believers, as he later was in Medina, but rather with reforming the beliefs and practices of his fellow Meccans. "Reforming" is a more appropriate term than "converting," because the Quran also reveals, as we have seen, that the worship of Allah was already well established there before Muhammad. What was at question, then, was not simply belief in or worship of Allah, which the Quraysh certainly did, but the Meccans' "association," as the Quran calls it, of other deities with Allah, a practice that seemed to accept the existence of other gods in the "exalted assembly" while at the same time denying that they had any autonomous power, though perhaps they could help men if God so willed. So it appears, at any rate, in some parts of the Quran:

Say: Call upon those whom you assert [to be gods] apart from Allah. They do not have so much as the weight of a mote in the heavens nor on the earth. They have no partnership in either of them, nor does He depend on any of them for support. Intercession will avail nothing with Him except for him to whom He gives permission. (Quran 34:22–23)

Some verses of the Quran openly concede the existence of such gods, simply pointing to the fact that they are Allah's creatures (25:3) and that, rather than being Allah's partners, they are His servants:

What, do they associate (with Allah) that which creates nothing, but are themselves created, and which have no power to help them, nor (even) to help themselves. . . . Those on whom they call other than Allah are [His] servants just as you are. If you are speaking the truth, just call on them and let us hear them answer you! Do they have feet, so that they walk, or hands, so that they pick things up, or eyes, so that they see, or ears, so that they hear? Go, call on your "god-partners" and let them do their worst to me, without let-up. (Quran 7:191–195)

Finally, Allah's position vis-à-vis the other gods whose existence even the Quran seems to acknowledge is illuminated by one of the epithets applied to Him, together with a self-gloss, in Sura 112, itself a basic statement of Quranic monotheism:[69]

Say: He is Allah: One;
He is Allah: the samad.
He has neither begotten, nor was begotten,
And no one is equal to Him.

(Quran 112)

Sacrifices

Like their Semitic and Arab fellows elsewhere in the Near East, the Arabs of the Hijaz used sacrifice as a primary way of forging and maintaining a relationship with the realm of the divine. "To every people," the Quran says, "did We appoint rites of sacrifice that they might celebrate the name of God over the sustenance He gave them from animals" (22:34). This is said with clear approval, but immediately preceding these

verses is a considerably more obscure passage, though apparently on the
same subject:

> But if someone holds in esteem the (sacrificial) tokens (sha'a'ir) of
> God, that esteem should come truly from piety of the heart. In them [the
> sacrificial animals?] you have benefits for an appointed term, but then
> their place (of sacrifice) is toward the Ancient House. (Quran 22:32–33)

Then follow more precise directions on the benediction and the consum-
ing of the animal sacrifice, again reflecting on what seems to have been
the current practice:

> For your benefit We have made the sacrificial camels one of the signs
> from God; there is much good for you in them. So pronounce the name
> of God over them as they line up (for sacrifice), and afterwards as they lie
> slain, eat of them and feed such as already have food and such as beg in
> humility. Thus have We made animals subject to you, that you might be
> grateful. (Quran 22:36)

The sacrifice of animals, which disappeared out of the Mecca Haram in
Islamic times but continued to be practiced at Mina during the Hajj,[70]
was but one form of sacrifice known to the Arabs. The Arab authorities
tell us of animals simply consecrated to the gods and kept within their
sacred precincts without being sacrificed, and the Quran seems to refer
to the practice of animal offerings as part of a repertoire of pagan ritual
practices:

> And was it not God who made the (custom of) a slit-ear she-camel, or
> a she-camel let loose for free pasture, or sacrifices for twin births, or stal-
> lion camels (freed from work)? (Quran 5:106)

Each devotee offered his own victim. Although animals sacrificed in the
desert sometimes might be simply left behind, as they often were at Mina
throughout Islamic times, in town the animal was usually cooked and
eaten as part of a common meal, a practice that created problems for
Muslims as it had earlier for Christians. Among the things forbidden to
the believer by the Quran is "that which has been sacrificed upon a stone
(nusub)" (5:4). Such stones (ansab) are described as "abominations" and
the "work of Satan" (5:93). These are familiar objects indeed, already
known from the story of Jacob's betyl in Genesis (35:14). Stones on which
one poured out the blood of sacrifice were widely used among the ancient
Arabs, not only as here in the vicinity of the Ka'ba, but even as tombstones and boundary markers for sacred enclosures.[71] With the coming of
Islam, their use constituted a form of idolatry, and the believer might not
share in the food.

Pilgrimage and Other Festivals

From our perspective, which is shaped by the Quran's own view, the best-known pagan ritual at Mecca was the pilgrimage. The Quran did not qualify it as pagan, of course—it was affirmed as a genuine remnant of Abrahamic practice—but beyond question it was performed, in one form or another, by both Meccans and visitors to their shrine city before Muhammad received the revelations that were to incorporate it into Islam. Only at a relatively late date, when the triumph of Islam was assured, were pagans prevented from making pilgrimage (Quran 9:17–18). "The months for the pilgrimage are matters of common knowledge," the Quran declares (2:197), as surely they were.

The pre-Islamic pilgrimage was not a single act but a complex of rituals joined in a manner, and for reasons, we cannot easily discern. The later Muslim tradition "harmonized" the Islamic version of the complex by identifying each of its elements with some incident in the Abraham legend, which was itself enriched by association with otherwise inexplicable practices in the Hajj ritual. The construction of the Kaʿba is described in the Quran as the work of Abraham and Ishmael (2:127), and the circumstantial evidence suggests that this may have been a common belief among the pre-Islamic Quraysh. Yet there is no evidence, Quranic or circumstantial, that such a claim was made by Muhammad or had been accepted by the pagan Quraysh for the various Hajj rituals. Their association with Abraham appears to have occurred well after the Hajj had been embraced as an acceptable and meritorious way for a Muslim to worship God (Quran 2:197; 3:97).

Absent the Abrahamic motif, the Hajj of Muhammad's Mecca disintegrates into an obscure series of acts centering not on Mecca but on the mountain called Arafat, eleven miles east of the city. The Hajj, it has been maintained, originally had nothing to do with Mecca, as even the Islamic version of the ritual testifies: the climax of the Muslim Hajj was and is the "standing" at Arafat, followed by a procession to Mina and sacrifice there, after which the pilgrim was free to remove the ritual vestments.[72] More, it was common knowledge that not the Quraysh but the Sufa, and later the Tamim, held the religious offices, the so-called "permission" (*ijaza*), at Arafat and Mina.[73] And not only was Mecca not part of the original Hajj; there may have been no trading in the city in connection with its own rituals. Such, at any rate, one might conclude from the fact that the famous pilgrimage fairs—and Mecca is never numbered among them—are associated with Arafat and Mina and that the Quraysh seem to play no major role in them.[74] Thus the Meccan ritual was at some point joined to the Hajj, probably by Muhammad himself.

The Quran brings up the question of whether Muslims, who focused their religious orientation toward Mecca and were not accustomed to linking commerce with ritual, were permitted to indulge in trade, as did the Hajj habitués of Arafat and Mina. In this context the revelation preserved in Quran 2:198 was made public: "It is no fault for you if you seek the bounty of the Lord." There is little doubt that these verses refer to the pilgrimage season. Someone apparently had objected to mixing commerce and the pilgrimage ritual, a practice for which Muhammad then announced God's explicit permission. We obviously do not know everything behind the objection,[75] but what does seem reasonably clear is that previously pilgrimage trading had been restricted to the fairs, of which Mecca apparently was not one.[76] After the revelation of this verse at Medina, Mecca was sanctioned as a pilgrimage trading center, even though the Muslims could not take full advantage of the permission until the capture of Mecca shortly before Muhammad's death.[77]

If the Hajj was not Meccan, the Quraysh had their own holy days, including the spring festival called ʿumra and celebrated in the month of Rajab.[78] In Islamic times the Umra lost its seasonal aspect with the ban on intercalation, and some of its distinctive character—its sacrifices, for example[79]—disappeared in its combination with the Hajj.[80] But it preserved its special, and peculiarly Meccan, identity well into Islamic times, as we shall see.

The Muslims later made a careful distinction between ʿumra—a word whose exact literal meaning is unclear—and hajj or pilgrimage properly so called, but it may not always have been thus. On the model of the two Jewish spring and fall haggim of Passover and Sukkoth, to which both Arab festivals appear to be closely related, the Umra and (Muslims') Hajj were both originally hajj. It may well have been Muhammad himself who determined that the Arafat ritual was the "Great Hajj" and the Umra the "Lesser," a distinction nowhere apparent in pre-Islamic times.

The distinction between Umra and Hajj is already present in the Quran (2:197), but the latter ritual, which became an obligation for every Muslim, may be a composite of several different cult activities—some at Mecca, some at shrines outside the city, woven, whether by Muhammad or by someone earlier, into a single liturgical act. The "running" between Safa and Marwa, for example, originally belonged to neither the Umra nor the Hajj, and some Muslims in fact protested its inclusion in either, objections that were presumably silenced by the revelation of Quran 2:158.

There is no evidence that Muhammad substantially altered any of the basic rituals of the Meccan pilgrimages, whereas he did modify the chaotic "overflowing" (ifada) from Arafat and the time of the departure from Muzdalifa for Mina.[81] So we may assume that the donning of special clothing and the entering into a taboo state was practiced in pre-Islamic Mecca as it was elsewhere in the Semitic world. The ritual in the Haram had chiefly to do with a circumambulation of the Kaʿba, which in Islamic days included the "greeting of the Black Stone," a gesture of touching, pressing, or kissing with abundant precedents in pre-Islamic practice, though of a very different import, as we shall see. Outside the Haram, ritual required the devotee to run back and forth, another type of "circumambulation,"[82] between the two hills of Safa and Marwa, the sites of the well-known idols of Asaf and Naʾila in pre-Islamic days. This latter ritual ended with the offering of sacrifices at Marwa.[83]

Pilgrimage Fairs

Sura 106 of the Quran, the one called "The Quraysh," played a critical role, perhaps *the* critical role, in the later Muslims' understanding of their ancestors at Mecca and, through them, on the modern interpretation of the entire Meccan enterprise before Islam.

> For the covenants of security of the Quraysh,
> The covenants (covering) the journey of winter
> and of summer,
> Let them worship the Lord of this House,
> Who provides them with food against hunger and
> security against fear.
>
> (Quran 106)

This is the currently standard translation/interpretation of the sura, which might be paraphrased as: "Because the Lord granted (or perhaps guaranteed) the treaties enjoyed by the Quraysh, treaties which have made possible their annual commercial journeys, let the Quraysh recognize this and worship the Lord of the Kaʿba, who has, through these treaties and their consequences, provided the Quraysh with both sustenance and security." This is intelligible in English, but the Arabic of the sura has posed serious linguistic and syntactical problems that have bothered commentators from the beginning.[84] And not everyone read the celebrated "two journeys" of Sura 106 as an expanded opportunity for trade. The commentator al-Razi (d. 1209) for one thought that the "journey of winter and of summer" referred to the travel of pilgrims to Mecca, the one referring to the Umra of the month Rajab and the other to the Hajj of the month Dhu al-Hijja.[85]

If it was a guess, it may have been an inspired one. Muslim commentators, who lived in an era and a society without intercalation and so without seasonal festivals, would have had difficulty imagining the seasonal pilgrimages, as all such were in pre-Islamic days. Such pilgrimages would

surely have been "eased" if they took place under the authority and protection of the now saintly Quraysh. Thus, on this reading of Sura 106,
every year, twice a year during the sacred months, pilgrims were drawn to
Holy Mecca on pilgrimage, and their fee of homage was the supply of
provisions on which the Quraysh and the other Meccans lived. Trade
enters nowhere in this equation, particularly not the long-distance trade
read by some of the commentators into the second verse of the sura.

Trade may have been a background issue, however, or rather the
Quraysh's participation in it. Some members of Muhammad's audience
appear to have opposed it, or such seems to be the sense of the already
cited Sura 2:198: "It is no fault for you if you seek the bounty of the
Lord." Detailed prescriptions regarding the pilgrimage "in the well-
known months" immediately precede and follow that verse. Muslim historians had a good deal of information on the circumstances and places
where the "Lord's bounty" was reaped by interested parties, namely, the
holy-day fairs (*mawasim*). That trade should be tied to the pilgrimage was
natural to most of the participants, save perhaps to the puritanical *Hums*,
who, as we shall see, had a fierce and exclusive devotion to Mecca. Peoples
who for reason of danger or distance did not normally associate came
together under the protection of the truce of God to worship and, it
seems clear, to trade.

Azraqi's is the most detailed sketch of the market fairs:

> The Hajj was in the month of Dhu al-Hijja. People went out with their
> goods and they ended up in Ukaz on the day of the new moon of Dhu
> al-Qa'da. They stayed there twenty nights during which they set up in
> Ukaz their market of all colors and all goods in small houses. The leaders
> and foremen of each tribe oversaw the selling and buying among the
> tribes where they congregate in the middle of the market.
>
> After twenty days they leave for Majanna, and they spend ten days in
> its market, and when they see the new moon of Dhu al-Hijja they leave
> for Dhu al-Majaz, where they spend eight days and nights in its markets.
> They leave Dhu al-Majaz on the "day of tawarih," so called because they
> depart from Dhu al-Majaz for Urfa after they have taken water (for their
> camels) from Dhu al-Majaz. They do this because there is no drinking
> water in Urfa, nor in Muzdalifa.
>
> The "day of tawarih" was the last day of their markets. The people who
> were present at the markets of Ukaz and Majanna and Dhu al-Majaz were
> merchants, and those who wanted to trade, and even those who had
> nothing to sell and buy because they can go out with their families. The
> non-merchants from Mecca left Mecca on the "day of tawarih." (Azraqi
> 1858: 129)

It is not easy to make sense of this description, particularly in its relationship to the pilgrimage. Although the actual location of the markets is

uncertain, all the places mentioned seem to be close to Mecca—though, significantly, not *in* Mecca—and to be connected to the Hajj.[86] And the sequence seems carefully arranged, possibly by the Quraysh, so that no two occasions coincided: from the first to the twentieth of Dhu al-Qaʿda was the fair of Ukaz; from the twenty-first to the twenty-ninth, that of Majanna; from the first to the eighth of Dhu al-Hijja, that of Dhu al-Majaz; on the ninth and tenth the Hajj took place; and finally, from the eleventh to the thirteenth, the fair of Mina.[87]

Pilgrims on the pre-Islamic Hajj thus traded at various locations in the vicinity of the Hajj sites and, it seems likely, at Mina and Arafat as well, before performing their rituals, a practice that did not extend, as we shall see, to Mecca. Thus the wealth of the pre-Islamic Quraysh had nothing to do, as it certainly did in the Islamic era, with trading with pilgrims at Mecca during the Hajj season. If Meccans traded, they did so elsewhere, at the fairs outside of Mecca—fairs they did not control[88]—or else as a function of the regional trading network set up as a result of arrangements with the bedouin and the Quraysh's own status as a holy tribe, a condition that had been formally institutionalized not long before Muhammad's birth by the confederation known as *Hums*.

The *Hums*

The Meccan historian Azraqi provides a succinct definition of the pre-Islamic religious sodality that the Muslims later remembered as *Hums*:

> We are the people of the Haram. We do not leave the Haram. We are Hums, and the Quraysh become Hums and all who are born to the Quraysh. Humsis and the tribes that became Humsis with them were so called because they were strict fundamentalists in their religion, and so an ahmasi [sing.] is a man who is religiously conservative.[89] (Azraqi 1858: 115)

Ibn Ishaq adds many more historical and ritualistic nuances to the portrait:

> I do not know whether it was before or after the Year of the Elephant [traditionally, 570 c.e.] that the Quraysh invented the idea of Hums and put it into practice. They said, "We are the sons of Abraham, the people of the holy territory, the guardians of the temple and the citizens of Mecca. No other Arabs have rights like ours, or a position like ours. The Arabs recognize none as they recognize us, so do not attach the same importance to the outside country as you do to the sanctuary, for if you do, the Arabs will despise your taboo and will say 'They have given the same importance to the outside land as to the sacred territory.'" So they [the Hums] gave up the halt at Arafat and the departure from it, though they recognized that these were institutions of the Hajj and the religion of

Abraham. *They considered that other Arabs should halt there and depart from the place, but they said, "We are the people of the sanctuary, so that it is not fitting that we should go out from the sacred territory and honor other places as we, the Hums, honor that; for the Hums are the people of the sanctuary." They then proceeded to deal in the same way with the Arabs who were born within and without the sacred territory. Kinana and Khuzaʿa joined them in this.* (Ibn Ishaq 1955: 87)

The *Hums* were, then, fellow tribesmen of the Quraysh, the Kinana, the Khuzaʿa, and the Amir ibn Saʿsaʿa. They had embraced, or perhaps had even newly embraced, what is called "the religion of Abraham," which the members closely identified with the cult of the Kaʿba in Mecca, even to the exclusion of the other pilgrimage rituals, chiefly the Hajj, which was focused on places like Mina and Arafat.[90] On this view, and we have no reason to doubt it, the original Hajj had nothing to do with the "religion of Abraham," and the Quraysh as *Hums* did not recognize the Hajj because some of its rituals took place outside the Haram. This passage from Ibn Ishaq seems to draw the *Hums'* definition of the Haram somewhat short of Arafat.

The Hums used to say, "Do not respect anything profane and do not go outside the sacred area during the Hajj," so they cut short the rites of pilgrimage and the halt at Arafat, it being in the profane area, and would not halt at it or go forth from it. They made their stopping place at the extreme end of the sacred territory at Namira at the open space of al-Maʾziman, stopping there the night of Arafat and sheltering by day in the trees of Namira and starting from it to Muzdalifa. When the sun turbaned the tops of the mountains, they set forth. They were called Hums because of the strictness of their religion. (Ibn Ishaq 1955: 89)

These limited cult excursions outside of Mecca may have been by way of concession to some of the bedouin members of the sodality or to newcomers who found it difficult to break old habits. Other reports stress the *Hums'* narrower definition of their sacred zone as the area immediately around the Kaʿba, as in this from Muqatil ibn Sulayman:

The Hums—*they were Quraysh, Kinana, Khuzaʿa and Amir ibn Saʿsaʿa—said: "Safa and the Marwa do not belong to the sacred sites of Allah." In the Age of Barbarism there was on the Safa an idol named Naʾila and on the Marwa an idol named Asaf.[91] They [the Hums] said: "It is improper for us to make a turning (tawaf) between them," and therefore they did not make a turning between them.* (Muqatil, Tafsir, ms. 1.25b[92])

If we are to believe this, the *Hums* attempted, perhaps not entirely successfully,[93] to exclude even Safa and Marwa, within a stone's throw from the Ka'ba, from their own particular rites. Or perhaps not. Muslim commentators continuously sought to supply the historical background for the Quran's great number of verses without context. One such verse directly addresses Safa and Marwa and what appears to be a group of Meccans who hesitated to accept the cult there:

Safa and Marwa are among the indications of Allah. It is therefore no sin for him who is on pilgrimage to the House of God, or visiting it, to go round them. (Quran 2:158)

This is a classic example of a Quranic answer without the question. We, and Muqatil ibn Sulayman, must supply it: "Is it a sin to perform the *tawaf* around Safa and Marwa?" And its two possible implications: Is it or is it not permissible in your new religious system to continue the current practice of performing the "turning" between Safa and Marwa? Or, as a member of the *Hums* might ask: Must we discontinue our present "Abrahamic" practice and revert to the old pagan custom of running between Safa and Marwa? Muqatil's report neatly supplies the context of the Quran's unasked question: Muhammad was breaking with the *Hums'* characteristic limitation of Allah's ritual to the Ka'ba alone.

Confining cult rituals to the Haram of Mecca was only one aspect of *Hums* observance. There were also dietary and domestic taboos and a great deal of emphasis upon the clothes connected with the ritual:[94]

The Hums went on to introduce innovations for which they had no warrant. They thought it wrong to eat cheese made of sour milk or clarify butter while they were in a state of ritual taboo. They would not enter tents of camel-hair or seek shelter from the sun except in leather tents while they were in this state. They went further and refused to allow those outside the Haram to bring food in with them when they came on the great or little pilgrimage. Nor could they circumambulate the House except in the garment of the Hums. If they had no such garments they had to go round naked. If any man or woman felt scruples when they had no Hums garments, then they could go round in their ordinary clothes; but they had to throw them away afterwards so that neither they nor anyone else could make use of them. The Arabs called these clothes "the cast-off." They imposed all these restrictions on the Arabs, who accepted them and halted at Arafat, hastened from it, and circumambulated the House naked. The men at least went naked, while the women laid aside all their clothes except a shift wide open back and front. (Ibn Ishaq 1955: 87–88)

When the Quraysh let an Arab marry one of their women, they stipulated that the offspring should be an ahmasi following their religion. . . . The Hums strictly observed the sacred months and never wronged their protégés therein nor wronged anyone therein. They went round the

Ka°ba *wearing their clothes. If one of them before and at the beginning of Islam was in a state of taboo, if he happened to be one of the house-dwellers, that is, living in the houses or villages, he would dig a hole at the back of his house and go in and out by it and not enter by the door. . . . The year of Hudaybiyya the Prophet was entering his house. One of the Ansar was with him and he stopped at the door, explaining that he was an ahmasi. The Apostle said "I am an ahmasi too. My religion and yours are the same," so the Ansari went into the house by the door as he saw the Apostle do. (Azraqi 1858: 115)*

If the report of Muhammad's claim that he too was a member of the *Hums* has any credibility, it must refer to his claim to be an adherent of the "religion of Abraham." At Medina at least, he did not venerate the Quraysh or exclude Arafat from Islamic ritual, nor did he appear to practice any of the *Hums'* clothing taboos described by Azraqi.[95]

It is possible to approach the belief system of the *Hums* from another side. Among the liturgical chants called *talbiyya*—"We are present (*lab-bayka*), O Lord, We are present"—is one that purported to be the ritual cry of the *Hums*.[96] In it Allah is addressed not only as "Lord of the Ka°ba," as we might expect, but also as "Lord of Manat, al-Lat, and al-Uzza," and even as "Lord of Sirius." Both sentiments are expressed in the Quran: the first in references to the goddesses as the "daughters of Allah," a notion that was embraced on at least one occasion, that of the "Satanic verses"; and the second as part of a kind of credo (Quran 53:49) associated with a scriptural monotheist. Allah, we seem to be told in this *talbiyya*, was not the only god. But He was assuredly the master of the other gods, another sentiment exactly echoed in the Quran:

Do they attribute to Him as partners things that can create nothing but are themselves created? No aid can come from them, nor can they even aid themselves. If you call them for guidance, they will not obey. As for you, it is all the same whether you call upon them or hold your peace. In truth, those whom you call upon besides Allah are servants (of Allah) like yourselves. (Quran 7:191–194)

MUHAMMAD AND THE HAJJ

The Muslims of the first and second century after the Hijra looked back upon time of their ancestors before the revelation of Islam and labeled it the "Age of Barbarism." They laid upon it their own version of a "sacred history" that is merely hinted at in the Quran; the religious traditions of Mecca were to a large extent rewritten, or misrepresented, or simply forgotten in the light of new revelation that had annulled the beliefs and practices of an earlier age. Those beliefs and practices were, however, the milieu that, if it did not produce Islam, certainly bore witness to its birth, and so to attempt to reconstruct it is nothing less than to supply the context out of which Muhammad and God's Quran came.

The Religion Called *Tahannuth*

When Ibn Ishaq attempts to explain how and where Muhammad received his first revelations, he cites a tradition that lifts one corner of the veil that covers most of what might be called religion in pre-Islamic Mecca:

> The Prophet used to sojourn on Mount Hira for a month every year.[97] That was the tahannuth which the Quraysh used to practice in the period of the Age of Barbarism. The Prophet used to sojourn during that month every year, feeding the poor who called upon him.[98] After the conclusion of that month of sojourn, before entering his house, he would go to the Ka'ba and circumambulate it seven times or as many times as it pleased God. When the month came when God wished to grant him His grace, in the year when God sent him and it was the month of Ramadan, the Prophet went out to al-Hira as was his custom for his sojourn. With him was his family. (Ibn Ishaq 1955: 105)

The traditionist Bukhari (d. 870 C.E.) offers another, somewhat different version of this report, transmitted on the authority of Aisha, the Prophet's wife, who was not yet born when the event occurred.

> Then he was made to cherish solitude and he sojourned alone in the cave of al-Hira and practiced tahannuth a number of nights before he returned to his family; and he used to take provisions for it [the sojourn]. Then he would go back to Khadija and take provisions for a similar (period of sojourn). So things went till the Truth came upon him when he was in the cave of Hira. (Bukhari, The Sound 1.5[99])

There was, then, no complete agreement among the early authorities on either *tahannuth* or the Prophet's own practice, whether it was a shared annual custom or Muhammad's private devotion, whether he was solitary or accompanied by his family, whether or not it was in a cave, whether the devotions included feeding the poor.[100] Modern opinion, which early on noted these obviously important traditions about Muhammad's religious background, had no greater conviction than its medieval antecedents. But other texts, not generally noted in this connection, have come to light, and they somewhat enlarge our understanding of the pre-Islamic *tahannuth*. One describes Abd al-Muttalib as the man who initiated the practice.

He was the first who practiced tahannuth *at Hira. . . . When the moon of Ramadan appeared he used to enter Hira and did not leave till the end of the month and fed the poor. He was distressed by the iniquity of the people of Mecca and would perform circumambulation of the Ka'ba many times. (Baladhuri,* Ansab al-Ashraf *1.84[101])*

Another tradition from the same source speaks more generally of the Quraysh:

When the month of Ramadan began people of the Quraysh—those intending tahannuth—*used to leave for Hira and stayed there a month and fed the poor who called on them. When they saw the moon of Shawwal they (descended and) did not enter their homes until they had performed the circumambulation of the Ka'ba for a week. The Prophet used to perform it [this custom]. (Baladhuri,* Ansab al-Ashraf *1.105[102])*

Tahannuth was, then, a Quraysh practice in the month of Ramadan somehow connected with Mount Hira—how or why we do not know. It included both deeds of charity, such as feeding the poor or freeing slaves, and ritual acts, such as the circumambulation of the Ka'ba. It was, in a sense, a novelty, an innovation, or at least a complex of practices restricted to a few of the Quraysh. Nor was it the only unexpected turn in the religious life of Mecca. Another had to do with the cult of the Lord of the Ka'ba, Allah.

Pre-Islamic Monotheism

Allah, we can be sure, was neither an unknown nor an unimportant deity to the Quraysh when Muhammad began preaching his worship at Mecca. What is equally certain is that Allah had what the Quran disdainfully calls "associates": other gods and goddesses who shared both his cult and his shrine. The processional chant of the pagans of the Age of Barbarism was, we are told, "Here I am, O Allah, here I am; You have no partner except such a partner as You have; You possess him and all that is his."[103] The last clause may reflect what we have already seen was an emerging tendency toward henotheism, the recognition of Allah as the "high god" of Mecca. But it was not sufficient for Muslims, who put in its place their own manifestly monotheistic hymn: "Here I am, O Allah, here I am; You have no partner; the praise and the grace are Yours, and the empire; You have no partner."

On the prima facie witness of the Quran, it was Muhammad's preaching that introduced this new monotheistic urgency into the Meccan cult. The Quraysh are relentlessly chastised for "partnering God"; and from what we otherwise know of Muhammad's Mecca, the charge is not unjust. But a closer look reveals that the matter was by no means so simple. While he was still at Mecca,[104] Muhammad had begun to invoke the example of Abraham, as in this verse that establishes the continuity of the "religion of Abraham" through the line of the prophets to his own preaching:

> He has established for you the same religion that He enjoined on Noah—and which We revealed to you—and that He enjoined on Abraham, Moses and Jesus—namely, that you remain steadfast in the religion and make no divisions in it. (Quran 42:13)

The "religion of Abraham," to use a phrase that Muhammad began to invoke later at Medina, must not have been an unknown concept at Mecca. There are traditions that others in the city had connections with Abraham, connections that centered, as Muhammad's own did, on the Meccan Ka'ba, the House that Abraham built.[105] The statue of Hubal was inside the building during the Age of Barbarism, but the ritual performed there was the Abrahamic one of circumcision.[106] A great many Abrahamic associations, all of them pre-Islamic, clustered around the Ka'ba.[107]

The origin of these associations is difficult to trace through every stage of their development, but there are scattered signs along the way. It was widely known that the pre-Islamic Arabs circumcised their young, though not on the eighth day as the Jews did, and Josephus was confident that he knew where they had gotten the custom: the Arabs "circumcise after the thirteenth year because Ishmael, the founder of their nation, who was born to Abraham of the concubine (Hagar), was circumcised at that age."[108] Josephus was not telling his readers something of which they were unaware: that the Arabs were descended from the biblical Ishmael and had lapsed from their original faith into forms of idolatry was a commonplace in the history of both the post-Exilic Jews and the Christians,[109] though it is not nearly so certain that Muhammad shared this idea.[110]

The *Hanifs*

In emphasizing the Abrahamic strain in Islam, the Quran calls Abraham a *hanif,* a somewhat mysterious term,[111] but one that the Quran contextually identifies with *muslim* in referring to Abraham. Like Abraham himself, a *hanif* is explicitly distinguished from Jews or Christians on the one hand and from idolaters or "associators" on the other, all summed up in a single verse of the Quran:

Abraham was not a Jew, nor yet a Christian, but was a hanif, a muslim, and was not one of the "associators." (Quran 3:67)

And it is precisely in Abraham's footsteps as a *hanif* that Muhammad and his followers are commanded to worship God:

They say: "Become Jews or Christians if you want the guidance." You say: "No, I prefer the religion of Abraham the hanif, who was not one of the 'associators.'" (Quran 2:135)

God speaks the truth: follow the religion of Abraham, the hanif, who was not one of the "associators." (Quran 3:95)

Who can be better in religion than one who submits (aslama) his self to God, does good and follows the religion of Abraham the hanif, for God took Abraham as a friend. (Quran 4:125)

Muslim scholars took the word and its abstract noun, *hanifiyya*, in two senses: first, as a synonym for historical Islam, the religion revealed to Muhammad and practiced by Muslims; and second, in the sense that the Quran meant it, as a form of "natural" monotheism of which Abraham was the chief, though not the sole, practitioner. In this latter sense, the Muslim tradition recalled that there were in Mecca and environs just such monotheists without benefit of revelation before Islam. Ibn Ishaq presents them in what is obviously a schematized setting:

One day when the Quraysh had assembled on a feast day to venerate and circumambulate the idol to which they offered sacrifices, this being a feast which they held annually, four men drew apart secretly and agreed to keep their counsel in the bonds of friendship. They were Waraqa ibn Nawfal . . . ibn Jahsh . . . Uthman ibn Huwarith . . . Huwarith . . . and Zayd ibn Amr. . . . They were of the opinion that their people had corrupted the religion of their father Abraham, and that the stone they went around was of no account; it could neither see, nor hear, nor hurt, nor help. "Find yourselves a religion," they said; "for by God you have none." So they went their several ways in the lands, seeking the hanifiyya, the religion of Abraham.

Waraqa attached himself to Christianity and studied its Scriptures until he had thoroughly mastered them. Ubaydallah went on searching until Islam came; then he migrated with the Muslims to Abyssinia, taking with him his wife who was a Muslim, Umm Habiba, the daughter of Abu Sufyan. When he arrived there, he adopted Christianity, parted from Islam and died a Christian in Abyssinia. . . . After his death the Prophet married his widow Umm Habiba. Muhammad ibn Ali ibn Husayn told me that the Apostle sent Amr ibn Umayya to the Negus to ask for her and *he married him to her. He gave her as a dowry, on the Apostle's behalf, 400 dinars.*

Uthman ibn Huwarith went to the Byzantine emperor and became a Christian. He was given high office there.

Zayd ibn Amr stayed as he was: he accepted neither Judaism nor Christianity. He abandoned the religion of his people and abstained from idols, animals that had died, blood and things offered to idols.[112] He forbade the killing of infant daughters, saying that he worshiped the God of Abraham, and he publicly rebuked the people for their practices. (Ibn Ishaq 1955: 98–99)

This and similar accounts of "natural" monotheists have not been universally accepted by modern scholars. Some are doubtless the result of special pleading—for example, the stories surrounding Waraqa ibn Nawfal, Khadija's cousin, who serves as a kind of John the Baptist in the accounts of Muhammad's early revelations. But others ring quite true, particularly when they have to do with persons known to have opposed Muhammad to the end.[113] And if they are true, we have another important clue to the existence of what Johann Fück identified as "a national Arabian monotheism which was a preparatory stage for Islam and which, in any examination of the possible stimuli that made themselves felt on Muhammad, cannot be ignored."[114]

Two prominent opponents of Muhammad who are also described as *hanifs* are Abu Amir Abd Amr ibn Sayfi and Abu Qays ibn al-Aslat.[115] The first was a prominent Aws leader at Medina who was identified with the man behind the mysterious affair—mysterious to us, though doubtless well known to the Quran's audience—of the "mosque of schism" built at Medina "in preparation for one who warred against God and His Apostle aforetime" (Quran 9:107). According to Ibn Ishaq, Abu Amir used to practice *tarahhub* and was called *al-rahib*, both apparent references to the practice of some kind of Christian asceticism.[116] Other accounts connect his *hanifiyya* with beliefs and practices close to Jewish ones.

It appears, then, that *hanifiyya* was in fact the "religion of Abraham" extoled in the Quran, to which were connected, as we might well expect, a veneration of the Meccan Ka'ba, doubtless as the Holy House built by Abraham, and, perhaps crucially for the development of Islam out of this matrix, a devotion to the Quraysh as the authentic guardians of the sacred precinct in Mecca.[117] Where the *hanifs*, and Muhammad, may have differed from the Quraysh was in their refusal to "associate" other gods with the Lord of the Ka'ba, a difference that was apparently acceptable to the Quraysh. What eventually separated Muhammad from the *hanifs* was their view of the Quraysh. Far from accepting the Quraysh as the un-

touchable guardians of the Haram, Muhammad repudiated and attacked
them.

One *hanif* who had a direct and important connection with Muhammad was Zayd ibn Amr, the Meccan who resisted not only Judaism and
Christianity but even Islam. For for that very reason, reports about Zayd,
especially ones that put him in conflict with the Prophet, enjoy a higher
degree of probability than many other *hanif* stories. Ibn Ishaq's *Life* pre-
serves some of Zayd ibn Amr's poetry, and at least one poem gives us
some idea of how he rebuked the Quraysh for their idolatry. Both the
images and the ideas are similar to those expressed in the Quran—what
might perhaps be described as biblical monotheism—and apparently met
with equally negligible success.[118]

Ibn Sa'd reports a tradition concerning Zayd and how he worshiped:

> This [the Ka'ba] is the qibla of Abraham and Ishmael. I do not worship
> stones and do not pray toward them and do not sacrifice to them, and do
> not eat what is sacrificed to them, and do not draw lots with arrows. I will
> not pray toward anything but this House till I die. (Ibn Sa'd, Tabaqat
> 3.380)

If this sounds remarkably like the Prophet's own preaching—though
Muhammad may have wavered briefly on the prayer-direction—it is
likely Muhammad who learned it from Zayd rather than vice versa. According to a famous, though much edited, tradition,[119] the young Muhammad was the pagan and Zayd ibn Amr was the monotheist. That was
sometime before the beginning of the Prophet's revelations. In this version of the tradition the report comes from Zayd ibn Haritha, who was
present and later told the story to his son.

> The Prophet slaughtered a ewe for one of the idols (nusub min al-
> ansab); then he roasted it and carried it with him. Then Zayd ibn Amr
> ibn Nufayl met us in the upper part of the valley; it was one of the hot
> days of Mecca. When we met we greeted each other with the greeting of
> the Age of Barbarism, in'am sabahan. The Prophet said: "Why do I see
> you, O son of Amr, hated by your people?" He said, "This (happened)
> without my being the cause of their hatred; but I found them associating
> divinities with God and I was reluctant to do the same. I wanted (to
> worship God according to) the religion of Abraham." . . . The Prophet
> said, "Would you like some food?" He said, "Yes." Then the Prophet put
> before him the (meat of the ewe). He [Zayd ibn Amr] said: "What did
> you sacrifice too, O Muhammad?" He said, "To one of the idols." Zayd
> then said: "I am not the one to eat anything slaughtered for a divinity
> other than God." (al-Khargushi, Sharaf al-mustafa[120])

This tradition, in one form or other, is likely to be true, because it flies in the face of later Muslim sentiments about the impeccability of the Prophet even prior to his call. It confirms the information passed on by Ibn al-Kalbi, that Muhammad offered a ewe to al-Uzza "in accordance with the religion of the people."[121]

There were, then, monotheists at Mecca before Islam, and Muhammad, the man who practiced *tahannuth* on Mount Hira, would eventually be reckoned one of them. But what of the other beliefs and practices of Meccan paganism? Did Muhammad share them as well? On the face of the Quran's testimony, it would appear so. In some verses of the early Sura 93 and in the context of Muhammad's attempt to reassure himself, the Quran comes as close to providing a biographical sketch of the Prophet as it ever does.

> Did He not find you an orphan and give you shelter?
> Did He not find you erring and give you the guidance?
> Did He not find you in need and make you rich?
>
> (Quran 93:6–8)

Verse 7 is closest to our purpose here. The Arabic words for "erring" (*dalla*) and "guidance" (*hada*) leave little doubt that the "error" was not simply that Muhammad was confused but that he was immersed in the same reprehensible practices in which the Quraysh persisted even after God had sent the "guidance" to them as well.[122] Although this interpretation is confirmed by the story of Zayd ibn Amr's admonition and the tradition from Ibn al-Kalbi,[123] and there are other remarks and notices to the same point, the Muslim tradition found it increasingly difficult to accept that Muhammad had been, perhaps for most of his life before his call, a pagan. The doctrine of Muhammad's impeccability, grounded, like its Christian counterpart, Mary's perpetual virginity, on the principle of *quod decet*, began to affect exegesis. About a century after the Prophet's death, it was driving the older traditions of Muhammad's pre-revelational paganism out of the commentaries.[124]

The same point emerges from an investigation of the reading of another early sura, 108, which begins: "We have granted you the abundance, so pray to your Lord and sacrifice." The later exegetical tradition either understood "sacrifice" as a mere gloss on "pray" or else insisted that it was the Hajj sacrifice at Mina. But nothing in the Quran suggests that. And in fact, the Meccan suras never mention the Hajj. Sura 108 must clearly be read in conjunction with the firm repudiation of paganism in 109:

> Say: O you who are unbelievers, I do not worship what you worship, nor will you worship what I worship; And I will not worship what you

have been worshiping, nor will you worship what I worship. To you your
religion and to me mine. (Quran 109:1–6)

This is Muhammad's break with Meccan paganism, announced after the
beginning of his revelations and perhaps referring to his discontinuation
of the practice of making the Hajj,[125] but not, it would appear from Sura
108, of the customary sacrifices at Mecca.[126]

The Quraysh Rebuild the Ka'ba

In 605 C.E., when, if we follow the traditional chronology, Muhammad
was thirty-five years old, a memorable event occurred in Mecca: the reconstruction of the Ka'ba, the only stone building in that town. We follow Ibn Ishaq's account:

> The Quraysh decided to rebuild the Ka'ba when the Apostle was
> thirty-five years of age. . . . They were planning to roof it and feared to
> demolish it, for it was made of loose stones above a man's height, and
> they wanted to raise it and roof it because men had stolen part of the
> treasure of the Ka'ba which used to be in a well in the middle of it. The
> treasure was found with Duwayk, a freedman of the Banu Mulayh ibn
> Amr of the Khuza'a. The Quraysh cut his hand off; they say that the
> people who stole the treasure deposited it with Duwayk. . . .
> Now a ship belonging to a Greek merchant had been cast ashore at
> Jidda and became a total wreck. They took its timbers and got them ready
> to roof the Ka'ba. It happened that in Mecca there was a Copt who was
> a carpenter, so everything they needed was ready at hand. Now a snake
> used to come out of the well in which the sacred offerings were thrown
> and sun itself every day on the wall of the Ka'ba. It was an object of terror
> because whenever anyone came near it, it raised its head and made a rus-
> tling noise and opened its mouth, so that they were terrified of it. While
> it was thus sunning itself one day, God sent a bird which seized it and
> flew off with it. Thereupon the Quraysh said, "Now we may hope that
> God is pleased with what we propose to do. We have a friendly craftsman,
> we have got the wood and God has rid us of the snake." . . .
> The people were afraid to demolish the temple, and withdrew in awe
> from it. Al-Walid ibn al-Mughira said, "I will begin the demolition." So
> he took a pick-axe and went up to it, saying the while, "O God, do not
> be afraid.[127] O God, we intend only what is best." Then he demolished
> the part at the two corners. That night the people watched, saying, "We
> will look out; if he is smitten, we will not destroy any more of it and
> we will restore it as it was; but if nothing happens to him then God is
> pleased with what we are doing and we will demolish (the rest of) it." In
> the morning al-Walid returned to the work of demolition and the peo-

ple worked with him, until they got down to the foundation of Abraham. They came upon green stones like camel's humps joined one to another. . . .

I was told the Quraysh found in the corner a writing in Syriac. They could not understand it until a Jew read it for them. It was as follows: "I am Allah the Lord of Bakka. I created it on the day that I created heaven and earth and formed the sun and the moon, and I surrounded it with seven pious angels. It will stand while its two mountains stand, a blessing to its people with milk and water," and I was told that they found in "the place" (of Abraham) a writing, "Mecca is God's holy house; its sustenance comes to it from three directions; let its people not be the first to profane it." . . .

The tribes of the Quraysh gathered stones for the building, each tribe collecting them and building by itself until the building was finished up to the Black Stone, where controversy arose, each tribe wanting to lift it to its place, until they went their several ways, formed alliances and got ready for battle. The Banu Abd al-Dar brought a bowl full of blood, then they and the Banu Adi ibn Ka'b pledged themselves unto death and thrust their hands into the blood. For this reason they were called the "blood-lickers." Such was the state of affairs for four or five nights, and the Quraysh gathered in the mosque and took counsel and were equally divided on the question.

A traditionist alleged that Abu Umayya ibn al-Mughira, who was at that time the oldest man of the Quraysh, urged them to make the first man to enter the gate of the mosque umpire in the matter of the dispute. They did so and the first one to come in was the Apostle of God. When they saw him they said, "This is the trustworthy one. We are satisfied. This is Muhammad." When they came to him and informed him of the matter, he said "Give me a cloak," and when they brought it to him, he took the black stone and put it inside it and said that each tribe should take hold of an end of the cloak and they should lift it together. They did this so that when they got it into position he placed it with his own hand, and then building went on above it. (Ibn Ishaq 1955: 84–85)

Ibn Ishaq's is not the only version of the Ka'ba project.[128] According to al-Azraqi, Mecca's premier local historian, there was a particularly destructive flood in that year—not an implausible event, given the history of the town.[129]

Downpours were many, and Mecca had its share of torrential rains and floods. One of these flooded the Ka'ba and its walls were cracked to the point that the Quraysh were afraid on the one hand to use the place and on the other to destroy or rebuild it for fear that some evil would befall them. (Azraqi 1858: 107)

An Egyptian ship was wrecked near Shuʿayba, then the nearest port to Mecca on the Red Sea. One of the survivors was a Greek or Coptic carpenter, or perhaps more generally an artisan, named Baqum (Pachomios) who was capable of putting a new roof on the Kaʿba. The Quraysh, Muhammad among them, cooperated by collecting stones for the new edifice.

When it came time to tear down the remains of the old building, a certain anxiety arose, and it was done only by a divine sign—a bird flew over and removed the serpent that had protected the sanctuary and its treasure for more than 500 years. One of the older Quraysh, who explained he had nothing to lose, began the work, but the others held back until they saw that nothing had happened. Nothing, that is, until they reached the Abrahamic foundations. When they tried to remove these lightening struck and an earthquake shook Mecca. They left them alone. The four factions among the Quraysh each built its own side. It was on that occasion that the door, formerly on ground level, was raised. When it was time to replace the stone they had to summon "Amin," the trustworthy Muhammad, to adjudicate. He used his mantle as described by Ibn Ishaq and all were satisfied.

Baqum then built the roof and inside made pictures of the Prophets, including Abraham and Mary and the Child Jesus. The "golden gazelle" and treasures which were kept in the house of Abu Talha during the reconstruction and the idols, stored in the Zamzam, were returned to their accustomed places inside the Kaʿba.

Elsewhere Azraqi supplies some additional details on the representations inside the reconstructed Kaʿba, which now included "pictures of trees and pictures of angels."

There was a picture of Abraham as an old man and performing divination by the shaking of arrows, and a picture of Jesus son of Mary and his mother, and a picture of angels. On the day of the conquest of Mecca, the Prophet entered the House and he sent al-Fadl ibn al-Abbas to bring water from Zamzam. Then he asked for a cloth which he soaked in water, and ordered all the pictures to be erased, and this was done. . . . Then he looked at the picture of Abraham and said, "May God destroy them! They made him cast the divining arrows. What does Abraham have to do with divining arrows?"

Ata ibn Abi Rabah said that he saw in the House a decorated statue of Mary with a decorated Jesus sitting on her lap. The House contained six pillars . . . and the representation of Jesus was on the pillar next to the door. This was destroyed in the fire at the time of Ibn al-Jubayr. Ata said he was not sure that it was there in the time of the Prophet but he thought it was. (Azraqi 1858: 111)

The Prophet at Medina

In the year 610 of the Christian era, when he was, according to the traditional chronology, forty years of age, Muhammad received his divine call to prophecy. After some hesitation he followed his supernatural vocation and began to preach the message of the Oneness of God and the certainty of a Final Judgment to his fellow Meccans. Revelation followed revelation—they were all finally collected in the Quran—but he enjoyed little success in his native place. Indeed, it is not unlikely that he would have been killed by his increasingly implacable enemies had he not won some following in Yathrib, an oasis some 270 miles to the north, and accepted an offer to migrate there in 622 C.E. At Yathrib, later called Medina, "The City (of the Prophet)," Muhammad enjoyed political success, and with it power, the power to enact policies regarding his new religious insights. One of the most striking and significant of these was his divinely inspired decision to change the direction of prayer. Earlier he had, like the Jews, faced Jerusalem in prayer; but shortly after his arrival in Yathrib-Medina, and probably in reaction to a Jewish refusal to accept his prophetic claims, he changed the prayer-direction (*qibla*) for all Muslims away from Jerusalem and toward the Ka'ba in Mecca.

THE UMRA FULFILLED

Did the change of the *qibla* betoken some modification of Muhammad's attitude toward the rituals at Mecca? We cannot know. Muhammad was cut off from both the city and its rituals for six years after his migration to Medina. Not until 628 C.E., amid growing signs of the success of his mission, did he take action: somewhat abruptly, he announced his intention of making the Umra that year. He did not, however. He was blocked at a place called Hudaybiyya, where the Quraysh finally agreed that he might freely return to the city the following year. Muhammad turned and equally abruptly led a successful raid on the Jewish oasis of Khaybar.

The point of Hudaybiyya was not forgotten, however, in the successful flush of Khaybar. Muhammad still intended to make the Umra.

When the Messenger returned from Khaybar to Medina he stayed there from the first Rabi' until Shawwal, sending out raiding parties and expeditions. Then in Dhu al-Qa'da—the month in which the polytheists had prevented him from making the pilgrimage (in the preceding year)—he went out to make the "fulfilled pilgrimage" in place of the 'umra from which they had excluded him. Those Muslims who had been excluded with him went out in A.H. 7 [February 629 C.E.], and when the Meccans heard it, they got out of his way. The Quraysh said among themselves, "Muhammad and his companions are in destitution, want and privation."

A man I have no reason to suspect told me that Ibn Abbas said: "They gathered at the door of the Dar al-Nadwa to look at him and his companions, and when the Prophet entered the sanctuary he threw the end of his cloak over his left shoulder leaving his right upper arm free. Then he said, 'God have mercy on a man who shows them today that he is strong.' Then he embraced and kissed the stone and went on trotting, as did his companions, until the point where the temple concealed him from them, and when he had embraced and had kissed the southern corner he walked to kiss the Black Stone. Then he trotted in the same fashion for three circuits and walked the rest."

If the somewhat tortured manner of expressing the ritual actually performed by the Prophet on the occasion of this Umra suggests that other considerations were later steering the passage, Ibn Ishaq immediately confirms the suspicion: early on, likely in the generation after Muhammad, there had been a debate about the ritual of circumambulation, or perhaps only the "embracing and kissing" (istalama) part of it.

Ibn Abbas used to say, "People used to think that this practice was not incumbent on them because the Prophet only did it for this clan of the Quraysh because of what he had heard about them until the Farewell Pilgrimage, when he adhered to it and the sunna carried it on." (Ibn Ishaq 1955: 530–531)

The issue of the ritual of a Muslim Hajj was determined, then, at least according to Ibn Abbas's report, by Muhammad's "customary practice" (sunna), here defined by his ritual acts during the famous Farewell Pilgrimage in March 632 C.E, the only pilgrimage the Prophet ever led in person.

Circumambulation was not the only legal problem connected with the Umra of February 629. There is strong evidence that Muhammad offered the customary animal sacrifices on this occasion.[130] And more, he took another wife, an act that was, according to one report, consummated while the Prophet was in a state of *ihram* or ritual purity, when normally all sexual acts were forbidden.[131] Ibn Ishaq allows the reader to have it both ways.

The Messenger married Maymuna daughter of al-Harith on that journey when he was in a state of ihram. (His uncle) al-Abbas ibn Abd al-Muttalib gave her to him in marriage [and probably became a Muslim at the same time]. The Messenger remained three days in Mecca. Huwaytib ibn Abd al-Uzza with a few Quraysh came to him on the third day because the Quraysh had entrusted him with the duty of sending the Messenger out of Mecca. They said, "Your time is up, so get out from among us." The Messenger answered, "How would it harm you if you were to let me stay and I gave a wedding feast among you and prepared food and you came too?" They replied, "We don't need your food, so get out." So the Messenger went out and left Abu Rafi' his client in charge of Maymuna until he brought her to him in Sarif. (Ibn Ishaq 1955: 531)

The Hajj of Year 9

The Apostle remained there [in Medina] for the rest of the month of Ramadan and Shawwal and Dhu al-Qa'da. Then he sent Abu Bakr in command of the Hajj in the year 9 (of the Hijra) to enable the Muslims to perform their Hajj while the polytheists were at their pilgrimage stations. Abu Bakr and the Muslims then duly departed. (Ibn Ishaq 1955: 617)

The rest of this chapter of Ibn Ishaq's *Life* is devoted to a lengthy explanation of another momentous change in the relations between Muslims and non-Muslims, a change signaled, the tradition asserts, in the verses of Sura 9 revealed on this occasion. Which verses, however, and in what order is a highly complex and difficult question:[132]

A declaration of immunity from God and His Apostle is given to the pagans with whom you have contracted alliances.

Go about safely in the land for four months and know that you cannot frustrate God, and that God is about to humiliate unbelievers.

And a proclamation from God and His Apostle on the Day of the Great Pilgrimage—that God and His Apostle dissolve treaty obligations with the pagans.

Except those pagans with whom you made treaties and who have not afterward failed you in any regard and have not supported anyone against you. As for them, respect their treaty till the end of their term. God loves those who obey.

And when the sacred months are passed, kill the pagans wherever you find them, and take them and surround them and lie in wait for them in every spot. But if they repent, and observe the ritual prayers and pay the alms-tithe, then leave them alone. God is forgiving, compassionate. (Quran 9:1–5)

There was a final caution sounded in Sura 9. If the nonbelievers were excluded from the pilgrimage, would this not threaten the livelihood of the Muslims of Mecca?

It is not for the pagans to operate [or "visit"] the shrines of God while they witness against their own souls to disbelief. The works of such bear no fruit; they shall dwell in fire. The shrines of God shall be operated [or "visited"] by such as believe in God and the Last Day, establish ritual *prayer, contribute the alms-tithe and fear God. It is they who are the truly guided. . . .*

O believers, truly the pagans are unclean; so let them not approach the sacred shrine after this year (of grace) of theirs. And if you fear poverty (as a result), God will enrich, if He wills it, out of His own bounty. For God is all-knowing, all-wise. (Quran 9:17–18, 28)

These Quranic announcements were made, according to the traditional chronological sequence, upon Muhammad's return from Tabuk in 630 C.E., and they mark his final break with paganism. Previously, the Prophet had conducted political relations with the pagans, or "associators" (*mushrikun*), as he invariably calls them. He had concluded treaties with them, and non-Muslims had even taken part in his raids and shared the booty that came from them.[133] No longer. The pagans were to be granted a respite of four months; thereafter they would be killed wherever the Muslims encountered them.[134]

There was, of course, another option: they might convert and become part of the new, entirely Muslim political order. The community (*umma*) had been redefined, as we have just seen, to include only Muslims, and the terms of membership mandated the institution of liturgical prayer (*salat*) and the payment into the community treasury of the *zakat*, an alms-tithe to the Muslims but transparently a tax to those being threatened with conversion or extinction.

Later Muslims were somewhat uncertain about many elements of this tradition, including precisely who made the announcement.[135] Some traditionists said it was Abu Bakr or Abu Hurayra; others, as might be expected in a community where the division between Sunni and Shi'ite ran deep, maintained that it was Ali ibn Abi Talib:

Abu Bakr, during the pilgrimage which he conducted, before the Pilgrimage of Farewell, sent Abu Hurayra, among others, to announce on the day of the sacrifice that no polytheist would make the Hajj and that no naked person would perform the tawaf. (Bukhari, The Sound 5.212)

The consequence is set out in another tradition:

Abu Bakr broke the treaties of the peoples in that year, and in the year of the Pilgrimage of Farewell during which the Prophet made his pilgrimage, no pagan performed the Hajj. (Bukhari, The Sound 4.124)

And again, on the reputed testimony of Abu Hurayra, and in a manner calculated to save the Abu Bakr version and yet assert Ali's claim:

Abu Bakr sent me among the heralds which he sent during that pilgrimage, on the day of sacrifice to announce at Mina that no pagan would perform the Hajj after that year and that no naked person would perform the circumambulation. Meanwhile the Prophet sent after us Ali ibn Abi Talib, ordering him to announce the temporary immunity. Ali announced with us the immunity to the people at Mina on the day of sacrifice and that no pagan would perform the Hajj after that year and that no naked man would perform the circumambulation. (Bukhari, The Sound 6.81)

And finally, according to Azraqi, it was on the occasion of his reentry into Mecca in 630 that Muhammad also reestablished the boundaries of the greater *haram* of Mecca, which went back to Abraham's day but had been tampered with by the Quraysh. They were set at one hour out on the Medina road; three hours on the Yemen road; five hours on the Ta'if road; three hours on the road to Iraq; and four hours on the Jir'rana road. These were renewed by Muhammad's second successor, Umar, and then once again by Umar's successor, Uthman.

The Pilgrimage of Farewell

The months for the Hajj are well known. If anyone undertakes that duty during them, let there be no obscenity, nor wickedness nor wrangling during the Hajj. And whatever good you do, God knows it.

Take provision with you for the journey, but the best of provisions is righteous conduct. So fear Me, you who are wise. (Quran 2:197)

The Quran had thus simply commanded that the Hajj be made, "during the well-known months"; that it was "a duty men owe to God," everyone, that is, "who is able to afford the journey" (3:97). The command was, then, a plain and direct one, doubtless on the correct assumption that the parties addressed were well acquainted with this pre-Islamic ritual. But as we have seen, the rite was complex even at the beginning, and its complexities assured that a later generation of Muslims would have a host of questions on the subject. The Quran had already addressed some of them, the case of an interrupted pilgrimage, for example:

Complete the Hajj or Umra in the service of God, but if you are prevented, send a sacrificial offering from what is available; do not, however, shave your heads [that is, signal the completion of the obligation] until the offering reaches the place of sacrifice. But if any of you becomes ill (after formally beginning the rites) or has a scalp ailment (requiring shaving), he should compensate by either fasting or feeding the poor. (Quran 2:196)

As the verse itself reveals, the ritual complexities of the Hajj might be considerable (later they spawned an entire guild of guides to assist the pilgrim through them). As on other issues, the answers were sought among the *hadith*, the reported utterances of the Prophet himself, and more particularly those that clustered around the so-called Farewell Pilgrimage in 632 C.E.

We know little of Muhammad's connection with Meccan rituals, including the Hajj, either before or after his call to prophethood, though it seems safe to assume that he took part in the rituals of his native city.[136] Once removed to Medina, he was obviously in no position to participate in any of the cultic observances in Mecca and its vicinity, not, at any rate, until the month of Dhu al-Qaʿda (February) 629, when, as we have seen, he was permitted to perform the Umra as part of a general political settlement concluded at Hudaybiyya. Mecca fell in January 630. Although Muhammad performed the Umra in March of that year, he did not participate in the Hajj. In March 631 the Hajj was led by Abu Bakr, and Muhammad was once again absent. Thus it was not until Dhu al-Hijja (March) in 632 C.E., the year of his death, that Muhammad went on what was to be his first and final Hajj as a Muslim.[137]

Needless to say, the details of this pilgrimage were later lovingly recalled: they served as the foundation of all future performances of this ritual, which is a solemn obligation upon all Muslims.[138] But despite all this apparent attention, ambiguities remain. Various suras of the Quran, notably the second, third, and ninth, contain detailed prescriptions concerning both the Hajj and the Umra and their relationship; and there is a disagreement, as we shall see, among the traditionists on whether these were delivered in connection with Abu Bakr's Hajj of 631 or on the occasion of the Prophet's own Farewell Pilgrimage in 632.

What there is no disagreement about in the tradition is that the Prophet delivered a discourse on the occasion of his final pilgrimage and that it covered instruction on the performance of the pilgrimage as well as detailed prescriptions on a great variety of subjects. Ibn Ishaq preserved one version in his *Life of the Messenger of God*:

> In the beginning of Dhu al-Qaʿda the Messenger prepared to make the pilgrimage and ordered his men to get ready. Abd al-Rahman ibn al-Qasim from his father, from Aisha, the Prophet's wife, told me that the Messenger went on pilgrimage on the 25th of Dhu al-Qaʿda [20 February 632 C.E.]. (In its course) the Messenger showed men the rites and taught them the customs of the Hajj. (Ibn Ishaq 1955: 650)

The pilgrimage was in fact a pre-Islamic custom of long standing, with its own rituals and customs. The Prophet took what he found, discarded some elements of the cult, reshaped others, and integrated whatever was suitable into a new, specifically Muslim Hajj. At the end of Muhammad's sermon, for example, Ibn Ishaq records a tradition that shows the Prophet clarifying and redefining the sacred territory, the "stations," connected with the pilgrimage.

Abdullah ibn Abi Najih told me that when the Apostle stood on Arafat he said: "This station goes with the mountain that is above it and all Arafat is a station." When he stood on Quza on the morning of Muzdalifa he said: "This is the station and all al-Muzdalifa is a station." Then when he had slaughtered in the slaughtering place in Mina he said, "This is the slaughtering place and all Mina is a slaughtering place."

Then Ibn Ishaq adds his own concluding summary, reprising what he had said at the outset:

The Apostle completed the Hajj and showed men the rites and taught them what God had prescribed as to their Hajj, the "standing," the throwing of stones, the circumambulation of the temple and what He had permitted and forbidden. It was the pilgrimage of completion and the pilgrimage of farewell because the Apostle did not go on pilgrimage after that. (Ibn Ishaq 1955: 652)

If Ibn Ishaq chose not to include in his *Life* many details of how the Prophet "showed men the rites and taught them" the customs of the Hajj, the details of that instruction were preserved in the canonical collections of *hadith*, like these on the subject of *ihram*, the state of ritual purification:

Ibn Umar said (on the authority of the Prophet), the months of the Hajj are Shawwal and Dhu al-Qaʿda and the first ten days of Dhu al-Hijja. And Ibn Abbas said, it is the custom (of the Prophet) that a man shall not enter the state of ritual purity (ihram) except in the months of pilgrimage. (Bukhari, The Sound 25.34)

The state of *ihram* is a highly complex one and raised many uncertainties, beginning with where precisely the taboo state should be entered:

Ibn Abbas said that the Prophet—may God bestow peace and blessings upon him—appointed for the people of Medina [that is, people coming from Medina] Dhu al-Hulayfa as the place where they should enter the state of ihram; for the people of Syria, Juhfa; for the people of Najd, Qarn al-Manazil; and for the people of the Yemen, Yalamlam. These are for them and for those who come upon them from other places, for those who have taken a decision to perform the Hajj and Umra. And for whoever is on the nearer side of these points, the appointed place (for ihram) is where he starts, so that for the people of Mecca it is Mecca. (Bukhari, The Sound 25.7)

Ibn Umar reported about the Prophet—may God bestow peace and blessings upon him—that a man once asked him, what should a man wear in the state of ihram? He answered, "He shall not wear shirt, nor turban, nor trousers, nor headgear, nor any dyed cloth; and if he cannot find footwear, then let him wear leather stockings, but cut off so that they may be lower than the ankles." (Bukhari, The Sound 3.53)

Ibn Abbas said, someone in a state of ihram may smell sweet-smelling plants, and look in a looking-glass, and use comestibles as medicines, like olive oil and butter; Ata said, he can wear a ring and carry a purse. When Ibn Umar made the circumambulation while in the state of ihram he girdled his middle with a cloth. Aisha's opinion was that there was no harm in wearing underpants. (Bukhari, The Sound 25.18)

Ibn Umar reported that he heard the Prophet—may God bestow peace and blessings upon him—forbidding women in the state of ihram the wearing of gloves, a veil, and dyed garments, and (adding) that besides these they might wear whatever they liked of garments colored with safflower, or made of silk, or ornaments or trousers or shirt. (Abu Dawud, The Custom 11.29)

Aisha said, we went out intending only the Hajj, and when we reached Sarif I began menstruating. The Messenger of God—may God bestow peace and blessings upon him—came to me and I was weeping. He said, "What is the matter with you? Are you menstruating?" I said I was. He said, "This is a matter that God has ordained for the daughters of Adam, so do what the (other) pilgrims do, except do not circumambulate the House." (Abu Dawud, The Custom 6.1)

Although they cannot be dated with precision, the Quran too has verses that seem to offer clarification on ritual points of the pilgrimage. Sura 22, for example, presents extensive and detailed instruction on the sacrifices performed during the Hajj and specifically addresses the question—which remains, as often, unasked in the body of the Quran but unmistakably underlies the answer—as to whether it is permitted to eat the flesh of the animals offered for sacrifice:

You are permitted (to eat) the sacrificial animals, except those specified (as prohibited), but shun the abomination of idols and shun the word that is false.
In them [the sacrificial animals] you have benefits for a term appointed; in the end their place of sacrifice is near the Ancient House.[139] To every people did We appoint a place of sacrifice, that they might celebrate the name of God over the sustenance He gave them from animals. (Quran 22:33–34)

For your benefit We have made the sacrificial camels one of the signs from God; there is good for you in them. So pronounce the name of God over them as they line up (for sacrifice), and afterwards as they lie slain, eat of them and feed such as already have food and such as beg in *humility. Thus have We made animals subject to you, that you might be grateful.*

It is not their meat or their blood that reaches God; it is your piety that reaches Him. He has thus made them subject to you, that you may glorify God for the Guidance He has given you.[140] *(Quran 36–37)*

HAJJ AND UMRA

Among the other consolidations attempted by the Prophet during his Pilgrimage of Farewell was the combination of the two previously independent rituals of the Umra and the Hajj, a topic already touched upon in the Quran. The verse in question seems to envision an interrupted Umra being attached to a Hajj:

And when you are in a state of security, if anyone wishes to resume (tamatta') the Umra into the Hajj, he must make an offering such as he can afford; but if he cannot afford it, he should fast three days during the Hajj and seven days on his return, ten days in all. This is for those whose household is not in the Sacred Precinct. (Quran 2:196)

That would obviously never do as a general instruction, and the *hadith* attempted to fill out the picture, like this portmanteau specimen passed down by Ibn Umar and preserved by Bukhari:

On the Farewell Pilgrimage the Messenger of God—may God bestow peace and blessings upon him—profited by combining the Umra with the Hajj. . . . So he performed the circumambulation when he arrived in Mecca. The first thing he did was to kiss the corner (in which the stone was embedded), then he ran the first three turns around the Ka'ba and then walked the next four. When he had finished the circumambulation of the House, he said two "prostrations" of prayer near the Station of Abraham. Then he pronounced the taslim formula, and when he had finished he went to Safa and made the circumambulation of Safa and Marwa seven times, after which nothing that was forbidden to him in the state of ihram was lawful for him until he had completed the Hajj, had sacrificed his animal on the Day of Sacrifice, and returned and once again circumambulated the House: then everything that was forbidden to him in the state of ihram became lawful for him. (Bukhari, The Sound 25.104)

The Umra, we have seen, was primarily a Meccan feast that consisted chiefly in a ritual circumambulation of the Ka'ba and the sevenfold "running" between Safa and Marwa, and it was brought to a formal end by the sacrificing of animals at Marwa, whereafter the pilgrim shaved his head and left the purified state.[141] It was a solemn and independent ritual, or rather, complex of rituals, since the rites of the Ka'ba and those of Marwa and Safa might themselves once have been distinct. Whatever the case, the rites of the Umra and the Hajj were distinct rituals in the eyes of Muhammad and of the early Muslims, and they were apparently celebrated by the Arabs at two different seasons of the year, the Umra in the fall and the Hajj in the spring,[142] as they were in the year Muhammad made his Farewell Pilgrimage.

ISLAMICIZING THE HAJJ

The process of converting the Umra and the Arafat festivals from a pagan into a Muslim ritual was not accomplished of a sudden at the pilgrimage of 632. The Medinese suras of the Quran are filled with instruction and remarks linking Abraham and Ishmael not merely with the Ka'ba but with the rituals of the Hajj as well. Attention has already been drawn to the following verses of Sura 22, which appear in the form of a command to Abraham after he had finished building the Ka'ba.

Announce to the people the pilgrimage. They will come to you on foot and on every lean camel, coming from every deep and distant highway that they may witness the benefits and recollect the name of God in the well-known days (ayyam ma'lumat) over the sacrificial animals He has provided for them. Eat thereof and feed the poor in want. Then let them complete their rituals and perform their vows and circumambulate the Ancient House.

Such is it [the pilgrimage]. Whoever honors the sacred rites of God, for him is it good in the sight of his Lord. (Quran 22:27–30)

The Quran merely suggests. The later Muslim tradition hastened, as we have already seen, to fill in the details explaining how Abraham, and indeed Adam before him, had initiated the Hajj.[143] Whatever modifications Muhammad undertook, the tradition asserted, represented a restoration of the original form of the Hajj.

The third verse of Sura 9 of the Quran, which has already been cited in connection with the Hajj of year 9 (630 C.E.) contains what it itself announces is a formal proclamation (*adhan*):

And a proclamation from God and His Apostle on the Day of the Great Pilgrimage—that God and His Apostle dissolve treaty obligations with the pagans. If you repent, it is better for you. But if you turn your backs, then know that you cannot frustrate God. Inform those who disbelieve of a painful punishment.

Although the surrounding verses might plausibly be assigned to the pilgrimage led by Abu Bakr in 631 C.E., this one appears to be the fulfillment of the prior warning that *thereafter* the pagans would be excluded from the Hajj. Here the pagans are informed of the ban. The presence of pagans at a Hajj during which Muhammad himself led the Muslim contingent doubtless troubled many of the ancient authorities, who preferred to keep all forms of paganism distant from the Prophet. More disturbingly for the traditional assignment of this verse to the pilgrimage of the previous year, there is no very convincing reason for calling Abu Bakr's the "Great Hajj." The ancient commentators sensed the difficulty as well.

CHAPTER II

Mecca and
the Ways Thither

CHANGES IN THE HARAM

THE FIRST TWO successors of the Prophet at the head of the new and rapidly expanding Muslim community ruled by what might reasonably judged a consensus of that community. But with the accession of Uthman (r. 644–656 C.E.), the third of these Caliphs, as they were called, the divisive forces of ambition and dissatisfaction made their violent appearance. Uthman was murdered by political rivals, and his successor, Ali (r. 656–661), likewise came to a violent end at the hand of an assassin. Other members of the same Umayyad family to which Uthman had belonged then ascended to power, a long series of them between 661 and 749 C.E. They ruled not from Medina, however, but from Damascus. The Holy Cities were in effect abandoned politically, to be possessed, inevitably, by the forces of opposition to the regime.

Rebuilding the Ka'ba

The passage of power from the first Umayyad, Mu'awiya (r. 661–680), to his family was not an easy one. At Mu'awiya's death there was opposition to the accession of his son Yazid, opposition that eventually led to insurrection by members of the family of Ali under the banner of the Prophet's own grandson Husayn, the younger son of Ali and Fatima. Yazid destroyed the unfortunate Husayn and his supporters at Karbala in Iraq in 680, an event that won him the undying hatred of the Alids and their supporters everywhere. Yazid himself died in 683 and was succeeded by his thirteen-year-old son Mu'awiya (II), whose rule lasted only forty days. The weakness of an unpopular ruler all but invited revolt, and Umayyad governors were expelled from Basra and Kufa. In Mecca, amidst a rising tide of insurrection, Abdullah ibn al-Zubayr, the son of an early hero of Islam, proclaimed himself the genuine Caliph.

Ibn al-Zubayr had revealed his designs even before the death of Yazid, and the ailing Caliph in Damascus had sent against him an army under the command of Husayn ibn Numayr. The Umayyad forces took Medina from Ibn al-Zubayr's supporters without much difficulty, and then in August 683 they began the siege of Mecca. Stones and torches were cast down upon the city from the nearby slopes of Abu Qubays. Ibn al-Zubayr's troops took shelter in tents inside the Haram. The tents took fire, and soon the Ka'ba itself was in flames.[1]

After two months of siege, news arrived from Damascus of the death of Yazid and the uncertainties of the succession. The troubled Syrian army soon moved off; and in the peaceful interval that followed, Ibn al-Zubayr took thought of rebuilding the Ka'ba.

When the army of al-Husayn ibn Numayr left Mecca on the 24th of Rabi' I in the year 683, Ibn al-Zubayr called upon the elite of the people and questioned them on whether he should tear down (and rebuild) the Ka'ba. Many of them advised him against tearing it down. It was 'Abdullah ibn Abbas who said that he should leave it as is, as the Prophet had, because he feared that (destroying it) would set a precedent for future generations to tear it down and rebuild it. So he advised him (merely) to renovate it instead.

Ibn al-Zubayr answered: "By God, there is no one among you who will not mend the house of his parents, so how do you wish me to do otherwise with God's House, when I watch it fall apart piece by piece? When even the pigeons sit on its walls, the stones fall down."

Ibn al-Zubayr asked around for advice for days, and finally he resolved to tear down the building. He wished to be the one to rebuild it, according to what the Prophet said, on the foundations of Abraham and in the manner in which the Prophet had described it [that is, Abraham's Ka'ba] to Aisha.

The problem, of course, was that sometime before his first revelations Muhammad himself had participated in the reconstruction of the Ka'ba by the pagan Quraysh in a manner somewhat different from Abraham's original. It was on that occasion, according to a tradition transmitted by Aisha, that Muhammad said, "If your people [the Quraysh] had not just recently given up their pagan beliefs, I would have destroyed the Ka'ba and rebuilt it, restoring what they had omitted." It was on those grounds, then, that Ibn al-Zubayr decided to proceed.

He wanted to build it with wars.[2] He sent to the Yemen for the wars but was told that it breaks and disintegrates and rather to build it with gypsum mortar. And he was told that the gypsum from San'a was the best and so he sent 400 dinars to buy gypsum from San'a and ordered that it be done quickly. He then asked some learned men from Mecca where the Quraysh got their stones and he was told of their stone quarry and so he got all that he needed.

When the stones were collected and he was ready to begin the demolition, the Meccans evacuated the city and went to Mina, where they stayed because they were afraid a punishment would befall them for demolishing it. When Ibn al-Zubayr ordered the work of demolition to begin, no one dared to do it. When he saw this, he climbed it himself, took up the pick and started dismantling it himself. When the rest saw that nothing had happened to him, they got up to assist him.

They demolished it with the help of the people, and by the time the sun was descending, the building walls were leveled to the ground on all sides. This took place on Saturday, the fifteenth of II Jamada in the year 64 [8 February 684 C.E.]. . . . Ibn al-Zubayr, since he was asked by name not to leave them without a qibla, put up around the Ka'ba a wooden frame to which he attached cloth curtains so that the people could circumambulate outside it and pray.

The burning question, of course, was: Would the new, rebuilt Ka'ba be authentic? Ibn al-Zubayr invoked the best possible testimony on both his right to undertake the project and the size and shape of the new construction.

Ibn al-Zubayr said: I bear witness that I have heard Aisha say: The Prophet said: "Your people [the Quraysh] diminished the House when they built it because they could not afford the expense (of rebuilding it on Abraham's foundations). So they reduced it by some cubits in the direction toward the Hijr. And but for the fact that till recently they were unbelievers, I would myself demolish the Ka'ba and restore the reduced dimensions. I would also make two doors for it (opening) down at ground level, one toward the east for people to enter and one to the west for people to exit. And do you know [Muhammad continued] why your people raised the door (above ground level)?" Aisha said she did not. Muhammad said: "To make sure that no one but whom they wished would enter it. If they disliked a certain person's entering it, they would allow him to climb up and then, when he was about to enter, they would push him away and he would fall to the ground. If it should ever seem good to your people to demolish the Ka'ba (and rebuild it), come let me show you how much they cut off on the side toward the Hijr." And Muhammad showed them about 7 cubits.

A chance discovery then added an additional note of verification to Ibn al-Zubayr's project to restore the Ka'ba to its original form. The very foundations of Abraham's edifice were unearthed:

When Ibn al-Zubayr had leveled the Ka'ba, he discovered the foundations of Abraham which extended into the hijr about six cubits and ten inches and were constructed like the linked necks of camels or intertwined fingers so that if the hijr was moved, all the other corners would move with it.

He started building on that foundation and put the threshold of the door of the Ka'ba atop one layer of marble close to ground level, and he located the back door in the same manner—the threshold consisted of the long green marble stone—this (latter) in the back of the Ka'ba close to the Yemeni corner. And the building went on behind the curtains even as the people were circumambulating outside it. The building reached the height where the Black Stone[3] had to be put in its place. Ibn al-Zubayr, when he was demolishing the (old) House, had wrapped the Stone in a brocade and then placed it in a chest which he kept in his residence in the Dar al-Nadwa. He had also taken all the decorations that were in the Ka'ba and put them in the Ka'ba vault in the house of Shayba.

When the (new) building reached the level of the Black Stone, Ibn al-Zubayr ordered that it be placed between two courses of stone . . . , carved out to match (the size of the Black Stone). When the place was prepared, Ibn al-Zubayr ordered his son Abbad ibn Abdullah along with Jubayr ibn Shayba to put the Stone in a cloth. Ibn al-Zubayr instructed them: "When I begin praying the noon prayer, you carry it out and put it in its place." . . . When the prayer was begun and Ibn al-Zubayr had made his first prostration, Abbad came out of the Dar al-Nadwa carrying the Stone, and Jubayr ibn Shayba was with him. They passed through the rows of people praying and entered the curtain surrounding the building. The one who put the Stone in its place was Abbad ibn Abdullah and he was assisted by Jubayr ibn Shayba.

The Stone had been cracked by the fire into three parts. (In addition) a splinter had chipped off it and it was preserved by some of the Banu Shayba for a long time after that. Ibn al-Zubayr held it together with silver nails, except for the splinter from off its top, whose position is clear at the top of the Stone. The length of the Stone (rukn) is two cubits and it occupies the thickness of the Ka'ba wall. The rear face inside the wall is carved something like a molar tooth with three roots. Ibn Jurayj said: "I heard some who described the color of its rear face inside the wall. Some said it was rosy, others said it was white." (Azraqi 1858: 140–144)

A later visitor to Mecca, the Spanish poet and *littérateur* Ibn Abd Rabbihi (d. 940), passed on a tradition about an inspection of the Black Stone in Ibn al-Zubayr's day:

A narrative has been related on the authority of a Meccan who traced it up to the learned doctors of that city through an uninterrupted chain of transmitters, to the effect that they examined the Black Stone at the time when Ibn al-Zubayr pulled down the house and extended it. They measured its length and found it to be three cubits. They also found it to be *of an intensely white color except on its external side. Its blackness is said to have been due—and God knows best—to the touches and kisses it has received from the pagan Arabs and to (their) smearing it with blood. (Iqd 3.298 = Shafiʿ 1922: 428)*

Azraqi's narrative continues:

He built the Kaʿba twenty-seven cubits in height and it consisted of twenty-seven courses of stone, and the thickness of the wall is two cubits. Inside he put three pillars, while in the Age of Barbarism the Quraysh had six pillars. Ibn al-Zubayr sent to Sanʿa for the marble known as balaq and he put it on the apertures that are on the ceiling for light. The entry to the Kaʿba used to be by a single-panel door, but he made a double door with a height of eleven cubits from the ground to the top, and he made the back door the same size. . . . Inside he made a wooden ladder at the Syrian [northwestern] corner whereby to ascend to the roof. When Ibn al-Zubayr was done building it, he aromaticized it inside and out, top to bottom, and he draped it with (the Egyptian linen cloth known as) qubbati. (Azraqi 1858: 145)

"A GATE OF PARADISE": THE DISCOVERY OF THE TOMB OF ISHMAEL

Another remarkable event occurred during the reconstruction of the Kaʿba, nothing less than the discovery of the burial place of Ishmael in the *hijr*, the area at the northwestern face of the Kaʿba:

Abu al-Walid told us that he had heard from his grandfather, who heard from Khalid ibn Abd al-Rahman, (a tradition going back to) al-Mubarak al-Hassan al-Anmati, to wit, "I saw Umar ibn Abd al-Aziz in the hijr and I heard him say that once Ishmael had complained to God of the heat of Mecca. God revealed to him that 'I will open a gate of Paradise for you in the hijr. A breeze will blow upon you from it from now until the Day of Judgment.' And that was the place in the hijr where Ishmael died." Khalid said that the opinion was that the area between the roof-gutter and the western opening of the hijr is where his tomb is located.

Abu al-Walid told us that he (further) heard . . . that Ibn al-Zubayr had the hijr dug up and discovered a basket of green stones. He asked the Quraysh about them but none of them knew anything. So he sent for Abdullah ibn Safwan and asked him. Ibn Safwan said, "That is the tomb of Ishmael, so do not move it." So Ibn al-Zubayr left it where it was. (Azraqi 1858: 219–220)

When the constructions were complete, Ibn al-Zubayr and his followers performed the Lesser Pilgrimage with great pomp and splendor,[4] though with some innovations:

When he circumambulated around the Ka'ba, Ibn al-Zubayr touched all four corners, saying, "The touching of these two corners, the Syrian and the western, was abandoned (by the Quraysh) because the house was incomplete (without the space included from the hijr)." The House remained as Ibn al-Zubayr built it, with people touching all the (four) corners as they circumambulated, and entering the House through the eastern door and exiting through the western door, with the doors fixed at ground level, until Ibn al-Zubayr was killed. (Azraqi 1858: 144–145)

Despite Ibn al-Zubayr's political insurrection, the Hajj continued to be conducted under a truce amidst the hostilities. At the pilgrimage of 688, we are told, four different standards were shown at Arafat without bloodshed: those of Ibn al-Zubayr, the Kharijites, and the Shi'ites, and finally, that of the Umayyads' Syrian troops, which were attempting to dislodge the rebel from the Holy City.[5]

THE SIEGE-HAJJ OF 692

Initially, Ibn al-Zubayr's insurrection had been directed against a sickly and ineffective Yazid, but two years later the Caliphate was in the hands of Abd al-Malik ibn Marwan (r. 685–705 C.E.). In 691 he entrusted the suppression of the revolt to al-Hajjaj ibn Yusuf (661–714 C.E.), a loyal and tough soldier and administrator who had already crushed resistance to the Umayyad regime in Iraq and Iran.

Abd al-Malik ibn Marwan entered Kufa after (the rebel) Mus'ab was killed. He remained there for some days, then directed an army (to proceed) against Ibn al-Zubayr in Mecca. He placed al-Hajjaj ibn Yusuf al-Thaqafi at its head. Al-Haytham ibn al-Aswad al-Nakha'i came (to Abd al-Malik) and said, "O Commander of the Faithful, direct this Thaqafi servant to take care with the Ka'ba. Order him not to startle off its birds and not to tear asunder its veils and not to bombard its stones (with the mangonel), but rather to corner Ibn al-Zubayr in (Mecca's) ravines and tunnels until he dies there of hunger or leaves it and is deposed." Abd al-Malik told al-Hajjaj, "Do that, avoid the Haram and camp in Ta'if."

Al-Hajjaj set out and reached Ta'if. He then wrote to Abd al-Malik, "If you ignore Ibn al-Zubayr, keep your hands from him, and do not order me to contest with him in battle, then his numbers and equipment will increase. So permit me to do battle with him." Abd al-Malik wrote back to him, saying, "Do whatever you think is appropriate." Al-Hajjaj then ordered his men to prepare to make the Hajj. He then came from Ta'if and sent forward the front part of his army, who set up the mangonel (manjaniq) on Abu Qubays. (Baladhuri, Ansab al-Ashraf 5.357–358)

The move, we are told, was a deception. The rest of the troops thought they were going to make the Hajj; only when they reached Mina did they realize that a catapult had been set up to bombard the city. Abd al-Malik meanwhile sent the commander Tariq ibn Amr with an additional five thousand men to join the two thousand under Hajjaj's command. They arrived in January 692, and the siege of the city began at the end of March.

The eighth day of Dhu al-Hijja, and so the formal opening of the Hajj, fell on 1 May 692. The siege was lifted, or at least the bombardment was stopped, and both sides made gestures at undertaking the pilgrimage.

Al-Hajjaj led the pilgrimage that year since Ibn al-Zubayr was besieged. Tariq ibn Amr's arrival in Mecca (for the pilgrimage) took place on the new moon of Dhu al-Hijja. Al-Hajjaj did not circumambulate the Ka'ba, nor did he go to it in the ihram. He wore a sword but (like a pilgrim) did not approach women or use perfume until Abdullah ibn al-Zubayr was killed. Ibn al-Zubayr sacrificed camels in Mecca on the day of sacrifice [the tenth of Dhu al-Hijja], but neither he nor his companions performed the pilgrimage that year because they did not stand at Arafat.[6]

According to al-Waqidi . . . from the father of Sa'id ibn Muslim, who said: "I made the pilgrimage in the year 72 [692 C.E.]. We came to Mecca and entered it from the upper part of the city. We found the forces of Hajjaj and Tariq between al-Hajun [the site of the cemetery of Mecca] and Bir Maymun. We circumambulated the Ka'ba and (performed the 'running') between Safa and Marwa. Then Hajjaj led the pilgrimage. I saw him making the 'standing' at the hills of Arafat, on horseback, wearing a coat of mail and a neck protector. Then he went back. I saw him turn off toward Bir Maymun. He did not circumambulate the Ka'ba. His men were armed. I saw that they had a great deal of food, and I saw a caravan coming from Syria carrying food: biscuit, barley meal, and flour. I saw that his forces had plenty to eat." (Tabari, Annals 2.830–831 = Tabari XXI: 207–209)

As soon as the pilgrims departed, the fighting resumed. Ibn al-Zubayr, we are told, did not lack for allies, some of them, like the bedouin volunteers, not much to his liking. Some were sent away. Others abandoned him, including the Abyssinians, who grew weary of the fighting, and the Kharijites, radical sectarians whose cursing of the Caliph Uthman the renegade Ibn al-Zubayr, for all his anti-Umayyad sentiment, found intolerable. His supplies, moreover, were running short, and the bombardment from the slope of Abu Qubays was having an effect.

Hisham ibn Urwa's father said, "The stones of the mangonel were thrown at the Ka'ba until the kiswa became rent like the openings at the bosom of a woman's blouse. A dog was hurled by the mangonel at the Ka'ba and it toppled a pot in which we were cooking bulgar. We took the dog and found that it was fleshy (and so we ate it); it was more filling for us than the bulgar."

Uwana said that the Ka'ba was hit so often that it became shaky and fragile. A cloud with lightning and thunder appeared in the sky and a bolt of lightning hit the mangonel, burnt it and killed twelve of the people operating it. That terrified the Syrians and they stopped fighting. Al-Hajjaj said, "I am a native of the Tihama, and it is a land where thunder-bolts are frequent. So do not be frightened of what you see. (Generations) before you used to make offerings and a fire would be sent down and it consumed the offering. That was a sign that the offering had been ac-cepted." He then brought up another mangonel and the bombardment continued. (Baladhuri, Ansar al-Aashraf 5.362)

The Syrians pressed in until Ibn al-Zubayr and his men were cornered in the Haram. Tabari's account continues, here based on the alleged testi-mony of an eyewitness:

I saw the gates (of the Haram) filled with Syrians on Tuesday, and Ibn al-Zubayr's forces gave up their watch stations. The enemy outnumbered them and set men, a commander and troops from one country, at every gate: troops from Hims held the gate facing the door of the Ka'ba; troops from Damascus held the Banu Shayba gate; troops from the Jordan held the Safa Gate; troops from Palestine held the Banu Jumah Gate; and troops from Qinnisrin held the Banu Sahm Gate. Al-Hajjaj and Tariq were together at the lowest part of the hollow [the valley bottom] and Marwa. Ibn al-Zubayr would attack sometimes in one area and some-times in another. (Tabari, Annals 2.849 = Tabari xxı: 229)

The morning of Tuesday, the 17th of I Jumada [4 October 692], al-Hajjaj seized the gates from Ibn al-Zubayr. Ibn al-Zubayr had spent most of the night praying. Then he sat with his legs braced against his belly with the shoulder belts of his sword and slept lightly. He awoke at dawn and said, "Give the call to prayer, Sa'd." The latter thereupon gave the call to prayer beside the Station (of Abraham).

After his prayers and a brief address to his troops, Ibn al-Zubayr once again took up his arms.

He attacked the enemy and got as far as Hajun. A brick was hurled at him and struck him in the face; he was shaken by it and his face began bleeding. . . . Then the enemy gathered together against him.

So Ibn al-Zubayr fell, and it was Tariq ibn Amr who provided his epitaph:

When the news (of Ibn al-Zubayr's death) reached al-Hajjaj, he prostrated himself. Together with Tariq ibn Amr, he went and stood over
him. Tariq said, "Women have borne none manlier than he." Al-Hajjaj
said, "Will you praise one who disobeys the Commander of the Faithful?"
"Yes," said Tariq. "He has freed us from blame; were it not for his (valor),
we would have no excuse. We have been besieging him for seven months.
He had no defensive trench, no fortress, no stronghold; yet he held his
own against us as an equal, and even got the better of us whenever we met
with him." Their words were reported to Abd al-Malik, who declared
Tariq right. (Tabari, Annals 2.850–851 = Tabari xxi: 229–232)

THE RESTORATION OF AL-HAJJAJ

So the Haram was once again in the hands of the Umayyads, though with
considerable damage to the shrine. Almost immediately, the question of
the reconstructed Ka'ba arose. Abdullah ibn al-Zubayr's head was sent to
Damascus, together with a request for instructions.

When al-Hajjaj entered Mecca he wrote to Abd al-Malik ibn Marwan
that Ibn al-Zubayr had added to the House what does not belong to it,
and that he had introduced into it a second door. Abd al-Malik wrote
back to him, "Close the western door that was opened by Ibn al-Zubayr,
and tear down what he has added to it from the hijr, and use the material
to restore the building to the way it was." Al-Hajjaj demolished six cubits
and one span of it from (the part) next to the hijr, and he rebuilt it on the
diminished foundation of the Quraysh, and closed it with the material
from the demolition. He closed up the door that was in the back of the
building and left everything else untouched. (The result is that) to this
day everything in the building was built by Ibn al-Zubayr except for the
wall in the hijr, which was built by al-Hajjaj. He closed off the door that
was in its back as well as the area from under the threshold of what is
today the eastern door down to ground level, (a space which) measures
four cubits and one span. This is all of what al-Hajjaj built. The step
inside (the Ka'ba) and the double door that are there today were also built
by al-Hajjaj. (Azraqi 1858: 145–146)

The struggle over the Ka'ba was one of authenticity—one door or two,
ground-level or elevated entry, connection with or separation from the
semicircular *hijr* wall to the northwest—matters we are in no position to
judge. In question was not Muhammad's Ka'ba, of course—the Prophet
had nothing to do with the design of the building—but the extent to
which the Quraysh in pre-Islamic days had departed from Abraham's design. There were traditions one way and the other on the subject, though
we cannot say whence they arose. The point was conservatism, preserving
the received architectural tradition, much as Zerubbabel and the return-

ing Israelites attempted to do vis-à-vis the Temple of Solomon.[7] The Haram has been remodeled many times, most recently and massively by the Saudis in 1957; but the Ka'ba in its midst, what the nineteenth-century Dutch Orientalist Snouck Hurgronje called "a monument of old Arabia preserved with antiquarian solicitude," remains much the same structure it became when Muhammad assisted in its reconstruction. The changes introduced by Ibn al-Zubayr are only a vivid memory.[8] Even Abd al-Malik and his son al-Walid (r. 705–715), both prodigious builders in the Abode of Islam, contented themselves with simply beautifying the Haram. Uthman's low outer wall was raised and turned into a covered portico—as it has remained, in one form or another, ever since—and adorned in some parts with gilt, marble facing, and mosaics.[9]

Harun and Zubayda

The fall of the Umayyads finally came about in 749 C.E., and they were succeeded by the Abbasids. The Abbasids too ruled their empire far from the Holy Cities; but unlike the Umayyads, they made frequent pilgrimage there and put huge sums into the expansion and adornment of both Mecca and Medina. The chroniclers of both the city, like Azraqi, and of the Abbasid Caliphs, like Tabari, are filled with stories of the Abbasids' architectural and personal investment in the Hijaz cities and the Hajj, and the most generous and pious among them were the celebrated Harun al-Rashid (r. 764–809 C.E.) and his almost equally celebrated wife, Zubayda. The historian Mas'udi (d. 956) quotes an earlier historian's summary of their generosity:

> Harun al-Rashid was scrupulous in fulfilling his duties as a pilgrim and in waging Holy War. He undertook public works, the construction of wells, cisterns, and forts on the road to Mecca as well as inside that latter city and in Mina, Arafat, and Medina. . . . The epitome of generous charity in this same reign was manifested in the person of Umm Ja'far Zubayda, the daughter of Ja'far and the granddaughter of (the Caliph) Mansur. This princess had numerous caravanserais built in Mecca and she filled this city and the pilgrim road which bears her name with cisterns, wells, and buildings that still stand today. (Mas'udi, Muruj 8.294)

The tracks across steppe areas are generally determined by the pace of the traveler and the presence or absence of water near the limits of a day's march. Water sources are scattered thinly over much of the peninsula, and so transhumance, travel, and even commerce were possible across the steppe, from the Iraqi sown lands, for example, into the Hijaz, or from the Persian Gulf littoral into the lava lands of Syria.[10] The coming of Islam, which soon turned Medina into a capital city and Mecca into the object of pilgrimage, put a new premium on crossing the steppe. At first we hear few details of it, though people must have been passing to and fro between Mecca and Medina and the new settlements in Syria and Iraq, whether with an army or on pilgrimage. But it is not surprising to discover, when details are given—on Ali ibn Abi Talib's march from Medina to Kufa in 656, for example, or his son Husayn's 679 trek from Mecca to his own destruction in Iraq—that most followed the same line of "stations" that later constituted the central section of the main pilgrimage route between Kufa and the Hijaz: Rabadha, Hajir, Fayd, Zarud, Tha'alabiyya, Zubal, and Aqaba.[11]

There are not many signs that the Umayyads paid particular attention to this route. Their power was, after all, based in Syria and not Iraq. But with the accession of the Abbasids in 749 and the shift in power from Damascus to Baghdad, there was a new interest in facilitating the passage between Kufa (along with Basra further south, the jumping-off point for the voyage across the steppe) and the Holy Cities of the Hijaz. In 751, the very first of the Abbasid line, al-Saffah (r. 749–754), ordered that fire signals and milestones (amiyal) be established all the way from Kufa to Mecca.[12] All we know about Mansur's (r. 754–775) efforts is that he built some forts along the route, but al-Mahdi (r. 775–785) was active in clearing and leveling the way to the Holy Cities. The passage could be made so quickly—at least under demonstration circumstances—that al-Mahdi had ice delivered to him in Mecca from Iraq during his pilgrimage in 776.[13]

In 777 al-Mahdi undertook a grander and more practical enterprise on behalf of the Iraqi pilgrims.

> In this year [161 A.H. = 777–778 C.E.] al-Mahdi ordered the building of castles [qusur, fortified posts] on the road to Mecca more extensive than the castles that Abu al-Abbas (al-Saffah) had built from Qadisiyya to Zubala, and he ordered that Abu al-Abbas' castles should be enlarged, and he left the staging posts that Abu Ja'far (al-Mansur) had built as they were. He ordered the building of reservoirs at each watering place and the renewal of milestones and cisterns and the building of watering troughs with the reservoirs. He put Yaqtin ibn Musa in charge of this, and he continued with it until the year 171 [787–788 C.E.].[14] (Tabari, Annals 3.486)

Finally, al-Mahdi connected Mecca with the Yemen by the imperial post service (barid).[15]

> In this year [166 = 781–782 C.E.] al-Mahdi ordered the establishment of the post between the city of the Prophet [Medina] and Mecca and the Yemen by mule and camel, and the post had not been established there before. (Tabari, Annals 3.517)

One reason for the early Abbasids' interest in the Hajj route from Iraq was their own penchant for leading the Hajj in person. Harun, for example, began his reign with the avowed intention of leading the pilgrimage to Mecca and the holy war against the Byzantines in alternative years.[16] He did not achieve his scheme, but he did make the pilgrimage on six (or, according to others, nine) separate occasions.[17] His final one in 804 was, as it turned out, the last Hajj ever performed by a Caliph. His wife, Zubayda, made five or six pilgrimages, the first in the company of Harun, when, in fulfillment of a vow, he made his notorious Hajj of 790 entirely on foot, though the path across the steppe was cushioned for him with woolen mats spread out along the way.[18]

Husband and wife were both lavish in their gifts to the Holy Cities, but Zubayda's name in particular is attached to two projects long remembered by grateful pilgrims: her provision of abundant drinking water for Mecca, and her improvements along the Kufa-Hijaz route. We are far better informed on the queen's waterworks than on her benefactions along the pilgrims' way, but her name is firmly attached to that latter, and later pilgrims and travelers called the route from Kufa to the Holy Cities simply "Zubayda's Way" (*darb Zubayda*).[19] We are told that she built water tanks, wells, residences, and rest stops at ten sites, and perhaps more, along the way, and three major stations were named after her.[20]

THE PATHS TO MECCA

The medieval Abode of Islam appears to be filled with travelers, not merely the rich and the powerful like Harun and Zubayda, but simple pilgrims attempting to fulfill their religious obligation to make the Hajj to Mecca at least once in their lives. They are mostly mute, those plain Hajjis, but some at least of the Muslims in constant motion across the Islamic lands were considerable literary men who later fashioned their journeys into books. But they too were often pilgrims as well, and three of the most important of them have left circumstantial accounts of not only Mecca but also, since they were professional travelers, of the ways thither. All three of them—Nasir-i Khusraw (Hajj of 1050), Ibn Jubayr (Hajj of 1184), and Ibn Battuta (Hajj of 1326)—will be cited at length in this chapter and the following.

Whereas travel literature is a personal statement, there also exists in Arabic a body of geographical writing not limited to personal experience but committed to the more general purpose of describing the entirety of the Abode of Islam, with a particular emphasis on its roads and their stations. The very earliest example of the genre, by Ibn Khurdadhbih (d. 893–894), is in fact called *The Book of Routes and Provinces*, as are many of its successors, including those of Istakhri (ca. 951) and Ibn Hawkal (ca. 977). Some are rather dry repertoires; but others, like the *Book of Countries* by Ya'qubi (d. 891–892) and the *Finest Structure in the Knowledge of Climes* by al-Muqaddasi (d. 988–989), are filled with social, historical, and architectural information of great interest, though the description of any given place is generally more succinct than that by one of the professional travelers.

All of these authors were obviously interested in the Holy Cities and Holy Land of Islam, though from different perspectives. Ibn Hawkal, for example, here attempts to lay out the routes and distances between the Holy Cities of Mecca and Medina and other centers in the Abode of Islam:

> These then are the distances in the interior (of Arabia). From Kufa to Medina is about twenty stages. From Medina to Mecca is a distance of ten stages by the main road. From Kufa (directly to Mecca) is a route which is about three stages shorter (than if you go by way of Medina): at the entry to the native place of the Naqra this road turns from the direction of Medina to end up at the native place of the Banu Sulaym, then to Dhat Irq and then to Mecca. The road from Basra to Medina is eighteen stages and crosses the Kufa road in the vicinity of the native place of the Naqra. The road from Bahrayn to Medina is about fifteen stages; that from Raqqa is about twenty stages . . . and the distance is the same from Damascus to Medina and from Palestine to Medina. From Egypt to Medina, following the coast, is twenty stages. Travelers (from Egypt) meet those coming from Syria at Aila. Pilgrims from the Maghrib join the Egyptians, but at times their respective caravans travel separately, though with common way-stations. (Ibn Hawkal 1964: 1:39)

"Stages" is, of course, a rather imprecise measure of distance. It is, presumably, the distance covered by a caravan in one day. That distance is generally reckoned at twenty-four or twenty-five miles, where a mile is counted at a thousand paces. The distance can be converted into time if we accept Richard Francis Burton's equation:

> I have estimated the pace of a Hijazi camel, laden and walking in caravan line, under ordinary circumstances, at two geographical miles an hour. A sandy plain or a rocky pass might make a difference of half an hour each way, but not more. (Burton 1893: 1:244)

To maintain this pace, then, the caravan traveler was in the saddle—or litter—for twelve hours out of every twenty-four. We return to Ibn Hawkal:

> The pilgrims from Egypt and Palestine, when they have passed Midian [the northwestern Hijaz], have a choice of two routes to arrive at Medina.

The first is by Bada and Shaghb, a fortress in the desert which the Umayyads had granted to Zuhri and where his tomb is located, and from there you reach Medina by way of Marwa. The other route goes along the coast and comes to Juhfa, where there meet the pilgrims from Iraq, Damascus, Palestine and Egypt. The route from Raqqa is no longer used in our day, and there are only very small groups of Arab [perhaps here = bedouin] pilgrims who accomplish the pilgrimage in small units. With that exception, all the other routes are used for passage. (Ibn Hawkal 1964: 1:39–40)

From Aden to Mecca takes nearly a month of travel. There are two routes: one along the coast, which is the longer. This is the Great Road of the Tihama. Whoever takes it passes through San'a, Sa'da, Jurash, Bisha, Tabala and so arrives at Mecca. The other route, different from the Tihama way, goes by way of the flatlands and it is called Sudur. It follows the edge of the mountains for about twenty stages; it is thus the shorter. It passes through the tribes and settlements of the Yemen and is the way taken by notables.

The inhabitants of the Hadramawt and Mahra cross their land to reach the main route between Aden and Mecca, and this traverse takes twenty-two stages, with the result that their entire trip (to Mecca) lasts more than fifty days.

The route from Oman crosses the desert and is a difficult one by reason of the desolation of the region and the lack of inhabitants. Their only way (of getting to Mecca) is going by sea to Jidda because if you go across the flatlands of the coast of Mahra and the Hadramawt as far as Aden or the Aden route, the trip is too long. So it is only rarely used. The same is true of the way from Oman to Bahrayn: it is a bad road and is little practical because of the internal quarrels among the Arabs (along the way). (Ibn Hawkal 1964: 1:49)

This is a large view of the Hajj routes, calculated in the main from their distant points of origin. But the greatest difficulties of the trip were not so much in those outlying stages as in the interior routes of Arabia, and particularly, as we shall see below, within the Hijaz itself.

THE WAYS FROM IRAQ

We begin with the great pilgrim roads from Iraq to Medina and Mecca. The chief Iraqi point of departure for the nine-hundred-mile trek to the Holy Cities was Kufa. There the pilgrim struck out upon the already noted Darb Zubayda, "Zubayda's Way," so called because of the improvements financed by Harun al-Rashid's queen in the early ninth century.[21] As we have seen, the Iraqi path to Mecca across the north Arabian steppe began to draw official attention and, quickly, royal investment under the early Abbasids. Milestones, fire beacons, wells, cisterns, forts, and rest stations dotted the various stages along the route. Even before Zubayda, the way from Iraq to Mecca and Medina was clearly the best furnished—and most carefully protected—of all the Hajj roads.

Its protection may also have been the road's curse. The increased ease and speed of the journey and the very public examples of the early Abbasid Caliphs, who often made the pilgrimage in person, all encouraged a growing number of pilgrims to make the long journey through central Arabia. And with the growth in the number and wealth of the pilgrims inevitably came the increased attention of the predatory bedouin who lived along the route. Serious trouble began to be reported as early as the Caliphate of al-Wathiq (r. 842–847 C.E.), and thereafter the Sulaym, Asad, Hilal, Tayy, Harb, and Khafaja bedouin all show up in the historians' accounts of troubles along the way.[22] The remedies were the standard ones: send troops or money. But the obvious vulnerability of this long thin line through the desert, with its exposed water sources, meant that such measures would be only partially successful.

To the bedouin depredations in the ninth century were added the somewhat more ideologically motivated attacks of the Qarmatians in the tenth.[23] The Qarmatians, who in 930 C.E. took and sacked Mecca and carried off the Black Stone,[24] were bold enough and strong enough to attack not only passing pilgrim caravans but even the fortified stations built to protect those voyagers.[25] With the accession of the Buyids in Iraq, and particularly Adud al-Dawla (r. 978–982), the threat to the pilgrims along the Darb Zubayda appears to have abated, and the work of restoring the facilities at imperial expense was taken up again.

In the course of time, there came to be two routes from Iraq, depending on whether one took up the journey across the desert at Kufa or Basra. The first, the Darb Zubayda, passed through Fayd just to the south of Hayl in the Jabal Shammar region; the more southern Basra route passed by Dirʿiyya, the later Saudi capital. The two routes came together at Dhat Irq, two days out of Mecca to the northeast.[26]

The itineraries, stop by stop, are laid out in the various "Roads of the Realm" books of the ninth century, but a far more graphic appreciation is provided by actual travelers over those roads, as we shall see. The Iraqi caravan set out, then, from Kufa or Basra and generally crossed the Najd to Medina, though an Iraq-Mecca route was not unknown. For the rest of the circuit, Medina to Mecca and return, the caravan kept its integrity, though it was possible to switch into and out of it. Ibn Jubayr, for example, arrived from Egypt by boat, went up in nondescript company to Mecca, and, after completing his Hajj there, joined the Iraqi caravan in

1184 for its trip back to Medina and subsequently remained with it on its return to Baghdad. Ibn Battuta, on the other hand, came to Medina in 1326 with the Syrian caravan from Damascus. He continued with that company on the Darb al-Sultani to Mecca (see below), but for his return he switched to the Iraqi caravan, with whom he went back to Medina and thence on to Kufa and Iraq.

The Panorama of the Iraqi Caravan

Both Ibn Jubayr and Ibn Battuta left panoramic views of the Iraqi caravan after their departure from Mecca for Medina. Here is Ibn Jubayr's description:

This assemblage of people of Iraq, Khurasan and Mossul, as well as those of other countries who have joined them to accompany the Amir of the Hajj, made up a crowd whose number is known to God alone. The vast plain (at Khulays) was filled with them, and the flat immensity of the desert was too narrow to encompass them. You could imagine the earth attempting to maintain its balance under the crowd's heaving and waves streaming from the force of its currents; you could picture in this crowd a sea swollen with waves, whose waters were the mirages and whose ships were the camels, their sails the lofty litters and round tents. They all went forward gliding in and out of a great rising of clouds of dust, their sides colliding as they passed. On the immense extent of the plain you could see the thrust of a crowd filled with pain and fright and the knocking together of litters. Who has not seen with his own eyes this Iraqi caravan has not experienced one of the genuine marvels of the world worth the effort of describing and whose telling can seduce the listener by its marvelous character.

Consider what happens if one of the travelers assigned to a section of the caravan should have to leave it without taking note of a landmark to guide him back to his place. He would lose his way, would perish, and be reckoned among those lost in the desert. Occasionally distress of this type brings one of the travelers to the tent of the Amir to request his assistance. The latter sends one of his information officers, one of those who have been appointed to pass on his orders, to find out the traveler's name, the name of his cameleer and of his country, and then to take him up behind him on his camel and make a circuit of the noisy mob. This officer announces all that in a loud voice, pointing out the lost person, giving the name of his cameleer and country until, perchance, the cameleer happens upon him and takes the man back into his own hands. If it does not happen that way, that is the end of the man's arrangement with his cameleer, unless he later happens upon him by chance along the way.

Another marvelous thing about this caravan is that, despite its huge size, which constitutes it a world unto itself, after the baggage has been unloaded and people are in their campsites, once the Amir has the drums called kus sounded to signal the departure, between that moment and the one when the camels are loaded with their packs, their saddles and their riders, the interval is no longer than the time it takes to twice say "No." Scarcely have they been sounded the third time and the animals are on the road. This is the result of firm planning and the detailed precautions that are taken for the trip.

This caravan travels at night to the light of torches, which people on foot carry in their hands, and you will not see one litter which is not preceded by a torch. Thus people travel as it were among wandering stars which illuminate the depth of the darkness and which enable the earth to compete in brightness with the stars of heaven. (Ibn Jubayr 1949–1951: 213–215/Ar. 184–186)

As we shall see, Ibn Battuta came to Mecca with the Syrian caravan from Damascus; but he left eastward, in the company of the Iraqi caravan headed across the Darb Zubayda:

On the twentieth day precisely of Dhu al-Hijja [17 November 1326] I went out of Mecca in company with the commander of the caravan of Iraq, the Pehlewan Muhammad al-Hawih,[27] a man of Mossul, who occupied the office of commander of the pilgrims after the death of Shaykh Shihab al-Din Qalandar. Shihab al-Din was an open-handed and worthy man, who was held in high honor by his sultan, and used to shave his beard and eyebrows after the fashion of the Qalandaris.[28]

When I left Mecca (God Most High ennoble her) in company with the above-mentioned Amir Pehlewan, he hired for me the half of a double litter as far as Baghdad, paying its cost from his own purse, and took me under his protection.

We went out to the Bottom of Marr, after performing the farewell circuit with a host of men of Iraq, Khurasan, Fars and other eastern lands, of uncountable multitude, (so many that) the earth surged with them (as the sea surges) with dashing waves, and their advance was like the march of high-piled clouds. Anyone who left the caravan for natural want and had no mark by which to guide himself to his place could not find it again for the vast number of people. Included in this caravan were many water-carrying camels for the poorer pilgrims, who could obtain drinking water from them, and other camels to carry provisions (for distribution) as alms and to carry medicines, potions and sugar for those who should be attacked by illness. Whenever the caravan halted, food was cooked in great brass cauldrons, called dasts, and supplied from them to the poorer pilgrims and those who had no provisions. With the caravan was also a number of spare camels for the carriage of those unable to walk. All this was due to the benefactions and generosity of Sultan Abu Sa'id. . . .

This caravan contained also animated bazaars and great supplies of luxuries and all kinds of food and fruit. They used to march during the night and light torches in front of the file of camels and litters, so that you saw the countryside gleaming with light and the darkness turned into radiant day. (Ibn Battuta 1958: 249–250)

Joining the Persian Caravan at Hayl (1879)

In January 1879, Wilfrid and Lady Anne Blunt were guests of Muhammad ibn Rashid, the powerful Amir of Hayl and the Jabal Shammar. During their stay there was camped outside the town a caravan of Persian Hajjis returning from Medina to Najaf, the shrine-tomb of Ali in Iraq. The Blunts hastened to join its protection for their ongoing voyage of discovery.

We left Hayl by the same gate at which we had entered it, what seemed like years before, but instead of turning towards the mountains, we skirted the wall of the town, and further on palm gardens, which are its continuation, for about three miles down a ravine-like wadi. Then we came out on the plain again, and . . . halted for the last time to enjoy the shade, for the sun was almost hot, before joining the pilgrim caravan, which we could see like a long line of ants traversing the plain between us and the main range of Jabal Shammar.

It was, without exception, the most beautiful view I ever saw in my life, and I will try to describe it. To begin with, it must be understood that the air, always clear in Jabal Shammar, was this day of a transparent clearness, which probably surpasses anything seen in ordinary deserts. . . . For this is the very center of the desert, four hundred miles from the sea, and nearly four thousand feet above sea level.

Before us lay a foreground of coarse reddish sand. . . . Across this sand lay a long green belt of barley, perhaps a couple of acres in extent, the blades of the grain brilliantly green, and just having shot up high enough to hide the irrigation furrows. Beyond this, for a mile or more, the level desert fading from red to orange, till it was again cut by what appeared to be a shining sheet of water reflecting the deep blue of the sky—a mirage, of course, but the most perfect illusion that can be imagined. Crossing this, and apparently wading in the water, was the long line of pilgrim camels, each reflected exactly in the mirage below him with the dots of blue, red, green or pink, representing the litter or tent he carried. The line of the procession might be five miles or more in length; we could not see the end of it. Beyond again rose the confused fantastic mass of the sapphire colored crags of Jabal Aja, the most strange and beautiful that can be imagined—a lovely vision. (Blunt 1881: 307–309)

We were in front of the Hajj when we came to this tell (Tell al-Sayliyya), and we waited on top of it while the whole procession passed us, an hour or more. It was a curious spectacle. From the height where we were, we could see for thirty or forty miles back over the plain, as far as Jabal Aja, at the foot of which Hayl lies. The procession, three miles long, was composed of some four thousand camels (nor was this the whole Hajj caravan), with a great number of men on foot beside. In front were the dervishes walking very fast, almost running; wild, dirty people, but amiable, and quite willing to converse, if they know Arabic; then a group of respectably dressed people walking out of piety.... Sometimes they chant or recite prayers. All these devotees are very rude to us, answering nothing when we salute them, and being thrown into consternation if the greyhounds come near them, lest they should be touched by them and defiled.

Some ways behind these forerunners comes the berak, or banner, carried in the center of a group of mounted dromedaries magnificently caparisoned and moving on at a fast walk. These most beautiful creatures have coats like satin, eyes like those of a gazelle, and a certain graceful action which baffles description. Not even the Arabian horse has such a look of breeding as these thorough-bred camels. They are called na'a-miyya because one may go to sleep while riding them without being disturbed by the least jolting.

After the banner comes the mass of pilgrims, mounted sometimes two on one camel, sometimes with a couple of boxes on each side, the household furniture. The camels are the property of the bedouin, mostly Shammar.... They follow their animals on foot, and are at perpetual wrangle with the pilgrims, although, if they come to blows, Ibn Rashid's police mounted on dromedaries interfere, deciding the quarrel in a summary manner.

The Persian riding on a camel is the most ridiculous sight in the world. He insists on sitting astride, and seems absolutely unable to learn the ways and habits of the creature he rides; and he talks to it with his falsetto voice in a language no Arabian camel could possibly understand.... The better class of pilgrims, and of course all the women except the very poor, travel in litters—panniers, of which a camel carries two—covered over like a tradesman's van with red or blue canvas. One or two persons possess tahterevans, a more expensive kind of conveyance, which requires two mules or two camels, one before and one behind, to carry it. In either of these litters the traveler can squat or even lie down and sleep. The camels chosen for the litters are strong and even-paced; and some of these double panniers are fitted up with a certain care and elegance, and the luxury of

Persian rugs and hangings. A confidential driver leads the camel, and servants sometimes walk beside it. One of the pilgrims keeps a man to march in front with his nargileh, which he smokes through a very long tube sitting in the pannier above. (Blunt 1881: 316–319)

A Visit to the Persian Caravan Camp

As we shall see below, the British travelers William Palgrave and Richard Burton both had occasion to meditate on the fortunes of Shiʿite pilgrims in Arabia in the mid-nineteenth century. Palgrave also had the opportunity to visit the Persians' camp outside of Burayda and note how business was conducted in the Hajj camp town:

At this hour [shortly after sunrise] we would often thread the streets by which we had first entered the town (of Burayda), and go out betimes to the Persian camp, where all was already alive and stirring. Here are ranged on the sand baskets full of eggs and dates, flanked by piles of bread and little round cakes of white butter; bundles of firewood are heaped close by, and pail of goats' milk or camels' milk abound. And amid all these sit rows of countrywomen, haggling with tall Persians or with the dusky servants of Taj Jahan, who in broken Arabic try to beat down the prices, and generally end by paying only double what they ought.

Not a few Burayda townsmen are here, chatting or bartering, and Bedouin, switch in hand. If you ask any chance individual among these latter what has brought him hither, you may be sure beforehand that the word camel in one or other of its form of detail, will find place in the answer. Criers are going up and down the camp with articles of Persian apparel, cooking pots and ornaments of various descriptions in their hands, or carrying them off for higher bidding in the town. For what between the extortions of Muhanna and the daily growing expenses of so long a sojourn at Burayda, the Persians were rapidly coming to the end of their long purses and short wits, and had begun selling off whatever absolute necessity could dispense with as superfluous, to obtain wherewithal to buy a dish of milk or a bundle of firewood. Hence their appearance was a ludicrous mixture of the gay and the ragged, of the insolence of wealth and the anxious cringe of want; they were, in short, gentlemen in very reduced circumstances, and looked what they were. (Palgrave 1883: 175–177)

THE SYRIAN HAJJ

We know more about the Syrian caravan than the Iraqi one because it started at a more considerable place (Damascus), had a longer continuous history, was led in Mamluk and Ottoman times by the Governor of Syria, and is, for its later stages, well documented in the court archives of the city. Finally, there were more foreigners in Damascus than in either Kufa or Basra, non-Muslims who found in the Hajj an exotic caravan phenomenon worth commenting upon.

Coming and Going in 1432

One of those foreigners was Bertrandon de la Brocquière, himself a Christian pilgrim to the East and recently arrived in Damascus from Jerusalem in 1432:

> On the day after my arrival (in Damascus) I saw the caravan return from Mecca. It was said to be composed of 3,000 camels; and in fact it was two days and as many nights before they had all entered the town. This event was, according to custom, a great festival. The Governor of Damascus, attended by the principal persons of the town, went to meet the caravan out of respect to the Alcoran, which it bore. This is the book of law which Muhammad left for his followers. It was enveloped in a silken covering, painted over with Moorish inscriptions; and the camel that bore it was in like manner decorated all over with silk.

This sounds something like the empty palanquin called the Mahmal, better known to us from the Egyptian caravans (see below), though certainly borne by the Syrian one as well.

> Four musicians and a great number of drums and trumpets preceded the camel and made a loud noise. In front and around were about thirty men, some bearing cross-bows, others drawn swords, others small harquebuses, which they fired off every now and then.[29]
> Behind this camel followed eight old men mounted on the swiftest camels, and near them were led their horses, magnificently caparisoned and ornamented with rich saddles, according to the custom of the country. After them came a Turkish lady, a relation of the Grand Seigneur, in a litter borne by two camels with rich housings. There were many of these animals covered with cloth of gold.

In what follows, Bertrandon, or his source, has got the facts badly garbled. The tomb of Muhammad was not in Mecca—as often asserted in medieval Europe—but in Medina, and the house of God built, according to Muslim tradition, by Abraham was in Mecca, not Medina.

> The caravan was composed of Moors, Turks, Berbers, Tartars, Persians and other sectaries of the prophet Muhammad. These people pretend that, once having made a pilgrimage to Mecca, they cannot be damned. Of this I was assured by a renegade slave, a Bulgarian by birth, who be-

longed to the lady I have mentioned. He was called Hayauldoula, which signifies in the Turkish language "servant of God" [actually, "Life of the Realm"] and claimed to have been three times to Mecca. I formed an acquaintance with him because he spoke a little Italian and he often kept me company in the night as well as in the day. In our conversations I frequently questioned him about Muhammad and where his body was interred. He told me he was at Mecca; that the shrine containing the body was in a circular chapel, open at the top, and that it was through this opening the pilgrims saw the shrine; that there were among them some who, having seen it, had their eyes thrust out because, they said, after what they had just seen the world could no longer offer them anything worth looking at. There were in fact in this caravan two persons, one of them sixteen and the other twenty-two or twenty-three years old, who had thus made themselves blind. Hayauldoula told me also that it was not at Mecca where pardons for sin were granted, but at Medina, where St. Abraham built a house that still remains. The building is in the form of a cloister, of which pilgrims make the circuit.

Bertrandon joined the caravan cortege as it continued north from Damascus:

I will describe the order of its march. The caravan has a very large drum, and the moment the chief orders the departure, three loud strokes are beaten. Every one of them then makes himself ready and, when prepared, joins the file without uttering a word. Ten of our people would, in such cases, make more noise than a thousand of theirs. Thus they march in silence, unless it be night or that anyone should sing a song celebrating the heroic deeds of their ancestors. (Bertrandon de la Brocquière = Wright 1848: 301–302, 309)

Ibn Battuta Sets Off from Damascus on the Hajj

The Muslim traveler Ibn Battuta went to Mecca in the same Syrian caravan a century before Bertrandon watched its reentry into Damascus. After an abortive attempt to reach the Hijaz by one of the Egyptian routes (the one followed by Ibn Jubayr in 1184 up the Nile and thence east to Aydhab on the Red Sea), Ibn Battuta finally began afresh from Damascus in Syria in 1326 C.E. It is a mercy that he did so, for a great deal of Ibn Batutta's account of the Holy Cities is lifted, often word for word, from his predecessor Ibn Jubayr, and it seems likely that he would have done the same with the Red Sea crossing. Here, however, Ibn Battuta is on his own.

When the new moon of Shawwal appeared in the above-mentioned year [1 September 1326], the Hijaz caravan went out to the outskirts of

Damascus and encamped at the village called al-Kiswa (ten miles south of Damascus), and I set out on the move with them. The commander of the caravan was Sayf al-Din al-Juban, one of the principal amirs, and its chief justice was Sharaf al-Din al-Adhruʿi (from Adhruʿ) in the Hawran. . . . My journey was made with a tribe of bedouin Arabs called al-Arajima, whose amir was Muhammad al-Rafiʿ, a man occupying a high position among the amirs. We marched from al-Kiswa to a place called al-Sana-mayn, a big place [twenty miles south of Kiswa], and marched on from there to the township of Zurʿa [the modern Ezra, fifteen miles south of Sanamayn], a small place in the district of Hawran. After a halt in its vicinity we traveled on to the town of Busra [twenty-seven miles south of Ezra]; it too is a small place. It is the usual practice to stop there for four nights, so that any who have remained behind at Damascus to finish off their business may make up on them.

This extended halt outside the starting point to enable the travelers to organize themselves, a common practice of large caravans, later took place at Muzayrib, nearer to Damascus. The growing number of pilgrims, and the journey's increasing administrative and mercantile complexity—Muzayrib became a considerable market—may have required a stop somewhat closer to the metropolis.

It was at Busra that the Apostle of God, May God bless him and give him peace, came before his mission, while engaged in trading on Kha-dija's account, and in the town (there is shown) the place where his she-camel couched, over which a great mosque has been erected. The inhabitants of the Hawran flock to this town (with their produce) and the pilgrims supply themselves here with provisions for the journey. They travel next to the Pool of Ziza [twenty miles south of Amman], where they stop for a day, then go on to al-Lajjun, where there is running water, and thence to the castle of al-Karak. (Ibn Battuta 1958: 158–159)

Ludovico di Varthema Departs Damascus in 1503

In 1503, on the 8th day of April, the caravan being set in order to go to Mecca, and I being desirous of beholding various scenes . . .

So begins the extraordinary account of the first European to visit the Muslim holy cities of the Hijaz. We know nothing about Ludovico di Varthema except what can be gleaned from his travel account, which was first published in Italian in 1510 and subsequently in many European languages. A Venetian, the son of an Italian physician, likely a former soldier, and a married man with children, he traveled "to behold the various kingdoms of the world. . . . And inasmuch as all countries have been very much laid open by our people, I deliberated in my own mind that I should see those which had been least frequented by the Venetians." This intent carried him first to Alexandria, thence to Cairo, by sea again to Beirut, inland to Aleppo, and, in 1503, to Damascus:

... and not knowing how to set about it, I formed a great friendship with the captain of the Mamluks of the caravan, who was a Christian renegade, so that he clothed me like a Mamluk and gave me a good horse, and placed me in company with the other Mamluks, and this was accomplished by means of the money and other things I gave him. (Varthema 1863: 16)

Although he does not say so, it is thus palpably certain that Varthema, like so many of his Christian European successors, went to Medina and Mecca in the disguise of a Muslim. Indeed, there was only one other way to go: as a genuine Muslim.

Varthema has another distinction. Most of the Europeans who followed him, from Pitts to Burton, went by the Red Sea route from Egypt to Yanbu or Jidda. Varthema was the first and, until Burckhardt went part of the way in 1812 and Doughty accompanied the Hajj caravan from Damascus to Mada'in Salih in 1876, the only European to go overland through Syria to the Hijaz. His account continues:

In this manner we set ourselves on the way, and traveled three days to a place called Muzayrib, and there we remained three days, in order that the merchants might provide themselves, by purchase, with as many horses as they required.

On the 11th [that is, the 14th] of April, the said caravan departed Muzayrib; there were 35,000 camels, about 40,000 persons, and we were 60 Mamluks in guard of the said caravan. One third of the Mamluks went in advance of the caravan with the standard, another third in the center, and the other third marched in the rear. . . . From Damascus to Mecca is a journey of forty days and forty nights; thus, we set out from Muzayrib in the morning and traveled for twenty hours. At that point certain signals made by the captain were passed from band to band that the whole company should stop where they found themselves, and they pass twenty-four hours in unloading and feeding themselves and their camels. And then they make signals, and the camels are immediately laden again. And you must know that they give the said camels for food only five loaves of barley-meal, uncooked, and each a [ball of paste meal] of about the size of a pomegranate, and then they mount on horses and journey all night and all the following day for the said twenty-two hours, and then for twenty-four hours do as before. And every eight days they find water, that is, by digging in the earth or sand; also, certain wells and cisterns are found, and at the end of eight days they stop for one or two days, because the said camels carry as great a burden as two mules, and they only give the poor animals drink once in every three days. When we halted at the said waters we always had to fight with a vast number of Arabs, but they never killed more than one man and one lady, for such is the baseness of their minds that we 60 Mamluks were sufficient defense against 40,000 or 50,000 Arabs; for pagans, there are no better people with arms in their hands than are the Mamluks. You must know that I had excellent experiences of these Mamluks during the journey. (Varthema 1863: 16–19)

It is not easy, or sometimes even possible, to follow the precise stages of Varthema's southward journey; but somewhere in the difficult country around Aqaba, perhaps in the notorious chasm of the "Steps of Aqaba," the fatal dangers of the Hajj voyage became real indeed:

Then we passed that valley, which was at least twenty miles, and there died there from thirst thirty-three persons, and many were buried in the sand who were not quite dead, and they left only their faces uncovered.

The caravan had already had experience of bedouin in the vicinity of Muzayrib, but their encounter here at the entry to Midian was far more threatening.

Afterwards we found a little mountain, near which was a well, whereat we were well pleased. We halted upon the said mountain. The next day, early in the morning, there came 24,000 Arabs, who said we must pay for their water. We answered that we could not pay, for the water was given by God. They began to fight with us, saying that we had taken their water. We fortified ourselves, and made a wall of our camels, and the merchants stood within the said camels, and we were constantly skirmishing, so that they kept us besieged two days and two nights, and things came at last to the state that neither we nor they had anything to drink. They had completely surrounded the mountain with people, saying that they would break through the caravan.

Not being able to continue the fighting, our captain consulted with the Moorish merchants and we gave them (the Arabs) 1,200 ducats of gold. They took the money and then said that 10,000 ducats of gold would not pay for their water, and we knew that they wanted something else besides money. So our prudent captain arranged with the caravan that all those men who were capable of bearing arms should not ride on the camels, and that each should prepare his arms. The morning having come, we put forward all the caravan, and we Mamluks remained behind. We were in all three hundred persons, and we soon began to fight. One man and one woman were killed by bows on our side, and they did us no further harm. We killed of them 1,600 persons. Nor is it to be wondered at that we killed so many of them: the cause was that they were all naked and on horseback, without saddles, so that they had a difficulty in turning on their way. (Varthema 1863: 20–21)

Ibn Battuta on the Road in Syria and Arabia

We shall encounter Varthema later at both Medina and Mecca, but we now return to Ibn Battuta's narrative of his own Hajj journey through what is today southern Jordan:

The caravan stopped outside al-Karak for four days, at a place called al-Thaniyya, and made preparations for entering the wilderness. Thence we traveled to Ma'an, which is the last town in Syria, and descended through the Pass of al-Sawan into the desert.

Though Ma'an later became an important market town on the Syrian caravan route, it was in Ibn Battuta's day the pawn of the bedouin tribes that surrounded it like a hostile sea. The "Pass of al-Sawan" was probably the same dangerous descent referred to by Varthema.

After a march of two days we halted at Dhat Hajj, a place of subterranean waterbeds with no habitations, then on to Wadi Baldah (but there is no water in it), and then to Tabuk. This is the place raided by the Apostle of God [in 631 c.e.]. It has a spring which used to yield a scanty supply of water, but when the Apostle of God went down to it and used it for his ablutions, it gave an abundant flow of running water and continues to do so to this day.

The huge caravan encamps near to the spring referred to, and every one of them slakes his thirst from it. They remain here four days to rest themselves and water the camels and lay in supplies of water for the fearsome wilderness between Tabuk and al-Ula. It is the practice of the watercarriers to take up their positions at the side of the spring, and they have tanks made of buffalo hides, like great reservoirs, from which they water the camels and fill the large waterbags and the ordinary waterskins.[30] Each amir or person of rank has a (private) tank from which his camels and those of his retinue are watered, and their waterbags filled; the rest of the people arrange with the water-carriers to water the camel and fill the waterskin of each person for a fixed sum of money.

The caravan then sets out for Tabuk and pushes on speedily night and day, for fear of this wilderness. Halfway through is the valley of al-Ukhaydir, which might well be the valley of Hell, God preserve us from it. One year the pilgrims suffered severe distress in this place, by reason of the simoom (or "poison") wind which blows here, their water supplies dried up, and the price of a drink of water rose to a thousand dinars, but both seller and buyer perished. The story of this is inscribed on one of the rocks of the valley. Going on from there, the caravan halts at the Pool of Muʿazzam, a vast basin called after al-Malik al-Muʿazzam of the house of Ayyub [Sultan of Damascus, 1218–1227], in which the rain-water collects in certain years, but which is generally dry in others.

On the fifth day after leaving Tabuk, they reach the well of al-Hijr— the Hijr of Thamud [now Mada'in Salih]—which has an abundance of water, but not one of the pilgrims draws from it, however violent their thirst, following the example set by the Apostle of God (God bless him and give him peace), when he passed it by on his way to Tabuk. . . . At this place are the dwellings of Thamud, in some hills of red rock. They are hewn out and have carved thresholds, such that anyone seeing them would take them to be of recent construction. Their bones lie crumbling inside these houses, "verily in that is a warning example" (Quran 3:11). The place of the kneeling of the she-camel of Salih (on him be peace) is between two hills there, and in the space between them are the traces of a mosque, in which the pilgrims perform a prayer.[31]

From al-Hijr to al-Ula is half a day's journey or less. Al-Ula is a large and pleasant village [eighteen miles south of Mada'in Salih], with palm gardens and watersprings at which the pilgrims halt for the space of four nights. They provision themselves and wash their clothes, and also deposit here any surplus of provisions they may have, taking with them only the amount of their strict necessities. The inhabitants of this village are trustworthy persons. This is the limit to which the Christian merchants of Syria may come, and beyond which they may not pass, and they trade in provisions and other goods with the pilgrims here.

The caravan then sets out from al-Ula and encamps on the day following the resumption of its journey in the valley known as al-Itas (?). It is a place of violent heat, in which the fatal simoom wind blows. It blew up one year on the caravan, and none but a few of the pilgrims escaped with their lives. . . . After this they encamp at Hadiyya, which is a place of subterranean waterbeds in a valley; they dig pits in it and the water comes up, but brackish. On the third day they alight outside the sanctified city (of Medina), the holy and illustrious. (Ibn Battuta 1958: 160–163)

THE HAJJ ROUTE FROM EGYPT

The normal overland route from Cairo to the Hijaz was the same path whose "stations" are described by most of the Arab geographers, whose work in fact chiefly consists in enumerating such stops along the way. The route was divided into thirty-four stages, each about twenty-eight to thirty miles in length. The journey was not continuous, however: with a couple of rest periods of a few days en route, it took roughly forty days to go out and about the same time to return.

The pilgrims collected at Birket al-Hajj a few miles north of Cairo and then, after about four days, generally proceeded in no particular order to Ajrud, a marshaling ground about fifteen miles northwest of Suez. There the Caravan Commander began to arrange this amorphous crowd into what would be their order of march (see below), and thereafter no one was permitted to leave the ranks without permission.

One or two hours after sunrise, the pilgrims, now constituted a caravan, proceeded either south to Qulzum (Suez) or, more generally, directly eastward. The routes came together again at Thughrat Hamid and then crossed the Sinai through Qala'at al-Nakhl to Aqaba.[32] This constituted only one-quarter of the "Egyptian Way": from Aqaba the caravan descended to al-Bad', remained close to the coast as far south as Rabigh, and then joined the Sultan's Way between Medina and Mecca.

The Duration

As in the case of the Syrian caravan, we have substantial and continuous records for the pilgrimages from Cairo to Mecca. A rough estimate of its average duration, as has been said, would be about three months for the round trip: forty days out and forty back. The Mahmal, the decorated, camel-borne palanquin that signified Egyptian sovereignty, generally left Cairo sometime around the twentieth of Shawwal; its return depended on the conditions, human and natural, along the route, but the twenty-second or twenty-third of Muharram was considered fairly standard.[33]

The eleventh-century Persian traveler Nasir-i Khusraw gives us his own calculations for the journey out, by land and by sea, starting from Suez:

Whoever wants to go to Mecca from Egypt must go east. From Qulzum [Suez] there are two ways, one by land and one by sea. The land route can be traversed in fifteen days but it is all desert and three hundred parasangs long [about 1,050 miles]. Most of the caravans from Egypt take that way. By sea it takes twenty days to reach al-Jar, a small town in the Hijaz on the sea. From al-Jar to Medina it takes three days. From Medina to Mecca it is one hundred parasangs [about 350 miles]. (Nasir-i Khusraw 1986: 43)

The time it took for the caravan to travel from Cairo or Damascus to Mecca was subject to outside influences as well, one of which was the commercial interests of the carriers. Although such influences were not so apparent in Nasir's day, they became increasingly important as the commercial life around the Red Sea quickened. The following story, told by Selim Sawwaf, one of the last of the camel contractors for the Damascus caravan, to Christine Phelps Grant in Damascus in 1935–1936, illustrates the degree to which the caravan had passed from government to private control:

The camel-masters originated a law which was, at least in more recent times [ca. 1875–1910], ruthlessly enforced: namely, that the entire trip should never take more than forty days and forty nights to perform. Five days, not counted in the forty, were spent in Medina, but that was the only exception countenanced. No halts of more than one hour were allowed by day, and a great part of the journey was performed by night. Sometimes, if the caravan accomplished a thirty mile stage with exceptional speed, in less than the allotted time (in, for example, ten or nine hours instead of twelve), a halt of two or three hours was granted at the first watering place encountered therein. Otherwise, on every third day, an hour's rest at some village was arranged. But that was all. Were a person to fall ill, or to die, or a woman to weaken under the strain, even so, no exception could be made to this stringent regulation. Once embarked upon the pilgrimage, it behoved the pilgrim to persevere to the bitter— sometimes very bitter—end. Anyone who failed in this self-imposed duty, and was unable to travel, was left behind: even, upon occasion, to the mercy of the marauding Bedouin.

When at last they reached their objective and finally arrived at Mecca, the caravan stayed there for more than three weeks. Only a short time was exacted in the Holy City for religious purposes (all the prescribed duties of the Hajj, that is to say, could be performed within three, or at most six days), but a long rest was allowed the pilgrims: partly for the purposes of trade and commerce, and partly so that both men and beasts might have a chance to recuperate from the long and exhausting trip.

The return journey was made exactly as the outgoing one had been, in forty days, the only change in the routine being a shortened stay at Medina. According to Selim Sawwaf, the camel-owners and contractors were solely responsible for this forty-day test of endurance; and the reason he gave was that a great and disproportionate expense should be incurred by them for every extra day spent on the road, beyond the time they had contracted for. . . . The lines in the Quran (2:196) which urge pilgrims to "hasten quickly" when they approach the Holy Places . . . also furnished the camel-masters with a religious argument and pretext for insisting on the maximum speed during the entire journey. (Grant 1937: 229)

The Pilgrimage of Nasir-i Khusraw (1048)

Nasir-i Khusraw, a Persian bureaucrat from eastern Iran, began his journeys in 1045 C.E. Although he made the Hajj four times in the course of the next few years, it was the fourth one, when he went from Cairo via

Aydhab and Jidda to Mecca in 1049, that he turned into a book. It is a pity he chose to describe that particular way—he had previously (1048) come from Medina and would return again from Jerusalem with the Syrian caravan—because Ibn Jubayr left us a far more detailed account of that same route.

THE HAJJ ANNOUNCEMENT IN CAIRO

Nasir had his own interest in detailing the journey he did. He provides, for example, the earliest account (1048) of the formal Hajj preparations in Cairo, with the Sultan formally and officially in control.

It is customary for a representative of the Sultan to appear in the mosques in the middle of the month of Rajab and proclaim the following: "O company of Muslims! The Pilgrimage season is at hand, and the Sultan, as usual, has undertaken the outfitting of soldiers, horses, camels and provisions." During Ramadan the proclamation is repeated, and from the first of Dhu al-Qaʿda the caravan moves out. The daily disbursement to the soldiers (accompanying it) for fodder is one thousand Maghribi dinars, over and above the twenty dinars each man receives per diem for the twenty-five days until they reach Mecca, where they stay for ten days. Thus, with the twenty-five days it takes them to return, they are gone for two months, and sixty thousand Maghribi dinars are spent for provisions, not counting miscellaneous disbursements for rent, bonuses, stipends and camels that die.

In the year 1048 C.E. an edict of the Sultan [al-Mustansir, Fatimid ruler of Egypt, 1036–1094] to this effect was read to the people: "The Prince of the Faithful proclaims that in this year, owing to drought and the resulting scarcity of goods, which has caused the deaths of many, it is unwise for pilgrims to undertake the journey to the Hijaz. This we say in Muslim commiseration." Therefore the pilgrimage was held in abeyance until the next year, although the Sultan did send the covering for the Kaʿba as usual, which he does twice a year. This very year, since the covering was being sent via the Red Sea, I went along. (Nasir-i Khusraw 1986: 58–59)

A QUICK TRIP TO THE HIJAZ

Nasir-i Khusraw made his first and very hurried visit to Mecca in 1048. Although it constituted an official pilgrimage, it was very much shorter than the Hajj he would complete in 1050.

On the 18th of April 1048 C.E. I left Egypt and we reached the Red Sea (at Qulzum) on the 25th. From there we traveled for fifteen days by boat until we arrived at a town called al-Jar. From there it is a four-day journey to Medina, which is a town with damp and salty soil on the edge of the desert. It has running water, though not much, and is a palm grove. . . .

We stayed in Medina for two days; then, as time was short, we left. The road leads to the east. Two stations outside of Medina is a mountain and a defile called Juhfa, which is the miqat for Syria, the Maghrib and Egypt—the miqat being the place where the pilgrims put on the ihram [the ritual pilgrimage garb]. They say that one year many pilgrims had stopped there when suddenly a flash-flood swept down and killed them all, which is why it is called Juhfa ["sweeping away"]. From Medina to Mecca is one hundred parasangs [approximately 350 miles], but the road is rocky and it took us eight days.

On Sunday 23 May 1048 we arrived in Mecca and entered through the Safa Gate. As there had been a drought in Mecca that year, four pounds of bread cost one Nishapuri dinar. The "sojourners" were leaving the city, and no pilgrims had come from anywhere at all. On Wednesday, with the help of God, we completed the pilgrimage rites at Arafat. Afterwards we stayed at Mecca for only two days. . . .

When I returned to Egypt, it had been seventy-five days (since I left). This year thirty-five thousand people came to Egypt from the Hijaz; and since they were all hungry and naked, they received clothing and a pension from the Sultan until the next year, when the rains came and food was once again plentiful in the Hijaz to support these people. The Sultan gave them all clothing and gifts and sent them back home. (Nasir-i Khusraw 1986: 59–60)

The Nile Route and the Red Sea

At the beginning of the twelfth century c.e. the Western intruders called Crusaders held not only Jerusalem but also large areas of northern and coastal Syria and even areas east of the Jordan. There they built the fortress of Montreal (1115) in the oasis of Shawbak and another called "Petra of the Desert" (1142) three hours east of the Dead Sea, with lesser posts at an even further remove from these bases. By 1116 c.e. the Seigneurie of Montreal extended all the way to the Gulf of Aqaba and included the fortress of Aila there.

Thus, between 1116 and 1187 the Frankish Crusaders controlled the land routes between Syria and Egypt. If a caravan wished to try the passage, it had to detour far to the east of the Crusader fortresses in the Transjordan and then try to slip through the net south of the Dead Sea. The economic consequences were considerable, of course. But more to the point, the Frankish presence in southern and eastern Jordan forced the Syrian Hajj caravans far out into the desert and constrained the Egyptians, who were by then normally crossing the Sinai and passing through Aqaba into the Hijaz, to scout for entirely new routes. That is why the author of our best eyewitness account of a medieval pilgrimage to Mecca, the Spaniard Ibn Jubayr, had to make the difficult overland journey from the Nile to the Red Sea coast at Aydhab.

Ibn Jubayr was not the first to describe the passage over land from Qus to Aydhab and then the voyage to Jidda. The route into Upper Egypt had been mentioned in the previous century by the travelers Ibn Rusteh and, as we have seen, Nasir-i Khusraw, who gives a somewhat perfunctory description. It was in fact a somewhat round-about way of getting to Mecca. The overland trip from the Nile to the Red Sea was difficult and dangerous, and Aydhab had the well-merited reputation of being one of God's least favored places. But what made the route attractive, indeed necessary, was the Crusader presence in Sinai and east of the Red Sea. Thus, for about two hundred years (1062–1266), Aydhab replaced Aqaba as the transit port of Red Sea traffic, both commercial and religious. Once the Crusaders were gone and the Muslim Mamluks firmly in control, the Sinai route became popular once more. Aydhab was destroyed by the Mamluk Sultan Barsbay in 1426, and the port never recovered; later commerce on the western shore of the Red Sea went instead to Suwakin farther south.

Ibn Jubayr was born at Valencia or Xativa on 1 September 1145. He left Granada on 1 February 1183 and did not return until 25 April 1185. In the interval he had visited Alexandria and Cairo, gone up the Nile to Qus, crossed the desert to Aydhab, voyaged over the Red Sea to Jidda, spent more than eight months at Mecca, and completed the Hajj and Umra in 1184.

Ibn Jubayr left Mecca on 5 April 1184 in the pilgrim caravan to Iraq, spent five days visiting Medina, and then followed the classical route to Baghdad, where he stayed only five days before going on to Mossul. From there he passed into Syria at Aleppo, went up the Orontes Valley to Hama and Homs, and then reached Damascus, where he remained for two months (July–September 1184). After visiting Tyre, he embarked at Acre in October and did not reach Messina until December, after a long and difficult crossing that ended in a shipwreck. Ibn Jubayr remained three and a half months in Sicily awaiting favorable winds, then without further adventures reached Cartagena on 18 April 1185, whence he returned to Granada.

We begin not with the beginning of Ibn Jubayr's work but with his arrival in Aydhab, a port town on the African coast of the Red Sea and the maritime point of departure for travelers to the Hijaz.

On the afternoon of Saturday we entered Aydhab, an unwalled city on the shore of the Sea of Jidda; its houses are for the most part mud huts, though one sees some few more recent constructions of masonry. It is one of the most frequented ports in the world since ships from India and

Yemen end their journey there and depart again, to say nothing of the
ships of pilgrims departing and returning. It is situated in a wilderness,
without vegetation, and one eats there nothing that has not been imported. The inhabitants enjoy, nonetheless, an easy life, thanks to the
pilgrims. First, they profit directly from each pilgrim because they collect
a fixed tax on all the provisions carried by these latter, though it is not
very high when compared to the tribute which was in existence until it
was abolished by Salah al-Din. . . .[34] Second, they make money on the
pilgrims by reason of the jalba, which are their boats. They exact considerable sums for carrying the pilgrims to Jidda and bringing them back
when they have finished their pilgrimage. There is no one among the
better-off citizens of Aydhab who does not have one or two jalbas which
bring them in a large income. (Ibn Jubayr 1949–1951: 78–79/Ar. 69)

Ibn Jubayr is normally an objective and dispassionate reporter. Or he was
until he reached his destination on the Red Sea:

The people of Aydhab treat the pilgrims in an unspeakable manner:
they load them into their jalbas, one made to sit atop the other, and they
pack them in as if they were cages filled with chickens. What impels them
to act in this way is their greed and their desire to rent their skiffs. They
make up the purchase price on one trip and so they have little care what
the sea does after that.

Of all the lands of God, the one that most merits a scourge where the
sword has replaced the whip is indeed this one. For anyone who is able, it
is better not to visit it but rather to join, via Syria and Iraq, the Amir of
the Baghdad caravan. And if the pilgrim cannot do this on his way out, he
may use it at least at the end of the Hajj, when the pilgrims disperse. He
should make his way with the Amir al-Hajj to Baghdad and thence to
Acre. He can go from there, if he wishes, to Alexandria or Sicily, or anywhere else. . . . And if his trip is extended by this detour, this is little
compared to the price he would pay at Aydhab and its vicinity!

The people who live there belong to a tribe of blacks called the Beja,
who have a sultan chosen from among their number, who lives with them
in the neighboring mountains. Sometimes they come into the town to
speak with the governor. . . . This race of blacks lives worse than animals,
and is their inferior in intelligence; they have no religion save the formula
asserting God's uniqueness, which they pronounce to display that they
are Muslims; that apart, there is nothing in their beliefs or in their conduct which is either acceptable or licit. Men and women go around completely naked, with only a ribbon to conceal their sexual parts; and for the
most part they do not even bother with that. They are, in a word, an
immoral people and it would be no sin to call the curse of God down
upon them.

On Monday, the 25th of Rabi' I [18 July 1183], we boarded a jalba to make the crossing to Jidda. But we remained that day in port because the wind had fallen and the sailors were absent. The next day, Tuesday morning, we hoisted sail under the benediction of God and with the hope of His favorable assistance. The extent of our stay in Aydhab, not counting that Tuesday, was twenty-eight days; it will be held in our account before God, for the miserable life we led there, the horror of our situation, the undermining of our health because of the lack of appropriate nourishment. What is one to expect from a city where everything is imported, even the water, and water of a type that renders thirst more pleasant to the heart. Who would blame someone who turns away from the city saying, "Foul water, the sky in flames." Staying there is one of the deepest pits with which the way to the Holy House, may God increase its glory, is strewn. May He increase the rewards of the pilgrims for what they have endured, particularly in this evil city. . . . May He free the pilgrims from a stay there by rendering usable the direct way to His Holy House, that is, from Cairo by way of the Aqaba or Ayla to the Holy City of Medina, a short trip during which the sea is on his right and the Jabal Tur [the traditional Mount Sinai] is on his left. The Franks have a strongly guarded fortress in the vicinity, which prevents us from following this route. (Ibn Jubayr 1949–1951: 81–83/Ar. 71–73)

Ibn Battuta tried to pass the same way in 1326 but found it impossible:

At length, after traveling fifteen days (overland from the Nile), we reached the town of Aydhab, a large town, well supplied with fish and milk; dates and grain are imported from Upper Egypt. Its inhabitants are the Bejas, black-skinned people who wrap themselves in yellow blankets and tie headbands, each about a fingerbreadth wide, around their heads. They give daughters no share in their inheritance. . . . One third of the city belongs to (the Sultan of Egypt) al-Malik al-Nasir, and two thirds to the king of the Beja, who is called al-Hadrabi.

On reaching Aydhab we found that al-Hadrabi, the sultan of the Beja, was engaged in hostilities with the Turks [that is, the Mamluk troops of the Sultan of Egypt], that he had sunk their ships and the Turks had fled before him. It was impossible for us to make the sea-crossing, so we sold the provisions we had made ready, and returned to Upper Egypt. (Ibn Batutta 1958: 68–69)

The Sinai Route

Ibn Jubayr ended his description of Aydhab with the prayer, "May God free the pilgrims from a stay there by rendering usable the direct way to His Holy House." His prayer was answered in 1266, when the Mamluk

Sultan Baybars sent the ceremonial curtain (*kiswa*) for the Ka'ba by the Sinai route, which thereafter became once again the normal pilgrimage route from Egypt to Medina and Mecca, though Central and West African pilgrims continued to use what was for them the shorter Red Sea land-sea route.

THE EGYPTIAN HAJJ CARAVAN DEPARTS (CA. 1575)

We can observe the departure of the Egyptian caravan in the company of the anonymous European who was with it sometime about 1575 and whose account was included by Hakluyt in his *Voyages*:

The Captain (of the Caravan) and all his retinue and officers resort unto the castle [that is, the citadel] of Cairo before the Pasha, which gives every man a garment, and that of the Captain is wrought with gold, and the others are served according to their degree. Moreover he delivers unto him ye Chisva Talnabi [Kiswat al-Nabi], which signifies in the Arabian tongue the "garment of the Prophet." This vesture is of silk, wrought in the midst with letters of gold, which signify: la illa ill' alla Mahumet Resullaha: that is to say, there is no god but God and his ambassador Mahumet. This garment is made of purpose to cover from top to bottom a little house in Mecca standing in the midst of the Mesquita [mosque], the which house, they say, was builded by Abraham or by his son Ishmael. After this he delivers to him a gate made of purpose for the aforesaid house, wrought all with fine gold and being of excellent workmanship, and it is a thing of great value. Besides he delivers unto him a covering of green velvet made in the manner of a pyramid, about nine palms high, and artificially wrought with most fine gold, and this is to cover the tomb of their prophet within Medina.

These precious objects are carried in procession from the Pasha's residence on the Citadel to a mosque near the Bab al-Nasr. They are stored in this mosque until the pilgrim caravan begins to form at Birca.

Then the Captain departs with his company, and taking the vestures out of the Mesquita (at the Bab al-Nasr), carries the same to the aforesaid place of Birca, where the Captain having pitched his tent with the standard of the Grand Signor over the gate, and the other principal tents standing about his, stays there some ten days and no more. In which time all those resort thither that mean to follow the Caravan in this voyage to Mecca. Where you shall see certain women which intend to go on this voyage accompanied with their parents and friends mounted upon camels, adorned with some many trifles, tassels and knots, that beholding them in same a man cannot refrain from laughter.

The last night before their departure they make great feasting and triumph within the Caravan, with castles and other infinite devices of fireworks, the Janissaries always standing about the tent of the Captain with such shouting and joy that on every side the earth resounds, and this night they discharge all their ordnance, four or six times, and after the break of day upon the sound of a trumpet they march forward on their way.

It is to be noted that from Cairo to Mecca they make 40 days journey or thereabout, & that same great days' journeys. For the custom of the caravan is to travel much and rest little, and ordinarily they journey in this manner. They travel from two o'clock in the morning until the sun rising, then having rested till noon, they set forward, and so continue till night, & then also rest again, as is abovesaid, till two of the clock. And this order they observe till the end of the voyage, never changing the same, except in some places, whereof we will hereafter speak, where for respect of water they rest sometimes a day and a half, and this they observe to refresh themselves, otherwise both man and beast would die. (Anon. Hakluyt 1927: 3:179–180)

SECURITY PRECAUTIONS

The precautions described by the anonymous pilgrim making the Hajj from Cairo in the last quarter of the sixteenth century have particularly to do with the last three-quarters of the journey, from Aqaba southward along the Red Sea hinterland.

And because the caravan goes always along the Red Sea bank, which in going forth they have on their right hand, therefore the two hundred Janissaries parted into three companies go upon their left hand well armed and mounted upon camels bound one to another, for upon that side is all the danger of thieves, and on the other side no danger at all, the Captain of the Caravan always going about his people, sometimes on one side and sometimes on the other, never keeping any firm place, being continually accompanied by the Chaus and 25 Sipahi, armed and mounted upon dromedaries, and 8 musicians with viols in their hands, which cease not sounding till the captain take his rest, upon whom they attend, until such time as he entereth his pavilion, and then licensing all his attendants and followers to depart, they go each man to their lodging. (Anon. Hakluyt 1927: 3:180)

We cannot identify the exact stopping places from this account, nor indeed from any of the medieval geographers, who supply copious names but never quite identical ones.[35] In any event, this route, like all the other overland paths, fell into increasing dissuetude with the growth of maritime traffic across the Red Sea and then into almost complete oblivion as steam replaced sail. This, for example, is how British intelligence rated the last stages of the Egyptian overland way, those from Aqaba southward to Rabigh, in the opening years of the twentieth century:

The track southward from Aqaba is the Egyptian Hajj route, and, as such, has been provided by wells at all stages; but since it has ceased to be followed by the Mahmal, or by any large body of pilgrims under official escort, the wells and rest-stations have fallen into decay, especially on the Midian coast. Otherwise it is easy going, and as far as Yanbu is comparatively safe from any but irresponsible footpads. From Yanbu onwards, security depends on the attitude of the Zubayd Harb (bedouin). (Hogarth 1917: 82)

Africans on the Hajj

John Lewis Burckhardt explored large tracts of Nubia before working his way eastward to Suwakin, where he took ship to Jidda in July 1814. In the region called Taka, between the Nile and the Red Sea in what is today the Sudan, he paused to take stock of the African pilgrims in his company and their ways to the Holy Cities of Arabia.

We had now with us eighteen or twenty Takayrna, or Negro pilgrims. Takruri, the singular of this name, is not derived from a country called "Takrur," as is generally supposed in the East, and which has misled all the Arabian geographers, but from the verb takurrar, to multiply, renew, to sift, to purify, to invigorate, i.e. their religious sentiments, by the study of the sacred book, and by pilgrimage. The appellation is bestowed on all Negroes who come west, in search of learning . . . or for the Hajj, of whatever country they may be. They do not call themselves by this name of Takruri, which many assured me they had not heard of till they reached the limits of Darfur. All these pilgrims can read and write a little; . . . I never found any of them quite illiterate. After making some progress in the schools of their country—schools being met with in all the Muslim countries of Africa—they proceed to Mecca for the Hajj, or in order to study the Quran and the commentaries upon it, in that place and Medina; or to Cairo, for the same purpose; but the greater part go for the Hajj; at present there are not more than twelve in the mosque al-Azhar in Cairo, and I did not find above double that number in the great mosque of Mecca. . . .

The greater part of the Takruris who visit Mecca come from the schools of Darfur, the principal of which are at Konjara, in the neighborhood of Kobba. Those from the most western countries who pass this road are from Bahr al-Ghazal and Bagarma. All the black Hajjis from the west of Bagarma, from Burnu as far as Timbuctu, either travel with the Fezzan, or great Maghribi pilgrim caravan, or proceed by sea from the coast of Barbary. Their motives for undertaking the journey are partly a sincere desire to fulfil the precepts of their religion, and partly the ambition of enjoying afterwards the credit which the Hajj confers in their own country upon those who have performed it, and which of course is in proportion to the difficulty of the journey.

The Takruris seldom travel alone, at least they never set out alone on their journey; they generally form parties of about a dozen, and as opportunity offers, join some caravan on the road, or proceed by themselves. Their usual route to Mecca is by Assiut, by Shendi or by Sennar (on the Blue Nile). Those from the most western countries meet at Darfur; after which, only such as can afford to travel with the Darfur caravan, which requires capital sufficient to buy camels and provisions for the journey through the desert, repair to Assiut, from whence they proceed to Jidda by way of Qusayr (on the Red Sea).

The pilgrims who go by Sennar come from Kordofan and pursue their journey by three different routes; to wit, 1) through the interior by the Mogren (river) to Taka, and from thence to Suwakin; I do not over-rate the number who pass this way at five hundred annually; . . . they never travel in large parties, but a few are seen almost daily passing along the banks of the river. . . . From Taka they proceed with the caravans (across country) to Suwakin, where they wait till they find a ship to convey them to Jidda. The usual fare is from one to two dollars.

Distance is scarcely ever taken into consideration by these pilgrims, nor indeed by any bedouin or traders in these countries; fatigue they care little about; loss of time, still less; one object only occupies their attention, under the two forms of direct gain and the saving of expense. . . . It will readily be conceived that the danger and fatigue incident to the journey prove fatal to great numbers of the pilgrims: perhaps one-sixth fall victims to their zeal. The greater part of the diseases by which they are attacked on the road arise from their being almost destitute of clothing; many perish in the desert through want and fatigue, and others are murdered; but as all who die on the road are looked upon as martyrs, these contingencies have little effect in diminishing the annual numbers, or in diverting others from their purpose. Although the greater number of the pilgrims are stout young men, yet it is not rare to see women following their husbands to the Hajj; and almost incredible as it may seem, one of the men who joined our caravan at Taka was blind. He . . . was continually led by a stick, which one of his companions held in his hand as he marched before him. I saw this man afterwards begging in the mosque at Mecca, and again at Medina, sitting on the threshold of the temple, exclaiming, as he appealed to the charity of the Hajjis, "I am blind, but the light of the word of God and the love of His Prophet illumine my soul and have been my guide from the Sudan to this tomb." He received very

liberal alms, and would probably return to his home richer than he left it.
(Burckhardt 1819: 406–408)

THE INTERIOR ARABIAN ROUTES

At the beginning of the First World War the British intelligence and diplomatic venture in Cairo known as the Arab Bureau collected all the information then available on the Hijaz and published it in 1917 under the title of *Handbook of the Hijaz.* Its main author was the archeologist David Hogarth (1862–1927)—the British, like the Germans, quite un-selfconsciously combined archeology and intelligence gathering in the Middle East before the war—Britain's principal authority on Western Arabia. In that same year Hogarth's protégé T. E. Lawrence, another former archeologist, went to the Hijaz and set in motion what came to be known as the "Arab Revolt."

Among other things, the *Handbook* considered the passages across the Hijaz, which were, as the author noted, none other than the routes of pilgrimage:

> *The presence of the goals of Muslim pilgrimage in Hijaz causes tracks to converge on it from all quarters. . . . The points toward which all main tracks are directed are Medina and Mecca. . . . The tracks come from the center (Hayl, Qasim, and Riyadh), from the north (Syria and Egypt), from the west coast and from the south (Asir and Yemen). None of these reaches Mecca and Medina without crossing some desert and more steppe, and, except between Jidda and Mecca and along the coast line, all encounter hilly country and some difficult mountain passes. In general, the Hijaz routes are among the least safe of the Arabian peninsula from nomad attack. (Hogarth 1917: 84)*

By 1917, the great bulk of the pilgrims arrived in Arabia by sea and disembarked, if they were from Egypt or from Syria-Anatolia via Egypt, at Yanbu on the coast opposite Medina. If they were among the increasing number of pilgrims coming from India and Indonesia, they likely landed, together with African pilgrims crossing over from Suwakin, at Jidda, the port of Mecca. Thus the importance of the two east-west passages: Yanbu to Medina and Jidda to Mecca.

Yanbu to Medina

The route from Yanbu to Medina was identical for much of its extent with the Darb Sultani from Medina to Mecca, which veered off to the south toward the end (see below). The English soldier George Forster

Sadleir came down by it in 1819 after his epic trek from Qatif on the east coast of Arabia across the peninsula to Medina:

September 15th (1819) —Marched from Bir Ali (the first stop on the west after leaving Medina) at 7 A.M., our route westerly through the mountains. About two miles from Bir Ali we came to the spot at which two Turks had been wounded a few days previously. Two mountains of very difficult ascent command this pass within pistol-shot. Here the bed-ouin have been posted awaiting the arrival of any solitary traveler who might chance to pass, and whom they might be capable to overpower. Continuing our route through the valley, we found . . . the rocky mountains of a more considerable elevation. We arrived at 5 P.M. at a spot which was marked by a small white tower on the top of a mountain to the west, at the floor of which we found a deep well of good water.

September 16th —Marched at 5 A.M.; continued our route through the mountains in the same valley. These mountains are high, rocky and barren . . . the road gravelly and good; the mountains to the southwest impassable. We halted at 12 at a solitary well which afforded but a scanty supply of water, the demand for which became very pressing before evening.

September 17th —Marched at 4 A.M., and continuing our route through the valleys as yesterday; we reached Judayda at 12. It is a miserable village of huts built of stone; one part of the village is built up against the side of the mountain, but the lower village, which has several date gardens, lies in the hollows. . . . The sun does not shine in the valley more than three hours a day, which renders it a very unhealthy spot. The tribes which reside in the mountains . . . have made paths along the tops of the mountains where they can assemble a large force, and the entrance to their valley was once strongly defended. . . . On the advance of Tussun Pasha (against the Wahhabis in Medina in 1812) they defended their valley so resolutely that he did not effect his passage without the loss of many men. We proceeded on to the village of Hamra, which we reached at 12, and here found a tolerable supply of water.

September 18th —Marched at 4 A.M. Almost every person had to complain of the loss of camels or baggage or horses. The Turks [the Turco-Egyptian military detachment with whom Sadleir was traveling] never place any guard or watch during the night, and during last night the thieves had been particularly active. . . . At 7 A.M. we crossed a hill from which we descended by a very rugged, difficult, rocky road, which here divides into two branches: the one turning off to the south [that is, the Darb Sultani] runs to Mecca and Jidda and unites with the one which leads from Humra to the above places; the other road is that which we followed to the west, and which led us to Bir al-Sultan, where we arrived at 11 A.M. The well was very deep and full of good water. . . . We en-

camped in a small sandy plain. The road to Badri is to the south of this range. There the two caravans of pilgrims, the Egyptian and Damascus, always join and proceed to Mecca.

September 19th —Halted this forenoon to forage the camels. The Magribi bedouin (accompanying us) were sent on in advance to enable us to proceed with the more ease in the afternoon. We marched at 3 P.M., continued our route till daybreak, when we emerged from the hills and halted at Malka, the wells of which are brackish.

September 20th —Marched from Malka. Hence the country assumes a new aspect, and opens into an extensive plain bounded to the west by the Red Sea. Arrived at Yanbu at 10 A.M. (Sadleir 1866: 108–110)

The Routes between Mecca and Medina

The obligation of the pilgrimage had only to do with the rites at Mecca, of course, but the overwhelming number of pilgrims included Medina, with the Prophet's own mosque and his tomb within it, on their itinerary. Pilgrims coming down by land from Syria, and most of those from Iraq, stopped at Medina on their way to Mecca. For Egyptian pilgrims, the African voyagers coming across the Red Sea, and those arriving from the Yemen, a visit to Medina might more conveniently follow the Hajj. Richard Burton rapidly surveys the various ways of passing between the two Holy Cities.

Four roads lead from Medina to Mecca. The Darb al-Sultani or "Sultan's Highway" follows the line of the coast; this general passage has been minutely described by my exact predecessor.[36] The Tariq al-Ghabir, a mountain path, is avoided by the Mahmal and the great caravans on account of its rugged passes; water abounds along the whole line, but there is not a single village and the Subh bedouin who own the soil are inveterate plunderers. The route called Wadi al-Qura is a favorite with the dromedary caravans; on this road are two or three small settlements, regular wells, and free passage through the Banu Amr tribe. The Darb al-Sharqi or "Eastern Road," down which I traveled, owes its existence to the piety of the Lady Zubayda, wife of Harun al-Rashid. That munificent princess dug wells from Baghdad to Medina and built, we are told, a wall to direct pilgrims over the shifting sands. There is a fifth road, or rather mountain path, concerning which I can give no information. (Burton 1893: 2:58)

Of the four ways enumerated by Burton, the "Sultan's Way" was doubtless the major route from Mecca to Medina and vice versa. It was traveled in the Middle Ages by two of our most detailed reporters, Ibn Jubayr in 1184 and Ibn Battuta in 1326. Although it was a strenuous trip, neither traveler suggests that it was particularly dangerous.

Ibn Jubayr had finished his Hajj and had already made arrangements to pursue his further travels to Baghdad and Mosul; hence he journeyed from Mecca to Medina with the same Iraqi caravan whose company he would subsequently share from Medina to Baghdad:

Sunday evening, April 1st (1184), we went to join company at the camp of the Iraqi amir at al-Zahir, which is about two miles from Mecca. We had just fixed the rental of our mounts as far as Mosul, which is ten days beyond Baghdad. . . . We spent three days at al-Zahir, renewing each day our concourse with the venerable House and repeating our farewells to it.

On the afternoon of the 3rd the camp was struck, slowly and gently, out of regard for slower pilgrims and the stragglers; it was moved to Marr Bottom, about eight miles from the place we had left. . . . From the day we had arrived in Mecca on the 4th of August 1183 to the day of our departure from al-Zahir, the 3rd of April 1184, our stay at Mecca had lasted eight and a third months, and, taking into account the differing number of days in the months, two hundred and forty-five happy and blessed days. . . . By God's generosity we had been deprived of seeing the Sacred House on only three days out of that number: the day of Arafat, the day of sacrifice and . . . the day of our departure for al-Zahir. May God provide in his generosity that this is not our last contact with the sacred soil.

From there we left, after the noon prayer on Thursday, for Marr Bottom, a fertile valley with many palm trees, where a flowing spring provides running water which irrigates the soil of this region. The valley embraces a wide area, with numerous villages and springs. Fruit is exported from here to Mecca. (Ibn Jubayr 1948–1949: 210/Ar. 182)

On Friday there was an unexpected delay. One of the royal personages in the caravan, the daughter of Amir Mas'ud, ruler of "the passes of Cilicia, Armenia and the neighboring areas of the land of Rum," was missing from the caravan, though she had departed with it. The commander of the caravan ordered a delay until she could be found. The "gaudy princess" turned up finally on Saturday, without explanation, it appears, though speculation about where she had been, and why, was rife.

We were under way again on Saturday, April 9th (1184), and camped near Usfan, where we passed part of the night and where we made our morning prayer, at dawn on Sunday. The place is situated on a plain between two mountains with copious wells, which bear the name of the Caliph Uthman—may God be pleased with him. . . . There is an ancient fortress with strong towers, but it is unoccupied; age has left its mark on it and it has been ruined by the absence of upkeep and a progressive delapidation. We passed several miles beyond this place and then camped at the height of the heat to rest. Soon after the noon prayer we left for Khulays, where we arrived on the evening of the same day. This place too is located on a plain with numerous palm trees. There is a sturdy fortress atop the mountain which dominates the plain, and in the plain itself another fortress, which has fallen into ruin. There is a flowing spring whose water has been diverted into underground canals. The water is taken from them through openings like well-mouths; caravans there replenish their supply of water since it is lacking along the way due to the constant dryness. The caravan passed Monday morning there, busied with the watering of the camels and providing drink for themselves.

At noon on Monday, immediately after the prayer, we left Khulays and resumed our march, which stretched out to the very last moment before the time of the night prayer. We halted and had enjoyed only a brief sleep before the drum sounded again. We broke camp and marched until afternoon of this day, when we made a rest stop until the beginning of the noon prayer of Tuesday. We left this halting-place for a valley called Wadi al-Samk ("Valley of the Abyss"), a name which seems hardly appropriate to the place. We arrived there at the very end of the time for evening prayer, and we remained there on Wednesday to replenish our water supplies: water is found there in pools or sometimes by digging in the sand.

We left at the beginning of the noon prayer of Wednesday, and during the night crossed a steep, rocky bluff, where we lost many camels; we halted in the plain, where we slept for part of the night. There followed a trek across an immense desert area extending as far as the eye could see, a stretch of sand where the camels no longer had to walk in line since the way was so broad. We made a rest halt in the middle of the day, Thursday, the 14th of April (1184); we were then two stages from Badr. In the beginning of the afternoon we resumed our march and camped for the night at a place near Badr; we were on our way again and reached Badr before the second half of the night.

Badr was not merely a stopping place. Here Muhammad won his famous victory, quite unexpectedly, over the Muslims' pagan persecutors from Mecca, as Ibn Jubayr does not fail to remark:

Badr is a large town, with palm-groves that run one into the other. There is a fortress high atop a mountain; its approach is via the bottom of a valley between the mountains. Badr has a flowing spring. The site of the pool before which took place the battle in Islam which glorified the faith and cast down the polytheists is occupied today by a palm-grove, and the place where the martyrs fell is behind it. The Mount of Mercy upon which the angels descended (Quran 3:134) is on the left as you go from Badr to al-Safra. Opposite this hill is the Mount of the Drums, which looks like an elongated sand-dune, and it is so called because of a widely held tradition that there is heard there every Friday the sound of drums as a perpetual reminder of the Prophet's victory there. The site of the shelter in which the Prophet stayed is at the foot of this hill, and the battleground in front. In the palm-grove of the pool there is a mosque and what is said to be the place where the Prophet's camel knelt. One of the bedouin who live at Badr confirmed that the drums were heard on the hill, but that this took place on Mondays and Thursdays, which caused us great surprise. No one knows the truth of the matter save God Most High.

It is one march from Badr to al-Safra, and the road that leads there follows a valley between mountains, where there are continuous palmgroves and numerous springs; in all, an excellent road. At al-Safra there is a stout fortress, and nearby a number of others, particularly two called The Twins, one named "The Hassanite" and the other "The New Fort."

The month of Muharram [14 April 1184]. May God make us part of His blessing and that of His new year [580 A.H.]. The new moon appeared on Saturday night as we broke camp from Badr to al-Safra.... We camped again after the time of the evening prayer and so we were there Saturday morning to salute the new crescent moon. We made a rest halt so that our water could be replenished and people relax until the afternoon prayer. From there to Medina the Blessed there is, God willing, three days' journey.

We left there on Saturday afternoon, and our journey lasted until just after the time of the night prayer. We followed a way along a valley, hemmed in continuously by mountains. We camped for the night into Sunday, only to leave again in the middle of the night and continue our journey into the morning, when we paused at the "Well Marked with a Standard" to rest from the heat of the day. It is said that Ali ibn abi Talib fought the Jinn there; it is also called al-Rawha. These wells are extremely deep and it is barely possible to touch the bottom; the water comes from a spring.

We took the road again a little after the mid-afternoon prayer on Sunday and continued until the end of the time for the evening prayer, when we camped at the Pass of Ali—upon him be peace. We left there in the middle of the night, by way of Turban, for al-Bayda, from which you can see Medina the Blessed. We camped on the morning of April 16th at the Wadi Aqiq, at the side of which is located the mosque of Dhu al-Hulayfa, where the Prophet donned the ihram for pilgrimage. Medina is five miles distant, and the territory of Medina extends from Dhu al-Hulayfa to the tomb of Hamza and to Quba. What can first be seen from here is the tall white minaret of the Mosque of the Prophet.

We left immediately after the noon prayer on Monday, April 16th, and camped outside the radiant city, the white land honored by Muhammad, the prince of Prophets. (Ibn Jubayr 1949–1951: 212–218/Ar. 184–189)

In 1326 Ibn Battuta traveled this route in the opposite direction, with a copy of Ibn Jubayr obviously near at hand.

Then came our departure from Medina to go to Mecca. We halted near the mosque of Dhu al-Hulayfa, where the Apostle of God—God bless him and give him peace—assumed the pilgrim garb. It is at a distance of five miles from Medina, of whose sacred territory it forms the limit, and not far from it is the Wadi al-Aqiq. Here I divested myself of my tailored clothes, bathed, put on the garment of my consecration and made a prayer of two bowings. I entered the pilgrim state under obligation to carry out the rites of the Greater Pilgrimage [the Hajj] without conjunction.

"Without conjunction": that is, without combining the Hajj with the Umra. The practical effect of this limited intention is that if he later decided to perform the Umra, Ibn Battuta would have to go out to one of the stations marking the boundary of Mecca's sacred territory and declare a new intention of making the Umra.

In my enthusiasm I did not cease crying Labbayka Allahumma through every valley and hill and rise and descent until I came to the Pass of Ali—upon him be peace—where I halted that night. We set out from there and encamped at al-Rawha, where there is a well known as Bir Dhat al-Alam ("the Well Marked with a Standard," also known as "the Wells of Ali"), and it is said that Ali—upon him be peace—fought with the jinn at this well. Then we continued our march and encamped at al-Safra, which is a cultivated and inhabited valley in which there is water, palm gardens, buildings, and a fortified grange, occupied by the Hassani Sharifs and others. There is a large fort in this place also, and in the neighborhood are a number of forts and contiguous villages. (Ibn Battuta 1958: 184–185)

We continued our journey from this place and encamped at Badr . . .

Here there is no pretense: Ibn Battuta simply copies word for word Ibn Jubayr's notes on the historical topography of Badr. Ibn Battuta then resumes in his own voice:

We went from Badr into the desert known as the Flat of Bazwa, which is a wilderness where the guide wanders from the way, and friend has no thought to spare for friend—a three nights' journey. At the end of this march is the vale of Rabigh, in which pools are formed by rain and hold the water for a long time. From this point, which is just before al-Juhfa, the pilgrims (coming southward along the coastal road) from Egypt and the Maghrib enter the pilgrim state.

We set out from Rabigh and marched for a space of three days to Khulays. We passed through the defile of al-Sawiq, which is situated at a distance of half a day's journey from Khulays, and a very sandy place. The pilgrims make it a point of supping a certain barley gruel there and bring it with them from Egypt and Syria for this purpose; they serve it out to people mixed with sugar, and the amirs fill the watering tanks with it and serve the people from them. It is related that when the Apostle of God (God bless him and give him peace) passed through this place his Companions had no food with them, so he taking some of its sand gave it to them and they supped it (and found it to be) this barley gruel.

We then camped at the pool of Khulays, which lies in an open plain and has many palm groves. It possesses a strongly built fort on the top of a hill, and on the plain there is another fort in ruins. There is a gushing spring at this place, for whose waters channels have been made in the ground so that they flow to the cultivated lands. The lord of Khulays is a Sharif of the Hassani line. The bedouin of that neighborhood hold a great market there, to which they bring sheep, fruits and condiments.

We marched next to Usfan, in an open plain between hills, where there are wells of spring water, one of which is attributed to Uthman ibn Affan—may God be pleased with him. The laddered way, which is likewise attributed to Uthman, is half a day's journey from Khulays; it is a narrow pass between two hills, and at one part of it there is a pavement in the shape of steps, and traces of old buildings. . . . We then marched to Usfan [or Asfan] and encamped in the Bottom of Marr, also called Marr al-Zuhran [and later, and presently, called Wadi Fatima], a fertile valley with numerous date palms and a gushing spring of flowing water which serves for the irrigation of that district. From this valley fruit and vegetables are brought to Mecca, may God Most High ennoble her. We set out again at dawn from this blessed valley, with hearts full of gladness at reaching the goal of our hopes, rejoicing in our present condition and future state, and arriving in the morning at the City of Surety, Mecca, may God Most High ennoble her. (Ibn Battuta 1958: 186–187)

The Last Stage: From Jidda to Mecca

For most pilgrims, the journey from the sea to inland Arabia began at Jidda, the port of Mecca and a city that never failed to make an impression, though only rarely a favorable one. Ibn Jubayr's is one of the earliest pilgrim appreciations of Jidda, and a relatively neutral one at that, though it will be recalled that he arrived there from Aydhab on the Egyptian shore, a town the usually imperturbable Ibn Jubayr found truly trying.

The city of Jidda is situated on the shore of the sea; its houses are for the most part mud bungalows. There are some inns there built of stone and clay, at the top of which there are some rooms of mud, like the ones we call ghorfa. These inns have roofs where one seeks rest at night due to the great heat. There are visible in this city ancient ruins that demonstrate that this was once a considerable city. There are traces of its ancient walls that still exist today. There is a place there with an old and lofty domed shrine (qubba); it is said that this was the resting place of Eve, mother of the human race, when she came to Mecca, and that they built this edifice to testify to the bestowed blessing and the merit of this place.[37] God knows best about all that.

The inhabitants of this city, which is close to both mountain and desert, are for the most part descendants of the Prophet, Alids, Husaynids, Hasanids, Jaᶜfarids—may God be pleased with their noble ancestor. They are in a state wretched enough to wring pity from the stones. They are engaged in all the lower occupations: renting camels, if they have any, selling milk or water or other goods, like the dates they garner here and there, or the wood they go out and gather. At times it is their women, themselves sharifas [Meccan aristocracy], who do this work.

Outside the city some old water installations bear witness to the antiquity of its foundation. It is said that this was a Persian city. It has cisterns hollowed out of the hard rock; these are many in number and are joined one to the other: they maintain that there are 360 cisterns outside the city and the same number inside. We saw with our own eyes a great number of them, without being able to determine exactly how many of them there are. (Ibn Jubayr 1949–1951: 85–87/Ar. 75–76)

The road between Jidda and Mecca was by all accounts the best known and best serviced of all the caravan routes within the Hijaz, as British Intelligence attested early in the twentieth century:

We have ample detail about the Jidda-Mecca road. It is the most traveled track in Arabia, protected by blockhouses at intervals, and well supplied by halt stations. The first few miles lie over sandy plain, after which the track passes through a range of low hills to the plain of Bahra. Thence it leads over dusty undulating country to the main ridge of Western Arabia, in a foothill valley of which, running north-east from the range, lies the Holy City at a mean altitude of no more than 700 feet. . . . Mecca donkeys are the best riding animals for this road, and very good animals can do the journey in six or seven hours. The track is unmade, unmetalled and unbanked; but it has been trodden to a very fair surface, and is not interrupted by natural obstacles. A motor car could probably pass over it all. . . . Guns have often been wheeled over it. (Hogarth 1917: 86)

Hogarth's was not the first time-distance estimate of this well-traveled route. Burckhardt, for example, offered this guess in 1814:

I traveled several times afterwards between Mecca and Jidda, in both directions. The caravan's rate of march is here very slow, scarcely exceeding two miles an hour. I have ridden from Mecca to Jidda on an ass in thirteen hours. The distance may be fairly estimated at . . . about fifty-five miles. (Burckhardt 1829: 58)

The Iranian pilgrim Farahani, whom we shall meet again, was far more exact in 1885:

It is twelve farsakhs from Jidda to Mecca. (The rate per) farsakh, insofar as I have been able to determine it with a watch, is this: One who travels mounted on horseback goes one farsakh per hour. Mules or pack horses . . . an hour and a half. A file of camels . . . an hour and forty-five minutes. Thus one reaches Mecca from Jidda in twelve hours if one goes mounted on ambling-paced pack horses or donkeys. It takes from sixteen to eighteen hours if one goes by pack-mule and litter. If one goes by litter and camel-train, it is a twenty-one-hour trip without stopping. (Farahani 1990: 205)

Speed often depends on motive, and we have an account of what must have been one of the fastest recorded transits—traditional style—of those fifty-five-odd miles. Leon Roches, on a secret mission for the French government, stood in his Muslim garb among the throng of pilgrims at Arafat in 1841. Suddenly a cry went up: "Yo, a Christian! Seize the Christian, the infidel son of an infidel!" Quickly Roches was indeed seized by a pair of strong arms, trussed, gagged, and thrown across a saddle horse, head down on one side, feet dangling on the other. He could see nothing. An hour later the gag was removed and he was held seated upright in the saddle as the Sharif's men escorted him to safety in Jidda. And, says Roches, with some satisfaction:

It took those cavalrymen roughly six hours to cover the seventy-six kilometers, seventy-six, that separate Jidda from Mecca. (Roches 1904: 342)

Roches probably did not miss a great deal inside his bag. The road was not very interesting, though it did have its pleasant traditions, as discovered by the Dutchman Snouck Hurgronje, a temporary resident of Mecca at the end of the nineteenth century and a careful observer of the city's mores.

The custom of stone throwing has of old maintained itself outside the Mina Valley, where Islam has legalized the throwing on to three stone heaps. The tomb of Abu Lahab is (likewise) still to the present day stoned. On the Jidda-Mecca road between Jidda and Bahra there are two stone heaps to which the passer-by of the lower class always contributes his stone. The legend is that a pastrycook in Mecca asserted that he could by fast running take a plate of fresh baked cakes hot to Jidda, but forgot to add the reservation "God willing." So when he arrived at that spot he was struck dead as a punishment. The other heap is explained by a similar legend of a pastrycook running from Jidda toward Mecca with a plate of tarts. Whence the two heaps are called "The Cakes" and "The Tarts." (Hurgronje 1931: 96)

1. The Harbor of Al-Wajh: Boat Conveying the Pilgrims and the
Mahmal to Their Steamer.

2. Quarantine Island: Abu Saʿd near Jidda.

3. The Employees and the Officers of the Mahmal in Jidda, 1321 A.H./1904 C.E.

موكب المحمل الشامي في جبل عرفات

4. The Egyptian Mahmal and Soldiers in Pilgrimage Garb.

5. The Syrian Mahmal and Soldiers in Pilgrimage Garb.

6. Procession of the Mahmal at Jidda
and the (falsely ascribed) Mausoleum of Hawa (Eve).

7. The Mahmal and the Director of the Pilgrimage Caravan in his Ihram Dress.

8. A Photo of the Soldiers Dressed in Ihram Clothes
in Mina in 1321/1904.

9. Sheikh with Pilgrims from Suwakin.

CHAPTER III

The Medieval Hajj

(1100–1400 C.E.)

THE POINT OF Ibn Jubayr's visit to Mecca was not simply to see and describe another interesting place in the Abode of Islam. Indeed, it was not a "visit" at all. Rather, he was performing one of the religious obligations resting upon all Muslims physically and financially capable of performing it: the ritual of the Hajj.[1] We return, then, to Alexandria and the beginning of Ibn Jubayr's entry into the area, and follow him now not so much as a traveler as a pilgrim.

IBN JUBAYR ON THE HAJJ IN 1183–1184

Saladin's Abolition of the Pilgrims' Tax

In 1169 C.E. Salah al-Din, the new sultan in Syria, attacked Egypt and in 1172 delivered it out of the hands of the Shi'ite Fatimids and into the nominal sovereignty of the Sunni Caliph in Baghdad. Saladin, as he is more commonly known in the West, where his reknown is connected with his conquest of the Crusader kingdom in Jerusalem in 1187, did not, of course, surrender the actual power—he and his descendents continued to rule Egypt down to 1250—but the two-century Fatimid Shi'ite threat to both the Caliphate and the Holy Places of the Hijaz was over. In 1174 the new Sultan's brother conquered the Yemen, and thenceforward Saladin and the Sunni Caliph were named in the public prayers in Mecca. Although the Sharifs were left in place as titular masters of the Holy Cities, the Two Harams were actually ruled by Saladin's governor in the newly conquered Yemen.

Saladin enjoys the same reputation for justice in the Muslim chronicles as he does in the European ones. His name was particularly fragrant in the Hijaz because one of his first acts as sovereign of the Holy Places was to remove the indirect—and illegal—taxes that had been imposed on pilgrims,[2] as Ibn Jubayr noted with approval:

> Among the titles of honor that will give this sultan [Salah al-Din] access to God, among the fair actions that will assure him a noble memory, spiritual as well as temporal, one should recall that he abolished the tolls

which, in the form of a regular tax, pilgrims had to bear during Fatimid times. By being constrained to its payment pilgrims suffered a painful vexation and experienced a kind of unbearable affront. It occurred that certain among them had no further reserves to assure their subsistence or simply had no further resources. They were constrained nonetheless to pay, seven and a half dinars the head . . . even though they were incapable of doing so. They had in consequence to suffer extremely ill treatment at Aydhab, a city which well deserves its name [adab = chastisement]. One type of punishment they had invented was to hang them by their testicles, or some other frightful thing. . . . At Jidda equal or worse tortures awaited those who had not paid the tax at Aydhab and whose names were not accompanied by a notice of payment. The Sultan Salah al-Din abolished this evil usage and compensated for this tax with its equivalent in victuals and other things. He appropriated for this compensation the entire tax of a given locality and he made certain that it arrived in the Hijaz in its entirety. (Ibn Jubayr 1949–1951: 61–62/Ar. 55)

Taxation and the Hajj Caravan

Salah al-Din's action, so warmly praised by Ibn Jubayr, was only a tempo-rary solution to a problem that continued well into the twentieth century. The pilgrims were performing a religious obligation, it is true, but they were also a potential source of income in every area through which they passed, as special taxpayers to rulers, as toll payers to anyone who could control a bridge or a pass or a city wall, as customers to every entrepreneur and merchant along every foot of the way, and as simple objects of extor-tion to any highwayman, generally bedouin, in out-of-the-way places, of which there were many along every overland Hajj route. We shall see abundant examples of all these means of separating the pilgrims from their money or possessions, but here we confine our attention to the ques-tion of official taxes and tolls.

ATTEMPTS AT CONTROL

Taxing pilgrims was regarded as illegal by all Muslim jurists, and those were the levies that Saladin abolished. But what a ruler decided in Cairo or Damascus was not necessarily what prevailed in the Hijaz. Only after Mamluk Baybars made himself master of the Hijaz, and particularly after he led his own "private" pilgrimage in 1268 C.E., was there an attempt to curb the Meccan rulers' practice of taxing the caravans. These were not capitation taxes but imposts on a great number of products, an *ad valorem* duty on the goods of the merchants with the caravan—which was proba-bly legal but was an obvious inhibition on trade—and a flat charge per camel for the ordinary pilgrims.

Even the Mamluk Sultans could not closely supervise what went on in Mecca, and so it was thought that the best way to wean the princes of Mecca away from these pilgrim revenues would be for the Sultan to make up their losses from his own purse. Accordingly, in 1269 Baybars promised an annual gift of 20,000 dirhams for Mecca in exchange for an end to the pilgrim imposts. It was a noble endeavor, but apparently it barely survived his death in 1286 C.E. Soon there was talk of the camel tax again, now at a charge of 50 dirhams per camel. In 1319 C.E. the Sultan Qala'un had once again to insist on the abolition of pilgrim taxes in the Hijaz. This time the balm for the rulers of Mecca took the form of a settlement upon them of the income of certain villages of Egypt and Syria.[3]

The sad saga continued. In 1359 Sultan Hassan took a new tack. He sent troops to the Hijaz to ensure that his orders forbidding taxes on the pilgrims were observed. After a year of demonstrations, inspired no doubt by the Sharif himself and the other notables of Mecca, Hassan withdrew the troops. The Sharif, for his part, canceled the taxes on food and on the retail merchants; henceforward, only the wholesale spice traders had to pay duty. The entire agreement was ratified in 1365 by a contract, which was posted on the Ka'ba. The Sharif was to be compensated by an annual payment of 160,000 dirhams.[4]

We leap forward half a millennium, to Mecca in the late nineteenth century. The reporter is a resident of the city, the Christian Snouck Hurgronje:

Failing regular taxes, the Prince, that is, the Grand Sharif, and the Resident, that is, the Turkish Governor, can only in indirect ways get for themselves a part of that which the Meccans, and especially the shaykhs [the pilgrim guides], earn. Pilgrims who are not Turkish subjects have to pay for a Turkish government pass for their journey from Jidda to Mecca, which pass is quite useless to them, the cost of forming a concealed tax on the pilgrims. (As for the Turkish subjects,) they ask from the pilgrims in Jidda "free contributions," for example, for the maintenance of the Meccan aqueduct and the construction of a Jidda one. (Hurgronje 1931: 78)

SHEARING THE SHEARERS

If it was illegal to tax the pilgrims, there was nothing to prevent the government from skimming out of the wallets of the chief beneficiaries of the tourist trade, the professional guild of guides. In an Ottoman Empire still innocent of an income tax, this required the application of a familiar technique, extortion—a tricky business, because the guides had in effect lifetime tenure. Snouck Hurgronje describes the conditions in 1884:

The licenses given to shaykhs are a means of shearing those shaykhs themselves. From of old the "masters" of a guild require, besides their admission into the guild by the guildsmen, the recognition also of the local ruling powers. Like the admission, so the recognition also was good for life, if the person did not forfeit the position by his misconduct. Now this exception makes it possible for the Grand Sharif to threaten such a one with a withdrawal of the license unless he secures himself with presents. Until a short time ago, except for such measures taken against some individuals, the license once acquired and properly paid for was inalienable; only at a shaykh's death did his successor again have to pay, and the corporations gave beside on certain feast days, on when for instance they had to ask for an audience, presents to the ruler of the town. In these last years, however, the Prince and the Resident have sometimes applied a general bleeding process to all the guild alike.

When, in the opinion of these gentlemen, the shaykhs who are exploiting a particular class of pilgrims seem to be making more than enough money, then they in accord with the chief shaykh (who in such matters can raise no objections) introduce a new ordinance for the guild by which ordinance all licenses have to be renewed. This renewal, however, costs every shaykh some hundreds of dollars, and these men are thus compelled to discount their gains in advance. And now the chief shaykh has an opportunity, by giving under the new ordinances some advantages to his friends over their competitors, to do a little private business on his own account, but he must again make deductions from the profits of this private business as soon as the higher authorities have wind of it. (Hurgronje 1931: 78–79)

MAUVAIS TYPES IN THE HIJAZ

We are once again with Ibn Jubayr on his Hajj in 1183–1184, though the subject is timeless.

The inhabitants of areas of the Hijaz and elsewhere are mostly divided into sects and parties. They have no faith and profess various doctrines. They think to treat the pilgrims worse than they would treat the tributary "protected minorities" [the Jews and Christians]. They take away most of the goods they have collected for their own use. They strip them bare and plot to get hold of everything they possess. . . . If God had not brought some comfort to the Muslims in this region by the hand of Salah al-Din, . . . one would have despaired that the evil should have ever dissipated. It was he who abolished the taxes imposed on pilgrims and who replaced them with money and food which he sent to Mukhtir, the amir of Mecca. When this contribution, established for the benefit of the Meccans, is delayed in arriving, the amir begins once again to harass the pilgrims and declares his intention of barring the way to them, under the pretext that tribute must be paid. Thus chance would have it that we were held up at

Jidda while someone went to debate the question with the Amir Mukhtir. Finally his orders arrived: the pilgrims were not to enter the sacred territory of God unless they would guarantee that there would arrive the money and supplies that Salah al-Din had promised to supply; otherwise he would not surrender his taxes upon the pilgrims. Those were his words, as if the sacred soil of God belonged personally to him and he had the power to open it or not to the pilgrims! Glory to Him who changes and transforms the laws!

What Salah al-Din gives in place of the taxes on pilgrims amounts to 2,000 dinars and 1,000 ardabs of grain . . . to say nothing of properties which he set aside in the Saʿid (district) of Egypt and the Yemen for the benefit of the Meccans and to the same purpose. If this just ruler Salah al-Din had not been detained far away in Syria by the war against the Franks, the amir would not have pursued such a policy with regard to the pilgrims. The Islamic country that most deserves being purified by the sword and of being washed clean of its impurities and filth by blood spilled in the path of the Lord is this land of the Hijaz whose peoples share not in the honor of Islam and have possessed themselves of the goods and the blood of pilgrims. If there are in Spain jurists who hold that they are no longer obligated to the pilgrimage, their teaching is justified by these facts and by the treatment to which pilgrims are subjected, all without God's permission. (Ibn Jubayr 1949–1951: 87–88/Ar. 76–78)

As Nasir-i Khusraw describes some of the problems he encountered or heard about in 1049, it becomes apparent that the pilgrimage could be as hazardous as it was expensive:

A large caravan from the Maghrib ["the west," that is, Morocco] had come to Medina, and at the gates of Medina some Arabs had demanded protection money from them on the way back from the Pilgrimage. A fight broke out leaving more than two thousand Maghribis killed, and not many ever returned home.

In connection with what follows, it should be recalled that Nasir, traveling lightly and presumably rather quickly, covered the one hundred parasangs (approximately 350 miles by his measure) from Medina to Mecca in eight days.

On this same pilgrimage a group from Khurasan had come by land by way of Syria and Egypt and then by boat to Medina. On the 6th of Dhu al-Hijja, as they still had 104 parasangs to Arafat, they had said that they would give forty dinars to anyone who could get them to Mecca within the three remaining days in order for them to perform the Pilgrimage. Some Arabs came forth and got them to Arafat in two and a half days:

they took their [the Khurasanis'] money, tied them each to a fast camel and drove them from Medina. When they arrived at Arafat, two of them had died still tied to the camels; the other four were more dead than alive. At the afternoon prayer, as we were standing there, they arrived unable to stand up or speak. They finally told us that (en route) they had pleaded with the Arabs to keep the money they had given them but to release them, as they had no strength to continue. The Arabs, however, heedless of their entreaties, kept driving the camels forward. In the end the four of them made the Pilgrimage and returned to Syria. (Nasir-i Khusraw 1986: 61)

ENTERING THE STATE OF *IHRAM*

With the approach of the assembly to the sacred territory of Mecca, each pilgrim had to perform the first of the prescribed ritual acts connected with the Hajj, entry into the state of ritual purification (*ihram*). For Ibn Battuta, traveling southward from Medina, that took place at Dhu al-Hulayfa, five miles outside of Medina.[5]

Externally, what Ibn Battuta and his companions did was to trade their everyday clothes for a special garment. But the procedure was far more than a simple exchange. As explained by al-Ghazali (d. 1111), onetime professor at the prestigious Nizamiyya Madrasa in Baghdad, whose influential *Revivification of the Sciences of Religion* was more responsible for spiritualizing the ritual obligations of Islam than any other work, each act of the Hajj was a complex of understanding and intention.

You must know that the first (important) point about the Hajj is its understanding; I mean the understanding of the place of the Hajj in the (religion) of Islam. Then follows an eagerness for it [the Hajj], the decision to make it, a detachment from whatever might hinder it, the buying of the ihram garment, of provisions, the procuring of a means of transport, and the departure on the journey across the desert. Then comes the point (for the donning) of the ihram with the chant of Labbayka, and arrival at Mecca for the completion of all the (ritual) acts described earlier.

An important theme throughout the *Revivification* is that of intention: it is not so much the performance of an act as the purity of one's intention that gives it spiritual value:[6]

As for the decision (to make the Hajj), the (would-be pilgrim) must know that through his decision he intends to leave his family and home and leave aside desires and pleasures in order to visit the Lord's House, and thus to glorify even more the majesty of the House and of the Lord of the House. He must also know that he has decided on a sublime and momentous thing, and that he who is seeking a great thing must make great sacrifices. He must make his decision solely for the sake of God and remote from the blemishes of hypocrisy and the enhancement of one's own reputaiton. He must be certain that from among his intentions and acts only the sincere are acceptable, and that it is an abominably vile deed to have the House and the Haram of the King as a destination when the purpose of the visit is other than Him. He must therefore amend his decision out of sincerity, and sincerity is achieved by the avoidance of all hypocrisy and self-serving. He must be careful not to exchange that which is better for that which is worse.

The most powerful effect of the pilgrimage, Ghazali argues, is that it is, or should be, a preparation for death, and it is in connection with the *ihram* that he sounds the note most clearly.

As for buying the ihram garment, at that moment he should reflect on the shroud and how he will (one day) be wrapped in it. He will wear the ihram garment when he reaches the Lord's House, but it may be that his journey there will never occur. What is sure is that he will face God wrapped in his shroud. And just as he may not look upon the Lord's House except in clothes different from what he usually wears, so after death he cannot see God but in a dress different from his worldly dress.

When the incoming pilgrim arrives at the formal boundary points of the Meccan Haram, he performs the first of the ritual acts of the Hajj: he dons the pilgrim garment and utters the famous cry called the *talbiyya*, "At Your service, O Lord; at Your service." This formula, whose frequent and loud repetition upon entering the sacred territory is an essential part of the Hajj ritual, is doubtless of pre-Islamic origin. Although its original significance is by now unclear, what it meant for the Muslim was something akin to "At Your Service, O God!"[7]

Ghazali continues:

As for donning the ihram and uttering the talbiyya from the Haram boundaries onward, let him understand that it signifies answering the summons of God. Thus you must hope that you will be acceptable and take a care that your talbiyya be not answered with a rejection. You must stand there hesitating between hope and fear and repent with all your might and power, relying on God's grace and generosity, for the moment of the talbiyya is the beginning of something momentous. . . .

While raising his voice in the talbiyya at the boundary point, let him who is doing so remember how he answered God's call, "And proclaim among men the Pilgrimage" (Quaran 22:27), and remember as well the trumpet's summons to all humans, how they will be gathered together

from their graves; how they will assemble in crowds in the courtyard on
Judgment Day to answer God's call; how they will be divided into those
who will be made new (to God) and those who are hated, those who are
accepted and those who are rejected. (Ghazali, The Revivification 1.7.218–
220)

We witness the *ihram* ritual, if not the intention, in the company of an
anonymous traveler with the Egyptian caravan sometime about 1575.

> With the next morning by the sun rising, the Caravan arrives at Be-
> drhonem [Badr Hunayn in the Hijaz], in which place every man washes
> himself from top to toe, as well men as women, and leaving off their
> apparel, having each one a cloth about their privities . . . and another
> white one upon their shoulders, all which can go to Mecca in this habit
> do so and are thought to merit more than the other, but they which
> cannot do so vow to sacrifice a ram at the mountain of pardons. And after
> they be washed, it is not lawful for any man or woman to kill either flea
> or louse with their hands, neither to take them with their nails, until they
> have accomplished their vowed orations at the mountain of pardons
> aforesaid.[8] (Anon. Hakluyt 1927: 3:185)

After a Sea Voyage (1685 or 1686)

By land, the pilgrim could approach Mecca not only from Medina but
also from the Yemen or from Iraq, each of which had its own place where
the state of ritual purification had to be entered. If the pilgrim approached by sea, the donning of the garb depended on where one disembarked. When Joseph Pitts came to Mecca in 1685 or 1686, he landed at
neither Yanbu nor Jidda but at Rabigh between them, where he made
particular note of the change in clothes.[9]

> A few days after this [that is, after more than twenty days on the Red
> Sea] we came to a place called Rabbock [Rabigh, north of Jidda], about
> four days' sail this side of Mecca; where all the hagges (excepting those of
> the female sex) do enter into hirrawem or ihram, i.e. they take off all their
> clothes, covering themselves with two hirrawems or large white cotton
> wrappers. One they put about their middle, which reaches down to their
> ankles; the other they cover the upper part of their body with, except the
> head. And they wear no other thing on their bodies but these wrappers;
> only a pair of gimgameea [jamjamiyya], i.e. thin-sol'd shoes, like sandals,
> the over-leather of which covers only the toes, their insteps being all
> naked. In this manner, like humble penitents, they go from Rabbock till
> they come to Mecca to approach the temple; many times enduring the
> scorching heat of the sun till their very skin is burnt off their backs and

arms and their heads swoll'd to a very great degree. Yet when any man's health is by such austerities in danger and like to be impaired, they may lawfully put on their clothes, on condition still that, when they come to Mecca, they sacrifice a sheep and give it to the poor. During the time of their wearing this mortifying habit, which is about the space of seven days, it is held unlawful for them so much as to cut their nails or to kill a louse or a flea, tho' they see them sucking their blood; and yet, if they are so troublesome that they cannot well endure it longer, 'tis lawful for them to remove them from one place of the body to another.

During this time they are very watchful over their tempers, keep a jealous eye upon their passions, and observe a strict government of their tongues, making continual use of a form of devout expressions. And they will also be careful to be reconciled and at peace with all such as they had any difference with; accounting it a very shameful and sinful thing to bear the least malice against any. They do not shave themselves during this time. (Pitts 1949: 21–22)

Two Nineteenth-Century Views

These early descriptions of the entry into the *ihram* state are rather perfunctory, either because something well known was being described or else, in the case of Pitts, because he was not entirely sure of the significance of what he witnessed. In the nineteenth century, however, there was no lack of interest or detail concerning this ritual. Like Ibn Battuta many centuries before, Richard Burton approached Mecca with the Syrian caravan coming down from Medina. There was a pause at the station called Zariba.

Having pitched the tent and eaten and slept, we prepared to perform the ceremony of al-Ihram, assuming the pilgrim garb, as al-Zariba is the miqat, or the appointed place. Al-Ihram, literally meaning "prohibition" or "making unlawful," . . . is applied to the ceremony of the toilette and also to the dress itself. . . . It is opposed to ihlal, "making lawful" or "returning to laical life." The further from Mecca it is assumed, provided that it be during the three months of Hajj, the greater is the religious merit of the pilgrim; consequently, some come from India and Egypt in this dangerous attire.

Between the noonday and the afternoon prayers a barber attended to shave our heads, cut our nails and trim our mustachios. Then, having bathed and perfumed ourselves—the latter is a questionable point . . .

None of these acts is part of the actual ceremony of the *ihram*.[10] In fact, as will appear below, they are some of the practices that will henceforward be forbidden to the pilgrim for the duration of the taboo state.

... we donned the attire, which is nothing but two new cotton cloths, each six feet long by three and a half broad, white, with narrow red stripes and fringes. . . . These sheets are not positively necessary; any clean cotton cloth not sewn in any part will do equally well. Servants and attendants expect the master to present them with an ihram. One of these sheets . . . is thrown over the back, and, exposing the arm and shoulder, is knotted at the right side. The other is wrapped round the loins from waist to knee, and knotted or tucked in at the middle, supports itself. Our heads were bare, and nothing was allowed upon the instep. It is said that some clans of Arabs still preserve this religious but most uncomfortable costume; it is doubtless of ancient date, and to this day, in the regions lying west of the Red Sea, it continues to be the common dress of the people.

The wife and daughters of a Turkish pilgrim of our party assumed the ihram at the same time as ourselves. They appeared dressed in white garments; and they had exchanged the lisam, that coquettish fold of muslin which veils without concealing the lower part of the face, for a hideous mask, made of split, dried and plaited palm-leaves, with two "bulls'-eyes" for light. The reason why this "ugly" must be worn is that a woman's veil during the pilgrimage ceremonies is not allowed to touch her face.

Then follow the "Intention" and the "Invocation." The former states that in this instance, unlike Ibn Battuta, Burton's party explicitly intended to perform both the Umra and the Hajj on this single occasion:

After the toilette, we were placed with our faces in the direction of Mecca, and ordered to say aloud, "I vow this ihram of the Hajj and the Umra to Allah Almighty." Having thus performed a two-bow prayer, we repeated, without rising from the sitting position, "O Allah! Verily I purpose the Hajj and the Umra, then enable me to accomplish the two, and accept them both of me, and make both blessed to me."

There followed the talbiyya, or exclaiming—"Here I am, O Allah, here I am. No partner hast Thou; here I am. Verily the praise and grace are Thine, and the empire. No partner hast Thou; here I am." And we were warned to repeat these words as often as possible, until the conclusion of the ceremonies.

Then Shaykh Abdullah, who acted as director of our consciences, bade us be good pilgrims, avoiding quarrels, immorality, bad language and light conversation. We must so reverence life that we should avoid killing game, causing an animal to fly, and even pointing it out for destruction; nor should we scratch ourselves, save with the open palm, lest vermin be destroyed or a hair uprooted by the nail. The object of these ordinances is clearly to inculcate the strictest observance of the "truce of God." Pilgrims, however, are allowed to slay, if necessary, "the five noxious ones," to wit, a crow, a kite, a scorpion, a rat, a biting dog. We were to respect the sanctuary by sparing the trees, and not to pluck a single blade of grass.

*As regards personal considerations, we were to refrain from all per-
fumes and unguents; from washing the head with mallow or with lote
leaves; from dyeing, shaving, cutting or vellicating a single pile or hair;
and though we might take advantage of shade, and even form it with
upraised hands, we must by no means cover our sconces. For each infraction of these ordinances we must sacrifice a sheep—the victim is sacrificed
as a confession that the offender deems himself worthy of death: the
offerer is not allowed to taste any portion of his offering—and it is commonly said by Muslims that none but the Prophet could be perfect in the
intricacies of the pilgrimage. (Burton 1893: 2:138–141)*

The Shiʿite Persian pilgrim Mirza Muhammad Farahani, who made the
Hajj in 1885, provides his own, more legalistic list of the requirements of
the *ihram* state. As he himself notes, there were variations on details not
only between Sunni and Shiʿite but even among the various Sunni legal
schools:

*The essential part of the ihram is taking off the ordinary dress, putting
two pure white robes on oneself and reciting the talbiyya. Some of the
Shiʿite ulama have said there are twenty-four things which are forbidden
to a person in a state of ihram; some reckon twenty-two and a few sixteen.
(Farahani 1990: 203–204)*

The precise prohibitions to be observed by the pilgrim while in this formal state of consecration vary considerably from school to school.[11]
Burton gives his own (Shafiʿite) list,[12] while Farahani's Shiʿite version
includes sixteen interdictions: hunting; sexual pleasure with or from
women; intentional emission of sperm; use of perfume; use of ointments; lies, foul language, swearing; looking in a mirror; wearing knotted,
seamed, or sewn clothes, boots or stockings, rings for ornamentation; covering the head or ears; deliberately drawing one's blood; seeking shade (to
this day a Shiʿite peculiarity); cutting the hair or nails; killing or removing
lice from one's body or ticks from an animal; killing any living thing
except mice and scorpions; cutting grass or trees of the haram; wrestling
and fighting.[13]

THE PILGRIMAGE TO ARAFAT
(13 MARCH 1184)

Once again we are in the company of Ibn Jubayr, who has been presented
with a marvelously illuminating moral paradigm based on a simple question: When exactly does the month of Dhu al-Hajj begin in the Hijri year
579? The answer is apparently simple: with the appearance of the new
moon; or better, with the *observance* of the appearance of the new moon.

The Affair of the New Moon

The month of Dhu al-Hijja. May God allow us to share in its blessings! The new moon appeared on Thursday, corresponding to the 15th of March. Its observation was for the people an extraordinary event, a wonderful opportunity for altering the truth, for pronouncing false statements which even inert nature was ready to contradict as a lie. All were on the lookout during Thursday night, the thirtieth day of the month; but the sky of the horizon was covered by a mist and there were heaped up clouds right up to sunset, when a red glow of twilight appeared in the sky. People were hoping that a break would appear in the sky permitting them to see the new moon. From time to time someone would cry out a takbir [the cry "God is great!"], and the docile crowd would respond with one of its own, with everyone standing there motionless looking at what they could not see and pointing out that which they had imagined.

All of this arose from their great desire that the "standing" of Arafat should take place on a Friday, as if the pilgrimage only had a religious value when the waquf fell on Fridays. People invented false sightings. A group of Maghribis—may God purify their acts!—some Egyptians, notable people, all testified before the Chief Justice that they had seen the new moon. But he dismissed them out of hand, violently rejected their testimony and declared them shameful for offering him lies. . . . The justice Jamal al-Din showed a great deal of firmness and judgment in this matter of the false witnesses. He was praised for it by the educated and congratulated by men of good sense. And that was only right. The rites of pilgrimage are of great importance for Muslims . . . and if accommodations were permitted, pious zeal would disappear and the religious conscience would be weakened.

Testimonies regarding the new moon rested in suspense until the day when reports of its appearance on Thursday night, which would be the 15th of March, multiplied; testimonies offered by pious and conservative people, Yemenites and others coming from Medina. But the justice stayed firm in his refusal to listen to such witnesses and to postpone his decision until the arrival of the courier who would announce the coming of the Iraqi caravan so that he might be informed of the position of the Caravan Commander on this subject. . . . On (the following) Wednesday, the seventh of this month (of Dhu al-Hijja) the courier arrived. The coming of the courier brought peace and tranquillity to the troubled, since he arrived with good and comforting news: he announced that the new moon had been seen on the (previous) Thursday. The news spread quickly, and the fact received sufficient support that the qadi had to deliver his sermon on that same day, according to the established custom, on the seventh of Dhu al-Hijja, after the noontime prayer. He instructed the faithful on their ritual obligations, and then he informed them that the following day would be the day of the ascent to Mina, that is to say, the day of tarwiyya; that the "standing" would take place on Friday and that, according to the noble tradition reported of the Prophet, it was worth seventy (ordinary) "standings," since the superiority of this "standing" over that of other years was similar to the superiority of Friday over other days. (Ibn Jubayr 1949–1951: 193–198/Ar. 167–170)

When the Persian notable Farahani made the pilgrimage in the summer of 1885, the issue was still much the same, though perhaps somewhat more accurately identified.

One reason that the Sunnis want Arafat to fall on a Friday is to obtain a Greater Pilgrimage.[14] Another is because if Arafat falls on a Friday, the judges will get a bonus from the government because there are more vows and prayers (connected with) the Greater Pilgrimage. In every (period) of seventy years, Arafat must fall on Friday ten times. But for the considerations (just cited), they move the day of Arafat to Friday every three years. This year too they moved Arafat to Friday. (Thus) they left Arafat at sunset on Friday. That Sharif and the Pasha had also submitted to this and left. The Shiʿites, who numbered about six thousand and were mostly subjects of Iran, spent Saturday at Arafat since no one had seen the (new) moon. (Farahani 1990: 252–253)

Mina

We return to Ibn Jubayr, now at Mina.

On Thursday the crowd went up early to Mina and from there continued on the way to Arafat. If one were following the sunna, the night would have been passed at Mina, but this year they passed it over by necessity, in their fear of the Banu Shuʿba who were attacking the pilgrims along the way to Arafat. The Amir Uthman [prince of Aden] fulfilled on his own initiative in these circumstances an effort, let us say rather an act of Holy War, which gave hope for the forgiveness of all his sins, if it so pleases God. What he did was advance at the head of his well-armed companions as far as the defile between Muzdalifa and Arafat, to the place where the way is hemmed in between two mountains. It was from one of them, on the left as you proceed toward Arafat, that the Banu Shuʿba used to descend to despoil the pilgrims. In this canyon between the two mountains the amir had a round tent set up after he had sent in advance one of his companions who rode on horseback to the top of this precipitous mountain. We were much in awe of this latter's deed, but our admiration went more particularly to his horse which had scaled a slope where a gazelle would not have found footing. The crowd of pilgrims was then secure, thanks to the intervention of the amir, who thus gained a double reward, one for making the pilgrimage and the other for Holy War, since it was surely such to assure the security of God's "delegates" on such a day. People continued to go up without interruption throughout that day and the next night, as well as all through Friday. Thus there assembled at Arafat a crowd such as only God could estimate their number.

Muzdalifa is situated between Mina and Arafat, and as far from Mina as that latter is from Mecca, that is, about five miles. From Muzdalifa to Arafat it is the same distance, or a little less. It is called "the holy place of the sacrifices," and also "the assembly." Thus it has three different names.

About a mile before it is found the Wadi al-Muhassir, which it is customary to cross quickly; it is the boundary between Mina and Muzdalifa, since it is exactly equidistant from both. Muzdalifa is on flat terrain extending between two mountains. It is surrounded by reservoirs and basins built to hold water at the time of Zubayda, may God have mercy on her. In the middle of this plain there is an enclosure, in the center of which rises a domed shrine; at the top of this dome there is an oratory to which you ascend by steps on both sides. People crowd around to get up there and make their ritual prayer there during the night they pass at Muzdalifa. (Ibn Jubayr 1948–1951: 198–199/Ar. 171–172)

At Arafat

Arafat too is situated on a plain, which extends as far as the eye can see, so as to serve as a rendezvous for all creation. This immense plain is surrounded by many mountains. At the end of the plain is located the "Mount of Mercy" on which and around which takes place the "standing" of the faithful. In the foreground two markers somewhat resembling milestones indicate that what is beyond that, on the other side of Arafat, is profane terrain and that which is inside is sacred territory. . . .

The Mount of Mercy is isolated from the other mountains, located in the middle of the plain. It is made entirely of discrete rocks. It was difficult of access until Jamal al-Din, whose benevolence has been mentioned previously, had gentle steps made on all four sides, by which it is possible to go up even with loaded animals. He paid a great deal for the work. At the top of the mountain is a domed shrine which is called after Umm Salima, though no one knows the genuine attribution. In the middle of this domed shrine is an oratory where the faithful crowd around to make prayer. This venerated oratory is surrounded by a vast platform, a magnificent belvedere which dominates the Arafat plain.

Going from there in the direction of the prayer-direction [that is, toward Mecca] one finds a wall where prayer-niches have been made and in front of which the faithful come to perform their ritual prayers. At the foot of this mountain, on the left as you face in the prayer-direction, there is a house of ancient construction, whose upper part has lofty chambers with arcades; the name of Adam is connected with it. On the left, facing the direction of prayer, one sees a rock which is the place the Prophet took as his station, and which is on top of a flat rock. Around the Mount of Mercy and the venerated house there are water basins and cisterns. Also to the left of the house and quite near it is a small oratory.

Near the two markers and on your left as you face the prayer-direction, you see an ancient and vast oratory from which survives a wall on the prayer-direction side and to which is attached the name of Abraham; the preacher makes the sermon there on the day of the "standing"; then the prayers of noonday and late afternoon are combined into one. (Ibn Jubayr 1948–1951: 200–201/Ar. 173)

THE "STANDING" AT ARAFAT

The gathering of the faithful at Arafat was completed on Thursday and over the night into Friday. In the last third of this same Thursday night the amir of the Iraqi caravan arrived and set up his camp on the vast plain, on the right side of the Mount of Mercy as you face the direction of prayer. But the prayer-direction at Arafat is on the west: it is in this direction that the Ka'ba is situated vis-à-vis Arafat. The morning of this Friday there was at Arafat an assemblage that can only be equaled by the Final Gathering. . . . Some truthful elders among the local population with experience of the Holy House said that they had never seen a more numerous crowd at Arafat, and my own opinion is that not since the time of Harun, who was the last Caliph to make the Hajj, has there been a similar gathering in Islam.

After the two prayers of noontime and mid-afternoon had been combined this Friday, the faithful made their "standing" in adoration, in humility and in tears, begging the favor of the Most High. Cries of "God is great!" arose and a tumult of voices went up in invocation of God. . . . The crowd remained there, their faces burned by the sun, until its orb had disappeared and the prayer of sunset had arrived. The amir of the pilgrimage appeared in the midst of his soldiers dressed in coats of mail; they made the "standing" near the rocks around the small oratory I have already mentioned. The Yemeni Sarwa had set up their "standing" camp in the places on Arafat that had been designated for them and which they had transmitted from father to son from the time of the Prophet without one tribe ever intruding upon the space of another. This year they assembled in numbers never seen previously. Similarly, the Iraqi amir had come accompanied by a suite the likes of which he had never brought before. He was accompanied by a crowd of non-Arab princes, Persians, Khura-

sanis, women of illustrious birth whom they called khatuns and women who were the daughters of princes. The mass of non-Arabs was beyond counting.

For the "flight" (nafr) they followed the example of the Maliki prayer-leader because Malik's rite requires that the "flight" not be made until the sun has disappeared and the time of the sunset prayer has come.[15] There were Yemeni Sarwa who made the "flight" before that. When the moment had come, the Maliki imam made a gesture with his two hands and came down from the place where he had made his "standing"; the crowd surged forward on their "flight" with an enthusiasm that made the earth tremble and the mountains shake. (Ibn Jubayr 1948–1951: 201/Ar. 173–175)

THE PILGRIMAGE À LA GRANDE LUXE

What caught Ibn Jubayr's particular attention in the enormous spectacle at Arafat was the camp of the commander of the Iraqi caravan.

The camp of the Iraqi commander provided a marvelous spectacle. Its order was perfect, the installations superb, with its round tents and admirable enclosures, the magnificent likes of which are not to be seen. The commander's tent has the most important appearance; it had around it an enclosure like a wall of cloth, like the cloister of a garden or the decorated summit of a dwelling. Inside were round tents, all black on white, with embroidered borders resembling banks of flowers. . . . This enclosure, which was like a wall, had four lofty gates like those in the most powerful fortresses, and through them one entered into the various vestibules and elbowed passageways. Then one came to a large open space where the tents were raised. Thus the amir seemed to live in a walled city. (Ibn Jubayr 1948–1951: 202–203/Ar. 176)

The rich, as always, had a very different experience of the pilgrimage, at least in its externals.

There are also round tents that are carried on the backs of camels and serve to shield one from the sun. . . . They are built on wooden constructions which are called qashawat . . . and which are like hollow boxes. Similar to the cribs of children, these boxes are used indifferently by men and women and are filled with soft drapery where the traveler is seated, as if taking his ease in a large and pleasant cradle. There is a second on the other side which serves as a counter-weight, and the round tent covers both. They are carried in this fashion, sound asleep, without even knowing they are traveling; or they do as they please. When they arrive at a stop that has been fixed for them, if they are people accustomed to good living or luxury, one has already put up their linen enclosure, they are brought in on their mounts and stairs are placed down to help them dismount. Thus they pass from the shade of the pavilion of their palanquin to their

round tent of their station stop without being discommoded by contact
with the air or by ugly attacks by the sun. But take care of these searches
for well-being. These people, when they travel, no matter how long its
extent, undergo no pain; they suffer no fatigue from the length of their
passage or from the great distance to their goal. There is far less comfort
for the pilgrims carried in maharat, litters like the shaqduf . . . which is,
however, wider and bigger. . . . Those who cannot have these conveniences suffer from the fatigue of the journey, which is part of the punishment of the future life (and hence remitted if one suffers it on the pilgrimage). (Ibn Jubayr 1948–1951: 203–204/Ar. 176–177)

From Arafat to Muzdalifa

We return with Ibn Jubayr to Muzdalifa, the Hajj station closer to Mecca:

The faithful left (Arafat) after the setting of the sun, as was already said.
They arrived at Muzdalifa toward the time of the last nighttime prayer
and there performed both nighttime prayers, according to the custom of
the Prophet. The mashʿar al-haram was completely lit that night with
brilliant wax candles, and as for the mosque itself, it had become one large
light. Looking at it, one could well believe that the stars of the heaven had
come down there. It was the same on Friday night for the Mount of
Mercy and its mosque, since the non-Arabs of Khurasan and other pilgrims of the Iraqi caravan are the most moved to bring candles and use
them in profusion to illuminate the venerated sanctuaries.

The pilgrims passed that night, that is, Saturday, in the sacred place
(mashʿar al-haram). After the dawn prayer they leave for Mina after having made a wuquf and an invocation (duʿa). All of Muzdalifa is place for
a wuquf save the Wadi Muhassir through which one hastens on the way
to Mina. . . . It is at Muzdalifa that the pilgrims generally collect the pebbles for the stoning; this is the recommended ritual, though some collect
them around the mosque of al-Khaʾif at Mina: there is latitude for either
practice. (Ibn Jubayr 1948–1951: 204–205/Ar. 177)

The Day of Sacrifice

When the pilgrims arrive at Mina they hasten to fulfill the stoning of
The Slope with seven rocks. Then they sacrifice a large or a small animal
and they are freed from all the prohibitions save those of women and
perfumes. . . . This stoning is done at sunrise on the day of sacrifice, and
it is then that the pilgrims generally accomplish their turnings of the
"flight"; there are, however, some who remain there till the second day,
and some others until the third, which is that of the going down to
Mecca.

The second day, the day after the sacrifice, at sunset people go to throw seven stones at the first pillar, and the same number at the one in the middle; at both they take their stand to make an invocation; likewise at the Pillar of the Slope, but without making a station: all of that in imitation of the Prophet. On these two days the Pillar of the Slope takes the last place, while on the day of sacrifice it was the first and the only; no other had a share with it.

On the second day after the sacrifice, when the pillars have been stoned, the preacher pronounces the sermon in the mosque of al-Kha'if, then he pronounces together the midday and later afternoon prayers. This preacher had come with the Iraqi commander; he was invested by the Caliph with the offices of preacher and Chief Justice of Mecca, according to what was said. This person had the name of Taj al-Din, and the most obvious thing about him was his stupidity and blundering: his sermon was the perfect expression of it; his language was not even syntactical.

On the third day the last of the faithful hastened to come down to Mecca after having completed all forty-nine of the stonings. . . . It was once traditional to pass three days at Mina after the sacrifice to complete the throwing of seventy stones, but in our times it was common practice to reduce the time to two days. . . . All of which came from the fear brought on by the Banu Shuʿba. (Ibn Jubayr 1948–1951: 205–206/Ar. 177–178)

As the pilgrimage ritual wound down, the discipline born of piety began to yield to the more common passions of large crowds.

The day of the going back to Mecca there was a brawl growing out of a quarrel between the blacks of Mecca and the Turks in the Iraqi caravan. There were wounds, swords unsheathed, bows drawn, arrows let fly; goods were pillaged, since Mina is, during those three days, a market for the wealthy: everything is sold there from precious pearls to the largest glass beads, all types of objects and from the whole world over; it is the place where people congregate from all countries. But God averted the dangers of this quarrel by suppressing it quickly. (Ibn Jubayr 1948–1951: 206–207/Ar. 178)

The Renewal of the Veil of the Kaʿba

Saturday, the day of sacrifice (at Mina), there was brought by camel from the camp of the Iraqi commander to Mecca the covering for the holy Kaʿba. The new justice walked before it with a garment of Sawad cloth sent by the Caliph. Flags floated over his head; drums were beat behind him. . . . The covering was placed on the venerated roof above the Kaʿba.

On Tuesday, the 13th of this blessed month, the Banu Shayba undertook to unfold it, a cloth of bright green, possessing a beauty to enchant all who looked upon it. Above there was a large strip of red embroidery with inscriptions; on the side that faced the venerated Station of Abraham and where the holy door opened, that is, on its blessed face, one read, after the bismillah: "The first house that was founded for men . . . " etc. (Quran 3:90) and on the other sides the name of the Caliph and invocations on his behalf. (Ibn Jubayr 1949–1951: 207/Ar. 178)

One ancient custom that took on a new importance during the Abbasid era was that of covering the Ka'ba, a stone building for as long as we know anything of it, with some kind of fabric. The origins of the tradition—and its motives—are lost, but the later Muslim tradition preserved the memory of Yemenite kings sending ceremonial coverings for the Ka'ba along with their sacrificial offerings.[16] Those sacrifices were made in honor of the Lord of the Ka'ba, so it is likely that they, and the ritual covering of the Ka'ba, took place during the Meccan pilgrimage *par excellence*, the so-called Umra that occurred during the month of Rajab. The Umra survived as a colorful but minor festival in Islam, as we shall soon see; but the re-covering of the Ka'ba, together with much else from that holiday, was transferred to the Muslims' Hajj.

The early history of the custom under Islam is traced by the Meccan historian Azraqi:

Abu al-Walid said that he had heard . . . that Umar ibn al-Khattab used to strip the Kiswa off the House every year and he used to give it to pilgrims so they could use (pieces of) it as coverlets on long nights. My grandfather told me that he had heard . . . that the Ka'ba was covered in pre-Islamic times by the donations of the people from Anta', Aksiyya, Karar, and Anmat, and there were piles and piles (of cloth). But when the Muslims adorned and covered the Ka'ba (with funds) from the State Treasury, the covering became less and less.

It used to be decorated during the Caliphates of Umar [r. 634–644 C.E.] and Uthman [r. 644–656 C.E.] with "Qubbati," a kind of cloth made in Egypt, except that one year Uthman (also?) used a Yemeni cloth called "Rawdan," and he was the first to drape the Ka'ba with two kinds of cloth. . . . Shayba ibn Uthman related that all the cloth from the pre-Islamic period was removed because the Muslims did not want there anything touched by the polytheists because of their baseness. (Azraqi 1858: 179–180)

Thus, according to Azraqi, Umar was the first Muslim ruler to interest himself in the covering of the Ka'ba, though only out of necessity. In Umar's day the Banu Shayba, the traditional custodians of the Ka'ba,

advised the Caliph that the cumulative weight of the cloths, which apparently were draped one over the other year after year, was causing damage
to the roof of the structure. Umar gave his permission to remove and
replace them, and he himself sent a new veil of Egyptian manufacture.[17]
The tradition may have been tendentious—it does provide defensible
grounds for the later custom—but whatever the case, the practice is attested to for Umar's successors, specifically Uthman.

It was in the reign of Umar's Umayyad relative Mu'awiya (r. 661–680)
that the Banu Shayba began to sell the remnants of the veil from the
previous year.[18] There must have been some opposition to this practice, at
least initially, because one of the Shaybids had to get the *vendere licet*
from no less an authority than Aisha herself. She seems to have consented,
though with the stipulation that proceeds go not into the purses of the
Banu Shayba but to some pious cause "in the path of God."[19]

At the beginning of the ninth century the covering for the Ka'ba, now
sent regularly with the Iraqi caravan by the Abbasid Caliphs in Baghdad,
became embroiled in the Shi'ite politics that characterized that era. A
certain Abu Saraya, a self-proclaimed protector of the House of Ali, sent
one of the Alids, Husayn ibn Hassan al-Aftas, to Mecca, where he managed to depose the Abbasid governor. Once in power, Husayn stripped
the Holy House of its coverings and replaced them with a new one bearing the embroidered legend, "By order of al-Asfar ibn al-Asfar Abu Saraya,
protector of the family of the Prophet, a covering for the Holy House of
God, which has been cleansed of the covering of the usurpers, the sons of
Abbas. Written in 199 [814–815 C.E.]."[20] There is no indication of the
color of this covering, but it was likely either white or green, colors identified with the Alids and their claims, rather than the black associated with
the Abbasid dynasty.

The Englishman Richard Burton saw the Ka'ba in the summer of 1853,
when he came to Mecca in disguise. The *kiswa*, the large cloth used to
cover the building, had just been replaced, at the end of the pilgrimage as
was then customary, by a new one brought from Cairo:

> The Ka'ba had been dressed in her new attire when we entered.[21] The
> covering, however, instead of being secured at the bottom to metal rings
> in the basement, was tucked up by ropes from the roof, and depended
> over each face in two long tongues. It was of a brilliant black, and the
> hizam, the zone or golden band running round the upper part of the
> building, as well as the "face-veil"—the gold embroidered curtain cover-
> ing the Ka'ba door—were of dazzling brightness. (Burton 1893: 2:211).

The making of the present specimen, Burton explains, was the hereditary
right of the Bayt al-Sadi family, which crafted it in a cotton factory in
Cairo.

The *Kiswa* is composed of eight pieces—two for each side of the Ka'ba—the seams being concealed by the *hizam*, a broad band which at a distance looks like gold. It is lined with white calico and is supplied with cotton ropes. Anciently, it is said, all the Quran was interwoven in it. Now it is inscribed "Verily the first of houses founded for mankind (to worship in) is that at Bakka, blessed and a direction to all creatures" (Sura 3), together with seven chapters, namely "The Cave," "Maryam," "The Family of Amran," "Repentance," "Ta Ha," "Ya Sin" and "Tabarak." The character is called *Tumar*, the largest style of Eastern calligraphy, legible from a considerable distance. The *hizam* is a band about two feet broad, and surrounding the Ka'ba at two-thirds of its height. It is divided into four pieces, which are sewn together. On the first and second is inscribed the "Throne verse," and on the third and fourth the titles of the reigning Sultan. These inscriptions are, like the door curtain, gold worked into red silk by the Bayt al-Sadi. (Burton 1893: 2:215)

THE UMRA OF RAJAB

The traveler Ibn Buttuta sets out a traditional version of the origins of the Umra, the so-called "Lesser Pilgrimage":

The Meccans also give this Umra the name of the "Umra of the Eminence" because they commence the rites of pilgrimage on this occasion from an eminence in front of the Mosque of Aisha, God be pleased with her, and at a distance from it of a bowshot, close by the mosque called by the name of Ali, God be pleased with him. The origin of this ceremony goes back to Abdullah ibn al-Zubayr, God be pleased with him and his father. When he had completed the building of the sacred Ka'ba, he went out, walking barefooted, to make an Umra accompanied by the citizens of Mecca. The date was the 27th of Rajab. He went as far as this eminence, and having begun the rites of pilgrimage from there made his way by the track of al-Hajun to the Ma'la (quarter), whence the Muslims entered Mecca on the Day of Conquest. This Umra has therefore remained a traditional practice among the people of Mecca down to the present day. The "day of Abdullah" was celebrated, for he himself provided a large number of animals for sacrifice upon it, and the chiefs of the Meccan families and other citizens of means did the same, and the people continued for several days to eat and to give to eat, in gratitude to God Most High for the furtherance and help which He had granted to them in building His Holy House exactly as it had been in the days of al-Khalil [that is, Abraham], upon whom be the blessings of God. (Ibn Battuta 1958: 235–236/Ar. 383–384)

The Umra in Rajab, it is certain, long antedated Ibn al-Zubayr and, indeed, antedated Islam itself. What Ibn al-Zubayr did was to provide some uneasy scholars with a justification for a practice that was, in Islamic times at least, of doubtful orthodoxy. A whole body of tradition surrounds the question of the extent to which Muhammad would permit the pre-Islamic practices to continue under the new dispensation, and most particularly the sacrifices. The Prophetic tradition that prohibits "sacrifice of the firstlings (of the flock) or of animals slaughtered in Rajab" was obviously intended to ban sacrifice on the Lesser Pilgrimage. But as often happens on disputed questions, a precisely contradictory tradition makes the *atira* an obligation, where *atira* is explained as the sacrifice of a ewe, a common practice in Rajab in pre-Islamic times. And again: "Upon the people of every house there is an obligation every year (to slaughter) a victim (on the Sacrificial Feast at Mina) and an *atira* (of Rajab)." These opposing traditions were eventually resolved by a harmonizing one, this time reported on the authority of Ali: "The Sacrificial Feast (of Mina) abrogated every (other) sacrifice, the fasting of Ramadan abrogated all (other) fasting."[22]

Nasir-i Khusraw Explains the Rites of the Lesser Pilgrimage

Although the Hajj obligation could not be fulfilled on any but the prescribed days in the month of Dhu al-Hijja, the Umra could be performed at any time, and many, if not most, pilgrims combined its rituals with those of the Hajj. A separate "intention" had to be made for each, however. Nasir-i Khusraw explains:

For people who have come from faraway places to perform the minor pilgrimage [the Umra], there are milestones and mosques set up half a parasang [a little over a mile] from Mecca, where they bind on their ihram. "To bind the ihram" means to take off all sewn garments and to wrap on a seamless garment about the waist, and another about the (upper) body. Then in a loud voice they say, "Labbayka, Allahumma, labbayka" ["At Your service, O God, at Your service"] and approach Mecca. When anyone already inside Mecca wants to perform the minor pilgrimage, he goes out to one of the markets (outside the city), binds his ihram, says the Labbayka and comes back into Mecca with the intention to perform the minor pilgrimage.

Having come into the city, you enter the Haram Mosque, approach the Kaʿba, and circumambulate to the right, always keeping the Kaʿba to your left. Then you go to the corner containing the Black Stone, kiss it, and pass on. When the Stone has been kissed once again in the same manner, one circumambulation has been completed. This continues for seven circumambulations, three times quickly and four slowly. When the circumambulation is finished, you go to the Station of Abraham opposite the Ka'ba and stand behind the Station. There you perform two prostrations called the "circumambulation prayer." Afterwards you go to the well of the Zamzam, drink some water, or rub some on the face, and leave the Haram Mosque by the Safa Gate.

Just outside this gate are the steps up Mount Safa, and here you face the Ka'ba and say the prescribed prayer, which is well known. When the prayer has been said, you come down from Safa, and go from south to north through the bazaar to Marwa. Passing through the bazaar, you past the gates to the Haram Mosque where the Prophet ran and commanded others to run also. The length is about 50 paces, and on either side are two minarets [or pillars]. When the people coming from Safa reach the first two minarets, they break into a run until they pass the other two at the other end of the bazaar. Then they proceed slowly to Marwa. Upon reaching the end, they go up to Marwa and recite the prescribed prayer. Then they return through the bazaar and repeat the run until they have gone four times from Safa to Marwa and three times from Marwa to Safa, making seven runs the length of the bazaar.

Coming down from Marwa the last time, you find a bazaar with about twenty barber shops facing each other. You have your head shaven and, with the minor pilgrimage completed, come out of the Sanctuary. (Nasir-i Khusraw 1986: 68–69)

The "Running" of the Masa'a

As Nasir noted, one of the central rituals of the Umra was to run up and down the street called the Masa'a between the two eminences of Safa and Marwa. Ibn Jubayr supplies some additional details:

Every foreign visitor to Mecca—may God ennoble it—makes a Lesser Pilgrimage upon his arrival there. It is recommended to him to enter by the Shayba Gate, make seven turns around the Ka'ba, and leave by the Gate of al-Safa. He makes his way between the two pillars which al-Mahdi had set up there as an indication of the way followed by the Prophet to reach al-Safa. . . . Between the Yemeni corner (of the Ka'ba) and these two pillars there are forty-six paces, and between them and the Safa Gate, thirty paces; from the Safa Gate to al-Safa, seventy-six paces. Al-Safa has fourteen steps and is surmounted by three lofty arcades. The upper level is broad, like a bench. Between al-Safa and al-Marwa the way is surrounded by houses and is seventeen paces broad. Between al-Safa and the green pillar is as was said; the marker is a green pillar that owes its color to its being painted; it is toward the corner of the minaret which is in the eastern corner of the mosque, along the edge of the depth of the valley going toward al-Marwa and on the left of the faithful who is making the "running." It is from there that he takes up the rapid pace of the "running," as far as the two green markers, which are also green pillars like the preceding, one at the Ali Gate in the wall of the Haram and on the left as you go out that gate; the matching one is in the wall of a house next to that of the Amir Mukhtir [the Sharif, or hereditary ruler of Mecca]. Each of the two pillars has a placard fixed like a crown atop it. I found this inscription traced in golden letters on it: "Al-Safa and al-Marwa are among the rites of God," and so forth (Quran 2:153), and then: "This marker was ordered put up the servant of God and His Caliph Abu Muhammad al-Mustadi bi-amrillah, Commander of the Faithful—may God exalt his victory—in the year 1177."

Between al-Safa and the first marker there are 93 paces, and from this to the other two, 75: this is the length of the running course, going and returning, from the single marker to the double one and back again to the single marker. Finally, from the two markers to al-Marwa it is 325 paces. Thus the total number of paces that one covers in making the "running" from al-Safa to al-Marwa is 493. The number of steps at al-Marwa is five; there is only a single arcade there and its breadth is the same as that at al-Safa, 17 paces. (Ibn Jubayr 1949–1951: 126–127/Ar. 106–107)

The Local Festival of Rajab

Many Muslims, with appropriate intention, perform the Umra in conjunction with the Hajj. It is, however, a quite separate ceremony, with its own rituals. There was, moreover, a special Umra—perhaps the original one—celebrated in month of Rajab, three months before the Hajjis began arriving. Down to the nineteenth century, it was an elaborate and festive affair, and had, in some of the most famous pages of Ibn Jubayr's book, the distinct flavor of a local Meccan holiday.

For the people of Mecca this blessed month (of Rajab) brings one of the most venerated annual ceremonies, the greatest of their holidays. They have never neglected it, either in the past or today; they pass on the tradition from father to son and claim that it goes back to the Age of Barbarism; thus they call it the "breaker of the lance-tips" since it was one of the sacred months when it was forbidden to take up arms.

The time fixed for this celebration is the night when the new moon appears as well as the morning that follows it. Preparations take place several days in advance. We shall give a brief description of what we saw. After the mid-afternoon prayer on Wednesday, that is, during the evening of the sighting of the new moon, we saw the open spaces and the streets of Mecca filling up with palanquins fastened atop camels, draped, some of them with all sorts of silk fabrics, others with fine linen stuff, according to the wealth and luxury of their owners; everyone put on a public display according to his means. They begin to pass out of the city toward Tanaʿim [one of the boundaries of the sacred territory of Mecca], the sacralization point for the faithful making the Umra. Then all the palanquins roll like a flood through the ways and crowded quarters of Mecca. The camels that bear them are decorated in various ways; as if they were victims marked for sacrifice, they are garlanded with magnificent scarves of silk and other stuffs.

At times the curtains that cover the palanquins trail to the point of dragging along the ground. The most remarkable of the ones we saw was the palanquin of the Sharifa Jumana, daughter of Fulayta [Sharif of Mecca, 1123–1132] and the paternal aunt of the Amir Mukhtir, since the ends of her curtains trailed in waves upon the ground; then other palanquins of the harem of the amir, and of those of his officers, and then still others, whose number I cannot say since it was impossible to count them. They appeared in all their brilliance on the backs of camels, as if round tents had been fixed there. To see them one would have thought it was the encampment of a tribe that had built its housing with all magnificence. On this night of Thursday there was no one, Meccan or stranger, "God's neighbor," who did not leave to make the Umra. We were among the crowd that went out, eager to win the blessing of this magnificent night. We had great difficulty in clearing our way to the mosque of Aisha through the crush of the crowd and the obstacles created by the palanquins. Fires were lit along both sides of the way, burning torches were carried before the camels of the palanquins belonging to the women of the Meccan aristocracy, which served as another mark of distinction.

We fulfilled the Umra; we made the turns (around the Kaʿba) and then we went on the "running" between Safa and Marwa while the night was passing. Along the entire course you could see only lamps and fires, with an overflow of men and women in palanquins, who were making the saʿy. We succeeded only by threading our way between their palanquins and the legs of their camels, so great was the crush, and the palanquins knocked against each other. We were present there at one of the most extraordinary nights of this world here below. Who has never seen it with his own eyes has never seen a true marvel, a marvel that would make him think of the spectacle on the Day of the Resurrection, so great was the number of people there in their pilgrim garb, crying Labbayka, calling upon God and humbling themselves before Him.

On this night the sacred Haram was completely filled with lamps which sparkled with light. From the time that it had been proclaimed, with the support of the Amir, that the new moon had been seen, that latter ordered that the drums be beaten and the trumpets sound to signify that this was indeed the night of the feast. The morning of Thursday night he went out to make the Umra with a cortege the likes of which could not be recalled. The people of Mecca came out to accompany him down to the last man, woman, and child. They went out in order, tribe by tribe, quarter by quarter, all decked out with their arms, on horse and on foot, in a crowd so large that the onlooker was astonished. If all these people had come from different countries it would be astonishing enough. But what is one to say when they are all from the same city! That is the most tangible proof of the blessing of this city.

They went out in marvelous order: the knights advanced on their horses and made display of their arms; those on foot leaped one at the other and made play of each other, their arms in hand, lances, sabres, shields of leather. They pretended to thrust with their lances, to strike with their swords, to protect themselves with their shields, behind which they took shelter. This battle made an extraordinary spectacle indeed. Some threw their lances and caught them in their hands while the point was coming straight down upon their heads and they were in a position where they could not turn away. Others threw their swords in the air and then caught them by the handle as if they had never left their hands.

Finally the Amir appeared, surrounded by his officers and preceded by his sons, who are still quite young men. Before him the standards waved; drums and tambourines accompanied him; he was surrounded by majesty. The mountains, streets, and passages were filled with spectators, with the crowd of the "neighbors of God." When the Amir reached his place and did what he had to do, he took the return path. The soldiers were drawn up in order before him, they with their war games and the people with their acrobatics. A band of bedouin Arabs was mounted on red thoroughbred camels, an incomparably beautiful sight; they raced their camels against horses before the Amir, raised their voices to celebrate his praises and call God's favor down upon him right up to the time when he reached the sacred mosque.

He completed his turnings around the Ka'ba, preceded by Quran readers, and the muezzin of the Zamzam raised his voice to wish him a happy feast day, praising and praying for him. When he finished his turnings, he made the multazam prayer, then arrived at the Station (of Abraham), behind which he made his prayer; for they had brought it [the stone] out of the Ka'ba for him and had placed it under its wooden dome, behind which he made the ritual prayer. When he had finished that latter, they took off the dome that covered the Station so that he could touch and make contact with it. Then they re-covered it with its dome.

Then the Amir went to the Safa Gate to come to the place for the "running." A cortege formed in front of him. While he completed the "running" on horseback his officers surrounded him and he was preceded by lancers on foot. (Ibn Jubayr 1949–1951: 150–154/Ar. 119–120)

The Ka'ba was normally opened every day during the month of Rajab. But on the twenty-ninth of that month there was a special ceremony.

The 29th (of Rajab), which was a Thursday, was reserved exclusively for the women. They emerge from each of their lodgings after many days' preparation, similar to the ones made before visits to the noble tombs. There is not, on that day, a single women in Mecca who does not present herself at the Sacred Mosque. The Banu Shayba, after they come to open the noble door, according to custom, hasten to leave the Ka'ba and leave it empty for the women. Men too leave the area of the circumambulation and the Hijr. There remains not a single man around the Blessed House. The women hasten so quickly to enter that the Banu Shayba are scarcely able to go down from the Noble House through the midst of them. The women form themselves in lines and then get all mixed and tangled as they try to get in all together. There are cries, shouts, tahlils, takbirs, and their jostling repeats the spectacle of the Yemenite Sarwa bedouin during their stay in Mecca. . . . After continuing thus for half a day, they sort themselves out into circumambulating and visiting the Hijr; they find peace in kissing the Black Stone and touching the corners of the Ka'ba. It is for them a great day, their day, brilliant and radiant. . . . Usually, when they are with the men, they are left apart; they look upon the Noble House without being able to go in; they contemplate the Black Stone but do not touch it at all. In all that, which is their lot, it is only looking, and chagrin confuses and shakes them; they are permitted only the circumambulation, and that segregated. So this particular day, which comes round again every year, they celebrate as the noblest of feasts and they make elaborate preparations. (Ibn Jubayr 1949–1951: 160–161/Ar. 137–138)

Rajab was also the occasion of the annual washing out of the Ka'ba, and this too was a perquisite under the profitable control of the Banu Shayba:

The next day [the day after Ladies' Day, twenty-ninth of Rajab] the Banu Shayba address themselves to washing the Sacred House with the blessed water of Zamzam; the reason is that many of the women brought with them small children and their food. This washing is necessary not only out of respect but also from a care to avoid the impressions that might enter the hearts of those whose judgment is not strong enough to prevent their seeing there an accident of soiling to this noble edifice, to this place specially marked for sanctity and veneration. When the water from this washing begins to flow many men and women hasten to wash their faces and hands with it to gain the attached blessing; at times too they collect it in jars prepared for this end, all without disquieting themselves as to why this washing was being done in the first place. But there are some who do not, since they do not regard what is being done as licit or justified. What do you think then of the blessed water of Zamzam that is poured out in the interior of the Sacred House and spreads as far as its venerated corners, then flows up against the Multazam and the Black Stone which one touches out of veneration? Is it not then worthy that mouths seek it and that not only hands and feet but faces too be moistened with it? (Ibn Jubayr 1949–1951: 161/Ar. 138)

We have another, more elaborate account of this same ritual. The year is 1807, and the reporter is the early nineteenth-century pilgrim—or spy— Ali Bey al-Abbasi:

On Thursday the 29th of January (1807) and the 20th of the month of Dhu al-Qaʿda, the Kaʿba was washed and purified, with the following ceremonies. Two hours after sunrise, the Sultan Sharif went to the temple accompanied by about thirty persons and twelve negro and Arabian guards. The door of the Kaʿba was already open and surrounded with an immense number of people. The staircase was not placed. The Sultan Sharif got upon the shoulders and heads of the multitude and entered with the principal shaykhs of the tribes. Those below wished to do the same, but the guards prevented them by beating them with their sticks. I stayed at a short distance from the door, to avoid the crowd, and in a short time received an order from the Sharif of the well to advance to the door, where he stood making signs to me. But how could I get through the crowd that stood between us?

All the water carriers of Mecca were advancing with their vessels full of water, which they passed from hand to hand, until they reached the guards at the door. They also passed a great number of very small brooms, made of the leaves of palm trees, in the same manner. The negroes began to throw the water upon the marble pavement of the Kaʿba: they also cast rose water upon it, which, flowing out at a hole under the door, was caught with great avidity by the faithful. But as it did not run out fast enough to satisfy the wants of those at a distance who were desirous to obtain it, they cried out for some of it to drink and to wash themselves with; the negroes with cups and with their hands threw it in quantities over them. They were civil enough to pass a pitcher and a cup full of it to me, of which I drank as much as possible and poured the rest over myself; for although this water is very dirty, it is a benediction of God, and is besides much perfumed with rose water.

I made a last effort to approach: several persons raised me up, and, after walking upon the heads of several others, I arrived at the door, where the negro guards helped me get in.

I was prepared for the operation; for I had on only my shirt, an over-garment of white wool without sleeves, my turban and the cloak that covered me.

The Sultan Sharif swept the hall himself. Immediately after I entered, the guards took off my cloak and presented me with a bundle of small brooms, some of which I took in each hand; and at the instant they threw a great deal of water upon the pavement, I began my duty by sweeping with both hands, with an ardent faith, although the floor was quite clean and polished like glass. During this operation the sharif, who had fin-ished, began to pray.

They gave me afterwards a silver cup, filled with a paste made of the sawdust of sandalwood, kneaded with the essence of roses; and I spread it on the lower part of the wall, that was incrusted with marble, under the tapestry which covered the walls and the roof; and also a large piece of aloe wood, which I burned in a large chafing dish, to perfume the hall.

After I had finished all these things, the Sultan Sharif proclaimed me Khadim Bayt Allah al-Haram, or Servant of the Forbidden House of God; and I received the congratulations of all the assistants. . . . They gave me a small quantity of the sandalwood paste and two of the small brooms as interesting relics, which I kept most carefully. The negroes helped me down upon the people, who also assisted me to reach the ground, and addressed compliments of felicitation to me. I then went to the Maqam Ibrahim to say a prayer. They returned me my cloak, and I went home completely wet. (Ali Bey 1816: 2:58–59)

MEDINA THE RADIANT

Most pilgrims used the occasion of the Hajj to visit the Prophet's tomb at Medina, and Ibn Jubayr was no exception. He arrived in Medina on 16 April 1184 in the company of the Iraqi caravan coming up from Mecca.

Ibn Jubayr at Medina

Immediately upon their arrival, the pilgrims went directly to the Proph-et's mosque to pay their initial respects.

The evening of that same day we went into the sacred mosque to visit the pure and venerated tomb. We delivered our greeting standing before it, piously touching the dust of its sacred walls. We prayed in the "Gar-den," the space that extends between the holy tomb and the pulpit; we touched the wood of the venerable pulpit trod by the foot of the Prophet and touched the surviving fragment of the palm tree which whimpered *for him. This latter is enclosed in a pillar which is in front of the "Garden" between the tomb and the pulpit, on your right when you face the pulpit. We then joined the assembly in making the late afternoon prayer. Fortunately we had on this occasion a certain freedom in our movements since people were mostly engaged in seeing to their baggage and setting up their tents. Thus we were able to achieve the object of our desire and go right into this venerated monument and offer our due greetings to the two Companions of the Prophet who lie there, the "Just One" [Abu Bakr] and "The Discerner" [Umar]. (Ibn Jubayr 1949–1951: 218–219/Ar. 189)*

THE MOSQUE OF THE PROPHET

Afterwards there was time for more careful observation, beginning with the mosque building itself.

The blessed mosque is rectangular in shape and surrounded on all four of its sides by galleries which enclose it. The center is entirely filled by a courtyard, where the soil is covered with sand and pebbles. The qibla [south] side has five aisles running from west to east, and the north side the same; the eastern side has a gallery of three aisles and that on the west four.

The venerated mosque is 196 paces long and 126 wide; there are 290 columns on which the ceiling rests immediately, without benefit of any arches to support it. . . . They are made of stones dressed piece by piece, put together and cut with the hollow joint within; molten lead is poured in the joints to insure the stones' being joined into a single, compact pillar. They are covered with a coating of whitewash which renders them bright and smooth and gives them the appearance of marble. (Ibn Jubayr 1949–1951: 219/Ar. 190)

THE TOMB OF THE PROPHET

Ibn Jubayr had already mentioned "the Garden," "the space that extends between the holy tomb and the pulpit." The word *Rawda*, or "Garden," is used in two senses: first, as the entire area running across the southern gallery of the mosque, from the Gate of Peace on the west to the Prophet's tomb on the east; and second, as in the next passage, as the area containing the tomb, or rather, the tomb building, proper. At a later period the term *Rawda* was used exclusively for the first area, and the tomb building was designated as "the Chamber" (*al-Hujra*).

The sacred "Garden" is on the extreme south side (of the mosque), toward the east. It occupies, in the (northerly) direction toward the courtyard, two entire galleries and a little more than four spans of the third. It has five corners and five faces; its shape is unusual and difficult to express. Its four (accessible) faces are exactly different from the prayer-direction so that no one can take any one of them for his prayer-direction since he would thus deviate from the (true) prayer-direction. I was told by the shaykh . . . Abu Ibrahim Ishaq ibn Ibrahim al-Tunsi that this construction notion was Umar ibn Abd al-Aziz's, for fear lest the faithful might make the tomb building a mosque for the ritual prayer.

From west to east the tomb building has the width of two galleries, and the interior of this space is divided into six aisles. The length of its southern face is 24 spans and the eastern face 30 spans; between the eastern and the northern corners is a face of 39 spans; between the western and the southern corners, 24 spans. On this latter side an ebony coffer, worked with geometric designs in sandalwood, and plated with silver so that it shines like a star, is placed to the right of the head of the Prophet; it measures 5 spans in length, by 3 wide, by 4 high. On the side which connects the northern and the western corners there is an opening covered with a veil; it is said that this is the place where the Angel Gabriel descended.

All (five) of the sides of this venerated tomb building extend to a total of 272 spans. They are covered with marble marvelously dressed and well arranged. This marble facing covers a little less than a third of the walls' height. Above it, and covering another third, is a coating of musk and perfume that is blackened and cracked with age. The upper part of the walls is a wooden wainscotting that goes up to the ceiling, since the ceiling of the blessed "Garden" is connected with that of the mosque. Hangings end at the border of the marble. They are blue-green in color with eight- and four-sided geometric designs. Within these polygons are traced white circles and dots.

On the wall facing toward Mecca there is a silver nail opposite the face of the Prophet to mark his venerated visage, and people stand in front of it to say their greetings. At his feet is the head of Abu Bakr the Just, and the head of Umar touches the shoulders of Abu Bakr the Just. For the greeting you stand with your back to the direction of prayer and facing toward Muhammad. The greeting made, you turn toward your right toward Abu Bakr and then toward Umar.

In front of this (southern) wall about twenty silver lamps are hung, and two golden ones. To the north of the holy Garden is a small depression in marble with a prayer-niche on its prayer-direction side. It is said that this was the chamber of Fatima, and indeed her grave as well. God alone knows the truth. (Ibn Jubayr 1949–1951: 219–221/Ar. 190)

The doubt was occasioned by the fact that the tomb of Muhammad's daughter was also shown in the nearby Baqiyyaᶜ cemetery.

THE PROPHET'S PULPIT

Ibn Jubayr next describes the Prophet's pulpit, and here he reverts to the other meaning of "Garden" (*rawda*), here called the "little Garden": the space between the pulpit and the tomb, rather than the tomb building itself.

> To the right of the venerated "Garden," at a distance of forty-two paces, is the venerated pulpit. . . . There are eight paces between this place and the "little Garden" which is between the tomb and the pulpit and which is the object of a Prophetic Tradition according to which it is "one of the gardens of Paradise." The faithful come to this "little Garden" to perform their prayers, and with good reason. Opposite it, on the Mecca side, is a pillar which is said to cover the remains of the palm-tree trunk which whimpered for the Prophet, and a piece of it is still visible in the middle of the pillar; people kiss it and seek out the blessing they would obtain by touching it and rubbing their cheeks against it.
>
> The venerated pulpit is somewhat less than the height of a man, five spans wide and five deep; it has eight steps. It has a door in the form of a wooden lattice which is kept closed and opened (for the sermon) on Fridays; it measures four and a half spans. The pulpit is covered with ebony. At its top you can see the place where the Prophet sat; it is covered with an ebony plank which is not fixed to it but merely prevents anyone's sitting there. People put their hands in to touch it and then pass their fingers over their own clothes to get the blessing that comes from touching this venerated seat. (Ibn Jubayr 1949–1951: 221–222/Ar. 191–192)

Reconstructions

In Ibn Jubayr's day the mosque in Medina was still that built and decorated by the Umayyad Caliph al-Walid and his deputy, the future Caliph Umar ibn Abd al-Aziz, in 770 C.E. It had undergone minor alterations since then, but the ground plan and decor remained intact until the middle of the thirteenth century. Then, on the first night of Ramadan in the year 1256, one of the watchmen of the mosque accidentally set a fire.

> The fire spread across the roof of the mosque and then to everything under it: the pulpit of the Prophet, doors, cupboards, grills, chests, to such an extent that there remained not a single piece of wood, or at least none that was not damaged; likewise with books, copies of the Quran and the "clothing" of the sacred tomb. . . . The only thing to escape the flames was the domed edifice built by Nasir li-Din Allah [r. 1180–1225] as the treasury of the sanctuary . . . because this qubba stood in the middle of the courtyard of the mosque, and, as well, by reason of the blessing of the

sacred copy of Uthman's Quran (which it contained). . . . The columns of the mosque remained standing in place, bending like date palms when the wind blew. The lead of some of them melted, however, and they toppled. (Samhudi, Khulasat, 165)

The task of rebuilding fell to—or rather, was quickly embraced by—the Caliph Mustaʿsim (r. 1242–1258) in Baghdad, who in the following year sent money, workers, and materials. A portion of roof was rebuilt, chiefly over the tomb and the rest of the southern, or *qibla*, end of the prayer-hall. It was one of the last acts undertaken by any Abbasid Caliph in Baghdad. The following year the Mongols took the city, and both the Mamluk Sultan of Egypt and the ruler of the Yemen hastened to associate themselves with the Medina project. The Mamluk Sultan Baybars (r. 1233–1277) completed the roof, and his Yemeni counterpart supplied a new pulpit to replace the old.[23]

In the two hundred years that followed, the Mamluks continued to add to the repairs and adornment of the mosque.[24] The tomb of the Prophet received special attention: a wooden grill around the outside in 1269 (it was already surrounded by a stone wall, as we have seen, in 770 C.E.); a wooden cupola on the roof over the tomb in 1279; and then in 1476 a masonry cupola over the tomb itself, a construction that did not quite reach the roof of the mosque.[25]

Then a new disaster befell the mosque. On the night of 15 November 1481 lightning struck the southeastern minaret, which toppled over in flames and set the rest of the mosque afire. This time it was not merely the roof and the wooden appurtenances within that were destroyed. Many columns toppled, and first the arches between them and then the very walls began to collapse. The destruction was almost complete.[26] The Mamluk Sultan Qaʾit Bey (r. 1468–1498) invested heavily in the reconstruction, which was done on the grand scale. Four hundred workers were sent from Egypt with equipment, supplies, and materials and began rebuilding the mosque. The southern, or *qibla*, wall was rebuilt from its foundations, and the eastern wall was pushed back to enlarge the passage between it and the tomb of the Prophet.[27] What emerged when the work was completed in 1487 was an entirely new building, different in both form and decoration from the mosque built by Walid and Umar ibn Abd al-Aziz in 770.[28]

Varthema at Medina

As we have already seen, the first European known to have penetrated the Muslim Holy Land of the Hijaz, and to have left an account of the venture, was the Italian Ludovico di Varthema. The year is 1503:

We arrived in two days' time at the city which is called Madinat al-Nabi. Near that city, at a distance of four miles, we found a well by which the caravan halted for a day, and at this well each person washed himself and put on clean linen to go into the said city, which contains about 300 hearths and is surrounded by walls made of earth. The houses within are constructed with stone walls.

The country round the said city lies under the curse of God, for the land is barren, with the exception that about two stones' cast outside the city there are about fifty or sixty feet of palm trees in a garden, at the end of which is a certain conduit of water which descends at least twenty-four steps, of which water the caravan takes possession when it arrives there.

A story long current in Europe, though unknown even to Muslim legend, was that the tomb of the Prophet was (1) at Mecca and (2) miraculously suspended in the air. The Arabian explorer Carsten Niebuhr heard the latter story in the late eighteenth century, as we shall see, and termed it "ridiculous." Two and a half centuries earlier Varthema was able to refute it by the testimony of his own eyes:

Now some who say that the body of Muhammad is suspended in the air at Mecca must be reproved; I say that it is not true. I have seen his sepulcher in this city, Madinat al-Nabi, in which we remained three days and wished to see everything. The first day we went into the city, at the entrance by the door of their temple, which they call Meschita [that is, masjid or mosque], and each of us, small or great, was obliged to be accompanied by some person who took us by the hand and led us to where Muhammad was buried. (Varthema 1863: 25–26)

The mosque is made square in this manner: being about 100 paces long and 80 wide, and it has around it two doors on three sides, and the roof made arched, and there are more than 400 columns of burnt stone, all whitened, and there are about 3,000 lighted lamps burning on one side of the arches. On the right side, at the head of the mosque, there is a square tower, about five paces on every side, which tower has a cloth of silk about it. At the distance of two paces from the said tower there is a very beautiful grating of metal where persons stand to see the said tower; and on one side, on the left, there is a little door which leads you to the said tower, and in the said tower there is another little door, and by one of the doors there are about 25 books, and on the other side there are 25 books, which are those of Muhammad and his companions, which books declare his life and the commandments of his sect. Within the said door there is a sepulcher, that is, a pit, under ground, wherein are placed Muhammad, also Ali and Abu Bakr and Uthman and Umar and Fatima.

Varthema either misheard or was misinformed. By unanimous tradition, the Prophet's cousin and son-in-law Ali was buried at Najaf in Iraq, and the third Caliph, Uthman, lay outside the mosque in the Baqiyyaᶜ cemetery.

Then Varthema, the safely returned author, not the would-be Hajji, adds his own Christian comment on Muslim sectarianism. There were books, he noted, stored round the tomb.

These said books treat about each of his people, that is, of the said captains [the first Caliphs]; and it is on this account it is said that this canaille cut each other to pieces, for some wish to act according to the commandments of one, and some of another; and thus they do not know how to make up their minds; and they kill each other like beasts about these heresies, for they are all false. (Varthema 1863: 26–28)

Varthema then continued on to Mecca, where we shall follow him below.

Under New Auspices

Every Mussulman, as is well known, is obliged, once in his life, to visit Mecca and perform acts of devotion in the sacred places. (Niebuhr 1792: 2:36)

So begins, succinctly and accurately, the brief account of the Hajj that Carsten Niebuhr incorporated into the narrative of his explorations in Arabia in 1761–1762. He did not visit Mecca itself, but he acquired enough information about this central Islamic ritual to give his European readers a plausible account of at least its externals. He continues:

If this law were strictly observed, the concourse of pilgrims would be immense; nor could the city contain such crowds from every country in which the Mahometan religion has been introduced. It may be presumed, therefore, that none but such as are more than ordinarily devout discharge this duty.

Few as the caravans are, in proportion to the number of the Mussulmans, even those few are composed, in great part, of persons who go upon other motives than devotion, such as merchants who think this the safest opportunity for the conveyance of their goods, and the most favorable for the sale of them; purveyors of all sorts who furnish the pilgrims with necessaries; and the soldiers paid by the caravan for escorting them. From this it happens that many persons have seen Mecca several times without ever visiting it upon any but views of interest.

The most considerable of these caravans is that of Syria, commanded by the Pasha of Damascus. At a certain distance from Mecca it joins that from Egypt, which is second in numbers, and is conducted by a Bey, who takes the title of Amir Hajji. A third comes from the Yemen; and a fourth, still smaller in numbers, from the country of Lashsᶜa. A few pilgrims come from the Red Sea and from the Arabian settlements on the coast of Africa. The Persians join that which is from Baghdad, and is conducted by a Pasha. His post is lucrative, for he squeezes large sums from the Persian heretics. . . .

I had occasion to speak of the ihram, and of the place where pilgrims are obliged to assume that garb of humility. I may add that they must proceed without delay to Mecca as soon as they arrive at the border of the sacred territory. . . . If he has not been present from the commencement at the celebration of all the ceremonies, and performed every appointed act of devotion, he cannot obtain the title of Hajji, an honor much coveted by the Turks because it confers substantial privileges and commands respect to those who bear it. The rarity of this title in Mahometan countries is a proof of how negligently the law enjoining pilgrimage is observed. (Niebuhr 1792: 2:36–39)

Niebuhr's report on the Hajj is impressionistic at best. A far more detailed picture of the caravans that annually converged on Mecca can be obtained from much more exacting sources. In 1517 the armies of the Sultan of Istanbul drove the Mamluks from their domains in Syria and Egypt, and thus the Ottoman Turks, pious and powerful Sunni Muslims, became not only the political masters of most of Arab Islam but also the "Servants of the Two Holy Sanctuaries," as their proud titulature proclaimed. *Al-Haramayn*, the "Two Sanctuaries," were of course Mecca and Medina, and to the Ottomans fell both the considerable honor of governing the two holiest cities of Islam and the substantial burden of protecting and subsidizing them, their inhabitants, and the ever larger number of pilgrims performing the Hajj.

In the Ottoman era, for the first time, a full-scale portrait of the Hajj, often down to minute details, can be drawn from archival sources. The imperial administrative bureaus in Istanbul concerned themselves with the Hajj from about 1550 onward, producing a continuous flow of information until about 1683, when the pressure of other events turned bureaucratic attention elsewhere.[1]

THE SYRIAN PILGRIMAGE

Financing the Syrian Hajj

In addition to the records of the central administrative bureaus in Istanbul, another new and important archival source of the era is provided by the provincial budgets of Egypt and Syria, where the underwriting of the annual Hajj caravan constituted a major, and growing, expense.[2] From those budgets, for example, we learn that ever-increasing sums of money were allocated by the Damascus Amir al-Hajj for something called *vacibürreaye* camels, apparently mounts provided at government expense for Istanbul dignitaries, palace ladies, ambassadors, and the like, whose perquisites included a free trip to Mecca and back. It was not an inconsiderable expense, and as Ottoman resources declined, the number of those who claimed *vacibürreaye* increased, until finally the government began reducing the allowances for such mounts until they eventually reached purely symbolic levels.[3]

In the Ottoman Empire the Hajj was, then, an annually budgeted enterprise; that is, the Sultan, through his ministers and agents, attempted
to calculate expenses in advance and to match them against anticipated
revenues. The chief assessor was the *Bashdefeterdar* in Istanbul, the Sultan's Treasury Minister, who drew up a detailed annual budget for the
Hajj, listing both income and expenses.[4] These figures then became part
of the state record, and the Grand Vizier was so advised.

At that point the executive arm went into action. The Grand Vizier
was requested to issue the appropriate documents authorizing the Governor of Damascus, who was the chief collecting and disbursing officer of
the Syrian Hajj, to begin the collection of taxes for this purpose. This is
one such authorization, issued on 15 March 1749:

> *To ensure the safe departure and return, with God's help, of the joyful*
> *pilgrims who will travel in 1749 on the Damascus pilgrimage route under*
> *the supervision of the present governor of Damascus and Commander of*
> *the Pilgrimage, the honorable vezir, Hajji Esat Pasha,[5] the following ex-*
> *penses are recorded: wages and extras for 1,500 mercenary footsoldiers and*
> *cavalrymen; camels and other expenses; rental of camels for 400 Damas-*
> *cus local troops; basic and supplementary payments to Arab tribes: adding*
> *up to 309,341 piasters. Of this sum, 94,040 piasters are set aside as special*
> *funds.[6] . . . Besides this, there is also the sum of 215,300 . . . piasters item-*
> *ized and raised by promissory note from the areas named below. Accord-*
> *ingly, upon your excellency's approval, these will be recorded in the chief*
> *comptroller's office and the necessary certificates, copies and orders per-*
> *taining to the stated sums will be written. Orders to proceed are requested*
> *from your excellency. (Istanbul, Prime Minister's Archives, 15 March*
> *1749[7])*

These were not special taxes but merely part of the province's ordinary
tax revenues—chiefly from land taxes and the poll tax levied on non-
Muslims—earmarked for the pilgrimage, what has been justly called the
"annual equivalent of a military campaign."[8] The Hajj budget was then
simply deducted from the tax total due to be sent annually to Istanbul,
the so-called *irsaliyya*.[9] And if for any reason the funds from this source
proved insufficient, other resources could be and were called upon: the tax
revenues from another province, for example, or the government's dues
from its tobacco monopoly.[10]

The budgeted income and expenses are revealing; but, in the manner
of all such documents, they conceal as well. Payments made to the bedouin were often buried in "general expenses," and some costs seem to
remain about the same over long periods even though we know that steep
inflation occurred.[11] We are not sure how the bureaucrats dealt with these
problems, but what seems fairly clear is that they employed bookkeeping

devices to reduce the "book value" as opposed to the actual level of the pilgrimage expenses.[12]

Another method of keeping up with constantly rising expenses—the caravan costs accounted for a larger and larger percentage of the total expenditures of the province of Damascus—was for the Governor of Damascus to go each year to certain areas within his jurisdiction and collect—or extort—the government's dues in person,[13] a procedure that became increasingly critical in meeting the expenses of the pilgrimage. Finally, the Ottoman government could no longer undertake to meet the Hajj expenses in their entirety. A fixed sum was allocated to the annual caravan, and whatever additional sums were needed had to be provided by individuals, who were sometimes induced, it appears, by the promise of appointment as Caravan Commander.[14]

The Organization of the Damascus Caravan

Although some commissioning and investiture formalities took place in Istanbul, the imperial Hajj caravan proper began and ended in Damascus. And so, from the beginning of the Ottoman era, it was perfectly natural that the official upon whom the responsibility for its organization and safe conduct should fall was the Governor of Damascus.

The first Ottoman Governor of Damascus was Janbirdi al-Ghazali, a Mamluk of the old regime and a man of some piety, it appears, as well as an experienced administrator.[15] Soon after assuming office in February 1518, he began the long and difficult process of subjugating the Turkman nomads who threatened the caravan all the way from Damascus to Aqaba.[16] It took two years, but he was apparently successful. By 1520 caravans were traveling from Damascus to Mecca without incident, now protected by the same tribes that had once been their predators.[17]

In the end, Ghazali may have been more troublesome than the bedouin he suppressed. He revolted against his Ottoman sovereigns, and although the Turks put down their recalcitrant vassal and regained Damascus, their hold on the long frontier was once again weakened. In 1521 the new Governor of Damascus bought the safety of the Hajj caravan from the bedouin, setting a dangerous and expensive precedent between the government and its nominal subjects.[18]

The imperial Hajj caravan had several components in addition to pilgrims. In the first instance, it was from the beginning a government-sponsored and -run enterprise, and so it had at its head a government official, called the *Amir al-Hajj*, or Caravan Commander. With him were various officials to whom he delegated one or other of his duties in running this complex operation. And because a chief concern of this convoy was security, there was a military escort made of up various components. Finally, there were the "passengers": not merely the pilgrims, as one might suppose, but also, because this was perhaps the only secure way of making this particular journey, a variety of merchants—including the Amir al-Hajj himself—who had business in the Hijaz and used the caravan as a method of conducting it.

The military escort varied in size and composition. In the sixteenth century it was made up of a hundred "sepoys" (*sipahis*), or mounted troops, professional soldiers who held government land throughout the province in return for this service, and two hundred janissaries from the Damascus garrison. The system did not work very well. If many of the sepoys simply refused to report for service, the government showed itself increasingly willing to accept cash in lieu of service for the land grants. In the end, the caravan escort was provided by troops hired for the occasion at government expense.[19]

All of these personnel, as well as the pilgrims, were under the immediate supervision of the Caravan Commander. At first the Ottomans appointed senior Mamluk officials like Ghazali from Damascus or from other nearby cities to head the annual caravan to Mecca. Then, in 1571, there was a change in policy. Local notables holding the governorships of Ajlun, Gaza, Karak, and Nablus, for example, also led the pilgrimage, and at first quite successfully,[20] though with dimishing fiscal satisfaction to the imperial government. Finally, in 1708, the Ottomans established what would henceforward be the standard policy toward the administration of the Hajj: the Governor of Damascus would serve as the *Amir al-Hajj* for the annual trek from Damascus to Mecca and back.[21]

Like his Cairo counterpart, the Damascus Caravan Commander had extensive powers. Indeed, in the Hijaz he in fact outranked not only all the imperial officials attached to the caravan but even the Ottoman Governor of Jidda, the Sharif of Mecca, and the Egyptian Amir al-Hajj himself. It was this extensive authority that enabled the Sultan to establish his political will, through the Caravan Commander, in the Hijaz. This meant in practice the investigation, disciplining, or deposition of the Sharif of Mecca at the Sultan's pleasure.[22]

Like many before and since, a number of Ottoman pilgrims committed their impressions of the Hajj to writing. Few of them have been published,[23] but the most important is available: the account of the Syrian Hajj of 1672 by the celebrated Ottoman traveler Evliya Chelebi.[24] On 19 February 1672 Chelebi joined the heavily armed Damascus caravan being led by the Governor of the province, Husayn Pasha. It was a turbulent time in the Hijaz. In the preceding year the new Ottoman Governor of Jidda, Hassan Pasha, had arrived on the scene, preceded by rumors that he had been ordered to depose the Sharif and institute direct Ottoman control of Mecca. His orders in reality, as described by Chelebi, were likely no more encouraging to the Sharif and his relatives: "to repair the holy sanctuaries, to collect from all the Sharifian families and their dependencies the requisite dues and taxes, and to regulate and reform the Holy Cities."[25] The case was not unusual: it was neither the first time nor the last that the Commander of the imperial Hajj caravan and the troops who accompanied him were used to "regulate and reform the Holy Cities."

THE CARRIAGE AND CARE OF PILGRIMS

Save for a few pious and hardy souls who made the trip on foot, the pilgrims and the small army of guardians, functionaries, servants, and merchants traveled principally by means of camels. Which meant that each year outside of Damascus, Cairo, and Baghdad an enormous number of camels had to be collected and assigned to the Hajjis and others who proposed to go to Mecca. The supply of these camels was thus an important economic factor both for the state, which operated the caravan and its support system, and for the individual pilgrims, who were generally responsible—the poorest were usually given mounts—for supplying their own transportation.

Generally speaking, the camels for the Damascus caravan were provided by villages in southern Syria or by tribes on the Syrian steppe around Palmyra. The delivery point was not Damascus but at what we have already seen was the chief staging point of the caravan, the market town of Muzayrib, about sixty miles south of the Syrian capital.[26] The owners did not disappear, however, once the transaction was completed. Many of them accompanied the caravan on its way south, we are told, close enough to be in the shadow of the caravan's protection, but far enough to dissociate themselves from it, if that seemed wise.[27]

Brokerage Corporations

Villagers and bedouin sold or leased their camels to both the government and the individual pilgrim, but individuals did not usually go out and strike a deal with someone who chanced to own a camel. Both the pilgrim in need of a single animal and the Caravan Commander in search of thousands to bear himself, his party, his troops, and all the Hajj's provisions dealt with corporations of "travel agents," *muqawwims*, who contracted to provide both animals and personnel. The operations of these corporations are detailed in the records of the Damascus courts, where the Chief Justice certified the contracts and adjudicated the frequent disputes that arose from them. So deeply, and perhaps justifiably, did the pilgrims fear being left in the lurch by their transportation agents somewhere upon the long and dangerous way between Damascus and Mecca that the chiefs and all the agents were constrained to appear in court and pledge a collective guarantee of the individual contracts.[28]

Burckhardt explains how the system worked from the viewpoint of the pilgrim intending to join the caravan at Damascus:

> The greater part of the pilgrims usually contract for the journey with one of the great undertakers, or Muqawwims, as they are called; this agreement is only for a beast of transport and for water; as to eating, the pilgrims generally mess together at their own expense, in bodies of about a half dozen. The Muqawwims, on agreeing to furnish a beast of burden, are bound to replace whatever may die on the road, and are therefore obliged to carry with them at least one unloaded camel for every loaded one. It is a general practice of the Muqawwims to obtain as large sums as possible on account from the pilgrims who engage them for the journey. They generally agree among each other upon the sum to be demanded, as well as the moment at which it is to be called for; so that if the pilgrims resist the imposition, the Hajj sometimes remains encamped on the same spot for several days, the Muqawwims all refusing to proceed, and feeing the Pasha for his connivance at their injustice. On their return to Damascus, if they have already extorted from the pilgrims in the course of the journey more than the amount of their contract, as often happens, they generally declare themselves to be bankrupts, and then the value of a few camels is all that remains to pay their debts to the pilgrims.

As might be imagined under the circumstances, providing one's own transportation was not much encouraged.

> Those pilgrims who do not engage the Muqawwims, as is generally the case of those who come from Armenia and the borders of the Black Sea, perform the journey somewhat cheaper upon their own beasts; but they are ill-treated on the road by the Muqawwims, are obliged to march last in the caravan, to encamp on the worst ground, to fill their water-skins the last, and are often even avanized by the Pasha.[29] It is difficult to conceive the wretched condition of the greater part of the Hajjis, and the bad conduct of the troops and the Arabs. (Burckhardt 1822: 243–244)

When the Hijaz Railway began operations in 1908, it effectively ended the caravan trip between Damascus and Medina. We are instructed on how the camel brokerage system worked in its final days by one who was engaged in it.

> There lives in Damascus today [1935–1936] a certain silk merchant, by the name of Selim Sawwaf, who formerly owned 2,000 camels and was a contractor for the Hajj caravans. Between 1875 and 1910, Selim Sawwaf

made thirty trips to Mecca, and on the basis of his long experience he gave (to the author) the following information concerning the supplying of the great caravans. Camel "owners," according to him, had always been in the habit of buying their camels each year, as cheaply as possible, from the desert Arab who raised them. Then they hired out these animals, at the highest possible price, to prospective Hajjis and convoy officials; and sold them at a profit, on their return to Damascus.

Possibly the Pasha of medieval Damascus once had a monopoly on this lucrative trade . . . but fortunately for Selim Sawwaf, there was no government monopoly in his day. In order to take part in contracting for the pilgrims, a single owner, or perhaps a collective group of camel owners, acting as a unit, had to contribute a minimum "share" of 200 camels. The potential market of the Muqawwims, or camel-masters, depended directly upon the numbers of pilgrims to be convoyed. These numbers varied year by year, varied so greatly that, within the thirty years' experience of this particular contractor, the demand for camels had fluctuated between four thousand, in some years, to as many as twenty thousand in others. (Grant 1937: 229)

Transportation Costs for the Pilgrim

How much did it cost the pilgrim to fulfill his religious obligation by this overland route? It is only in the eighteenth and nineteenth centuries that estimates of that figure take on a note of reality. The Damascus court records, which preserve the contracts between pilgrim and carrier, and the careful accounting of the pilgrims themselves enable us to make some kind of assessment. In about the middle of the eighteenth century, the court records show, the pilgrim paid a broker about 70 piasters to travel to Mecca: 40 for food and transport, 5 for a place in the two-sided litter atop the camel, 15 for luggage (the weight allowance for food and provisions was about 126 pounds), 5 for water, and 5 for the camel driver. The return cost more, as much as 110 piasters, either because of the greater weight of goods purchased at Mecca by merchants and pilgrims or because of the greater danger of attack that such freighted caravans courted.[30] And what was the actual value of the roughly 200 piasters spent on such a round-trip journey? A great deal apparently. In the mid-eighteenth century that amount was somewhat more than enough to buy an average-size Damascene house, for example, and ten times the annual salary of an imam-teacher in the mosque there.[31]

A half century later, the figure of 200 piasters for the round-trip was nothing more than a golden memory. Burckhardt's estimates, based on information collected at Muzayrib in the spring of 1812, show the effects of inflation:

As far as the Pasha is concerned, the affairs of the great (Damascus) caravan were generally well managed; but there still reigned a great want of economy, and the expenses of the Hajjis increased every year. Of late years, the hire of a single camel from Damascus to Mecca has been 750 piasters; as much, and often more, was to be paid coming back; and the expenses on the road, and at Mecca, amounted to at least 1,000 piasters, so that in the most humble way, the journey could not be performed at less than 2,500 piasters, or £125 sterling. (Burckhardt 1822: 243)

The government had also to supply camels, and this was the responsibility of the Caravan Commander. In addition to providing mounts for his own staff of officials and retainers and for the ill and halt, he had to ensure carriage of the supplies for men and beasts, the gifts to the bedouin on the way, and the provisions for the people of the Hijaz. That surely involved thousands of camels annually,[32] and where great numbers were involved, there was also the opportunity for great profit. In Syria professional breeders raised camels for this particular occasion of the Hajj, and more than once the Governor of Damascus was advised by Istanbul to take action against some of the more unscrupulous camel factors. On one occasion the Ottoman government thought to try breeding its own camels, and some land round Busra in Syria was set off for that purpose. The experiment lasted no more than a year.[33]

The pilgrimage obligation was fulfilled in a few short days at Mecca, Mina, and Arafat, but the Hajj, as a government enterprise, took the better part of a year.[34] It began with the Finance Minister's preparation of the Hajj budget in the third month of the year. In the seventh month the stipends and other entitlements for the Holy Cities and their residents were despatched from the capital for Damascus. In the eighth and ninth months the Governor of Damascus and the Amir al-Hajj made a tax-collecting descent on the cities of the southern areas of the province. The caravan finally departed from Damascus between the twelfth and the twentieth of Shawwal, the tenth month of the lunar year. It was followed by the departure of the relief caravan, the *jurda*,[35] in the next month, or even in Dhu al-Hijja, the last month of the year, when the pilgrimage rites were being performed in Mecca. Both caravans, the Hajj and the *jurda*, arrived back in Damascus in Safar, the second month of the new year.

Damascus, like Cairo and Baghdad, was an assembly point for pilgrims from much farther afield. Pilgrims from the Maghrib and West Africa converged on the Egyptian capital, while at Baghdad there collected the Iraqi Hajjis and the pilgrims from Iranian Islam. But the trek across the Syrian and Arabian desert, through a terrain and across a population hostile to the traveling Shiᶜite, was an especially perilous one, particularly because there was little official protection. The eighteenth-century rulers of Iran attempted to form their own caravans for the benefit of the Persian pilgrims, but the Ottoman Sultan, who controlled much of the territory through which the caravan would eventually have to cross, was unwilling to share either his responsibilities or his privileges with another ruler, particularly a Shiʿite one, and so the proposals came to nothing.[36] As a result, large numbers of Persians preferred to cross Upper Mesopotamia into Syria, and thence to Aleppo, where they could join others traveling south to join the Damascus caravan.[37] There they found assembling not only their coreligionists from northern Syria but also "Rumis" from Anatolia and, indeed, the entire network of Turkish Islam.

As always, it is difficult to number the pilgrims on the road to Mecca, particularly the motley assembly that collected in Damascus. Occasionally a Muslim or European observer will make a stab at an estimate, especially if the caravan is notable for its size or other circumstance. Thus a Jesuit who witnessed the caravan of 1739 put its size at somewhere between 15,000 and 20,000 souls. Constantin Volney, a Frenchman much inclined to statistics, guessed the number in the notorious caravan of 1757—it had been grievously attacked by bedouin (see below)—at 60,000, while Turkish sources numbered 70,000 to 100,000 faithful. Volney thought the more usual total was between 30,000 and 50,000.[38]

Another, more illuminating, if not necessarily more accurate, approach to the problem of numbers is through the Ottoman tax registers, which from the fifteenth century indicate whether a person bore the title of *Hajji*, that is, had made the pilgrimage. The results of an analysis of the data from a number of Anatolian towns have been described as "rather disconcerting." Contrary to what might have been expected, the percentage of Hajjis, which ran about 9–10 percent during the reign of Muhammad the Conqueror (1451–1481), when the Holy Cities were under Mamluk sovereignty, declined to under 5 percent during the reign of Sulayman (1522–1566), when the Ottomans not only controlled the Hijaz but invested large sums of money in enterprises there. A decision to make the Hajj was obviously based on far more complex considerations than simply who ruled there.[39]

Garrison Life on the Ottoman Darb al-Hajj

South of Deraʿa in southern Syria, as the caravan made its slow way into what is today Jordan, settlement grew thinner and the presence of nomads more threatening. Not only their summer pasture lands drew them; the annual migration of a lumbering and richly laden caravan was a sharp incentive for the bedouin to try their fortunes against whatever protection the caravan could muster. One powerful carapace was gold, as we shall see. But in addition to buying off the predators, the Ottomans, from the very beginning of their reign, attempted to protect the route by systematically establishing garrisons of varying sizes in fortified places at the watering and resting stops all along the Darb al-Hajj. Selim I ordered the construction of forts at Sanamayn, Muzayrib, and Tell Farʿun, all on the Hajj route but all still fairly close to Damascus. By 1563 important additions to the system extended far further south and indeed into the Hijaz itself: Qatrana, Maʿan, Dhat al-Hajj, Tabuk, Ukhaydir, al-Ula, and finally, in 1576, Hadiyya, forty-two hours or four halting places away from Medina.[40]

After this initial building surge, Ottoman attention appears to have turned elsewhere; but when, at the beginning of the eighteenth century, the governors of Damascus were made directly responsible for the pilgrimage, funds were once again invested in securing the Darb al-Hajj. In 1708–1709 extensive repairs were carried out on the station and water supply at Hadiyya; then in 1730–1733 a castle and cisterns were built at Mudawwara between Maʿan and Tabuk, and a bridge constructed across the always dangerous bed of the Wadi Hassa. Later a fort was built at Madaʾin Salih, with additional installations between 1779 and 1780.[41]

The troops to fill these fortresses were drawn from the Damascus garrison or, more accurately, garrisons. From 1660 onward, there were two often contentious and always competing corps of regular troops in Damascus: a body of locally recruited carabiniere, called the "local janissaries," and troops sent down from Istanbul, the "imperial janissaries." Both were posted to garrison duty in the forts along the Darb al-Hajj, though assuredly not to the same places. Local janissaries manned the forts at Sanamayn, Qatrana, Karak, Madaʾin Salih, and Ukhaydir, while the imperial troops served at Muzayrib, Unayza, Muʿazzam, and Maʿan.[42]

The size of the Damascus troop pool, local and imperial, fluctuated over the years, but what remained consistent was the notion that a certain number of the whole—in 1720, for example, 390 out of a total of 883 local janissaries—should be assigned to garrison duty in connection with the Hajj. More, they served on a rotating basis, every other year in some places, every fourth year in others. So the tour of duty lasted a year at a time, the new troops going out with the year's caravan, those whose tour was over returning with the same caravan on its way back to Damascus.[43]

Another, and far more mischievous, constant in this garrison duty along the Hajj route was the pay of those same troops. Whatever the original purchasing power of five aspers a day—a soldier's pay in 1553—imperial policy held in check this particular budget item by not raising wages for more than two hundred years. What that meant—and this was doubtless understood in Istanbul—was that the soldiers were permitted, at least tacitly, to reimburse themselves from other sources. And so they did, by all reports, chiefly by buying provisions cheap from the locals in the neighborhood of the fortress and selling them dear to the pilgrims, or else illegally selling to the local bedouin the provisions sent down by the government for the use of the pilgrim caravan when it passed. It was, Burckhardt, remarked, a way of making a fortune.[44]

By 1800, then, on paper at least—the paper of the imperial chanceries in Istanbul—an impressive network of manned and provisioned fortresses stretched all the way from Muzayrib seven hours outside of Damascus to beyond Hadiyya in the vicinity of Medina.[45] So we are informed by the archival documents that note the allotments for both construction and repairs, and so too by the travelers who passed that way and remarked on what they saw and where they stayed.

Among the earliest of those travelers were Mehmed Edib, the Ottoman Hajji who went to Mecca along that route in 1779–1780,[46] and John Lewis Burckhardt, who passed that way about ten years later. Burckhardt, an explorer who was supposed to be looking for the sources of the Nile, attempted to describe what an Ottoman Hajj "castle" was:

The name of qal'at or castle is given on the Hajj route, and over the greater part of the desert, to any building walled in and covered, and having, like a Khan, a large courtyard in its enclosure. The walls are sometimes stone, but more commonly of earth, though even the latter are sufficient to withstand the attack of Arabs.

Al-Fahlatayn [or Nakhlatayn] is the last castle. At all these stations small castles have been built, close to the basins in which the rain water is collected. If there are any wells, they are within the walls of the castle, and the water is drawn up by camels in order to fill the basin, on the arrival of the Hajj. The pilgrims, in order to lighten their loads, generally leave in every castle a small parcel of provisions, which they take on their return. The castles are garrisoned by four or five men of Damascus, who are shut up there the whole year until they are relieved by the passage of the caravan. It often happens that only one man is left alive of the number; the others having been killed by the Arabs, or having died from the effects of the confinement, for the fear of the Arab seldom permits them to issue out of the castle. Each of these castles has a mughaffir, or protector, among the neighboring tribes, to whom the Pashas pay a certain tribute. The office of these guardians, who are usually inhabitants of the Maydan or suburb of Damascus, is very lucrative on account of the presents and small contributions made to them by the pilgrims. (Burckhardt 1822: 659–660)

The Englishman Charles Doughty passed down the Syrian "Pilgrims' Way" in 1887, at a low ebb of Ottoman power in the Arab lands. Like others before him, he stopped at the "castles," or kellas, along the way:

The kellas are fortified water stations weakly garrisoned; they may have been built two or three centuries, and are of good masonry. The well is in the midst of the kella; the water, raised by a simple machine of drum and buckets, whose shaft is turned by a mule's labor, flows forth to fill a cistern or birket without the walls. Gear and mules must be fetched down with the Hajj from Damascus upon all the desert road, to Mada'in Salih. The cisterns are jealously guarded; as in them is the life of the great caravan. No Aarab (nomads) are suffered to draw of that water; the garrison would shoot out upon them from the tower, in which, closed with an iron-plated door, they are sheltered themselves all the year from the insolence of the nomads. The kellas stand alone, as it were ships, in the immensity of the desert; they are not built at distances of camps, but according to the opportunity of water; it is more often two or even three marches between them. The most difficult passage of the pilgrim road before Medina, is that four or five marches in high ground, next above Mada'in Salih; where are neither wells nor springs, but two ruined kellas with their great birkets to be filled only by torrent water, so that in some years, in a nearly rainless country, they lie dry. A nejjab or post, who is a Bedouin dromedary-rider is therefore sent up every year from Mada'in Salih, bringing word to Damascus, in Ramadan before the pilgrimage, whether there be water run in the birket at Dar el-Hamra, and reporting likewise the state of the next waters. . . . In years when the birket is empty, some 1,500 girbies are taken up in Damascus by the Hajj administration, to furnish a public supplement of five days, water for the caravan: these water skins are loaded betwixt the distant waterings, at the government cost, by Bedouin carriers.

The caravaners pass the ruined and abandoned kellas with curses between their teeth, which they cast, I know not how justly, at the Hajj officers and say "all the birkets leak and there is no water for the hajjaj; every year there is money paid out of the treasury that should be for the maintenance of the buildings; the embezzling pashas swallow the public silver; we may hardly draw now of any cistern before Ma'an, but after the long marches must send far to seek for it, and that we may find is not good to drink." Turkish peculation is notorious in all the Hajj service, which somewhat to abate certain Greek Christians, Syrians, are always bursars in Damascus of the great Mohammedan pilgrimage: —this is the law of the road, that all look through their fingers. The decay of the road is also, because much less of the public treasury is now spent for the Hajj service. The impoverished Ottoman government has withdrawn the not long established camp at Ma'an, and greatly diminished the kella allowances; but the yearly cost of the Hajj road is said to be yet 50,000 pounds, levied from the province of Syria, where the Christians cry out, it is tyr-

anny that they too must pay from their slender purses for this seeking hallows of the Moslemin. (Doughty 1888: 47–48)

We get one of our final glimpses of this Ottoman fortress network from Marcel Castiou, who went down the Syrian Darb al-Hajj in the first years of the twentieth century. The "castles" were spaced, by his reckoning, about thirty-four miles apart, and he describes them as "ancient massive constructions" about sixty feet square and manned, in this Turkish twilight, by one bedouin family and occasionally four or five Turkish soldiers. Typically, there were two *birkehs*, or cisterns, nearby, one for the pilgrims and one for their animals. In dry seasons carriers had to be hired out of the imperial allotments to fill the reservoirs from nearby wells.[47]

THE BEDOUIN PROBLEM

The term "Arabs" in Burckhardt's summary complaint cited above is, as often in these texts, not an ethnic designation but a reference to the bedouin, those nomads of Sinai, Syria, and Arabia who preyed on the caravans that passed each year through their midst.[48] As Burckhardt continues, there is no doubt who these bothersome "Arabs" are:

The Bedouin are particularly dexterous at pilfering; at night they sometimes assume the dress of the Pasha's infantry, and thus introduce themselves unnoticed among the camels of the rich Hajjis, when they throw the sleeping owner from his mule or camel, and in the confusion occasioned by the cries of the fallen rider, drive off the beast. (Burckhardt 1822: 244–245)

An unpleasant business, surely, but the conduct of these particular bedouin seems almost playful compared to what some of their brothers under the black tents were capable of.

Who Are the Bedouin?

Ludovico di Varthema was the first Westerner to notice a phenomenon that very few subsequent travelers from Europe would fail to remark: these nomadic predators of the Hajj called bedouin, who had their own characteristic style of life. His experience of them was at Muzayrib, not very far out of Damascus.

You must know that they ride, for the most part, without saddles, and in their shirts, excepting some of their principal men. Their arms consist of a lance of Indian cane ten or twelve cubits in length with a piece of iron

at the end, and when they go on any expedition they keep as close together as starlings. The said Arabians are very small men, and are of a dark
tawny color, and they have a feminine voice and long, stiff and black hair.
And truly these Arabs are in such vast numbers that they cannot be
counted; and they are constantly fighting among themselves. They in-
habit the mountain and come down at a time when the caravan passes
through to go to Mecca, in order to lie in wait at the passes for the purpose of robbing the said caravan. They carry their wives, children and all
their furniture, and also their houses, upon camels, which houses are like
the tents of soldiers, and are of black wool and of a sad appearance.
(Varthema 1863: 18)

It was not until the Danish expedition to Arabia in the 1760s that a full-
scale portrait of the bedouin manner of life emerged, now cloaked, however, with some of the liberal political ideas of that era in Europe. Carsten
Niebuhr went about collecting information about the bedouin rather
than living among them, as Doughty, for example, was later to do; but he
knew enough to sketch their peculiar tribal organization, beginning with
the distinction between the city Arabs and the bedouin:

The Arabs settled in cities, and especially those in sea-port towns, have
lost somewhat of their distinctive national manners by their intercourse
with strangers; but the bedouin, who live in tents and in separate tribes,
have still retained the customs and manners of their earliest ancestors. They are the genuine Arabs, and they exhibit, in the aggregate, all
those characteristics which are distributed respectively among the other
branches of their nation.

I have repeatedly noticed the different acceptations in which the word
shaykh is used. Among the bedouin it belongs to every noble, whether of
the highest or the lowest order. Their nobles are very numerous and compose in a manner the whole nation; the plebeians are invariably actuated
and guided by the shaykhs, who superintend and direct in every transaction. (Niebuhr 1792: 2:158–159)

Each (shaykh) governs his family with power almost absolute. All the
shaykhs, however, who belong to the same tribe, acknowledge a common
chief, who is called shaykh al-shuyukh, Shaykh of Shaykhs, or Shaykh
al-Kabir, and whose authority is limited by custom. The dignity of the
Grand Shaykh is hereditary in a certain family, but the inferior shaykhs,
upon the death of a Grand Shaykh, choose the successor out of his family,
without regard to age or lineal succession, or any other consideration except superiority of abilities. This right of election, with their other privileges, obliges the Grand Shaykh to treat the inferior shaykhs rather as
advocates than as subjects, sharing with them their sovereign authority.

The spirit of liberty, with which this warlike nation are animated, renders them incapable of servitude. (Niebuhr 1792: 2:18–19)

Niebuhr's account was widely read in Europe, but the Dane's vision of bedouin life reached an even wider audience through Edward Gibbon, who relied heavily upon it in his treatment of the origins of Islam in Chapter L of *The Decline and Fall.*

Payments to the Bedouin

Niebuhr too remarks on one of the most familiar of bedouin practices: exacting money from those who passed their way.

Every Grand Shaykh justly considers himself as absolute lord of his whole territories, and accordingly exacts the same duties upon goods carried through his dominions as are levied by other princes. The Europeans are wrong in supposing sums paid by travelers to the Grand Shaykhs to be merely a ransom to redeem them from pillage. The Turks, who send caravans through the desert to Mecca, have submitted to the payment of these duties. They pay a certain sum annually to the tribes who live near the road to Mecca; in return for which the Arabs keep the wells open, permit the passage of merchandise, and escort the caravans. (Niebuhr 1792: 2:165)

If that is the way it appeared to Niebuhr from his Arab sources, the view was somewhat different in Damascus. Year after year the annual Syrian Hajj had to thread its way through the gauntlet of hostile and rapacious bedouin, who emerged just outside the gates of Damascus and retreated only before the portals of Mecca. Bedouin harassment was fairly constant throughout the history of the Hajj, and certain sectors of the route were particularly vulnerable.[49]

Defense against the bedouin had always been beyond the powers of the pilgrims themselves. They were in fact already dependent upon those same desert dwellers to provide the only transportation capable of taking them to Mecca and back, the camel. Responsibility for guaranteeing the pilgrims' security in the fulfillment of this religious obligation thus fell upon the government, the self-styled "Servants of the Two Sanctuaries," but called by the local people, considerably more offhandedly and not always affectionately, simply "the regime" (*al-dawla*). The large sums involved were well worth spending, thought Charles Doughty, who traveled down the Pilgrims' Way to Arabia in 1887.

A yearly loss to the empire is the surra or "bundles of money" to buy a peaceful passage of the abhorred Bedouins: a half part of Western Arabia is fed thereby, and yet it were of more cost, for the military escort to pass "by the sword." The destitute Bedouins will abate nothing of their yearly pension; that which was paid to their fathers, they believe should always be due to them out of the treasurers of the "Sooltan," and if any less be proffered them they would say "The unfaithful Pashas have devoured it!" the pilgrimage should not pass, and none might persuade them, although the Dowla (Sultan's Empire) were perishing. . . . Malcontent, as has often been seen, they would assault the Hajj march or set upon some corner of the camp by night, hoping to drive off a booty of camels: in warfare they beset the strait places, where the firing down of a hundred beggarly matchlocks upon the thick multitude must cost many lives. (Doughty 1888: 49)

Despite Doughty's sour assessment, the regime appears to have done its best, both by attempting to garrison the route itself—a not terribly effective tactic along a lengthy road chiefly through desert—and by either buying off or co-opting the bedouin along the way, to make it more profitable for them to refrain from plundering the caravan than not.[50] The result was something of a stand-off. The government generally paid its handsome tribute, and so long as it did, the bedouin restricted themselves to what might be called a tolerable level of plundering.

The payments were not made without plan or reason. As we have already seen, they were a budgeted part of the government's Hajj expenses. How they were distributed depended on the judgment of the Caravan Commander. Many of the bedouin along the way were too few, too weak, too intimidated, or too distracted to make trouble, and they received nothing. The most generous payments, not unnaturally, went to the most powerful and the most aggressive of the tribes. The arrangement was constantly being tested on both, or rather, all three, sides. The government obviously had an interest in paying as little as possible and so experimented with cutting back stipends. Its chief local official, the Amir al-Hajj, had a similar, though differently motived interest, and the Caravan Commanders often withheld part of the allocated payments—not so much to test the bedouin as to line their own pockets. And finally each tribe had continually to assert its own terrifying credibility vis-à-vis Istanbul and to maintain its position versus other desert rivals for the coveted position of "Hajj protector."[51]

So the dangerous game went on, the commander inevitably paying the bedouin their first installment on the way out, and then making a calculated guess as to whether the caravan could make it back to the safety of Damascus without disgorging the other half. And the bedouin, well aware of the game, greedily watched the caravan staggering back north, now loaded with tempting merchandise from the marts of the Hijaz.[52]

The Bedouin Attack of 1757

When the system broke down, trouble quickly followed. In the eighteenth century the chief tribe of bedouin between Damascus and the northern Hijaz was that of the Banu Anayza. These relative newcomers to the area had displaced some of the other tribes, including from their former favor in the Sultan's heart and purse. It was the discontent of the Banu Sakhr, and their attempt to reestablish themselves, that provoked one of the eighteenth century's most explosive encounters between the bedouin and the Hajj.[53]

The first signal of trouble was the report that reached Damascus in September 1757 that the Banu Sakhr had attacked and scattered the southward-bound *jurda*, or relief caravan, between Qatrana and Ma'an. This was serious news: it meant that the main caravan, now on its return from Medina, was exposed to a terrible danger. This much was clear both in Damascus and to the Amir al-Hajj, Husayn Pasha, Governor of the Damascus Province, who by then had reached Tabuk with his charges. The Banu Sakhr, he was told, awaited him on the route ahead. After an unsuccessful attempt to buy them off, the Amir, who as usual had been counting on the *jurda* for resupply at Tabuk, had little choice but to forge ahead in the hope that help was on the way from Damascus. To remain at Tabuk was simply to starve to death.

The caravan left Tabuk, and, as threatened, the Banu Sakhr fell upon it at Hallat Amrar between Tabuk and Dhat Hajj. The possessions and supplies of the Hajjis were carried off; many of the pilgrims were killed on the spot; and many later died of thirst, starvation, and their wounds. Among them was the sister of the Sultan, but not Husayn Pasha, who managed to escape but never again dared to return to Damascus.

It was an atrocious and public calamity, and the blame fell not so much on the bedouin perpetrators—perhaps because nothing better could be expected from them, but more likely because they were well beyond any revenge or reprisal—as on the officials held responsible, and in the first instance the mayor of Damascus, also the Pasha's deputy, who had not gone speedily to the caravan's aid at the first report of trouble. When the news of the disaster reached Damascus on 31 October 1757, there was a storm of indignation at the mayor, who four days later did lead a relief column southward, too late to save the pilgrims, obviously, but just in time perhaps to save his own skin.

The repercussions were next felt in Istanbul itself. In addition to the turmoil surrounding the installation of a new Sultan, the city was in the grip of an inflationary rise in the price of food staples and experiencing other forms of social unrest.[54] It was an already explosive situation, and when the news of this new, ill-omened calamity arrived—ill-omened because this particular caravan was carrying relics of the Prophet for public veneration in the capital—the explosion occurred, set off by the stirring of palace politics.[55] Aboukouf, the Chief Eunuch of the Imperial Harem and a man of obvious importance in the dispensation of the empire's posts and patronage, was accused of having placed his protégé Husayn Pasha, "an obscure man and neither loved nor feared by the bedouin," in the post of Governor of Damascus and so of having brought on the disaster. Aboukouf was beheaded and his head hung from the gate of the Seraglio so the public could see and presumably be appeased because the culprit had been found and justice done.

The Ottomans' defensive techniques for the Egyptian caravan were essentially the same as those for the Syrian one.[56] Some bedouin were attached to the caravan as its "guardians," with the assumption that they would not then attack it. Even if that assumption proved true, their very proximity suggested thievery as an appealing alternative to pillaging. So the bedouin guardians were not only paid but guarded against as well. In addition, there were regular and stipulated payments from the imperial treasury to the tribes along the route—never, of course, regarded as tribute by the paymaster, but rather as gifts. The payees presumably did not much care what the pay-off was called so long as it was delivered, and they would certainly have agreed to mention the Sultan in their prayers, had they prayed.

Just as on the Syrian Darb al-Hajj, however, there was the ever-present danger that the greed of a local official, notably the Caravan Commander, would prompt him to withhold the payment to the bedouin for his profit. This was a risky business indeed. There was a large sum to be kept if this gamble succeeded; but if it did not, the lives of the pilgrims were forfeit.[57] The Amir al-Hajj was a crucial figure in the success or failure of a pilgrimage Hajj caravan.

THE EGYPTIAN PILGRIMAGE

As it had for the Mamluks, the pilgrimage caravan continued to be useful to the Ottomans for the delivery of goods and funds to the Hijaz. Moreover, Mecca was still a convenient place of exile or, in this case cited by the Egyptian diarist Ibn Iyas, just of brief respite, since this gentleman's Hajj was going to rid the Egyptians of the presence of someone "who had done good for no one." The year is 1522.

The Chief Military Justice left for Mecca the Noble by the sea route. He was accompanied, on his departure from the Citadel, by the Prince of Amirs, the Commandant of the Citadel Khayr al-Din, together with some Ottoman officers. This trip by the Chief Military Justice was going to rid the Egyptians of his presence since he had done good for no one. It was he who was responsible for the suppression of the four justices,[58] who had been stripped of their administrative responsibilities; he had forbidden notaries to sit on tribunals and had curtailed their studies; he had forbidden the assistants of the four justices to become involved in judicial affairs. . . . He had offended everyone with his regulation of marriage contracts, on which he had imposed a tax. . . . He had bothered women by forbidding them to go around in the markets or riding a donkey. At the time of his departure from Egypt women were chanting the refrain, "Hey, hey, let's role in the hay. The Army Judge has gone away."

It was known that the Prince of Amirs allocated to the Justice, just as he was about to depart for Tur, 10,000 dinars over and above what had been given him on his arrival from Istanbul. Also at the moment of the departure of the Justice for the Hijaz, the Sultan Sulayman sent him, through an Ottoman minister, a sum of 40,000 dinars to defray the expense of putting back into order a spring that had ceased to supply Mecca, to rebuild the Dome of the Oil in the Haram, as well as for the construction of a minaret in the Prophet's sanctuary (at Medina). (Ibn Iyas 1955–1960: 2:450–451)

The Cairo Caravans

Early in September 1522 the overland caravan of that same Hajj departed. Here it is styled, after its most prominent feature, the "Mahmal Caravan."

The Mahmal left Cairo with great éclat; it was an outstanding ceremony. The Commander of the Mahmal Caravan was the Amir Janim Dawlatbay, governor of the Fayyum, who was performing this office for the third time. He crossed Cairo in solemn procession, with a battalion drawn up in parade order, as in the past, from troops of the Commanders of a Thousand. In it were six carriages drawn by draft horses, each bearing a copper cannon with ball, since the Hijaz route was not very safe due to the depradations of the bedouin.

By order of the Prince of Amirs, the covering of the holy Ka'ba had been sent by sea to Mecca, as well as the money gifts for the various pious people who had retired at Mecca or Medina. The Chief Justice of the Army carried these gifts of the Sultan with him when he embarked for Mecca, a precaution he had taken to avoid the attacks of the Arabs along the land route, since the official way to the Hijaz was dangerous during troubled times. (Ibn Iyas 1955–1960: 2:458)

The pilgrimage time of the previous year had fallen in the dead of winter, which occasioned some particular hardships for the Egyptian caravan, as Ibn Iyas also tells us:

The pilgrimage returned to Cairo, led by the Amir Janim, Commander of the Mahmal Caravan. The pilgrims had suffered a great deal from a shortage of foodstuffs and the deaths of many camels. On their departure from Aqaba the cold had become intense and the wind blew with gale force. A large number of pilgrims died there: between Aqaba and the arrival in Cairo there were probably about 80 deaths. Others remained seriously ill because of the cold and the wind, which their bodies had not the strength to resist. (Ibn Iyas 1955–1960: 2:414)

Here an eyewitness describes the departure of the Cairo caravan sometime about 1575. After the fall of Baghdad to the Mongols in 1258, Cairo remained, together with Damascus, one of the two great marshaling points for the departure of the Hajj caravans to Mecca. While Damascus was the assembly point not only for Syrian pilgrims but also for those from Anatolia and even Iraq and Iran, Cairo was, as the anonymous reporter of 1575 describes, the jumping-off point for Hajjis collecting from all across North Africa and sub-Saharan Africa—"Takruris," as they were called— who had either come down the Nile to Cairo or had joined one of the North African caravans across the Sahara.[59]

As touching the Caravan which goes to Mecca, it is to be understood that the Mahumetans observe a kind of Lent continuing one whole moon, and being a moveable ceremony, which sometimes falls high, sometimes low in the year, called in their tongue Ramadan and their feast is called Bayram. During this time of Lent all they which intend to go to Mecca resort unto Cairo, because twenty days after the feast the Caravan is ready to depart on the voyage; and thither resort a great multitude of people from Asia, Graecia and Barbaria to go on this voyage, some moved by devotion, and some for traffick's sake and some to pass away the time.

Now within a few days after the feast they which go on the voyage depart out of the city two leagues unto a place called Birca, where they expect the Captain of the Caravan. This place has a great pond caused by the inundation of the Nile, and so made that the camels and other beasts may drink therein; whereof, namely, of mules, camels and dromedaries, there are at least forty thousand, and the persons which follow the Caravan each year are about fifty thousand, a few more or less according to the times. Moreover, every three years they renew the Captain of the Caravan, called in the Arabian tongue Amarilla Hajji [Amir al-Hajj], that is, Captain of the Pilgrims, to whom the Grand Signor [the Ottoman Sultan] gives every voyage eighteen purses, containing each of them six hundred twenty and five ducats of gold, and these be for the behoove of the Caravan and also to do alms unto the needful pilgrims.

This Captain, besides other servingmen to follow him, has also four Chausi [kawass] to serve him. Likewise he has with him for the security of

the Caravan four hundred soldiers, to wit, two hundred Sipahi or horse-
men mounted on dromedaries and two hundred Janissaries riding upon
camels. . . . The charge of these is to cause the Caravan to march in good
array when need requires; these are not at the commandment of any but
of the Captain of the Caravan. Moreover, the Captain has for his guide
eight pilots, the office of whom is always firm and stable from heir to heir,
and these go before guiding the Caravan and showing the way, as being
well experienced in the place, and in the night they govern them as the
mariners, by the stars. (Anon. Hakluyt 1927: 176–177)

Although the Cairene and Damascus caravans both filled the same basic
functions—the transportation and secure escort of pilgrims to and from
Mecca in order to perform the ritually ordained Hajj—their practices
differed in a number of important respects. Damascus, as we have seen,
had a secondary caravan, the *jurda*, to travel out, meet, and support the
returning Hajj caravan. Cairo, on the other hand, sent forth a secondary
caravan *before* the main Hajj cortege. This preliminary caravan left Cairo
three or four months earlier, in the month of Rajab—it was called the
Rajabiyya, or "Rajab caravan"—and allowed the pilgrims to spend a
longer time in the Holy Cities and so perform the various optional litur-
gies at Mecca and Medina in a more leisurely and careful fashion.[60]

The Mahmal

As Henry Maundrell noted in connection with the Damascus caravan,
both it and the Cairene cortege prominently featured the curious empty
camel litter known as the "Mahmal."[61] It was a large and decorated palanquin built on a wood frame and then covered with black, green, or red
silk.[62] Inside were a copy of the Quran and an expensively made carpet,
both the gift of the ruler, and the latter intended as a new covering for the
tomb of the Prophet at Medina. The camel that bore the Mahmal, a
carefully chosen prime animal, was thereafter freed of ever bearing another burden.

Although we have some idea of when the custom began—probably in
Egypt, though not necessarily as an Egyptian custom, and the other versions were derived ones—no one is at all certain what it meant.[63] Some
connected this carrying of an empty litter with an old bedouin custom of
bearing a maiden into battle as a kind of tribal totem, while others have
seen in it a kind of royal tent or pavilion, the royal presence, so to speak,
without the royal person. Whatever the case, the Mamluk Sultan Baybars apparently first introduced the custom into the Cairo caravan in
1266 C.E.,[64] and thereafter it was a fixture—indeed, the centerpiece—of
the annual Hajj cortege leaving the Egyptian capital.

The Mahmal was not only a religious symbol; it was a token of sovereignty and a mighty talisman of honor for the ruling house. The Governor of Damascus led the Syrian caravan, with the Mahmal, in person in 1672. As he stood awaiting the pilgrims at Muzayrib in February amidst worsening weather, he finally decided that he risked missing the assembly at Arafat if he waited any longer. His words at Muzayrib were recorded by Evliya Chelebi, a Turkish traveler who was making the Hajj that year, and they reflect how the governor, and the Ottomans generally, viewed their obligation toward the pilgrimage:

> I am not appointed to carry the pilgrims. I am responsible only for getting to Mecca (on time) with the sacred Mahmal and the two treasure caravans, the waqf of God, from Egypt. And should the Egyptian Mahmal arrive in Mecca without the sacred Mahmal from Damascus, then this would cause a new problem for the honor of the Ottoman dynasty. However much it may hurt my own honor, I must take care of the sacred Mahmal. And if there were only serviceable mules available, I would load them up with the treasure of the Mahmal. And if we were three overnights behind, I would, by God's help, reach (Mecca) in one night and would enter directly into the sacred precincts. (Chelebi 1935: 273[65])

If we know that Sultan Baybars began the custom in 1266, probably as part of his program to underline Egyptian sovereignty in the Hijaz, the custom ended for much the same reason, as we are informed by Harry St. John Philby apropos of his description of the Hajj of 1931.

> The word mahmal, literally meaning "carrier," is used in connection with the pilgrimage to signify the ceremonial camel-borne canopies or litters which were annually sent down with the pilgrimage caravans from Damascus and Cairo by or on behalf of the Turkish Sultan and the Egyptian Khedive respectively in token of the sovereignty claimed by them—the Khedive being of course the Sultan's viceroy at any rate up to the time of the Great War—over the holy cities of the Hijaz. It is believed that this custom originated in the preparation made on a certain occasion long ago for the visit to Mecca of an Egyptian (or Turkish) princess, who was in the end unable to make the journey but insisted on sending her sumptuous litter filled with valuable gifts for the shrines of Mecca and Medina by way of proxy.
>
> Since then the Mahmals had been regarded as an official symbol of the authority of the Sultan-Caliph and his viceroy until 1926, when the conquest of the Hijaz by the Wahhabi ruler and his assumption of the royal title deprived the canopies of all significance—the Damascus Mahmal, which Charles Doughty accompanied down into Arabia in 1876, had indeed been discontinued long before the advent of the Wahhabis. Never-

theless, the Egyptian Mahmal was duly sent to the Hijaz in 1926 and installed at Mina during the pilgrimage. Its presence was, however, resented by the fanatical Wahhabis and a disturbance ensued, in which shots were exchanged. That was the end of the Egyptian Mahmal and the beginning of a decade of coolness between the Saudi and the Egyptian governments. At the end of this period, however, the quarrel was made up to the mutual satisfaction of both parties, and in token thereof, the Egyptian Mahmal visited the Hijaz once more, but only once. It was not allowed to proceed further than Jidda, and having served its purpose as an outward and visible sign of the reconciliation of the two governments, was thereafter discontinued in deference to Wahhabi sensibilities on the initiative of the Egyptian government. (Philby 1946: 26–27)

The Organization of the Caravan

The annual caravan (or caravans) from Cairo to Mecca was, like its Damascus counterpart, an enormous enterprise. As we have seen, it is possible to piece together bits of information on the Damascus caravan in Ottoman times from various judicial archives. In the case of the Cairo cortege, we have, apart from pilgrims' descriptions, the additional advantage of possessing administrative handbooks prepared precisely for the officials charged with the staggering task of organizing these annual caravans. The pilgrims may be better witnesses, for the latter, like all practical handbooks, more often reflect the way things should be rather than the way they were. But if the proper allowances are made, these highly detailed manuals provide invaluable information on the makeup and regulation of the Egyptian caravan in late Mamluk and early Ottoman times. The most important of these handbooks is undoubtedly that written by Abd al-Qadir al-Ansari al-Jazari, an official who spent most of his adult life (1517–1553) in the Ottomans' Bureau of Pilgrimage in Cairo and who often traveled with the caravans.[66]

THE CARAVAN COMMANDER AND HIS STAFF

Whatever its origin, a Hajj caravan, according to Jazari and every report we have, was under the charge of an official already noted in connection with the Syrian caravan and called the *Amir al-Hajj* or "Caravan Commander." This prestigious and responsible position, we also know, could enrich its holder. He was a government appointee, and at the beginning of the Ottoman regime the honor was generally bestowed on a grandee from Istanbul. Then, in the early eighteenth century, with the resurrection of the Mamluk military aristocracy in Egypt, one of the latter usually led the Egyptian caravan. His duties are simply described: (1) to organize the caravan, which included the acquisition and distribution of supplies;

(2) to escort and protect the pilgrims to and from the Holy Cities; and (3) to receive and deliver contributions in cash and kind for the *Haramayn*, or the Two Sanctuaries, and to supervise their distribution there.

The Ottomans began their sponsorship of the Hajj, as one might expect of a new and somewhat parvenu regime, with prodigal liberality, and within thirty years they were looking for ways to reduce this particular budget item. The money in question, or rather, the resources, whether the value was large or small, was placed in the hands of the Amir al-Hajj. Some of it was for the various perquisites for this high and responsible office, but the great bulk was for what might be called operating expenses. The Amir was given cash, grain, and clothing, some of it as pay for his suite and troops, some as supplies and subsistence for those same people, and some as stipulated "gifts" for the bedouin along the way. He drew arms and ammunition from the state arsenal, though all of the arms and the unused ammunition were supposed to be handed back on his return.[67] In the Ottoman system all these outlays except the specific honorifics earmarked for the Amir himself, robes of honor, for example, had to be accounted for. Whether they were is another question. How much of the allotted sums the Amir did *not* pay to the bedouin could not be known, nor how much he realized from the sale of the state provisions supplied for his own men or animals. But what was obviously not reported was the pay-back side of the ledger: what the bedouin or rulers or Mecca paid to the Amir al-Hajj simply to get their hands on what they, or "the regime," thought was due to them. It was, by any reckoning, an enormously profitable enterprise for the Caravan Commander.[68]

The Ottoman accounting system provides us with a far better picture of where the money came from than where it actually went. The Amir's ever-increasing expenses in operating the Hajj caravan were subsidized from the income from state lands earmarked precisely for this purpose, from supplemental funds from the state treasury, funds which increased in truly staggering increments,[69] and finally, as we learn from the estate settlement of Sulayman Jawish, even from the notable's own funds.

Sulayman Jawish was commander of the Egyptian caravan in 1739 C.E., and his estate settlement, with its careful receipting of salaries, provides important information on the makeup of the Egyptian Hajj caravan in the second quarter of the eighteenth century. Among those in the direct employ of the Amir, the largest contingent were the cameleers, some of them attached to the Sultan's service, some of them bedouin recruited for the occasion, who accounted for nearly 57 percent of the salary expenditure.[70] The next largest item was the pay of the water bearers, who received a tip in addition to their pay and who represented 13 percent of the salary budget. Next were the *akkams*, the baggage handlers and tent men, who also were tipped. They received 12 percent of all the salaries, while the torchbearers got a little over 10 percent for their care of the torches during the long night marches. Ranged below these major groups of employees were the grooms, muleteers, and shepherds. Finally, there were cooks and bakers and the all-important coffee dispensers.[71]

Once the caravan was upon its way, the powers of the Caravan Commander were almost absolute. But they were not unshared. No man, no matter how autocratic or gifted, could run a Hajj caravan unaided. Chief among the Caravan Commander's associates was the *dawadar*, a combination chief of staff, paymaster, and executive assistant. He made sure that the Amir's commands were both delivered and carried out, dispensed to the bedouin their allocations (and received something in return), had the final say in police matters, oversaw security during the night march when the Amir slept, and finally, served as the go-between for petitioners to the Amir.

The *dawadar* was also responsible for reporting all cases of injustice to the Amir, but infractions of religious law were heard and adjudicated by the *Qadi*, or Islamic justice, assigned to the caravan.[72] In that same connection, because cases in Islamic law were decided not so much by evidence as by the testimony of certified reliable witnesses, two such notarized witnesses (*shuhud*) were likewise attached to the Hajj cortege.

The ongoing administrative business of the caravan was handled by a kind of secretarial department that bore the same name as the ministries of Muslim states, namely, *Diwan*, though this mobile version was obviously far more modest in scope and personnel than its counterparts in Cairo. It eventually had its own budget and statutes and was run by a ministerial secretary (*katib*), a post held by Jazari's father and then, at the latter's death in 1538, by Jazari himself.

A parallel institution had the important responsibility of overseeing the livestock, on whose well-being the very existence of the caravan depended. These animals bore the supplies of both the pilgrims and the Pasha's suite and troops, as well as their own fodder. To add to the complication, these beasts were generally leased rather than owned by the government. There were opportunities for both extortion and possibly fatal malfeasance in these supervisory positions, and Jazari, who spent an entire lifetime worrying about such matters, worried a great deal about this particular "Department of Transport."[73]

"IN WHAT ORDER THE CARAVAN TRAVELLETH"

It is possible, on the basis of the handbooks, to reconstruct the order of march of the caravan. Jazari, for example, tells us that in the case of the Egyptian caravan it was in 1405 that the Amir al-Hajj first decided that the pilgrims would proceed in parallel columns. These and all other matters of procedure and arrangement were obviously in the Caravan Commander's hands, though he was willing to listen to suggestions on occasion, especially, as we have seen, if there was a profit to be made in some modification of the caravan's progress.

Speaking generally, however, first in the order of march came a kind of advance party consisting of the supply camels carrying provisions for men and beasts, then scouts, the Amir's personnel, whose first task was to set up the Commander's tent and other facilities at the next stop, and cooks and bakers, so they too could get a head start on the enormous task of feeding this crowd. The caravan proper—and here the double file began—was led by the notables, military and civil, most of them in litters and carefully segregated from the rest of the Hajjis.

Next followed the strongboxes carrying the considerable funds and valuables that went out with each caravan: gifts, bribes, pay for the military and the bedouin along the way, plus all the pension funds and other perquisites that the government undertook to pay to the authorities and citizens of the Holy Cities. This treasure was surrounded by heavily armed cavalry and followed by the royal standard accompanied by additional soldiers and the inevitable Turkish band.[74]

Next in the order of march were the women on Hajj and the tents and provisions provided gratis for the poor from the funds of a charitable foundation. There followed the merchants, those who provided the necessary and profitable service of buying and selling to the pilgrims. Then came the great mass of pilgrims, followed, finally, by a rear guard of regular soldiers and bedouin, whose functions included rounding up, escorting, and, if necessary, waiting for stragglers.

This order of march, as has been remarked, comes from an administrative manual and so probably represents more of an ideal than a reality. What the reality was like, we can learn in detail from the anonymous pilgrim of circa 1575:

> The manner and order which the caravan observeth in marching is this. It goeth divided into three parts, to wit, the forward, the main battell, and the rearward. In the forward go the 8 pilots with a Chaus,[75] which hath four knaves and each knave carrieth a sinew of a bull, to the end that if occasion requireth, ye bastinado may be given to such as deserve the same. These knaves cast offenders down, turning up the soles of their feet made fast to a staff, giving them a perpetual remembrance for them and the beholders.
>
> This Chaus is as the Captain of the forward (guard), which commandeth lights to be carried before when they travel at night. Also there go in this forward 6 Santones with red turbans upon their heads, and these eat

and ride at the cost of the Captain of the caravan. These Santones, when the caravan arriveth at any good lodging, suddenly after they have escried the place, cry with a horrible voice saying, good cheer, good cheer, we are near to the wished lodging. For which good news the chiefs of the company bestow their benevolence upon them. In the forward goeth very near the third part of the people of the caravan, behind which go always 25 Sipahi armed with swords, bows and arrows to defend them from thieves.

Next unto the forward, within a quarter of a mile, followeth the main battell, and before the same are drawn the said six pieces of ordnance, with their gunners, and fifteen Sipahi archers. And next unto these cometh the chief physician, who is an old man of authority, having with him many medicines, ointments, salves and other refreshings for the sick, having also camels with him for the sick to ride on, which have no horse nor beast.

Next unto him goeth one camel alone, the fairest that can be found; for with great industry is found the greatest and the fairest which may be found within the dominions of the Grand Signor. This camel is also decked with cloth of gold and silk, and carrieth a little chest made of pure Legmame made in likeness of the ark of the Old Testament; but, as is abovesaid, made of pure Legmame, without gold or any other thing of cost. Within this chest is the Alcoran all written with great letters of gold, bound between two tables of massy gold, and the chest during their voyage is covered with silk, but at their entering into Mecca it is all covered with gold, adorned with jewels, and the like at the entrance to Medina. The camel aforesaid which carrieth the chest is compassed about with many Arabian singers and musicians, always singing and playing upon instruments.

After this follow fifteen other most fair camels, each one carrying one of the aforesaid vestures, being covered from top to toe with silk. Behind these go twenty other camels which carry the money, apparel and provisions of the Amir al-Hajj, captain of the caravan.

After followeth the royal standard of the Grand Signor, accompanied continually with the musicians of the captain and five and twenty Sipahi archers, with a Chaus before them, and about these marvelous things go all the people and camels which follow the caravan.

Behind these, less than a mile, followeth the rearward, whereof the greater part are pilgrims: the occasion whereof is, for that the merchants always seek to be in the forward for the security of their goods, but the pilgrims which have little to lose care not though they come behind. Behind these always go five and twenty other Sipahi well armed with another Chaus their captain, and forty Arabians all archers for guard of the rearward. (Anon. Hakluyt 1927: 3:180–182)

Jazari, so voluble in laying out the formalities of the late Mamluk and early Ottoman Hajj, is much more reticent when it concerns the realities. But he was not, after all, a historian. And so when it comes to the number of pilgrims, the skillful bureaucrat makes no attempt to provide totals or even averages, but only offers chance remarks on extraordinary circumstances.[76] Thus we are told that the gathering at Arafat was particularly large in 1279 C.E.: 40,000 Egyptians and an equal number of pilgrims from Syria and Iraq. The numbers obviously must be treated with caution; what can be said is that somebody remembered that there were more people than usual on Hajj in 1279.

More revealing, because they are likely to be more accurate, are Jazari's equally random figures about animals. Unlike people, camels were leased for the Hajj and so had to be accounted for. The preliminary, or Rajab, caravan that left Cairo in 1431 was thought large with 1,500 camels, as was that in 1444 with 4,000. What, then, was normal? Or, if the main Iraqi caravans of 1395 and 1428 were thought small with 500 and 400 camels, respectively, are we to take as normal the one that came from Baghdad in 1383 with 4,000? A Christian pilgrim, James of Verona, claims to have run across a Hajj caravan in the Sinai in 1335 that numbered 17,000 people and 6,000 camels.[77]

IRANIANS MAKE THE HAJJ

In the late nineteenth century, as we shall see, some Iranians chose to enter the Hijaz by a circuitous sea route, but the more common path for Iranians journeying to Mecca was one or another of the caravan routes. They might proceed across Mesopotamia to meet the caravan assembling in Damascus, but a more direct way was either to join the caravan in Baghdad or, if their numbers were sufficiently great, to compose their own caravan for the trip along the Darb Zubayda. In any event, the Persian pilgrimage had its own particular problems. From the sixteenth century at least, Muslim pilgrims from Iran were overwhelmingly Shiʿites and so the objects of scorn and disdain from the Sunni rulers and populations through whose lands they had to pass en route to Mecca.

Shiʿite Trials

Although the experience for a Shiʿite on the road to Mecca was almost always a trying one, the situation became even more threatening in the nineteenth century, when the fundamentalist Sunni Wahhabis controlled

most of central Arabia and even, for a brief period, the Holy Cities themselves. William Palgrave, a onetime Jesuit, encountered one such group of
Shi'ites at Burayda, in the heart of Wahhabi territory, in 1867.

A few paces farther on, our way opened out on the great plain that lies
immediately under the town walls (of Burayda) to the north. This space
was now covered with tents and thronged with men of foreign dress and
bearing, mixed with Arabs of town and desert, women and children, talking and quarrelling, buying and selling, going and coming; everywhere
baskets full of dates and vegetables, platters bearing eggs and butter, milk
and whey, meat hung on poles, bundles of firewood, etc. stood ranged in
rows, horsemen and camel-men were riding about between groups seated
round fires or reclining against their baggage; in the midst of all this med-
ley a gilt ball surmounted a large white pavilion of a make that I had not
seen since I had left India some eleven years before, and numerous smaller
tents of striped cloth and certainly not of Arab fashion clustered around.
These tents belonged to the great caravan of Persian pilgrims, on their
return from Medina to Mashhad Ali by the road of Qasim, and hence all
this unusual concourse and bustle. Taj Jahan, the relict of Asaph Dawlah,
a name familiar to Anglo-Bengali readers, was the principal personage in
the band, and hers was the gilt-topped tent. . . . The rest of the caravan
was composed partly of Persians proper, natives of Shiraz, Isfahan and
other Iranian towns, and partly of a still larger number belonging to the
hybrid race that forms the Shi'i population of Mashhad Ali, Karbala and
Baghdad. All of course were of the sect just mentioned, though very diverse in national origin. Along with them, and belonging to the first or
genuine Persian category, was a person scarcely less important than the
Begum herself, namely Muhammad Ali al-Shirazi, native of Shiraz, as his
denomination implies, and representative of the Persian government at
Mashhad Ali, actually commissioned by orders from Teheran with the
unenviable office of director or headman of this laborious and not over-
safe pilgrimage. . . . The total of the caravan amounted to two hundred,
or rather more.
They had assembled at Riyadh in Najd, where they had arrived, some
from the northerly rendezvous at Mashhad Ali and others from that of
Abu Shahr—often corrupted on maps into Bushire—whence they had
crossed the Persian Gulf to the port of Ujayr, and thus passed on to Hufuf
and Riyadh. Here Faysal [the Saudi ruler of Riyadh], after exacting the
exorbitant sum which Wahhabi orthodoxy claims from Shi'i heretics as
the price of permission to visit the sacred city and the tomb of the
Prophet, had assigned them for guide and leader one Abd al-Aziz Abu
Butayn, a Najdean of the Najdeans, who was to conduct and plunder
them in the name of God and the true faith all the rest of the way to
Mecca and back again. (Palgrave 1883: 159–160)

The Iranians had other options. The Rashidi rulers of Hayl and the Jabal Shammar tried to draw Persian pilgrim caravans through their territory, in part to defy the rival Wahhabis and in part to make a profit. The policy was not often successful, it appeared.

The way by central Najd is more direct, and for that reason preferable to the Persians, on condition of having tolerable immunity from danger and pillage. . . . Faysal, overjoyed to draw this silver stream to his mill, waived the motives of bigotry and national hatred which had more than once led his predecessors to refuse the most advantageous offers when made by heretics. . . . Still he felt himself bound in conscience to make the unbelievers pay roundly for the negatively good treatment which he thus consented to afford, and took his measures accordingly.

Forty golden tomans was fixed as the claim of the Wahhabi treasury on every Persian pilgrim for his passage through Riyadh, and forty more for his safe-conduct through the rest of the empire: eighty in all. On his side, Faysal was to furnish from among his own men a guide invested with absolute power in whatever regarded the special arrangement of the march, and we may without any breach of charity suppose that the king's servant could do no less than imitate the good example of his master in fleecing the heretics to the best of his ability. Every local governor on the way would naturally take the hint and strive not to let the "enemies of God"—for this is the sole title given by the Wahhabis to all but themselves—go by without spoiling them more or less. So that, all counted up, the legal and necessary dues levied on every Persian Shiʿi while traversing Central Arabia and under Wahhabi guidance and protection, amounted, I found, to about 150 golden tomans, equalling nearly 60 pounds sterling, no light expenditure for a Persian, and no despicable gain for an Arab.

Besides this, seeming casualties might occur, helping to shear the wool still closer, nay, sometimes taking off the skin altogether. Such was the case with the hapless Persians at the very time of our meeting. Their conductor, Abu Butayn, had taken from them whatever custom entitled him to by way of advance payment and charged the disconsolate Taj Jahan more especially at the rate of her supposed wealth rather than any fixed precedent. But he had done more, and by dint of threats and bullying of all descriptions, including blows administered by his orders to the Persian commissioner, and in his own tent, had managed to get countless extras out of those entrusted to his guidance, till he had filled his saddle-bags with tomans and loaded his camels with plunder.

But on his return along with his injured proteges from Medina, whither he had led them to complete their devotions and his own profit, Abu Butayn began to fear lest they should lodge a complaint against him at Burayda, which lay on their road, the more so that Muhammad,

Faysal's third son, was now there in person, and that he should ultimately be forced to refund his ill-gotten wealth, not indeed to its Shi'i owners, for of that there was little danger under Wahhabi arbitration, but to the Riyadh treasury. . . . He resolved on the very worst course possible for him, namely that of anticipating investigation by flight. So when the pilgrims arrived at Ayun . . . Abu Butayn absconded, money and all, and took refuge in the rebel town of Unayza, leaving Taj Jahan . . . and the rest to find their way out of Arabia by themselves as best they could. . . . At Burayda they had fallen into the clutches of a genuine Wahhabi and lay at all the tender mercies of the most wicked and heartless of all Najdean governors, Muhanna al-Anayzi. . . . At this man's orders were now Taj Jahan and her fellow-pilgrims.

He had before our arrival already detained them for a good fortnight under the walls of Burayda, while he put every engine of extortion into play against them, and awaited from Faysal some further hint as to the conduct he was to hold with these "enemies of God." (Palgrave 1883: 160–162)

September closed, and then finally Muhanna selected a guide to lead Taj Jahan and the associates of her pilgrimage to the banks of the Euphrates. The Persians duly paid the price of their deliverance and departed on the northwestern track, having about twenty-five days' march before them, and slender provisions. However, during my stay at Baghdad in the following Spring I was happy to learn that they had at last arrived in safety. (Palgrave 1883: 192)

The Shi'ites in the Holy Cities

The Shi'ites' problems were by no means ended once they reached the Holy Cities. Richard Burton had befriended some Persian pilgrims along his way to Mecca in 1853. He saw them again after his arrival in Medina, one evening at the tomb of the Prophet.

My old friends the Persians—there were about 1200 of them in the Hajj caravan—attracted my attention. The door keepers stopped them with curses as they were about to enter, and all claimed from each the sum of five piasters, while other Muslims were allowed to enter the mosque free. Unhappy men! They had lost all the Shiraz swagger, their mustachios dropped pitiably, their eyes would not look anyone in the face, and not a head bore a cap stuck upon it crookedly. Whenever an "Ajami," whatever might be his rank, stood in the way of an Arab or a Turk he was rudely thrust aside, with abuse muttered loud enough to be heard by all around.

One of the points at issue between the Sunni Arabs and Turks and the Shiʿite Persians was the refusal of most of the latter to recognize the legitimacy of Muhammad's first three successors, Abu Bakr, Umar, and Uthman, to the advantage of the fourth Caliph, Ali, of whose "party" (*shiʿa*) they were. The first two of that unacceptable triumvirate, Abu Bakr and Umar, were buried next to Muhammad in the very same tomb building at Medina. And nearby was the tomb of Fatima, daughter of Muhammad and the highly venerated wife of Ali.

All eyes followed them as they went through the ceremonies of the visitation (of the tomb), especially as they approached the tombs of Abu Bakr and Umar—which every man (of them) is bound to defile if he can—and the supposed place of Fatima's burial. Here they stood in parties, after praying before the window of the Prophet's tomb: one read from a book the pathetic tale of the Lady's life, sorrows and mourning death, while the others listened to him with breathless attention. Sometimes their emotion was too strong to be repressed. "Ay, Fatima . . . O thou injured one, alas, alas!" burst involuntarily from their lips, despite the danger of such exclamations; tears trickled down their hairy cheeks, and their brawny bosoms heaved with sobs. A strange sight it was to see rugged fellows . . . sometimes weeping silently like children, sometimes shrieking like hysteric girls, and utterly careless to conceal a grief so coarse and grisly, at the same time so real and true. . . . Then the Satanic scowls with which they passed by, or pretended to pray at, the hated Umar's tomb! With what curses their hearts are belying those mouths full of blessings! How they are internally canonizing Fayruz, the Persian slave who stabbed Umar in the mosque, and praying for his eternal happiness in the presence of the murdered man! Sticks and stones, however, and not infrequently the knife and the saber, have taught the Persians the hard lesson of disciplining their feelings; and nothing but a furious contraction of the brow, a roll of the eye, intensely vicious, and a twitching of the muscles about the region of the mouth denote the wild storm of wrath within. (Burton 1893: 1:434–435)

Later on, at Mecca, Burton observed one of his own party dashing furiously around the Kaʿba, all the while "foully abusing every Persian in his path." The incident recalled other stories about the Persians in that place:

In 1674 some wretch smeared the Black Stone with impurity, and everyone who kissed it retired with a sullied beard. The Persians, says Burckhardt, were suspected of this sacrilege, and now their ill-fame has spread far. At Alexandria they were described to me as a people who defile the Kaʿba. It is scarcely necessary to say that a Shiʿa, as well as a Sunni, would look upon such an action with lively horror. The people of Mecca, however, like the Medinese, have turned the circumstance to their own advantage, and make an occasional "avanie" [that is, they impose an entirely illegal and arbitrary tax, in this case upon the Persians]. Thus nine or ten years ago, on the testimony of a boy who swore that he saw the inside of the Ka'ba defiled by a Persian, they rose up, cruelly beat the schismatics, and carried them off to their particular quarter, the Shamiyya, forbidding their ingress into the Ka'ba. Indeed, till Muhammad Ali's time, the Persians rarely ventured upon a pilgrimage, and even now that man is happy who gets over it without a beating. (Burton 1893: 1:168n.1)

Even at Arafat, the heart of the Hajj, certain distinctions set apart Sunni and Shi'ite, as explained by Hossein Kazemzadeh, a Shi'ite who made the pilgrimage in 1910–1911:

Sunni pilgrims always ascend the hill of Arafat, whether to perform the ritual prayer or to call after their friends or parents who could not make the pilgrimage with them. You can see people there crying out for those absent ones as if they wanted to make them appear. They believe that they are heard by those whom they are calling after here on this sacred mount where Adam and Eve were recognized and where, God willing, they too will be in the following year.

The Shi'ites do not go up the mount; their religious practice recommends against making one's prayers there. They prefer to pray standing at the foot of the mountain, on its right side, while the Sunnis are toward the left. But the Persians have their own manner of summoning to the pilgrimage. With their finger they trace on the ground a circle in the name of whomever they wish to see come to the holy places. At times some pious souls, wishing to make the pilgrimage a second or a third time, even trace a circle in their own name. This is a widespread custom, and every time a pilgrim departs for Mecca, his friends and relatives emotionally and tearfully say to him at his departure, "Do not forget me at the foot of Mount Arafat." (Kazemzadeh 1912: 214)

Mohammed Farahani and Hossein Kazemzadeh

Mirza Mohammed Hosayn Farahani left his home in Teheran on 16 July 1885 to perform the Hajj. He traveled via Qazvin and Rasht to Enzeli, thence by steamship to Baku, and by railway from Baku to Batum via Tiflis; from Batum he sailed across the Black Sea to Trabzon, Samsun, and Istanbul, and from Istanbul via Rhodes to Alexandria; again by rail he went to Suez, by steamship to Jidda (27 August 1885), Mecca (3 September), Medina (22 October 1885), then Yanbu, Sinai, and once again Suez, by canal to Ismailiyya, Port Said, Izmir, Istanbul, and then the same way home, where he arrived on 21 January 1886. Like many of his literary predecessors, he left a long, circumstantial account of his travels that includes a kind of census cum description of the pilgrims to Mecca in the year 1885.[78] Twenty-five years later another Persian, Hossein Kazemzadeh, likewise made the Hajj and commented on many of the same groups observed by Farahani. As Iranians, both men were, not unnaturally, quite circumstanial in their descriptions of their fellow countrymen on Hajj. Here is Kazemzadeh:

> Every year from 1000 to 8000 Iranian pilgrims come to Mecca the Exalted. All of them are subjects of the eminent government of Iran. They are of the Shi'ite sect except for a few who come from Kurdistan and some of the ports of Fars who are Sunnis. There is a consul on behalf of the Iranian government in Jidda. Sometimes he is permanently stationed in Jidda, such as previously (was the case with) Ahmad Bayki, who was for years the consul stationed in Jidda. Other times he is there on a temporary basis; that is to say, he comes to Jidda three months before the pilgrimage season and leaves two months after the end of the pilgrimage. . . . A privilege that the consul of Iran has—beyond the consuls of other countries—is that since he is a Muslim he can enter Mecca, Medina, Arafat etc. and accompany the (Iranian) subjects everywhere.
>
> Each of the Iranian pilgrims who enters the Hijaz via Jidda pays the consul in Jidda one and a quarter Levant dollars . . . for a visa. If the consul learns that a pilgrim who is an Iranian subject dies in the Hijaz he takes part of his estate. A tenth of whatever is involved in litigation also goes to the consul. For each camel the Iranian pilgrims hire to either Sa'diyya or Mecca, a fee goes to the consul, the pilgrim guide and the camel broker. For every camel that is hired from Mecca to Medina or Yanbu another sum will also go to the consulate.

Kazemzadeh offered some closer and more critical observations of his fellow Persians:

> The Persian pilgrims are generally well behaved, but among those who come from the southern provinces around the Persian Gulf there are misers and quarrelsome types. With their disputes, their complaints and their evil conduct they turn all the customs and port officials against them, while the northerners, who are peaceful and modest, are everywhere respected. The southern Persian pilgrims act in the same way with respect to their consul; they are always attempting to avoid getting a visa for their passports and to have themselves exempted from taxes.
>
> Most of the (Persian) consul general's time is taken up with resolving disputes; almost always these arguments occur between southern pilgrims and caravan leaders who spend hours on end discussing pointless issues.

*The northern pilgrims, who are more generous, and perhaps better edu-
cated and more reasonable, resort to the consul only when they cannot
resolve their problems on their own. They regard it as shameful to be
summoned to the consulate in the wake of a complaint or a piece litiga-
tion against them. (Kazemzadeh 1912: 193–194)*

We turn to Farahani's account:

*This year [1885], a few more than three thousand pilgrims had come
from Iran to Mecca the Exalted. That is to say, eight hundred came by the
Syrian route, of whom fifty had died of thirst and pestilence. About one
hundred people came via the Mountain Route by clandestine means or in
disguise. Twelve hundred people came by way of Bushihr, Bandar Abbas
and Baghdad and entered via Jidda. Also a few more than a thousand
came by way of Istanbul and entered via Jidda and Yanbu. About seven
hundred of these pilgrims were Hajjeh-furushes, ʿakkam, dervishes and
paupers, so no one got any profit from them. There were a few more than
two thousand (actual) pilgrims. The Iranian pilgrims, compared to other
pilgrims, were better (provisioned) and organized, in respect of expenses,
housekeeping necessities, tents and so on. (Farahani 1990: 191)*

Shiʿites and Dissimulation

Farahani's personal experience was apparently rather remote from that of
his fellow countrymen, but he did reflect on what it meant to be a Shiʿite
on pilgrimage in overwhelmingly Sunni Arabia. Should the Shiʿite, for
example, resort to the much-discussed practice of "dissimulation" and attempt to pass as a Sunni in that possibly hostile environment?

*The city (of Mecca) has about sixty Shiʿites who are often pilgrim
guides who associate with the Iranians and (who) may be descendants of
Husayn. These Shiʿites do not practice dissimulation (taqiyya) very much
at the present time. They clearly and openly practice Shiʿism. . . . Previously, the people of Mecca, on the pretext that Noah's ark came to rest on
Mount Judi on (the day of) Ashura [the Shiʿite day of morning for the
martyrdom of Husayn], and the Muslims had thus been saved from the
brink of destruction by Noah, held festivals on Ashura and brought out
instruments to play and sport. After the reign of Sharif Abd al-Muttalib
(ibn Ghalib),[79] since Sharif Abdullah[80] and the present Sharif Awn were
not hostile toward Shiʿism,[81] this practice was abolished and stopped out
of respect for the death of the Prince of Martyrs (Husayn).
Previously, in Mecca the populace greatly persecuted the Iranian pilgrims who were Shiʿites, so they had to practice complete dissimulation.
These days, because of the weakness of the Ottoman government and the*

European style law which is practiced there, and the strength of the Iranian government, this practice is completely abandoned. There is no persecution of Iranians. If they do not practice dissimulation, no one of them will be bothered. They show complete respect for the Iranians, especially those who do not show meanness in expenditures and appearance.

In Mecca, Medina and along the way, I wore Iranian garb everywhere. I put an Iranian hat on my head, and I never practiced dissimulation. Yet, not only did but no one ever bother me physically or verbally, I was afforded complete respect. My opinion is that in this day and age, dissimulation is unlawful, and one must not curse the (first four) Caliphs. Changing dress and concealing the Ja'fari [Shi'ite] rite results in nothing but hardship and hypocrisy. All the Sunni people know that the Iranians are of the Ja'fari rite and that their rite differs from the Sunnites in methodology and substance. They consider the dissimulation of the Iranians an instrument of hypocrisy. (Farahani 1990: 227–229)

THE CARAVAN AS MARKETPLACE
IN EARLY OTTOMAN TIMES

The Hajj was not merely a religious obligation; it was from the earliest times an annual fair, a merchandising opportunity of the first magnitude, and not only at Jidda and Mecca but even upon the road. One of the first accounts of its commercial functions under the Ottomans comes from the anonymous pilgrim who traveled to Mecca in 1575.

The Caravan carries with it six pieces of ordnance drawn by twelve camels, which serve to terrify the Arabians, as also to make triumph at Mecca and other places. The merchants who follow the Caravan, some carry for merchandise cloth of silk, some coral, some tin, others wheat, rye and all sorts of grain. Some sell by the way, some at Mecca, so that everyone brings something to gain by, because all merchandise that goes by land pays no custom, but that which goes by sea is bound to pay ten in the hundred. (Anon. Hakluyt 1927: 178)

The avoidance of maritime custom dues was doubtless a powerful incentive to use the Hajj caravan for the transport of goods from Mecca, or to be more precise, Jidda. But it would not have availed merchants much unless the caravan offered a secure way of transporting such goods.

Two types of merchandising are in question here. The small merchants were the sellers: they carried their goods with them, and their market consisted of the pilgrims en route. The great merchants were the buyers: they went to Jidda to meet the ships filled with Indian and other Eastern goods—spices, textiles, precious stones, and coffee—which they then carried to markets in Damascus and Cairo for sale there.

By the mid-eighteenth century this Eastern trade had become an international political issue.[82] Up to that time, goods had been carried from India to Jidda in Turkish ships, but then ships of the British East India Company, now firmly established in India, took over the transport, against the ineffective protests and impotent threats of the Ottomans. If the East India Company had had its way, Jidda would have been excluded entirely, and the goods would have been carried by ship directly to Suez. But a course that made commercial good sense to the East India Company would have eliminated the importance of the caravan (and its entrepreneurs) as a trading instrument and, even more to the point, the Sharif of Mecca, who had an immense investment (and equally immense return) in the trade going through his port city of Jidda. Nor did the idea much appeal to another party that preferred that the trade go overland to Damascus rather than to Cairo via Suez: the British Levant Company.[83]

The Pilgrims as Traders

One fairly common way for a pilgrim to finance his Hajj expenses was to become a trader, whether he made his normal livelihood in that fashion or not. There were always things to be bought and sold along the route, and no shortage of buyers or sellers, as John Lewis Burckhardt tells us:

Few pilgrims, except the mendicants, arrive without bringing some productions of their respective countries for sale; and this remark is applicable as well to the merchants with whom commercial pursuits are the main object as to those who are actuated by religious zeal; for to the latter the profits derived from selling a few native articles at Mecca diminish in some degree the heavy expenses of the journey. The Maghribis, for example, bring red bonnets and woolen cloaks; the European Turks shoes and slippers, hardware, embroidered stuffs, sweetmeats, amber, trinkets of European manufacture, knit silk purses etc.; the Turks of Anatolia bring carpets, silks and Angora shawls; the Persians cashmere shawls and large silk handkerchiefs; the Afghans tooth-brushes . . . made of the spongy boughs of a tree growing in Bukhara, beads of yellow soap-stone, and plain coarse shawls manufactured in their own country; the Indians, the numerous productions of their rich and extensive region; the people of the Yemen snakes for the Persian pipes, sandals and various other works in leather; and the Africans bring various articles adapted to the slave trade.

The Hajjis are, however, often disappointed in their expectations of gain; want of money makes them sell their little adventures at the public auctions, and often obliges them to accept very low prices. (Burckhardt 1829: 256–257)

Another insight into the mercantile quality of the Hajj is provided by the Ottoman *terke defteri* (estate settlements) of those who had died during the pilgrimage and whose possessions had thus to be catalogued and evaluated for testamentary purposes. These inventories list what has been called the "trousseau of the pilgrim," the collection of "clothing and primary necessities the pilgrim took with him, as well as the objects of piety and other merchandise he carried in the expectation of making an offering or equally likely of doing some business; and finally, the nature and type of the means of payment at the disposition of the pilgrim-merchant."[84]

One illuminating example is that of Mehmed Agha, a prosperous land-owner of Crete who died in 1705 on the way to Mecca. His baggage was modest indeed compared to his fortune, "a frugality that may have owed something to convenience, a precaution against theft, or perhaps religious humility,"[85] but the list gives a notion of what personal goods a pilgrim carried with him early in the eighteenth century: a fur-lined cloak (his most expensive article of clothing), as well as other outer wraps, two body shirts, a pair of boots, a coverlet, and a napkin. Mehmed Agha's other equipment was equally inexpensive and included a small basin, four platters, two plates, and a drinking cup. Finally, he also carried with him a kind of cardboard desk and a basket.

Mehmed Agha died outbound to Mecca. An examination of the possessions of those who died on the return voyage reveals the dimensions of the trade in "objects of piety" that went on the holy cities. They are very much what we might expect: prayer-beads (often in quantities that suggest possible resale at home), copper flasks with Zamzam water, and, an expensive item, shrouds steeped in that water.[86]

The Professionals

All the available information indicates that the merchants of Damascus, and particularly of Cairo, used the relative security of the annual Hajj caravan not simply to sell to pilgrims along the way but also to transport goods and funds to Mecca to conduct business, either directly or through agents in the Hijaz, with factors from the East. On the way out, they carried with them chiefly European textiles, foodstuffs, and a notable amount of coinage. On the return from Mecca they had, as we might expect, spices, drugs, coffee, and Indian textiles.[87]

The caravan was not the only transport between Cairo and Mecca, of course, and it is not always easy to estimate how much merchandise was carried overland and how much by Red Sea shipping. But in the course of the eighteenth century, and particularly toward the end, when there were repeated and serious problems with the bedouin along the land route,[88] the balance seems to have begun tipping in favor of the maritime passage.

We receive another perspective from the estate settlement of the Cairene merchant Sulayman Jawish, who was going to serve as Amir al-Hajj in 1739. He had stockpiled quantities of cereals at various stations along the way to Mecca. These were clearly intended as fodder for the animals in the caravan, but the very large surpluses stored in places like Aqaba and Jidda suggest something else: Sulayman Jawish was obviously engaged in the commercial sale of grain in the Hijaz, a trade that traditionally underwrote the purchase there of coffee and spices, the chief commercial imports into Egypt. And the connection with the Hajj caravan probably exempted him from the normal duties on such goods.[89]

The same suspicion attaches to the large sums of money Sulayman Jawish intended to carry with him, almost all of it in Spanish silver piasters, roughly 407 pounds of precious metals. The money may have been intended to buy Eastern products like coffee for resale in Egypt, or it may have belonged to Cairo merchants who were using the relatively secure opportunity of the Hajj caravan for the transfer of funds to the Hijaz.[90]

A great deal of our information has to do with professional traders in the Mecca enterprise, but it is likewise true that merchants from elsewhere were among those most likely to make the pilgrimage. And, as we have been instructed by Burckhardt, all classes of pilgrims often became merchants for the occasion, buying at home and selling en route, or buying at Mecca and selling at home.[91] The Swedish naturalist and explorer Fredrick Hasselquist, writing of Cairo in the middle of the eighteenth century, is quite explicit:

All do not go to Mecca out of devotion, and there are a number of people who make the pilgrimage only from a hope for gain. They buy from the French in Cairo cloth, red dye, spices, lead, copper, false pearls which they sell in Arabia, to say nothing of a prodigious quantity of German crowns and Spanish piasters which they take with them. They use them for coffee, Meccan balm, myrrh, incense, . . . drugs, Chinese porcelain, fabrics of cotton, silk, gold and silver, turbans, etc., from which the bey [the Amir al-Hajj] derives a considerable profit since he is the one who determines the time the caravan will be en route and remain at Mecca. Since this latter is very brief, when the merchants cannot wind up their business, they request the bey to defer their departure a few days, which he grants them in return for a sum they pay by the day and to which they all the more easily assent since the profits they make are so great. (Hasselquist, Travels in the Levant [1760][92])

THE RED SEA CROSSING

A more direct, and generally easier, route from Egypt to the Hijaz was by sea, the course we earlier observed Ibn Jubayr following. Some of the African pilgrims continued to cross over to Arabia from Suwakin or Qusayr, but in Ottoman times the most common port of embarkation was Suez. And it was to Suez that Carsten Niebuhr and the members of the Danish expedition to Arabia headed once their preparations were complete in Cairo.

The Danish Expedition of 1761

The prospect of crossing the Red Sea was viewed with at least some apprehension by the Danes, not so much because of the sea, as Niebuhr explains, but because of the men who sailed upon it:

> Although from pirates properly so-called, there is little to be feared in the Arabian Gulf, yet, so unskillful are the mariners in these latitudes, that they dare not venture any distance from the coasts. This timorous mode of sailing might expose a single vessel to the robbery of the Arabs; to avoid which the ships sail in little fleets; four always setting out together, that they may join to defend themselves. . . .
>
> We were recommended to the masters of two ships that were to make the voyage. Although now accustomed to living with Mahometans, yet, in our passage to Jidda, we suffered a degree of uneasiness which we had not felt upon occasions of greater danger. Some Greeks had hinted to us that the Mussulmans thought Christians unworthy of making this voyage in the company of the pilgrims who were journeying to the holy city; and on that account we should not go aboard with shoes on our feet. Some of the pilgrims, indeed, looked upon us little less unfavorably than a Capuchin going to Jerusalem would regard a Protestant.
>
> To avoid the company of Mahometans, we had hired an apartment (on board) which we thought the best. In a chamber opposite to ours lodged a rich black eunuch who was going to Mecca, and, useless as it could not but be to him, was accompanied by his seraglio, like a Turkish lord. In a large apartment under ours were forty women and slaves, with their children, whose crying and noise gave us no little disturbance. Every one of the other passengers had hired a place upon the deck, where he remained with his bales and parcels around him, having only a small space vacant in the middle. Our Greek sailors, who were very unskillful, were perplexed by these encumbrances, and could not go about to manage the vessel without trampling upon the goods of the merchants, which produced endless disputes.

Our vessel, though large enough to have carried at least forty guns, was very deeply laden. Besides her own freight, she towed after her three large shallops and one small; the three larger were filled with passengers, horses, sheep and even women of pleasure. . . .

To avoid any disagreeable encounters with the other passengers, we had taken care to go first on board. We had yet several days to wait till the governor (of Suez) should inspect the ships, to see whether or not they were overladen. This duty he never fails to perform, for a sum of money is payable to him from each vessel upon the occasion, which constitutes part of his revenue. At length, after all these delays, the four ships weighed anchor about midnight, on the 10th of October [1761]. (Niebuhr 1792: 212–215)

The first stop was Tur, on the coast of Sinai, where in a small neighboring village called Jebil, or Jubayl, lived all the pilots who made the Suez-Jidda run. They normally received 500 crowns for the voyage, in addition to something extra for training apprentice pilots in the art "which consists merely in distinguishing where the sand-banks and beds of coral lay." The convoy eventually made its way down the western coast of Sinai to Ras Muhammad, the point from which it was necessary to sail across open water to the Arabian shore.

The Europeans think this is the safest route as there is not, through the whole (passage), one rock on which a ship can be wrecked. But the Turks think themselves undone whenever they lose sight of land. So many misfortunes happen, indeed, from the ignorance of their seamen that they have reason for their fears.

In our passage we found ourselves in danger of a worse misfortune than shipwreck. The females who were lodged under us more than once suffered linen, which they were drying, to catch fire, in consequence of which the vessel must have burned if we had not been alarmed by their screams and hastened to their assistance. The second time when this happened our captain was enraged and sent down an inferior officer into the seraglio to beat the women for their carelessness. The infliction of punishment produced, at first, no small noise among them; but it was followed by four and twenty hours of sweet silence. Those women were indeed extremely troublesome and indiscreet. Hearing their voices so very near to us, I was tempted to look through a chink, and saw three or four of them naked and bathing. (Niebuhr 1792: 218–219)

When we came near the small isle of Qassani the Turks began to express their joy at having escaped the dangers of such a passage, and having so nearly reached the coast of Arabia. Cannons and muskets were fired; the ship and the boats were illumined with lamps and lanthorns, and all was exultation and jollity. The sailors went round with a box, asking a dole from the passengers; every one gave some trifle, and they then threw into the sea—not the money—but the box in which they collected it.

Continuing our course, we incurred considerable danger in doubling a cape surrounded with banks of coral because our pilot was drunk. He had frequently asked us for brandy on pretense that he could not see the hills, or the outline of the coast, unless his sight was cleared by the drinking of a little strong liquor. We had refused him for fear of giving offence to the other Mussulmans; but we soon saw that they were not so scrupulous, for the Captain sent to us every morning for a quarter of a bottle of brandy for his pilot. The Greek merchants might perhaps have made him drunk by adding to the dole which he received daily from us.

We arrived soon after at Yanbu, a walled town near the sea and having a safe harbor. Not having seen a single house since we left Tur, we felt no small pleasure at the sight of Yanbu. Such as meant to take Medina, on their way to Mecca, went on shore here. Three of our party also landed, and took their sabres in their hands, like the other passengers. An inhabitant of Yanbu, supposing them Turks, gave them the salutation of peace, salam alicum, and entered familiarly into conversation with them. But learning that they were Franks, he became vexed at having profaned his form of salutation by addressing it to Christians, and passionately railed at the insolent audacity of these infidels who dared to wear arms in Arabia. But the other Arabs not seconding his complaint, my fellow travelers came on board without meeting with any other unpleasant incident.

After pausing only a single day at Yanbu, the Danes' ship sailed on. It passed Cape Wardan and cast anchor near Rabigh, "a permanent habitation of a body of Arabs, who live there in tents." It was also at Cape Wardan that the pilgrims arriving by sea donned the *ihram*.

This is a piece of linen which is wrapped around the loins. The rest of the body is naked; and in this state they proceed through the rest of the pilgrimage, till they have visited the Ka'ba. The only other garment they are suffered to wear is a linen cloth upon their shoulders, which hangs down in the fashion of a scarf. But many, under the pretext of indisposition, retained their ordinary dress. (Niebuhr 1792: 221–223)

At length, on the 29th of October [1761], we arrived in the harbor of Jidda. The same reason which had induced us to enter the ship before the other passengers, disposed us to remain in it till they had all gone ashore. Every one was eager to get away with his goods as soon as possible, and to conceal them as much as they could from the officers of the customs. They were particularly at pains to conceal their ready money, which pays two and a half percent of duty. . . . All who had been this way in the former year, and were now returning from the city, complained bitterly of the harshness with which they were treated by the customhouse officers. We were therefore perplexed about our ready money, not that we were unwilling to pay the duties, but we were afraid of being plundered by the Arabs. As the Mahometans are unacquainted with use of letters of exchange, we had been obliged to carry with us Venetian sequins, the whole sum that we intended to expend on our journey. After various thoughts, we resolved to put our money in the bottom of our medicine chest, reserving only two hundred sequins, where we expected the officers of the customs to search. Our stratagem succeeded, and no person offered to move our medicines. (Niebuhr 1792: 224–225)

Navigating the Red Sea

Richard Burton, disguised as a Perso-Afghan Pathan, made the crossing from Suez to Yanbu in 1853 under sail in a traditional pilgrims' *sambuk*, of which he has left a very assured description:

Our pilgrim ship, the Silk al-Dhahab or the "Golden Wire," was a sambuk of about fifty tons, with narrow, wedge-like bows, a clean waterline, a sharp keel, and undecked, except upon the poop, which was high enough to act as a sail in a gale of wind. She carried two masts, raking imminently forwards, the main being considerably larger than the mizzen; the former was provided with a huge triangular lateen, very deep in the tack, but the second sail was unaccountably wanting. She had no means of reefing, no compass, no log, no sounding lines, no spare ropes, not even the suspicion of a chart.

The first look at the interior of our vessel showed a hopeless sight. Ali Murad, the greedy owner, had promised to take sixty passengers in the hold, but had stretched the number to ninety-seven. Piles of boxes and luggage in every shape and form filled the ship from stem to stern, and a torrent of hajjis were pouring over the sides like ants into the East Indian sugar-basin. The poop too, where we had taken our places, was covered with goods, and a number of pilgrims had established themselves there by might, not by right.

Burton's own appeal to might over right materialized in the person of Sa'ad, a redoubtable black who was a former slave and soldier and Burton's companion on the pilgrimage. His presence was felt immediately on the poop:

With our little party to back him he speedily cleared the poop of intruders and their stuff by the simple process of pushing or rather throwing them off into the pit below. We then settled down as comfortably as we could: three Syrians, a married Turk with his wife and family, the Ra'is or captain of the vessel, with a portion of his crew, and our seven selves, composing a total of eighteen human beings, upon a space certainly not exceeding ten feet by eight. The cabin—a miserable box about the size of the poop, and three feet high—was stuffed, like the hold of a slave ship, with fifteen wretches, children and women, and the other ninety-seven were disposed upon the luggage or squatted on the bulwarks. (Burton 1893: 1:188–190)

The French traveler Charles Didier made the same voyage in the same type ship a year later:

My vessel was one of those called a sambuk on the Red Sea. Sixty feet long and fifteen feet wide, it was not decked except at the stern, where there was a sort of poop-deck under which an enclosure had been arranged which was honored with the title of "cabin," and was just big enough to hold our two mattresses and nothing else. It was there that we slept; by day we lived in the open air, on the poop. The sambuk also proceeds under oars but has two quasi-lateen sails; one of them, to the fore, billows right out when the wind fills it, and forms a sort of hemispherical balloon before the prow. . . . The vessel was constructed of an extremely hard wood from India called saj. . . . Our sambuk enjoyed an excellent reputation; it was rightly reputed to be an excellent vessel and Shaykh Abd al-Afar, her owner, a rich Jidda merchant, had nothing but praise for her. I congratulated myself on finding her. Besides the Ra'is, it carried a crew of ten, plus a little black slave, agile and vivacious, who doubled as ship's boy and servant to everybody.

Didier had probably read his predecessors' accounts; he was, in any event, prepared for the worst:

This sea is one of the most difficult known to mankind: cut and crossed in all directions by submarine currents, bristling with reefs and banks of coral, it lies wide open to violent squalls which the proximity of coast and mountain make very frequent and very sudden; thus shipwrecks are common occurrences, despite the excessive caution and timidity shown by the mariners.

Leaving Tur at dawn, we were favored by a very fair wind all day long and soon rounded Ras Muhammad, the farthest cape of the Sinai Peninsula. In the evening the wind, though still fair for us, rose to a worrying degree of violence, and the sea was so rough that we were cruelly tossed in our cockle-shell. I have said that the Red Sea barques never sail at night, and we certainly maintained this custom in seeking a haven from the bad weather. By this time it was impossible. We had reached the Gulf of Aqaba, all of which had to be crossed before we could find shelter, or even an anchorage; we therefore had to go on sailing at night, despite the ever increasing fury of the waves and the roughness of the wind.

Without a compass—for I could scarcely honor with that name the clumsy wood-mounted needle that was little consulted in daytime and not even lit at night, directionless in the midst of darkness, we went sailing on at venture, carried wherever the hurricane willed. Despairing of mastering it, and not even trying to, the crew had stopped handling the ship. Plunged into inaction, even terror, they left the steering of her entirely to Allah and commended themselves, some silently but others in lamentation, to all the saints in the Muslim Paradise.

This mortal extremity lasted all night, a long winter night, and the breaking of day, far from putting an end to it, did no more than extend it, for the weather was even worse and the storm lasted till nightfall. Only then did we enjoy a brief respite; only then could I finally get away from my mattress and my prison. As the most trying things customarily offer compensations, the storm, which was chasing us along on course, at least had the advantage of making us run a good deal of our way in a very short space of time. At nightfall we dropped anchor a few yards off a small sandy desert island called Na'aman, located close in to the coast on which stands Dhiba, a large village in Arabia Petraea that is renowned for the excellence of its well. (Didier 1985: 45–48)

Didier was unmistakably a landlubber, and Burton too, though a most experienced traveler, had done most of his voyaging on land. A professional sailor, J. R. Wellsted, a British lieutenant of the Indian Navy, crossed the same waters in 1834, sent out by the East India Company as part of a survey of the entire Red Sea. He was aboard a British warship, the *Palinurus*, but it too almost came to grief in the Gulf of Aqaba, first on a hidden reef and then under the force of a destructive storm.

It was, during the four days we remained there [in a sheltering cove near the tip of Sinai]—the gale, especially at night, blowing with such violence that we could have carried no canvas to it—some consolation to reflect that we had been saved in a dark night from encountering, in an unknown and narrow sea, its full fury by the reef which, in the first instance, had so nearly proved our destruction.

Wellsted thought he knew the cause of the unusual ferocity of the wind and seas: the wind-tunnel effect of the Jordan rift:

Within the Gulf it is not difficult to trace the causes of the unusual violence of the wind nor the high and dangerous swell which it creates. On looking over a map of this portion of the globe, we perceive that one straight and continuous valley extends from the Dead Sea to the entrance of the Sea of Aqaba. The northerly wind, which prevails during the greater part of the year, naturally takes the direction of this valley. Finding no other outlet, however, than its southern termination, it acquires there an extraordinary force and strength; and although the body of water exposed to its influence is not greater than in some large rivers, yet, having none of their sinuosities, the course of its waves is uninterrupted to the entrance of the straits, and finding but a small outlet, the water returns by a violent effort in a powerful current. *(Wellsted 1838: 2:132–133)*

After the initial rough weather, Didier found the rest of the voyage much to his liking:

The following day made up for the gusty trials of the one before: the wind, still fair for us, had resumed more humane proportions, and the sea, still swelling in the morning, gradually calmed down. The crew had taken fresh courage and, having nothing to do, started singing. . . . That evening we made landfall at Wajh. . . . Informed of our arrival, the neighboring Bedouin, Arabs of the Billi tribe, brought us victuals of every description: eggs, mutton, milk, fish, even bread, so plentifully that it was easy for us to renew and refresh our provisioning for the voyage. The weather was splendid: the sea was entirely calmed and was lapping on the shore, whilst flocks of seagulls skimmed across the surface of the waves.

This little town serves as the port for a castle of the same name, located two or three leagues inland, on the great caravan route from Cairo to Mecca. Much farther north, five or six days' march away and fourteen days from Aqaba, on another caravan route—that from Damascus—there are, if I can credit local reports about them, really extraordinary ruins. The place is called Mada'in Salih, "Towns of the Prophet Salih." . . . What is this unknown town, buried in the heart of the desert? Who founded it? Who lived in it? Who destroyed it? Its existence is a problem and its fate a profound mystery: silence broods over its past as it does over its ruins.

The three days following, which were the 3rd, 4th and 5th of February, we did not come to land anywhere, and we stayed quite a long time away from the coast, sometimes even losing sight of it. By night we hove to out at sea. During those three days the weather was magnificent: the sky cloudless. . . . The coast of Africa had been invisible for a long time, but that of Arabia was in sight throughout the first day, edged with a line of reddish mountains whose long ridges and saw-toothed peaks kept my gaze entranced with the variety of their forms. *(Didier 1985: 48–50)*

Crossing from Africa

John Lewis Burckhardt came to Jidda from the African shore after ascending the Nile and exploring parts of Nubia. His point of embarkation was Suwakin, on the coast of what is today the Sudan and throughout the medieval period the chief port for those passing from Africa to the Hijaz, whether for commerce or pilgrimage. When Burckhardt reached it in 1814, having come overland from Shendi with a slavers' caravan, the town was not at the apogee of its prosperity.

10. The Northwestern Arch of the Kaᶜba and the Praying Places of the
Four Caliphs in the Mosque. The Pilgrims Praying in their
Afternoon Worship.

11. A Copy of a Letter in the Same Size as That Written on the Band of the Kaʿba.

12. A View of Zamzam with Pilgrims Drinking from It.

13. Pilgrims round the Ka'ba Kissing the Black Stone.

14. The Sanctuary at Mecca.

15. Prayers Around the Kaʿba.
(Note the shrouds, which have been washed in Zamzam water, laid out to dry in the sun.)

16. The Kaʿba.

17. Keeper of the Zamzam Well.

PORT SUWAKIN

*Suwakin is situated at the extremity of a narrow bay, about twelve miles
in depth and two in breadth. Toward the bottom of the bay are several
islands, upon one of which the town is built. . . . The harbor is on the east
side of the town, and is formed by a prominent part of the continent. The
arm of the sea on the west side affords no anchorage for ships of any
size. . . . The town upon the island is built in the same manner as Jidda:
the houses have one or two stories, are constructed of blocks of coral, and
have a neat appearance. . . . On the southeast side of the town, near the
harbor, some ancient walls indicate the former existence of fortifica-
tions. It is within the precincts of these walls that the Agha resides, and
the ships generally anchor under the windows of his house. Two or three
rusty iron guns lie dismounted upon the rubbish of the ruined walls,
which at present afford not the slightest protection to the town. The
Agha's house is a mean building, but it commands a fine view over the
bay towards the sea: near it are some warehouses and a wharf, at which
were lying the shattered hulls of several small ships, for nobody has here
the means or skill to repair vessels once damaged. The number of houses
in Suwakin is about six hundred, of which two-thirds are in ruins, for the
coral with which they are built soon decays unless constantly kept in
repair.*

*The Turkish government is represented in Suwakin by a custom house
officer, who lives on the island, and who bears the title of Agha. He commands the town but his power is greatly circumscribed. . . . The Agha has
no other means of maintaining what little authority he possesses than by
living on good terms with the (local) Amir, whom he either permits, or
aids, to extort sums from weak individuals in Qayf in order that he may
receive the Amir's assistance in the collection of customs on the island.
. . . The customs are levied upon all merchandise imported, principally
India goods and spices destined for the Sudan markets, and upon all the
imports from the Sudan which are shipped to Jidda for other countries,
consisting chiefly of slaves, horses and tobacco; two dollars are paid on
every slave and three on every horse.*

*The inhabitants of Suwakin have no other pursuit than that of com-
merce, either by sea or with the Sudan. They export the commodities
which they receive from the African continent to all the harbors of the
Hijaz and the Yemen down to Mokha, but chiefly to Jidda and Hudayda.
In Jidda they have a quarter of the town allotted exclusively to themselves,
where they live in huts made of rushes, like those of Qayf. . . . Besides the
articles of trade from Shendi and Sennar, namely, slaves, gold, tobacco,
incense and ostrich feathers . . . they furnish nearly the whole of the Hijaz
with water-skins, leathern sacks, and leather in hides; the water-skins are
bought up in the five principal towns of the Hijaz, as well as in the open*

country; the sacks are bought by the bedouin only, who use them to carry their provisions in. These articles form a very profitable branch of trade, for, as cattle in general are very scarce in the Hijaz from the want of pasturage, and as great numbers of water-skins are wanted for the pilgrims to Mecca, the skin sewed up is worth as much at Jidda as the sheep is worth in Suwakin. (Burckhardt 1819: 431–439)

A PASSAGE TO JIDDA

A small ship, one of those called Say in the Red Sea, had begun to load, and I informed the Agha of my intentions to take my passage on board of it. . . . The Agha ordered the master of the ship to give me a free passage and to put aboard some provisions for me, consisting of dates and sugar, the best articles of his own store room. We embarked on the evening of the 6th of July [1814]. When I saw the great number of people assembled on board, I repented having taken my passage in this ship; but I soon understood that from this time till the month of the Hajj (November) every vessel that sailed from Suwakin would be equally crowded with passengers. . . . One hundred and four persons, including the crew, were to be accommodated; of these fifty were Takruri men and women [West African pilgrims] and fifty were slaves belonging either to black or Suwakin merchants, who were on board. During the night about fifteen persons were sent on shore, to whom the Rais [the captain] returned their fare, which they had paid in advance, but there were still eighty-nine persons on the ship when we sailed the next morning.

We sailed after sunrise. It is the practice in all parts of the Red Sea to sail at this hour, and to anchor in a port in the afternoon; the mariners never depart from this custom till they are obliged to stand over to the opposite coast. The ignorance of the Arabians in navigation obliges them to this. Conscious of their want of skill, and of the insufficiency of their vessels, they avoid encountering an open sea or an adverse wind. The smaller ships have neither logs nor compasses on board, or, if they have, never make much use of them.

We had a fair westerly wind this morning. The blacks were all sick, no person had room sufficient to stretch out his limbs, and we were confined the whole day in the same position; the sailors were obliged to walk over the passengers to do their work, and the whole vessel was a scene of confusion and quarreling. . . . The passengers go on shore every evening, and often pass the night there. As we had no boat, and the vessel could not always be brought in close to shore, we were sometimes obliged to wade or swim to the beach.

The Takruris went and filled their water-skins at the well, and after their return the captain obliged them to go a second time to bring a sufficient quantity for the ship's company. These poor people were on all *occasions extremely ill-treated, although not one of them owed his passage to the captain's charity; the Suwakin people and sailors cursed and beat them repeatedly in the course of the day, and obliged them to do the ship's work, while they themselves sat at their ease smoking their pipes; the water and provisions of the poor pilgrims were constantly pilfered by the crew, and they were crowded into as narrow a space as three persons would be in the seat of a carriage intended to carry but two. The ship's company and merchants had every morning and evening fresh bread baked in a small oven on the prow, while the Negroes, who were never allowed to make use of the oven, fasted the whole day till they could cook their supper on shore. . . . For three or four months previous to the time of the Hajj Suwakin is full of Takruris, and they would be much more numerous were it not for the ill treatment they meet with from the people of Suwakin and the dangers of the passage across the Red Sea; the dread of which, more than the journey to the coast, discourages great numbers from coming. (Burckhardt 1819: 456–462)*

On 14 July the ship finally reached Jabal Mukawwar:

The passage across the sea is usually begun at this island, as from its being in a more northerly latitude than Jidda, and thus affording the full advantage of the northerly winds, as from the passage across being quite free from hidden shoals and reefs, which otherwise might render the navigation dangerous during the night. It requires generally two days and one night to perform the passage. (Burckhardt 1819: 469)

July 15th —A favorable wind sprung up this morning, and we steered for the open sea. A compass was brought from amongst the ship's lumber, but merely for form's sake, for the pilot and captain quarrelled which was the true north. Towards evening the wind increased, when the sailors exchanged the large sail for the smaller. When night set in, the brilliant light on the surface of the water, wherever it was agitated, greatly astonished the Negroes, who endeavored in vain to obtain an explanation of this phenomenon from the sailors. We passed a cold, uncomfortable night, no one having room enough to sleep in. The bold travelers of the desert betrayed great fear in the open sea, to the great amusement of the people from Suwakin.

July 16th. Early in the morning we decried the coast of Arabia; the ignorance of the pilot now became evident, for instead of finding ourselves off Jidda, as we might have been, had he steered by compass, we were at least fifty miles to the south of it. We entered a small bay in full sail. . . . We found the beach to be entirely barren, and without wells or springs to a considerable distance; no bedouin were any where visible. We were now in great distress for water. . . . The wind was foul, and we had no reasonable hope of reaching Jidda in less than two days. The Suwakin ships seldom arrive at Jidda with pilgrims without their having suffered from a want of water, the number of pilgrims on board being so great that it is impossible for them to carry a supply for more than three days without a sacrifice of other conveniences, which they are unwilling to make. . . . In the evening the great part of the Takruris left the ship to proceed by land to Jidda. . . . We were obliged to remain here at anchor till the following day.

July 17th. About noon we sailed with a southerly breeze, and at sunset the vessel was moored to a coral reef at some distance from the shore. There was an almost total eclipse of the sun this morning. . . . According to Muslim law, every Muslim repeated a prayer of two bowings, that is, the "Prayers of the Eclipse," which done, kettles, swords, shields and spoons were beaten against each other while the eclipse continued.

July 18th. It was calm this morning, and the sailors were employed at the oars; but they became so fatigued with rowing that we entered about mid-day a harbor. . . . There was not a drop of water in the vessel; a well was said to be in the mountains behind the shore, but no one on board knew exactly in what part; and though we were so near Jidda as to hear the report of some guns in the evening, yet there was the probability of our still remaining on board several days and thus suffering all the pangs of thirst. I desired therefore to be set ashore upon a raft. . . . A Greek passenger and two Suwakin men with their slaves followed. We walked the whole night along the barren beach, which was covered with a saline crust, till we fell in with the high road leading along shore towards Yemen; about an hour from Jidda we reached a bedouin encampment, where we refreshed ourselves and safely entered the town in good health. In the course of the morning of the 19th we smuggled into Jidda the slaves who had walked with us; those landed from ships pay a duty of a dollar a head. The vessel arrived the day following, July 20, 1814. (Burckhardt 1819: 472–474)

ALI BEY IN MECCA (1807)

Early in 1807 there landed in Jidda a princely pilgrim from the west with a great train of servants, scientific instruments, and such other apparatus of learning as recalled the liberal days of the Moors. He called himself Ali Bey al-Abbasi . . .

So we are introduced to one of the two chief reporters—the other is John Lewis Burckhardt—on the state of the Holy Cities of the Hijaz in the crucial years at the beginning of the nineteenth century. The introduction is by another expert on the Hijaz, David George Hogarth, the chief

British Orientalist in the years before the First World War and the author of *The Penetration of Arabia*. Hogarth continues on the subject of "Ali Bey":

He made the obligatory visit to Mecca in state, and tried, after taking ship to Yanbu, to go up to Medina also; but he was turned back by the Wahhabis. He returned to Egypt, and having journeyed thence by way of Syria and Turkey to Europe, reported himself in Paris in 1813. A year later a narrative of travels, translated from his Spanish manuscript, was published in Paris.

This man was in reality Domingo Badia y Leblich, who had set out from Cadiz in 1803. . . . Bankes publishing the narrative of . . . Finati in 1830 [see below] suggested that Ali Bey was a Jew, and claimed positive knowledge that he was a spy of Napoleon. Nor is it improbable that the emperor . . . did dispatch this man through Morocco and Tripoli to Mecca in order to gather information about the attitude in the eastern world to the new Arab movement, and to see if this could not be guided in any way to a furtherance of his own designs on Egypt, Syria and the East. (Hogarth 1904: 79–80)

Hogarth later had an opportunity to consult the Catalan edition of Ali Bey's travels, which provided more biographical details:

Ali Bey definitely substituted a political for a scientific purpose after being some time in Morocco; he was received by Napoleon on his return to Europe and entered the service of Joseph Buonaparte, whose fortunes he followed. He set out once again for Mecca via Damascus in 1818 but died on the road, two marches from Muzayrib, of dysentery (but a malicious suggestion was made subsequently that there had been foul play, prompted by British intrigue). As a cross was found under his vest, he was denied burial, and must be accounted a genuine Christian throughout. His effects and papers were stolen, but in part redeemed by the "English lady Ester Stenoff" (Hester Stanhope?). See Viatjes di Ali Bey etc., Barcelona 1888. (Hogarth 1904: 96n.)

While he was in Mecca, Ali Bey proved so genuine a Muslim and so thoroughly worthy of his illustrious pretension in speech and conduct that he was accorded not only unusual honor and privileges but full liberty to use scientific instruments and take notes. Thus he was the first European to describe the roads between Mecca and Medina and the Red Sea coast.[93]

Ali Bey Arrives at Mecca

The self-styled Ali Bey entered Mecca on 23 January 1807, barely two weeks before the Wahhabis, the warriors of the house of Saʿud in central

Arabia who had recently been converted to a form of Muslim fundamentalism and who were now arriving in the Holy City on pilgrimage.

At midnight between Thursday and Friday the 23rd of January 1807, or the 14th of the month of Dhu al-Qaʿda in the year 1221 of Hegira, I arrived, through the favor of divine mercy, at the first houses of the holy city of Mecca, fifteen months after my departure from Morocco. . . .

The moment I entered I performed a general ablution, after which I was conducted in procession toward the temple, with all my people, by a person appointed for that purpose, who, as he walked along recited different prayers in a loud voice, which we repeated together, word for word, in the same tone. I was supported by two people because of my extreme weakness.

In this manner we arrived at the temple, making a tour by the principal street to enter at the Bab al-Salam or Gate of Health, which they look upon as a happy auspice. After having taken off our sandals we entered in at this blessed gate, which is placed near the northern angle of the temple. We had already traversed the portal or gallery, and were upon the point of entering the great space where the house of God, al-Kaʿba, is situated, when our guide arrested our steps and, pointing with his finger towards it, said with emphasis, Shuf, shuf, al-bayt Allah al-Haram, "Look, look, the house of God, the prohibited." The crowd that surrounded me; the portico of columns half hid from view; the immense size of the temple, the Kaʿba, or house of God, covered with a black cloth from top to bottom; the silence of the night; and this man speaking in a solemn tone; all served to form an imposing picture, which will never be effaced from my memory. (Ali Bey 1816: 2:50–51)

The Arrival Ritual

On his entry into Mecca, Ali Bey set himself to the completion of the series of rituals prescribed for every newly arrived pilgrim.

The pilgrims go seven times around the Kaʿba, beginning at the black stone, or the eastern angle, and passing the principal front, in which is the door; from whence turning to the west and the south, outside the stones of Ishmael [the Hijr]. Being arrived at the southern angle, they stretch out the right arm; when, having touched the angular marble with the hand, taking great care that the lower part of their garment does not touch the uncovered base, they pass it over the face and beard, saying, "In the name of God, the greatest God, praises be to God"; and they continue to walk toward the northeast, saying, "Oh great God! Be with me! Give me the good things of this world, and those of the next." Being returned to the eastern angle, they raise their hands as at the beginning of the canonical prayer, and cry, "In the name of God, the greatest God." They afterwards say, with their hands down, "Praises be to God," and kiss the black stone. Thus terminates the first tour.

The second is like the first, except that the prayers are different from the angle of the black stone to that of the south; but they are the same from the latter to the former, and are repeated with the same forms during the seven rounds. The traditional law orders that the last rounds should be made in a quick step.

At the end of the seventh, and after having kissed the black stone, they recite in common a short prayer, standing near the door of the Kaʿba, from whence they go to a sort of cradle called Maqam Ibrahim, or the place of Abraham, situated between the Kaʿba and the Bab al-Salam, when they recite a common prayer. They then go to the well of Zamzam, and draw buckets of water, of which they drink as much as they can swallow. After this they leave the temple by the Bab al-Safa, or the gate of Safa, from whence they go to a small street facing what is called Jebel Safa, or the hill of Safa.

At the end of this street, which is terminated by a portico composed of three arches upon columns, ascended by steps, is the sacred place called Safa. When the pilgrims have arrived there, they turn their faces toward the gate of the temple and recite a short prayer standing.

The procession then directs its course through the principal street and passes a part of Jebel Marwa, or the hill of Marwa, the pilgrims reciting some prayers at the end of the street, which is terminated by a great wall. They then ascend some steps, and turning their faces toward the temple, the view of which is interrupted by the intervening houses, recite a short prayer standing, and continue to go from one hill to the other seven times, repeating prayers in a loud voice as they proceed, and short ones at the two sacred places, which constitute the seven journeys between the two hills.

These being completed, there are a number of barbers in waiting to shave the pilgrims' heads, which they do very quickly, at the same time saying prayers in a loud tone, which the former repeat after them word for word. This operation terminates the first ceremonies of the pilgrimage to Mecca. (Ali Bey 1816: 2:50–53)

THE WAHHABIS IN MECCA

Though he stumbled upon it all unknowing, Ali Bey was present at a historical moment in the history of Mecca, and indeed of all Arabia. He was in the city when the Wahhabis, the dreaded puritan "Brethren" from central Najd and Qasim who had taken and pillaged both Mecca and

Medina barely a year before, returned in force to perform the Hajj of 1807. Thus he is our earliest witness to these Islamic reformers who dominate the history of the Hijaz for the next few years and in whose hands the eventual fate of all Arabia would rest.

On the same day [3 February 1807] a part of the army of the Wahhabis entered Mecca to fulfill the duties of pilgrimage, and to take possession of this holy city. It was by chance I saw them enter.

I was in the principal street about nine o'clock, when I saw a crowd of men coming; but what men! You must imagine a crowd of individuals, thronged together, without any covering than a small piece of cloth around their waist, except some few who had a napkin placed upon the left shoulder, that passed under the right arm, being naked in every other respect, with their matchlocks upon their shoulders, and their khanjears or large knives hung to their girdles.

All the people fled at the sight of this torrent of men and left them the whole street to themselves. I determined to keep my post, not being in the least alarmed; and I mounted upon a heap of rubbish to observe them better.

I saw a column of them defile, which appeared composed of five or six thousand men, so pressed together in the whole width of the street that it would not have been possible to have moved a hand. The column was preceded by three or four horsemen, armed with a lance twelve feet long, and followed by fifteen or twenty men mounted upon horses, camels and dromedaries, with lances like the others; but they had neither flags, drums nor any other instrument or military trophy during their march. Some uttered cries of holy joy, others recited prayers in a confused and loud voice.

They marched in this manner to the upper part of the town, where they began to file off in parties, to enter the temple by the gate Bab al-Salam.

A great number of children belonging to the city, who generally serve as guides to strangers, came to meet them, and presented themselves successively to the different parties, to assist them as guides in the sacred ceremonies. I remarked that among these benevolent guides there was not one man. Already had the first parties begun their turns around the Ka'ba, and were pressing toward the black stone to kiss it, when the others, impatient no doubt at being kept waiting, advanced in a tumult, mixed among the first; and confusion being soon at its height, prevented them from hearing the voices of their young guides. Tumult succeeded to confusion. All wishing to kiss the stone precipitated themselves upon the spot, and many of them made their way with their sticks in their hands. In vain did their chiefs mount the base near the stone, with a view to enforce order: their cries and signs were useless; for the holy zeal of the house of God which devoured them would not permit them to listen to reason nor the voice of their chiefs.

The movement of the circle increased by mutual impulse. They resembled at last a swarm of bees, which flutter confusedly round their hive, circulating rapidly and without breaking order round the Ka'ba, and by their tumultuous pressure breaking all the lamps which surrounded it with their guns, which they carried upon their shoulders.

After the different ceremonies round the house of God, every party ought to have drunk and sprinkled themselves with the water of the miraculous well; but they rushed to it in such crowds, and with so much precipitation, that in a few moments the ropes, the buckets and pulleys were ruined. The chief, and those employed at the Zamzam abandoned their post; the Wahhabis alone remained masters of the well; and giving each other their hands, formed a chain to descend to the bottom, and obtained the water how they could.

The well required alms, the house of God offerings, the guides demanded their pay, but the greater part of the Wahhabis had not brought any money with them. They acquitted themselves of this obligation of conscience by giving twenty or thirty grains of a very coarse powder, small pieces of lead, or some grains of coffee.

These ceremonies being finished, they commenced shaving their heads; for they all had hair an inch long. This operation took place in the street; and they paid the barbers in the same coin that they had paid the guides, the officers of the temple, etc. . . .

Having returned home, I found that fresh bodies of Wahhabis were continually arriving to fulfill the duties of their pilgrimage. But what was the conduct of the Sultan Sharif during this period? Being unable to resist their forces, he hid himself, fearing an attack from them. The fortresses were provisioned and prepared for defense; the Arabian, Turkish, Maghribi and Negro soldiers were at their posts; I saw several guards and sentinels upon the forts' several gates were walled up; all was ready, in short, in case of aggression. But the moderation of the Wahhabis and the negotiations of the Sharif rendered these precautions useless. (Ali Bey 1816: 2:60–63)

The Pilgrimage Caravan of 1803

The Wahhabis were so called after their founder, Muhammad ibn Abd al-Wahhab (d. 1792). Though this movement of Islamic reform might have been successfully propagated through preaching, the conversion of the Sa'ud family of Najd added a fierce political energy to Abd al-Wahhab's teachings, an energy whose effect soon spread from the family's domains around Riyadh to nearby Jabal Shammar and even to al-Jawf. Because of their position in the center of Arabia, the Saudis could prey upon the caravans coming across the pilgrim routes to Mecca from Iraq and Iran.

In the late eighteenth century those caravans were the responsibility of the Ottoman Sultan, and although from 1790 onward his Mesopotamian vassals were exhorted to take action against the Wahhabis, nothing was accomplished. Even the Sharif of Mecca, never an advocate of any species of reform, came to terms with the movement and agreed in 1799 and 1800 to allow the Amir Saʿud personally to accompany the Persian caravan to Mecca. The Amir, it was said afterwards, devoted more energy to pillaging the caravan than to protecting it. Saʿud did not take kindly to the charge: in April 1800 he fell upon the Shiʿite tomb-shrine of Karbala in Iraq—the site of the martyrdom of Ali's son Husayn—and sacked and ruined it.

That was the beginning of all-out war, and fired-up Wahhabi troopers were soon on the routes toward Iraq, Syria, and the Hijaz. The Syrian Hajj caravan in particular was vulnerable to Wahhabi marauders at almost any point along its extended route, and the French consuls in Damascus begin to report, year after year, the misfortunes of the pilgrims.

In February 1803 the Wahhabis took Taʾif and blocked the march of the Syrian pilgrimage, led that year by Abdullah, Pasha of Damascus. The French consul Louis Alexandre Olivier de Corancez describes the events in his *Histoire des Wahhabis*:

Abdullah, however, the Pasha of Damascus and chief of the caravan, was already on the road to join the pilgrims. When he arrived at Muzayrib at two days' march from Damascus, he learned that the Wahhabis had just taken Taʾif and were marching against Mecca. He sent some Tatars to carry this news to Constantinople, while he himself continued on the way, uncertain of what treatment he might expect. But he found no obstacles. It was only four days from Mecca that a party of 400 Wahhabis presented themselves to him, and under the pretext of having him pay the dues which had hitherto been given to the bedouin, demanded a sum of money four times greater than was normal. Abdullah Pasha refused to pay. Obliged to defend himself, he defied the Wahhabis and killed 150 of their men. (Corancez 1810: 32)

In the end the pilgrims were permitted to enter Mecca, but on Wahhabi terms. They were limited to three days in the city, to prevent, it was said, their plotting with the Sharif of Mecca.

The caravan of 1803 experienced extremely harsh treatment at Mecca. Each pilgrim had to pay to the Wahhabis the sum of eight piasters, a shameful and previously unknown imposition. To increase the outrage,

Sa'ud made a new distinction between Arabs and Osmanlis [the Ottomans]. The latter paid a double tax, happy to have bought even at this price entry into Mecca, which the Wahhabis could have forbidden to them. But that prohibition would have deprived the Wahhabis of considerable revenue. It was to preserve this that Sa'ud permitted to the pilgrims the free fulfillment of all the ceremonies prescribed by their religion and that he made each one of them the pretext for a new tax. (*Corancez 1810: 71*)

Then, at the end of the pilgrimage of 1803, the Wahhabis made their first mass entry into Mecca. The holy places were "purified," the Sharif deposed, and the Sultan's name defiantly dropped from the Friday prayers, which constituted a formal denial of sovereignty. But for all his defiance, Sa'ud still felt threatened—incorrectly as it turned out—by a mass attack from Iraq, and so Mecca was abandoned before the end of the year.

The Pilgrimage to Arafat (17 February 1807)

We turn now to Ali Bey's account of the pilgrimage of 1807, the one he shared with the Wahhabi tribesmen.

The grand day of the pilgrimage to Mount Arafat being fixed for Tuesday the 17th of February [1807], I left the city the preceding afternoon. . . . At two o'clock I passed the barracks of the Negro and Maghrebi guards, which are situated at the northern extremity of the town. Afterwards, turning toward the east, I saw a large country house belonging to the Sharif, and soon obtained a view of the celebrated Jebel Nur, or Mountain of Light. It was upon this spot that the Angel Gabriel brought the first chapter of the Quran to the greatest of prophets. This mountain, which presents the appearance of a sugar-loaf, rises above the others that surround it. There was a chapel formerly upon its summit, which was an object that the pilgrims visited; but the Wahhabis, having destroyed it, have posted a guard to prevent them from ascending and saying their prayers, which Abd al-Wahhab has declared to be superstitious.

The town of Mina, called by some Mona, is composed of a single street which is so long that it took me twenty minutes to pass through it. There are several handsome houses in it, but the greater number are in ruins and without roofs. There are several dwellings of dry stone, about five feet high, which they let to pilgrims during the time of Easter.[94]

About four o'clock they pitched my camp upon the eastern side of Mina, in a little plain, where there is a mosque surrounded by a wall that resembled a fortification. The country lies in a valley, between mountains of granite rocks that are perfectly bare. The road, which is very level upon a sandy bottom, was covered with camels, with persons on foot and on horseback, and with a great number of litters of the same form as my own.

A detachment of Wahhabis, mounted on dromedaries, which I saw at the foot of the Jebel, arrived and encamped also before the door of the mosque. This was followed by several others, also mounted, so that in a short time the plain was covered. About sunset the Sultan of the Wahhabis, named Saʿud, arrived and his tents were pitched at the foot of the mountain, a short distance from mine.

A caravan from Tripoli in Barbary; another from the Yemen; a great number of Negro pilgrims from the Sudan and Abyssinia; several hundred Turks from Suez; a great many Maghribis, who came by sea; a caravan from Bassora; others from the East; Arabs from Upper and Lower Egypt; those of the country in which we were; and the Wahhabis: we were all now assembled and encamped together, or rather, one upon the other, in this little plain, where the pilgrims are obliged to encamp because tradition relates that the holy Prophet always encamped here when he went to Arafat.

The caravan from Damascus had not arrived; it had, however, set out with troops, artillery and a great number of women, to convey the rich carpet which is sent every year from Constantinople to the sepulcher of the Prophet at Medina, which present the Wahhabis look upon as a sin. This caravan was close to Medina when the Wahhabis went and met it and signified to the Pasha of Damascus, the Amir al-Hajj, that they could not receive the carpet which was destined for the sepulcher, and that if he wished to continue his journey to Mecca, he must previously send back his soldiers, his artillery and the women; so that by transforming themselves into true pilgrims, they would experience no impediment to the continuation of their journey. The Pasha, not willing to conform to these conditions, was desirous of retracing his steps. Some pretend to say that they [the Wahhabis] required a large sum of money from him, but others deny that fact.

On Tuesday the 17th of February 1807, the 9th of Dhu al-Hijja, in the year 1221 of the Hijra, at six o'clock in the morning, we all set out toward the southeast. At a short distance we passed a house of the Sharif; and at seven we arrived at Muzdalifa, a small chapel with a high minaret situated in a small valley; after leaving which, we defiled through a very narrow passage between the mountains and traversed a second valley to the southeast, which lay at the foot of Mount Arafat, where we arrived at nine. (Ali Bey 1816: 2:64–66)

The Ecumenical Experience of Arafat

Even in this much diminished Hajj season Ali Bey got some sense of an ecumenical Islam that the "standing" at Arafat seems to bring to so many pilgrims.

Mount Arafat is the principal object of the pilgrimage of the Mussulman; several doctors assert that, if the House of God [the Ka'ba in Mecca] ceased to exist, the pilgrimage to Arafat would be completely meritorious and would produce the same degree of satisfaction. This is my opinion likewise.

It is here (at Arafat) that the grand spectacle of the pilgrimage of the Mussulman must be seen—an innumerable crowd of men from all nations, and of all colors, coming from the extremities of the earth, through a thousand dangers, and encountering fatigues of every description, to adore together the same God, the God of nature. The native of Circassia presents his hand in a friendly manner to the Ethiopian, or the Negro of Guinea; the Indian and the Persian embrace the inhabitants of Barbary and Morocco; all looking upon each other as brothers, or individuals of the same family united by the bands of religion; and the great part speaking or understanding, more or less, the same language, the language of Arabia. No, there is not any religion that presents a spectacle more simple, affecting and majestic! (Ali Bey 1816: 2:66–67)

The Heart of the Hajj

Ali Bey now takes us step by step through the formal ritual of what was understood by all Muslims to be the heart of the pilgrimage, though here with some Wahhabi modifications.

Arafat is a small mountain of granite rock, the same as those that surround it: it is about 150 feet high, and is situated at the foot of a higher mountain to the east-southeast, in a plain about three-quarters of a league in diameter, surrounded by barren mountains. It is enclosed by a wall and surrounded by staircases, partly cut in the rock and partly composed of masonry. There is a chapel upon its summit, which the Wahhabis were then in the process of pulling to pieces. It was impossible for me to visit it because individuals who follow the same rite as myself, that is to say, the Maliki, are forbidden to ascend to the top, according to the instructions of the Imam, the founder of the rite. It was for that reason that we stopped, when we were half way up, to recite our prayer. At the foot of the mountain there is a platform erected for this purpose, called the Jama'a al-Rahman, or the Mosque of Mercy, upon which, according to tradition, the Prophet used to say his prayer.

Near the mountain are fourteen large basins, which the Sultan Sa'ud has put into repair. They furnish a great abundance of excellent water, very good to drink, and which serves also for the pilgrims to wash themselves with upon this solemn day.

The ritual commands that, after having repeated the afternoon prayer, which we did in our tents, we should repair to the foot of the mountain and await there the setting of the sun. The Wahhabis, who had encamped at great distances . . . began to approach . . . and in a short time I saw an army of 45,000 men pass before me, almost all of whom were mounted on camels and dromedaries, with a thousand camels carrying water, tents, fire-wood and dry grass for the camels of their chiefs. A body of two hundred men on horseback carried colors of different kinds fixed upon their lances. . . . It was impossible for me exactly to distinguish the Sultan (Sa'ud) and the second chief, for they were naked [that is, they were dressed in the ihram, the simple white clout and shoulder cloth of the pilgrim] as well as the rest. However, I believe that a venerable old man, with a long white beard, who was preceded by the royal standard, was Sa'ud. This standard was green, and had, as a mark of distinction, the profession of his faith, La illaha ill' Allah, "There is no other god but the God," embroidered upon it in large white characters.

The mountain and its environs were soon covered by Wahhabis. The caravans and detached pilgrims afterwards approached it. Notwithstanding the remonstrances of my people, I penetrated among the Wahhabis to their center, to be able to obtain a nearer view of the Sultan; but several of them with whom I conversed assured me that this was impossible, since the apprehension of a death similar to that which occurred to the unfortunate Abd al-Aziz, who was assassinated, had occasioned Sa'ud to multiply the number of his guard.

It is customary that an Imam of the Sharif should come every year and preach a sermon on the mountain. The one that came this day was sent back by Sa'ud before he commenced and one of his own Imams preached in his stead. The sermon being over, I observed the Wahhabis making signs of approbation; and they cried outrageously.

We waited upon the mountain for the period of the sun's setting. The instant it occurred, what a tremendous noise! Let us imagine an assemblage of eighty thousand men, two thousand women and a thousand little children, sixty or seventy thousand camels, asses and horses, which at the commencement of night began to move in a quick pace along a narrow valley, according to ritual, marching one after the other in a cloud of sand, and delayed by a forest of lances, guns, swords, etc.; in short, forcing their passage as best they could. Pressed and hurried on by those behind, we took only an hour and a half to return to Muzdalifa, notwithstanding it had taken us more than two hours to arrive in the morning. The motive of this precipitation ordered by the ritual is that the prayer of the setting sun ought not to be said at Arafat but at Muzdalifa, at the same time as the night prayer, which ought to be said at the last moment of twilight, that is, an hour and a half after sunset.

We set out the next day, Wednesday, the 18th of February, the 10th of the month of Dhu al-Hijja, and the first day of Easter, at five o'clock in the morning to go to encamp at Mina. We alighted immediately after our arrival and went precipitately to the house of the devil, which is facing the fountain. We had each seven small stones the size of gray peas, which we had picked up expressly the evening before at Muzdalifa to throw against the house of the devil. . . . As the devil has had the malice to build his house in a very narrow place, not above 34 feet broad, occupied also in part by rocks, which it was requisite to climb to make sure of our aim when the we threw the stones over the wall that surrounded it, and as the pilgrims all desired to perform this ceremony immediately upon their arrival, there was a most terrible confusion. However, I soon succeeded in accomplishing this holy duty, though with the aid of my people; but I came off with two wounds in my left leg. I returned afterwards to my tent to repose myself after these fatigues. The Wahhabis came and threw their little stones also, because the Prophet used to do so. We offered up the Paschal sacrifice this day.

Before saying the noon prayer [on the next day, Thursday, 19 February 1807], we went to throw seven small stones against a little stone pillar, about six feet high and two square, which is placed in the middle of the street at Mina and is said to have been built by the devil. We threw also seven stones at a pillar similar to the former, which is also reported to have been constructed by the same architect. It is placed about 40 paces distance from the other.

We set off on our return to Mecca on Friday, the 20th of February, the 12th of the month of Dhu al-Hijja, and the third day of Easter, after having repeated the ceremony of the seven stones.

Upon our entering the town we went to the temple, where we took seven turns around the House of God; and after having said the prayer and drunk the water of Zamzam, we went out at the Safa Gate to complete our pilgrimage by making the seven journeys between Safa and Marwa, as upon the night of our arrival; having completed which we felicitated each other on at last having finished the holy pilgrimage.

This solemn act was formerly accompanied by several other customs and forms of devotion added by different doctors or pious souls. But the Wahhabis have suppressed them, thinking them superstitions. There remained now but a few, which I observed in all their extent. (Ali Bey 1816: 2:67–73)

CHAPTER V

Through European Eyes: Holy City and Hajj in the Nineteenth Century

ON MAKING THE HAJJ UNDER PRETENSE

By the end of the Umayyad era, Mecca, if not Medina, was distinctly a holy place, a condition underlined not only by its enlargement and architectural adornment but also by the progressive limitation of access to the Two Harams. Jews and Christians were marked from the beginning as "Peoples of the Book" who enjoyed a privileged status under Islam. That privilege did not extend to dwelling in the Hijaz, however. According to tradition, it was the Caliph Umar (r. 644–654) who expelled them from what was coming to be regarded as a Muslim "Holy Land," citing as the basis for his action a Prophetic saying that "No two religions must remain in the land of the Arabs."[1]

The "land of the Arabs" was obviously a somewhat elastic term. The jurist Shafiʿi (d. 820) extended it in a somewhat broad fashion: "The Hijaz is Mecca and Medina, Yamama and their neighborhoods."[2] But there were exceptions, even early on. Non-Muslims were prohibited from the Meccan and Medina Harams, but they might remain in other localities, particularly along the coast, for three days for purposes of trade.[3] By the nineteenth century, foreign powers had established consular offices in Jidda,[4] a fact that required a certain adjustment of both rules and perceptions, as we are told by Hossein Kazemzadeh, a Persian pilgrim of 1910–1911:

> It is forbidden for Christians, and even their consuls, to go outside the walls of Jidda or to enter the Holy Cities under any pretext whatsoever. Even when it is a matter of installing or maintaining technical or industrial apparatus, or for public works (in those places), only Muslims are used. The few Christians who have visited them, like Gervais-Courtellemont, Burckhardt, Roches, Burton, Snouck-Hurgronje, etc., managed to enter only by disguising themselves as Muslims so as to escape the notice of the Turkish police and mingle with the thousands of pilgrims from various lands.

This rigorous prohibition is based in the first instance on religion [Islam] which absolutely forbids non-believers to enter the cities where the House of God and the tomb of the Prophet are located, and then there is the difficulty in protecting such (non-Muslims) from the bedouin and fanatics. There is another reason as well, of a political nature, namely, the desire to conceal from strangers what happens in those cities and to prevent them from exercising their influence there, which is, from a legal point of view, entirely legitimate.

Christians who do dare to enter these forbidden places run the risk of being assassinated, an act for which the Turkish government would bear no responsibility. But despite all that, it is relatively easy for the consuls to leave Jidda. They are constantly walking along the beaches and occasionally go fishing, accompanied by their kavasses and the guards which the local authority grants to them. Moreover, I have met at Mecca Young Turks who have told me that they regret this strict prohibition, adding that they will try to call the attention of the competent authorities to the possibility of mitigating its rigor. (Kazemzadeh 1912: 170–171)

John Lewis (or Johann Ludwig) Burckhardt (d. 1817), an Anglicized Swiss, was possibly the best reporter on the East in the course of the entire nineteenth century. When Burckhardt embarked upon his commissioned journey to the Near East in 1809, he and his sponsors had agreed that his only hope of penetrating deep into West Africa—his goal was to explore the sources of the Niger—was to assume the guise of a Muslim returning from pilgrimage. He put on his new identity in Malta on his way out to Syria in 1809, and although he was not at first entirely or everywhere convincing, Burckhardt had a long apprenticeship in both language and manners in Syria and Egypt before the persona of "Shaykh Ibrahim" was put to its closest test in the city of Ta'if.

John Lewis Burckhardt as a Muslim

Burckhardt was at Ta'if, east of Mecca, during Ramadan in 1814, attempting to get the permission of Muhammad Ali, then in residence there, to visit Mecca and Medina. He sent a go-between, a certain Bosari, to see the Pasha and make a preliminary test of the terrain:

In the evening Bosari went privately to the Pasha at his women's residence, where he only received visits from friends or very intimate acquaintances. In half an hour he returned and told me that the Pasha wished to see me rather late that evening in his public room. He added that he found seated with the Pasha the Qadi of Mecca, who was then in Ta'if for his health; and that the former, when he heard of my desire to visit the holy cities, observed jocosely, "It is not the beard alone which *proves a man to be a true Muslim," and turning to the Qadi, he said, "You are a better judge in such matters than I am." The Qadi then observed that, as none but a Muslim could be permitted to see the holy cities, a circumstance he could not possibly suppose me ignorant of, he did not believe that I would declare myself to be a Muslim unless I really was. (Burckhardt 1829: 70–71)*

Burckhardt's interview with Muhammad Ali, with the Qadi, or Islamic Chief Justice, also present, was somewhat inconclusive—the Pasha appears to have been chiefly interested in European politics. He was invited to return the next day; but before the second interview, he called upon the Qadi.

The Qadi Sadiq Effendi was a true eastern courtier, of very engaging manners and address, possessing all that suavity of expression for which the well bred natives of Stambul are so distinguished. After we had exchanged a few complimentary phrases, I mentioned my astonishment on finding that the Pasha had expressed any doubts of my being a true Muslim, after I had now been a proselyte to that faith for so many years. He replied that Muhammad Ali allowed that he (the Qadi) was the best judge in such matters, and added that he hoped we should become better acquainted with each other. He then began to question me about my Nubian travels. In the course of conversation literary subjects were introduced: he asked me what Arabic books I read and what commentaries on the Quran and on the law; and he probably found me better acquainted, with the titles at least, of such works than he had expected, for we did not enter deeply into the subject.

While we were thus conversing the call to evening prayers announced the termination of this day's fast. I supped with the Qadi and afterwards performed the evening prayers in his company, when I took care to chant as long a chapter of the Quran as my memory furnished at the moment. After which we both went to the Pasha, who again sat up part of the night in private conversation with me, chiefly on political affairs, without ever introducing the subject of my private business. (Burckhardt 1829: 72–74)

The business dragged on, and although he was eventually permitted to go on his way to Mecca, neither with nor yet quite without official sanction, Burckhardt thought he knew why the Pasha hesitated.

I was evidently considered in no other light than as a spy sent to this country by the English government, to ascertain its present state and report upon it in the East Indies. This, I presume, was the Pasha's own opinion: he knew me as an Englishman, a name I assumed during my travels (I hope without any discredit to that country), whenever it seemed necessary to appear as a European, because at that time none but the sub-

jects of England and France enjoyed in the East any real security: they were considered as too well protected, both by their governments at home and their ministers in Constantinople, to be trifled with by provincial governors. . . . Afraid as he then was of Great Britain, he probably thought it imprudent to treat me ill, though he did nothing whatever to forward my projects. (Burckhardt 1829: 74)

I am still ignorant of the Pasha's real opinion concerning my sincerity in professing the Muslim faith. He certainly treated me as a Muslim, and I flattered myself that the boldness of my conduct at Ta'if had convinced him that I was a true proselyte. As to the Qadi, who was a shrewd Constantinopolitan, most people supposed that the Porte had sent him to watch the proceedings of Muhammad Ali and give information accordingly to the Sultan; and it struck me that his behavior towards myself was connected with an intention of accusing the Pasha, on his return to Constantinople, of having protected a Christian in his visit to the holy places, a crime which would be considered unpardonable in a Pasha. Muhammad Ali, on his return to Cairo . . . took frequent opportunities, and indeed seemed anxious, to convince Mr. Salt and Mr. Lee, His Majesty's and the Levant Company's consuls, as well as several English travelers of note who passed through Cairo, that he knew perfectly well in the Hijaz that I was no Muslim, but that his friendship for the English nation made him overlook the circumstance and permit me to impose upon the Qadi. He entertained a notion, suggested to him by some of his Frank counselors at Cairo, that in some future account of my travels, I might perhaps boast of having imposed upon him, like Ali Bey al-Abbasi, whose work had just been received at Cairo, and who declares that he deceived not only the Pasha but all the ulama or learned men, of Cairo. To Muhammad Ali it was of more consequence not to be thought a fool than a bad Muslim. (Burckhardt 1829: 82)

If Burckhardt was uncertain of Muhammad Ali's real opinion of his sincerity in professing Islam, we are equally uncertain about that profession. He does not tell us whether in fact he was converted—there is no account of any formal ceremony—nor does he deny it. Other adventurers pretended Muslim birth, usually in some far distant Islamic land, and there is the occasional convert, sincere or otherwise. Burckhardt kept his own counsel.[5]

The Compleat Traveler Prepares for His Caravan Journey

Burckhardt took pains not only with his persona as "Shaykh Ibrahim"; as an experienced traveler, he knew that important details of kit and baggage likewise had to be attended to. At Esne in Egypt, Burckhardt prepared for his journey in a caravan across the Nubian desert, a voyage that would later carry him eastward to the Red Sea and eventually to Jidda and Mecca. He had both a camel for his baggage and a donkey for his own carriage. Once equipped, he moved south to Daraou, a town "ten hours to the north of Aswan on the Nile" and the jumping-off point for caravan traffic to Nubia.

> Arrived at Daraou, I had an opportunity of seeing the preparations of my fellow travelers, and of observing that mine was not regulated by that strict economy which served as a rule to the others. My baggage and provisions weighed about two hundred weight. The camel, however, was capable of carrying six hundred weight. The water for my use on the road was to be contained in two small skins slung across the saddle of the ass. My camel therefore could carry four hundred weight more, the freight of which, at five dollars per hundred weight, was worth twenty dollars. (Burckhardt 1819: 166)

It would provoke comment, Burckhardt thought, if he passed up this opportunity of turning a profit on his camel. Rather than subject himself to either the notice or the inconvenience of constantly loading and unloading the camel, he sold the beast and rented cargo space from the new owner.

> I appeared at Daraou in the garb of a poor trader, the only character in which I believe I could possibly have succeeded. It may not be superfluous to inform the reader in detail of the contents of my baggage and my provisions; at least it has always been with me a great desideratum in reading books of travels to collect such information for my own use.
> I was dressed in a brown loose woolen cloak, such as is worn by the peasants of Upper Egypt . . . with a coarse white linen shirt and trousers, a white woolen cap tied round with a common handkerchief as a turban, and with sandals on my feet. I carried in the pocket of my cloak a small journal book, a pencil, pocket-compass, pen-knife, tobacco purse, and a steel for striking a light. The provisions I took with me were as follows: forty pounds of flour, twenty of biscuit, fifteen of dates, ten of lentils, six of butter, five of salt, three of rice, two of coffee beans, four of tobacco, one of pepper, some onions, and eighty pounds of grain for my ass. Besides these I had a copper boiler, a copper plate, a coffee roaster, an earthen mortar to pound the coffee beans, two coffee cups, a knife and a spoon, a wooden bowl for drinking and for filling the water-skins, an axe, ten yards of rope, needle and thread, a large packing-needle, one spare shirt, a comb, a coarse carpet, a woolen cloth of Maghribi manufactory for a night covering, a small parcel of medicines, and three spare water-skins.

I also had a small pocket Quran, bought at Damascus, which I lost afterwards on the day of the pilgrimage, the 10th of November 1814, among the crowds at Arafat, a spare journal book and an inkstand, together with some loose sheets of paper, for writing amulets for Negroes. My watch had been broken in Upper Egypt, where I had no means of getting another. . . . The little merchandise I took with me consisted of twenty pounds of sugar, fifteen of soap, two of nutmeg, twelve razors, twelve steels, two red caps and several dozen of wooden beads, which are an excellent substitute for coin in the southern countries.

I had a gun, with three dozen cartridges and some small shot, a pistol and a large stick, strengthened with iron at either end and serving either as a weapon or to pound the coffee beans, and which, according to the custom of the country, was my constant companion. My purse, worn in a girdle under my cloak, contained fifty Spanish dollars . . . and I had besides sewed a couple of sequins in a small leather amulet tied around my elbow, thinking this to be the safest place of secreting them. (Burckhardt 1819: 167–168)

Later, at Berbera in Nubia, Burckhardt reflected more generally on the manner of travel in those parts:

The success of a traveler in this part of the world depends greatly, I may say wholly, upon his guides and fellow travelers, and their being well disposed toward him. If he is not thoroughly acquainted with the language of the country, it will be very difficult for him to select proper persons as his guides and companions, or to elude the snares laid for him by villainy or treachery; it is vain to suppose that fortune will throw in his way honest or friendly people, who are too scarce ever to be calculated upon in preparing for a journey through these countries. The traveler must consider himself as surrounded by some of the most worthless of the human race, among whom he must think himself fortunate if he can discover any less depraved than the rest, whom he can place some degree of confidence in, and make subservient to his views, which can only be done by identifying their interest with his own safety.

Above all, he must never be seen taking notes. I am fully convinced that if I had ever been detected by my companions with my journal in my hand, it would have given rise to the most injurious reports, and blasted all my hopes of success. While traveling through the desert, I took my notes with much more ease than during my stay at Berber. Being mounted on a good ass, I used to push ahead of the caravan and then alight under some tree or rock, where I remained, unobserved, apparently occupied only in smoking my pipe, until the caravan came up; but at Berber, and Shendi also, I was often at a great loss how to withdraw from the persons who surrounded me in the house where we lodged; and it was unsafe to walk so far from the village into the fields so as not to be observed. The having persons thus continually hanging about me was the most disagreeable circumstance attending my stay in these countries. I might have escaped it in some measure perhaps, by taking a lodging for myself, which I could have readily procured, but then I should have been entirely unprotected in the house of a stranger, who might have proved worse even than my companions; I should also have been unmercifully annoyed the whole day by visitors begging presents, and the little baggage I had would have been much less secure. (Burckhardt 1819: 241–242)

The "Lion of Algeria": Leon Roches

Leon Roches was born in Grenoble in 1809, studied the law there, and in June 1832 followed his father as an immigrant to the newly conquered territory of Algeria. Shortly afterwards he became smitten with a thirteen-year-old Muslim girl, whose parents thought it would be the better part of prudence to remove her from Roches's outstretched arms into an appropriate arranged marriage. Nothing came of the still-lingering liaison—the girl died later in the warfare that was still endemic in Algeria—but it whetted Roches's interest in things Arab and Islamic. He threw himself into the study of Arabic, which eventually drew him into the mystique surrounding the romantic figure of Abd al-Qadir, the would-be liberator of Muslim Algeria. Roches thought it possible to work a reconciliation between Abd al-Qadir and France, and he began to assume the identity of a Muslim as a means of entering the great man's circle.

The masquerade succeeded. "Umar ibn Rusha" passed as a Muslim convert and worked his way into both the circle and the heart of Abd al-Qadir. The two apparently became friends—Abd al-Qadir even arranged a marriage for his new young friend—and Roches began to understand the depth of Abd al-Qadir's sentiments against the infidel. In October 1839, however, when Abd al-Qadir decided to break his treaty with France and declare open warfare, Roches had to choose between his friend and his country. He blurted out to Abd al-Qadir that he was not a Muslim. The puzzled Abd al-Qadir at first did not understand, but when he finally realized what Roches was confessing, he quietly said, "I leave the punishment of your soul to God. As for your body, remove it from my presence. Be gone and be careful never to repeat in a Muslim's presence the blasphemy that I just heard because I could no longer be responsible for your life. Be gone."[6]

It was a crushing personal blow, but it did not cause Roches to despair entirely of a reconciliation between France and its new Muslim subjects. He thought he understood the problem, that it was a matter of religion:

I had come to the conclusion that most of the Arab tribes whose self-interest might have caused to rally to the French cause were prevented from doing so by reason of the fact that the Quran threatened with eternal damnation those Muslims who consented to live under Christian sovereignty. And it was those same verses of the Holy Book of Islam that Abd al-Qadir relied upon to induce the people of Algeria to a Holy War.

Yes, but an attentive reading of the Quran and certain of its commentaries can lead to a directly contrary thesis. Thus, when a Muslim people has resisted a Christian invasion to the extent and length their resources permit, and when they recognize the uselessness and dangers of this resistance, well known commentators have maintained the position that in such a case one should end the struggle and accept the sovereignty of the conquerors if those latter permit them the free exercise of their religious rituals.

France had, then, a large stake in procuring from a council, let us call it, of Islam's most eminent ulama, a ruling that would authorize the people of Algeria to live under French sovereignty. (Roches 1904: 229)

In the next years Leon Roches crossed the Islamic world, from Oran to Qayrawan to Cairo and on to Mecca and Taʾif in pursuit of this *fatwa*, or legal ruling, on behalf of France. He did in fact get his wish, first at an assembly in Qayrawan in August 1841, then an identical decree from an assembly at the al-Azhar in Cairo in November of that same year. For this latter, Roches once again donned his Muslim attire.

I could easily have passed in their eyes as an Algerian Arab, but had I chanced to encounter somebody who might recognize me, I would have stood convicted of fraud and my character and mission fatally compromised. (The French consul) M. Fresnel thus concealed my origins and said only that I was a convert to Islam and had been charged by the spiritual leaders of Algeria to obtain this fatwa that would help put an end to the war.

The *fatwa* was approved formally by the ulama—and privately by Muhammad Ali, Viceroy of Egypt, with whom Roches had had an earlier audience.

I was then virtually obliged to present myself at Mecca since the delegate of the Tajini Sufis (in Algeria) had declared publicly to the assembly that his master wished to give as great an authority as possible to the decrees of the ulama of Qayrawan and Cairo and that consequently he, the delegate, was going to Mecca to present the decrees to a supreme assembly of the ulama of the East and the West who were meeting in the Holy City on the occasion of the pilgrimage. (Roches 1904: 268)

I had at first thought to join, in the guise of a poor pilgrim, the great caravan that left from Cairo and made the journey (to Mecca) in sixty days. But my friends dissuaded me from this since I would arrive in Mecca only two days before the pilgrimage ceremonies began and there would be no time to present M. Fresnel's letter of introduction to the Sharif or to visit the ulama who had to approve the decree.

Once again I turned to my wise old friend Shaykh Tunsi. . . . He had the peculiar talent of being able to invent combinations that were simultaneously profitable to his interests and were of assistance to my mission. Thus, by a happy chance, he discovered that his brother-in-law the Mufti . . . was once again going on pilgrimage to the Holy Cities of Islam with his wife and his slaves. . . . My learned professor gave me to understand that this was an incomparable opportunity and he drew up an agreement whereby his brother-in-law undertook to include me in his little caravan and to board me and launder for me throughout the course of our journey to Mecca and during our stay in the city, down to the end of the ceremonies, in exchange for which I agreed to pay half the total expenses accruing from the transport, lodging, laundry and food for the Mufti, his wife, his four slaves and myself. This was expensive payment for the services my traveling companion could render me, but his title of Mufti and Hajji and his knowledge of the country and the obligatory pilgrimage ceremonies would greatly facilitate the fulfillment of my mission.

Since I was bound to arrive in Mecca some time before the pilgrimage ceremonies in order to present to the Sharif the letters or recommendation that had been given me by various Abyssinian princes, his brothers-in-law and M. Fresnel, and to get in touch with the ulama . . . I had to hasten my departure and find the means of accomplishing our trip as quickly as possible. To this end we could have gone to Suez or Qusayr and thence taken ship to Jidda. But in addition to the repugnance which my traveling companion had for embarking on the frightful boats that cross the Red Sea, he was also obliged to go to Medina, where he had acquaintances. And I too, perhaps even more than my Mufti, wanted to visit the city where the Prophet of Islam lay buried.

It was agreed then with Shaykh Tunsi and my companion on the road that, instead of waiting for the departure of the great Egyptian caravan on . . . the 14th of December . . . we would join the caravan of the Awlad Ali, an immense tribe occupying the coast between Derna and Alexandria, the ancient Cyreniaca, and whose transit from the fort of Ajrud (at the entrance to Sinai), where we would join them, to Yanbu, the point nearest to Medina, would take twenty-five or twenty-six days. The Mufti got in touch with the representative of the Awlad Ali in Cairo whom he charged with selecting a muqawwim for us. The muqawwim is a kind of pilgrimage agent who, in consideration of a sum agreed upon in advance, rents to the pilgrims the camels necessary for their transport, themselves and their baggage, and is obliged to provide food and water throughout the trip.

Finally, on November 6, 1841, Sayyid al-Hajji Hassan, his wife, his two Negroes, his two Negresses, Sayyid al-Milud ibn Salim al-Lughwati, the deputy from the Tajini brotherhood and his servant, and myself left Cairo with our dozen camels and our agent, a bedouin with the build of Hercules, armed to the teeth, mounted and escorted by four Nubians charged with leading our camels, whether at night or over difficult terrain. . . . The Mufti, despite his peaceful pursuits, made sure that we were armed, and even his two Negroes of whose courage and devotion he was assured. (Roches 1904: 269–274)

At Ajrud they joined the Awlad Ali, who numbered four hundred pilgrims and a thousand camels.

We left Ajrud on November 9th; the way seemed rather monotonous until the point when we entered the mountains to the west of Aqaba, at a distance of about 250 kilometers from Cairo and some kilometers north of the northernmost point of the gulf of the Red Sea called "The Sea of Aqaba." There I was struck by the terrifying appearance of the precipitous rocks in the midst of which we had to pass with the greatest of difficulty. It has the appearance of the abyss.

We generally traveled during the night and rested during the day. The gait of my camel was so fatiguing that I made part of the journey on foot, and since I was wearing a kind of slipper with very thin soles, my feet became bloodied during the rocky sections, which was quite often. . . . After passing through the wilderness of Sin and the terrible mountains of Aqaba I felt an inexpressible sense of well-being at our arrival, on the tenth day, at Maghayyir Shaʿib, a valley where palms and other fruit trees of all sorts form charming oases.

On December 2nd, in the morning, twenty-six days out of Cairo, we arrived at the station called Yanbu-the-Palms or Inland Yanbu, and we took our delightful ease in the shade of the magnificent date-palms. Our caravan then divided. Roughly a half continued on its way to Mecca; the other half went with us to Yanbu-on-the-Sea where pilgrims had need to do a little business and thence embark for the voyage to Jidda. (Roches 1904: 275–278)

Richard Burton on Disguise

Richard Francis Burton, who made the pilgrimage from Egypt in 1853, was a far more self-conscious voyager than Burckhardt and considerably less the idealist than Roches, and so his reflections on performing the Hajj under the pretense of being a Muslim are at the same time more personal,

more argumentative, and even somewhat more defensive than those of
the others. The preface to the third edition of his *Personal Narrative of a
Pilgrimage to al-Madinah and Mecca* notes the disapproval leveled at
Burckhardt and others for such a "violation of conscience," as one unhappy critic called the assumption of a Muslim identity. Burton of course
disagreed, for reasons we shall see shortly, and he was particularly upset by
the moral censures of an earlier traveler in Arabia, William Gifford Palgrave, which he cites:

> *Passing oneself off for a wandering Darweesh, as some European ex-
> plorers have attempted to do in the East, is for more reasons than one a
> very bad plan. It is unnecessary to dilate on that moral aspect of the pro-
> ceeding which will always first strike unsophisticated minds. To feign a
> religion which the adventurer himself does not believe, to perform with
> scrupulous exactitude, as of the highest and holiest import, practices
> which he inwardly ridicules, and which he intends on his return to hold
> up to the ridicule of others, to turn for weeks and months together the
> most sacred and awful bearings of man toward his Creator into a deliber-
> ate and truthless mummery, not to mention other and darker touches—
> all this seems hardly compatible with the character of a European gentle-
> man, let alone that of a Christian. (Palgrave 1865: 1:258–259)*

Odd sentiments indeed, Burton remarked, to be coming from the mouth
of "a certain Father Michael Cohen," former Jew, former Catholic, former Jesuit, former intelligence agent in the pay of Napoleon III. A little
like "Satan preaching against sin," he thought. Burton proceeded vigor-
ously to the defense of his own assumption of a Muslim identity, a defense in part moral and in part pragmatic, but inevitably highly personal:

> *Many may not follow my example; but some perchance will be curious
> to see what measures I have adopted, in order to appear suddenly as an
> Eastern upon the stage of Oriental life; and as the recital may be found
> useful by future adventurers, I make no apology for the egotistical sem-
> blance of the narrative. (Burton 1893: 1:4–5)*

> *The home reader naturally inquires, Why not travel under your En-
> glish name? For this reason. In the generality of barbarous countries you
> must either proceed, like Bruce, preserving the "dignity of manhood,"
> and carrying matters with a high hand, or you must worm your way by
> timidity and subservience; in fact, by becoming an animal too contempti-
> ble for man to let or injure. But to pass through the Moslem's Holy Land,
> you must either be a born believer, or have become one; in the former
> case you may demean yourself as you please, in the latter a path is ready
> prepared for you. My spirit could not bend to own myself a burma, a*

renegade—to be pointed at and shunned and catechised, an object of suspicion to the many and of contempt to all. Moreover, it would have obstructed the aim of my wanderings. The convert is always watched with Argus eyes, and men do not willingly give information to a "new Moslem," especially a Frank: they suspect his conversion to be feigned or forced, look upon him as a spy, and let him see as little of life as possible. Firmly as was my heart set upon traveling in Arabia, by Heaven! I would have given up that dear project rather than purchase a doubtful and partial success at such a price. Consequently I had no choice but appear a born believer, and part of my birthright in that respectable character was toil and trouble in obtaining a tazkira.[7] (Burton 1893: 1:22–23)

It remained for Burton to choose the precise identity he would assume:

After long deliberation about the choice of nations, I became a "Pathan." Born in India of Afghan parents who had settled in the country, educated at Rangoon, and sent out to wander, as mem of that race frequently are, from early youth, I was well-guarded against the danger of detection by a fellow-countryman. To support the character requires a knowledge of Persian, Hindustani and Arabic, all of which I knew sufficiently well to pass muster; any trifling inaccuracy was charged upon my long residence in Rangoon. This was an important step; the first question at the shop, on the camel, and in the mosque, is "What is thy name?" the second "Whence comest thou?" This is not generally impertinent, or intended to be annoying; if, however, you see any evil intention in the questioner, you may rather roughly ask him, "What may be thy maternal parent's name?"—equivalent of asking, Anglice, in what church his mother was married—and escaping your difficulties under the cover of the storm. But this was rarely necessary. I assumed the polite, pliant manners of an Indian physician, and the dress of a small Effendi (or gentleman), still, however, representing myself to be a Darwaysh, and frequenting the places where Darwayshes congregate. "What business," asked the Hajji,[8] "have those reverend men with politics or statistics, or any of the information which you are collecting? Call yourself a religious wanderer if you like, and let those who ask the object of your peregrinations know that you are under a vow to visit all the holy places in al-Islam. Thus you will persuade them that you are a man of rank under a cloud, and you will receive much more civility than perhaps you deserve," concluded my friend with a dry laugh. The remark proved his sagacity, and after ample experience I had not to repent having been guided by his advice. (Burton 1893: 1:44–46)

"To support the character requires a knowledge of Persian, Hindustani and Arabic, all of which I knew sufficiently well to pass muster," Burton remarked with uncharacteristic modesty. He was in fact an extraordinary linguist, indeed, an intimidating one.[9] Finally, just before leaving Mecca, his pilgrimage completed, Burton once again reflected on the danger inherent in what he had done.

> The amount of risk which a stranger must encounter at the pilgrimage rites is still considerable. . . . It is true that the Frank is no longer, as in Captain Head's day [circa 1829], insulted when he ventures out the Mecca Gate of Jidda; and that our Vice-Consuls and travelers are allowed, on condition that their glances do not pollute the shrine, to visit Ta'if and the regions lying eastward of the Holy City. And neither the Pasha nor the Sharif would, in these days, dare to enforce, in the case of an Englishman, the old law, a choice thrice offered between circumcision and death. But the first bedouin who caught sight of a Frank's hat would not deem himself a man if he did not drive a bullet through the wearer's head.
>
> At the pilgrimage season disguise is easy on account of the vast and varied multitudes which visit Mecca exposing the traveler only to "stand the buffet with knaves who smell of sweat." But woe to the unfortunate who happens to be recognized in public as an Infidel, unless at least he could throw himself upon the protection of the government. (Burton 1893: 2:239–240)

A note at this point makes it clear that Burton had given some thought to what he would do if detected: "The best way would be to rush into a house; and the owner would then, for his own interest as well as honor, defend a stranger till assistance could be procured. . . . Amidst, however, a crowd of pilgrims, whose fanaticism is worked up to the highest pitch, detection would probably ensure his dismissal at once *al numero de' piu*. Those who find danger the salt of pleasure may visit Mecca; but if asked whether the results justify the risk, I would reply in the negative."

Tips for Imposters

The prospect of "passing" in the Muslim society of the Holy Land did not seem quite so formidable to another Englishman, A.J.B. Wavell, who, as we shall see, was one of the first to perform the Hajj on the Hijaz Railway in 1908. Here he speaks of his stay in Damascus prior to setting out:

> It was not the twentieth day of Ramadan, and as we did not propose to start for Medina for about another month, it was worth while making ourselves comfortable. I felt that in view of what was before us the time was none too long for me to get at home with Eastern life to the extent necessary. It was essential that I should have at my fingers' ends certain phrases, quotations and greetings, with the appropriate answers to them;

that I should be able to go through the various Muslim ceremonies, in and out of the mosque, without making mistakes, and get so far accustomed to wearing and arranging my clothes, and doing other things in the conventional way, that I should not in any ordinary circumstances be conspicuous.

It is these multifarious customs and ceremonies that constitute the real obstacle to a European passing himself off as a Muslim born and bred— for they are common to Islam the world over, and a bad mistake would emphatically give him away. No matter how Eastern his appearance might be, how carefully he might be dressed, and how adept in the language, if after taking a bath someone said to him "Naiman" and he did not know the answer, he would stamp himself for an "Effrengi" [a "Frank," a European] as surely as if he walked down the "street called straight" in a sun helmet and a spine pad. A bad mistake when praying, visiting a tomb, or even in the responses during a service, might easily prove fatal. In fact, to pass successfully for any length of time, constant watchfulness as well as previous practice is essential. It is in these matters and not in the language or the disguise that the real difficulty is experienced.

There are nearly as many white men at Mecca as there are men black or brown in color. Syrian "Arabs" not infrequently have fair hair and blue eyes—as likewise have some of the natives of the holy cities themselves. I was once asked what color I stained myself for this journey. The question reveals the curious ignorance that lies at the bottom of the so-called race prejudices of which some people are so proud. You might as well black yourself all over to play Hamlet. (Wavell 1912: 40–41)

The same point that neither color nor dress was the problem was made, somewhat more amusingly, by John Keane, who was in Mecca in 1877– 1878 with what were apparently only the flimsiest of pretenses toward disguise:

After a week or ten days (in Mecca) I found I could walk about the crowded bazaars without attracting notice, my fair complexion exciting no curiosity among the chequered masses, nor my ignorance of Arabic giving me any inconvenience where so many nationalities were gathered, speaking more languages than I will stay to enumerate here, only mentioning that you may jostle against a Tartar, Malay, Negro and Turk round any Hindi tea-stall. Nor does the style of your get-up make any difference, except that it is advisable not to be too "swell" in order to avoid attracting beggars, but otherwise the Archbishop of Canterbury doing the circumambulation of the Ka'ba in his miter and robes would not occasion a passing remark, and would be placed nowhere by twenty much more wondrously attired figures. There was always something about that procession around the Ka'ba that made me think of it as Madame Tussaud's male waxworks out for a walk—the many varieties of costume, the stolid expressionless and the peculiar Tussaud complexion, were all there. (Keane 1881: 19–20)

Wavell continues:

If the object be simply to visit Mecca, or any other place, in secret, I should say that the simplest way of doing it would be to go disguised as a pauper—with five pounds in one's pocket, some dirty clothes, and nothing more. If, however, the expedition is to last any length of time, the objections to this are sufficiently obvious, and so far as many interesting sides of life in the country are concerned, the traveler would return very little wiser than when he started. Most people would prefer to amuse themselves in some other way. (Wavell 1912: 41–42)

And then, after his successful stay in Mecca, when he sounds for all the world like a travel agent:

I would advise anyone who wants to see Mecca to go at the pilgrimage season because it is easier to get there for one thing, and much more interesting for another. I do not think the measures I adopted as regards language, disguise, and so forth can be much improved upon. In any case, I strongly recommend the traveler to enter the country in disguise and not wait to assume it till after his arrival at the port. Neglect of this obvious precaution has led to several would-be pilgrims being found out at Jidda and ignominiously sent back. While in Mecca the traveler must be careful to avoid the society of pilgrims from the country to which he is supposed to belong, and he should not on any account allow his professional guide to come to his house; indeed, it is better if possible not to employ the same one twice. The less he has to do with them in any way the better—they are too sharp.

With due observance of these precautions, a passable knowledge of Arabic and Muslim ceremonial, and proper vigilance, the pilgrimage to Mecca may be made in disguise without running any risk worth mentioning. (Wavell 1912: 179)

Personality or sheer bravado? Or both? It is difficult to say. But in the twentieth century, when travel was quicker and easier, and Arabia was filling up with an army of foreign bureaucrats, journalists, mercenary soldiers, and hucksters, and even an occasional European convert to Islam, it was more of a question, as you approached the portals of Mecca, of having your papers in order.

The responsibility for issuing and verifying those papers most often fell upon the European consulars in Jidda, the main entry to Mecca, where representatives of Britain, France, the Netherlands, and Italy attempted to protect their thousands of Muslim subjects on Hajj from being robbed, kidnapped, press-ganged into the Hijazi army, or sold into slavery, but not, generally, to sort out who among their European visitors was a Muslim and who was not. The British consul Reader Bullard attempted to explain why in May 1924:

A young Englishman from British Malaya, Mr. J. H. Bamber, who had professed Islam for three years and bears the Muslim name of Abd al-Hamid came to Jidda with pilgrims from Penang, but was not allowed to go to Mecca. He might perhaps have got through, but he was foolish enough to have two passports with him, one the British passport on which he had left England after the war, the other the ordinary pilgrim passport giving his Muslim name. This was meat and drink for that spy maniac, King Husayn [Sharif of Mecca, 1908–1916; King of the Hijaz, 1916–1925]. Mr. Bamber was kept in Jidda while his papers were being sent to Mecca for examination, and was then, despite letters of recommendation from the Shaykh al-Islam of Kedah State and other persons of importance, told to leave as quickly as possible.

I refused to enter into Mr. Bamber's claim that as a Muslim he had a right to go to Mecca, and confined my assistance to watching that he suffered no ill-treatment and facilitating his departure. It is probably good Muslim law that any person who repeats the simple Muslim confession of faith is entitled to go to Mecca, but it is a religious question into which it would be unwise for this agency to enter, even if the circumstances had not given the Hijaz authorities ground for suspicion. Whether Caliph or not, King Husayn is the highest authority, spiritual and temporal, in Mecca, and the question of who may or may not go to Mecca may well be left to him and Muslim public opinion. There is in Jidda a Dutchman who has professed Islam for five or six years, but has not yet been allowed to go on pilgrimage. The excuse the king gives is that to give way would strengthen the accusation that he is subject to European influence. The case of Lord Headley [a British convert who was allowed to go to Mecca] he explains away by saying that Egypt had already received him as a Mahometan, though everyone else here believes that he was allowed to go to Mecca because the king had information that he was not only devastatingly stupid, but also completely under the control of the Imam of the Woking Mosque.

Whatever the grounds of the king's decision, it is in fact much more difficult for a European professing Islam to go to Mecca than it used to be. Snouck Hurgronje, the great Dutch Orientalist, not only went to Mecca without hindrance, but stayed there for some time and even taught in a mosque, and not many years before the war an Englishman called "Hajji Abdullah" Williams, who was subsequently well known in

Iraq, found no difficulty in getting to Mecca as a convert. It would be well that the authorities concerned should not issue a passport to Jidda to any Mahometan pilgrim of European birth unless the applicant has first obtained permission from the Hijaz Government to go to Mecca. Lord Headley estimates that there are in England at least 10,000 people who are genuine, though at present unavowed, Muslims; it would be exceedingly awkward if they all came on the pilgrimage and were treated in the same way as Mr. Bamber. (Foreign Office Papers E5217/424/91[10])

One such "Mahometan pilgrim of European birth" to whom a passport had been issued without prior consultation with the ruler of Mecca was the Frenchman Edouard Dinet. A painter in the "Orientalist" school, Dinet had converted to Islam during the First World War and then in 1929 made the Hajj in company with a native North African Muslim, one Sliman Ben Ibrahim Baâmer. Their joint account reveals some of the fear and anxiety that surrounded the venture even for a doubtlessly sincere convert and even in the twentieth century.

It was then (at Jidda) that a serious incident occurred which almost put a premature end to our journey. One of us, the Orientalist (painter) Dinet, though he had embraced Islam fifteen years previously under the name of Nasir al-Din, is of European origin, a fact mentioned on his passport, and for that reason the port police were refusing to allow him to disembark. But his collaborator Sliman ben Ibrahim, an Arab and Muslim by birth, pushed energetically from behind and so forced their way through the barriers of the police, whom he calmed down by his vehement protests. Thus, after we had been pushed and tugged in every direction we arrived at the office of one of the high functionaries of the port. We handed over to him the letters of recommendation of the illustrious Muslims who personally guaranteed our sincerity. The names of the signatories of those letters and of those to whom they were addressed produced a favorable impression and we were given permission to lodge with an official guide in the Muslim city; further, we were promised that our letters would be delivered as quickly as possible to their addressees.

The French vice-consul, M. Gault, whom we visited, was much relieved when he learned of the happy outcome of the affair, but he made no effort to conceal from us his own opinion that we had no chance of obtaining authorization to make the pilgrimage since King Ibn Saʿud doubted the sincerity of Europeans who converted to Islam and had forbidden them access to the Sacred Territories; indeed, he cited to us cases exactly analogous to our own. (Dinet & Sliman ben Ibrahim 1930: 16–17)

Dinet did after all receive permission to make the Hajj, but that by no means relieved his anxieties.

If, after we got into the venerated sanctuaries, one of us, the Orientalist Dinet, was recognized as a Rumi, that is to say, a European,[11] in the midst of a crowd unusually excited by religious fervor, he ran terrible risks since in the tumult it would be impossible for him to prove the sincerity of his Islamicization . . . , and the police, however well organized in the Hijaz, would arrive too late. M. Gault, the French vice-consul, did not conceal his profound uneasiness about this. He reminded us of earlier excesses committed by a fanatical population at Jidda: the assassination of the French and English consuls, and, more recently, the stoning of the French consulate. As for Dinet, he did not fear death in the Sacred Territory since for a sincere believer this is one of the most beautiful deaths possible. (Dinet & Sliman ben Ibrahim 1930: 20–21)

CHARLES DOUGHTY ON THE HAJJ

One Christian traveler who made no attempt whatsoever to conceal his identity, even in extremely dangerous and threatening circumstances, was the Englishman Charles Doughty. He traveled by a simple creed:

The traveler must be himself, in men's eyes, a man worthy to live under the bent of God's heaven, and were it without a religion: he is such who has a clean human heart and long-suffering under his bare shirt; it is enough, and though the way be full of harms, he may travel to the ends of the world. (Doughty 1888: 95)

The Hajj of 1876 Departs from Damascus

Doughty's adventure in Arabia began in 1876 in Damascus, when the city was filled with the commotion and excitement of the impending departure of the Hajj caravan.

There is every year a new stirring in this goodly Oriental city [of Damascus] in the days before the Hajj; so many strangers are passing in the bazaars, of outlandish speech and clothing from far provinces. The more part are of Asia Minor, many of them bearing over-great white turbans that might weigh more than their heads; the most are poor folk of solemn countenance, which wander in the streets seeking the bakers' stalls, and I saw that many of the Damascenes could answer them in their own language. The town is moved in the departure of the great Pilgrimage of the Religion and again at the home-coming, which is made a public spectacle; almost every Moslem household has some one of their kindred in the caravan. In the markets there is much taking up in haste of wares for the road. The tent makers are most busy in their street, over-

looking and renewing the old canvas of hundreds of tents, of tilts and the curtains for litters; the curriers in their bazaar are selling apace the water-skins and leathern buckets and saddle-bottles, matara or zamzamiyya; the carpenters' craft are laboring in all haste for the Hajj, the most of them mending litter-frames. In the Peraean outlying quarter, el-Maydan, is cheapening and delivery of grain, a provision by the way for the Hajj cattle. Already there come by the streets, passing daily forth, the akkams with the swaggering litters mounted high upon the tall pilgrim-camels. They are the Hajj caravan drivers, and upon the silent great shuffle-footed beasts, they hold insolently their path through the narrow bazaars; commonly ferocious young men, whose mouths are full of horrible cursings; and whoso is not of this stomach, him they think unmeet for the road. The mukowwems or Hajj camel-masters have called in their cattle (all are strong males) from the wilderness to the camel-yards of Damascus, where their serving-men are busy stuffing pillows under the pack-saddle frames and lapping, first over all the camels' chines, thick felt blankets of Aleppo, that they should not be galled; the gear is not lifted till their return after four months, if they may return alive, from so great a voyage. The mukowwems are sturdy, weathered men of the road, that can hold the mastery over their often mutinous crews; it is written in their hard faces that they are overcomers of evil by the evil, and are able to deal in the long desert way with the perfidy of the elvish Bedouins. It is the custom in these caravan countries that all who are to set forth, meet in some common place without the city. The assembling of the pilgrim multitude is always by the lake of Muzayrib in the high steppes beyond Jordan, two journeys from Damascus. Here the hajjis who have taken the field are encamped, and lie a week or ten days in the desert before their long voyage. The Hajj Pasha, his affairs despatched with the government in Damascus, arrives the third day before their departure, to discharge all first payments to the Beduw and to agree with the water-carriers (which are Bedouins) for the military service.

The open ways of Damascus upon that side, lately encumbered with the daily passage of hundreds of litters, and all that, to our eyes, strange and motley train, of the oriental pilgrimage, were again void and silent; the Hajj had departed from among us. (Doughty 1888: 41–42)

Getting Under Way

The new dawn appearing we removed not yet. The day risen the tents were dismantled, the camels led in ready to their companies, and halted beside their loads. We waited to hear the cannon shot which should open that year's pilgrimage. It was near ten o'clock when we heard the signal gun fired, and then, without any disorder, litters were suddenly heaved and braced upon the bearing animals, their charges laid upon the kneeling camels, and the thousands of riders, all born in the caravan countries, mounted in silence. As all is up the drivers are left standing on their feet, or sit to wait out the latest moments on their heels: they with other camp and tent servants must ride these three hundred leagues upon their bare soles, although they faint; and are to measure the ground again upward with their weary feet from the holy places. At the second gun, fired a few moments after, the Pasha's litter advances and after him goes the head of the caravan column: other fifteen or twenty minutes we, who have places in the rear, must halt, that is until the long train is unfolded before us; then we strike our camels and the great pilgrimage is moving. There go commonly three or four camels abreast and seldom five; the length of the slow-footed multitude of men and cattle is nearly two miles, and the width some hundreds of yards in the open plains. The hajjaj were this year by their account (which may be above the truth) 6,000 persons; of these more than half are serving men on foot; and 10,000 of all kinds of cattle, the most camels, then mules, hackneys, asses and a few dromedaries of Arabians returning in security of the great caravan to their own districts. (Doughty 1888: 45)

Doughty's majestic style masks the excitement of the moment in Damascus. Burton, for his part, arrived in the Hijaz by sea from Egypt, and so his first experience of the pilgrimage caravan, in this case too the Syrian one, came on his way from Medina to Mecca. Its mounting in Medina seemed anarchy itself:

Towards evening-time the Manakha [the open space just outside the wall of Medina] became a scene of exceeding confusion. The town of tents lay upon the ground. Camels were being laden and were roaring under the weight of litters and cots, boxes and baggage. Horses and mules galloped about. Men were rushing wildly in all directions on worldly errands, or hurrying to pay a farewell visit to the Prophet's tomb. Women and children sat screaming on the ground, or ran too and fro distracted, or called their vehicles to escape the danger of being crushed. Every now and then a random shot excited all into the belief that the departure gun had sounded. (Burton 1893: 2:54)

But once the caravan was fairly under way the impression was quite different:

There is a kind of discipline in these great caravans. A gun sounds the order to strike the tents, and a second bids you move off with all speed. There are short halts, of half an hour each, at dawn, noon, the afternoon, and sunset for devotional purposes, and these are regulated by a cannon. ... At such times the Syrian and Persian servants, who are admirably expert in their calling, pitch the large green tents, with gilt crescents, for the dignitaries and their harims. . . . A short discharge of three guns denotes the station, and when the caravan moves by night a single cannon sounds three or four halts at irregular intervals. (Burton 1893: 2:71)

The appearance of the caravan was most striking as it threaded its slow way over the smooth surface of the low plain. To judge by the eye, the host was composed of at fewest seven thousand souls, on foot, on horseback, or bestriding the splendid camels of Syria. In Burckhardt's day there were 5,000 souls and 15,000 camels. Captain Sadleir, who traveled during the (Wahhabi) war [1819], found the number reduced to 500. The extent of the caravan has been enormously exaggerated in Europe. I have heard of 15,000, and even of 20,000 men. I include in my 7,000 about 1,200 Persians.

There were eight gradations of pilgrims. The lowest hobbled with heavy staves. Then came the riders of asses, of camels and mules. Respectable men, especially Arabs, were mounted on dromedaries, and the soldiers had horses; a led animal was saddled for every grandee, ready whenever he might wish to leave his litter. Women, children and invalids of the poorer classes sat upon (an arrangement of) rugs and cloths spread over the two large boxes which form the camel's load. Many occupied Shibriyyas; a few, Shugdufs; and only the wealthy and noble rode in Takht-rawan.[12]

The morning beams fell brightly upon the glancing arms which surrounded the stripped Mahmal—on the line of march the Mahmal, stripped of its embroidered cover, is carried on camel-back, a mere framework—and upon the scarlet and guilt conveyances of the grandees. Not the least beauty of the spectacle was its wondrous variety of detail: no man was dressed like his neighbor, no camel was caparisoned, no horse was clothed in uniform, as it were. And nothing stranger than the contrasts: a band of half-naked Takruri [black Africans] marching with the Pasha's equipage, and long-capped and bearded Persians conversing with tarbush'd and shaven Turks. (Burton 1893: 1:64–66)

Doughty on the Syrian Darb al-Hajj

Doughty was a member of the caravan cortege as it snaked its slow way southward from Damascus:

The Darb al-Hajj is no made road, but here a multitude of cattle-paths beaten hollow by the camels' tread, in the marching thus once in the year, of so many generations of the motley pilgrimage over this waste. . . . Commonly a shot is heard near mid-day, the signal to halt; we have then a short resting-while, but the beasts are not unloaded and remain standing. Men alight and the more devout bow down their face to say the canonical prayers toward Mecca. Our halt is twenty minutes; some days it is less or even omitted, as the Pasha has deemed expedient, and in easy marches may be lengthened to forty minutes. "The Pasha (say the caravaners) is our Sooltan."

The Hajj alighting, there come riding in from the horizon, with beating of tambours, the Sayal troopers, our rear guard, and after them the squadron of Ageyl, which follow the Hajj caravan at two miles distance, and wheeling they go to alight all round our ranges of military tents. Also troopers march at the head of the caravan, with the Pasha and two field pieces borne upon mules' backs; other few, and sorry looking men they are, ride without keeping any order by the long flanks of the advancing column.[13] (Doughty 1888: 47–49)

That [cannon] shot is eloquent in the desert night, the great caravan rising at the instant, with sudden untimely hubbub of the pilgrim thousands; there is a short struggle of making ready, a calling and running with lanterns, confused roaring and rucking of camels, and the tents are taken up over our heads. In this haste aught left behind will be lost, all is but a short moment and the pilgrim army is remounted. The gun fired at four hours after midnight startled many wayworn bodies; and often there are some so weary, of those come on foot from very great distances, that they may not waken, and the caravan removing they are left behind in the darkness. Hot tea, ready in glasses, is served in the Persian lodgings, also the slave will put fire in their nargilies (water pipes) which they may "drink," holding them in their hands as they ride forward. Hajjis on horseback may linger yet a moment, and overtake the slow-footed train of camels. There are public coffee sellers which, a little advanced on the road, cry from their fires to the passengers. . . . They pour their boiling pennyworths to any that, on foot, can stand a moment and drink and comfort the heart, in the cold of the morning. Some others sell Damascus flat-bread and dried raisins by the way side: they are poor Syrians who have found this hard shift to win a little every year, following the caravan with small wares, upon an ass or a camel, for a certain distance, to the last Syrian station Maʿan, or even through the main deserts, where afterward they sell dates, to Medina and Mecca. (Doughty 1888: 57–58)

Burton found the night march particularly difficult and frustrating.

On Saturday, the 3rd September [1853], the hateful signal awoke us at one A.M. In Arab travel there is nothing more disagreeable than the night-march, and yet the people are inexorable about it. "Choose early darkness for your wayfarings," said the Prophet, "as the calamities of the earth (serpents and wild beasts) appear not at night." I scarcely find words to

express the weary horrors of the long dark march, during which the hapless traveler, fuming, if a European, with disappointment in his hopes of
"seeing the country," is compelled to sit on the back of a creeping camel.
The day-sleep too is a kind of lethargy, and it is all but impossible to
preserve an appetite during the hours of heat. (Burton 1893: 2:67–68)

The uncomplaining Doughty resumes:

From Damascus there are many pious women pilgrims to Mecca, but
now for the most part they take the sea to Jedda; the land voyage is too
hard for them, and costly for their families; and he is mocked in the raw
Hajj proverbs that will lead his querulous hareem on pilgrimage. Nevertheless the Hajj Pasha will have sometimes with him a pious housewife or
twain. Their aching is less which are borne lying along in covered litters,
although the long stooping camel's gait is never very uneasy. Also many
pairs of cradle litters are borne upon mule-back, which is good riding, and
even upon pack horses.

I might sometimes see heaving and rolling above the heads of men and
cattle in the midst of the journeying caravan, the naked frame and posts
of the sacred Mahmal camel which resembles a bedstead and is after the
fashion of the Bedouish woman's camel-litter. It is clothed on high days
with a glorious pall of green velvet, the prophet's color, and the four posts
are crowned with glancing knops of silver. . . . In this standard litter of
the Hajj is laid eth-thob, the gift of the Sultan of Islam, that new silken
cloth, which is for the covering of the Ka'ba at Mecca, whereof "Abraham
was the founder." I saw this frame in the stations, set down before the
Pasha's pavilion; I saw also carried in our caravan a pair of long coffers in
which were the mast-great tapers for the shrine of Muhammad. And looking upon the holy Hajjaj it is a motley army, spotted guile is in their
hearts more than religion; of the fellowship of saints on the earth are only
few in their company. A wonder it was to me to see how the serving men,
many of them of citizen callings, in which at home they sit still, can foot
it forty days long to Mecca and Mina. . . . Water is scant and commonly
of the worst; and these Syrians dwelling in a limestone country are used to
be great drinkers of the purest water. Marching all day they hardly taste
food but in the night stations, where they boil themselves a great mess of
wheaten stuff; they seldom buy flesh meat with money out of their slender purses. But after the proverb, men know not all their sufferance but in
the endeavor, also we may endure the better in company. There are very
few who faint; the Semitic nature, weak and quick metal, is also of a
wonderful temper and long suffering in God. And every soul would hal-
low himself (even though he be by man's law a criminal) in seeking
"God's house": in returning again the sweet meditation upholds a man of
seeing his home, his family, his friends. (Doughty 1888: 99–101)

Bedouin Thievery

As we have seen, one of the chief threats to the pilgrim en route to the Holy City, even to those within the protection of a large caravan, was predation by the bedouin tribes through whose midst they had to travel. If the local nomads were deterred from falling upon the caravan by the superior strength or firepower of the accompanying troops, they sometimes simply attached themselves to the slowly traveling column and served themselves as opportunity presented itself. Joseph Pitts described the ordeal in 1685 or 1686, and, on Doughty's testimony, things had not greatly improved by the late nineteenth century.

El-Awf (a great clan of Harb) are bitterly accused of outrages made upon the pilgrims marching betwixt the Haramayn, though their sheykhs receive a yearly surra from the government caravans of Syria and Egypt. The Bedouin inhabitants of that flaming wilderness are more miserable than beggars. Of the Awfi sub-tribe Lahabba it is said, that such is their cursed calling by inheritance! —to rob the Hajj caravans. They have no camels, for in that fearful country they could not maintain them: their booths are in the mountains, where they possess only a few goats. Every year they descend at the Hajj season; and they hope, of that they may lay their hands on in those few days, to feed themselves and their inhuman households till the time be come about again. Lahabbies taken in the manner excuse themselves, saying, "they fear Ullah! that the trade is come down to them from their fathers: and how else might they live in this dira, wherein the Lord has cast them? —and they and their wives and little ones! They do but take somewhat from the pilgrims for their necessity, and wellah, it is an alms."

These robbers have been many times denounced, by the Turkish officers, to the Bab el-Aly (the high ingate—after the Oriental speech—to the Sultan's government, which we call the Porte, and ridiculously the Sublime Porte); but the answer is always one— "That although the detriment be such as they have set forth, yet are those offenders neighbors of the Rasul, and the sword ought not to be drawn between Moslemin, within hearing of the Neby." (Doughty 1888: 174)

ON FIRST ARRIVING IN MECCA

At length the unaccustomed and anxious European traveler, after he had put on the *ihram* at the outer boundaries of the sacred territory, entered Mecca straightway and, once within the city, headed directly for the Haram, or "Great Mosque" as it was more often called.

Impressions of the Haram

Many of the early European accounts of the Haram are simple and dispassionately detailed. But two non-Muslim travelers at least allowed their emotions to break through into the accounts of their first glimpse of that holy place. Burton was an emotional traveler to begin with, though the emotions were not always positive, as will be seen in his reaction to the Prophet's mosque in Medina. The Haram at Mecca, however, provoked something different.

There at last it lay, the bourn of my long and weary pilgrimage, realizing the plans and hopes of many a year. The mirage medium of Fancy invested the huge catafalque (of the Ka'ba) and its gloomy pall with peculiar charms. There were no giant fragments of hoar antiquity as in Egypt, no remains of graceful and harmonious beauty as in Greece and Italy, no barbarous gorgeousness as in the buildings of India; yet the view was strange, unique—and how few have looked upon that celebrated shrine! I may truly say that, of all the worshipers who clung weeping to the curtain, or who pressed their beating hearts to the stone, none felt for the moment a deeper emotion than did the Hajji from the far north. It was as if the poetical legends of the Arab spoke truth, and that the waving wings of angels, not the sweet breeze of morning, were agitating and swelling the black covering of the shrine. But, to confess humbling truth, theirs was the high feeling of religious enthusiasm, mine was the ecstasy of gratified pride. (Burton 1893: 2:160–161)

Burton returned to the Haram later that same evening:

The moon, now approaching the full, tipped the brow of Abu Qubays and lit up the spectacle with a more solemn light. In the midst stood the huge bier-like erection, "black as the wings which some spirit of ill o'er a sepulcher flings," except where the moonbeams streaked it like jets of silver upon the darkest marble. It formed the point of rest for the eye; the little pagoda-like buildings and domes around it, with all their gilding and fretwork, vanished. One object, unique in appearance, stood in view—the temple of the one Allah, the God of Abraham, of Ishmael, and of their posterity. Sublime it was, and expressing by all the eloquence of fancy the One Idea which vitalized Islam and the strength and steadfastness of its votaries. (Burton 1893: 2:172–173)

A.J.B. Wavell seemed determined, like the "Javanese and Chinamen" he observed at Medina in 1908, "to be astonished at nothing," but at Mecca he lost some of his European detachment and disdain, as he himself confesses.

Having installed ourselves thus comfortably (in lodgings at Mecca), and done justice to a very good lunch served on a table in European style, with plates, knives and forks, we determined to go to the Haram at once to perform the "tawaf," after which we should be able to exchange the Ihram for our regular clothes. . . . Abd Wahid and I went together, duly performing our ablutions before starting. Twenty minutes' walk brought us to the Haram, and passing through we found ourselves at last in the great square that encloses the little group of buildings we had come to see. Before our eyes was the Ka'ba, its black covering almost startling in its contrast with the dazzling white of the sunlit pavement. From it our awe-struck gaze traveled in turn to the plain masonry dome that covers Zamzam's holy well, to the strange objects that mark the "maqams" of Muhammad, Abraham and Ishmael, and the curious stone hut of the Shafi'i sect; and then passed onwards to lose itself in the twilight of the surrounding colonnade.

The outstanding impression left by the whole scene is that of the unu-sual. It is not beautiful, it could not fairly be called majestic, but it awes one by its strangeness.

Wavell then retreated somewhat more remotely behind the impersonal pronoun:

One feels instinctively that one is looking at something unique: that there can be nothing else in the world the least like it. Whether the genius loci resides in the edifices themselves or in their arrangement, or whether it is auto-suggested by the tremendous belief concerning the small square building in the middle, I cannot decide, but it is there. Be the explanation what it may, the effect is almost uncanny. (Wavell 1912: 130–131)

Arrival Ceremonies

Immediately after his entry into Mecca on 23 December 1841, Leon Roches and his companions performed the usual arrival ceremony: seven turns around the Ka'ba, counter-clockwise, the first three at a quasi-trot, "to commemorate the flight of Muhammad from Mecca to Medina."

At each circuit you touch with your hand and kiss the Black Stone; we pressed our breasts against the wall of the Ka'ba in the space between the door and the Black Stone; and there, with our arms raised toward heaven, in a loud voice we asked for forgiveness for our sins. Then we made prayers and bowings beside the Station of Abraham. Finally we went into the room where the Zamzam well is located and there made additional prayers and had several drinks of the water. Thus ended the ceremonies required inside the mosque. (Roches 1904: 301)

There followed the sevenfold "coursing" between Safa and Marwa, after which the pilgrims had part of their heads shaven. It was then possible to remove their pilgrims' dress, retire and relax until the morrow. But one of Roches's companions suggested they proceed directly to the Umra instead of waiting for the next day. It was agreed:

> We went out to the "Umra," an oratory about 6 km. from Mecca on the Medina road. It was there, according to tradition, that Muhammad preferred to pray. We went as far as this oratory reciting certain prayers, remained there in prayer while we rested and then returned to Marwa chanting verses of the Quran. The barbers finished shaving our heads, and we had to go seven more times between Marwa and Safa and seven more times around the Ka'ba, until finally we reentered our caravanserai exhausted with fatigue. We had certainly covered more than forty kilometers during that day, and we had eaten nothing but a few dates and biscuits and drunk a few cups of tea. (Roches 1904: 302)

It is interesting to compare this rather dry account with the reactions of someone who was performing an actual pilgrimage, in this instance one Ashchi Dede Ibrahim Khalil, a seventy-year-old Ottoman bureaucrat who made the Hajj in 1898:

> On Wednesday, the 6th of Dhu al-Hijja God granted us an easy entry into Mecca the Venerated. After going straight to the Shaykh Mahmud quarter and setting up our tents there, we all came to the house of our guide, Shaykh Abbas Effendi. Following the meal after the evening prayer, we performed the night prayer there; then . . . with the guide in front of us and repeating the required prayers, we went straight to the Gate of Peace and through it into the Haram to the House of God. But how we went! I went like one who had been raised from the dead and was going to the place of judgment. The sacred enclosure was more awe-inspiring and dreadful and crowded than the place of judgment. With great difficulty, we went first to the Black Stone. Forced to push and shove people in order to touch the Black Stone, I thrust my head into the sacred opening as if with my last desperate effort. Rubbing my face and eyes and beard on it, and weeping the while, I made my face clean and bright as I rubbed it on the Black Stone. Pulling from behind, they tugged my head from the opening like [that of] a lifeless corpse. I stood there a moment and my wits returned to me.

Ashchi Dede was temporarily separated from his group but was discovered and rescued from the crush by the son of their guide, who then took the pilgrim by the hand and led him through the rest of the arrival ritual.

Thus with this *Hijazi* beloved holding my hand and me holding tightly to his, I circumambulated Mecca the Venerated [that is, doubtless, the Ka'ba] seven times, repeating the required prayers; then, leaving the mosque, we came and went between al-Safa and al-Marwa seven times. But how I came and went! I was not in control of myself, but Shaykh Abbas' son took me about. . . . Everything was twofold because we entered the consecrated state intending to perform the "combined pilgrimage" [both the Hajj and the Umra]. I had circumambulated the Noble House fourteen times and done the "running" (sa'y) fourteen. . . . While I remained oblivious of it through the joy of that night, the resulting pains in my knees and ankles gave me anguish for the next day or two. (Findley 1989: 494–495)

THE HARAM AND ITS DENIZENS

In the center of the town there stood in 1814, as it had for as far back as memory served, the sacred precinct of the Haram, and in its midst, the Ka'ba.

Where the valley is wider than in other interior parts of the town, stands the mosque, called Beitullah, or al-Haram, a building remarkable only on account of the Ka'ba, which it encloses; for there are several mosques in other places in the East nearly equal to this in size and much superior to it in beauty.

The Ka'ba stands in an oblong square, two hundred and fifty paces long and two hundred broad, none of the sides of which run quite in a straight line, though at first sight the whole appears to be of a regular shape. This open square is enclosed on the eastern side by a colonnade: the pillars stand in a quadruple row: they are three deep on the other sides, and united by pointed arches, every four of which support a small dome, plastered and whitened on the outside. . . . Among the four hundred and fifty or five hundred columns which form the enclosure, I found not any two capitals or bases exactly alike: the capitals are of coarse Saracenic workmanship; some of them, which had served for former buildings, by the ignorance of the workmen have been placed upside down upon the shafts. I observed about half a dozen marble bases of good Grecian workmanship. A few of the marble columns bear Arabic or Kufic inscriptions, in which I read the dates 863 and 762 (A.H.) [1459, 1362 C.E.]. . . . Those shafts formed of the Mecca stone, cut principally from the side of the mountain near the Shubayka quarter, are mostly in three pieces, but the marble shafts are of one piece. Some of the columns are strengthened with broad iron rings or bands, as in many other Saracen buildings *in the East; they were first employed by Ibn Zahir Barquq, king of Egypt, in rebuilding the mosque, which had been destroyed by fire in* A.H. *802 [1399–1400* C.E.*].*

This temple has been so often ruined and repaired that no traces of remote antiquity are to be found about it. On the inside of the great wall which encloses the colonnades a single Arabic inscription is seen, in large characters, but containing merely the names of Muhammad and his immediate successors: Abu Bakr, Umar, Uthman and Ali. The name of Allah, in large characters, occurs in several places. On the outside, over the gates, are long inscriptions, in the Thaluth character, commemorating the names of those by whom the gates were built, long and minute details of which are given by the historians of Mecca. The inscription on the south side, over Bab Ibrahim, is most conspicuous: all that side was rebuilt by the Egyptian Sultan al-Ghuri in A.H. *906 [1500–1501* C.E.*]. Over the Bab Ali and the Bab Abbas is a long inscription, also in the Thaluth character, placed there by Murad ibn Sulayman in* A.H. *984 [1576* C.E.*] after he had repaired the whole building. Qutb al-Din has given this inscription at length; it occupies several pages in his history and is a monument of the Sultan's vanity. This side of the mosque having escaped destruction [by a disastrous flood] in 1626, the inscription remains uninjured. (Burckhardt 1829: 134–136)*

The Servants of the Shrine

This large and complex edifice with the Ka'ba in its midst had to be cared for and the annual flood of pilgrims eased on their rounds of the sacred places located there. The Haram was the largest employer in the Meccan economy, and in all eras of Mecca's history permanent employees were attached to the Haram and its buildings. Only in the early nineteenth century do we first get some real sense of the size and composition of that body of "servants of the shrine."[14] We begin with Ali Bey's account, written at almost the same time Burckhardt was there.

The following are the persons attached to the temple: The principal chief, called the Shaykh al-Haram; the chief of the well of Zamzam, called Shaykh Zamzam; forty eunuches, who are negroes and are the guardians and servants of the House of God: they wear, as a sign of distinction, a large caftan or shirt of white cloth bound with a belt above their ordinary clothes and a large white turban on their heads: they also generally carry a reed or wand in their hand; a great number of attendants and water-carriers, whose business it also is to take care of the mats that are spread in the evening upon the ground in the court and the galleries of the temple. There are also an infinite number of other persons employed, such as lamp-lighters, lamp-trimmers, the servants of the Maqam Ibrahim, of the little ditch of the Ka'ba, of the several places of prayer of the four rites, of the minarets, of Safa and of Marwa; as also a number of porters who take care of the sandals (left at) the different doors. All these are charged to take care of the places to which they are attached, and to keep them clean. There are besides the public criers or muezzins of the minarets; Imams and private muezzins of the four rites; the Qadi and his people; the choristers; the munkis, or observer of the sun, to announce the hours of prayer; the administrator and servants of the black cloth, the Tob al-Ka'ba; the keeper of the keys of the Ka'ba; the mufti, guides, etc. etc., so that one half the inhabitants of Mecca may be considered as employed about the temple and have no other support than their wages,[15] which arise from charity, or the casual gifts of pilgrims. It is upon this account that when a pilgrim arrives all the inhabitants fix their eyes upon him, strive to render him services and honors against his inclination, and take the greatest interest in his welfare by trying to open the doors of heaven for him by their prayers and mystical ceremonies, each according to his rite.

Formerly the numerous caravans which arrived from all quarters of the globe where the religion of Islamism was practiced provided for all the wants of the city by the abundance of alms which they left. But now that the number is diminished, and the pilgrims are not in a state to contribute to the expenses, the number of persons employed being always the same, devotion and the practice of religion have become very dear, because those employed attach themselves to the pilgrim, whom they believe to be rich, so that he cannot quit without leaving 1,500 or 2,000 francs in alms and remuneration to them and the temple. There are not any of the pilgrims, even the poorest, who undertake the journey at the expense of public charity, or who beg their way, that are not obliged to leave them some crowns.

The gifts being individually given, each person catches what he can in public and in private, except the black eunuchs and the attendants at the Zamzam, who form two corporations. However, notwithstanding this species of organization, with their registers and their chests of receipts in common, each individual of both bodies tries to conceal and keep as much as he can in private.

The caravans also brought formerly large gifts from their respective countries, on the part of their countrymen; but there comes hardly anything now. The chief of the country too [the Sharif?] used to contribute a part of their [the servants of the shrine] subsistence; but being now impoverished by the revolution of the Wahhabis, far from giving, he takes all he can get. The Sultan of Constantinople furnishes negro eunuches for guards to the Ka'ba, for the choir and for the muezzins.

Some changes had very recently taken place at Mecca, changes that doubtless had an effect on the local economy.

The pilgrims once had several stoppages to make, which provided many benefits for those employed; but the Wahhabis have abolished all. The mosque and chapel where the Prophet was born; Jebel Nur, where he received the first revelation from heaven; the house of Abu Talib, where he passed part of his life; several places where he used to pray; the mountain of Qubays, where the miraculous black stone descended; the chapels of Sitna Fatima, the daughter of the Prophet, of Sidi Mahmud and other saints, all no longer exist. The pilgrims are consequently deprived of the spiritual merit they would have acquired by making their pious visits to these holy places; and the good inhabitants of the Holy City have lost the temporal wealth which resulted from these acts of devotion. (Ali Bey 1816: 2:91–93)

Burckhardt adds his own details to the economic portrait of the Haram and its servitors:

The service of the mosque occupies a vast number of people. The Khatibs, Imams, Muftis, those attached to the Zamzam, the muezzins who call to prayers, numbers of ulama, who deliver lectures, lamplighters, and a crowd of menial servants, are all employed about the Beitullah. They receive regular pay from the mosque, besides what they share of the presents made to it by hajjis, for the purpose of distribution; those not made for such purpose are reserved for the repairs of the building. The revenue of the mosque is considerable, although it has been deprived of the best branches of its income.

The income of the mosque must not be confounded with that of a number of Makkawis, including many of the servants, which they derive from other pious foundations in the Turkish empire, known by the name of Surra, and of which a great part still remains untouched. The donations of the hajjis, however, are so ample as to afford abundant subsistence to the great number of idle persons employed about the mosque; and as long as the pilgrimage exists, there is no need to apprehend their wanting either the necessaries or the luxuries of life.

Burckhardt begins with the traditional clan of the Banu Shayba and their chief, the keeper of the keys, whom we shall observe more closely below.

The first officer of the mosque is the Na'ib al-Haram, or Hares al-Haram, the guardian who keeps the keys of the Ka'ba. In his hands are deposited the sums bestowed as presents to the building, and which he distributes in conjunction with the Qadi; under his directions also the repairs of the building are carried out. I have been assured, but do not know how truly, that the Na'ib al-Haram's yearly accounts, which are countersigned by the Sharif and the Qadi and sent to Constantinople, amount to three hundred purses, merely for the expenses of the necessary repairs, lighting, carpets, etc. and the maintenance of the eunuches belonging to the temple. This office happens at present to be held by one of the heads of the only three families descended from the ancient Quraysh who remain resident at Mecca. (Burckhardt 1829: 156)

The Eunuches

Next to him [the Na'ib al-Haram] the second officer of the mosque in rank is the Agha of the eunuches, or, as he is called, Aghat al-Tawashiyya. The eunuches perform the duty of police officers in the temple;[16] they prevent disorders, and daily wash and sweep, with large brooms, the pavement round the Ka'ba. . . . The number of the eunuches now exceeds forty,[17] and they are supplied by Pashas and other grandees, who send them, when young, as presents to the mosque; one hundred dollars are sent with each as an outfit. Muhammad Ali presented ten young eunuches to the mosque. At present there are ten grown-up persons and twenty boys. . . . Extraordinary as it may appear, the grown-up eunuches are all married to black slaves, and maintain several male and female slaves in their houses as servants. They affect great importance, and in case of quarrels and riots, lay freely about them with their sticks. Many of the lower classes of Mecca kiss their hands on approaching them. . . . The eunuches have a large income from the revenues of the mosque and from private donations of the hajjis; they also receive regular stipends from Constantinople, and derive profit from trade; for like almost all the people of Mecca, and even the first clergy, they are more or less engaged in traffic; and their ardor in the pursuit of commercial gain is much greater than that which they evince in the execution of their official duties, being equalled only by the eagerness with which they court the friendship of wealthy hajjis.

Most of the eunuches, or tawashiyya, are negroes; a few were copper-color. Whenever negro hajjis come to Mecca, they never fail to pay assiduous court to the tawashiyya. A tawashiyya, after having been once attached to the service of the Ka'ba, which confers on him the appellation of tawashiyyat al-Nabi (the Prophet's eunuch), can never enter any other service. (Burckhardt 1829: 156)

The eunuches of the Haram were, Snouck Hurgronje noted dryly, "often strongly built but seldom amiable people."

The Banu Shayba

Even before Islam, Mecca was a city of vested interests, most of them scrupulously observed by all concerned. Islam brought an enormous increase in the fortunes of Mecca, and so of the share of income enjoyed by the possessors of special privileges in and around the Haram. Among the most ancient were the Banu Shayba, an old Meccan family who had charge of the Ka'ba in pre-Islamic times and still enjoyed that privilege when Ibn Jubayr made the Hajj in 1183–1184 and when Snouck Hurgronje lived in the city exactly eight hundred years later.[18]

In Ibn Jubayr's time the Banu Shayba had full control of the Ka'ba. They were the descendants, he explains, of a Companion of the Prophet and were "charged with the preservation of the House"—to open or close it on the great feast days and, if the price were paid, on other occasions. The concession must have been enormously profitable and, as a consequence, a trifle dangerous.

On Friday, the 24th of this month [February 1184], in accordance with an order from the Amir Mukthir, the chief of the Banu Shayba, Muhammad ibn Isma'il, was arrested; his home was looted and he was stripped of his charge of the Holy House by reason of the weaknesses of which he stood accused and which were unacceptable in someone responsible for the House. (Ibn Jubayr 1949–1951: 189/Ar. 163–164)

When the Ka'ba was opened on the Monday following, it was a cousin of the cashiered man who presided. But then, on the very next day, Ibn Jubayr was amazed:

The disgraced chief of the Banu Shayba appear(ed), proceeding slowly with pomp and ostentation in the midst of his sons, holding on his hand the key of the Ka'ba, which had been returned to him. . . . We asked how it was possible that the disgraced man had been returned to his office, and this despite the evidence of the weaknesses with which he had been charged. We were told that he had been reinstated thanks to 500 Meccan dinars which he had borrowed and paid. We will be long astonished at this. (Ibn Jubayr 1949–1951: 192/Ar. 166)

The arrangement was in no wise modified, and the door of the Ka'ba, whose key remained in the hands of the Banu Shayba, more often than not stood open for the payment of a fee. This was a kind of extortion, and outraged pilgrims on occasion greeted the arrangement with violence. The affair was to some extent settled in 1222, and in the usual way: the Egyptian Sultan undertook to pay the Banu Shayba an annual fixed sum to keep the door open, and passage free, for everyone in the pilgrimage season. And yet the arrangements seem hardly different in 1884:

As the Muslim does not need the intervention of a priest for any religious act, very few are in a position actually to put a tax on the use of a
holy place. So the exploitation of the Ka'ba is the privilege of the old
noble family of the Shayba; they do a trade in the used kiswa, the great
holy covering of the Ka'ba, of each year, selling small scraps of it as amulets, and on the days when the Ka'ba is opened to the public—the numbers and dates of the days vary . . . according to the will of the authorities.
The 10th of Muharram, the 27th of Rajab, the 15th of Shaban, and some
days of the Ramadan and Hajj months are the commonest opening
days—or on the rare days when a rich stranger pays a large sum for an
extra opening, the Shaybas receive money presents from the rich and
from nearly all strangers entering. A Meccan says as in joke, when he sees
a Shayba smiling, "The Ka'ba must be open today." On these and some
other occasions the (mosque) eunuches also get something, and a whole
swarm of various other people follow the visitor with superfluous service.
(Hurgronje 1931: 21)

The Frenchman Leon Roches came disguised to Mecca in 1841, was admitted to the Ka'ba, and left with the same impression: worship was a
privilege that had to be paid for, and not once but many times:

The Ka'ba is opened only three times during the year. Since one of
these solemn occasions was fixed at the 15th of Dhu al-Qa'da, which cor-
responded in this year of 1841 to December 29th, we had the opportunity
of being present. My pious Mufti companion was constantly congratulat-
ing me on this happy coincidence. "Think of it," he said to me, "you are
going to share in the abundant blessings that God pours out upon the
pious faithful who are able to go inside the dwelling of Abraham."

On the 29th of December, at the moment the sun began to gild the
tops of the minarets of the mosque, the eunuches approached the step-
ladder up to the Ka'ba and the Agha opened its door. Scarcely was it
opened when the pilgrims, who had collected in the courtyard of the
mosque well before the dawn prayer, thrust themselves into the interior of
this venerated place, and this despite the eunuches' efforts and the blows
of their staffs. My companions and myself, following the advice of our
guide, allowed the crowd to go ahead, and after three long hours of waiting we were able to enter, though still with some difficulty. Inside the
Ka'ba we were supposed to make certain prayers, accompanied with bowings, but that was entirely impossible: we were so tightly packed in that
we could scarcely breathe.

The inside is a simple room whose roof is supported by two columns.
The door provides the only light. The ceiling and the upper parts of the
supporting walls are hung with a rich silk stuff with beautiful inscriptions
in silver. The lower sections are faced with marble on which are striking

inscriptions in gold relief. The pavement is of vari-colored marbles. . . . A large number of lamps, of very fine workmanship and made, so they say, of solid gold, hang from the ceiling on golden chains. . . .

You must pay when you go up the ladder guarded by the eunuches, pay on entering, pay on leaving, when the Agha presents the key of the door to be kissed, pay when you go down the ladder, pay, always pay. It is sad to see the treatment given the poor pilgrims who cannot satisfy the cupidity of the innumerable functionaries attached to the mosque.

At midday the Ka'ba was closed, after it had been carefully swept and washed out by the eunuches. Many of the pilgrims went and piously presented themselves to be drenched by the water which poured out of the door. At the exit from the mosque there are a great many shops where are sold the remnants of the hangings of the Ka'ba, which are much in demand by the pilgrims. Also on sale are representations of the mosques and holy places of Mecca and Medina. There is no pilgrim, however poor, who does not bring his family and friends a pious souvenir of his pilgrimage. (Roches 1904: 306–307)

Finally, there is the entirely different, and somewhat puzzling, perspective of Giovanni Finati, an Italian soldier-convert who had served with Muhammad Ali's armies in the Hijaz and who was in Mecca in 1815:

I have already spoken of the little square building, whose walls are covered with hangings of black and gold, and which is called the Ka'ba. Once in the year, and once only, this holy of holies is opened, and as there is then nothing to prevent admission, it appears surprising at first to see so few who are willing to go into the interior, and especially since this act is supposed to have great efficacy in the remission of all past sins. But the reason must be sought for in the conditions which are annexed, since he who enters is, in the first place, bound to exercise no gainful trade or pursuit, nor to work for his livelihood in any way whatever; and next he must submit patiently to all offenses and injuries, and must never again touch anything that is impure or unholy.

Since it is not easy to find in the same person sufficient competence, with sufficient forbearance at the same time, and self-denial to fulfill these conditions, the number who enter the Ka'ba is very limited. Those who are disposed to smile at such superstitions may recollect that the conditions under which a novice enters upon any of the monastic orders in Italy differ little from these, except in being stricter and more binding; yet what numbers are always ready to profess them! Is this from a greater indifference there to the pleasures of this life, or from a more assured confidence in the reward, or from a more lax interpretation and observance of the vow? I have not myself seen enough of European monasteries to be able to answer this question. (Finati 1830: 1:266–269)

The Zamzamis

Both Ali Bey and Burckhardt called attention to the Zamzamis, or "men of the Zamzam," who for many pilgrims were probably the most ubiquitous of the servants of the Haram. Snouck Hurgronje describes how their service was organized toward the end of the nineteenth century.

The management of the Zamzam well was the hereditary charge of the Abbasids. Since the time when these abandoned their claim, the building, within which is the mouth of the well surrounded by a thick wall, is open to everyone, and nominally everyone can climb onto the wall and let down a leather bucket over the iron railing into the well. However, poor and serviceable men always occupy the places when the water is drawn, and they do not demand any reward. As a matter of fact, there is a great guild of "Zamzamis" who monopolize the distribution of the well water. Anyone who wants to have the water poured over him, or to get it "quite hot" from the well, goes himself to the building, and so do the Meccans whenever they want to have their jars filled. . . . All the Zamzamis have and keep in the mosque (1) their great clay jars, resting on wooden stands with metal cups fastened to the jars by chains, (2) their earthen cooling jars of which many dozens already filled are kept lying in the shadiest corners of the mosque. Both kinds of vessels are institutions managed by the Zamzamis.

Nominally anyone can bestow one of either kind of jars for the public use and charge anyone, for a reward, for the regular filling and proper distribution. It is traditional, however, to commit these services to the Zamzamis only, and the latter, though they formally bind themselves to do for the general benefit of the public the work for which they are paid, yet for intimate motives serve as a rule only among those strangers who are their customers. Generally the pilgrim gives, shortly after his arrival, at least one dollar to the Zamzami who has been recommended to him, and for the dollar the latter buys a cooling jar, inscribes on it the name of the pious founder, and adds it to the jars under his care. Thenceforward he constantly comes to meet the pilgrim with his jar, and does not fail as occasion serves to call his attention to the desirability of a more extensive pious foundation. He offers him his services for pouring water over his body, for which he expects a special reward. He tells him how the mats and carpets that he spreads out for worshipers in the mosque are pious foundations and are beginning to be worn and to need renewal. . . . He who spends freely gets every day his filled jar brought into his house, and especially in the month of fasting are such jars brought round in great numbers so that the inmates of the customer's house, as well as himself, may break their fast with Zamzam water. . . . Moreover, the procuring of tin and glass vessels filled for export with Zamzam water brings the well servants great profit. . . . *This is one of those profitable trades which at-tract so much attention on the part of the Government that a man can secure for himself the Government's protection in their practice only by a license from the Grand Sharif, which license is not granted for nothing.* (Hurgronje 1931: 21–22)

Leon Roches learned of another source of "tipping" in 1841:

> In speaking of the rapacity of the Meccans attached to the service of the mosque, I forgot to mention one of their means of pilgrim extortion which had been pointed out to me by my companions. "You see the shape of the containers (a kind of amphora) in which the water-porters carry the water of the Zamzam? They come to a point at their base so that they would not stand upright, a position in which the pilgrims could drink from them, if the porters did not support them between their hands. In this way no drop of water enters the throat of a Hajji without a remuneration being given to the water-porters." (Roches 1904: 307–308)

As for the water itself, most Europeans found it distasteful, mildly so or distinctly so:

> The produce of the Zamzam is held in great esteem. It is used for drinking and religious ablution, but for no baser purposes; and the Mec-cans advise pilgrims to break their fast with it. It is apt to cause diarrhea and boils, and I never saw a stranger drink it without a wry face. [George] Sale[19] is decidedly correct in his assertion: the flavor is salt-bitter, much resembling an infusion of a teaspoonful of Epsom salts in a large tumbler of tepid water. Moreover, it is exceedingly "heavy" to the digestion. (Burton 1893: 2:163)

The Guild of Guides

Of all those who made their living off the Haram or annual pilgrim, Burckhardt reserved his special, and unusual, disdain for the professional guides who had been, from the beginning, part of the Meccan landscape.

> The idlest, most impudent and vilest individuals of Mecca adopt the profession of guides (mutawwif or dalil); and as there is no want of these qualities and a sufficient demand for guides during the Hajj, they are very numerous. Besides the places which I have described in the town, the mutawwifs accompany the Hajjis to all the other places of resort in the sacred district, and are ready to perform every kind of service in the city. But their utility is more than counterbalanced by their importunity and knavery. They besiege the room of the Hajji from sunrise to sunset and will not allow him to do anything without obtruding their advice: they sit

down with him to breakfast, dinner and supper, lead him into all possible expenses that they may pocket a share of them, suffer no opportunity to pass of asking him for money; and woe to the poor ignorant Turk who employs them as his interpreter in any mercantile concern. . . . Some of the dalils are constantly stationed near the Ka'ba, waiting to be hired for walks round it; and if they see a pilgrim walking alone, they often, unasked, take hold of his hand, and begin to recite the prayers. They charge for this service about half a piaster; and I have observed them bargaining with the Hajji at the very gate of the Ka'ba, in the hearing of everybody. The poorer dalils are contented with a fourth of a piaster.

Many shopkeepers and people of the third class send their sons, who know these prayers by heart, to this station, to learn the profession of dalil. Those who understand the Turkish language earn great wages. As the Turkish Hajjis usually arrive by way of Jidda in parties of from eight to twelve who have quitted their homes in company and live together in Mecca, one dalil generally takes charge of the whole party and expects a fee in proportion to their number. It often happens that the Hajjis, on returning home, recommend him to some other party of their countrymen who, on reaching Jidda, send him orders to provide lodgings for them at Mecca, to meet them at Jidda, to superintend their short journey to the holy city, and to guide them in the prayers that must be recited on first entering it.

Some of these dalils are constantly found at Jidda during the three months immediately preceding the Hajj; I have seen them on the road to Mecca, riding at the head of their party, and treated by them with great respect and politeness. A Turk from Europe or Asia Minor who knows not a word of Arabic is overjoyed to find a smooth-tongued Arab who speaks his language, and promises all kinds of comforts in Mecca, which he has been taught to consider a place where nothing awaited him but danger and fatigue. A dalil who has twelve Turkish Hajjis under his care for a month generally gains as much as suffices for the expenses of his house during the whole year, besides new clothing for himself and all his children.

Some of these dalils have a very singular office. The Mohammedan law prescribes that no unmarried woman shall perform the pilgrimage; and that even every married woman must by accompanied by her husband, or at least a very near relation. . . . Female Hajjis sometimes arrive from Turkey for the Hajj; rich old widows, who wish to see Mecca before they die; or women who set out with their husbands and lost them on the road by disease. In such cases the female finds at Jidda dalils, or as this class is called, muhallil, ready to facilitate their progress through the sacred territory in the character of husbands. The marriage contract is written out before the Qadi, and the lady, accompanied by her dalil, performs the pilgrimage to Mecca, Arafat and all the sacred places. This, however, is understood to be merely a nominal marriage, and the dalil must divorce the woman on his return to Jidda. If he were to refuse a divorce, the law cannot compel him to it, and the marriage would be considered binding; but he could no longer exercise the lucrative profession of dalil. (Burckhardt 1829: 193–195)

Snouck Hurgronje observed another "marriage game" at Mecca and the role the guild of guides played in it.

We should have included the women among the guilds of exploiters of pilgrims. . . . They not only help their husbands faithfully in their business, but also work on their own account. Pilgrims who spend a few months on the pilgrimage, and those too who settle down in the country for a few years, generally wish to marry. As they habitually bring a full purse with them into the Holy City, the demand is answered by a plentiful supply. . . . Meccan women can easily get rid of distasteful marriage bonds, and we can now understand why continual change in marriage is pleasing to most of them. Their wares in the pilgrim market are their charms; the oftener the charms are made the subject of new contracts, the better for business. The relation between demand and supply in Meccan society is strongly influenced by the concourse of strangers. A Meccan man, it is true, does not allow himself to become beguiled by the daughters of Mecca the way a stranger does, but the demand on the part of strangers makes it easy for the Meccan women to stipulate for great advantages for themselves.

The foreigner who chooses to become a citizen of Mecca is besieged on all sides by offers of marriage. However capricious his taste may be, the go-betweens always have in stock what he wants. Even if he insists on paying a small dower, there is sure to be a widow or unpretentious woman who is not exacting on this head, and if he is disinclined to costly entertainments, he can content himself with a small (marriage) feast for which he has to pay little. Indeed, women are to be found who on the same evening after the conclusion of the marriage contract will come to the man's house without further ceremony. Sly women rely upon the fact that their experience and skill in dealing with men of different kinds will enable them in a few days to befool the husband. . . . If all goes well, the man will spend within half a year on the wife's whims, or on the dress and upkeep of her poor relations, the money that he reckoned enough for all his needs for a couple of years. When the purse is empty, the woman at once begins to show the unpleasant side of her nature, until at last her husband, unconsciously complying with her wishes, pronounces the form of divorce over her. He must then give her support for three (additional) months, and so she has full time to seek a new wedded position with the *help of her friends. . . . Of course, she is not always lucky. In this business too there are disappointments and bankruptcies. (Hurgronje 1931: 88)*

And, one presumes, even an occasional successful marriage. We return to Burckhardt on the subject of guides.

I believe there is not any exaggeration of the number in stating that there are eight hundred full-grown dalils, besides boys who are learning the profession. Whenever a shopkeeper loses his customers or a poor man of letters wishes to gain as much money as will purchase a slave, he turns dalil. The profession is one of little repute, but many a prosperous Mak-kawi has, at some period of his life, been a member of it. (Burckhardt 1829: 196)

Burckhardt arrived in Mecca at a difficult time for the Holy City and the pilgrimage; he came, moreover, as an individual, and from the rather unusual direction of Ta'if. All of these circumstances explain, to some degree, his reaction to the Meccan guides. Snouck Hurgronje, on the other hand, could observe the system rather than be subjected to it—he was living at Mecca—at a time when the political situation was considerably more settled and the competition among the guides for scarce pilgrims was long past. But the institution had also changed: as described by both Snouck in 1884 and in the following year by the Persian Farahani, the guides constituted a formal and well-organized guild whose adversary was no longer the impecunious pilgrim but the equally impecunious government, Sharifian and Turkish, of the Hijaz.

No matter how exactly the stranger may have studied the ceremonies of the great and small pilgrimage—and most do not study them—he can in no case dispense with the help of a man familiar with the local conditions; and the same may be said of the voluntary visits to holy spots. Immediately on his arrival on Arabian soil, that is generally in Jidda, he needs a guide, to take charge of him at the outset, to show him Eve's tomb, and later to hire for him camels and drivers for the journey to Mecca. If the pilgrim is not an Arab, the guide must also serve him as interpreter, and also, in Mecca, in house hiring, making ordinary purchases and so forth, he would meet with the greatest difficulties if he attempted to make his way without the official go-between. At least during the first weeks of his stay, he can make no step, enter into no relations with others, have recourse to no official, without the help of the mu-tawwif, properly the guide for the perambulation of the Ka'ba, but used in common parlance for strangers-guide in general.

There are small guides who carry on their business with the help of their families, their servants, or, as occasion arises, some hungry friends. Those in a larger way deal personally only with the most important cases, and especially look after their rich customers, but leave the real work to a whole army of sons, younger relatives, slaves and permanent and temporary employees. There are even mystics and learned men who give only their honored names so that their obscurer kinsmen may act under their style and title and then give them a share of the profits. (Hurgronje 1931: 23–24)

The work of the guide began before Mecca, in fact, as soon as the seaborne pilgrim—as more and more of them were in the late nineteenth century—landed at Jidda.

Each guide puts his services at the disposal of the pilgrims of a particular nation or even of a particular province whose language he speaks and with whose peculiarities he is familiar, for without such knowledge the guiding of pilgrims would be difficult and the exploitation of them would not be successful enough. From his business connections he gets information when a ship is approaching with pilgrims for him on board. To meet important guests he goes himself to Jidda, or sends his son there to supervise the reception which they get from his agent, the representative which all guides have in Jidda; the less important he commits at once to the agent's charge. At the unloading of the little boats which carry the pilgrims from the roadstead to the shore, the guides or their men are in attendance. They hire the porters who carry the pilgrim's luggage into the town, and they take an active part in the distribution of gifts to the customs officers. They are able quickly to take the measure of their customers, to find out what accommodation they need and for how long, and in what things they take most interest, and from the beginning they fix on the lodging that will best suit each customer out of those which they have to dispose of. (Hurgronje 1931: 24–25)

There is at Jidda the final obligatory visit to the grave site of the "many yards long Mother of Mankind," the hiring of camels, and the donning of the *ihram*. The pilgrim is then at last off to Mecca, accompanied by his guide.

In two days they reach Mecca. Here they at once perform the Umra, for which no special time of the year is fixed, and then put off the strange costume. For the ceremonies one or more personal conductors are assigned. These are according to the literal sense the guides; when acting in the employ of others they are called "showers," or, if young to the work, "apprentices." The "showers" in fact show them what to do in all circumstances, and direct the course of their charity, which always flows on these occasions. . . . With the Arabs it is in general the custom that in every transaction the third party, who may have taken part in the business only with a few words of recommendation, should get a small present; why then should not the guide who has disposed of his customer's purse to good purpose get his percentage of its outgoings: of the house rent, the price of food and other commodities, the sums which pilgrims bring with them on the Hajj for the representatives of their dead relations, the cost of the donkey ride to Tanaᶜim, where the pilgrim dons pilgrim dress for additional Umras, or to the cemetery and of the reward of the guides who are taken on there? Of all these items they somehow get their share.

For the Hajj, again the guide makes all arrangements. He provides camels, tents, provisions and fuel for the journey to Arafat and back; provisions and sheep for sacrifice are also bought in the Mina valley through the guide. On each detail of the pilgrimage an assistant of the guide instructs the pilgrims who are committed to his care, speaking to them in their own language and reciting to them the proper formulae which they have to utter. Both before and after the Hajj pilgrims go to Medina to visit the tomb of Muhammad: this visit is in all cases not obligatory, and is at the most only an annex to the great pilgrimage. Also for this journey to Medina the guides hire camels with their appurtenances. (Hurgronje 1931: 25–26)

It is, Snouck assures us, a genuine guild of experts, institutionalized and self-protective.

It can now be understood how important the guild of guides is for Mecca, where the Hajj must yield the daily harvest. He who would achieve success in the trade needs the help of many people and a favorable time; he, on the other hand, who has got success has very many persons at his disposal who without his help cannot get their share. On the numerical importance of the guild we can form an idea when we remember that the exploitation of only the Java (Malay) pilgrims occupies 180 guides with their numerous hangers-on. Over all is the Shaykh of the Guides who represents the most general interests of the body, protects traditions against attack, and, on the other hand, must also help the government in the introduction of new measures. However, the guides of each nationality form by themselves again a more or less closed group: the pilgrims have not only their own language, but also their own customs, their own preferred holy places; and all this naturally gives rise to special business circles and special interests. So the guides of the Turks, Egyptians, Maghribis, Indians, Malays etc. each form a small guild of themselves under their respective guild masters.

The guild master decides about the admittance of new members, and so it is considered whether competition will not be made too severe by the increase in number, and further whether the candidate has acquired claims by honorable conduct and proved capacity. Other considerations too are put in the balance. The guild master, himself a creature of the government, can hardly reject a candidate who is recommended by high officials; others recommend themselves with equal emphasis by their influential position or by the important presents which they hand to the Shaykh as an introduction to their candidature.

To confirm the admission of a new member, a little guild feast is given to which all the guildsmen are invited by the candidate. The feast is called "The Enmastering." Before the whole assembly the candidate says: "I ask our Shaykh for (leave to practice) the profession which is allowed by God"; whereupon the guildsmen reply: "Who is our Shaykh?" When he has mentioned the latter by name, the guild master asks whether he will obey him and be a good guild-brother to his "sons." His affirmative answer is followed by the recitation of the "Fatiha" [the opening sura of the Quran]. ((Hurgronje 1931: 26–29)

For all its exclusivity, the guild could not ensure its own monopoly, and there were around the edges of the enterprise "gypsy guides" ready to catch up whatever the guild members might have overlooked.

As the guild system is founded on tradition only, anyone is theoretically free to render such services to the pilgrims for money, but in practice the undertaking would be met by such difficulties that a man of good position would not expose his ease and good name to so great a danger. The men of the guild would rise against him like one man. The consideration which they have for one another in spite of all their mutual jealousy would be forgotten in dealing with an interloper. In secret and in public he would meet nothing but enmity, and no pilgrim could be advised to trust himself to such a "blackleg." . . . There is a like state of things in every guild, but in none are the traditional rules so strictly observed as in this most important and most numerically strong of all guilds. There are, however, interlopers, but these are such as would be found unworthy of admittance in the corporation, and their clients are only such pilgrims as are too poor or, like many Maghribis, too stingy to pay proper remuneration. These interlopers are called jarrars and lie in wait for their prey at the entrance of the town and in or near the mosque. When pilgrims arrive from a country whose inhabitants so seldom travel to Arabia that they have no special guides here, the guild master decides to whom they are to belong for exploitation. Such pilgrims can of course apply to the Government when the decision does not please them. (Hurgronje 1931: 27)

THE PILGRIMAGE OF 1842

As might be expected, Ali Bey, the would-be Muslim grandee, offers one perspective on the pilgrimage, while Leon Roches, in a somewhat humbler disguise and coming from what was already a colonial North African environment, gives quite another. Here Roches observes the procession of the caravans to Arafat in the Hajj year of 1842.

The Procession to Arafat

We were ourselves obliged to put on the Ihram once again since on the next day all the pilgrims must go in procession to Arafat, or "Place of Recognition." On this hill, according to the Arab tradition, Adam and Eve recognized each other after having wandered for a hundred years apart. Here take place the most important ceremonies of the pilgrimage.

On January 21st, at sunrise, the Syrian pilgrims went in procession across the city, the Mahmal at their head, accompanied by the Turkish soldiers who had escorted the caravan. The Pasha of Damascus and his brilliant escort came immediately behind. In the procession there were litters covered with rich stuffs and carried by camels richly caparisoned and decorated with tassels and bells. A crowd of the local inhabitants who did not have to go to Arafat acclaimed them as they passed.

After the Syrian pilgrims marched the western pilgrims who had come with the Egyptian caravan. They too were preceded by a Mahmal and the Amir al-Hajj, followed by a cavalry troop and a few hundred regular troops. In the midst of this immense cortege there could be seen a great many . . . palanquins mounted on the backs of camels for the portage of women.

All the pilgrims joined the Syrian and Egyptian caravans, including those who had arrived earlier, as well as the population of Mecca and Jidda who were taking part in the ceremonies; all of them forming an endless procession, and all of them chanting verses of the Quran at the tops of their voices. . . .

The procession took the route which we had earlier taken on our way to Ta'if. It enlarged or contracted according to the size of the valleys through which we passed, but for the rest, there reigned the disorder customary to all great assemblies of Arabs. (Roches 1904: 331–333)

On the Plain of Arafat

The procession passed through Mina and entered the plain of Arafat.

The Syrian caravan camped at the base of the hill called Jabal Arafat, about 200–300 meters to the southwest. The Egyptian caravan camped at the same distance toward the southeast. At some distance directly to the south the principal people of Mecca and Jidda set up their tents, and a little farther away, and toward the southeast was the camp of the Indians and the mendicant pilgrims. Still farther to the east was that of the bedouin. The place of these camps has become fixed over a long period of time. A market is set up just about in the middle of the plain occupied by the pilgrims.

The sun had set by the time we arrived, and the night was cold and dark. I cannot describe the spectacle of these various camps illumined by fires lit before the tents of the important or the rich. The brightness of the fires made visible the phantom shapes of the thousands of pilgrims who had arrived late and were going from tent to tent in search of their camping place. The calls of these unfortunate people, the religious invocations, the joyous cries of the people of Mecca beating time with their hands, the jangling cries of the coffee men and the strolling merchants, all these sounds, accompanied by the lugubrious complaints of more than 20,000 camels, made for a concert from hell.

The 9th of Dhu al-Hijja [22 January 1842], a day I shall never forget, an artillery salvo announced the dawn prayer. On all sides the muezzins of the various encampments made the call to prayer in their echoing soprano voices. We have no idea of this in Europe or western Africa; it is only beyond Cairo that the call of the muezzins becomes a ravishing melody.

When day came I saw under a new light the various encampments that occupied an area of from five to six kilometers north to south and about two kilometers wide. The tents were lined up to make almost straight streets, which swarmed with tightly packed crowds of people. In the middle of the camps of the great caravans I noticed cavalry men armed with rifles and lances practicing their maneuvers, while the two Turkish and Egyptian battalions and some regular troops were doing their exercises. Thousands of camels were feeding on the brush from the seared hills that bordered the valley. (Roches 1904: 334–335)

Atop the Mount of Mercy

In the company of a guide . . . I went up to the top of Mount Arafat the better to enjoy the spectacle. The mount is a hill of granite that the Arabs also call "the Mount of Mercy." It rises in the northeast of the plain near the surrounding mountains but separated from them by a rocky valley. Its sides are sloped, and its height appeared to me about 60 meters above the level of the plain. On the side of the mount steps have been cut in the rock. After you have climbed up this way you come to a spot called "the Place of Our Lord Adam." The Muslim tradition says that it was there that the Angel Gabriel taught Adam how to pray to God.

At the top of this plateau, and at the same height, but twenty meters to the east, there is a platform where the preacher takes his place. At the very top of the hill, a pavement, once covered by a dome which has since been destroyed by the Wahhabis, marks the place where the Prophet prayed at the time of the Pilgrimage. All about it are stretched handkerchiefs to hold the offerings of pilgrims. . . . Large reservoirs are built at the foot of Mount Arafat and serve to water the gardens (of the Sharif's country house nearby). They are filled from the aqueduct that goes to Mecca.

Once, my guide told me, the entire plain of Arafat was irrigated and cultivated.

Before the hour of prayer all the pilgrims had to make their ablutions near to the reservoirs filled from the aqueduct. Those who were in tents closed them during the (ablution) ceremony, but those who were not had to do their washing in public. Since I was in this latter group, I ran a great danger since I had not made a formal abjuration (of Christianity) and so had not been constrained to accept the stigma of Islam.

Roches was not, then, circumcised.

Had anyone noticed? What happened afterwards gave me reason to think someone had, even though I had taken all possible precautions since I was terrified at the prospect of the tortures that a fanatic and barbarous mob would inflict on me if they recognized that I was a Christian. (Roches 1904: 335–337)

In any event, the canon sounded and the call of the muezzins echoed in the plain and over Mount Arafat, whose sides were literally covered with the most devout pilgrims in their efforts to get close to the preacher. This latter, mounted on a richly caparisoned white camel, and dressed in a great white shawl with a long rod in his right hand, halted motionless on the platform I described before. It was there, they said, that Muhammad preached to the first Muslims. Quite near, and a little behind, was stationed the Sharif on a magnificent steed, surrounded by a large escorting party and by Negroes bearing his impressive green standards fringed with silver and gold which floated in the breeze over his head and that of the preacher, who is normally the Chief Justice of Mecca.

At the first discharge of the cannon all the tents were struck. The camels were stood up, loaded and lined up at the foot of Arafat. The caravans, Mahmals to the fore, occupied the front rank, and behind them the Pasha of Damascus drew up his escort and his regular troops; by their side was the Amir of the Cairo caravan with his soldiers and Egyptian horsemen, and finally the pilgrims of the Yemen occupied the last row.

The muezzin's echoing voice announced the mid-afternoon prayer for the third time and soon the most perfect silence settled over this so recently noisy and disorderly crowd. The preacher began his sermon. It was impossible to understand his words. I could make out his invocations to God, however, and at each one of them he slowly raised his hands to heaven, a gesture imitated by the sixty thousand in attendance, who repeated the striking declaration Labbayka, Allahumma, labbayka! "Here we are, O Lord, here we are!"

And yet, though I marveled at this grandiose scene, . . . the majesty of the ceremony of Mount Arafat, like all those in Mecca, was undercut by

*the antireligious attitude of a great number of pilgrims and Meccans who
had gathered in the cafés on the opposite side of the mountain and joked,
smoked and got involved in fierce arguments. The coffee men and even
some women came during the ceremony and offered coffee and cakes up
and down the lines of pilgrims. (Roches 1904: 337–339)*

Then occurred what the pretended convert from Algiers had most
dreaded: discovery.

*The sermon lasted until sunset. When the cannon signalled the end of
the ceremony it was almost night. There was a lot of commotion about
me. I heard cries, among which I could make out the words, "Yo! A
Christian! Seize the Christian, the infidel son of an infidel!" Then, all of
a sudden, I was seized by a pair of powerful arms, gagged and trussed in
such a way that I could neither see nor hear and could breathe only with
difficulty. I thought my last hour had come and I commended my soul to
God. (Roches 1904: 339)*

There was a happy ending, relatively speaking. News had been brought to
the Sharif that reports were abroad of a foreign spy among the pilgrims.
He knew immediately that it was Roches, who had been sent on a secret
mission by the French government and with whom the Sharif had had
cordial meetings a few days earlier in Ta'if. The Sharif's men were alerted
to what might happen if an identification was made, and so when the cry
went up, it was they who carried him off, to safety, from Arafat all the way
to Jidda, where Roches was put on a boat and despatched to Qusayr
across the Red Sea.

BACK FROM ARAFAT

The abrupt end of Leon Roches' pilgrimage at Arafat meant that he never
witnessed the other essential ceremonies that took place on the way back
to Mecca. Burckhardt is now our guide as we turn back toward Mina.

Mina

*Mina is a narrow valley extending in a right line from west to east and
varying in breadth, enclosed on both sides by steep and barren cliffs of
granite. Along the middle, on both sides of the way, is a row of buildings,
the far greater part in ruins: they belong to Meccans or bedouin of the
Quraysh, by whom they are either let out, or occupied during the three
days of the Hajj and left empty during the rest of the year, when Mina is
never inhabited. Some of these are tolerable stone buildings, two stories*

high; but not more than a dozen of them are kept in good repair. (Burckhardt 1829: 277)

Hossein Kazemzadeh, the Persian pilgrim who made the Hajj in 1910–1911, had a somewhat different perspective on this same stretch of terrain:

The road . . . is presently bordered on both sides by houses and shops. As a result the way has become too narrow for the passage of so many pilgrims attempting to go by at the same time and to perform the stoning ritual at the same time. The story is that it was the former Sharif Awn al-Rafiq who had, during the reign of (the Sultan) Abd al-Hamid, sold this public land and granted permission for buildings to be erected there. While the hundreds of thousands of pilgrims pass along this narrow way with their mounts and possessions, pausing some minutes before each of the stone pillars (for the stoning ritual), there are frequent accidents. Thousands of objects are lost or stolen, several people fall from their mounts, many of them are trampled upon or otherwise injured, and several actually killed. Each year more than fifty people lose their lives in this passage, and what adds to the danger is the fact that there is no official in charge of the transit. More, hundreds of camels are tied one to the next to form a single line. Several lines of camels enter on the passage at the same time, collide and jostle each other, get separated from the line and cause their load of pilgrim and his effects to fall off and cause bystanders to be injured by sharp objects. . . . No army in full retreat has ever presented a more disorderly appearance than this army of pilgrims over the course of a few hours. (Kazemzadeh 1912: 222–223)

The Stoning of Satan

On arriving at Wadi Mina, each nation encamped upon the spot which custom has assigned to it at every returning Hajj. After disposing of the baggage, the Hajjis hastened to the ceremony of throwing stones at the devil. It is said that when Abraham returned from the pilgrimage to Arafat and arrived at the Wadi Mina, the devil Iblis presented himself before him at the entrance of the valley, to obstruct his passage; then the Angel Gabriel, who accompanied the Patriarch, advised him to throw stones at him, which he did, and after pelting him seven times, Iblis retired. When Abraham reached the middle of the valley, he again appeared before him, and, for the last time, at its western extremity, and was both times repulsed by the same number of stones.

At the entrance to the valley, towards Muzdalifa, stands a rude stone pillar, or rather altar, between six and seven feet high, in the midst of the street, against which the first seven stones are thrown, as the place where the devil made his first stand. Toward the middle of the valley is a similar pillar, and at its western end a wall of stones, which is made to serve the same purpose. The Hajjis crowded in rapid succession round the first pillar . . . and every one threw seven small stones successively upon it; they then passed to the second and third spots . . . where the same ceremony was repeated. The stones used for this purpose are to be the size of a horse bean, or thereabouts, and the pilgrims are advised to collect them in the plain of Muzdalifa, but they may likewise take them from Mina; and many people, contrary to the law, collect those that have already been thrown. (Burckhardt 1829: 274–275)

The Sacrifice

Having performed the ceremony of casting stones, the pilgrims kill the animals which they bring with them for sacrifice; and all Muslims, in whatever part of the world they may be, are bound, at this time, to perform the same rite. Between six and seven thousand sheep and goats, under the care of the bedouin (who demanded high prices for them), were ready on this occasion. The act of sacrifice itself is subject to no other ceremonies than that of turning the victim's face towards the Qibla or Kaʿba, and to say, during the act of cutting its throat, "In the name of God, the Compassionate, the Merciful. God is Great!" Any place may be chosen for these sacrifices, which are performed in every corner of the Wadi Mina, but the favorite spot is a smooth rock on its western extremity, where several thousand sheep were killed in the space of a quarter of an hour.

As soon as the sacrifices were completed, the pilgrims sent for barbers, or repaired to their shops, of which a row of thirty or forty had been set up near the favorite place of sacrifice. They had their heads shaved, except those who were of the Shafiʿi sect, who shave only one-fourth of their heads here, reserving the other three-fourths till they have visited the Kaʿba, after returning to Mecca. They threw off the Ihram and resumed their ordinary clothes; those who could afford it put on new dresses, this being now the day of the feast. So far the Hajj was completed, and all the pilgrims joined in mutual congratulations and wishes that the performance of the Hajj might be acceptable to the Deity.

The pilgrims remain two days more at Mina. Exactly at mid-day on the 11th of Dhu al-Hajj, seven small stones are thrown against each of the three places where the devil appeared; and the same is done on the 12th of Dhu al-Hajj, so that by the three repeated throwings, each time of twenty-one stones, the number of sixty-three is cast during the three days. Many pilgrims are ignorant of the precise tenor of the law in this respect, as they are of several other points in the ceremonies of the pilgrimage, and either throw early in the morning the stones they should throw at midday, or do not throw the number enjoined. After the last throwing on the 12th the Hajj returns to Mecca in the afternoon. (Burckhardt 1829: 275–277)

By the twelfth of Dhu al-Hijja, the circumstances at Mina had become exceedingly grim, as Burton testified. He had, not surprisingly, a solution:

Literally the land stank. Five or six thousand animals had been slain and cut up in this Devil's Punchbowl. I leave the reader to imagine the rest. The evil might be avoided by building abattoirs, or, more easily still, by digging long trenches and ordering all pilgrims, under pain of mulct, to sacrifice in the same place. Unhappily, the spirit of Islam is opposed to these precautions of common sense. . . . And at Mecca, the headquarters of the faith, a desolating attack of cholera is preferred to the impiety of "flying in the face of Providence," and the folly of endeavoring to avert inevitable decrees. (Burton 1893: 2:224)

A later edition of his *Personal Narrative* enabled Burton to say "I told you so":

Since this was written there have been two deadly epidemics, which began, it is reported, at Mina. (Burton 1893: 2:224n.1)

Farewell

Freed of the fearful atmosphere of Mina, Richard Burton returned to the Haram, where at noon the pilgrims assembled for the Friday communal prayer at the House of God. This was the farewell ceremony of the Hajj, and Burton experiences, quite unexpectedly it appears, not one but a series of final transporting emotions:

After entering Mecca we bathed, and when noon drew nigh we repaired to the Haram for the purpose of hearing the sermon. Descending to the cloisters below the Bab al-Ziyada, I stood wonder-struck by the scene before me. The vast quadrangle was crowded with worshipers sitting in long rows, and everywhere facing the central black tower. The showy colors of their dresses were not to be surpassed by a garden of the most brilliant flowers, and such diversity of detail would probably not be seen massed together in any other building upon earth. The women, a dull and somber looking group, sat apart in their peculiar place. The Pasha stood on the roof of the Zamzam surrounded by guards in Nizam uniform. Where the principal ulama stationed themselves the crowd was thicker; and in the more auspicious spots there was to be seen but a pavement of heads and shoulders. Nothing seemed to move but a few dervishes, who, censer in hand, sidled through the rows and received the unsolicited alms of the faithful.

Apparently in the midst, and raised above the crowd by the tall pointed pulpit, whose gilt spire flamed in the sun, sat the preacher, an old man with a snowy beard. The style of head-dress called taylasan—a scarf thrown over the head, with one end brought round under the chin and passed over the left shoulder—covered his turban, which was white as his robes, and a short staff supported his left hand. Presently he arose, took the staff in his right hand, pronounced a few inaudible words and sat down again on one of the lower steps, while a muezzin, at the foot of the pulpit, recited the call to sermon. Then the old man stood up and began to preach. As the majestic figure began to exert itself there was a deep silence. Presently a general "Amin" was intoned by the crowd at the conclusion of some long sentence. And at last, towards the end of the sermon, every third or fourth word was followed by the simultaneous rise and fall of thousands of voices.

I have seen the religious ceremonies of many lands, but never—nowhere—aught so solemn, so impressive as this. (Burton 1893: 2:225–226)

Burckhardt did not leave Mecca with the Hajj caravan as so many pilgrims did, and so he had an opportunity to see the Holy City after the completion of all the ceremonies and the departure of most of the visitors.

The termination of the Hajj gives a very different appearance to the temple. Disease and mortality, which succeed to the fatigues endured on the journey, or are caused by the light covering of the Ihram, the unhealthy lodgings at Mecca, the bad fare and sometimes absolute want, fill the mosque with dead bodies, carried thither to receive the Imam's prayer, or with sick persons, many of whom, when their dissolution approaches, are brought to the colonnades, that they may either be cured by the sight of the Ka῾ba, or at least have the satisfaction of expiring within the sacred enclosure. Poor Hajjis, worn out by disease and hunger, are seen dragging their emaciated bodies along the columns; and when no longer able to stretch forth their hands to ask the passerby for charity, they place a bowl to receive alms near the mat on which they lay themselves. When they feel their last moments approaching, they cover themselves with their tattered garments; and often a whole day passes before it is discovered that they are dead. For a month subsequent to the conclusion of the Hajj, I found, almost every morning, corpses of pilgrims lying in the mosque; myself and a Greek Hajji, whom accident had brought to the spot, once closed the eyes of a poor Maghrebi pilgrim who had crawled into the neighborhood of the Ka῾ba to breathe his last, as the Muslims say, "in the arms of the Prophet and the guardian angels." He *intimated by signs his wish that we should sprinkle Zamzam water over him; and while we were doing so, he expired: half an hour afterwards he was buried. There are several persons in the service of the mosque employed to wash carefully the spot on which those who expire in the mosque have lain, and to bury all the poor and friendless strangers who die at Mecca.* (Burckhardt 1829: 162–163)

After describing all the Hajj ceremonies in detail, Burckhardt finally undertook to sum up this supremely important Muslim ritual for the benefit of his European readers.

The principal duties incumbent upon the Hajji are: 1. that he should take the Ihram; 2. be present, on the 9th of Dhu al-Hajj, from afternoon till sunset at the sermon preached at Arafat; 3. attend a similar sermon at Muzdalifa, at sunrise on the 10th of Dhu al-Hajj; 4. on the 10th, 11th and 12th of Dhu al-Hajj throw on each day twenty-one stones against the devil's pillars at Mina; 5. perform the sacrifice at Mina; or, if he is too poor, substitute for it a fast at some future time; and 6. upon his return to Mecca visit the Ka'ba and [if he is combining the Hajj and the Umra] visit the Umra.

The law makes so many nice distinctions, and increases so greatly the number of rules which are to guide the pilgrim at every step, that very few can flatter themselves with being quite regular Hajjis. But as no ritual police is kept up during the ceremony, everyone is completely his own master and assumes the title of "Hajji" whether he has strictly performed all the duties or not. It is enough for such that they have been at Arafat on the proper day—this is the least distinction, but a mere visit to Mecca does not authorize a man to style himself Hajji, and the assumption of this title without some further pretensions exposes him to ridicule. (Burckhardt 1829: 284–285)

A VISIT TO MEDINA

Hajj and Ziyara

As Carsten Niebuhr had pointed out and as Richard Burton now instructed his non-Muslim readers, a visit to Medina was not a part of the obligatory pilgrimage, or *Hajj*, which refers to the formal, time-tied ceremonies at Mecca. A journey to Medina constitutes rather a *ziyara*, a pious visitation, which had as its focal point the Prophet's Mosque.

The Masjid al-Nabawi, or Prophet's Mosque, is one of the Haramayn, or the "two sanctuaries" of Islam, and is the second of the three most venerable places of worship in the world; the other two being the Masjid al-Haram at Mecca (connected with Abraham) and the Masjid al-Aqsa of Jerusalem (the peculiar place of Solomon).

A visit to the Masjid al-Nabawi, and the holy spots within it, is technically called ziyara or Visitation. An essential difference is made between this rite and the Hajj or Pilgrimage. The latter is obligatory by Quranic order upon every Muslim once in his life; the former is only a meritorious action. Tawaf, or circumambulation of the House of Allah at Mecca, must never be performed at the Prophet's tomb. This should not be visited in the Ihram or pilgrim's dress; men should not kiss it, touch it with the hand, or press the bosom against it, as at the Ka'ba; or rub the face with dust collected near the sepulcher; and those who prostrate themselves before it, like certain ignorant Indians, are held to be guilty of deadly sin. (Burton 1893: 1:304–306)

The Tomb of the Prophet

Burckhardt, more impressed with the Medina mosque than Burton, describes the Prophet's tomb within.

Near the southeast corner (of the mosque) stands the famous tomb, so detached from the walls of the mosque as to leave between it and the south wall a space of about twenty-five feet, and fifteen between it and the east wall. The enclosure which defends the tomb from the too near approach of visitors forms an irregular square of twenty paces, in the midst of the colonnade, several of its pillars being included within it: it is an iron railing, painted green, about two thirds the height of the columns, filling up the intervals between them, so as to leave their upper part projecting above it, and entirely open. The railing is of good workmanship, in imitation of filigree, and is interwoven with open-worked inscriptions of yellow bronze, supposed by the vulgar to be of gold, and so close of texture that no view can be gained into the interior, except by several small windows, about six inches square, which are placed in the four sides of the railing, about five feet above the ground.

What appears of the interior (of this enclosure)[20] is a curtain carried round, which takes up almost the whole space, having between it and the railing an open walk of a few paces only in breadth. There is a covering (as the eunuches affirm) of the same stuff of which the curtain is made. This is a rich brocade of various colors interwoven with silver flowers and arabesques, with a band of inscriptions with gold characters running across the midst of it, like that of the covering of the Ka'ba. This curtain is at least thirty feet high: it has a small gate to the north, which is always shut, no person whatever being permitted to enter within its holy precincts, except the chief eunuches, who take care of it and who put on, during the night, the new curtain sent from Constantinople, whenever the old one is decayed, or when a new Sultan ascends the throne. The old curtains are sent to Constantinople and serve to cover the tombs of the sultans and princes.

According to the historian on Medina,[21] the curtain covers a square building of black stones, supported by two pillars, in the interior of which are the tombs of Muhammad, and his two earliest friends and immediate successors, Abu Bakr and Umar. As far as I could learn here, these tombs are also covered with previous stuffs, and in the shape of catafalques, like that of Ibrahim in the great mosque of Mecca.[22] . . . The historian says that these tombs are deep holes and that the coffin which contains the dust of Muhammad is cased with silver and has on the top a marble slab inscribed Bismillahi Allahuma salli alay ("In the name of God, bestow Thy mercy upon him").

Muslim tradition says that when the last trumpet shall sound, Isa (Jesus Christ) is to descend from heaven to earth and to announce to its inhabitants the great day of judgment, after which he is to die, and will be buried at the side of Muhammad in this Hijrah; that when the dead shall rise from their graves, they will both rise together, ascend to heaven, and Isa on that day will be ordered to separate the faithful from the infidels. In conformity with this tradition, the spot is pointed at through the curtain of the Hijrah, where the tomb of Isa will be placed. (Burckhardt 1829: 331–336)

When Leon Roches visited Muhammad's tomb in 1841, he saw, or rather, was shown, somewhat more than Burckhardt.

Near the southeast corner (of the mosque) is the famous tomb of Muhammad; eight or ten meters separate it from the walls of the mosque, and around the mosque the marble pavement has been replaced by very beautiful mosaics. The tomb is surrounded by a finely worked iron grill on which run inscriptions in gilt bronze. This grill forms an irregular square some 14 meters on each side, in one of which are engaged some of the pillars which support the arches of the mosque. It is about 15 meters high. Some few small windows are let into the grill about 1 m. 20 above the ground. On the south side are two large windows whose supports are plated over with silver and bear Arabic inscriptions in relief. It is there that the pilgrims recite the longest prayers. The tomb is illuminated by great windows of colored glass in the walls of the mosque. There are four entries let into the grill. Only one is opened and that gives entry to the guardians charged with cleaning and the lighting. The grilled enclosure is called "The Hejera" (The Refuge) in memory of the flight of the Prophet, whence also comes the name hejyre, the Muslim era.[23]

The construction over the tomb of the Prophet, which you cannot see, must be nearly the same height as the grill. It is completely covered by an immense silken tent embroidered with flowers and arabesques, with attractive Arabic inscriptions in golden relief forming a band in the middle of the tenting. A passage of three or four meters separates the tenting from the railing (of the grill). Only important personages are allowed into this passage; you can obtain this privilege by paying bakhshish to the custodians. But no one, we were told, was permitted to raise the tenting, in which is let an opening which gives entry to the interior of the mausoleum. This is patently false, and we were certainly not the only ones to have obtained this privilege whereby, by paying twenty dollars (110 francs) . . . we received permission not only to enter into the reserved passageway but even, when there was no pilgrim at the large windows, to raise the second tenting. This infraction lasted barely a minute, time enough to see three catafalques covered with rich drapes in a square room whose ceiling was supported by two pillars. Several golden lamps cast a feeble light on the rich drapes and the walls, which appeared almost black to our sight.

There, we were told by the custodians, . . . was the tomb of the Prophet Muhammad, buried deep in the earth. His body was inside a cedar coffin completely covered with silver leaf. The two other tombs, somewhat smaller, enclose the bodies of Abu Bakr, father-in-law of the Prophet, and of Umar ibn al-Khattab, the second Caliph. Next to the tomb of Muhammad there is a space with an open and empty tomb. It is destined to receive the body of Jesus, son of Maryam, whom God raised to heaven, body and soul. . . . In the space enclosed by the grill surrounding the mausoleum of the Prophet and the tenting which covers it is the tomb of Fatima, his daughter who had married Ali. The tomb of the Prophet was once surrounded, we were told, by magnificent presents donated by all the princes of Islam, and whose value was incalculable. But fires and the Wahhabis have destroyed or pillaged them, and there alone remain, we were told, some splendid golden urns. (Roches 1904: 284–286)

And finally, Burton on the tomb chamber:

The Hujrah or "Chamber," as it is called, from the circumstance of its having been Aisha's room, is an irregular square of from 50 to 55 feet in the southeast corner of the building, and is separated on all sides from the walls of the mosque by a passage about 26 feet broad on the south side and twenty on the east. . . . Inside there are, or are supposed to be, three tombs facing to the south, surrounded by stone walls without any apertures, or, as others say, by strong planking. Whatever the material may be, it is hung outside with a curtain somewhat like a large four-post bed. The external railing is separated by a dark passage from the inner, which it

*surrounds; and is of iron filigree painted of a vivid grass green, with a view
to the garden. Here carefully inserted in the verdure, and doubly bright
by contrast, is the guilt or burnished brass work forming the long and
graceful letters of the Suls [thuluth, a round cursive] character, and disposed into the Muslim creed, the Profession of Unity, and similar religious sentences.*

*On the south side, for greater honor, the railing is plated over with
silver, and silver letters are interlaced with it. This fence, which connects
the columns and forbids passage to all men, may be compared to the
baldacchino of Roman churches. It has four gates . . . they are kept constantly closed, except the fourth, which admits into the dark passage
above alluded to the officers who have charge of the treasures there deposited; and the eunuches who sweep the floor, light the lamps and carry
away the presents sometimes thrown in here by devotees. (Burton 1893:
1:314–316)*

Ceremonies in the Mosque at Medina

On first entering the mosque, which is generally done through the western entry called the *Bab al-Salam* or Gate of Peace, the pious visitor proceeds eastward across the Rawda partition (the more sacred sourthern end
of the mosque) toward the tomb chamber. After reciting two short suras
(109 and 112) from the Quran, he passes through the Rawda partition and
stands facing the first, or western, window of the tomb on its southern
side, his back to the southern, or prayer-niche, wall of the mosque. Burckhardt describes what follows.

*With arms half raised he addresses his invocations to Muhammad in
the words "Peace upon you, O Muhammad, Peace, O Envoy of God,"
etc. recapitulating about twenty of the different surnames and honorable
titles of Muhammad and prefixing each with "Peace be upon you." He
next invokes his intercession in heaven, and distinctly mentions the
names of all those relatives and friends whom he is desirous to include in
his prayers; it is for this reason that an inhabitant of Medina never receives a letter from abroad without being entreated, at the end of it, to
mention the writer's name at the tomb of the Prophet. If the pilgrim is
delegated on the pilgrimage for another, he is bound here to mention the
name of his principal.*

*After these prayers are said, the visitor is desired to remain for a few
minutes with his head pressed close against the window in silent adoration; then he steps back and performs a prayer of four prostrations.*

A similar ceremony occurs at the next two windows as well, those marking the tombs of Abu Bakr and Umar.

When this ceremony is finished, the visitor walks round the southeast corner of the Hijrah and presents himself before the tomb of Sitna Fatima, where, after four prostrations, a prayer is addressed to Fatima al-Zuhira, or "Bright-blooming Fatima," as she is called. He then returns to the Rawda, where a prayer is said as a salutation to the Deity on leaving the mosque, which completes this ceremony, the performance of which occupies at most twenty minutes. . . . . The ceremonies may be repeated as often as the visitor wishes, but few perform them all, except on arriving at Medina, or when on the point of departing. It is the general practice, however, to go every day at least once to the window opposite Muhammad's tomb and recite there a short prayer; many persons do it whenever they enter the mosque.

On every spot where prayers are to be said people sit with handkerchiefs spread out to receive the gifts of visitors, which appear to be considered less as alms than as a sort of toll; at least a well-dressed visitor would find it difficult to make his way without paying these taxes. Before the window of Sitna Fatima sits a party of women (Fatima being herself a female saint) who likewise receive gifts in their handkerchiefs. In the Rawda stand the eunuches, or the guardians of the temple, waiting till the visitor has finished his last prayer of salutation to wish him joy at having successfully completed the ziyara or visit, and to receive their fees. And the great gate of the Bab al-Salam is constantly crowded with poor, who closely beset the visitor on leaving the mosque; the porter also expects his compliment as a matter of right. The whole visit cost me about fifteen piasters, and I gave ten piasters to my cicerone; but I might perhaps have gotten through for half that sum. (Burckhardt 1829: 339–340)

How the ritual actually unfolded, and the effect that it had on the head and heart of a pious Muslim, is revealed in the memoirs of Ashchi Dede, the Ottoman bureaucrat who, as we have seen, made the pilgrimage in 1898. This account begins with his arrival in Medina—he had not yet been to Mecca—at the beginning of January 1898:

The chief guide had a fine and rather large selamlik with two or three rooms. . . . We spent the night there, and the next morning early we went to the bath known as the bath of the Prophet, performed our ablutions, and donned the garments appropriate to the place. That is, on our feet yellow outer boots and black slippers, a woolen outer robe over a white inner robe, and on the head a white turban wound over a soft felt cap.

Leaving their quarters, which were quite close to the Prophet's Mosque, Ashchi Dede and his group entered the building.

With the chief guide in front and we behind, reciting the appropriate prayers, we approached the grille (surrounding the tomb of the Prophet).

There we prayed for a long while. Then, going a few paces farther, we likewise recited prayers before (the tomb of) Abu Bakr, may God be pleased with him. After that we went one or two steps farther and repeated special prayers before (the tomb of) Umar, may God be pleased with him. Going from there to the lower end of the Prophet's Garden, we prayed similarly where the angels of the Divine Presence stood. Then, at the foot, we paid our respects to our mother Fatima, may God be pleased with her. Then going a few steps farther, we recited prayers and the sura Ikhlas (Quran 112) (out) through the Door of Gabriel for the souls of the Companions of the Prophet, their wives and children buried in the perfumed earth of the Garden of Baqi'a, may God be pleased with all of them. After that, passing before the special platform for the Aghas of the Noble Sanctuary,[24] facing toward Abbas, the uncle of the Prophet who is buried an hour away on Jabal Uhud, we again recited prayers and the Ikhlas. Then we again came before the presence of the Prophet, performed special prayers, withdrew one or two paces, faced the qibla, gave praise and thanks to God and rendered benedictions. (Findley 1989: 488–489)

A few days later, Ashchi Dede had occasion to return to the tomb.

On account of the approaching arrival of the Amin al-surra, they raised the inner curtains of the Prophet's tomb to sweep. Thus it became possible to observe the interior completely. Immediately summoning all my boldness and saying "If you please, O Messenger of God," I drew near to the grille. Kneeling down doglike (in humility), I looked upward through the window. The morning sun was just presenting its supplication through the tiny windows of the dome, the sides of the blessed tomb were veiled in satin, and the drapery was fastened with rings of iron to aloewood poles there. Thus there was an interval where the part above the poles, the upper part of the blessed tomb, could be seen. How that sacred place caught my eye! How it touched me! My soul attained the Beloved! My soul attained its Lord. My reason departed from my head and I arrived at the wilderness of possession. Giving way at my knees, I collapsed there like a lifeless dog. After a while, I recovered my wits, and my ardor quietened. Truly the spiritual light and the divine manifestations that I saw—praise be a hundred thousand times—remained imprinted on my poor heart. (Findley 1989: 491–492)

The Baqiyya' Cemetery

Burckhardt followed the pilgrim custom of going from the Mosque of the Prophet to the nearby cemetery that held the remains of many of Islam's early heroes.

On the day after the pilgrim has performed his first duties at the mosque and the tomb, he usually visits the burial-ground of the town, in memory of the many saints who lie buried there. It is just beyond the town-walls, near the gate of the Bab Juma, and bears the name of al-Baqiyya. A square of several hundred paces is enclosed by a wall which, on the southern side, joins the suburb, and on the other is surrounded with date-groves. Considering the sanctity of the persons whose bodies it contains, it is a very mean place, and perhaps the most dirty and miserable burial-ground in any eastern town of the size of Medina. It does not contain a single good tomb, nor even any large inscribed blocks of stone covering tombs; but instead, mere rude heaps of earth with low borders of loose stones placed about them.

The Wahhabis are accused of having defaced the tombs, and in proof of this the ruins of small domes and buildings are pointed out, which formerly covered the tombs of Uthman, Abbas, Sitna Fatima, and the aunts of Muhammad, which owed their destruction to these sectaries. But they would certainly not have annihilated every other simple tomb built of stone here, which they did neither at Mecca nor any other place. The miserable state of this cemetery must have existed prior to the Wahhabi conquest and is to be ascribed to the niggardly minds of the townspeople, who are little disposed to incur any expense in honoring the remains of their celebrated countrymen. The whole place is a confused accumulation of heaps of earth, wide pits, rubbish, without a single regular tomb-stone. . . .

The most conspicuous personages that lie buried here are Ibrahim, the son of Muhammad, who died in his youth; Fatima, his daughter, according to the opinion of many, who say that she is buried here and not in the mosque; several of the wives of the Prophet; some of his daughters; his foster-mother; Fatima, the daughter of Asad and the mother of Ali; Abbas ibn Abd al-Muttalib; Uthman ibn Affan, one of the immediate successors of Prophet, who collected the scattered leaves of the Quran into one volume; the "Martyrs," as they are called, who were slain here by the army of heretics under Yazid ibn Mu'awiya, whose commander, Muslim, in A.H. 60 (others say 62) came from Syria and sacked the town, the inhabitants of which had acknowledged the rebel Abdullah ibn Hantala as their chief; Hassan ibn Ali, whose trunk only lies buried here, his head having been sent to Cairo, where it is preserved in the fine mosque called al-Hassaniyya; the Imam Malik ibn Anas, the founder of the sect of the Malikites. Indeed, so rich is Medina in the remains of great saints that they have almost lost their individual importance, while the relics of one of the persons just mentioned would be sufficient to render celebrated any other Muslim town. (Burckhardt 1829: 362–363)

Burton was there in 1853.

There is a tradition that seventy thousand, or according to others a hundred thousand saints, all with faces like full moons, shall cleave on the last day the yawning bosom of al-Baqiyya. About ten thousand of the Ashab, the Companions of the Prophet, and innumerable Sadat [nobles] are here buried: their graves are forgotten, because, in the olden time, tombstones were not placed over the last resting places of mankind. The first of the flesh who shall arise is Muhammad, the second Abu Bakr, the third Umar, then the people of Baqiyya*, among whom is Uthman, the fourth Caliph, and then the incolae of the Jannat al-Ma*ala, the Meccan cemetery. The Prophetic Tradition, "whoever dies at the two Harams shall rise with the Sure on the Day of Judgment," has made these spots priceless in value. . . . It is a pity this people refuses to exhume its relics. . . .*

*The burial place of the Saints is an irregular oblong surrounded by walls which are connected with the suburb at their southwest angle. . . . Around it palm plantations seem to flourish. It is small, considering the extensive use made of it: all that die at Medina, strangers as well as natives, except only heretics and schismatics, expect to be interred in it. It must be choked with corpses, which it could never contain did not the Muslim style of burial greatly favor rapid decomposition, and it has all the inconveniences of "intramural sepulture." The gate is small and ignoble, a mere doorway in the wall. Inside there are no flower-plots, no tall trees, in fact none of the refinements which lighten the gloom of a Christian burial-place. The buildings are simple; they might even be called mean. . . . The ancient monuments were leveled to the ground by Sa*ud the Wahhabi and his puritan followers, who waged pitiless warfare against what must have seemed to them magnificent mausolea, deeming as they did a loose heap of stones sufficient for a grave. . . . The present erections owe their existence, I was told, to the liberality of the Sultans Abd al-Hamid and Mahmud. (Burton 1893: 2:131)*

CHAPTER VI

Steamships and Cholera: The Hajj in Modern Times

THE END OF THE TRADITIONAL HAJJ

IN JANUARY 1842 Leon Roches had a series of private interviews with the Sharif Muhammad ibn Awn at Ta'if. Roches here professes to give a near verbatim transcript of the Sharif's musings, which, even if not exact, must have reflected the mood in Mecca near mid-century.

Where Are the Pilgrims of Yesteryear?

"Where are the days," the Sharif said to me, "when the faith of Muslims drew to the Holy City hundreds of thousands of believers, who came from every quarter of the earth? Religious indifferentism is gradually overcoming Islam, and the number of pilgrims has decreased because of the falling-off of their faith. Previously six great caravans regularly arrived from all points of the compass. Our ancestors saw sovereign princes come to Mecca, followed by entire peoples; the last of the Abbasids, Musta`sim billah [r. 1242–1258] camped at Arafat with 130,000 camels. Once the pilgrimage was regarded as an act commanded by God Himself. Muslims took on as a pious duty the fatigues and privations of the overland journey. All remained pure during the pilgrimage period, and prayer and the reading of the traditions of the Prophet were their sole occupation. Today, scarcely forty or fifty thousand pilgrims visit the House of God. No more than three caravans come here, from Syria, from Egypt, and from the Yemen, and they are small, particularly the last. Most pilgrims come by sea, all engage in commerce, and the spirit of speculation has replaced piety in their hearts. And their conduct, alas, during the pilgrimage period! May God preserve your eyes from the sight of their shameful acts. (Roches 1904: 323)

If the pilgrimage was suffering, it was hardly the fault of the Sultan in Istanbul. Revenues from endowment lands continued to be allocated and gifts sent, official ceremonies for the departure of Hajj officials were regularly celebrated in Istanbul, and Damascus still glowed with excitement as the yearly preparations for the caravan drew near.

The Hajj formally began in Istanbul with the appointment of an Ottoman notable to be the *Amin al-Surra*, or "Master of the Purse," who was described in 1900 as "an official representing His Majesty, our master the Sultan, in transmitting the stipends of the imperial *surra* to their recipients, according to the lists the department of *waqfs* furnishes, copied from the records kept in the department."[1] The Istanbul ceremonies were long and elaborate, ending "in the middle of Ramadan, (when) the *Amin al-Surra* presents a petition to His Majesty the Sultan, asking permission to set forth. Then an imperial decree is granted and a steamship is prepared for them by the relevant Ottoman department, in which they sail to Beirut, which they reach (in about a week) early in the last decade of Ramadan. From Beirut they all proceed to Damascus."[2]

The Syrian Caravan

Until the advent of the steamship and the Suez canal made the sea voyage easier and safer, the Sultan's own Turkish countrymen generally traveled overland through Anatolia and joined the Syrian caravan forming in Damascus. And it was the Syrian caravan too that bore most of the Sultan's gifts to the Holy Cities and their inhabitants. Not unexpectedly, Istanbul paid special attention to this Syrian caravan, as the Anglicized Swiss John Lewis Burckhardt noticed from both Damascus and Mecca in the troubled times at the beginning of the nineteenth century:

The Syrian caravan has always been the strongest, since the time when the Caliphs in person accompanied the pilgrims from Baghdad. It sets out from Constantinople and collects the pilgrims of northern Asia in its passage through Anatolia and Syria, until it reaches Damascus where it remains several weeks. During the whole of the route from Constantinople to Damascus every care is taken for the safety and convenience of the caravan; it is accompanied from town to town by the armed forces of the governors; at every station caravansaries and public fountains have been constructed by former Sultans, to accommodate it on its passage, which is attended so far with continual festivities and rejoicings.

At Damascus it is necessary to prepare for a journey of thirty days across the desert to Medina; and the camels which had transported it thus far must be changed, the Anatolian camel not being able to bear the fatigues of such a journey. Almost every town in the eastern part of Syria furnishes its beasts for the purpose; and the great bedouin shaykhs of the frontiers of that country contract largely for camels with the government of Damascus. Their number must be supposed very great, even if the cara-

van be but thinly attended, when it is considered that besides those carrying water and provisions for the Hajjis and soldiers, their horses and the
spare camels brought to supply such as may fail on the road, daily food for
the camels themselves must be similarly transported; as well as provisions,
which are deposited in castles on the Sham [Syrian] route, to form a supply for the return. The bedouin take good care that the camels shall not
be overloaded, that the numbers wanted may thus be increased. In 1814,
though the caravan consisted of not more than four or five thousand persons, including soldiers and servants, it had fifteen thousand camels.

The Syrian caravan is very well regulated, though, as in all matters of
oriental government, the abuses and exceptions are numerous. The Pasha
of Damascus, or one of his principal officers, always accompanies this
caravan, and gives the signal for encamping and starting by firing a mus-
ket. On the route a troop of horsemen ride in front and another in the
rear, to bring up the stragglers. The different parties of Hajjis, distinguished by their provinces or towns, keep close together; and each knows
its never-varying station in the caravan, which is determined by the geographical proximity of the place from whence it comes. . . . Thus the people of Aleppo always encamp close by those of Homs etc. This regulation
is very necessary to prevent disorder in night marches. (Burckhardt 1829:
247)

Another, even more detailed account of the Syrian pilgrimage was written
in the first year of the twentieth century by Arif al-Munir. The immediate
purpose of his *Book of the Increasing and Eternal Happiness—The Hejaz
Railway* was to counter the opposition to a truly radical proposal being
discussed in Istanbul: the construction of a railway from Damascus to
Medina. But the book also contains a highly detailed account of the Syrian overland caravan, the last we possess before the railway, the motorcar,
and, finally, the airplane changed its character forever.[3]

The "Master of the Purse"

Arif is particularly detailed on the tasks delegated to the various officials
attached to the Hajj, the most important of which was doubtless the
Amin al-Surra, or "Master of the Purse."

In the past the Syrian pilgrimage caravan has had considerable importance. This was due to the fact that an imperial decree would arrive, appointing one of the greatest dignitaries in Istanbul as the amin al-surra on
behalf of the sultan. This was established by the late Ottoman Sultan
Selim I, as the bearer of gifts for the people of Sham [Damascus] and
Quds [Jerusalem] and the Haramayn [the "Two Sanctuaries," Mecca and

Medina]. On the 15th of Sha*ban several scholars, imams, chassis and some of the officials of the department of waqfs proceed to the anteroom of the imperial palace in Istanbul. The amin al-surra presents himself before His Majesty the sultan, the Victorious, the Commander of the Faithful. . . . As is customary, they gather there, then set out together in a large procession and go to Scutari. It was here that the "march of the purses" used to start when it proceeded to Damascus by land via Anatolia.

They remain there until mid-Ramadan. Then they request permission of the sultan to depart. When the imperial irade [decree] arrives nowadays they travel by sea to Beirut, and thence to Damascus. If the amin al-surra must attend to any such affairs in Beirut as cashing a bill of exchange, he would remain there to settle them; if not, he would proceed directly to Damascus. The Vali of Syria, in his administrative council, would have already started to provide for the needs of the pilgrimage to the Hijaz: establishing fees and prices for transportation, litters, sedans, seats and palfreys; appointing muqawwims, those entitled to rent tents and camels to the pilgrims, or bring them water; selecting one of them to be in charge of carrying the Mahmal, the surra, the amin al-surra, the jukhadar, and other officials of the pilgrimage, such as the superintendent. The muqawwim is the title of the chief camel-master. This is done with the knowledge [and consent] of the superintendent (muhafiz) of the pilgrimage who takes it from and returns it to Damascus. Formerly the superintendent used to be the Vali of the Vilayet of Syria. One of the duties ascribed to him was to accompany the pilgrimage to Mecca to supervise it, going and returning, in the same manner that the Vali of Tripoli in Syria [Lebanon] used to lead the relief convoy (jurdi) to meet the Syrian caravan with supplies.

Two or three days after the amin al-surra arrives (in Damascus) he starts distributing their due to those deserving the charity of the surra, whether in cash, in grain, clothes, slippers, shoes, snuff and other things, according to the written instructions he received in the ledger he received from the department of waqfs in Istanbul. Then a representative of those deserving the surra comes to Damascus from Jerusalem. He brings along legal proof of his being the representative entitled to obtain the charity allotted to the Jerusalemites. Then the Syrian and other pilgrims busy themselves to acquire provisions, clothes, riding animals, fodder, water skins, tents, and the like, that they need. The superintendent of the pilgrimage starts buying what he and his retinue would need in the way of provisions, ammunition and equipment. He also supplies information to the surgeon-physician the government has appointed to accompany the pilgrimage, to doctor and cure the pilgrims free of cost and supply them with free medicine. (Arif al-Munir 1971: 71–72)

The Mahmal Procession

The ceremonies continued. On the thirteenth of Shawwal, olive oil, the gift for the Haramayn from Kafr Susa and other villages in Syria, is collected and carried in procession across Damascus to be deposited in the Government House, "which serves as a depot for some of the things pertaining to the pilgrimage." A similar procession in the afternoon of the same day features the large beeswax candles prepared for the Haramayn.

The transport of special candles for the sanctuaries of the Holy Cities was a small part of a highly complex operation, but for the functionary charged with the task it was both an honor and a privilege. In 1898 that honor was bestowed on Ashchi Dede Ibrahim Khalil, an elderly and pious civil servant who had served the empire long and well, notably in Damascus. He recalled the event in his memoirs:

> Two years ago, when I was in Istanbul, the noble Trusteeship of the Treasure to be sent to Mecca and Medina [that is, the office of Amin al-Surra] for the year 1315 [1898] was entrusted to His Excellency, our soul and spirit, Mukhtar Effendi; and this shameless sinner . . . had firm intentions from that date on, setting by from my salary each month for necessary expenses (of accompanying him).

All preparations made, Ashchi Dede left his home in Edirne by train for Istanbul in January 1898.

> As soon as I got off the train, I went straight to the mansion of His Excellency, the Corresponding Secretary (of the Ministry of War) and paid my respects to him in the presence of the brethren there. He displayed extraordinary pleasure and said: "The office of steward (kethuda) (of the surra) was to have been entrusted to you, but what could be done when another was recommended by order from the palace? . . . Now there is a duty greater and more noble than the stewardship or anything else; and that is the sacred office of transporting twenty-five chests of white wax candles specially prepared and embellished for the Prophet's Garden in (the mosque at) Medina. So, then, I have entrusted this office to you. Ten men will accompany you. Take them, see to the safeguarding of the money that will be given to you to cover necessary expenses en route, and take care that the candles reach Medina. (Findley 1989: 482–483)

And so they did:

> Since it was a fulfillment of duty, praise be that the candles for the tomb of the Prophet were accepted as free of breakage, compared to those

of the year before. . . . They showed us the candles of the previous year. They were all in bits and completely broken. They had to be melted down and remade in Medina. That much breakage had not been seen (before). "What could we do? The qaʾim maqam [the district officer] at Yanbu got his hands on them; they wouldn't let us interfere. Turn them over to us and we'll send them," they said. No doubt the camel-drivers, putting them onto and off their camels, had reduced them to that state. In any case, if it please God, our humble service was acceptable to His Messenger. (Findley 1989: 490)

To return to the preparations in Damascus, on the fourteenth of Shawwal the standard (*sanjak*) of the pilgrimage is taken from its storage place at army headquarters and carried in another procession to the quarters of the Ottoman military commander. On the fifteenth, it is the turn of the Mahmal, which was kept in Istanbul and transported with the *Amin al-Surra* to Damascus for the pilgrimage. This was the most elaborate of the processions.

The military band sets forth first. It is followed by the cavalry which paces to guard the caravan; then a unit of mounted gendarmerie, then the sedans of the amin al-surra and the superintendent of the pilgrimage, then the ranking dignitaries—two by two—and the amin al-surra himself, bringing up the rear and bidding farewell to the crowd. All wear their official uniforms with their medals. Then comes the representative of the naqib al-ashraf [the dean of the linear descendants of the Prophet], wearing a green turban, while a few others wear green jubbas. The accoutrements of the naqib's mare and its reins are green; his servants also wear green turbans and green jubbas. The muezzins surround the Mahmal, most of them in front of it, then come the students of the military schools on its four sides. . . . They are preceded by the Mawlawi dervishes, followers of Jalal al-Din Rumi, in two long rows, with their shaykh riding in front, praising Allah's name. The camel with the standard paces behind the Mahmal. Sometimes the representative of the naqib al-ashraf has a difference of opinion with the shaykh of the Mawlawi dervishes concerning precedence, each desiring the other to precede him. Then the Akil [Bedouin escorts] march behind the Mahmal and the standard, carrying one or more flags and drums, which they play while they chant in their own style in groups answering one another while they ride their male and female camels. . . . The caravan proceeds thus, with an officer called the head of protocol (teshrifatji) in its midst. He watches over everyone, holding a written paper that lists the names of the riders and their ranks. If one of these rides either before or after his appropriate place, he makes him return to it.

The Mahmal procession advances through the densely packed streets of Damascus to the Bab Misr, later called the Damascus Gate and the site of the Hijaz Railway station. Ten minutes beyond is a small shrine called al-Asali, where tents have been set up and all the dignitaries have tea before returning to the city. The Mahmal and standard are then taken to Muzayrib to await the beginning of the march on the twenty-eighth or twenty-ninth of Shawwal. That, at any rate, is the way it once was.

All this was so in earlier times. Nowadays on the 3rd of Shawwal there are the festivities of the candles, while as a whole those of the oil have been canceled, despite the importance formerly attached to them. On the 4th of Shawwal there are the festivities of the standard, according to the previous custom. On the 5th the crowds and troops rejoice with the Mahmal; but the military commander, the Vali, the qadi and the mufti do not ride horses at the procession's head; rather, before the procession they ride to the station in their carriages wearing their official uniforms, both on the caravan's going and its return. They proceed to the tents at the aforementioned station of al-Asali and greet the amin al-surra. . . . They sit awhile, then leave in their carriages before the procession. In the same fashion (nowadays) most of the dignitaries do not ride in the procession at all. Some of them imitate the military commander and the Vali [the Ottoman governor], and also ride in carriages. This is a result of personal grudges and individual ambitions, which cannot be listed in detail here. (Arif al-Munir 1971: 76–79)

ARRANGEMENTS LARGE AND SMALL

Ever since they assumed sovereignty over the Hijaz and its holy places in the seventeenth century, the Ottoman Sultans had fulfilled their responsibilities of underwriting the costs of the annual caravans from Cairo and Damascus and of sending the expensive subsidies that had become part of the "entitlements" of many residents of the Holy Cities. Beyond that, they made little effort to control the pilgrimage as such. But with increased European commercial interest in the Red Sea, and with rising European concerns that the Hajj was the center and the Hajjis the carriers of fatal diseases into the heart of Europe, the Sultans began to show more concern for the holy places. They had little choice, perhaps: if the Sultans would not rule the Hijaz, then the European powers might, and perhaps even with the cooperation of the always pliant and opportunistic Sharifs of Mecca.

More stringent Ottoman control of the Hijaz was manifested in a number of ways. The governor's hand was strengthened, for example, by increasing the garrison troops in Jidda, and a form of Ottoman municipal government was imposed upon Mecca, which had previously been run simply as a sharifal fief. These purely internal measures attracted little outside attention, until the Turks insisted, in the wake of the assassination of Sharif Husayn in 1880 by a Baluchi tribesman,[4] that henceforward all foreigners entering Ottoman territory would be required to possess a passport and a visa.[5]

Costs to the Government

The visa requirement for foreign Hajjis probably brought some much-needed revenue into Ottoman coffers—the British indeed suspected that was the entire point of the exercise—but the price for the now traditional ceremony and the newly enhanced security was high. And because the Vali, or Ottoman governor, of Jidda had few resources of his own—there was a constant struggle with the Sharif over the disposition of the customs revenues of the port—the provincial administration that was to bear some of these costs instead, of necessity, drew from the imperial exchequer.

The chief expense by far within the Hijaz was security—meaning, because there were as yet no external dangers to the province, the support of the troops that protected the pilgrimage caravans that passed through it.[6] The imperial government's outlay was enormous, but Sultan could ill afford to take chances with either the safety of the caravan or the well-being of the notables of his Holy Cities. News of a disaster in the first or an unseemly scanting in the second would travel quickly all over the Abode of Islam with each season's returning pilgrims. So the caravans had to be fitted out and protected along the way with both a military escort and the wholesale distribution of subsidies and bribes to the bedouin, for which the Sharif often served as the intermediary.[7] Moreover, budget figures from the 1880s show that nearly 18,000 Turkish liras were spent on pensions and gifts for the religious and political elite of the Holy Cities, and another 25,500 and more paid for the distribution of foodstuffs, all in addition to the money annually budgeted for the upkeep of the two shrines and their servants.[8] Somewhat smaller amounts were forthcoming from the government of Egypt, which bore the additional expense of providing a new gold-embroidered *kiswa*, or covering, for the Ka'ba each year,[9] and from the vilayets, or provinces, of Beirut and Syria, which helped underwrite the costs of the Damascus pilgrimage.[10]

Costs to the Pilgrims

Although an impoverished pilgrim might expect to receive some government subsidy to help fulfill this pious obligation, most pilgrims bore the costs on their own shoulders. And, as Burckhardt details, these could be considerable for overland travelers.

The Hajjis usually contract for the journey with a muqawwim,[11] one who speculates in the furnishings of camels and provisions to the Hajj. From twenty to thirty pilgrims are under the care of the same muqawwim, who has his tents and servants and saves the Hajjis from all fatigue and trouble on the road: their tent, coffee, water, breakfast and dinner are prepared for them, and they need not take the slightest trouble about packing and loading. If a camel should die, the muqawwim must find another; and however great may be the want of provisions on the road, he must furnish his passengers with their daily meals. In 1814 the hire of one muqawwim, and the boarding at his table, was one hundred and fifty dollars from Damascus to Medina, and fifty more from Medina to Mecca. Out of these two hundred dollars, sixty were given by the muqawwim to a man who led the camel by the halter during the night marches, a precaution necessary in so great a caravan, when the rider usually sleeps, and the animal might otherwise easily wander from the path. In addition to the stipulated hire, the muqawwim always receives some presents from the pilgrim. On the return to Syria the sum is something less, as many camels then go unloaded.

Few travelers choose to perform the journey at their own risk, or upon their own camels; for if they are not particularly protected by the soldiery, or the chief of the caravan, they find it difficult to escape the ill-treatment of the muqawwim at watering-places, as well as on the march; the latter endeavoring to check, by every means in their power, the practice of traveling independent of them, so that it is rarely done except by rich Hajjis who have the means of forming a party of their own amounting to forty or fifty individuals. (Burckhardt 1829: 248–249)

In the late nineteenth century, and particularly after the opening of the Suez Canal, more and more pilgrims journeyed to Mecca via ship to Yanbu or Jidda. Not only Egyptians, but Syrians and Anatolians sailed from Beirut through the canal, and ever-increasing numbers of Indian and Indonesian pilgrims arrived from across the Indian Ocean. In addition to the long-haul fare to and from the port of embarkation (see below), the seaborne pilgrim faced numerous expenses once landed in the Hijaz: a transfer fee to get from ship to land in Jidda, at least overnight lodging in Jidda, local camel hire from Jidda to Mecca, and the costs of guides, lodging, and transportation at Mecca and Medina—all fees that were usually included in the "package" contracts for the caravan passenger.[12] The results might be well imagined. The Hijaz began to fill up with impoverished pilgrims from East Asia who had managed to get to Mecca but were then stranded. They were a problem for the Hijaz, where almost everyone was supported by a government dole to begin with, as well as for the colonial powers, Britain in India and the Netherlands in the East Indies, whose subjects these impoverished Hajjis were. Eventually no would-be pilgrim was permitted to leave the East Indies or Malaysia without a paid return ticket, and there was pressure on Great Britain to do likewise with Indian Muslims.[13]

Hossein Kazemzadeh, a Persian on Hajj in 1910–1911, took particular note of the wide gap between rich and poor among the Indians making the pilgrimage, though the contrast was doubtless true of other groups as well:

Indian pilgrims are of a very mixed character. Some are rich to the point of prodigality, others have barely the wherewithal to stay alive. You see rich people who will pay several pounds for a flacon of perfume, pour it all out on their heads and walk off; or who will pay several rupees for a glass of Zamzam water which, if they waited a few moments, they could have had for nothing. On the other hand, there are wretches in a state of total privation, lying nearly nude along the road, seeking some relief in the shade of the bushes called mughilan, the only vegetation which abounds in these deserts. Passers-by give something to eat to these unfortunates who are at the mercy of the sun and the sand, and occasionally some generous person will take them with them to Mecca on their camels.

The English and Dutch have put certain monetary conditions on the pilgrimage for their Muslim subjects, conditions which make the pilgrimage impossible for those with insufficient means to the end of avoiding such miseries; but for all that the poor can still be seen among those pilgrims. (Kazemzadeh 1912: 192–193)

We get some idea of how the poorest of the poor pilgrims fared aboard ship from Lieutenant J. R. Wellsted, the Indian Navy officer engaged in a survey of the Red Sea in 1835:

Attached to the caravans, and at the various stations, are a number of wretched beings, for the most part in the last stage of disease, and safely dependent on the precarious charity of their fellow travelers for the means of visiting and returning from the holy cities. To prevent their accumulation at the different ports, where they would probably engender disease, they are portioned out into separate parties by the governors, who compel the different boats and ships to furnish them with provisions, and convey them, free of expense, to the various ports whither they may be proceeding.

To evade this burden, the honest captains do not scruple to use every artifice, and the poor wretches are frequently enticed out of the vessel and left at the first place she may touch at. If that is near any port having a competent authority, he places them on board the next vessel; but if, as more commonly happens, they are landed on some unfrequented shore, a miserable death by thirst and starvation awaits them. (Wellsted 1838: 2:267–268)

Mulcting the Pilgrims

If it were simply a matter of travel expenses, the situation for the ordinary pilgrim would be grim enough; but in addition to those costs, however inflated they might be, there were the various extortion schemes apparently harbored by every reasonably adult Hijazi from the least of the guides right up to, and of course including, the Sharif himself. Perhaps the most notorious of the schemes was the one contrived, with the aid of a new technology, by Awn al-Rafiq (Sharif, 1882–1905). One Osman Bey, a confidant of the Sultan and the relative of the Sharif by marriage, used his printing press in Istanbul to produce 10,000 Qurans, which he then sold to the Sharif for 2,500 Turkish liras. The Sharif in turn forced every East Indian pilgrim to purchase one. When the Netherlands consul intervened, bookstores then had the honor of purchasing the remaining copies, at the Sharif's prices of course. The same scheme was floated again in 1888, although this time the guides were constrained to buy the Qurans, which they then sold to their pilgrim clients at triple their own purchase price.[14]

There is perhaps little to wonder at in this. As almost every observer of the Meccan economy has remarked, the pilgrims represented the only source of income in an impoverished land, and it mattered little to the Hijazis that the sources of their livelihood were fulfilling a religious obligation. Hossein Kazemzadeh reflected philosophically, and resignedly, on the condition in 1912:

The pilgrimage is the sole resource in these desert and lifeless lands which do not even possess local means of transport. Like the farmer who tries to get the maximum possible yield at his harvest, so these people, who have no other means of subsistence save what they can get from the pilgrims, always strive to get as much profit as they can during the pilgrimage period, which is for them what a harvest is for others.

It is in fact in this organization (of guides) and in this land that one can observe the struggle for survival. The inhabitants realize perfectly well that between pilgrimages they must necessarily remain inactive; they can produce nothing. Their attempts at monopoly resemble the feverish activity of the poorer classes in Europe on the eve of a general strike. Just as we see people there, if they do not have the means to buy expensive provi-

sions, hurry to snap up and stockpile food, charcoal, etc. against the days when a prolonged strike might deprive them of basic necessities, so too the residents of Mecca and Jidda, and particularly those who live off the pilgrimage, hasten to amass as many resources as they can for the days when nature, with its excessive heat, will render them incapable of providing for their own subsistence. That is the reason why people who are engaged in the pilgrim business attempt the most clever schemes to attract clients, including deceits and frauds and even the kind of competitive brawls that require the intervention of the authorities to restore order. (Kazemzadeh 1912: 154–155)

The Guides Revisited

Kazemzadeh offered his observations on the Meccan economy with an eye rather specifically on the guild organization of guides in the Hijaz. We have already seen how these aggressive ciceroni appeared to European observers. Muslim impressions were not entirely different, though perhaps, like Kazemzadeh's, somewhat more sympathetic to the motives that lay behind the conduct. If we look to his account and to that of Mirza Farahani, an Iranian notable who made the pilgrimage in 1885, it is apparent that the pilgrim trade had become considerably more internationalized through the nineteenth century with the introduction of the steamship and the opening of the Suez Canal.

In Mecca there are about thirty Shi'ite and Sunni pilgrim guides appointed by the Sharif of Mecca who have permits for leading pilgrimages. Usually they and their fathers have been pilgrim-guides for centuries. Each of them has seven or eight assistants and servants. Before the pilgrimage season begins, they go to the cities which are transit points for pilgrims such as Najaf, Bombay, Bushire, Bandar Abbas, Rasht, Istanbul and Odessa. They issue to everyone they locate who wants to go to Mecca the invitation: "You are without information about the practices and activities there; you must have someone knowledgeable and a pilgrim guide; you will not find (anyone) better than me." Of course, the pilgrims are beseeching God that they might have a knowledgeable man who will work hard on their behalf. Another thing they do is to promise some of the ʿakkam, hamleh-dars, and hajjeh-forushes (who are well known and come to Mecca every year) as follows: "I will give you one Levant dollar (which is about 6,000 Iranian dinars) for every pilgrim you bring for me." (Farahani 1990: 184)

Kazemzadeh describes who these local pilgrimage agents were and what they did:

The hamledar (caravan conductor) will escort the pilgrims. . . . He is a man who has made the pilgrimage several times, knows the routes, the Arabs [the bedouin] and their chiefs, and is experienced in traveling across the desert. . . . There are some of them who own hundreds of tents, camels, mules, donkeys, etc. and are rather rich.

In the caravan itself there are, in addition to the hamledar, servants called ʿakkams who are hired by the hamledar to serve the pilgrims, . . . chavushes, whose chief mission is to chant for the pilgrims poems in honor of the (Shiʿite) Imams, dervishes, . . . and hajjehforushes, literally, those who sell their pilgrimage, that is to say, who make the Hajj in the name of and at the expense of someone with whom they have contracted. (Kazemzadeh 1912: 144–146)

We return to Farahani's account:

After making these preparations, they return to Mecca near the beginning of the pilgrimage season. For their part, these ʿakkam, hamleh-dars, and hajjeh-forushes, with a view to making a profit for themselves, assure every pilgrim they see or know of the commendability of that pilgrim guide. . . .

Another thing they do is to send one of their agents or servants to every point of entry for pilgrims to the Hijaz . . . in order to watch out and assemble the followers there. . . . If the pilgrim is a notable, the pilgrim-guide goes out a day's journey or two to welcome him and also invites him home one night to give him supper. Thus, the pilgrim is totally dependent upon the pilgrim-guide and utterly at his mercy. If, for instance, he has any goods to sell, he is compelled to inform and seek the approval of his pilgrim-guide, who arranges with the buyer to get half of the money for those goods. And if, for instance, the pilgrim wants goods from there [Mecca] for gifts or to buy for commerce, (the guide will) go to the seller (and say) "Let that pilgrim buy at a high price." At least half of the profit goes to the guide. Or if, for instance, the pilgrim wants to go from Jidda to Saʿdiyya or Mecca, or to hire transports from Mecca to Medina or Yanbu, this, of course, must be done with the assistance of the pilgrim-guide.[15] Thus this year everyone who went from Jidda to the Saʿdiyya boundary paid eighteen Levant dollars to hire camels. Of these eighteen Levant dollars, seven is the fare for the camel that carries one, while for each camel the Pasha, the Sharif, the consul, the pilgrim-guide and the camel broker (mukharrij) take eleven dollars.

If (the pilgrim) wants to rent a place to stay in Jidda or Mecca, the pilgrim-guide has a role in that and will receive a share. If the pilgrim goes to Arafat or Mina, part of the charge for the beast of burden and the tent goes to the pilgrim-guide. If the pilgrim or someone in his party dies, a payment to the pilgrim-guide is expected for the vows and prayers which *are the special duty of the pilgrim-guide. In the end, if the pilgrim is poor and has little money, he must certainly give at least two Levant dollars . . . as remuneration to the pilgrim-guide. If he does not pay, or does not have the money, the matter will result in hostility, disputes and petitions to the Sharif, the governor and the consuls. It will be collected by force, violence or the imprisonment of the helpless pilgrim. If the pilgrim is wealthy and a dignitary, the pilgrim-guide will try as hard as he can to collect from one to ten lira from him. (Farahani 1990: 184–185)*

Certain of the Meccan *mutawwifs*, or guides, specialized in Persian pilgrims. They were, Kazemzadeh reports, generally Arabized Persians, and in 1910 there were seven, including a woman, "which shows that the charge is reserved to certain families who remain responsible even after the death of the primary agent." The seven had divided up the Iranian provinces among them and were responsible to the Sharif for the security of the persons and goods of their clients. Each had available houses and camels for lease to the pilgrims, at prices fixed by the government.

What is owed to the guide, apart from gifts and tips, is one majidiyya or four francs per pilgrim. To make the collection easier, this cost is added, by the permission of the Sharif, to the camel rental. The pilgrims also pay a tax of one majidiyya to the municipality of Mecca. (Kazemzadeh 1912: 153)

Pilgrimage Arrangements (1910–1911)

By the opening years of the twentieth century the pilgrimage system was highly organized and seemed to function quite smoothly:

When the time of the pilgrimage approaches people who intend to make the Hajj seek out companions to form a group or caravan. At the same time the hamledars, who will conduct the pilgrims on the way, arrive, each in the city or province of his clientage, and proceed to negotiate their contracts with the pilgrims and thus put together a caravan. It is the custom in some of the cities of Persia to summon the inhabitants to pilgrimage to Mecca by a herald called a chavush who chants religious songs in the streets of the city and exhorts the residents to make the pilgrimage. (Kazemzadeh 1912: 144)

As Kazemzadeh noted, contracts were solicited and signed in the pilgrim's home town well before departure.

Before describing the various types of contracts, it should be noted that the proceedings are not officially registered and that the government imposes no legal formalities in connection with them. The government requires only the mutual consent of contracting parties and will intervene only in the case of a dispute. . . . These contracts are made in the presence of a mulla who certifies the deed by placing his seal upon it, or even simply between the contracting parties without recourse to a mulla. (Kazemzadeh 1912: 148)

A pilgrim negotiating with a caravan leader could choose one of three types of contracts, as described by Kazemzadeh.

1. The simple contract or verbal agreement by which the pilgrims who have their own mounts, servants and supplies, or who are making the pilgrimage on foot, ask only to accompany the caravan in order to avoid making the journey alone.[16] In such cases it is the custom to give a gift to the caravan leader and tips to the caravan servants, even though there is no need of the services of these latter.

2. A contract for the rental of mounts, tents and service. This kind of contract can be written or verbal, and by it the caravan leader contracts to provide to the pilgrim such and such a mount, from this place to that, at a cost fixed by the contract, as well as whatever is necessary for the trip, upon payment of costs. The pilgrim is free to choose his own lodgings in the various cities en route, as well as during his stay at Arafat and Mina.

3. The contract called mukaffa. This contract must be drawn up in duplicate and signed by both parties. By it the caravan leader undertakes to provide everything necessary for the journey, from the day of departure to the return to Persia, both dates specified in the contract. Thus mounts, lodging, service, the costs of quarantine, the "brotherhood taxes," food, taxes on passports, etc. will all be picked up by the caravan leader. The pilgrim undertakes to pay, in two or three payments, the sum agreed upon. This sum varies according to distance, the route that is chosen, lodging and food, from between 150 and 400 tomans [600–1,600 francs].

This contract is the rarest and least certain for the pilgrim since it puts him entirely at the mercy of the caravan leader. . . . Generally the caravan leader wishes to discuss future terms in the middle of the journey, using pressure and even threats and the withholding of food, relying on the fact that in the middle of the desert there is no authority to constrain him to observe the terms already agreed upon.

Despite all the formalities, these contracts, the last in particular, are the subject of a great many disputes on both sides. (Kazemzadeh 1912: 148–149)

Earlier generations of pilgrims generally had to carry all their funds with them—and run the risk of losing the entire purse to thieves along the way—but by the nineteenth century the letter of credit had somewhat reduced the risk:

Usually pilgrims do not carry with them all the money required for the trip. Instead they provide themselves with barats or letters of credit to be cashed in at such and such a city. . . . A merchant or a commercial house with agents in a foreign city writes them a letter of credit ordering them to pay the sum of X to Mr. X who had paid the said sum to the writer. The endorser of the barat, before he makes the payment, verifies the identity of the bearer from his passport, the testimony of other merchants of the city, or by a certification of the (pilgrim's) Consul General if the bearer is not otherwise known. (Kazemzadeh 1912: 147)

Arriving at Jidda

When a boat enters the port of Jidda its arrival is publicly announced by a crier who goes around the various quarters announcing the arrival or departure of such and such a ship at such and such an hour. Then the guides' agents (wakil) and the landlords (khanedar) gather at the port. One man, who is called the "Iranian deputy" has the task of asking the pilgrims the name of their guide.[17] . . . When he has learned who they are, he points each one to the guide's wakil and directs him to follow where he leads. He repeats this question to each group and notes down in his notebook the number of pilgrims assigned to the wakil of each guide. Wakils and landlords each pay a fee of 2 piasters [40 centimes] for each pilgrim assigned to them. . . .

When the pilgrims have been divided up in this fashion, each agent sends a message to his guide to tell him the number of his pilgrims and the day of their departure from Jidda for Mecca so that this latter can send his servants to the gate of the city to receive them. . . .

The rental of rooms at Jidda has been fixed by the government at 2 piasters a day per pilgrim. Under the former regime the fee was up to 10 piasters a pilgrim, of which 5 went to the renter and the remainder was divided between the (pilgrim's) consul and local officials. No more than eight persons can share a room, although formerly there were more than twenty, packed in like sheep in stalls.

As for the rental of camels and other mounts from Jidda to Mecca, this is the charge of the camel-broker (mukharrij) designated by the Sharif. All the camel-drivers must be listed on his records, and the pilgrims or their caravan leaders or the wakils who wish to rent camels must present themselves to the camel-broker and pay the rate fixed by the government. . . . The camel driver receives his due from the broker, which amounts to about 5 piasters [one franc] per camel. (Kazemzadeh 1912: 155–157)

A Pilgrim's Handbook circa 1910

How little the Hajj had changed over the centuries may be judged from a Turkish handbook current in Constantinople in 1910. Kazemzadeh heard it being read aloud among the Turkestani pilgrims gathered in the capital.

During the march, never dismount from your camel, and at night, when the stopping-place has been reached, do not dismount until the camel-driver says to, since there are always suspicious people in these places.

When you do dismount, do not leave your luggage; those who do in order to relieve themselves, turning their back to the mountain and their eyes from their baggage, run the risk of having their throats cut or being robbed. That is why you should, in those circumstances, dig a hole in the sand near to where the baggage is and relieve yourself without embarrassment.

If you wish to sleep, it should be done in shifts so that someone can watch that people's possessions are not stolen or that the camels are not run off from the caravan by the Haramis.[18]

Never argue with the camel-drivers: if they are fed each day from the pilgrim's own provisions and if they are given the usual bakhshish, one's person and belongings will be secure.

Camels should be mounted before the departure of the caravan. A large number of pilgrims, and particularly the elderly who cannot move with agility, lose their camels, complain, seek out their companions and end up behind the caravan; they are simply delivering themselves up to brigands and Haramis.

To which Kazemzadeh added his own warning:

Those are the lessons that every pilgrim should learn before setting out. Inexperience and naiveté cause a great many accidents and expose the pilgrims to considerable danger en route. Sometimes there are malicious people who join the caravan and pretending to Islamic brotherhood, they give the pilgrims tobacco mixed with a substance that puts them to sleep, after which they rob them. (Kazemzadeh 1912: 197–198)

GETTING THERE: TRANSPORTATION
ON SEA AND LAND

As already noted, the sea route to the Hijaz became increasingly popular in the nineteenth century. There had always been crossings from Egyptian and African ports to the Hijaz coast, but by the mid-nineteenth century steamships were reducing the trip from Suez to Jidda, which took anywhere from thirty to forty days by sail, to a mere three. And by the end of the century there was another steamship service from the Persian Gulf to Jidda:

The pilgrims who pass by way of the Persian Gulf use the ships of the Persian maritime company called Nasiri, founded during the reign of

Nasir al-Din Shah by the merchants of Shiraz and Bushire—the share-holders are all Persians—and which presently [1911] operates a service be-tween Bushire and Jidda. The ships sail under the protection of the Brit-ish flag. The company has at present eighteen ships, which bear Persian names like Muzafferi, Humayun, Khusraw, Islami, Rahmani, Husayni, etc. The captains are generally English, though sometimes Indian. On each ship there are a number of Parsis who serve as secretaries and transla-tors, to facilitate the service and hear the complaints of the pilgrims. Each year the company's agent at Jidda gives away hundreds of free tickets to poor pilgrims and dervishes. (Kazemzadeh 1912: 151)

As the number of seafaring pilgrims increased, so too did the perils of the voyage. If steamships enabled more pilgrims to come more quickly and from longer distances to Mecca, the companies that owned or chartered them could make enormous profits. Ships, some of them of dubious sea-worthiness, were often crammed to the bulkheads with as many bodies as the human condition could bear. Food and particularly drinking water were often in short supply—pilgrims were expected to carry their own provisions and do their own cooking—and the only sanitary facility was the sea itself.

Everyone recognized the appalling circumstances of these voyages, and there were calls for government intervention. The Ottomans, who had no financial stake in the business, were eager to limit the number of passen-gers that could be carried per square foot or per deadweight ton, but the British, who almost monopolized the steamship business until the Dutch entered the trade in the 1870s, were reluctant. In 1886 the government of India appointed the firm of Thomas Cook & Son to be the sole agent for the transport of pilgrims from India to the Hijaz. Then, in the following year, it introduced the Native Passenger Ship Act, soon followed in the next year by similar "Pilgrim Traffic Regulations" from the Ottomans, both of which put severe limitations on the number of passengers permis-sible on any pilgrimage vessel and further mandated the presence of one or more physicians on ships of certain sizes.[19]

From Suez to Jidda

The Persian pilgrim Mirza Mohammed Farahani embarked upon one of the Red Sea steamships from Suez to Jidda in 1885.

We stayed at Suez Friday . . . Saturday . . . and Sunday. The morning of Monday, the twelfth of Dhu al-Qaʿda [23 August 1885], we took our baggage and belongings and went first to the door of the customs house, which is an enclosure beside the sea. We waited three hours at the door of the customs until all the pilgrims had come and gathered there. After that, the customs inspectors came and looked at the people's baggage. In spite of the fact that all of the pilgrims were being carried by rowboat from one particular place, nevertheless most of the baggage and freight was not inspected and was passed nonchalantly. They did not inspect our baggage. If someone had numerous dutiable goods, it was possible to give money secretly to one of the customs inspectors so they would not open the baggage.

After finishing with the customs, the pilgrims with baggage and goods immediately (left) the customs house enclosure and boarded rowboats. In accordance with Khedival decree, these rowboats which transport people must assemble before a trip one farsakh over water at a place which the government had built beside the sea. The rowboats with the passengers must line up in an orderly fashion. At this place there are ten or twelve Arab families who have built houses and have also pitched tents there (to serve) as coffee houses and groceries. They bring many watermelons and some other food items for sale there on the days the pilgrims depart. In this building there is an official on behalf of the Khedive. He also has four assistants. The day the pilgrims depart that official with his assistants come out of the building near noon. In the event that all the pilgrims who have come are arranged and waiting in good order on the sea in the rowboats, they then take off the passengers from every rowboat and, person by person, they first inspect one's Ottoman visa which was obtained in Istanbul. Then they inspect the health certificate that was obtained from the physician. One person also comes on board the rowboat and searches the baggage and freight (to see that) no one without a passport has been hidden under the baggage and freight. They very sternly prevent anyone without a passport from going unless he pays a considerable fee and gets a new passport from this same official.

Anyhow, this official looks at all the people in the rowboats. Meanwhile, he makes an inventory of how many rowboats (there are) and how many people have been transported in each rowboat and the amount of fares that have been collected. They give two-thirds of the fares to the rowboat owners and take one third as haqq miri, that is the government tax. (Farahani 1990: 172–173)

This apparently orderly procedure, with distinctly "modern" government bureaucrats supervising the pilgrims, contrasts sharply with medieval accounts of embarkation. It was the innovation of Muhammad Ali, Pasha of Egypt a half century earlier, as we are told by Lieutenant Wellsted of the Red Sea survey of 1835.

The regulations which Muhammad Ali has established at the different ports relative to the embarkation, passage and disembarkment of pilgrims, are salutary and judicious. The number of passengers assigned to each *vessel is limited in proportion to her size, which number she is on no account permitted to exceed. Many of the boats make several voyages during the season. To prevent confusion, or the exercise of any undue preference, a register is kept of the pilgrims as they arrive, and they are subsequently embarked in the same order. The amount of passage money cannot be fixed at any precise sum, since all pay according to their supposed means; but among the middle classes it may be averaged at six dollars from Suez, and four dollars from Qusayr (farther down the coast of Egypt). (Wellsted 1838: 2:264–265)*

We return to Farahani's account.

The steamship did not leave the night before Tuesday the thirteenth nor on Tuesday itself until two hours before sunset. It carried many passengers. About 1,000 people gathered on this boat, of whom 200 were Iranians and the rest were Ottomans, Egyptians and people from Bukhara. The women's place was on a special deck the sides of which had been screened off. The storerooms and boiler rooms were full of people. It was very crowded. They did not charge excess fare for extra baggage but they took (it) to the hold down below (where it) was stained or damaged. They are not as exacting on this ship as is the manner on the European steamships. Everyone cooks things everywhere on the ship. There is no prohibition of water-pipes or samovars.

Two hours before sunset the ship departed. Then someone came and took the steamship tickets that had been given to people. There were about thirty people who were without tickets and had boarded concealed. They stowed away dishonestly and did not pay the boat fare. They [the ship officials] did not interfere with several people they knew were without tickets owing to their poverty and impecuniosity.

This steamship is one of the Khedival steamships and is named the Mahalleh. Aside from the employees of the engine room who are English, the other employees are all Muslims. The steamer was more crowded because of this. Near the time of the pilgrimage, every steamship that goes from Suez to Jidda will be very crowded, especially the steamships which have agreed with the Istanbul companies to carry the passengers of the companies' steamships. (Farahani 1990: 173–174)

The steamships doubtlessly added both speed and safety to the pilgrims' journey, but there was also considerable uncertainty when it came to scheduling and connections. The Ottoman bureaucrat Ashchi Dede made the Hajj in 1898, well into the age of steam on the Red Sea, and discovered that patience was one of the pilgrim's requisite virtues:

On Monday, 16 Ramadan, toward morning, we boarded the train (at Alexandria), reached Suez at two in the evening and met the group. We intended to go by steamer to Yanbu the next day, but . . . by the decree of Providence we ended up going to Jidda instead of Yanbu. That is, we pulled out a ways from the port at Suez, then it became apparent that we were going to Jidda and afterwards to Yanbu. Although we protested, they answered: "There's no use protesting; this week the ship goes first to Jidda, from there to Suwakin, then to Yanbu. If you give fifty liras, then first to Yanbu." I smiled and said, "The saints, through the Corresponding Secretary (of the Ministry of War), gave me fifty Ottoman liras as travel expenses for the men who are accompanying me . . . and part of this has been spent. So we have no choice but to submit to events." Giving praise to God, and with no trouble at sea, we arrived safe and sound at Jidda on Friday 20 Ramadan at seven o'clock. (Findley 1989: 485–486)

While the steamer continued to Suwakin, Ashchi Dede and his companions remained in Jidda, where they visited, among others places, the tomb of Mother Eve. When the ship returned six days later, the Ottoman party reboarded and made the one-day voyage from Jidda to Yanbu. Here they were delayed, albeit in a very pleasant caravansary on the seashore, because of the feast of Bayram marking the end of Ramadan.

Last Views of Jidda

With the advent of steamship travel, most nineteenth-century pilgrims entered the Hijaz through the port of Jidda, a city now transformed by its expanded role in the pilgrimage. Hossein Kazemzadeh describes what it was like in 1910:

The city of Jidda has a Muslim population of nearly 25,000. In addition to the consuls of the European powers, some Christians are encountered there, employees of the maritime companies and the merchant houses or minor craftsmen. . . . The port is rather large, but rocks, which are sometimes visible at the surface of the sea, prevent easy access by ships, which cannot enter or leave the port once it is dark since they run the danger of being damaged by the rocks. . . . The ships generally anchor at a league or more offshore and travelers are brought ashore in large sailing vessels called sambuks.

There is nothing remarkable in the construction of the buildings: they are generally three or four stories high, built out of clay or wood. The bricks used in their construction are made of earth taken from the shore during low tide and left to dry in the sun for some days to make them, by the action of the sun, as hard and resistant as stone.

Because of the lack of water, the only forms of vegetation are several wild trees growing in the garden of the government palace and in that of the head of the municipality outside the city. As for drinking water, the locals use run-off water. Most of the houses have cisterns to collect rain-water, and when there is none, the bedouin bring in by camel-back water which they fetch out of cisterns dug into the flatlands. This water, which is yellowish in color and has an unpleasant smell, sells for 2 Turkish piasters [40 centimes] for a goatskin full.

There is also sea-water distilled at two plants, one at the port of Jidda— its water is not healthy because of the impurities that collect along the shore—and another on the island of Shaykh Sa˚id some kilometers distant from the port. The consulates have their drinking water brought from Suez on Egyptian ships that make a regular weekly run between Suez and Jidda. The distilled sea-water is sold in tin petrol cans at 40 paras the can. . . . There is also a machine for making ice installed a number of years ago, though it is still not in use. Each of the consulates has its own ice-making machine.

The most attractive quarter is that called the "Damascus quarter" and there the consulates, the houses of the local notables, the government palace, post office, telegraph etc. are all located. There is only one public bath and one pharmacy, both of them run by the municipality, which oversees the general condition of the city, and the streets are, as a matter of fact, cleaner than those of Mecca. The city supervisor, to illustrate the difficulty in keeping the streets clean, told me every day there enter or leave Jidda more than 5,000 camels. If each camel leaves three kilos of droppings a day, the city workers would have to clean up 15,000 kilos of manure every day. . . .

The goods on display in the market are covered with so many flies that you cannot tell the color of the goods without chasing them away. Since it would be too difficult to eat or drink something and at the same time chase away the flies with your hand, there is at the British Consulate a person specially hired to continuously move a great fan suspended in the middle of the consul general's room to chase the flies and freshen the air. In the evening, when the shops close, the flies go, like the merchants, to private houses to seek their prey there, and that is why it is impossible to sleep without being bitten unless the bed is enwrapped in a fly-net.

As for the intellectual life of Jidda, there is a newly built government primary school in the Damascus quarter where children study according to the methods adopted in Constantinople, and a club founded by the Committee of Union and Progress. . . . During the past year the CUP founded at Medina two new well-organized schools where hundreds of children receive a primary education. (Kazemzadeh 1912: 162–165)

Two of the last views of Jidda under the Sharifs—it came under Saudi control in 1925—are provided not by pilgrims but by Westerners of a new age, Harry St. John Philby, a professional soldier, and Amin Rihani, an Arab traveler-journalist from New York.

Philby came to Jidda from Najd at the behest of the British government. He and David George Hogarth, who had come over from Cairo,
were to meet with Sharif Husayn in early January 1918.

The city of Jidda is hemmed in by solid walls on the three land-faces to
north, east and south, and these are continued along the sea front, on
which side, however, are the customs houses and other official and commercial buildings, for the most part of modern construction and without
elegance, right down to the wharves along the fringe of the sea. Here in
the town hall Sulayman Qabil, the major or Ra'is baladiyya, and his officers carry out their official duties; and here too lie the great hostels in
which pilgrims from all parts of the world are accommodated, each according to his nationality, by enterprising agents from his own country,
during the days they spend at Jidda on the outward and return journeys.
Jidda is indeed a busy port with a floating population, whose numbers I
cannot conjecture.

Outside the southeastern corner of the city lies an extensive Takruri
[black African] settlement of reed huts, the haunt of laborers and artisans
come from the African coast in search of a living; and behind it on the
seashore is the Kanisa [literally, "the church"], as the Arabs call the little
cemetery in which are interred such Europeans as from time to time
death has overtaken during their sojourn on the inhospitable coast of the
Muslim Holy Land.

Inside the city is a truly eastern jumble of wealth and poverty; great
mansions of the captains of commerce and enterprise, with their solid
coral walls and wide expanses of woodwork tracery, side by side with hov-
els broken and battered with age; mosques great and small, with pointed
minarets tapering skyward amid masses of vast square buildings; and
crowded bazaars, with their lines of dark shops, protected from the sun by
central roofs, here of wood and canvas much the worse for wear, and there
of corrugated. Everywhere a contrast of light and shadow, splendor and
squalor, dust and dirt; and above it all flew the flags of many nations,
Great Britain, France, Italy and Holland, amid the countless emblems of
a united Arabia. (Philby 1922: 1:232)

When he wrote those lines, the British soldier must have had little reason
to believe that he would one day be numbered among Jidda's captains of
commerce, perhaps first in that company, and that he would dwell in the
greatest mansion of all, the baroque extravagance on Jidda's waterfront
known as the Bayt Baghdadi.

Amin Rihani spent a month in Jidda in 1922 as the guest of Husayn,
longtime Sharif of Mecca and then King of the Hijaz. The city somehow
seemed familiar.

Jidda did not seem new to me. I felt I had been there before, not with Burton and Burckhardt, however, but with one who had preceded them by about a thousand years. Ibn Jubayr of Granada, who made the pilgrimage to Mecca when Saladin, the mighty and good, was on the throne, is a chronicler of accuracy and courage. . . . If the Jidda of those days was a den of thieves who preyed upon the pilgrims, and if the high-road to Mecca was held by bands of bedouin who took from the pious multitudes what the Jidda thieves had overlooked, Ibn Jubayr said so in plain Arabic and protested to high heaven against the rank irreligion that nested in the Holy Places of Islam.

I do not know how much irreligion is still nesting in the dark and cobwebbed corners of Mecca and Medina; but the den of thieves and the bedouin bandits were not in evidence. The pilgrimage, in these happy days of Husayn the First, Sharif and King, was comparatively safe. But the Jidda of Ibn Jubayr, with this exception, had not changed. The same five-story houses with their attractive walled roofs for summer nights; the same narrow winding streets, which in places enable the housewives, through their balconies in opposite buildings, to borrow things from each other or to pull each other's hair; the same woodsheds in the markets and bazaars to shut out the fierce Arabian sun; the same squares and camels and litters for the transportation of pilgrims; the same hodge-podge of humanity which Islam brings together from every corner of the earth; the same bare-footed, half-naked Arabs carrying their only heritage of power and grandeur, a sword; the same winds that beat Jidda one day on the right cheek and one day on the left, the sword notwithstanding; the same fruits and vegetables the Wadi Fatima yields to a frugal population; the same watermelons whose delicious quality raised Ibn Jubayr to poetic heights of description—they are all still there. . . .

There are but a few things in the Jidda of today which Ibn Jubayr did not see; a condenser, for instance, which takes the salt out of sea water for the sake of the Europeans and a few of the sophisticated modern Arabs. Also the tables and chairs in the cafés—and the flies! Yes, there are stivy dens in Jidda where the bedouin might rattle his sword for a drink of uncondensed water, where a city tramp might doze over a narghila, and Takruri blacks, the porters of the town, are seen stretching their weary limbs and listening to the porter-gossip of the day. (Rihani 1930: 44–46)

The Way Home

His pilgrimage completed, Farahani stood at Yanbu in November 1885.

There is no steamship from Yanbu to Jidda. There are rowboats, launches and sailboats which do not have a schedule for their departure or how often they go. Occasionally a steamship passes by this port. From Yanbu to Jidda is 180 miles, and it takes from 17 to 20 hours by commercial steamship. . . . The companies know the schedule for the arrival of the pilgrims at Yanbu, and at that time there are steamships for whoever comes to Yanbu and there is no delay. For whoever comes later than that schedule, the ships that come to transport pilgrims will have loaded and left. Then there will be cause for delay.

In this year, when we arrived at Yanbu, about ten or twelve thousand pilgrims from various places had assembled at Yanbu and wanted to leave. Six steamships were also anchored there and were waiting for the pilgrims. Three passenger ships were going to Istanbul, two via Beirut, and two via Basra. At first, the deck-class fare to Istanbul was fixed at seven lira and the fare to Beirut at five lira. Then the pilgrims haggled with ship companies about the fare, and in the end the fare to Basra was four lira, to Istanbul five and three to Beirut. Cabin class to Istanbul was fourteen lira.

Farahani then offers some detailed information about the routes to the intermediary stops, first that to Beirut:

As for the pilgrims who went to Beirut, most were residents of Syria; a few were residents of Arab Iraq. About twenty Iranians went by that route. It was said they were members of the Babi sect who were going to Beirut and would go from Beirut to Acre to visit in Acre Mirza Hosayn Ali, the chief of the Babis, who is there.[20]

From Yanbu to Beirut, without stopping, takes six to seven days by steamship, and one arrives on the seventh day. However, nowadays it will take more than six days because the passengers to Beirut must stop two days for quarantine at the wadi [Tur] of Mount Sinai. From Beirut to Damascus by train takes twelve hours. For people who want to go from Beirut to Baghdad, it is two days by steamship from Beirut to Alexandretta, and from the port of Alexandretta to Aleppo overland by mule or pack horse in five days. From Aleppo to the river bank [of the Euphrates] is a trip of three days, and from the river bank to Baghdad by small steamer is a trip of five days.

As for the pilgrims who go via the ports of Bushihr, Basra and Baghdad, they go from Yanbu to Jidda in one day; from there by steamship to Bandar Jadaydeh in three days and from there to Aden in thirty hours. From Aden one reaches Muscat in five days; and from Muscat to Bandar Abbas in three more days. From there to Bushihr is a trip of forty-five hours. One goes from Bushihr to Basra . . . in one day. From Basra one takes a small steamer, enters the Shatt al-Arab and reaches Baghdad in five days. . . . So all together, it is a trip of twenty-two days at sea by steamship, without stopping, from Yanbu to Baghdad. . . .

Anyhow, having arrived at Yanbu on Wednesday, the 26th of the sacred month of Muharram [4 November 1885] . . . we took a boat from Yanbu and set out on the evening of Monday, the first of Safar [9 November 1885]. We took the Arab steamship which belongs to Saʿid Pasha, the former Khedive of Egypt, and is named the Mahalleh and set out. This steamship usually operates in the Red Sea, and also from Suez at the time to go to Mecca. Although it is old, its furnishings worn out, and it is not clean or orderly, still it is swift and large. If the wind is not unfavorable, it can go ten miles an hour. Since its captain and crew are Arabs and Muslims, and they are not harsh to the pilgrims, there were many pilgrims on this steamship. There were about 800 pilgrims. (Farahani 1990: 285–288)

Travel on Land

While sea transport became easier and swifter, the traditional overland route remained in the nineteenth century much as it had been in the sixteenth or the eleventh, a journey by camel and donkey over exceedingly forbidding terrain. Thus the hire of these animals was one of the main tasks facing the prospective pilgrim. Nor was it an easy one. As Farahani describes it, these essential means of transportation were in the often unscrupulous hands of one of the most tightly guarded monopolies in the Hijaz.

THE CAMEL BROKERS

In order for the pilgrims to hire riding animals throughout the Hijaz . . . a camel-broker (mukharrij) is designated by the Sharif for each national group of pilgrims. That is, six people have been designated as camel-brokers: one is the camel-broker for the Iranian pilgrims; another is the camel-broker for the Ottoman pilgrims; another is the camel-broker for the people of Java; another . . . for the Indian pilgrims . . . for the North African pilgrims . . . and for the Egyptian pilgrims. Their work is that they sit down together and take counsel and fix the hiring rates each year according to the situation. The hiring of riding animals by the pilgrims in every part of the Hijaz is with their knowledge, assignment and assistance. . . . Whatever the amount of the fare they determine is put into practice, and no one will disagree. For each camel a fee is expected for the Sharif, the consul, the pilgrim-guide and themselves and is added to the fare. . . . All of these camel-brokers have gotten very wealthy. (Farahani 1990: 194–195)

THE LOCAL HAJJ MARKET AT MAʿAN (1845)

Pilgrims traveling overland in caravans had to be supplied en route, and local markets, some of considerable size, sprang up along the Darb al-Hajj to meet the demand for provisions. In 1845 and again in 1848 Georg Wallin, a Swedish native of what was then the Russian Grand Duchy of Finland, explored the northern and western regions of Arabia. He crossed first the Syrian and then the Egyptian overland Hajj routes to Mecca. His description of one of the entrepots, Maʿan on the way down from Syria, graphically illustrates the consequences of the Hajj caravan for stops along its route.

Maʿan, now a city of some size in southern Jordan, was seated on the fringe land between the desert and the sown. Thus, in addition to its artificial, pilgrimage-induced economy, the town had to confront, successfully it seems, the perennial problem of agriculturalists settled athwart bedouin grazing land.

We immediately issued on the vast plain of the Syrian desert, into which the chain (of the Shara mountains) merges with a slow and sensible descent, and taking a full easterly direction, we reached in 5 hours the town of Maʿan. . . . The present town of Maʿan is one of the largest places on the Syrian pilgrims' way, containing about 200 families of 7 different clans, mixed up with immigrants from other villages in Syria. They are in general a healthy and well-built people, of the most prominent Syrian type, able to raise a force of 150, or, as others told me, of 300 well-armed and gallant young men. Trusting in this force, the inhabitants in our times have begun to make head against the claims of the nomads, either refusing altogether or abating the so-called "brother tax" which a great many shaykhs of the neighboring tribes of Shararat, Huwaytat and Anayza exact of them. This tax, levied by all genuine bedouin tribes, almost without exception, not only on every village in the desert, but also on others wayfaring and trading among them . . . is probably founded on the claims which the bedouin think themselves entitled to lay on the desert as their common inherited land. Every district of this common land has in course of time passed into the exclusive possession of one certain tribe, within the limits of whose dominion no other tribe, without special permission, is allowed to enter, no village tolerated to exist, and no stranger to pass without protection, bought by tribute from the masters of the soil. . . .

Now all settled cultivators are regarded by the bedouin as natural enemies, who are consequently not allowed to subsist in their land except under their protection, which protection they sell for as high a price as they are able to extort. But the more the settlement increases in power and wealth, the more they strive to repel or moderate the nomads' claims. . . . This resistance on the part of the villagers, and their standing their ground, seldom fails to be acknowledged by the bedouin, to whom nothing is so contemptible as cowardice and dependence, and generally goes a long way to making relations with them more intimate.

This is in fact the case at Maʿan, whose valiant and manly inhabitants

the bedouin esteem more than most other villagers. This greatly contributes to facilitate the intercourse between the two parties, and a livelier
trade than I witnessed in any other place on this route is carried on by
way of barter between Ma͑an and the surrounding desert. The articles
most wanted are clothes, gunpowder, lead, weapons, spices, coffee and
sugar, which latter luxury has in our times become in great request even
in the desert, and for these they give in exchange camels, sheep, wool,
butter and milk.

Were it not for the credit these tradesmen (of Ma͑an) allow the bedouin, the latter could procure themselves these necessaries much easier
and cheaper from the same markets whence the inhabitants of Ma͑an
purchase their wants, as well as most of the commodities they use for their
exchange trade. These markets are principally Hebron, Gaza and al-
Aqaba. Sometimes they go as far as to Damascus to the north or to Jawf
to the east. . . . The most important market, however, is the village itself
during the two days the Syrian pilgrimage caravan generally reposes here
on its way to and from Mecca. During the whole year the inhabitants lay
up in store for these four days, called "the season," all sorts of provisions
and forage for the pilgrims and their camels, which they generally very
profitably exchange for other wares.

As the greater part of the pilgrims like to combine mercantile speculations with the meritorious discharge of the religious duty of pilgrimage,
they take care to provide themselves with such commodities as will sell
along the way. On leaving Damascus they load their camels with materials of cloth and cotton, and other European manufactures, for which they
find a good market throughout Arabia, and on returning from Mecca
they carry with them coffee and spices, cloaks from Baghdad, and Persian
caps or Indian swords and daggers, all of which commodities are comparatively rare, and are in great request in the western parts of the peninsula.

There is besides, during these days, a great conflux of bedouin, gathering in the village from the adjacent desert, and thus these small and, during the rest of the year, generally very dull places on the pilgrim's way
present the aspect of the most stirring and crowded fair in Europe. All
things which can be disposed of are exhibited for sale or barter; everyone
is engaged in speculations of traffic and profit. . . . But it must be borne in
mind that this traffic with the pilgrims is the main source of their subsistence, and the greatest part of the inhabitants of Ma͑an do, in fact, in
these four days gain enough to suffice for the support of their families
during the rest of the year. (Wallin 1850/1854: 121–124)

GETTING FROM MECCA TO MEDINA

In the nineteenth century, then, the overland routes to and from the
Holy Cities of Arabia were much as they had always been. This or that
ruler in Cairo or Istanbul might invest in new water or defense facilities,

but the effects tended to be ephemeral. Each caravan had very much to look to its own safety and each pilgrim to choose wisely among the available options. In passing from Mecca to Medina, for example, the Hajji was confronted with a number of possibilities, each with its attractions and drawbacks, as described by Farahani:

> As for those who have not gone to Medina the Agreeable and must go there, they will go with one of these three caravans:
> The first way is to travel with the heavily guarded official caravan from Damascus.
> One is the Syrian caravan which is accompanied by the Pasha, the Amin-i Surra, soldiers and artillery and is orderly and regular. Everyone who goes with it is in complete security. However, these days few Iranians go via this route because of the long trip, the great trouble and the untold expense. The Syrian caravan sets out from Mecca from the 25th of the month of Dhu al-Hajj to the end of the month.

Another, more circuitous route was through the domains of the Rashidi "Amir of the Mountain" (the shaykh of the Banu Rashid, the paramount tribe of the region), that is, the Jabal Shammar, with its capital at Hayl:

> Another is the "Mountain Caravan." Every year the hamleh-dars of Arab Iraq conduct some Iranian and Ottoman pilgrims with the party of the Amir of the Mountain and convey his standard to Mecca in good order and regularity. This caravan leaves very early. Since it has a guardian, the way is secure. Less of the pilgrims' money is lost. The expenses for it are by comparison less than by the Syrian route. Nevertheless, it has some faults. . . . This year no more than fifty or sixty Iranian subjects had come via this route owing to a government prohibition, and those went secretly and in bedouin dress.[21] Nevertheless, the guides with Abd al-Rahman, the deputy of the Amir of the Mountain, who is the leader of the Mountain route pilgrims, came again to Mecca and invited the Iranian pilgrims to be conveyed via the Mountain route. Since most of the revenue of the Amir of the Mountain comes from the Iranian pilgrims, and the Iranian pilgrims have not come by this route for two years due to the government prohibition, it is a matter of great regret and remorse for the Amir of the Mountain. He behaved extremely well in every respect to the few Iranian pilgrims who had accompanied them. He wrote an explanation to the Iranian consul who was in Mecca through the intermediary of his agent Abd al-Rahman. He requested the release of the pilgrims to go via the Mountain route and made many promises, such as, "I will look after the pilgrims in every way, and no sort of injustice or disrespect will befall them."
> The pilgrim-guides also gave nearly 700 liras . . . for the release of the

pilgrims to go via the Mountain route. Nevertheless, because there was a prohibition, permission for the pilgrims to go by the Mountain route was not given. It is easy to seize, with utter severity, any of the Iranians who go by stealth with the Mountain hamleh-dars, return them to Mecca, and fine and imprison them. The amounts which accrue from this matter are the perquisite of the Iranian consul.

Since the profit of the Amir of the Mountain has been greatly reduced owing to this two-year prohibition, it is possible that this will effect benefits for the pilgrims who do go via this route. All sorts of guarantees about the tranquility of the pilgrims will be made, and then, because of that it will be the best route.

Then there was the safest and the best choice, the so-called "Flying Caravan":

> Yet another is the "Flying Caravan." The Flying Caravan is that by which one or two of the chiefs of the tribes of the Hijaz convey the pilgrims with the assistance of Bedouin camel drivers. They go by Medina the Agreeable, and from there to Yanbu or Jidda. These Bedouin chiefs offer guarantees for the safe arrival of the pilgrims with the knowledge of the consul in the presence of the Sharif of Mecca. They give two (of their own) people as pledge and hostages. If the pilgrims arrive safely, the Sharif releases these hostages. If not, he imprisons and punishes them. Thus most pilgrims of all nationalities go with this caravan.

If this caravan offered some degree of surety against attacks from without, the same was not true of the pilgrim's person and property within the caravan:

> There is no method in the departure of this caravan. It sets out from Mecca going to Medina group by group from the 20th of the month of Dhu al-Hijja to the end of the month. There is no order or regularity in anything about this caravan. There is much thievery from within and without it. Most of the camel drivers are thieves and robbers. Along the way if something is lost, it is the responsibility of the camel driver. Because of this few belongings of people are lost along the way. But after an individual arrives at the lodgings, if he is a little careless, they steal his belongings at once. If one night 100,000 tomans of pilgrims' belongings are carried off, or fifty pilgrims are killed, or if some of the thieves are killed, there is no judgment or calling to account. Usually the pilgrims stay awake from nightfall to morning, weapons in hand, saying "Keep away, keep away!"
>
> Thieves from Egypt, Syria and Arab Iraq come to Mecca especially for the pilgrimage season. They accompany these caravans until the pilgrims reach Jidda or Yanbu. A great amount of personal property is lost.

It was an expensive proposition to travel with this relatively safe caravan, and one of the reasons was the practice noted by all travelers across bedouin-controlled territory, the payment of the *khawah*, or "brotherhood tax."

One of the problems with this caravan is the matter of the toll which the tribes of the Harb collect in their territory (which is a place of passage for the caravan) from those passing through. This tax for passage is named the khawah. The Ottoman government contracts to pay the Bedouin a yearly amount on behalf of its citizens and the citizens of foreign countries. No one interferes with them. However, citizens of Iran must themselves pay the toll individually. The toll is added to the fare and is paid to the chief of the caravan who provided the hostages. If that chief does not covet the toll for himself and gives it rightly to the tribal chiefs, the caravan will arrive safely and they will not be hindered by anyone. If not, the chiefs of the Harb prevent the pilgrims from going in order to exact the toll. It will cause delays. Thus in earlier years, the pilgrims were delayed for a month or two months in Rabigh and elsewhere for this reason, and the chiefs of the caravan who had collected the tolls from the pilgrims fled. They charge ten Levant dollars per pilgrim for the toll.

Another difficulty with this caravan is that a large fare is charged the pilgrims. That is, for each camel that transports a pilgrim, something must go to the Sharif; something must go to the Pasha; something for the chief of that caravan; something for the pilgrim-guide of that pilgrim; something for the camel-broker; something for the consul; and something for the caravan-followers. All this is added to the fare, and the fare becomes very exorbitant. They charge seventy-one Levant dollars for the fare from Mecca the Exalted to Medina the Illuminated and from Medina to Yanbu, including one litter capable of transporting two pilgrims. They provide a cook and a pack for each litter. They charge twenty-two Levant dollars each for that pack and cook. In reality, the toll is not charged for that pack and cook. They charge the pilgrim passenger forty-six Levant dollars, including the toll, for the camel. For every seven pilgrim passengers one does not pay the toll. Anyone who wants to go from Mecca to Medina, and from Medina to Jidda, is charged on the same basis. At most, they will collect two or three Levant dollars per camel. . . .

Despite all these problems regarding this caravan, it is still the best of the caravans since one is more quickly delivered from the hands of the Bedouin. Most people these days go via this "Flying Caravan." (Farahani 1990: 248–249)

The "brotherhood" tax noted by Farahani, though transparently a form of extortion practiced on Iranian Shiʿites, did not lack its own brazenly preposterous rationalization. The Persian pilgrim Hossein Kazemzadeh, who made the Hajj in 1910–1911 and had to pay it, explains:

Between Mecca and Medina there are Arab tribes who exact tribute from the Persian pilgrims who pass through their territory. This tribute is called khawah or "the right of brotherhood." I have not been able thoroughly to study the origins of this tribute, and shall content myself with setting down what the Arabs and Persians have to say on the subject. It is believed that the Persians were obliged, according to an unwritten agreement from long ago, to pay this tribute in token of brotherhood and friendship. The Persians, living as they did a life of abundance and profiting from the natural riches of their land, would thus have wished to assist their Arab brothers—since all Muslims are brothers—by providing them with material assistance.

This is the way the Arabs explain the origin of this tribute, which is not very plausible since other Muslims in similar circumstances are not subjected to this tax. And, in addition, a voluntary act of charity can hardly be said to constitute an obligation. The Persians are of the opinion that after the conquest of Arabia by the Turkish sultans, who were never completely successful in subduing the Arabs and maintaining order in the country, Persian caravans made up entirely of Shi'ites and passing over these routes to Mecca were always exposed to the attacks of bandit tribes under the pretext that they were "Rafidis," and hence their enemies.[22]

Since the Turkish government is unable to chastise the bedouin and prevent massacres and pillaging, the Shi'ite or Persian pilgrims have attempted to deal directly with the Arab chieftains. These latter have proposed they pay an annual sum in tribute rather than undergo the fate to which they have been submitted for so many years. The Shi'ites accepted the offer and thus these sworn enemies have become brothers and the tribute imposed on them is called khawah or the "tribute of brotherhood."

There are forty-four tribes that exact this payment, twenty-four on the route to Yanbu and the rest on the others. When a Persian caravan has to pass through the territory of one of these tribes, it stops and the (Arab) chief comes to count the pilgrims. The tribute is four Turkish pounds [90 francs] per pilgrim for the entire transit and each tribe gets ten piasters [2 francs] per pilgrim. The . . . Arab caravan leaders have collected in advance the sum due from the pilgrims and have only to square their accounts with the Arab chieftain and hand over to him his due. (Kazemzadeh 1912: 159–161)

The Land versus the Sea Route

The way to Mecca no longer presented, as it had in Ibn Jubayr's day, a relatively simple choice: whether, for example, to leave Cairo by caravan across the Sinai or to travel up the Nile, cut across to Qusayr or Aydhab, and pass by boat to Jidda. From the 1830s, when steamships entered the Red Sea, there was a notable decline in the overland routes. After 1865 Persian pilgrims could, if they wished, take ship from one of the Persian Gulf ports and so avoid the overland trip through the Najd or the Jabal Shammar. With the completion of the Suez Canal, the sea route also opened up to Turkish and Syrian pilgrims who normally sailed from Beirut to Ismailia. Muhammad Ali had opened a canal between Alexandria and Cairo—this too was soon navigated by steamships—and a railway linked Cairo and Suez.

Tradition was strong, however, and even as others were deserting the caravan for the steamship, the Sultan's official cortege from Constantinople continued to travel overland. Few private pilgrims joined it, however, as the French consuls reported from Damascus:

> The Amir al-Hajj arrived in Damascus (from Istanbul) . . . accompanied by only two pilgrims. Each year fewer and fewer pilgrims take the land route to Mecca. This year it will certainly not amount to more than 500 souls. The expenses of the caravan meanwhile increase every year by 1,500,000 francs. . . . It is not clear why the Porte continues to suffer such considerable expenses when it would be an easy matter to send a steamship every year to Beirut to take the pilgrims to Alexandria. (Ministry of Foreign Affairs Papers: Damascus, 1864[23])

> The Mecca caravan entered Damascus on the thirteenth of May, and counted scarcely 200 pilgrims. The question is why the Porte continues to inflict itself with an annual expense of more than 25,000 purses when it would be so easy and so inexpensive to send to Jidda by sea the covering that the Sultan dispatches each year for the tomb of the Prophet (at Medina). (Ministry of Foreign Affairs Papers: Damascus, 1876[24])

Tradition finally yielded to economic considerations, at least in part. From 1866 onward, the *Amin al-Surra*, the Sultan's chief representative on the Hajj, came to Damascus by sea via Beirut, though from there on he traveled by caravan to Mecca.

Almost from the beginning, the most dangerous and, as steamship tariffs decreased, the most expensive part of the trip was the journey from Medina to Mecca, or, for those who came by sea to Mecca via Jidda and wished to visit the Prophet's tomb, from Mecca to Medina. Though more roundabout, it was safer and cheaper to travel from Mecca to Medina or vice versa by sailing between Yanbu and Jidda and reducing the caravan trips to the relatively safe Yanbu-Medina or Jidda-Mecca transits. Here the local resistance to sea transport became fierce and the politics highly complex.[25] Though the pilgrim might well prefer the sea route, many others, among them the Sharif, the bedouin, and the *Amin al-Surra* himself, had a stake in the camel rental business and/or the protection business. The Hajj memoir of the elderly Ashchi Dede, who made the pilgrimage in 1898, graphically illustrates the straits into which a pilgrim might be cast:

> Praise and thanks be to Him, on Tuesday 8 Shawwal, toward morning we set out in a caravan (from Yanbu) for Medina. As is known, they have what is called a shatuf [that is, shuqdhuf], which is a frame with a pair of seats, that is, it is a seat about the size of an iron single bedstead, made of datepalm branches, and protected against the sun with fabric and oilcloth on top. . . . We found ourselves companions with Mehmed Effendi. . . . He was a good [Sufi of the order of] Naqshbandi, absorbed in his own spiritual state. . . . I mounted the camel-litter with him on one side and my humble self on the other; we set out with a prayer that we might bow our shameful faces to the dust (at the tomb) of the Prophet of God, on whom be blessing and peace, and so make them clean and unsullied. We got about half the way, and came to a place in the wilderness known as the "Well of Abbas." There we remained one day and two nights. The reason for this was that the local (bedouin) shaykh wanted money to open the road.[26] They were not pleased about the caravan. Indeed, my heart grew weary with all the talk and I could find no peace. At last, by the beneficence of God, we escaped from there.
>
> The Hijaz road (from Yanbu to Medina) is a strange one. The stopping places are rather far apart; and one generally reaches the stopping places at night four or five hours after sundown. At that, what is called a stopping place will be a valley between two mountains. The camel drivers, helping people down from the camels, cry out that there are many thieves. In fact, there are not any thieves; they are the thieves. One had best not stray too far from his camel-litter. One even relieves nature right beside it. If one goes five or ten paces, he gets hit with a stick and is deprived of whatever he has. We saw a lot of this kind of thing. These places are not necessary for us. (Findley 1989: 486–487)

The last remark, the unguarded cry of a Turkish civil servant who had spent many years in Damascus dealing, at a distance, with the problem of rapacious Arab bedouin, summed up growing Ottoman frustration with its eyalet (subprovince) in the Hijaz. There was an equal store of anger and frustration on the other side as well, not so much on the part of the Arab bedouin and their shaykhs, who were merely trying to extort a living in the immemorial manner, as from the Sharif and merchants, who had little patience for either Ottoman corruption or its reform. After fulfilling their pious obligations in Medina, Ashchi Dede and his party made the even more difficult overland trek to Mecca. Precisely which of the several possible routes they followed is impossible to know from Aschchi Dede's illegible handwriting,[27] but the problem they encountered was the standard one.

The road had been blocked for five or six years, that is, since a great shaykh along that road had not been given his surras, he had not allowed any pilgrims along that route. But now it was desired to open that road in the name of His Excellency, the Corresponding Secretary (of the Ministry of War) and to pass that way with the mediation [or: protection] of some other shaykhs, and so we set out that way. Although the great shaykh sent a paper to the Amin al-Surra saying "I won't let you through here," it did not arrive until after we had left Medina and so did not reach the Amin. Consequently we were going our way, relying on the mediation [or: protection] of the other shaykhs, when all of a sudden, one or two days out, we entered that shaykh's frontiers. It got to be evening. Reaching a halting place and stopping, we set off a cannon. The shaykh heard the cannon's sound and asked, "What is this cannon?" They told him it was the arrival of the surras. "Strange, I wrote them a paper. They did not listen or pay attention." So saying, he flew into a rage.

The caravan descended from the mountain region to a valley where the ground was covered with slippery stones. Fear and anxiety began to overcome the company.

While we were in this state of dread, the sounds of weapons were heard from the soldiers in our front. In response, the soldiers at our sides sounded their bugles and shouted something with one voice. We supposed that the way before us was empty, that the soldiers were firing their weapons as a show of bravery, and that the soldiers at our side were saluting back with horns and crying "Long live the Padishah!"

At a certain point, we went beyond the frontiers of the man in question and fell upon the desert. At last, as everyone shared the good news, we reached safety and stopped at the halting place. We asked what had gone on and learned that, alas, it was not as we supposed. For the shaykh's men had fired on the soldiers from those high rocks; the latter had returned fire, and the bugles and the soldiers' shouts signaled "For shame! For shame! For shame!" When it became clear that there were several killed and wounded on our side and also losses from the Arabs, we became very sad. . . . Later the shaykh came to the tent to meet with the Amin al-Surra. The latter reprimanded and chastised him and made certain threats. The shaykh said, "Since five or six years they have not given me what is due me. I did this especially because you were relying on the other shaykhs." Then, praise God, His Excellency, after further admonitions, gratified the shaykh by promising him that he would get his back payments from His Excellency the Sharif of Mecca. (Findley 1989: 493–494)

18. A View of the Mahmal Passing through Aqaba on the Caravan Route of al-Wigh before the Station al-Khatala in 1326/1908.

19. A View of the Palanquins of Camels at Arafat.

20. A View of the Mahmal at Arafat in 1321/1909.

21. The Southwestern View of the Camp of the Pilgrims at Arafat.

22. The Mosque Khayf and Mina.

23. Mina.

24. The Door of Mercy on the Prophet's Mosque in Medina.

25. The Dress of the Imam on Friday at Medina.

زمزم أمامة

26 Arafat.

HEALTH AND THE HAJJ

When the first reliable statistics began to be kept in the nineteenth century, what had previously been a suspicion could be confirmed: a large number of pilgrims were indigent or came to Mecca enfeebled by age or the long journey.[28] The health dangers of collecting large crowds of such people in close quarters and under often unsanitary conditions are apparent, but it was not until the nineteenth century that an epidemic disease appeared in the Hijaz, in the form of cholera. Though long present in India, cholera was not reported outside the subcontinent until 1817 and 1823, when it appeared in island ports around the Indian Ocean. In 1831, *une année fatale*, as the historian Firmin Duguet calls it, the disease made its first appearance in Mecca; thenceforward, until well into the twentieth century, it was almost continuously present in the Holy Cities.

The Ottomans—and even the Sharif, according to his lights—attempted to address the problem and its grave effects in the Hijaz as best they could.[29] Only when cholera began to appear in Europe (in 1830 and 1837), and not until episodes of the disease were unmistakably connected with the Hajj, did other nations begin to pay attention. In 1847 France established a network of *medécins sanitaires* connected to its consulates in the chief cities of the Near East: Beirut, Damascus, Alexandria, Cairo, then Suez, Teheran, and Smyrna/Izmir. In Paris, in 1851, an international conference on the disease proposed the establishment of quarantines in eastern ports, but there was no discussion or even mention of the pilgrimage as such.[30]

Cholera in the Hijaz

In 1865 a major epidemic struck the Hijaz. It originated in Java and Singapore and was carried to Mecca by pilgrims, one-third of whom perished during the pilgrimage. By the time the Hajj was over, 15,000 of an estimated 90,000 pilgrims had died of cholera. When ships carrying returning Hajjis arrived at Suez, they reported to the local authorities that there were no instances of the disease, although more than a hundred corpses had been thrown overboard since leaving Jidda. That was in May. By June, the disease was raging in Alexandria—60,000 Egyptians died in three months—and later that same month it reached Marseilles and thence most of the cities of Europe. In November 1865 cholera was reported in New York City.[31]

At French urging, another international conference was convoked almost immediately, and when the representatives of seventeen nations met in Constantinople in February 1866, they directly addressed the question of the Hajj. The conferees acknowledged that cholera was endemic in the Ganges Valley of India and that it was invariably imported into the Hijaz. They prescribed that the number of pilgrims going to Mecca be limited and that their "quality" be improved by requiring a "means test," as the Dutch were already doing in their East Indian colonies.[32] They further recommended that quarantine stations be set up at Tur in Sinai and Wajh in the Hijaz, and eventually one on Qamaran Island at the southern end of the Red Sea; and they strongly urged the Ottoman Empire to institute criminal proceedings against anyone who gave false information to the health authorities. The Egyptian Quarantine Board went even further.[33] It required that all departing pilgrims show proof of both health and means of subsistence, that the numbers of passengers aboard ship be strictly regulated, and that all ships arriving from the east undergo an obligatory fifteen-day quarantine at Mokha and the same at Massawa. Any ship arriving at Jidda without having passed through the quarantines would be turned back. All returning caravans would pass through Wajh, where there would be a fifteen-day quarantine. For the returnees by sea, there would be an obligatory examination at Jidda or Yanbu. In case of doubt, ships would undergo inspection at Tur. If cholera was clearly attested among any of the passengers, all ships would undergo a fifteen-day quarantine at Wajh. Finally, throughout the pilgrimage, all ships, no matter what their certification or previous quarantines, would submit to a five-day inspection quarantine near Suez.[34]

A new corner had been turned in the relations of the European powers with the Hijaz. Since Roman times, Westerners had contemplated, and occasionally and not very successfully attempted, military intervention in the Hijaz. Commercial interests were generally the reason, and in the nineteenth century the French occupation of Egypt and the opening of the Suez Canal increased both European appetites and access to the Red Sea shores of Arabia. In 1865, however, fear replaced greed. The threat of devastating cholera epidemics invading Europe by way of the Hijaz succeeded in uniting rival European powers in a concerted *politique sanitaire* whose objective was regulation of the life of Western Arabia and, no less, of the most sacred ritual of Islam, the Hajj. As one French physician put it after the 1865 epidemic, "Europe realized that it could not remain like this, every year, at the mercy of the pilgrimage to Mecca."[35]

THE PILGRIMAGE OF 1893

If the object of these measures was to shield Egypt and Europe from infection carried by returning pilgrims, they were apparently a success. Cholera continued to rage throughout the east, however, and even in Mecca and Medina, where there were eight epidemics between 1865 and 1892.

The worst of all occurred in 1893, when nearly 33,000 pilgrims out of some 200,000 perished at Jidda, Mecca, and Medina.[36] One of the most graphic eyewitness accounts comes from a physician in Ottoman employ, a Dr. Oslchanictzki, who left behind an unpublished memoir:

I was sent from Qamaran to Jidda with a colleague to supervise the return of the pilgrims. All was quiet in the city, but we knew that at Mecca there was a veritable hecatomb of pilgrims; more than a thousand were being reported dead daily. An initial convoy of 5,000 camels brought 15,000 pilgrims to Jidda. The ill had to be kept outside the city and only the healthy were admitted. I went with my colleague to the place and we began our medical inspection, which lasted from 4 A.M. till noon. The sight was terrible: everywhere were the dead and the suffering, the cries of men, women and children mixed with the roaring of the camels, in short, a terrifying scene which will never be blotted out of my memory.

The next and following days there were new arrivals in the same sanitary conditions, as disastrous as they were heart-rendering. Our medical visitation was useless in saving the city, since, despite our vigilance, some of the ill got in and sowed the infection there. It would have required not two but twenty physicians and a considerable number of assistants to insure the isolation of the sick. We had at our disposal five large houses outside the city, while fifty would not have been enough for the task.

The city of Jidda became then a vast cemetery, and the most urgent and useful sanitary precautions consisted in burying the dead bodies that filled the caravansaries, mosques, cafés, houses and public places. There was this peculiarity. The burial of the cholera victims was no easy matter since the porters and workers refused to do it, even though richly rewarded. It required all the authority of the head of the municipality to force them. The latter was at our side throughout the epidemic serving tea to the ill and even medicines to those willing to take them; he . . . devoted himself to the task with little care of himself and a scorn of danger, the likes of which we found in no other city official, great or small.

We saw many cases of lightning-swift death, and—this is another still vivid memory— each evening we said farewell to each other, my colleague and I, before retiring, out of fear that we would never see the morrow. On disembarking from one of the ships in Jidda harbor, I passed on the water Mr. O., an English maritime agent who was embarking on that same ship. We greeted each other in friendly fashion on passing, but once on board the poor wretch was leveled by a sudden attack and left the ship a corpse. . . .

This epidemic lasted for a month at Jidda, that is, the time it took for all the pilgrims to come from Mecca to this port. And, like all the cholera epidemics in the Hijaz, it ended the day after the last one of them departed.

Due to a lack of physicians to accompany the pilgrims, I was designated to serve as such on board one of the last boats to leave Jidda, the British steamship Etna. We made our course by Yanbu where we took on board a thousand pilgrims just arrived from Medina: 215 of them were Circassians and the rest Moroccans. I had the Circassians lodged separately on the upper deck since the Moroccans allowed no one else in their company. Between Yanbu and Tur some of our crew were taken by cholera; the Circassians, who subsisted only on tea and biscuit brought from their homeland, had no casualties; as for the Moroccans, no one knew what happened to them since they permitted no visits, neither mine nor anyone else's. But on more than one occasion I could see from the upper deck three or four people collected around one of the sick and energetically massaging him, almost as if they were kneading or molding him; but I do not know if this treatment brought the dying back to life since, as I said, no one knew what was going on among them.

Our quarantine at Tur lasted for twenty days. In the harbor were other boats like our own which were unable to disembark their pilgrims to the quarantine quarters for lack of space. In addition, every morning we had the cruelest sight one could imagine: one or two corpses thrown from who knows what ship floating on the water. We could see the sharks attacking these human bodies and shredding them before our horrified gaze. (Memoir of Dr. Oslchanictzki[37])

By the time the next International Health Conference convened at Paris in 1894—under the name of the "Sanitary Conference on the Mecca Pilgrimage"—cholera in the Hijaz had become a full-blown political issue as well as a matter of health. The Ottomans were not enforcing the international regulations in their own territories, it was clear, and now the European powers, notably France, England, and the Netherlands, began to insist that they had a right to intervene directly in sanitary questions at Jidda. The disease afflicted more of their own subjects than those of the Ottomans, they claimed: of the pilgrims who had arrived by ship in Jidda for the Hajj of 1893, 13,477 were Ottoman subjects, whereas 82,900 lived under European sovereignty, though far from Europe, of course. When the Ottoman delegate protested that this was interference in the internal affairs of a sovereign state, he was told that it was a question not of national sovereignty but of basic human rights.[38]

The conference then proceeded to prescribe the most stringent controls to date on the pilgrimage traffic. Pilgrims were required to undergo medical examination and observation at their ports of embarkation, and a physician was required on all ships carrying more than one hundred Hajjis—two on ships carrying more than a thousand—with serious penalties for infractions. Finally, the conference established quarantine stations on Qamaran Island near the southern straits entry to the Red Sea and at the northern end of the Persian Gulf.[39]

THE PILGRIMAGE OF 1895

When the next International Health Conference met in Paris in 1895, the Ottoman delegates began the proceedings by announcing that their government would be taking firm action to improve both the quarantine facilities at Jidda and the general hygienic conditions at Mecca. Eventually some of these measures were carried out, though not extensively or quickly enough to have much effect on the pilgrimage of 1895. The same Dr. Oslchanictzki who was temporarily posted to Jidda in 1893 was once again on service there during the Hajj of 1895:

> The Board of Health in Constantinople[40] thought it necessary, to combat the spread of the plague, to have built at Jidda a large hospital as well as a number of lavatories at different points in the city and the port since the pilgrims were relieving themselves in the open streets. They also had fitted out near the Quarantine Office a pavilion to serve as a disinfecting area so that the clothes and bedding of the pilgrims could be disinfected before they embarked.
>
> But the mutawwifs [the guild of guides] stirred up the pilgrims and in one night the disinfection station and the steam baths were destroyed by pilgrims of Bukhara. On this same occasion there was an armed attack against a number of Consuls who were outside the city—by the Medina gate—near the hospital built by the Board of Health. The English Vice-Consul was killed,[41] and the Consuls of Russia and England and the Vice-Consul of France were wounded. The inquiry by the local authorities that followed pointed out that the attack was directed not against the Consuls but against the medical officers. Thus we were obliged to fulfill our duties accompanied by armed guards and to sleep nightly on board one of the ships in Jidda harbor so as to avoid unpleasant surprises. (Memoir of Dr. Oslchanictzki[42])

THE PILGRIMAGE OF 1908

Another physician, Dr. Salih Subhi, left a more detailed account of the main health facility in Jidda, the one built in 1895, which he saw in December 1908:

> The hospital is installed in a vast pavilion built of old wood and furnished with two large, moth-eaten sofas about 4 feet deep which extend

ong each of the long sides of the pavilion. This is the common bed for he entire pavilion. Every yard or so there is a hole about eight inches in diameter for the patients to relieve themselves; in each hole there is a lake or mountain of excrement.

The water jugs are all empty; the sick have no change of clothes, and their only cover is a blanket of flies so dense that it is impossible to see their face or skin. . . . No distinction is made among the sick: those with intestinal problems are bedded right next to those with the pox. (Memoir of Dr. Salih Subhi[43])

The year 1908 turned out to be one of the worst in the Cholera Era in the Hijaz. The pilgrimage was scheduled to begin on 17 January 1908, but already by early December cholera cases were reported in Mecca, Medina, Yanbu, and Jidda. France forbade its Algerian subjects to go on Hajj that year, but elsewhere no restraints were imposed. One official later recalled the scene as pilgrims began to pour into Jidda:

The great square between the Health Bureau and the City Hall where the pilgrims camped was distasteful to look upon. The entire area was covered with excrement, the remains of rotten vegetables and spoiled fruit, all of which gave off a sickening odor that made the air unbreathable. So many were the obstacles that the streets were unusable, and on more than one occasion I came across dying people right out on the street, deprived of all help.

The quarantine building was already full when news from the interior became more and more alarming. The Board of Health of Constantinople let go the pilgrims who had been in quarantine, and passage between Jidda and Mecca also became open; pilgrims from whatever port of origin could freely disembark and continue on their way to Mecca, where the cholera was on the increase.

The epidemic made deeper and deeper inroads. From the first day of the appearance of cholera the health authorities did not isolate the known cases; they were satisfied to disinfect their premises after having forbidden entry.

The number of dead increased daily and reached a peak during the pilgrimage ceremonies themselves, when in four days 1,381 people died at Mecca alone. The official report turned to Mina.

During the three days of the ceremonies the valley of Mina was the most disgusting sight imaginable. Filth and remains of animals were mingled with the hundreds of corpses that choked the valley. . . . More than one body was discovered in a state of putrefaction and others were thrown into the ditches that had been dug for the disposal of the (sacrificial) animals.

At Jidda, the return of the pilgrims resembled the flight of an army from slaughter.

With the arrival of the first (return) caravan from Mecca to Jidda, cases of cholera reappeared and increased in proportion to the growth in numbers. During the course of a week pilgrims arrived day and night in endless caravans, after having strewn the way (from Mecca) with corpses that became the prey of vultures and wild beasts. (Report of a Mission to the Hijaz[44])

The last of the great plague years connected with the Hajj was 1912; thereafter epidemic cholera disappeared from the Hijaz.

Health Problems at Arafat and Mina

Health hazards threatened at almost every step of the pilgrim's way, but they were the greatest where the most people were collected at one time—at Arafat, for example, at the climax of the Hajj ceremony:

The fountain of Ayn Zubayda passes through a narrow channel at the foot of Mount Arafat. At several points it is uncovered so that water may be drawn from it. But most of the pilgrims bathe and wash their clothes there as well. These men, who have not washed for months and who have not changed their clothes from their departure from home except to don the ihram, use this holy water not so much, I think, to make themselves clean as to immerse themselves or even to make the ritual ablutions. We ourselves have seen several pilgrims from Bukhara washing themselves in the same place from which drinking water was drawn. The government has sent five or six soldiers to prevent people from fouling this water or washing their clothes in it, but there is too much space for their surveillance to be effective.

Two basins have been dug, large enough for the pilgrims to bathe in, but the water is never changed, and it is safe to say that these two pools are genuine sources of infection. But hundreds of pilgrims dive into them, and some even rinse their mouths with the water in them. (Kazemzadeh 1912: 214–215)

The most terrible danger of all was encountered at Mina, after the ceremony at Arafat, where each pilgrim had to offer sacrifice:

Those who are performing the complete pilgrimage or those liable for expiatory sacrifices are obliged to sacrifice a male or female sheep or a male or female camel, as the case may be. But the sacrifice of a camel is rare; only the Sharif does such each year, and with considerable pomp. The sacrifice must be made in the name of a single individual rather than a pious act performed on one occasion on behalf of several people. Lambs to be sacrificed must be no less than six months old, sheep no less than a year and camels no less than five. The animal must not be totally or partially blind, nor lame, nor with broken horns, nor with its ears clipped, otherwise the sacrifice is invalid.

The animals are bought at Mina, whither they are brought by the thousands from all directions. The pilgrim can cut its throat himself, and that is more worthwhile, or delegate the task to another; but if it is delegated, the pilgrim must have his hand on that of his deputy. Religious custom recommends that the pilgrim eat a little of the flesh of the sacrificed animal and that the rest be distributed to the poor. (Kazemzadeh 1912: 220–221)

Richard Burton, it will be recalled, fumed over the sanitary conditions at Mina in the 1860s and 1870s in the wake of the prescribed sacrifices. Mirza Mohammad Farahani provides an eyewitness account of the situation in 1885:

After returning from stoning the pillars, they perform the sacrifice at that time, each whatever sacrifice he can. . . .

On this holiday about 200,000 sacrificial animals were slaughtered at Mina. They had prepared large pits as a place for performing the sacrifice. Nevertheless, they threw many of the sheep's heads and trotters, the guts, flesh and bones of the sacrificial animals amid the tents and along the road. It was made filthy everywhere as far as the Khayf Mosque. Even though two hundred black slaves, who are the street cleaners, work under the careful scrutiny of their supervisors and clean all the filth from the roads, and though they immediately pour a mixture of lime over the pits where the sheep are killed and cover them up, still the air is infected by the odor of carcasses to the extent that smelling it causes disease. For this reason, illness and plague first appear at Mina.

The government physicians keep a watch on Mina. Every day of these three days at Mina, they get a list from the undertakers and ascertain that each day a certain number have died and what illness was the cause. If the disease is contagious, they inform Istanbul and the frontier posts.

In Istanbul they determine at a meeting of the public health officials how many days there should be a quarantine and in what place. After it is determined that there is disease in Mina, they raise a yellow flag on top of the mountain as a sign of there being disease, so that the pilgrims will know what precautions to take. This raising of the yellow flag causes terror, and many die out of fear. If the disease is not contagious, still, out of precaution, they determine in Istanbul that the pilgrims should be quarantined for two or three days. Whichever way they go, they will have a quarantine, unless via the route to Bombay or Bushihr. (Farahani 1990: 241–242)

The precautions did not always work. The year 1885 was relatively trouble-free, but in 1893, when nearly 33,000 of somewhat more than 200,000 pilgrims perished, the situation at Mina was out of control. Dr. Qassim Izzedine, an Indian physician making the pilgrimage, describes the scene:

Along the streets (of Mina), amidst the movement of pilgrims who are performing their devotions with a praiseworthy resignation, you could see corpses being carried away and the suffering sick, and the same scene unfolded under the tents. Those assigned to wash the corpses could no longer carry on their duties. Several of them had died and the survivors found themselves worn out with fatigue. Three hundred corpses were piled up in the cemetery waiting to be buried. The men charged with the burial of the cadavers of (sacrificed) sheep had fled, and thousands of these cadavers lay exposed to the sun and putrefying.

Dr. Izzedine went out again the following day:

The corpses on the street were far more numerous than yesterday. Everywhere one could see the ill tied to the backs of camels. . . . The pilgrims were pensive and serious. No one cried out. The only sound was the savage cries of the camels.

The further you went from Mina, the more numerous became the corpses; a considerable number of pilgrims, who were not ill when they left, died on the way, their end hastened by the jolting of the camel ride and the heat of the sun. All these corpses were black. The pilgrims re-entered Mecca with their corpses and their sick. Within a few hours the plague gripped the city: it was found in every house and every quarter.

The 13th of Dhu al-Hijja [29 June 1893], the fourth day of the (pilgrimage) festival, the situation became more frightful. On that day the death toll reached extraordinary proportions (2,455). The dead were no longer buried; they were simply left in the streets. Some streets were choked with dead bodies. There were no more ill people to be seen, only corpses. But the pilgrims continued calmly to perform their devotions without complaint. It appeared to me that among this mass of pilgrims that I had before my eyes, the brain was no longer functioning. The pilgrims were like machines: they allowed themselves to be led; they no longer had any will of their own. They sensed only the need to leave. (Cassim Izzedine, Le Choléra et l'Hygiène à la Mecque, 64–66[45])

The situation had not greatly improved by 1911, when Hossein Kazemzadeh was at Mina.

For sanitary reasons ditches have been dug where the pilgrims are supposed to make their sacrifice and into which the animal should then be thrown, without either eating it or giving it to others. There are some soldiers there assigned to prevent the sheep from being carried away after they have been sacrificed and to make sure that all the animals have been thrown into the ditches. But this measure is never effective since most of the pilgrims perform the sacrifice in their tents or near to them, and there would never be enough officials to circulate in this vast valley and take action against infractions. Even the pilgrims who voluntarily bring their animals to be sacrificed at the ditches can carry them away again for the price of a few piasters to the soldiers assigned to oversee them. More, the pilgrims do not understand the point of the sanitary measures, having no sense of the danger from eating this meat in such excessive temperatures. On the contrary, they attribute to this meat sacrificed to God miraculous powers and even that of curing diseases! (Kazemzadeh 1912: 221)

Our last look at Mina dates from 1924, during the final pilgrimage conducted under the auspices of King Husayn. The reporter is a certain Dr. Salih:

The streams of blood, the garbage scattered everywhere, the animal pelts reserved for the state, the large number of animals sacrificed (roughly 20,000 daily), the Takruri beggars, men, women and children, struggling over the scraps of meat they could salvage, all contributed to a terribly moving and painful scene. Twenty soldiers formed a protective line to prevent any of the animals destined for sacrifice from entering into Mina proper. Burials in beds of lime took place only at night, and since there was not enough lime and the ditches were too shallow, there was everywhere the smell of putrefaction, which made the air unbreathable. (Memoir of Dr. Salih[46])

Quarantine Stations

From the first, the nineteenth-century international conferences convoked to deal with cholera epidemics had recommended the establishment of quarantine stations where signs of the disease could be detected, the persons and possessions of travelers disinfected, and the pilgrims held for some days—five in normal times, fifteen during epidemics—to give the disease a chance to run its course. On the initiative of the Egyptian Quarantine Board, established in 1831, such stations were set up in various places, chiefly at port facilities. The overland caravans served as their own natural "walking quarantines" to the same end.[47]

THE SUEZ QUARANTINE (1885)

The Persian pilgrim Farahani had a few occasions to experience some of the hygiene measures taken along the Hajj route. The first, at Suez on the way out to Jidda, was not impressive for its efficiency:

Another of the difficulties for the pilgrims at Suez is that the chief physician there on behalf of the Khedive must give health certificates to the pilgrims. As for the fee for writing the certificate, he charges three qorush-e saq and ten pareh per person, which is about one Iranian kran. However, it is not necessary that the physician see every pilgrim. That is, the method for obtaining (the certificate) is that one person goes and takes the money and gets the health certificates for ten or twenty people. (Farahani 1990: 171)

THE STATION AT TUR

This perfunctory stop at Suez on the way out to Mecca was intended merely for certification. Farahani encountered a genuine quarantine at Tur in Sinai on his return journey by steamship from Yanbu to Suez:

Wednesday, 11 November 1885 at nine o'clock, the steamship anchored at the wadi of Mount Sinai, which was the quarantine site this year. When the captain first informed the quarantine officials, ten or twelve rowboats came below the steamship and transported the pilgrims without charging a fare. Although the oarsmen took one qurush and a half from the pilgrims as a gratuity, this was not in addition to a fare. On land, they went on foot. A government building had been constructed on the edge of the landing. Most of its rooms were like very spacious storage rooms or halls.

The employees of the quarantine are as follows: one chief doctor, two (other) doctors, one inspector, one assistant inspector, one accountant, one official in charge of security, called the muhafiz, and two hundred foot soldiers.

These troops do not allow the pilgrims to wander around. As soon as all the people of a steamer have assembled in the open area in front of the building, they announce that the pilgrims must obtain tickets and enter the quarantine. The inspector, assistant inspector and accountant are seated in one of the rooms. All the pilgrims must pay them one and a quarter Levant dollars per person and take tickets. They charged some of them who are not knowledgeable about the operation of the quarantine from one and a half to two dollars for the tickets. . . . They gave printed tickets to each person, couple, ten people, or whatever. As soon as they had collected the money from all the pilgrims and given out the tickets, then the accountant stood at the door of the building with two soldiers and inspected the people's tickets. The pilgrims entered the building group by group. In some of the rooms of this building there is fumigating equipment like a sulphur burner. If people do not have a disease known to be contagious, they do not have to be fumigated.

At another door to the building by which the people exit, there is a vast plain. On that plain, four groups of military field tents had been pitched, so that each group was at an interval of one meydan [about one mile] from the next. Each group had three rows of white tents, and each row had twenty-five tents. So altogether there are three hundred tents. In front of each group of tents there were also six tents where the shop-keepers stayed. There were two coffeehouses and four grocer's tents. They also have fruits and sell everything at an exorbitant price. Those six shop-keepers are Arabs. There is also a tent in each group for two Jewish money changers and two Armenian butchers. Live sheep can also be obtained but they are extremely expensive.

Beside each group of tents there are also two iron water tanks. Each one has two or three spigots. They draw water from those spigots. The water is brought in continuously by government camels and poured into the tanks. They gave water, however much is desired, to the pilgrims for free. These four groups of tents are the collective property of the four steamers. Each steamer that comes to the quarantine must lodge all its passengers in one of those groups. Variously, every five, seven, eight or ten people will have one tent. There are thirty soldiers to take care of each group of tents. They watch out for the pilgrims' belongings at night, and by day they also insure that the people of one ship and group of tents do not mix with the group or the people of another ship. Thus, after our arrival at the quarantine, two other ships came which were visible from afar, but we did not see the people of those ships nor did they see us.

At one spot in the desert, near the government building, there are some trees, date palms, and a little greenery where ten or twenty tents have been pitched. It is the residence of the soldiers and the employees of the quarantine.

To sum up, it was noted earlier in the description of Arafat and Mina that this quarantine was set up by the Ottoman government's bureau of health in Istanbul. If there is no contagious disease, the period the pilgrims stay in the quarantine is 48 hours. If during the 48 hours, someone dies on land, the period will be renewed. Its employees are, however, [in the pay] of the Khedive of Egypt; the Sinai wadi is also part of the kingdom of Egypt. It seems that the service and fealty and obedience which the Khedive of Egypt renders to the Ottoman Empire is no more than using the moon and the star flag and this matter (of the quarantine). This quarantine in no way causes any loss or expense for the Ottoman Empire. Whatever they expend on it, they get back double from the pilgrims.

If there is an external air of efficiency about the Sinai quarantine, the reality lay not so deeply buried that Farahani could not detect it:

Exorbitant sums go to the employees of the quarantine. When officials are posted to the quarantine, it is as if they had been appointed officials

in charge of fleecing and plundering the pilgrims.[48] One of the circumstances that makes this clear is that the authorities of the quarantine, especially the chief doctor, take something from the captains of the steamers
not to make trouble: if someone dies during the two days stopped at the
quarantine, they don't renew the period and do not delay the steamer.
(Farahani 1990: 288–291)

In 1922 Amin Rihani, a Syrian Arab by origin, a Christian, and a New
Yorker, was going out to Jidda on a small steamer whose only other passenger was an Irish woman who had worked as a nurse for twenty years in
the Egyptian service, many of them at the quarantine station at Tur. Rihani's opinions of the place, then, likely came from this so-called Mother
of the Pilgrims:

The Quarantine Station at Tur, the second best in the world,[49] is, indeed, one of the guide posts of civilization east of Suez. It is international,
but its administration is in the hands of the Egyptian Government. On
that sun-baked sandy wilderness, not far from the village proper, it stands
out, a town by itself, hygienicly conceived and built; its wards and its
stores, its clinics and its disinfecting rooms, its soda-water factory and ice
plants—they recall the best in Europe. It can accommodate from two to
three thousand pilgrims at a time, the total number for the whole season
sometimes rising to forty thousand. The Egyptian pilgrims, returning
from Mecca, are first disinfected and then sent into wards for a period of
from three to ten days, according to the prevailing health conditions at
the time.
    No greater service to Islam, to the world, in fact, could be rendered by
medical science. Ever since the Tur Quarantine was established, about
thirty years ago [under international auspices], Egypt has not had a single
cholera epidemic. It is, moreover, teaching the Muslims sanitation and
hygiene. They first balked at the idea of a quarantine, resented the interference with the pilgrimage, and objected strongly to the disinfecting process; but they have gradually reconciled themselves to it, and now . . . the
first thing they ask for, when they arrive, is a bath. There may be something blasphemous in a disinfectant after a pilgrimage to the Holy Places,
"but health and well-being and cleanliness," said the Celtic "Mother of
the Pilgrims," "are enjoined by the Prophet." She knows the Muslim's
Book as well as her own. (Rihani 1930: 5–6)

QAMARAN ISLAND

Qamaran Island, only eleven miles long and five and a half wide, and a
mere four and a half miles from the Yemeni coast of Arabia, possesses "the
dubious distinction of having undergone more foreign occupations than
any part of the Arabian peninsula."[50] It is not difficult to understand why.

With a secure harbor just inside the Bab al-Mandab and with its own source of water, Qamaran beckons invitingly as a base and reprovisioning station to any maritime power covetous of controlling either the entry to the Red Sea or the southern Arabian coast. The Portuguese Afonso d'Albuquerque clung almost desperately to it early in the sixteenth century, and not long afterward Husayn al-Kurdi and Salman Pasha tried clumsily to hold it for the Mamluk Sultans, or perhaps for themselves. The Ottomans were somewhat more successful. They used the island in 1538 as a staging area for their conquest of the Yemen, and later as a refuge when their grip on the Yemen seemed to be slipping. In 1636 the Zaydi Imams of the Yemen drove the Ottomans out of their land and took over the island as well.

The beginning of the nineteenth century brought new players onto the tiny stage of Qamaran. The Wahhabis coveted the Yemen. The French, although driven out of Egypt in 1801, still had commercial ambitions in the Red Sea, and Qamaran Island seemed a likely base from which to pursue them. The two came to an agreement of sorts, which would have permitted the French a foothold on Qamaran, but the affair was botched, and the British East India Company intervened to dash French hopes. Muhammad Ali too briefly passed across the Qamaran landscape between 1819 and 1837, when the ruler of Egypt held the entire eastern coast of the Red Sea. And once again it was Britain, which had occupied Aden in 1839, that forced Muhammad Ali off the island and indeed out of the entire area.[51]

The Ottomans were back in the Yemen and on Qamaran in 1849, and it was their sovereignty over the island that made it a likely place for a quarantine station on the southern approaches to Mecca. The 1866 International Conference recommended just such a station to monitor ships and passengers arriving from India and the East, and shortly afterward the Turks sent a sanitary commission to find "a convenient spot on the Arab coast." They found Qamaran Island. But it was only after a number of other commissions had investigated more possibilities that a quarantine station was established on Qamaran in 1882, when it received 9,067 pilgrims. By 1897 the facility was capable of processing 6,000 pilgrims at one time. During the 1906–1907 pilgrimage season there was a staff of forty attached to the quarantine, and a total of 44,333 arrivals passed through Qamaran.[52] In 1884 an Indian Muslim doctor was appointed the British vice-consul for Hudayda and Qamaran, and he lived on the island during the pilgrimage season.[53]

Almost from the first outbreak of cholera, the European powers exercised direct or indirect control over the sanitary conditions affecting the Hajj. What must have appeared to be a permanent organization was put in place by the International Health Convention of 1926, which established a Paris office to coordinate the sanitary control of the Meccan pilgrimage in cooperation with the Egyptian Quarantine Board. The system remained in place until creation of the World Health Organization in 1948, one of whose objectives was to reexamine the Hajj controls. By then, however, the Saudis, who had taken over political and religious responsibility for the pilgrimage in 1926, regarded the arrangements established in that year as blatant infringements on Saudi sovereignty.[54] The World Health Organization agreed in principle to hand over complete control to the government of Saudi Arabia—the Egyptians would continue to run the Sinai quarantine—their only condition being the enlargement of the quarantine facilities in Jidda. The Saudis promised that such would be done, and the expanded facility was completed in 1956. Finally, in 1957, "65 years after the first effective health control was instituted by the International Sanitary Convention of Venice of 1892, the health administration of the Hajj became the sole responsibility of the Saudi Arabian Government."[55]

CHAPTER VII

The Great War
and After

THE HIJAZ RAILWAY

RAILROAD-BUILDING SCHEMES were in the air during much of the nineteenth century, and the Near East was not exempt from such plans. The British appear to have contemplated a railway from Port Said across the Sinai and the north of Arabia to one of their client ports on the Persian Gulf. If the plan was serious, it was never realized, but it may nonetheless have encouraged the Turks to enlarge their own thinking and take up a project that seems to have been first suggested in India in the late 1890s: a railway from Damascus to the Yemen.

It was an attractive idea at the time and under the political circumstances. The Ottomans, facing troubles in Arabia from the Yemen and the newly active Wahhabis in the Najd under Ibn Sa'ud, looked upon a railway as a cheap and convenient method of supplying and reinforcing Ottoman garrisons in Arabia. Such, at any rate were the findings of an imperial commission assigned to study the Wahhabi situation in Arabia. The commission's recommendation began to move toward realization in May 1900, when Abd al-Hamid issued, on the twenty-fifth anniversary of his Sultanate, an imperial decree appointing two commissions: one, a financial body in Istanbul under Izzet Pasha, a Syrian Arab who served as the second secretary to the Sultan, and the other, an executive committee with headquarters in Damascus, to be headed by the Governor of Syria. The chief executive officer was the Ottoman general Kazim Pasha, and the chief engineer from 1901 onward was the experienced German railway builder Heinrich Meissner.[1]

The financing of the project was novel indeed: the new railway was to be a *waqf*, an Islamic endowment, and by thus identifying it as an Islamic project rather than an Ottoman one, the Sultan was free to solicit donations from Muslims all over the world. And to further emphasize the Islamic quality of the enterprise, he promised that workers and materiel would all be from the Abode of Islam. Though the literal fulfillment of that pledge was clearly impossible—the tracks and cars came from Europe, and German engineers worked on the plans and construction[2]—to

a certain extent the promise was kept, particularly as it referred to working crews inside the Hijaz, where the bulk of the labor was done by Turkish army units.[3]

Actual construction began in September 1900, crews started laying rail
from Damascus southward and Dera'a northward. Year by year the main
line lengthened: in 1903, from Damascus to Amman; in 1904, as far as
Ma'an; in 1906, to Mudawwara; and to Mada'in Salih in 1907. There
were trunk lines as well, notably one from Dera'a to the Mediterranean at
Haifa. The one-thousandth kilometer was reached at al-Ula in September
1907, and exactly a year later—eight years after it was begun—the Hijaz
Railway reached to Medina, eight hundred miles from Damascus and as
far as it would ever go.

A Would-Be Hajji Rides the Rails

One of the very first travelers on the newly opened railway was, as we have
seen, A.J.B. Wavell, another Englishman bent on making the Hajj in disguise. In 1908 he made his way to the Hijaz Terminal in Damascus:

> The Hijaz railway station is situated on the eastern side of town some
> little distance out. . . . The train was due to start at eleven in the morn-
> ing—European time—but we were warned not to be later than nine, as it
> was expected to be very crowded. There are two classes, first and third.
> Seeing that the journey (to the Medina terminus) was to take four days at
> the least, and we were fairly affluent, I was strongly tempted to travel first
> class, especially as the difference did not amount to very much. Our
> Damascus friends however strongly opposed this extravagance. They said
> that even the "very best people" went third, and that it was nearly as com-
> fortable. I gave up the idea when I found that it would probably involve
> putting on a special carriage for me, for I naturally wished to make myself
> as inconspicuous as possible on arriving.

The third-class tickets to Medina cost £3 10s. sterling each, "not a great
deal for a journey of over a thousand miles," Wavell remarked. With more
than two hours still to wait, Wavell and his companions placed their luggage in one of the carriages and went off for tea.

> On returning to the train I found all confusion. The carriages consisted
> of plain wooden benches with a passage down the middle. These were in
> pairs facing one another with just room for two to sit on each. We had
> reserved four of them, but other passengers turning up had forcibly re-
> moved our things from two of them. . . . Our carriage was now absolutely
> jammed, as likewise were all the others. There was no room for anything,

and we were jammed up together with our belongings in a most uncomfortable way. Although we still had an hour to wait, we did not dare to leave again and sat in our places waiting for the train to start. As it was, many people arriving late were turned away for want of room. When, much to our relief, we did start, we were half an hour late.

Among those in our compartment were several Turkish officers in uniform, some Syrian pilgrims and some very dirty Moroccans. Next to us, on the other side of the carriage, were two Turks, father and son, whose only luggage appeared to be a gramophone. This ubiquitous instrument is very popular in the Hijaz and many Arabic records for it are now to be obtained—among them even passages from the Quran!

We traveled through open cultivated country till night fell. The Jebel al-Shaykh, a fine peak overlooking Damascus, well above the snow-line, was still visible the following morning. In the course of the first day we passed several large stations, but by the morning of the second we had entered the desert and thenceforward few inhabitants were visible. . . . We had brought what food we required—mostly hard-boiled eggs, bread and cakes, but what with the dust and the stuffy atmosphere we could hardly eat anything. Through the night we dozed at intervals, but sleep in our constrained position was difficult. The second day I had a bout of malarial fever, which lasted till we got to Medina, and did not enhance my enjoyment of the journey. The kindness of our fellow passengers in this emergency was remarkable. Seeing that I was ill, they insisted on crowding together so I could have room to lie down, as often as I would permit them to do so. The Turkish officers, who had a small charcoal brazier, cooked things for me when possible, and gave me fruit, of which we had foolishly lost our own supply.

On the third day there was a delay from nine in the morning until five in the afternoon: the relief engineer did not show up, and the incumbent refused to continue until he had had some sleep.

The engine driver being at last sufficiently refreshed, we started again. Another long night passed, and we were traversing a country broken up into fantastically shaped hills and covered with huge boulders of weird forms. . . . We were now in Arabia, and as we proceeded the aspect of the country became ever wilder. High mountain ranges appeared on either side, and the great pinnacles of rock became more twisted and uncanny in appearance. The track wound through gloomy gorges over which huge rocks hung menacingly.

About midday we reached Mada'in Salih. This is the boundary of the Hijaz province, and beyond it no one, not being a Muslim, is allowed to pass. When the railway was being built all the European engineers were discharged at this point and the work was carried on entirely by Turks and Arabs. *This place, which itself is simply a collection of tin shanties, is remarkable for the extraordinary rock dwellings. . . . These have been well described by the Arabian explorer Doughty and several others. (Wavell 1912: 54–55)*

The Great Railway War

The Young Turks, or, to give those Ottoman reformers their more formal name, the Committee of Union and Progress, desired a centralized Ottoman state and so were committed to the railway's extension to Mecca and the Red Sea ports. On the other hand, the newly appointed Sharif Husayn, whose only power base, apart from his own aristocratic legitimacy, was the bedouin of the Hijaz, strongly opposed it, as did the nomads. Similar opposition may have cost Husayn's predecessor his office, but the new Sharif judged, correctly, that he was far too deeply entrenched to suffer deposition from Istanbul.

That bedouin opposition to the railway was more than a matter of words became clear when the earliest railway passengers began to arrive in Medina. Wavell had an opportunity to experience it firsthand once the train he was riding passed into the Hijaz—and beyond the effective reach of the Ottoman government.

In the afternoon of this third day we reached a good-sized village surrounded by date palms—the first habitations we had seen since leaving Syria. Here we stayed for an hour and were able to replenish our provisions and get some coffee. All the stations south of Mada'in Salih are fortified with trenches and barbed wire, and the whole scene reminds one of South Africa at the time of the [Boer] war. There was fighting all along here while the railway was in course of construction, and the posts are still occasionally attacked by wandering tribes. We passed several wrecked engines that had run off the track owing to it not having been properly laid, and we were obliged to proceed very carefully. We were told that it was by no means unlikely that we should be attacked between this place and Medina—not by the belligerent tribes, but by bands of marauders whose object was merely robbery. We therefore looked to our weapons on restarting. We were due to arrive at Medina at noon the next day—Sunday.

Nothing happened during the night, and we were all much cheered by the reflection that it was the last we had to spend on that accursed train. I was also feeling much better, in spite, or perhaps because, of having had no medicine whatsoever. We were somewhat delayed, and it was not until one o'clock that the dull thudding of distant artillery fire told us that we were approaching our destination. The stations were now protected by considerable earthworks and had garrisons of a company or more. . . . A

little later, through a gap in the hills, there appeared the needle-like mina-
rets of the Prophet's mosque—then, as we emerged on to the plain, the
city itself. (Wavell 1912: 56–57)

Wavell may have missed the worst of the fighting. In May 1908 Medina itself was attacked by the bedouin, and only the arrival of substantial troop reinforcements from Damascus prevented the tribesmen from over-running the city.[4]

If the bedouin attacks up and down the line were intended to intimidate the Ottoman authorities, they succeeded. In 1910 the railway imposed a special surtax on tickets between Mada'in Salih and Medina, and in March 1911 the surtax zone was extended northward to Dera'a. The point of the tax was simple: the proceeds were paid to the bedouin shaykhs along the way to restrain them from attacking the railroad.[5]

Over its brief life as a public conveyance rather than a military transport, the Hijaz Railway proved a popular means of getting to the holy land. Whatever problems Wavell may have experienced paled in comparison to the hardships the caravan passenger was expected to tolerate. The price, two Turkish pounds, was only about a tenth of the cost of caravan carriage;[6] and even if the scheduled time of seventy-two hours between Damascus and Medina was only rarely achieved, the trip by rail was almost unimaginably shorter than the month or more spent on the caravan trek. Passenger figures for the railway's years of operation reflect all these factors. Total traffic, civilian and military, rose from 246,109 in 1908, the first year of operation, to 360,000 in 1913, the last full prewar year.[7]

In 1914, just before the outbreak of the First World War, the Ottomans made a major change in the legal status of the railway. From the beginning, the railroad's moneys, some of which were raised from Muslim donations throughout the Islamic world, were kept separate from the Ottoman state budget. But when the Ottomans approached the French in 1914 with a request to enter the Paris bond market, the French, among other conditions, proposed that a Frenchman serve as director of the Hijaz Railway. It was in an effort to counter this move that the railroad was transferred to the Ottoman Ministry of Pious Foundations. Thus, by declaring that the railroad was in effect an endowed religious foundation (*waqf*), the Ottomans guaranteed that, at least in terms of Islamic law, the Hijaz Railway could never be sold, divided, or administered by a non-Muslim.[8]

The Hijaz Railway was intended not only to provide the Ottomans with strategic flexibility in the disposition of their armed forces in distant provinces but also to introduce a new era in pilgrim transportation. The first objective was all too successfully achieved. In order to pin the Turkish garrison in Medina during the First World War, the British and their

Arab allies expended a good deal of their meager resources on destroying the rail link that the Turks had forged between their principal army corps and the beleaguered vilayet in Arabia.[9]

WARTIME PILGRIMAGES

In the last weeks of July and the opening days of August 1914 the European Powers were plunged into war—Britain, France, and Russia on one side and Germany with Austro-Hungary and its allies on the other. Formally, the Ottoman Empire was allied with neither side and might indeed have waited out the subsequent conflict unscathed: it was still the consistent policy of all the European states to preserve the integrity of the empire, if only against the rapacity of each other. The Ottoman Empire may indeed have been, as one historian has described it, "like a ruined temple of classical antiquity, with some of its columns still erect and visible,"[10] but within those ruins life still stirred, and perhaps imperial ambitions as well. And so in November 1914 the triumvirate of reformers who ran the state—Talat Bey, Enver Pasha, and Jemal Pasha—chose, with little or no consultation, to cast the fortunes of the Sultans' legacy with those of Germany.

Like many other Turks and Arabs, Sharif Husayn strongly opposed any talk of entering the war and wrote to the Sultan in August 1914 to that effect. As early as February 1914, however, the British in Egypt had made contact with Husayn's son during one of Abdullah's trips abroad. The objective was to detach the Sharif, and so also the Holy Cities of Islam, from allegiance to the Ottomans, who by then openly advocated Germany's cause. The Hijaz enterprise seemed ripe. Husayn, the most conservative of Ottoman vassals, had long been in conflict with the forces of reform at work in the empire, and his son Abdullah, on his father's behalf, had already begun conversations with emerging Arab nationalist groups in Syria. The Turks, for their part, had little love for or trust in their Arab subjects. When war was finally declared between Britain and Germany's Ottoman ally in November 1914, the British stepped up their attempts to win over Husayn.

The British principal in the approach to the Sharif was the High Commissioner for Egypt, first Lord Kitchener and then Sir Henry McMahon. McMahon in particular carried on a lengthy correspondence with the Sharif from 14 July 1915 to 10 March 1916, and the terms, promises, and understandings in those letters, explicit and implicit, would bedevil much of the postwar history of the Middle East. The Hijaz figures very little in the exchange, though both parties seem to have assumed that the Hijaz would be independent after the war and ruled by Husayn.

Whatever the later disagreements, there was a meeting of minds, British and Sharifian, in the summer of 1916. On 9 June 1916 Husayn's sons Faysal and Ali cut the railway near Medina, and on the next day the Turks were attacked throughout the Hijaz. In Mecca, Sharif Husayn publicly proclaimed what came to be called the Arab Revolt, and not long afterward he declared himself King of the Hijaz.

The Pilgrimage of 1916

British policy concerning the Sharif issued from the High Commisioner's residence in Cairo and ultimately from Whitehall, but the actual negotiations in the Hijaz were conducted chiefly by Ronald Storrs, who bore the title of Oriental Secretary to the High Commissioner. Storrs made his first visit to the Hijaz in May–June 1916. Strategy was discussed, as was the Sharif's request for troops, equipment, and a substantial British subsidy. Storrs was uneasy about "pouring into the yawning mouth of Jidda," as he put it, "a ceaseless stream of corn, cash and cartridges." Moreover, any such undertakings might be misinterpreted as an impingement on Arab independence. With these worries on his mind, Storrs sailed into the Hijaz on the flagship of the British Red Sea fleet, the *Eurylus*, which was carrying the *kiswa* to Mecca for the pilgrimage of October 1916. In his autobiography, Storrs quotes from the diary he kept on that occasion:

> *September 26, 1916. Passed through the dangerous but well bouyed Jidda reef about 3:30 to find Hardinge dressed and flying Egyptian flag at peak with green three crescented ensign—the flag chosen by Sharif Husayn to supersede the Ottoman-Egyptian flag with single crescent and star—at head to denote that she was carrying the Mahmal, which indeed was plainly visible on deck. The town under afternoon sun looked as if it were carved in ivory. . . . Colonel Brémond, of French Mission, tall, ugly, dirty, strong and very sympathetique, came aboard at 4:30. (Storrs 1945: 166)*

The Holy Cities of the Hijaz were still very much what they had been in the seventeenth or even the fourteenth century, but the twentieth was rapidly making somewhat disruptive, and somewhat comic, inroads, as Storrs noted.

> *Going down to telephone, rang up No. 1 Mecca. After a short pause I distinguished what I rightly took to be the tones of the Grand Sharif himself, bidding me a warm and affectionate welcome to Jidda. . . . At this moment three or four other voices became audible on the wire, and I remarked to the Sharif that in my opinion we were being tapped. He said it was quite impossible that this should be so at Jidda . . . (but) I immediately had the satisfaction of hearing him call through to Central*

in stronger language than I had expected from so holy a man, ordering them to cut off everybody's instrument in the Hijaz excepting his own and mine for the next half-hour. This was instantly done, and we conversed henceforth in a vacuum of death. (Storrs 1945: 167)

Storrs's mission was political, but the infidel British, as the present carriers of both the Mahmal and the *kiswa,* those venerable tokens of Meccan sanctity—and of Egyptian sovereignty—were now necessarily drawn into the preliminary Hajj ceremonials:

The Admiral [Wemyss] was officially invited to ride at the head of the procession through Jidda of the Holy Carpet itself, an honor that we prudently, if reluctantly, thought fit to decline. For like reasons and with infinitely sharper regret, I had to refuse the Grand Sharif's subsequent personal invitation that I should visit him in Mecca.

As soon as the barge came back, . . . the Admiral went on board the Hardinge to return the official morning visit of Fathi Pasha, the Amir al-Hajj, the General in Command of the Egyptian Mahmal and Pilgrimage. The General was . . . attired in his pilgrim's bath-towel costume and sandals, completed by an officer's belt, and the salute was played by a military band with conductor all similarly apparelled. (Storrs 1945: 168)

A FRENCH MISSION TO ARABIA

Earlier in 1916 Ronald Storrs had offered the opinion that it was in the best interests of the British that the pilgrimage of 1916, the first under Husayn as an independent ruler of the Hijaz, should "open as brilliantly as possible. Any row, scandal or epidemic would react swiftly and discreditably upon the management, and discourage or even annihilate subsequent bookings." That moment was now drawing near. But by the time the season of 1916 was at hand, Britain had a new and formally acknowledged partner in the Hijaz, one that had its own interests in the Hajj.

Since 1915 the British and French had been conducting joint naval operations on the Red Sea. Then, in August 1916, the French accepted a British invitation to join in "concerted but independent arrangements" and send a mission to the Hijaz. The conditions were laid down by the President of the French Council of Ministers on 2 August 1916, signed by General Graziani of the General Staff and General Roques of the Ministry of War, and summarized as follows by Colonel Edouard Brémond, the chief of the military side of the mission:

The reopening of the pilgrimage to Mecca, which has been closed down by the (British) blockade of Arabia and the danger of exposing natives (of other lands, notably the French colonies in North Africa) to contact with the Turks. This pilgrimage was the principal resource of the Sharif, but it would be limited nonetheless to 600 natives of Algeria, Tu-

nisia and Morocco because of the lack of transport and the anticipated expenses.

To profit from this occasion by designating to take part in the pilgrimage certain notable religious personages whose loyalty was beyond doubt, who would take to the Amir presents and subsidies, together with greetings from our Muslim subjects.

There would join this political delegation from Alexandria onward a French military mission made up exclusively of natives, whose chief would be delegated to ask of the Sharif what support he was expecting from France, in trained native personnel, arms, munitions and materiel.

To coordinate the activities of the political and military delegations, the President of the Council requests the appointment of a French officer who would be under order from the French Minister in Cairo.

This superior officer should first go to Alexandria with the Mission. He should then stay in contact with it, whether from Jidda or an Egyptian port on the Red Sea. He should organize at Suwakin, for example, a base to receive soldiers and technical personnel, native troops and war materiel assembled for eventual disposition by the Sharif.

The means, however limited, that can be put at the disposition of the Sharif should doubtless be such as to permit him to use still unorganized Arab forces and to neutralize extremely important enemy forces to the benefit of the military position of the Russians and English in Asia Minor and, in consequence, to those of France in the East. (Brémond 1931: 36–37)

To head this delicate and important mission, General Roques proposed then Lieutenant Colonel Brémond, a veteran of campaigns with native troops in French North Africa. According to Roques:

[Brémond] is notable for his complete understanding of Arabic, which he speaks and writes (he holds a certification in Arabic) and by his deep comprehension of a Muslim milieu, in which he has lived for several years. He is perfectly versed in Islamic affairs and is equally suitable for native political delegation and a military mission. (Brémond 1931: 38)

Both delegations, the military and the political, went off without much help from either the intelligence or the historical section of the General Staff, Brémond noted wryly. Just before their departure for Arabia, a British politician in Egypt chanced to make a remark that struck home with Brémond.

Lord Hardinge noted that the despatch of a French Muslim military mission would oblige England to do likewise and that it would be "very difficult to put together a Muslim mission from India." An avowal of a weakness of which there would be many other examples, French and British. And if we did less poorly than the English, we were far from doing well. Our obligation as protectors, as well as our interest as a land with a low birthrate, is to give to the Maghribis the capacity of living a modern French life. (Brémond 1931: 43)

THE PILGRIMS ARRIVE

On 15 September both French missions, the Muslim political delegation led by Sidi or Sayyid (Si) Kaddour Benghabrit and the military by Colonel Brémond, boarded a French cruiser, and at 5 P.M. on 20 September they were in the roadstead at Jidda, giving, and receiving in turn, a nineteen-gun salute. Various local dignitaries came aboard to greet them and invite them to a reception ashore on the next day.

The mission disembarked at nine the next morning and exhausted all the resources of local ceremonial: endless speeches at the dock, a procession through multi-colored and approving crowds, a banquet of 100 guests or more, telegrams and telephone calls of greeting from the Sharif. At the latter's instructions Colonel Brémond handed over to the Sharif's deputy the French subvention of 1,250,000 gold francs.

On September 24th our colors were once against raised above the French Consulate, which had been pillaged by the Turks (before they withdrew from Jidda) and at 6 o'clock, under the direction Si Kaddour Benghabrit and of Commander Cadi [the ranking Muslim officer of the military delegation] our missions left by camel, garbed in the ihram. The Grand Sharif had them received by various dignitaries at Hadda, and then again at the gate of Mecca. Our representatives passed through almost the entire population of the city to the sanctuary, then to the residence of the Amir, who was their host and had quarters prepared there. Si Kaddour was received in a private audience. . . .

Communications were handled remarkably. When the King had telephoned on September 22nd to announce the capture of Ta'if (by Abdullah), the Chief of Mission [Brémond] had telegraphed to Cairo that the pilgrims could come ahead to Jidda. The Orénoque put them ashore on the 25th to the number of 600. . . . Some of the Moroccan pilgrims who had known Colonel Brémond at Rabat in 1907–1908 greeted him with "al-Cabtan! the Captain!" when he came aboard.

The British presence was represented by both the Egyptians and the Indians, as the French was by the North Africans, but Colonel Brémond paid the former only passing attention.

Our pilgrims arrived (by camel and donkey) at Mecca on September 28th. The same day the Egyptian Mahmal was put ashore at Jidda with an escort of 500 Egyptian soldiers garbed in the ihram, with two cannons and two machine guns. . . . There were 900 Egyptian pilgrims with them.

Thousands of Indian pilgrims filled the streets; there was joy everywhere: "the harvest" had returned! Thanks to the actions taken by the Grand Sharif people everywhere came to Mecca in a previously unknown—and never seen again—atmosphere of tranquillity and security. (Brémond 1931: 50–52)

"FROM VERDUN TO THE KA'BA!"

The pilgrimage was officially scheduled for 8 October 1916, and it took place without the Turks, for the first time since 1833. There was talk that Jemal Pasha intended to send the Syrian Mahmal from Medina to Mecca with twelve thousand men and German support, and in fact, the Mahmal left Damascus and reached Medina on schedule. But the Sharif permitted it to travel no farther. The medical general who represented the Sultan had eventually to return to Damascus without even catching sight of Mecca.

Brémond continues:

Throughout the period of the Hajj Amir Husayn manifested continuous signs of his favor toward our representatives and pilgrims. He named Si Kaddour and Commander Cadi to assist in the annual cleansing of the Bayt Allah, a much appreciated honor. At the solemn prayer which followed the ceremony the Amir took up his position at the place, marked with a marble slab, where Muhammad had prayed and had Si Kaddour stand beside him, and then, before he gave the signal for prayer to begin, said to Commander Cadi in a loud voice, "From Verdun to the Ka'ba!" which made a deep impression on the thousands in attendance, since at that time everyone knew that if the Allies were not defeated, it was because the French, alone, had held at Verdun.

The pilgrimage left Mecca on the 6th for Mount Arafat where the Great Feast was celebrated on the 8th. The number of pilgrims was estimated at 30,000. The Grand Sharif was favorably received throughout. He had his band play the "Marseillaise" at Arafat in honor of the pilgrims and reviewed the troops of Aziz Ali al-Misri—one squadron, 2 infantry companies, 2 mountain batteries, composed of Turkish deserters or prisoners and an Egyptian detachment.

The success of the pilgrimage surpassed the most optimistic expectations, both the Amir's and ours.

There was, however, during the Hajj some anti-European, and particularly anti-French, propaganda from Egyptians. The editor of the Egyptian journal al-Manar, Muhammad Rashid Rida, had made an anti-French speech at Mina in the presence of the Amir in which he denounced

France's ambitions in Syria. But the Amir interrupted in an open manner and requested him to drop the subject. Muhammad Rashid also distributed to the pilgrims an Arabic broadside, published before the war, which accused France of wishing to destroy the Holy Places and carry off the Black Stone and the remains of the Prophet to the Louvre. . . .

On October 17, 1916, the Orénoque left Jidda with our pilgrims, who happily returned home. (Brémond 1931: 52–54)

Storrs too interested himself in the Hajj of 1916. His stay in the Hijaz fell about a week after the end of the pilgrimage, and he used the occasion to inquire how it had gone, a matter of some importance to the new Sharifian regime and no less to their British than to their French sponsors.

Gathered from inquiries about Mecca from various sources that 20,000 people had attended the Pilgrimage, which was an unqualified success. The Sharif himself had never expected anything like that number. The state of Mecca itself highly satisfactory, and the Jidda-Mecca-Ta'if road as safe as any in Egypt. Egyptian and Indian pilgrims very well treated and highly pleased thereat. Two Indians . . . were talking against the Sharif and had even stuck up insulting posters on to his palace. I believe the matter has been reported to the Indian Government. The French Mission was popular, but not much liked by the Sharif, who appears not to want the French to know "more than is necessary" of his country. . . . Sharif's prestige is very great, and Abdullah is the only member of his family not afraid of him, although he handles him with more diplomacy than the blunt and outspoken Faysal. The Egyptian army much admired and much praised. Living not expensive. . . . Shops all small, in hands of Meccans, Indians, Yemenis and Javanese. Practically no interest in the War or any exterior topic. (Storrs 1945: 177)

Nothing occurred so gratifying perhaps as having the "Marseillaise" played at Arafat, but Storrs and his superiors had reason to feel both relieved and satisfied at the Hajj of 1916.

The Pilgrimage of September 1917

The pilgrimage season of 1917 opened on a rather awkward note for Colonel Brémond. He had suggested detaching one hundred Muslim soldiers from French forces at Port Said to make the Hajj. The proposal provoked a reaction from no less than General Ferdinand Foch, Chief of the General Staff, an astonishing way of dealing with a rather small matter, Brémond thought.

Most of our Muslim soldiers [Foch responded], particularly those from Algeria, are not practicing (Muslims). They care very little, then, about making the pilgrimage to Mecca and see it only as an opportunity for temporarily escaping service in their units. Moreover, the simultaneous detachment of 100 men from the various units at the base will certainly work a hardship on good military order, which has to be taken into account so as not to interfere with the operation of this base during the course of the pilgrimage.

Foch thought that forty pilgrims would be quite enough for the occasion.

[The] delegation [should] be made up only of those who have agreed spontaneously and without pressure to make the pilgrimage and are chosen from among the most observant soldiers. It is, in fact, extremely important from a political point of view that the people of Arabia who have come over to our cause be exposed to only those African soldiers whose conduct is irreproachable and who are admirably motivated. (Brémond 1931: 170)

Brémond does not record his response, if any, and in the end seventy soldiers made the pilgrimage. But fourteen years later, in his memoirs, Brémond read his former commanding officer a lesson.

The number of Muslim soldiers in Egypt or Arabia who "care very little about making the pilgrimage" is few or none. Religious sentiment is in no way based on the way a religion is practiced; one might say the exact opposite is true: the most observant are the least religious. The country of our Maghribis is undoubtedly inclined toward religious piety . . . and this religious sentiment is one of the primary ways of affecting the Maghribis: a leader who has gained their respect and confidence by his conduct, his attitude, his private life, his moral posture, will never appeal to them in vain. The awkward aspect is that this strong sentiment can take the form of xenophobia; religions are like rivers: they irrigate, but at times they also inundate. One needs strong dams.

The value of the proposed military operation was demonstrated by the fact that it was copied first by Italy, and then by England, which sent 8,000 Indian soldiers in groups of 2,000. (Brémond 1931: 171–172)

POLITICS AND PRAYER

The lesson concluded, Brémond returns to the summer of 1917.

The month of Ramadan began on June 20, 1917. The English unloaded 4,000 tons of food supplies and twelve tons of Indian or Turkish coins. An Italian mission came from Massawa, brought by the cruiser Calabria, and it was received in Mecca by the King (Husayn) on July 6th. The King took various security measures in connection with the pilgrimage. He announced on July 30th on a visit to our Military Mission—he had come to Jidda four days earlier to make sure it was carried out—that all of our soldiers would be his guests, and that he would underwrite all the expenses of landing our civilian delegation, who would be put up by his Deputy. Colonel Wilson was given the use of a tug-boat for the duration of the pilgrimage and the English doctor Major Thompson arrived with three physicians and the materiel for a hospital of 100 beds.

The first convoy of pilgrims, 375 Sudanese, arrived in Jidda from Port Sudan . . . on June 1st. From this point on the arrivals took place almost daily. More than a thousand pilgrims came by sambuk from Massawa, some of them having spent more than twenty days in the passage because of storms and—these pilgrims carry their own food and drink—dying of hunger and thirst.

On September 3rd the liner Nera of the Maritime Services, which had left Suez on August 31st, brought the French delegation: 20 Algerians, 12 Tunisians, 21 Moroccans, a few unattached pilgrims, a few servants, to a total of 83 people. . . . The delegation was formally received by the King on September 10th at Mecca, and the imposing and dignified bearing of our delegates made an excellent impression. And they for their part were most flattered by the reception they were given.

The French military mission that had been discussed by Brémond and General Foch also arrived: thirty-five Muslim soldiers from the French Palestine Detachment and thirty-five from Port Said, Wajh, and Yanbu. They too were given a reception and a formal dinner.

The table service was done as follows: all the platters are placed on the table beforehand; three or four blacks stand on the table in bare feet and, kneeling before them, present the platters to the diners. It represents the dining custom of a time, not too distant, when people ate seated on the ground and requires servants who are ritually clean according to Islamic law.

The Egyptian Mahmal arrived at Jidda on September 14th aboard the Hardinge, accompanied by the (French) Suva, with the same ceremonial as in 1916; but there were only 200 Egyptian pilgrims. What happened was that Farouki, the King's agent in Cairo concerned himself only with the political scene in Syria. He totally ignored the religious element, whom he scandalized by often going about drunk and appearing in public with an Italian mistress. He did a great deal of harm to the Sharif's cause with public opinion in Egypt.

They were awaiting in Mecca the Imam Abd al-Rahman, the father of the reigning prince of Najd [of Abd al-Aziz ibn Saʿud], and the King had sent the Sharif Hamza . . . to meet him at Taʾif with all the available military personnel, since there was some uneasiness at Mecca on the actual intentions of the Wahhabis. . . . They waited in vain because the

Imam Abd al-Rahman had become so corpulent that he had to give up the idea of the trip after the first day. He had himself replaced by one of his sons, the Amir Muhammad, who arrived in Mecca on the night of the 21st, was received by the King on the 22nd and made Husayn a present of twelve riding camels, eight horses and a mule.

It should be remarked here that all Muslims have access to the Pilgrimage and the Holy Places, whatever their rite, orthodox or not, while the less tolerant Christians have been forced to segregate the Holy Places of Jerusalem.

The first ceremony took place at Arafat on September 26th, and on the 28th there took place in the King's tent an incident that caused a great sensation. . . . A group of Yemenis with a green flag—the color of the Zaydi Shiʿites of Yemen—attempted to come into the tent on the pretext of performing a dance. At a sign from the King the guard blocked their way; a maddened Yemeni then wounded one of the guards in the arm with a dagger. On the advice of the Chief Qadi, the King imposed a fine on the attacker. The unhappy soldier killed him outside the tent, however. The soldier was arrested, as well as the other Yemenis. This incident was later invoked by the Yemen as a reason for the break with the Hijaz in 1919. Public opinion saw it as an attempt on the life of the King.

The Pilgrimage returned to Mecca on September 29th; at its return, M. Cherchali (the head of the French civilian delegation) telephoned that all had gone well, but that everyone was ill—malaria was rampant in the Hijaz in 1917—including himself, and rather seriously. . . . He estimated the number of pilgrims at 70,000—the British Agency placed the number at only 53,000. It was still double the number of 1916. There were 30,000 people who had come from the Najd with Amir Muhammad and 10,000 from the Yemen, while no one had come from those two places in 1916. A Turkish air attack had been expected at Mina. There had been no political speech.

THE WAHHABI RANK-AND-FILE

Brémond and some of his men also got their first indirect taste of the Wahhabi rank-and-file, which they did not find particularly pleasant.

The Amir Muhammad ibn Saʿud and his party left Mecca on October 2nd. The impression these people produced on our nationals was unpleasant: genuine savages, taking everything they saw, by force if necessary; like apes, some said.

On the suggestion of the Chief of Mission, the President of the War Cabinet had telegraphed on September 16th to thank "His Majesty" for the reception given our soldiers, and on the 29th the King telegraphed to Colonel Brémond, "I do not know how to express my gratitude to the

*Government of the Republic for its sensitive attentions in my regard." . . .
As is obvious, there was always perfect harmony. The second pilgrimage
consolidated the gains of the first; there was no greater enthusiasm than in
1916, but the Hijaz had become accustomed to seeing us, in what was now
our place.*

*(Finally), it should be noted that our pilgrims were of the opinion that
they had fulfilled a duty of French patriotism rather than a religious obligation. Indeed, since the overland trip was impossible, and the imams of
the four rites do not consider the sea voyage obligatory when there is danger, there was no pilgrimage obligation in 1917. (Brémond 1931: 173–179)*

THE POSTWAR HAJJ

Late in 1918, as the war against Turkey moved toward an end far from the
Hijaz, the British became increasingly concerned about the political dis-
equilibrium caused by the disappearance of Turkish sovereignty from
Arabia. Because it was clearly in their own interests, the British had
"given" Husayn his independence by underwriting and then protecting
the Arab revolt in the Hijaz. The question now was whether they would
continue to protect Husayn's sovereignty in opposition to the ambitions
of another of their clients in the Peninsula, the considerably more self-
sufficient House of Saʿud. It was a question the British were not keen to
answer, but in the summer of 1918 it was already being asked in Whitehall.

The Saudis, like Husayn, pursued their own course of action during
the war, which was quite remote from anything going on in France or
even Palestine. In December 1916 they had signed a treaty with Britain
whereby the latter recognized Ibn Saʿud as the independent sovereign of
Najd, al-Hasa, Qatif, and Jubayl.[11] It was a temporary measure, and without any specifics regarding the boundaries of the Amir's realm. But in
1918, and despite Husayn's profound and expressed displeasure, it was still
the regulatory instrument between Ibn Saʿud and the British.

In October 1918 the British were urging the two rulers in Mecca and
Riyadh to resolve their growing territorial differences. Arrangements did
not work out—chiefly because of Husayn, it appeared—and in November of that year the British High Commissioner felt constrained to write
to the King in Mecca.

*Your Highness has said in a letter that it is "contrary to the interests of
the country to create disturbances between Mecca and the capitals of people like Ibn Saʿud." This, as your Highness is aware, is also the opinion of
His Majesty's Government, who, in the solicitude for your Highness's*

welfare and for the Arabs, would view with the gravest apprehension the outbreak of hostilities in Arabia, which they fear might even prejudice the political settlements which will be made in the near future.

At the end of September 1918, British and Arab forces had taken Damascus. With the signing of an armistice with a defeated Ottoman Empire at Mudros on 30 October 1918, a peace settlement did indeed appear to be rapidly approaching. The High Commissioner's letter continues:

> Your Highness can have no doubt of the sincerity of His Majesty's Government towards your Highness which precludes their showing partiality toward Ibn Sa'ud or anyone else to the detriment of your Highness's interests; and your Highness knows the terms of the existing agreement between His Majesty's Government and Ibn Sa'ud which safeguard his rights in his own territory. Amir Ibn Sa'ud has been officially informed that His Majesty's Government deprecate any action by him outside his country. They have also refused his recent application for additional war materiel, and, as suggested by your Highness, have required him to suspend further military operations—which were originally started at our suggestion—against the Turcophile Ibn Rashid (of Hayl). . . .
>
> Having regard to the foregoing considerations, and in view of your Highness's previous assurances, I find it difficult to believe that your Highness has refused to hold further communication with Ibn Sa'ud (which would be implied by a refusal to entertain his messenger and letter), and I hope your Highness will find means to remove any legitimate cause for misconception of your policy and disposition on the part of this Amir, who, although your Highness's inferior in prestige and material resources, is, nevertheless, a considerable factor in Arabian politics. (Foreign Office Papers 192618[12])

This deft combination of stroking and reprimand had little effect on Husayn: for as long as he ruled in the Hijaz, the King found it impossible to deal, either directly or indirectly, with his rival in Riyadh.

The Pilgrims of Najd

One issue that bedeviled Hashimite-Saudi relations throughout the postwar period was Husayn's refusal to permit Wahhabi pilgrims from Najd to make the Hajj. The British were, as usual, caught in the middle of this quarrel. On 22 May 1922 the British Agent in Jidda informed the Foreign Office that the King "absolutely refuses to accept Najd pilgrims by land." The spread of their Wahhabi ideology, the King alleged, made it highly likely that his enemies would stir up local riots. The consul suggested that the wisest course might be to prevail upon Ibn Saʿud not to send any of his followers that year.[13] In Baghdad, meanwhile, Sir Percy Cox, the British Political Officer, took up the matter with Faysal, the newly crowned King of British-mandated Iraq.

Faysal admits that the present dangerous situation is entirely the result of the mad obstinacy of his father, which has alienated his subjects as well as hostilized his neighbors; and he urges that influx of large numbers of Ikhwan [armed fraternities of bedouin "converts" to the Wahhabi creed] into the Hijaz at the present juncture will, in spite of assurances given, almost inevitably result in a conflagration which will extend to the Holy Places themselves, at a time when they are full of Muslims of all nationalities, whose lives would be in jeopardy. Consequence will be great consternation throughout Islam, and though His Majesty's Government would not in any way be responsible, it would react injuriously on their prestige and interest.

I then asked him what he thought could be done, and he replied that in his belief the only remedy was for us to appeal to Ibn Saʿud to stop his people going on the pilgrimage in the interests of Islam as a whole.

To which Cox added his own recommendations to Winston Churchill at the Colonial Office:

I suggest that appeal (to Ibn Saʿud), if made, should be made in the interests of Islam as a whole and the message should be in a form which we can publish if necessary. . . .

We could not well hold Ibn Saʿud responsible if the Hijaz voluntarily embraced Wahhabi faith in order to escape Husayn's intolerable misrule, but it is difficult to foresee what would be the effect on Islam and how far Great Britain would be taxed with responsibility for the resulting chaos. (Foreign Office Papers E5412/248/91[14])

London finally decided on a compromise: Ibn Saʿud was requested to limit the number of his pilgrims to a minimum,[15] and Husayn was warned that he must accept them. The King attempted to turn the situation to his own advantage, as described by Major W. E. Marshall, the British consul in Jidda:

Interviewed King Husayn today [11 June 1922] and gave him His Majesty's Government's warning about Najd pilgrimage.

At first he agreed to accept them provided that they were villagers and not nomads, and that they came via Medina in separate caravans of not more than 800 camels each, and not in one large party. . . . Afterwards he

said that all this was conditional on His Majesty's Government sending him four British aeroplanes and pilots to be under his orders during the pilgrimage.
I said that this was impossible. (Foreign Office Papers E5884/248/91[16])

Husayn finally acceded and on 10 July 1922 sent, via the British Agent in Baghdad, "friendly greetings to Ibn Saʿud" and promised a warm welcome to his Hajj emissary. Ibn Saʿud was likewise agreeable to limiting the number of pilgrims and of sending only townspeople and not the more fanatic tribesmen. He cabled to Jidda:

> I recognize importance of the matter, and you may rest assured that there will be no offense given by us; in fact, fighting in Holy Mecca is forbidden by Shariʿa. . . . I found in your telegram a hint that I should make peace with King Husayn. I am only too willing for good relations, and as proof thereof will send most friendly letter with Amir of Hajj. (Foreign Office Papers E6881/248/91[17])

The Najdi pilgrims arrived in Mecca on 30 July 1922, and all went well. There were about eighteen hundred of them, mostly townsmen, as Ibn Saʿud had promised, and though some one hundred were armed and carried a Wahhabi banner, Husayn, though nervous, chose to ignore it. They left on 12 August after being searched for gold, as the king's customs regulations stipulated; and what was discovered was taxed without incident.[18]

Reader Bullard, the British Consular Agent in Jidda from 16 June 1923 onward, was immediately plunged into the complex relationship embracing the Hijaz, Britain, and, as this was the summer of 1923, Turkey, whose postwar fate was being decided at a conference in Lausanne. The issues between the former Ottoman Empire and its erstwhile Vilayet of the Hijaz were many, but two were in the foreground in 1923: the return of the treasures of Medina that the Turks had removed to Constantinople in 1918, and the disposition of those endowments in Turkey whose income had been dedicated in perpetuity to the support of the Two Sanctuaries in the Hijaz.[19] Yet the peace treaty signed between the Entente and Turkey on 24 July 1923 contained not a single reference to either the treasures or the endowments.

One of the responsibilities of the British Agent in Jidda was to provide Whitehall with a detailed account of the annual Hajj, and on 18 December 1923 Reader Bullard filed his report on the pilgrimage of that year. He began by noting that 75,221 pilgrims had come by sea, nearly 20,000 more than in 1922, and that three-quarters of those new Hajjis were British subjects from India and Malaysia. Nearly two-thirds of the pilgrims had come by British flag vessels.[20] He continues:

Pilgrimage day was 23rd July. It is estimated that 100,000 pilgrims were present at Arafat on that day. This number includes local as well as foreign pilgrims. The first pilgrim ship arrived at Jidda on 27th January; the first pilgrims ship carrying pilgrims home left on 31st July, the last on the 19th October.

To relieve the congestion which inevitably results from the passage of so many pilgrims through a single small seaport within a few days, pilgrims are hurried off to Mecca the day after their arrival in Jidda. Their effects are cleared from customs by pilgrim guides, and often the pilgrims do not see their property from the time it leaves the steamer or the lighter until the moment when the camels are being loaded. It is then frequently found that something is missing, but the rush to get to Mecca is so great that few pilgrims wish to stay to make immediate investigations. According to the official notice, there are in the customs (at Jidda) some 300 packages awaiting claimants. The actual number is probably very much larger. (Foreign Office Papers E/25/11/91[21])

Nor is it likely, Bullard adds, that any pilgrim can return from Medina within the stipulated time to claim lost baggage.

International Intervention

Husayn was only somewhat more rapacious than his predecessors in the Sharifate. But they had enjoyed the enviable position of "protecting" the pilgrims from the Ottomans while simultaneously being supported by those same Ottomans and being themselves protected by the Turkish military from the more predatory among their own Arab subjects. Husayn had lost those advantages in throwing off Turkish sovereignty and so had little choice but to exact whatever he could from each season's "harvest" of pilgrims. There was a landing fee at Jidda, baggage and customs charges (the latter ranging up to 600 percent of the retail value of the goods), and an artificially high rate of currency exchange. Finally, the Sharif had a grasping hand upon all means of transport to and within the Hijaz; in the postwar period he even began purchasing used steamers out of various European services and so entered the Red Sea pilgrim trade.[22]

We have some detailed, though not entirely disinterested and not at all spiritual, descriptions of the postwar pilgrimages conducted under the auspices of King Husayn. There were occasional physical improvements: the Masaʿa, the street between Safa and Marwa where the pilgrims performed their "running," was roofed over, and the Haram and its vicinity were electrified, both in 1923.[23] But the overwhelming issue, though not necessarily one of Husayn's choosing, revolved around treatment of the pilgrims. The British consul in Jidda was required to report on all the affairs of the Hijaz; and the Hajj, which by then involved a great number of British (as well as French, Dutch, and Italian) colonial subjects, was obviously a matter of great interest to Whitehall.

A conference was held at the Foreign Office on 18 March 1919 to discuss the issues raised by the postwar Hajj in an independent "Kingdom of the Hijaz" and the nature and extent of Britain's role in it. Should the British, for example, "confine themselves, as in the past, to guarding the interests of British subjects, or are they to accept general responsibility for ensuring that King Husayn takes adequate precautions?"

The Meeting were of the opinion that, in view of the situation arising out of the Arab Revolt and by the support given by His Majesty's Government to King Husayn during the war, His Majesty's Government could not confine themselves, as in the past, to guarding the interests of British pilgrims. . . . It was considered that, although no responsibility could be accepted by His Majesty's Government for King Husayn's arrangements, it was, nevertheless, in the highest degree desirable, from the point of view of His Majesty's Government, that adequate precautions should be taken during the ensuing pilgrimage for the protection of the pilgrims both from the point of view of defense and sanitation. While there was no reason to encourage a bumper pilgrimage, it was essential that it should be successful, and that no handle be given to pro-Turkish and anti-Sharif propaganda.

The sentiments were undoubtedly reasonable, but reason had its price.

The Meeting were of the opinion that for this year, at any rate, King Husayn would require financial support to enable him, among other things, to carry out the necessary measures to ensure that the pilgrimage should be a success, and they considered that this support should, in the first place, be a charge on Imperial funds. . . . The expense of the necessary sanitary arrangements at Jidda and Yanbu was estimated at 6,000 liras for this year. As regards the defense measures . . . it was realized that, in the event of hostile aggression on the part of Ibn Saʿud, it might become necessary to contemplate the provision of further financial support.

It was understood, however, that the Treasury were strongly of opinion that any expenses on account of military defense should be met by King Husayn from the existing subsidy, which includes a very large sum for military purposes generally, and that pressure should be put upon him to take adequate precautions for the protection of pilgrims by threat of reducing or discontinuing the subsidy.

And there was, as usual, the always vexing question of quarantine: Who should be required to be examined, where, and under whose auspices?

It was considered that the pilgrims should be quarantined both on their inward and their outward journey at Qamaran, Tur, and Suwakin, and also at Jidda and Yanbu. It was agreed that the formation of a small inter-departmental committee consisting of one representative each from the Foreign Office, Egyptian Government, Government of India, and Local Government Board (Board of Health) was highly desirable for the purpose of working out in detail proposals as to sanitary arrangements.

The stations at Qamaran, Tur, and Sawakin were under the respective supervision of the governments of India, Egypt, and the Sudan, and so under eventual British control. At the quarantine stations of Jidda and Yanbu, however, arrangements were in the hands of King Husayn. He should have, the Conference suggested, "the supervision of the British Agent at Jidda, acting under the orders of the High Commissioner, Cairo." The arrangement was not so simple, of course. And finally, there were the overland routes from Damascus.

With regard to pilgrims proceeding by land, it was understood that the demolition of the Hijaz railway would in any case entail a road journey of about a month for pilgrims from Syria and Palestine. There was some difference of opinion whether this was in itself a sufficient safeguard, and it was foreseen that in the event of the outbreak of infectious disease at Mecca it might be necessary to impose quarantine for the return journey at some suitable point along the line. (Foreign Office Papers 45538[24])

The consuls kept a close watch on Jidda disembarkations, and their reports provide statistics on the seaborne pilgrims. By this count, 58,584 pilgrims arrived in Jidda for the pilgrimage of 1920, 57,255 for the Hajj of the following year, and 56,319 in 1922.[25]

"To Mecca, Smuggled in a Motor Car"

The British were necessarily concerned with large issues of policy, but on the Hijaz stage other players were making trial of lesser matters. As the nineteenth century's revolutionary means of transport began sinking into the desert sands north of Medina, one of the twentieth's preferred vehicles began to make its appearance in that same unlikely milieu. We have already met Amin Rihani, the naturalized Arab-American Christian who was the guest of King Husayn in Jidda in February 1922. One morning of Rihani's stay promised to be different from every other morning of his life.

Early in the morning we got into the King's motor car—the (King's son) Amir Zayd, the Foreign Minister Shaykh Fuᶜad, the Sharif Ali, Chief of the Harb bedouin, Constantine Yanni of the Aviation Department and I. But no one knew where we were going except the last mentioned of the party and the first. The Amir Zayd, the night before, had imparted to me the secret and thus deprived me of sleep. On the wings of magic, like Hasan of Basra, I traveled far, leaving a virgin footprint in the most sacred precinct of Islam. For has it once happened before what was to happen on the morrow?

The servants and guards who were packed into another car—a German spoil of war—were sent ahead of us; and an hour later, driving through the northern gate, past the market outside the city wall, and into the Jidda plain, we were on the ancient and present highway to Mecca. On the horizon in the East, about seven miles away, is a half-circle of hills, soft in expression, modest in gesture, behind which in the distance rise the rugged peaks of Ta'if.

In twenty minutes we had traversed the plain, passed Rughama, the first café on the road, and winding our way through a pass, were among the hills. Then spoke the Amir Zayd: "What matters it? Let us tell them. The Sharif Ali will lose his job if he speaks; Shaykh Fu'ad is entrusted with greater secrets of State; and Constantine, you will not betray a fellow Christian. . . . Yes, we are going to Mecca, billah! For the sake of Amin— the Amir Amin Khan from India—and no one need say a word about it.

To Mecca, smuggled in a motor car. This was indeed a novelty, the first adventure of its kind by a Christian traveler. I need not dwell on my joy of that day, although I preferred to be on a camel, one of a caravan, a Hajji Abdullah [Burton] or a Hajji Ibrahim [Burckhardt], a pilgrim among pilgrims. But that had been done before; and while the deception was still possible, it was not in my case necessary. Nor was it for that matter void of danger. On the contrary, there were four others inculpated with me; and when, in moments of conscience, as we motored through the hills, I contemplated my action—my willingness to let four companions share the responsibility with me—I felt a preference for the ancient deception.

The caravans go forth in the peace and security of Allah, and we, for the third time get stuck in the sand. We had debouched into another plain surrounded with hills, not higher than those we had passed, and lo, the other trombile, as the bedouin call the motor car, was ahead of us, apparently waiting for us. No: it was stuck, like our own, in the sand. We got out of our rut . . . and went to its rescue. A few of the bedouin had gathered round it and were making a feeble effort to push it ahead. . . . But the German trombile was in no humor for a spin. It snorted, whirred for a moment, and stopped again. Something more than sand was the matter.

We decided to abandon the German trombile. . . . The Amir Zayd ordered the lunch baskets to be moved into our car and told the servants to shift for themselves. . . . Not long after we had tried to make up for lost time did we stop again. I thought someone had fired upon us. But we were passing through a volcanic region . . . and a scabrous flint cut the tire two inches across. The Hindu chauffeur, eminently efficient, was not long, however, in making the change.

We passed by the principal station, midway between Jidda and Mecca, where the pilgrims stop for coffee and a smoke, and sometimes rest overnight. It is a street of tents made of straw or brushwood or timber, while here or there is a café built of stone. There are tables and chairs, and settees of rush or rope which the rich pilgrims may use as beds. But most of them sleep in the open on the sand. . . . The name of the place, Bahra, lake in Arabic, is supposed to be derived from the fact that there was once a lake in the vicinity.

At Hadda, the next station from Bahra, the King has a palm grove, and his tenants, meeting us at the gate, led us through to a spreading acacia tree, under which they had constructed diwans and spread them with carpets. Evidently they had been ordered to do the honors; for they told us His Majesty had telephoned twice to find out if we had arrived. He was worrying about us. But he knew even his best car has to be pushed and pulled out of the sand more than half a dozen times between Mecca and the sea. (Rihani 1930: 52–58)

The new technology of the *trombile* proved inadequate for the task. A disappointed Rihani had to turn back to Jidda.

"Move in a Common Faith toward a Goal Unique"

Rihani longed for the caravan experience. As he returned unsuccessful back along the Mecca-Jidda road in his *mawtah* car, he could still observe the crowds heading expectantly toward the Holy City in the centuries-old way.

Behold the ancient caravan, the first century saluting the twentieth. We meet with many of them on the road to Mecca. From Java and Sumatra, from India and Afghanistan, from Morocco and the African wilds, they seek the fountain of eternal life and bliss. Color and race and rank, like the distance of land and sea, yield to the supreme purpose, make the world of the pilgrim move in a common faith toward a goal unique, a shrine in the desert. And only a cup of brackish water to offer to the pious and the weary—brackish water, indeed, but from the Well of Zamzam—the well of eternal life and bliss.

At Yanbu and Jidda they land in multitudes of shifting squalor and picturesqueness. From every ship a scene, from every land a fashion. The

Takruri black, a giant with a rag around his loins; the fastidious Somali in florid gingham apron and white toga; the Javanese with their unveiled women in short skirts of gorgeous colors or just a piece of rich material clinging to their stunted forms; the gentlemen from India, in graceful folds of silk and cashmere, traveling third class with the multitude; the fellah of Egypt in red slippers and blue gallabiyya; the trans-Caucasian in a huge turban crowning a truculency of aspect unassuaged; and the Moroccan, graceful and stately and proud, in the ample folds of an immaculate white burnous—they are all brought together in the most democratic spirit by the faith that was born in the wilds of al-Hijaz. Zamzamward the caravan moves.

Across the desert, through the Najd hills and the Great Nafud, they come from Persia and Arabistan, from Bukhara and Baghdad, in caravans that link the plateau with the plain and the desert with the hills. The leader gives the word—a gun is fired—woh-haw!—the sun is setting—we start! And the camels grunt and gurgle and growl; and the pilgrims, after the sunset prayer, jam and hiddle and clamor for attention; and the copper utensils rattle in the pack; the sword of the Arab clatters at his side against his water can; and the old shaykh rates the impatient one for pulling in the tangle at his sleeve and beads; thus the caravan, slowly and tumultuously composed, moves to the tinkling of bells and the squeaking of saddles and the rhythmic cry of Allah! Allah! It slowly moves into the shadow and soon out of it, in a generous moon, toward the Holy City.

Exciting times they had, those pilgrims of old. Even up to the last days of the Turk, before the Husayn era of independence and the fear of the Most High was inaugurated, the pilgrim's faith was still subject to such spite as only Iblis could conceive. But the pilgrim withstood and endured; he came out of the fire of the Hijaz, moreover, pure and whole, and laden with divine grace. (Rihani 1930: 53–55)

In the twentieth century, viewed from the back seat of an automobile, the caravan experience had become what it was not even for the nineteenth-century European travelers who shared it: a colorful, romantic, and altogether sanctifying mode of travel. Although one could still see pilgrim caravans plying their slow way to Mecca in 1922, other modes of making the Hajj, not nearly so romantic or painful, were available in the twentieth-century Kingdom of the Hijaz.

Down the Syrian steppes and the lava-strewn waste they come, huddled in the cattle-cars of the Hijaz Railway; the engine puffing at its steam ration of war days; wheezing, coughing, uttering sibilants of despair; stopping for hours between stations, for a day and a night; waiting for Allah knows what at station points—the regular soldiers have something to do, perhaps with the bedouin bands—and filling the poor, wilted, dazed and crumpled-up Hajji with such longing for a camel, such visions of caravans moving in the moonlight to rhythms of devotion and delight, as only Allah in His mercy can assuage. But—marvel of constancy!—they reach Medina with the same faith, undiminished and unadulterated, that moved them from home. (Rihani 1930: 54–55)

Jidda-Medina-Yanbu-Jidda (1922)

The annual British consular reports on the Hajj were pieced together from various eyewitness accounts and summarized, however graphically, by an official who had not in fact been on the scene. The participants often gave another, even more illuminating perspective. For example, one Mohammed Beg, "Resident of Lahore," left this detailed account of the mostly overland trip he made from Jidda to Medina and back in 1922.

The caravan started (from Jidda) on the 20th August, 1922, for Medina. . . . We reached Asfan, when we heard that several foot passengers were looted and killed by the bedouin. We stopped at this place for the whole day and the night, in the latter part of which an Egyptian lady was attacked by the bedouin, but with a hue and a cry being raised, one of her relatives got a wound on his head, but there was no loss. The bedouin were firing from the hills, and we could see them moving about.

We went on till we left Qadima on the 25th August, and were proceeding in our shughdufs [double-slung litters] when all at once the camel train stopped and a great noise in the front was heard, and we could see the bedouin and the camel-keepers firing at each other. We were all thunderstruck, as bullets were passing over our heads like showers of rain. One bullet came in my shughduf, but by a miracle, after tearing some clothes, remained stuck in the bag tied to the side of the shughduf. . . . Our guide cut off the train of his caravan and took a side by-path to avoid the scene of the trouble, but still the caravan suffered at the hands of the bedouin, as two women were shot and died the following night and were buried at Rabigh the next day.

We reached Rabigh on the 28th at about 12 noon and were proceeding when there was trouble again and shots were fired from the surrounding hills, but we were passing rapidly through danger. I cannot say whether there were deaths or not as the train of camels was too long and I could not see what happened at the front or the rear. We reached Bir Hassan on the 30th and were detained for two days. We heard several shots during the night and the day following. . . .

On our way from Khalis to Bir Abbas on the 2nd of September we were again surrounded by the bedouin and shots were profoundly poured on us, but we did not stop and nothing can be said of what loss of life occurred here again. At this place we were detained for six days and consumed all our rations. We suffered a great deal from suspense, heat, exposure and at last were asked to pay a guinea (additional) each camel, but again it was found that the sum thus collected would not meet the demand of the Ahmadi tribe. The camel-keepers had also gone to their homes, which were in the vicinity of this camp.

Negotiations here were prolonged: the camel-keepers and the local bedouin were obviously in collusion. In the end, 13,300 gold pieces had to be collected from the pilgrims and sent to the Ahmadi tribesmen, who then permitted the caravan to continue—although, as Mohammed Beg noted, "There were several deaths here as well."

We left this place on the 6th September, but I am not sure of exact dates, as we had lost clue of dates and days, and after two hours of our departure from this camp we were again stopped by the bedouin and shots were being fired on us, but we went on and to my belief nothing occurred. During the night, which was dark, as we were going along, cries of women were heard and one of the women passed us running and crying that she was made to get down and the cameleer took away the camel. No one could help her. Another woman of our caravan died, and a man complained that he had lost 900 rupees during the night journey. We reached Medina on the 15th September, 1922. . . .

We were ordered to leave Medina soon after the Friday prayers, and brought out our belongings to where our shughdufs were standing, but we were again made to wait two days as it was said that the Sharif had not paid some money as an allowance to a tribe and told the tribe to get it from us. I cannot prove the veracity of this statement, but we had to wait there exposed to the sun and the dew in an open place after leaving the houses we had hired in the town.

On our leaving Bir Darwish in the afternoon of the 16th September at about 10 o'clock in the night we were again very severely attacked by the bedouin. Shots were poured like showers of rain upon us and the bullets passed our heads. It was a severe attack but we hurried on. I saw a camel dropping and an Egyptian lady shot. We arrived at Turra on the 18th September, and the Egyptian lady was buried here. I am not aware of any other loss of life, but it was said that four men died. A foot pasenger who met us the next day said that he was left behind and came at daybreak from where he had slept and saw a shughduf without riders and with beds and utensils lying about and a heap of mud, seemingly the grave of the occupants.

We arrived at Yanbu in the morning of the 23rd September, 1922. Here I and several others had no money left, and we had been without rations and managed by borrowing from each other. I had to borrow money from my guide. We hired a house; water was very dear. . . . When I and the others went to buy tickets for the steamer we were not allowed by the menials to go above (to the sales office) without paying money, and each and every one had to pay . . . at the entrance and similarly at the next story. . . . Bribery was common and openly asked, and we had to pay in all 25 rupees, each man for one ticket, including quarantine charges, and bribery at each step.

On the 29th September, 1922, at about 2 P.M., we were ordered to bring our luggage to the sea-side, which we did, and remained sitting in the sun till evening, when we were turned out, and we spent the night exposed to the wet climate. Next morning we had to take our luggage again to the sea-side, and hungry and thirsty we had to wait in the sun, but the gate-keepers would not allow anyone to go in until he was paid some money, and allowed one man only through a partly opened gate. We had to throw our luggage over an eight-foot railing, and our utensils, etc. were damaged.

At last, after paying different sums to officials, we were made to take our seats in the boat and taken to the steamer. We were hoisted up by our arms and thrown by our arm-pits in the second-floor of the steamer, without being allowed to take a drop of water or food. No pen can describe the misery men and women suffered in this black hole; men and women cried for water, and it was terribly hot, and both up and down floors were cram full, so that no one could move about, while sitting, even, was difficult. There was no accommodation for making water and w.c., and it was impossible to go up (to the deck). Men were falling on each other. I, with great difficulty, crawled up and trampled several to go to the captain, but he did not hear me. People now saw the difference between British rule and Mohammedan Government.

The thirty hours of misery over, with one or two deaths on board, we came to Jidda, where our luggage was thrown in boats, which came on shore at dusk, and here, fasting, hungry, thirsty, without going to the w.c. for thirty hours, we had to face another difficulty of picking out our luggage, as there was no light in the boat to enable us to find our things. God only can fathom the misery and trouble we went through in the night. (Foreign Office Papers E2478/120/91[26])

Public Health and Quarantine

Whatever its other dangers, the postwar pilgrimage continued to remain free of epidemics. The British Agent in Jidda reported in 1921:

The health of the pilgrimage throughout was good and the death-rate low. Some of the Javanese pilgrims who went to Medina before the Hajj suffered a good deal from the heat, and a considerable number died. With the exception of an outbreak of smallpox, and a few cases of typhoid fever, no infectious disease occurred. (Foreign Office Papers E656/656/91[27])

THE QUARANTINE AT JIDDA

As we have already seen, it was at the insistence of the European powers, in the face of recurring outbreaks of cholera spread from Mecca by returning Hajjis, that the Ottomans opened the first quarantine stations at Tur in Sinai for Egyptian arrivals and at Qamaran Island near the straits of the Bab al-Mandab for Indian Hajjis. Not to be outdone, King Husayn subjected the pilgrims to another scrutiny at his own quite unnecessary quarantine station at Jidda. Run by the notorious Thabit Pasha, the medical facilities were described as "both farcical and appalling . . . largely composed of an act of faith and one hypodermic syringe."[28]

Amin Rihani had arrived in Jidda by ship from Suez on 25 February 1922, invited, it would appear, by friends on Husayn's staff. His mission was a little vague,[29] but no sooner had he stepped ashore than he was met by the mayor of Jidda, and a phone call confirmed that Husayn had just left Mecca to come to Jidda and greet him in person. That same afternoon Rihani was in the presence of the man he described as "of all the Arab Kings, the most kingly, if not also the most spiritual and the least clannish."

> Here is not a hard-visaged Arab, severe and saturnine. Here is a suavity rather, with an undercurrent of sadness, and a serenity coupled with genial grace. . . . He is a descendent of the Prophet and he has lived twenty years in Constantinople. His charming personality, therefore, has two sources, innate and acquired, the Prophetic and the diplomatic. (Rihani 1930: 17)

The King, for his part, thought he was entertaining a famous and influential guest, and almost immediately he took Rihani to visit the medical pride and joy of his kingdom.

> King Husayn thought that his Quarantine—the Quarantine of Jidda—is the best in the world. . . . "Our Quarantine is incomparable. Come and see with your own eyes."
> His Majesty clapped for the servant and ordered the launch. He was ever thus, with rarely a program for the day, but always sudden and surprising. An excellent method to keep the servants alert and the soldiers on guard, but it does not always succeed in Arabia. The launch! And in a few minutes . . . a soldier came in to say that the launch was ready. Nothing else was. His Majesty put on his galoshes with his own hand and walked out without his black slaves, without his Secretary and without uttering a word of dissatisfaction.

. . . In an hour we were at the Island of Abu Saʿd. The pilgrims, seeing the royal launch, crowded round the landing. The Turks in baggy trousers—souvenirs of the old regime—shouted at them and tried to drive them back. King Husayn motioned, Nay, with his head and hand; and as soon as he landed he was besieged by them.

They shed tears of joy when they saw the Descendant of the Prophet. I have never seen such expressions of reverence, of devotion, of ecstatic servility; and as they crowded round this man, groveling, bending, whining words of worship, they seemed at a loss how to bow or kneel. Those that fell on both knees kissed the hem of his robe, others rubbed their faces against his shoes, others against his breast; and having done, they withdrew, but not their gaze, and stood at a little distance with outstretched hands. More than a King he was to them, and more than a Sharif; they stood before a revelation, as it were, a substantiation. The Prophet himself seemed to be patting their cheeks, their backs, their hands. I could see that the King was moved, and his words were few.

Rihani was on a carefully guided tour, it is true, but he did not appear to find the facilities "appalling."

The Quarantine consists of about ten buildings, mostly one story, each with two doors in the center facing each other. You enter into a vestibule on either side of which is a concrete floor about a foot high. There the pilgrims, after they have passed through the fumigation room, spread their mats and rugs and bedding, and pile their luggage as a partition between each other. In a sense, the place reminded me of Ellis Island. But here are no iron bars, no dark rooms, no stuffy sleeping quarters, no smelling berths, no heart-eating suspense, and no danger of deportation.

The utter lack of furniture made these buildings look so clean, so airy, so hygienic. The only complaint seemed to be about water. Had they had any previous knowledge of Jidda, however, their present thirst would be more supportable. They would accept it, one said, as a test of faith—the only one remaining, and lasting only three days. Those who have contagious diseases are removed from the steamer direct to another island not far from Abu Saʿd, with a hospital in it, and beds in the hospital, and doctors and nurses in charge; and they have little to do in the pilgrimage season, in spite of (the station at) Qamaran Island at one end of the Red Sea and Tur at the other. (Rihani 1930: 75–78)

The British agents at Jidda had quite another view, however: the suppression of epidemic diseases was the result of the European-controlled quarantines and owed nothing to the health facilities of the Kingdom of the Hijaz.

Reports received show that the medical arrangements of the Hashimite Government were totally inadequate, their hospitals insufficiently staffed and badly equipped, and with a deplorable and inexcusable lack of ordinary medicines. (Foreign Office Papers E656/656/91[30])

The consular report on the pilgrimage of 1923 echoes the same theme.

The health of the pilgrimage was good. There were no epidemics, thanks not to any measures taken by the Hijaz Government, but to the fact that the pilgrimage, following the revolution of the Muslim calendar, now takes place in mid-summer. There were a few cases of smallpox—the only infectious disease reported. Dysentery and diarrhoea were the prevailing maladies, and there were a considerable number of cases of sunstroke. . . . In the absence of proper government statistics, it is impossible to say how many pilgrims died, but the number must be large. . . . Many pilgrims who are almost too old to travel come on the pilgrimage, and of these a large proportion die. Many deaths are caused by exhaustion due to heat and malnutrition. (Foreign Office Papers E25/11/91[31])

And little or no improvement was made at the danger points where the pilgrims had perforce to congregate, Mecca and Arafat, as here reported in 1922 by an Indian physician.

In Mecca the streets are generally dirty, as there are few scavengers and no public latrines. There are no dustbins, hence the night soil [human excrement], sweepings and all other rubbish are thrown into the streets and from there they are only partially removed by scavengers. The meat, fish, sweet-meats, fruits and other prepared foods are exposed to dust and flies. The system for the disposal of excreta is a cesspool under each house, and this cesspool is emptied after the lapse of years. The smells that enter the houses from these cesspools are occasionally very offensive.

At Arafat the water channel of the Zubayda Canal runs underground through the camping area, but it is open at some places where the water is received in tanks for the use of the public. As all the people and animals have access to these tanks, the water soon becomes muddy and contaminated. There are few flies and few mosquitoes, but owing to the absence of latrines, human and animal excreta was so abundant that it was almost impossible to avoid soiling the feet or shoes.

At Mina, however, conditions appear to have been improved.

At Mina the water is protected. There are few flies and few mosquitoes. The slaughtering ground was kept in a fairly sanitary state, as the blood and offal were buried soon after the animals were slaughtered. The lack of latrines again led to extensive soiling of the ground. The death rate was low and the causes of death were exhaustion, debility and terminal diarrhoea in old people, dysentery and chronic lung diseases. There was no epidemic. (Foreign Office Papers E2478/120/91[32])

Despite the arrest of epidemic diseases, quarantines still operated at Tur in Sinai, on Qamaran Island just inside the Bab al-Mandab, and, finally, at the king's own facility at Jidda.

Twenty-four hour quarantine (at Jidda) was imposed on pilgrims from all except two or three boats. An exception was made on these few occasions because it was too rough for the doctor to go out to the ships comfortably on the day of arrival. This is unfair to the steamers, which lost a day and had to find another day's water for the pilgrims, and unfair to the pilgrims who received no refund and moreover had to pay as much to the lightermen for the three miles to shore as for the ten miles to the islands and back to land. It also shows what a farce the quarantine at Jidda is. Nevertheless, although we may know for certain that the object of the institution of quarantine at Jidda is to flatter the vanity and fill the pockets of an incompetent and corrupt administration, . . . the Indian argument, which this agency has not failed to use in the past, is that arrangements at Qamaran make quarantine at Jidda unnecessary. But 1) the Hijaz is not a signatory to the International Sanitary Convention, 2) King Husayn as an independent monarch claims the right to take such measures as he thinks necessary to keep epidemics out of the country, and 3) the neglect of the Quarantine Board at Alexandria to impose quarantine on pilgrims from Egypt, where plague is endemic, at Tur . . . justifies the establishment of a quarantine station at Jidda, which is then temptingly available for pilgrims from India and Java. . . . Quarantine is an uncomfortable business everywhere, and it is particularly exasperating to ignorant pilgrims who see their holy land only a few miles away yet unattainable. But it might be made much worse at Jidda (by lodging a complaint). The Hijaz official in charge of quarantine is a Turk of a particularly disobliging and obstructive kind,[33] who would think nothing of revenging a complaint by afflicting additional hardships on Indian pilgrims. (Foreign Office Papers E2478/120/91[34])

THE EGYPTIAN HOSPITAL AFFAIR

Public health and politics were closely linked throughout the nineteenth century, at least from the time when Hajj-spread epidemics invaded Europe and prompted the West to pressure the Sultan to take sanitary measures in his Arabian province, a response that was often interpreted in Istanbul as an infringement on Ottoman sovereignty. After the First World War, some of the parties had changed, but the issue remained the same. Britain and its protégé state in Egypt were applying the pressure, and it was the newly crowned King of the Hijaz who resisted in the name of national sovereignty. Reader Bullard included in his 1923 report one small skirmish, though a prolonged one, in that battle.

The desire of the Egyptian Government to send two small hospitals with the official Egyptian pilgrimage, one for Jidda and the other for Mecca, led to a diplomatic battle which is not yet over. It was very shortly before the time of the pilgrimage that the question was raised by the Egyptian Government, in a telegram addressed to the Hijaz Government. The latter replied that the Hijaz waqfs in Egypt [endowments in Egypt whose income had been pledged to the support of the Two Sanctuaries], which had been in dispute for a long time, must be settled first. . . . A final appeal was sent to Mecca through the British Residency in Cairo and this agency [in Jidda], but with no more success. . . . The Hijaz's Government's final offer was that the doctors, drugs, medical equipment etc. might accompany the Mahmal, "starting when the Mahmal starts, and halting when the Mahmal halts." This seems generous at first sight, but it must be remembered that the cortege in charge of the Mahmal embarks for Egypt about ten days after arrival, whereas many Egyptian pilgrims stay in the Hijaz for some months. (Foreign Office Papers E2478/120/91[35])

The Mahmal itself was a token of sovereignty, and so it too became part of the quarrel, as Bullard later explained in his memoirs.

The pilgrimage season of 1923 began with a quarrel between Egypt and the Hijaz, on the arrival in Jidda of a vessel bringing the Mahmal, the litter containing the Kiswa, which is the covering (not a carpet) for the shrine at Mecca.[36] The Kiswa is changed every year, and at that time the new one was provided by the ruler of Egypt. King Husayn refused to allow the Mahmal to be landed because it was accompanied by two small hospitals for Egyptian pilgrims. The King took this as a reflection on his administration and as derogatory of his independence. During the war the Government of India had sent medical services with its pilgrims, but when he had no further need of the Allies, King Husayn refused to allow these services to continue, although the Hijaz hospitals were little more than bare buildings and the King's own employees used to come to the Indian doctor at the Consulate for treatment. However, no arguments advanced by the Egyptians, or by the British Consulate, which was in charge of Egyptian affairs, had any effect on the King, and the Mahmal and the hospitals returned to Egypt. The King was in a strong position as he had a new Kiswa in hand—one sent down by the Turks during the war and never used.[37] (Bullard 1961: 126–127)

The quarrel with Egypt was patched (up in 1924) and the Mahmal arrived and was allowed to go to Mecca, with a medical unit. The truce, however, did not last. The King noticed that the name of the King of Egypt had been placed in one corner of the Kiswa and had it covered up.

This was discovered and photographed by the Egyptians and the Egyptian Amir al-Hajj made a scene. *Reports received in Jidda said that the Amir al-Hajj lined up his military escort in front of the Mosque in Mecca and made the band play the Egyptian National Anthem, and that he made slighting references to Hijazis, who, he recalled, had been trounced by the forces of Muhammad Ali a century before. (Bullard 1961: 136)*

Among the casualties of the dispute were the Egyptian soup kitchens at Mecca and Medina.

A measure which, if persisted, will mean hunger to many of the poorer pilgrims next year is the closing of the Egyptian takyahs at Mecca and Medina. These takyahs were founded by Muhammad Ali for the distribution of bread and alms to the poor, whether pilgrims or residents. The Mahmal dispute is probably the immediate cause of the suspension of this charitable work, but there was already disagreement before the pilgrimage season. The Ministry of Waqfs in Egypt voted a considerable sum for the alteration and extension of the takyah at Mecca, in order to make room for a pharmacy, a consulting-room and a free guest-house, and sent an engineer to Mecca to supervise the execution of the work. The Hijaz Government, however, not only refused to allow the work to begin, but even raised objections to the retention of the takyah in its present position. The reason given is that the takyah, which is in the main street and almost opposite the mosque, attracts a large crowd of indigent people, who wait about day and night for the distribution of food, and use the vicinity of the mosque in every respect as a private residence, but a mere passion for cleanliness is not sufficient to account for the selection of the Egyptian takyah, of all the crowded institutions which surround the mosque, as the object of attack. Anyhow, both takyahs have now been closed. (Foreign Office Papers E25/11/91[38])

Official Extortion

During the pilgrimage season of 1922, the King introduced something new into the panoply of charges levied against the pilgrims: customs dues on personal effects. W. E. Marshall, the British Consular Agent at Jidda, did what he could to alleviate the newest hardship.

Customs dues on pilgrims' effects were instituted for the first time, and at the beginning of the pilgrimage extortionate charges were made. The very clothes the pilgrims were wearing, if they were adjudged new by the customs authorities, were taxed, and on occasions the tax charged was 50% of the cost of the article. . . .
As the pilgrims were complaining bitterly about these customs charges,

I made representations to the Hashimite Government that customs dues on pilgrims' personal effects should be waived or moderated. In their reply the Hashimite Government notified me that the following articles brought by the pilgrims would be exempt from customs dues:

1. Rice, if not a full sack.
2. Oil, petroleum and sugar, if not a full tin.
3. Bread, called Kajib, syrups and coconuts in any quantity.
4. Ihram clothes, all used towels and five new ones for each person.
5. All perfumes for private use.
6. Flour, lentils and wheat, not more than one sack per person.
7. All ladies' ornaments, silks, etc. . . . .

Though the Hashimite Government did not in all particulars, especially with regard to foodstuffs, carry out these regulations strictly, conditions were greatly improved.

A further hardship imposed on the pilgrims was the customs dues of 50% levied on the import of Turkish mejidis [the principal Turkish gold coin]. No previous warning was given, and pilgrims from Bahrayn and Mesopotamia, who had brought mejidis, suffered considerable loss. A further order for the confiscation of all Maria Theresa dollars was given the customs authorities, and some pilgrims from the Yemen, who arrived with no other currency, were penniless. The matter was referred to King Husayn, who said that the money should be kept in the customs and returned to the pilgrims on their return journey. In the meantime these pilgrims were left in the country without any means of support. (Foreign Office Papers E2478/120/91[39])

One of Marshall's successors as consul, Reader Bullard, reflected in his memoirs on the pilgrimages he had witnessed. What the pilgrims had to put up with from guides, bedouin brigands, and royal officials seemed to him little more than official extortion:

The pilgrims suffered greatly from the rapacity of the pilgrim guides. No one is permitted to make the pilgrimage by himself: he is attached to an official pilgrim guide who knows the language of the country from which he comes. This facilitates the observance of the formalities and the ritual, but the hold it gives the guide over the pilgrim can easily be abused. (It also serves as a check on anyone attempting get into Mecca in disguise, for any peculiarity of speech, any suspicious detail of his history, is likely to be noticed by the guide, and even more by pilgrims in the same party who come from the area he professes to come from. Hence the elaborate history invented by Richard Burton to cover up his European origin.)

King Husayn deprecated anything likely to bring criticism on his regime, but he had as little control over the guides as he did over marauding tribes, and sometimes in his search for revenue he himself provoked legitimate complaints. A party of six hundred Indian pilgrims arrived at Yanbu from Medina expecting to find there a steamer that would take them home. A pilgrim steamer properly equipped was waiting at Jidda, but the captain was not allowed to go to Yanbu to pick up his passengers. Instead the six hundred-odd pilgrims were given passage to Jidda, for a consideration, on a steamer belonging to King Husayn which could perhaps have carried a hundred in comfort, and they spent twenty-two hours in misery.

The greatest scandal, however, arose from the robbery by desert tribes, deprived of their former subsidies, of caravans bound for Mecca. The bedouin were moderate in their demands in the early part of the 1923 season, lest pilgrims should be scared away, but a section of the last caravan was held up for three weeks, until a sum of about £4,000 had been paid in tolls. The pilgrims naturally demanded a refund from the Hijaz Government. To keep them quiet a sum of about £700 was paid, but that was all. King Husayn alleged that the pilgrims had insisted on taking the dangerous road, whereas it was clear that the guides, doubtless in collusion with the bedouin, had taken the most prosperous pilgrims by the most dangerous route, among them the grandmother of the Amir of Afghanistan, who had to pay the brigands £700. (Bullard 1961: 127–128)

Amin Rihani, the well-treated American guest of the King, was far more persuaded of the goodwill of the new government of the independent Hijaz than was the resident Bullard, who had to deal with that government on official levels. Rihani thought the government did its best to shield both the pilgrims and their faith from some of the ruder extortionist shocks that had awaited earlier generations of Hajjis. In fact, it had introduced one of the most revolutionary measures ever attempted in the Near East: a tariff of fixed prices.

As soon as the pilgrim lands in Jidda, he receives a circular printed in his own language in which his attention is called to the fixed tariff. Everything, from the boat in the harbor to the last ceremony of the Hajj in Mecca—board and lodging in the two cities, the trip to Mount Arafat, the Zamzam drink, the guide's fee, even the bakhshish [gratuity] is listed. This much and no more must you pay, O most worthy Hajji; and please report to the authorities any violation of the Tariff.

The only item he has to bargain for is the transportation to Mecca, because, the circular says, the fee depends on the availability of camels. But I do not think the circular is exact; for I suspect that the camel market cannot be controlled, and the cameleer remains a mercenary and an unrepentant one.

To the guides also, in spite of the tariff, all pilgrims are not the same.

There is, to be sure, a scale of desirability and favor, at the top of which stands the Javanese and at the bottom the blacks of Takrur. The guide or his agent has a tourist rather than a pilgrim in a Muslim of Java; but in a Takruri black there is nothing to attract a servant of the Ka'ba. He is as hard as stone, . . . works his way across, coming from Port Sudan empty-handed, carrying and fetching in Jidda, and after a few months, with his well-earned piasters in his bosom-pocket, he walks to the Holy City. . . . Between the two extremes there are different shades of liberality, of sanity and of sordidness. The Indian pilgrim reads well the tariff and keeps it in his pocket; the Egyptian reads it once and forgets it; the Syrian glances over it and tears it up. He knows better. He is, of all the pilgrims, most impervious to bunco. He is the "wise one." The Egyptian is perhaps as wise, but he is not so close-fisted as the Hajji from Syria. (Rihani 1930: 78–79)

THE WAHHABI PILGRIMAGE OF 1925

By the time the pilgrimage season of 1925 approached, the Kingdom of the Hijaz was in ruin. Husayn had been forced to abdicate, and though his son Ali still clung to Jidda, Ibn Sa'ud was in possession of Mecca. A final, and what seemed to all inevitable, attack upon Mecca's port might have been expected before the pilgrims began arriving. Instead, in March, Ibn Sa'ud issued an invitation to pilgrims to come to Mecca via the Hijaz ports already in his hands, Lith and Qunfudha. If this was a tacit admission that Ibn Sa'ud was not yet capable of taking Jidda, the news from other fronts was less cheering for King Ali: Wahhabi pressure was sensibly building up around Wajh, Yanbu, and Medina. When Rabigh, another access port for pilgrims, fell into Wahhabi hands, the Hijaz government promptly declared it under blockade. The strategy was ineffective—most of the incoming pilgrim ships sailed under British flags, and the single steamship that constituted the Hijazi blockade made no move to prevent them from entering the harbor—and by June ships were landing pilgrims at Wahhabi stations up and down the coast. Pilgrims disembarked at Jidda as well, and on 26 June King Ali rescinded his earlier policy and permitted them to pass through his lines and onto the road to Mecca. Bullard thought "the real reason was . . . that he feels beaten and wants to get what little credit he can before it is too late."[40]

Ibn Sa'ud, too, turned conciliatory on the eve of the pilgrimage and raised the siege of Jidda a trifle. On 20 June he sent the following communication to the foreign representatives at Jidda:

Although I am aware that your Governments have declared their complete neutrality in regard to the war in progress between Najd and Hijaz,

I think it necessary to give you an explanation about our military position and our plans for the future.

I have to inform you that I have decided, with the help of God, to adopt a quicker and stronger plan both for the siege of Jidda and the capture of other places. For military reasons it has been decided to change the present position of the army and to dispose it according to a new arrangement and plans drawn up for the purpose. . . . It is not to be understood that this transfer involves raising of the siege of Jidda; on the contrary, it will remain, we trust, under even stricter siege than before.

As to the question of pilgrims and public security in Mecca and on the roads leading to it from the ports of Rabigh, Lith and Qunfudha, I have to inform you, in order to forestall any attempt to make trouble, . . . that the most minute precautions are being taken for the safety of pilgrims, and that all preparations have been completed to ensure their comfort and tranquillity both for their journey (to Mecca) and for their return. (Foreign Office Papers E4126/10/91[41])

Eldon Rutter

The Hajj of 1925, the first under the political auspices of the House of Sa'ud, was also the first in more than a century to reflect the religious sensibilities of the "pietists" (*mudayyina*), the followers of Abd al-Wahhab, whom we have already seen in Mecca on pilgrimage. There was a privileged witness on hand at that occasion. Eldon Rutter, an English convert to Islam, was performing his first Hajj and so had an unparalleled opportunity to watch the old order yield to the new. At first, however, the new Muslim was aware only of his own feelings.

Through the forest of columns (of the Haram) I could dimly see the great gravel-strewn quadrangle, over four and a half acres in extent; and in its midst, covered by a black cloth which made it hardly defined in the darkness, stood the Bayt Allah, the House of God, the Ka'ba.

Under the arches of the cloisters, bare-footed, long-robed, silent figures were hurrying to take up their positions behind the imams. In all parts of the great quadrangle, worshipers were forming into long lines facing the Ka'ba, preparing to perform the morning prayer. Over the crest of the hill of Abu Qubays, the first faint light of dawn showed in the sky, like a transparent patch in a sheet of dark-blue glass.

"Look," said Abd al-Rahman, "The Sacred House of God!"

I walked forward to the edge of the cloisters, and looked out across the wide court of the Mosque towards the great black-draped cube—that strange building, in the attempt to reach which tens of thousands, perhaps millions, of human beings have prematurely forfeited their lives; and seeing which, unnumbered millions have felt themselves to be on the very threshold of Paradise. It stood, with the simple massive grandeur of a solitary rock in the midst of the ocean—an expressive symbol of the Unity of that God Whose house it is. Aloof and mysterious it seemed, reared up majestically in the center of the great open quadrangle; while round and round its base the panting Hajjis hurried eagerly, uttering their pitiful supplication, "O God, grant us, in the world, good; and, in the hereafter, good; and save us from the punishment of fire!" (Rutter 1930: 107–108)

It was only after Rutter finished his arrival rituals, as he sat chatting with some new Meccan friends, that the subject of the "pietists" arose.

"What happened when the mudayyina came into Mecca?" I asked him.

"There came four men wearing the ihram and riding camels, and they passed down the streets, which were deserted, and cried out the promise of security and that the people of Mecca—the Neighbors of God—were under the protection of God and of Ibn Saʿud. And all of us had locked and barred our doors. And in the second day there came two thousand of the mudayyina, ihramed and carrying rifles and swords and mounted on riding camels. Then they all performed the circumambulation of the Kaʿba and went out again to Al-Abta, the place of their camp. After a few days they broke into the palace of Sayyidna (Our Lord [King Husayn]), and tied up a donkey in his sitting place. And on the donkey's head they put the turban of Sayyidna. After that they drove the donkey, and he wearing the turban, out into the streets, and went around the city with him in front of them. Then they kicked the jewelled Stambuli coat of Sayyidna, and his jewelled state umbrella, into the market place with their feet, and sold them for five piasters." (Rutter 1930: 142–143)

On Friday of that same week, when he went into the Haram to pray, Rutter caught his first sight of the new sovereign of the Hijaz.

Prayers being over, many of the congregation proceeded to perform the circumambulation. Among these I observed a broad figure, over six feet in height, dressed in a yellow robe and carrying a black umbrella as a protection against the sun. He compassed the House with long deliberate strides, and at his heels pressed a motley crowd of bedouins. This was Abd al-Aziz ibn Saʿud, the bedouin lord of the desert and invader of the Hijaz. (Rutter 1930: 145)

At the Mount of Mercy

The Hajj proper began, and Rutter followed its rites with the others who had come to Mecca that season. Early in the morning of the ninth of Dhu al-Hijja the pilgrims approached Arafat.

For the last hour of our journey the dawn had been slowly lightening the clear sky to eastward, and now, as we left the enclosing walls of the narrow sandy bottom and emerged into the spacious plain, all the black jagged summits of the hills which fell away on either side of us were suddenly crowned with gold. Before our eyes extended a perfectly level plain, some four miles across from west to east, and nearly twice that distance from north to south. . . . Directly in front of us, in the center of the opposite mountain wall, as we approached from the west, was a towering conical peak, and a little way in front of this stood a small isolated hill some two hundred feet in height. This latter, which is called Jabal al-Rahma, is surmounted by a column built of granite blocks, cemented together and whitened. From the summit of the hill the Hajj sermon is preached and the column is a distinguishing mark to enable travelers to recognize the hill from a distance. . . . It stands in the northwestern corner of a square stoned-paved platform at the top of the hill. This platform measures seven yards by eight and in the middle of its northern side stands a prayer-niche.

The platform on the summit of Jabal al-Rahma is approached by a broad, roughly-constructed stairway leading up the southern slope of the hill. . . . The sides of the hill are very steep, and are covered with boulders of all sizes and shapes. . . . Jabal al-Rahma, or the Mount of Mercy, is frequently termed Jabal Arafat. At its base it measures some three hundred yards in length from northwest to southeast, and one hundred and fifty yards from southwest to northeast. (Rutter 1930: 156–159)

It was a strange place and a strange company. Meccans and Yemenis, Turks and Bukharans, Malays and Indians, Moors and Syrians; and this year, outnumbering all the rest collectively were the sour-visaged Najd Ikhwan [the Wahhabi "Brethren"]. All wore the ihram, save one or two of the pedlars and the bedouin camel-drivers. I estimated the number of the pilgrims assembled on the plain at seventy thousand. . . . There were probably twenty-five or thirty thousand Wahhabis present, most of whom sat out the hours of waiting beside their saddled camels, far out on the plain to the southwest of Jabal al-Rahma.

Somewhat before midday Rutter went to visit the Namira mosque situated on the Arafat plain. On returning, he caught his second glimpse of Ibn Saʿud.

On our way back to the tent we passed the burly figure of Ibn Saʿud, dressed in a couple of towels, bestriding a beautiful Najd horse which looked rather like a little animated rocking-horse under his long form. He was attended by four mounted guards carrying rifles. (Rutter 1930: 160–161)

A Drop in the Crime Rate

At sunset began the *ifada*, the tumultuous rush from Arafat back to Muzdalifa:

All over the wide plain a great fog of dust rose, obscuring the bases of the hills so that their peaks alone were visible. . . . Far out on the northern side of the plain rode the scattered hosts of the Najd Ikhwan—dim masses of hasting camelry, obscurely seen in the falling dusk. . . . Most of the Wahhabis, all of whom rode dromedaries, reached the gorge (to Muzdalifa) ahead of the other pilgrims and the Meccans. Some few, however, still continued to come out of the blackness behind us—lurching by at a fast trot on their great upstanding camels. As we proceeded I noticed several Wahhabis, ihramed like the rest, returning singly or in twos toward Arafat. Riding past at a walk, they scanned the crowd with piercing glances, paying particular attention to the foot travelers who were mixed indiscriminately among the camels and donkeys. These men were on police duty, searching for any sign of theft or other misdemeanor (such as smoking) among the crowd.

The days of the pilgrimage form the most prosperous season for Mecca's thieves, but this year few cases of theft occurred, on account of the deterrent influence of the merciless Wahhabis. The penalty in Islamic law for a first offense of theft is the cutting off of the robber's right hand. . . . On the following day, at Mina, I saw a wretched Hijazi bedouin come running down the village street. He held his right forearm with his left and only remaining hand. The stump of the other arm was dripping blood, the hand having just been severed. Seeing a cauldron of boiling clarified butter at which a stall-keeper was cooking kufta (meat balls), the maimed malefactor ran up to it and thrust his forearm into the burning grease. He held it there for a moment then drew it out and went quickly away, just in time to escape the impending blows of the stall-keeper. As he scuffled away, a gruesome object, which was suspended about his neck with a piece of string, swung from side to side. It was his severed hand. (Rutter 1930: 164–165)

Abd al-Aziz ibn Saʿud at Mina

The Hajj ceremonies continued with the "stoning" at Mina.

We went to stone the "Great Devil," which is a piece of wall built against a rock at the Mecca-ward end of the street of Mina. A continuous double stream of the poor and mad Wahhabis went by us with unnecessary energy on their bouncing camels as we walked down the sandy road. They came in at a fast trot, dodging all over the narrow street. The long *sleeves of their thawbs and the ends of their abayas flew loosely in the air, and from their saddles long tassels streamed and danced about their cam-els' knees. Arrived at the devils, they threw their stones without dis-mounting, and turning, rode wildly back again. Some of these had their women perched behind them on the animal's croup, while a few of the women rode alone, brandishing sticks and thwacking the ribs of their tall camels, like the men. All the Wahhabi women were shrouded from head to foot with a single black garment. Into this was sewn a piece of thinner material, also black, at the part which covered the face. This was to enable them to see and breathe to some extent. (Rutter 1930: 170–171)*

The sacrifice followed, and Rutter and his Meccan friends retired to their tent at Mina.

I asked Abd al-Rahman to come with me to join the crowd of bedouins and Meccans and Hajjis who were streaming from all parts of the valley towards the tent of Ibn Saʿud, in order to offer him their congratulations upon the completion of the Day of Arafat and the arrival of the Feast of Sacrifices. This proposition he deprecated, saying "We know nothing of the mudayyina, nor do we want to know anything of them." Eventually, however, he said he would go with me to the Amir's tent, and himself remain outside while I entered.

We made our way to the cope-stoned earthen platform where the tents of the Sharif of Mecca were formerly pitched at this season. Over the tents which now stood there flew the green flag of Najd. Before the entrance of the reception tent stood two black slaves, cloaked and kerchiefed like bed-ouins, and armed with Arab swords adorned with massive silver hilts. The visitors streamed into the tent in batches, shook hands with Ibn Saʿud, and wishing him a blessed feast, passed out at the further side. A few of them kissed him on the forehead, the shoulder, or the back of the hand.

Upon entering the tent, I could at first see very little save the jostling crowd. Soon these dispersed to the sides of the tent, or went out the fur-ther exit, and I saw at the opposite end a number of bedouins and Mec-cans sitting upon chairs and benches arranged in a semi-circle around the side of the tent. In the center of the curve, flanked by three or four of his military amirs, sat Abd al-Aziz ibn Saʿud. He wore no finery nor carried any weapon. Over a white linen undergarment he wore a simple cloak of yellow hair-cloth, and on his head a red-and-white cotton kafiyya, sur-mounted by a black hair-rope agal, bound with silver wire. His feet were bare, as he had shed his sandals at the edge of the carpet. He sat with an amiable smile on his face, and wearing black spectacles in order to lessen the effect of the sun-glare. He rose to take the hand of each of his visitors in turn, and returning our salutations and congratulations briefly and smilingly, he then immediately turned his attention to the next comer.

This lion of many desert battles, and the sovereign lord of more than half of Arabia, invariably rises to receive his visitors, whether prince or dervish.

Ibn Sa'ud was at that time some forty-five years of age. Although considerably over six feet in height, he is well and even gracefully proportioned. The features of his long Arab face are large and strong, the mouth somewhat coarse and thick-lipped, the eyes a trifle on the small side. His beard and moustache—the latter cropped short, the former in length a hand's breadth in the Wahhabi style—are inclined to sparseness. He speaks remarkable well, in an easy well-modulated tone, and uses slight, graceful gestures of the hands. Like many other people of energy, he is frequently very abrupt with his minions when they make mistakes or get in his way. Abd al-Aziz is not himself a religious fanatic, but he is an ambitious statesman; and in the latter capacity he does not scruple to make use of religious fanaticism for the purpose of attaining the objects of his ambition. . . . He is a relentless enemy while opposition lasts, but in the hour of victory is one of the most humane Arabs in history. (Rutter 1930: 173–174)

Wahhabi Iconoclasts

The Wahhabis generally made the Hajj in the same manner as other Muslims. It was only in the secondary rituals, where custom rather than prescription prevailed, that they differed fiercely with their coreligionists, and in no matter more strongly than in the cultus of the dead saint, even if the deceased were a prophet.

The Prophet's birthplace (mulid al-nabi) is chief among the places in and about the Holy City which form the objects of pious visitation. This is situated in the ravine called Shi'b Ali, near Suq al-Layl. It stands in one corner of an open space, some forty yards square, between the ancient houses, and consisted, before the advent of the Wahhabis, of a small square mosque surmounted by a dome and flanked by a short minaret.[42] . . . The mosque is divided by a wall into two chambers, each about thirty feet long by fifteen feet wide, and the right-hand one of these is again divided into two chambers of unequal size. The more westerly of these, which is the larger, stands on the site of the room in which Muhammad is said to have been born. A circular hole, nearly a foot in diameter, in the marble floor is shown as being the actual spot on which the Lady Amina gave birth to the future Prophet.

The Wahhabis, true to their principles, demolished the dome and the minaret of this building and removed the draperies and other ornaments from it. They also prohibited the hereditary custodians from sitting at its doorway to receive alms. Before their occupation of the Holy city, this placid occupation had furnished the principal source of income for a family of sharifs. Now, whenever the mulid al-nabi was mentioned in a gathering of Meccans, faces grew grave, and here and there among the company a bitter curse would be uttered against the Najdis. . . . It was dangerous to stand and look for long at this or any other sacred site or building, for a passing Wahhabi, seeing one so occupied, would be quite capable of laying about him with his camel-stick, calling down curses the while upon those who make supplication to the Prophet. The Wahhabis would have entirely prohibited visitation of the mulid, but the fact of its being a mosque enabled Abd al-Aziz to prevail upon the ulama to persuade the wild men that there was nothing unlawful about its being used for the purpose of prayer and meditation. Consequently they have left the gateway in the half-ruined walls un-obstructed, and Ibn Saʿud gained credit with them for having allowed the dome to be demolished, and credit from the foreign Hajjis for protecting the place from complete demolition. (Rutter 1930: 270–271)

Nor did the Wahhabis spare the cemetery of Maʿala, the burial place of many early Muslims and celebrated Meccans.

The famous cemetery of Maʿala occupies twenty or thirty acres of ground at the northern end of the Meccan valley. . . . Here, according to tradition, are buried the Prophet's mother Amina; his wife, Khadija; and his ancestors Abd Manaf and Abd al-Muttalib, together with a number of famous early Muslims. The mutawwifs [the official guides] have invented long supplications and pious exercises to be said at these tombs. These being outside the Prophet's practice are termed "innovation." The few tolerant men among the Wahhabis term these exercises "undesirable innovation," while the many intolerant Wahhabis call them rites of polytheism. . . . The tombs of these personages were formerly crowned with small but handsome domes, but these, without exception, have been demolished, together with most of the tombstones. The guardians of each tomb, who formerly derived considerable income from the Hajjis, now no longer dare spread their handkerchiefs on the ground to receive the pilgrims' alms. The cemetery is silent and deserted, save when a funeral party quickly bears in one more departed Muslim to join the millions whose dust lies there. (Rutter 1930: 274)

The Politics of Pilgrimage

The British were still uncertain what posture to take toward the new sovereign of western Arabia, an old ally who had defeated another old ally and former protégé. The success or failure of the first pilgrimage under

Saʿudi auspices, and the treatment of Indian Hajjis in particular, would be one factor in British considerations. Reader Bullard attempted to provide, from what his sources told him, an assessment of the historic Hajj of 1925.

Ibn Saʿud claims that 60,000 Najdis were present at Arafat for the Hajj. This figure may be an exaggeration, but all the pilgrims who have reached Jidda (on their way home) say that the Najdis were very numerous: "The plain was full of them." There were, of course, few pilgrims from overseas: they consisted mainly of about 2,500 who came from or via India through Rabigh, a few hundred from Syria, Turkey, West Africa, etc. who traveled via Massawa and Qunfudha, and an unknown but not large number of Sudanese and Nigerians who sailed from Massawa and other ports to Qunfudha.

All reports indicate that the pilgrimage was very healthy and that there was no epidemic of any kind.

The pilgrims from India who traveled to Mecca via Rabigh took five days on the road but arrived safe. The charge for camels was low, and no extortion was practiced by the camel-drivers. . . . Rabigh does very well indeed for a small number of pilgrims, but it would not meet the requirements of a normal season. The commanding officer of the H.M.S. Cornflower estimates that only four or five ships could lie at anchor in the harbor. . . . This would not do for a normal season when pilgrims pour in from seven or eight ports and when as many as twenty steamers lie at anchor in Jidda harbor waiting for pilgrims to return.

The Hijaz Government agreed to allow pilgrims returning from the Hajj to come to Jidda to embark. . . . About 200 British Malays and 1,000 Takrunis have reached Jidda (returning) from Mecca. One or two seem to have been robbed by Wahhabis along the road, but most of the parties saw no Arabs at all.

If the Indians, and so the British, were interested in the Hajj, there were other Muslim items on the menu, including a not unexpected visit to Ibn Saʿud from the Indian Caliphate Committee.

An Indian delegation consisting of representatives from the Caliphate Committee and the Committee of Ulama appear to have traveled to Mecca via Rabigh. According to the Umm al-Qura, the Mecca newspaper,[43] they seized the occasion of the Hajj feast (Id al-Adha) at Mina to exchange speeches with Ibn Saʿud. The leader of the delegation, . . . who began by praising the state of security on the road, said that they and the Muslim world were expecting the Holy Land to be cleansed of all impurity—especially from the stain of foreign suzerainty. They approved of Ibn Saʿud's plan not to rule over the Hijaz or to make it part of his do-

minions, but simply to clear it of Husayn and his sons, and of a project to call a conference of the Muslim world to deal with the question.

Ibn Saʿud replied at length, affirming his orthodoxy and addressing another somewhat delicate question:

He was completely independent in his territory (he said), and no one had the right to interfere in its affairs in any way whatsoever. It is true that there was a treaty between himself and a certain Power, relating to the safeguarding of certain interests essential to his territory. There was precedent for that in the times of the Prophet and the Orthodox Caliphs. God forbid that he should admit any foreign interference in his territory; such interference would be contrary to both his religion and his honor.

It was through God and his sword that he attained honor and glory; no State helped him, no Government carried him to success with its forces. The title by which his community and his people knew him was sufficient for him, whether he was called General or Amir or King.

Titles may not have meant much to Ibn Saʿud, but there was one he did not much favor:

He had recently urged a party of Meccans who came to see him not to put their trust in the title of Sharif, or in office or rank. Bilal the Abyssinian was preferable to the Prophet's uncle, Abu Lahab. (Foreign Office Papers E4547/10/91[44])

While Ibn Saʿud was performing his first pilgrimage in Mecca, his thoughts were already turned toward the final steps of his annexation of the Hijaz: the conquest of Medina and Jidda. The British, who had just recently created the Amirate of the Transjordan for Abdullah, were aware of the Amir's plans—there was no effort to conceal them. To forestall an additional Saudi move upon Aqaba, which was arguably a part of the Hijaz, they removed thence to Cyprus the person of the ex-King Husayn and took the further precaution of occupying Aqaba with their own armored cars.[45]

The "Saudi Hajj" of 1925 was not the last of the traditional pilgrimages, but it marked a watershed in the history of the Muslim Holy Land. The Hijaz had been in the hands of Husayn's ancestors for over a millennium, and it was they who controlled both the pilgrimage and the pilgrims who made it. But the transfer of sovereignty from Hashimite Sharif to Saudi prince appears far more profound to the observer than it was on the ground: Saudi justice and order was soon seen to be preferable to the greed and anarchy that had marked the reigns of Husayn and many of his predecessors. Under the Saudis, the Hajj was a safer and more secure enterprise; extortionate practices disappeared, and even the powerful guild of guides was curbed. But if the Saudis brought order, they also brought a new religious sensibility, that of Abd al-Wahhab and his creed of a strict, almost puritanical Islam. From the beginning of the Saudi tenancy of Mecca, the pious accretions of shrine and rites that had grown up around the Hajj over many centuries were stripped away. What was thought to be the pristine ritual was restored.

For the next twenty years the Hajj was conducted in security and even privacy, as the attention of the larger world that had discovered the Hijaz in the new geopolitics of the First World War turned its attention elsewhere. But only briefly. The Second World War did not rediscover the Muslim Holy Places but focused the Allies' attention on the Saudis' other extraordinary possession: the world's largest oil reserve. The consequences for the Hajj began to be felt in the immediate postwar era. The House of Sa'ud poured its new wealth into the refurbishing of the holy places and then into accommodations and facilities for the pilgrims, who now arrived in ever greater numbers by air. By 1957, the Meccan Haram was transformed—the Ka'ba alone excepted—into an enormous new shrine complex. (Similar renovations contiue at Medina.)

The Hajj remains the same religious act performed by Muhammad and prescribed to all Muslims, but under the Saudis it now unfolds in physical circumstances unrecognizable and almost unimaginable to the Hajjis of even the recent past.

Notes

INTRODUCTION

1. The lives and circumstances of the European visitors are rehearsed in a number of works. See, for instance: Hogarth 1904; Bidwell 1976; Freeth & Winstone 1978; Tidrick 1981; Trench 1986.

2. This more general and "anthropological" approach to the Hajj is explored by some of the authors collected in Eickelman & Piscatori (1990); cf. their annotated bibliography, pp. 256–263.

3. On the evolution of the term *rihla*, see Gellens (1990: 53) and El-Moudden (1990: 69–70). Netton 1993 connects *hijra*, *hajj*, and *rihla*.

4. Batanuni 1911 (on the Hajj of the Egyptian ruler Abbas Hilmi in 1910, with plans and early photos); Rif'at Pasha 1925 (an account by the Amir al-Hajj of the Egyptian caravan for the pilgrimages of 1901, 1903, 1904, and 1907, with hundreds of historic photographs).

5. See, for example, the works of Shaw, Rafeq, Barbir, and Ochsenwald cited in the body of the work.

CHAPTER I
ORIGINS

1. Firestone (1990: 63–71) analyzes the three major versions (those of Ibn Abbas, Ali, and Mujahid) of the "transfer to Mecca." On Tabari's account, see ibid., 67.

2. The space between the northwest face of the later Ka'ba and a low semicircular wall, the *hatim*, opposite it. See below.

3. Firestone 1990: 64, no. 7.

4. So Tabari, *Annals* 1.281, 283. The events on the occasion of one of these later visits is used to explain something else. When Abraham calls, Ishmael is off hunting, and so Abraham is greeted by Ishmael's wife, a woman of the Jurhum tribe. He asks for bread or wheat or barley or dates. She has none and offers instead milk and meat, which he accepts and blesses. "Had she brought bread or wheat or dates or barley," the commentator explains, "Mecca would have been the most plentifully supplied with these things of any place on God's earth" (ibid., 284).

5. Abu Qubays is a mountain rising above the valley of Mecca on the east.

6. Tabari, *Annals* 1.1131 = Tabari VI: 52.

7. The literal reference is to the removal of the growth of hair, fingernails, and so on, which could not be done while in the state of ritual pilgrimage purity.

8. Most of the Quranic texts referring to the Hajj have Muhammad and not Abraham as the speaker.

9. *Arafat* and the verb "to know" are etymologically linked in Arabic.

10. Compare the systematic analysis in Firestone (1990: 94–104).

11. On the "commemorative" as opposed to the "mimetic" quality of the Hajj ritual, see Graham (1983: 68).

12. Tabari, *Annals* 1.1093–1098. Cf. Ibn Ishaq 1955: 52–53.

13. Cf. Fahd 1968: 210, 212.

14. Cf. Nevo & Koren 1990: 24–25.

15. On this quality of the Ka'ba, see Hawting (1984) and below.

16. The area extends roughly from al-Hudaybiyya on the west to Arafat on the east, from al-Jir'ana mosque on the north to Adat Labn on the south.

17. Caetani 1905: 96.

18. 'arish; cf. Rubin 1986: 98. On the earlier speculation on the Ka'ba as a tent, see Wellhausen (1897: 73).

19. Fahd (1968: 204–205), following Wellhausen (1897: 73). On the Meccan tent tradition, see Azraqi (1858: 196) and Jahiz, Hayawan 3.44.

20. The four corners of the present Ka'ba—and we have no reason to think that the foundations were ever altered in its long history—are generally oriented toward the cardinal points of the compass. But the more particular orientation of the building is far more complex; see Hawkins & King (1982: 102).

21. Cf. Fahd 1968: 234.

22. There is a minor strain of tradition that denies this, but Hawting (1984: 234–235) thinks its motive was a fear that prayer within the Ka'ba might eventually devaluate or even replace the circumambulation around its exterior. Moreover, in the course of Islamic history there was a strong popular sentiment for an "open" Ka'ba (ibid., 238).

23. On the sanctity of Abu Qubays, see Rubin (1986: 120–121).

24. Azraqi 1858: 477–478.

25. Ibn Sa'd, Tabaqat 1.135. Cf. Lammens 1928: 102–103; Rubin 1986: 119.

26. Fakihi, Ta'rikh Makka, Ms. Leiden Or. 463:276a.

27. Azraqi 1858: 73–74. Tabari (Annals 1.1132) seems to suggest independently—if in fact the hajr al-rukn or "pillar- or angle-stone" of his text is the Black Stone—that it was there in the pre-Quraysh era.

28. Rubin (1986: 121) prefers to have the Black Stone (first?) built into the Ka'ba during its Qurayshite reconstruction at the time of the Prophet.

29. Cf. Fahd 1968: 205.

30. According to Azraqi (1858: 142–143, 220), the tombs of Ishmael and Hagar were "discovered" there during the reconstruction by Ibn al-Zubayr; cf. Rubin (1986: 109).

31. Rubin (1986: 99–101, 104): "It seems as if the main function of the entire enclosure containing the Ka'ba and the Hijr was to mark the boundaries of the sacred ground in which several idols were worshiped."

32. So Lüling 1981: 132ff.

33. Rubin 1986: 106.

34. Ibn Ishaq 1955: 183 (the Quraysh are discussing Muhammad); ibid., 264 (Muhammad is sleeping there).

35. Fahd 1966: 363–364; Rubin 1986: 112.

36. Ginzberg 1909: 1:350. Cf. Hawting (1982: 42) and, on the "gate of heaven" tradition, Azraqi (1858: 219–220).

37. Azraqi (1958: 197) remarks: "Bakka is the place where the sanctuary is situated and Mecca is the city." It may be conjectured that what he knew about the name "Bakka" is what we do, that single verse in the Quran. Cf. Yaqut 1.506; Fahd 1968: 213.

38. Kister 1971b: 479. Cf. Hawting 1982: 30–31.

39. Nor is there much agreement among the moderns. Wellhausen (1897: 76) and Gaudefroy-Demombynes (1923: 103) thought it was originally some sort of sacrificial stone, and Lammens (1924: 56) regarded it as a betyl.

40. Hawting (1982: 31): "I envision that the name first arose as a designation for the sanctuary because it was there that Abraham had stood in the presence of God; when the Meccan sanctuary was taken over, for reasons which are not clear Maqam Ibrahim could no longer be used as a name for the sanctuary as a whole and so it became attached to the stone which now bears its name, a literal interpretation of the root from which maqam is derived giving rise to the story which is most commonly used to explain why the stone is

called 'Maqam Ibrahim': it is a stone on which Abraham had stood while building the bayt."

41. Kister (1971b: 485) interprets this as a reading of the Hebrew Seba' ot in Hebrew.

42. Fakihi, Ta'rikh Makka, cited by Kister (1971b: 485–486).

43. Wellhausen 1897: 76. Fahd (1968: 210–212) derives the name from a Mesopotamian prototype, the goddess Ninurta.

44. Some of the wells in Mecca and vicinity are described by Azraqi (1858: 68–70). Cf. Rubin 1986: 115n.122.

45. Azraqi 1858: 289–290, 292–293. Cf. Rubin 1986: 110.

46. Cf. Hawting 1990: 77.

47. Wellhausen 1897: 77–78; Fahd 1968: 103ff.; Lüling 1981: 172–173.

48. Fahd 1968: 104; Lazarus-Yefeh 1981: 22.

49. According to Azraqi's reports (1858: 74–75), Qusayy placed one of the idols next to the Ka'ba and the other in the place where the well of the Zamzam was to be dug later. Others maintain that he put both idols by the Zamzam, where they remained until the conquest of Mecca. The divergence suggests that within a century after the coming of Islam, no one really knew where they had been.

50. Lammens 1928: 101–189.

51. The elementary form of these deities, once a warmly debated topic (cf. Henninger 1959: 14–15), does not concern us here.

52. The age of idolatry is long past for those who study idol worshipers, and so we can only very tentatively impose our conceptual patterns on the pre-Islamic Arabs performing sacrifice and other ritual acts before stones.

53. The most detailed Muslim study of pre-Islamic figurative art appears to have been in Jahiz's Book of Idols, now unfortunately lost, though its contents are described in the same author's Book of Animals, whence they are cited by Fahd (1968: 249).

54. Fahd 1968: 101 and 29.

55. Dussaud 1955: 41 and n.3.

56. Lammens 1928: 101–180.

57. There are in fact a number of hot springs in the Yarmuk Valley on the border between Syria and Jordan.

58. The names themselves appear to mean stones; cf. Fahd 1968: 105.

59. Other sources say that it came from northern Jordan.

60. Azraqi 1858: 111.

61. Cf. Fahd 1968: 101–102.

62. Henninger 1959: 11; Fahd 1968: 168ff.

63. Ibn al-Kalbi 1952: 19. Cf. Wellhausen 1897: 30.

64. Watt 1988: xxxiv–xxxv. Verse 26 of the same sura accepts such a role for the angels: "How many angels there are in heaven whose intercession is of no avail except when God gives leave to those whom He chooses and accepts."

65. Fahd 1968: 89.

66. Ibn al-Kalbi 1952: 12.

67. Wellhausen 1897: 217–224.

68. Henninger 1959: 12.

69. See the detailed analysis in Rubin 1984a.

70. The principal Quranic injunction to sacrifice occurs in Sura 108, which reads in its entirety: "Behold, we have given you abundance. So pray to your Lord and sacrifice. In truth, it is the one who hates you who is suffering loss." Despite its apparently straightforward command, the second verse raised considerable debate among the Muslim commentators, chiefly because it occurs in a Meccan sura and so apparently commands the Prophet to participate in a pagan ritual—possibly connected with the Hajj and possibly not—before the later "Islamicization" of the Pilgrimage. See Birkeland (1956: 76–78), who

remarks: "So it is a notorious fact that the Koran contains at least one Surah from a time *before* Muhammad had abandoned the performance of religious rites customary in Mecca" (85–86).

71. Wellhausen 1897: 101ff.; Goldziher 1889:211; Fahd 1968: 26.

72. Wellhausen 1897: 79–84; Crone 1987: 173.

73. Ibn Ishaq 1955: 49–50. Cf. Wellhausen (1897: 81) and the demur in Kister (1965: 155).

74. Kister 1965: 136n.1; Kister 1980: 37–38; Crone 1987: 176.

75. The commentators were not certain who raised the objection to mixing trade with the pilgrimage, whether the pre-Islamic Arabs or the early Muslims, but the preferred view is that it was the latter. See Crone 1987: 171 and n. 20.

76. The evidence is collected in Crone (1987: 170–174).

77. And which eventually led to the desertion and disappearance of Ukaz, Dhu al-Majaz, and Majanna, which, whatever their earlier commercial (and religious?) importance, were assigned no *ritual* role in the Muslim version of the Hajj. Cf. Azraqi 1858: 131; Crone 1987: 157n.49.

78. On the rituals of Rajab, see Wellhausen (1897: 74, 93); Gaudefroy-Demombynes (1923: 192–194); Goitein (1966: 92–93); Kister (1971a).

79. Wellhausen 1897: 94, 115–116.

80. Cf. Quran 2:158: "So if you *hajj* the House or ʿ*umra* . . ." (where both rituals are used as verbs), it is "no sin" to make a "turning" around Safa and Marwa, a ritual identified not with the pre-Islamic Hajj but with the Umra.

81. Gaudefroy-Demombynes 1923: 256–257, 264–265.

82. Wellhausen 1879: 76; Rubin 1986: 124–125.

83. Kister 1971a: 191n.2.

84. Birkeland 1956: 102–121; Shahid 1981: 430; Rubin 1984a: 177.

85. Rubin 1984a: 174n.59.

86. Cf. Crone (1987: 163n.74), with reference to Azraqi (1858): "Ukaz was located one *barid* from Taʾif on the Sanʿa road, Majanna one *barid* from Mecca, and Dhu al-Majaz one *farsakh* from Arafat (in its turn located about thirteen miles east of Mecca on the road of Taʾif." When Burckhardt (1829: 214) consulted the savants of Mecca in the early nineteenth century on the location of Ukaz, he received an answer entirely different from that offered by the historians.

87. Wellhausen 1897: 99–100.

88. Cf. Crone 1987: 155.

89. Kister (1980: 36) defines the *Hums* as "a group closely connected by ties of loyalty and allegiance to the Kaʿba, observing distinctive ritual practices during the Hajj and enjoying a special privileged position in Mecca." The word means "zealot" or "devotee," but one common derivation connects it with *al-hamsâ*, a name for the Kaʿba that refers to the gray stones from which it was built (Kister 1965: 139; Rubin 1986: 123), though it is just as likely the other way around, that the Kaʿba as *al-hamsâ* = the Kaʿba as "the *Hums'* thing."

90. Cf. Wellhausen 1897: 79ff.; Crone 1987: 173–176.

91. This is the reverse of the usual siting of these two idols.

92. Cited by Rubin 1986: 123.

93. Rubin 1986: 126.

94. Wellhausen 1897: 87.

95. Azraqi 1858: 121, 124.

96. Kister (1980: 36–37) remarks, "This may be a quite faithful exposition of their belief."

97. By Islamic times the verb "to sojourn" had taken on a technical meaning: to pass a

shorter or longer period of time in pious prayer and practices at one of the preeminent mosques of Islam, notably, though by no means exclusively, at either of the "Two Harams" of Mecca and Medina.

98. Guillaume (in Ibn Ishaq 1955: 105) has: "the Apostle would pray in seclusion and give food to the poor."

99. Cited by Kister 1968: 224.

100. Kister 1968: 226–227.

101. Cited in Kister 1968: 232.

102. Cited in Kister 1968: 233.

103. Azraqi 1858: 134. Cf. Kister 1980: 33–34.

104. On the older conviction that the "Abrahamic" aspects of Muhammad's preaching were a consequence of his confrontation with the Jews at Medina, see Beck (1952) and Rubin (1990: 99n.68).

105. The consensus opinion was that Muhammad prayed facing Jerusalem before changing his prayer-direction to the Kaʿba early in his stay in Medina (cf. Quran 2:142–144). But there is a persistent strain of reports that he prayed toward the Kaʿba even before he prayed facing Jerusalem; see Rubin 1990: 102.

106. Ibn Ishaq 1955: 67. Cf. Rubin 1990: 103–104.

107. Cf. Rubin 1990: 104–106; Firestone 1990: 143.

108. Josephus, *Antiquities* 1.12.2. On pre-Islamic Arab circumcision, see Wellhausen (1897: 174–176).

109. Jubilees 20:11–13 (cf. Rubin 1990: 106); BT Sanhedrin 91a. Sozomen, the church historian writing in southern Palestine no more than a century and a half before Muhammad, knew that Arabs counted Abraham in their ancestry and that "many among them still live in the Jewish fashion" (*Church History* 6.38.1–13).

110. See the elaborate documentation to the contrary presented in Dagorn (1981).

111. It is clearly a loan word in Arabic, but its obvious antecedent, the Syriac plural *hanpe*, is used by pre-Islamic Christian writers to designate "pagans" or "idolators" and so in precisely the opposite sense from that which invoked in the Quran.

112. Guillaume remarks (in Ibn Ishaq 1955: 99n.2): "The influence of this Jewish formula, taken over by early Christianity (Acts 15:29), is clear."

113. Watt, *Encyclopaedia of Islam* (2d ed.), art. "Hanif," thinks that many, if not all, such stories are retrospective Islamic projections for apologetic purposes. But among others, Fück (1936: 91) accepts some of them, as does Rubin (1990: 85–86), particularly when they concern men who opposed Muhammad: "The reports concerning these persons must be taken as authentic, because as already noted by Fück, no Muslim could have any interest in characterizing those opponents of the Prophet as *hanifs*."

114. Fück 1936: 91.

115. Studied by Gil (1987) and Rubin (1990: 86–88, 90–94).

116. Ibn Ishaq 1955: 278. Cf. Wellhausen 1897: 239.

117. Rubin 1990: 95–97.

118. Ibn Ishaq 1955: 100–101.

119. Kister 1970.

120. Cited by Kister 1970: 270.

121. Cf. Kister 1970: 275; Rubin 1990: 101.

122. See generally on this critical verse Birkeland (1956). For the meaning of *dalla* and *hada*, see ibid., 28.

123. In a tradition preserved by the later exegete Razi, and cited by Birkeland (1956: 29), Kalbi paraphrased this Quranic verse as "He found you an unbeliever (*kafir*) in a people of error and guided you."

124. Birkeland 1956: 29–30.

125. Birkeland 1956: 79.

126. Cf. Birkeland (1956: 85): "it is a notorious fact that the Quran contains at least one sura from a time before Muhammad had abandoned the performance of religious rites customary at Mecca."

127. The feminine form of the imperative suggests that the Kaʿba itself is addressed as "O God." On the consistent references to the Kaʿba as female, see Young (1993).

128. Azraqi 1858: 105–109. The building history of the Kaʿba is given in summary in Azraqi (1858: 307ff.) and on a number of occasions by Qutb al-Din (1857: 55ff., 146ff., 202, 207, 221ff.).

129. Rubin (1986: 99) cites reports that at the time of the Jurhum a kind of "barrier" (*jidar*)—the builders were called *jadara*—or dam was built near the Kaʿba. On the presence of similar constructions in what appear to be shrines in the Negev, see Nevo & Koren (1990: 28).

130. Wellhausen 1897: 77. Cf. Rubin (1986: 126): "In fact, some reports state that the Muslims performed the *tawaf* between Safa and Marwa during this Umra, while the pre-Islamic idols were still situated upon these hills: the pre-Islamic idols were not demolished until the conquest of Mecca in 630 C.E. (Azraqi 1858: 75, 77; Waqidi 2: 841–842)."

131. Cf. Schacht 1950: 153.

132. Bell (1937) is one not very convincing attempt at unpacking the enigma by cutting and pasting. Cf. Rubin (1982 and 1984b), who investigates the traditional interpretations.

133. Rubin 1984b: 17.

134. As Rubin (1984b: 18–20) points out, the announcement was necessarily an abrogation of earlier verses of the Quran (e.g. 2:190 and 8:61) prescribing a quite different treatment of the pagans. Sura 2:191, for example, prescribes war only against attackers. And there is also 60:8: "God does not forbid that you should be loyal and righteous toward those who did not fight you in religion and did not drive you out of your abode."

135. Bell 1937: 233–234; Rubin 1982: 258.

136. Cf. Tabari (*Annals* 1.1765): "The Prophet made three Hajjs, two before the Emigration and one after, (the latter also) with the Umra."

137. There was even some dispute on these matters. Cf. Tabari, (*Annals* 1.1765): "(A report from Ibn Umar had it that) the Messenger of God performed two Umras before performing the Hajj. When this report reached Aisha, she said, 'The Messenger of God performed four Umras. Abdullah ibn Umar knew that. One (of the Umras) was with the Hajj (of Farewell).'"

138. The standardization may have taken some time, however. As late as 716 C.E. the Caliph Sulayman seemed unsure of the details of the Hajj ritual. See Hawting (1993:36–37), citing a report of Yaʿqubi.

139. At the time of this verse the place of sacrifice was apparently still near the Kaʿba, as it had been throughout Islamic times. As we have already seen, during the Farewell Pilgrimage the Prophet limited sacrifice to the "slaughtering place" at Mina.

140. On the further implications of this "spiritualization" of sacrifice, see Graham (1983: 66–67).

141. Wellhausen 1897: 74, 93; Gaudefroy-Demombynes 1923: 192–198; Goitein 1966: 92–93; Kister 1987.

142. Cf. Rubin (1982: 244) and the literature cited there. On the likelihood that the Arabs' pilgrimage festivals of the seventh and twelfth months—the ordinal numbers are unimportant in this context—like the Israelites' Tabernacles and Passover *haggim*, were both originally equinoctial feasts, see Segal (1961: 80–82) and Ali (1954: 128).

143. Cf. Lazarus-Yafeh (1981: 44) on the not entirely successful attempts to connect various parts of the ritual with Abraham's sacrifice of Isaac/Ishmael.

CHAPTER II
MECCA AND THE WAYS THITHER

1. Cf. Wüstenfeld 1861: 131–133.
2. A Yemeni plant used as liniment and as a yellow dye. Here perhaps it was being used as a binding in a mortar.
3. Here as elsewhere the text says "pillar" or "column" when clearly it is the Black Stone that is being referred to.
4. According to the Meccan tradition, this occurred in February 685 C.E. and marked the beginning of the celebration of the Umra in the month of Rajab as the most splendid of all local Meccan holidays. Cf. Wüstenfeld (1861: 136) and Chapter III below.
5. Tabari, *Annals* 2.781–782.
6. Baladhuri (*Ansab al-Ashraf* 5.360) provides some additional details: "Ibn al-Zubayr and a group with him made their sacrifices at Marwa since they could not get out to Mina and Arafat. Al-Hajjaj had asked Ibn al-Zubayr for permission to circumambulate the House, but Ibn al-Zubayr denied him that since al-Hajjaj had denied his attendance at Arafat."
7. Another parallel suggests itself. Ibn al-Zubayr's concealment of the work of reconstruction behind a type of scaffolding so that the ritual might continue uninterrupted is reminiscent of Herod's similar strategy in his not so conservative rebuilding of the Second Temple.
8. Hurgronje 1888: 4. Cf. his striking remark apropos of the Ottoman reconstruction of the Haram in 1572–1577: "So entstand allmählich um die rohe Kaʿba, welche Muhammad noch als genügend für Allah und seine aus dem armsten Lande der Welt zusammenströmenden Gäste betrachtete, ein Tempel für den civilisierten Gott des späteren Islams" (16).
9. Cf. Grabar 1985: 4.
10. Musil 1928: 205.
11. Tabari, *Annals* 1.3138, 3143, 3144; 2.288, 290, 292, 293–294.
12. Tabari, *Annals* 3.81.
13. Tabari, *Annals* 3.484.
14. In August 781 al-Mahdi started across the steppe between Kufa and Mecca on his way to complete the Hajj. He paused at a way station called Aqaba near what is the present border between Iraq and Saudi Arabia, when "water became scarce for him and those with him, and he was afraid that what they carried would not sustain them and those with him. On top of that, he developed a fever so he returned (to Iraq) from Aqaba. He was angry with Yaqtin about the water because he was in charge of the cisterns. During their journey and on their return the people were severely afflicted by thirst until they were on the verge of perishing" (Tabari, *Annals* 2.502 = Tabari XXIX: 218).
15. Tabari, *Annals* 3.517.
16. Abbott 1946: 242.
17. Yaʿqubi, *Taʾrikh* 2.521–522; Masʿudi, *Muruj* 9.66–68; Tabari, *Annals* 3.701.
18. Masʿudi, *Muruj* 6.281; Tabari, *Annals* 3.575; cf. Abbott 1946: 242 and 101.
19. Musil (1928: 205–212, 235–236) has collected the literary evidence on the so-called Darb Zubayda, "Zubayda's Way." On Harun's own contribution, see al-Rashid 1978: 34.
20. Abbott 1946: 245; al-Rashid 1978: 35.
21. Abbott 1946: 258–260; al-Rashid 1978: 35.
22. al-Rashid 1978: 35.
23. al-Rashid 1978: 36.

24. Qutb al-Din 1857: 162–165.

25. Mas'udi, *Tanbih* 385–386, 375–376; Tabari, *Annals* 3.2269–2275.

26. Le Strange 1905: 83–84.

27. *Pahlawan* is a Persian term properly meaning "hero," "athlete," and was occasionally applied, like the Christian expression "athletes of God," to Sufis.

28. A kind of Sufi gyrovague, without a fixed convent or residence, and with a reputation for somewhat eccentric behavior.

29. This is one of the very first references to small arms in the Near East.

30. H.A.R. Gibb, Ibn Battuta's translator, notes here that "the large water-bag (*rawiya*) was made of several skins sewed together and carried on camels. The ordinary waterskin (*qirba*) is a goat-skin."

31. As the story is told, somewhat elliptically, in the Quran (11:64–71), the prophet Salih, one of their own number, preached the doctrine of Muslim monotheism to the Thamud and miraculously produced a she-camel from the rock as a divine sign authenticating his prophetic mission. The folk of al-Hijr, far from being convinced, slaughtered the camel. They were struck dead for their disbelief and their domiciles destroyed.

32. The central stations are studied in Tamari (1982).

33. Jomier 1953: 91.

34. See Chapter III below.

35. These are surveyed by Musil (1926: 321–326).

36. That is, J. L. Burckhardt.

37. The "bestowed blessing," in Arabic *baraka*, looms very large in Ibn Jubayr's visits to the Holy Cities, and he enumerates them as assiduously as a medieval Christian pilgrim to Jerusalem might tell off the indulgences attached to a visit to the holy places there.

CHAPTER III
THE MEDIEVAL HAJJ

1. And, though he does not mention it in his *Travels*, Ibn Jubayr undertook this particular Hajj to atone for his drinking of the forbidden wine at the Almohad court in Grenada. See Netton 1993a: 57–58.

2. See also Hurgronje 1888: 69–70 and Netton 1993a: 67–68.

3. Jomier 1953: 210–211. The information comes from Maqrizi, *Suluk* 1.579, 724; 2.197.

4. Jomier (1953: 211–212), citing chiefly Fasi (1857: 284–286).

5. Dhu al-Hulayfa thus constitutes a *miqat* (pl. *mawaqit*), one of the "stations" marking the frontier of the sacred territory, and so the place where one entered *ihram* (the state of ritual purity), symbolized by donning the pilgrim's garb, called in Arabic by the same term. On the *mawaqit*, see Gaudefroy-Demombynes (1923: 19–25).

6. Gaudefroy-Demombynes (1923: 168): "In Muslim teaching it is 'intention' (*niya*) that dominates every religious act and conditions its validity. . . . It is important to insist on this point, which is a universal one in Islam, since Muslim ritual has often been criticized for being mechanical, without understanding that such an 'automatism' in no sense conforms to Muslim teaching."

7. The formula is discussed at length by Gaudefroy-Demombynes (1923: 179–184).

8. The ablutions connected with the *ihram* are described by Gaudefroy-Demombynes (1923: 168–170).

9. The prescribed pilgrim garb is detailed by Gaudefroy-Demombynes (1923: 170–176).

10. On this point, see Gaudefroy-Demombynes (1923: 169).

11. See Gaudefroy-Demombynes (1923: 185–189).

12. Burton 1893: 2:284–286.
13. Farahani 1990: 204.
14. With appropriately greater blessings. See Gaudefroy-Demombynes (1923: 252) and Burckhardt (1829: 285).
15. On this pre-Islamic ritual, also called *ifada*, see Gaudefroy-Demombynes (1923: 256–257).
16. Gaudefroy-Demombynes 1954: 7–8.
17. Azraqi 1858: 180.
18. Azraqi 1858: 176, 180, 183. Cf. Tabari, *Annals* 1.1388, 3057.
19. Gaudefroy-Demombynes 1954: 11.
20. Tabari, *Annals* 3.984–988.
21. The Ka'ba as female has been treated by Young (1993).
22. On these traditions, and the entire question of Rajab, see Kister (1971a, esp. 192–194).
23. Samhudi, *Khulasat*, 166.
24. The changes are listed in résumé in Sauvaget (1947: 44–45).
25. Samhudi, *Khulasat*, 157 (roof dome), 158–162 (tomb dome).
26. Samhudi, *Khulasat*, 168. This was the fire that destroyed the original of Samhudi's manuscript history of Medina. It was in the room he occupied within the mosque. Cf. Sauvaget 1947: 46.
27. Samhudi, *Khulasat*, 169.
28. Sauvaget 1947: 48.

CHAPTER IV
UNDER NEW AUSPICES

1. Faroqhi 1988: 151.
2. For Egyptian budgets, see Shaw (1962 and 1968). The Syrian budgets have been used extensively by Bakhit (1982), Barbir (1980), and Rafeq (1966 and 1987).
3. Faroqhi 1988: 154–155.
4. Barbir (1980: app. 4) reproduces three such budgets from the Istanbul archives, those of 1733, 1749, and 1764.
5. Perhaps better known to his fellow Arabs of Damascus as As'ad al-Azm.
6. These special revenues were usually set aside for fortress and garrison maintenance.
7. Cited by Barbir (1980: 112–113).
8. Barbir 1980: 110.
9. Rafeq 1966: 70; Barbir 1980: 113.
10. Barbir 1980: 114–115.
11. Faroqhi 1988: 154.
12. Thus the same coin, the piaster, was valued at 120 aspers when it was collected but reckoned at 160 aspers when it was spent (Barbir 1980: 119–120). We cannot be sure about expenditure totals: although there was a unified income budget for the Hajj, there was no parallel single budget for expenses (Barbir 1980: 112).
13. Cohen 1973: 165–166. We have firsthand recollections of the terrors that such visits provoked in Jerusalem (Peters 1985: 544).
14. Faroqhi 1988: 155.
15. Before the Ottoman takeover, and after a long climb up the ladder of Mamluk administration, Ghazali had been governor of Hama, Safed, Karak, and Jerusalem (Bakhit 1982: 19n.91). It seems safe to assume that Ghazali's arrangements for the Hajj as Ottoman Governor of Damascus were little different in form, if not in scale, from those during the Mamluk era.

16. To avoid this threat, caravans occasionally used the obviously circuitous route from Damascus to Gaza and thence to Aqaba. On this way, see Popper (1955–1957: 1:48).

17. Bakhit 1982: 21.

18. Rafeq 1966: 53.

19. Bakhit 1982: 111–112; Rafeq 1966: 70.

20. Rafeq 1966: 54; Bakhit 1982: 108–109.

21. Rafeq 1966: 58.

22. Barbir 1980: 160–163.

23. Ilgürel (1975, 1976, 1978) provides an overview of Ottoman travel literature, including *menasik ül-Hajj* (pilgrimage guides). The account of Mehmed Edib, written in 1682, has been translated and published (Edib 1816–1817).

24. Chelebi 1897. Bilge (1979) includes extracts, some of them translations and some paraphrases, from this same volume.

25. Chelebi 1935: 679.

26. Chelebi 1935: 570–575; Rafeq 1987: 129–130 (with information drawn from Damascus court registers).

27. Burckhardt 1822: 245.

28. Rafeq 1987: 131.

29. The term *avania*, the Arabic *awaniyya*, was used to cover the multitude of arbitrary and often illegal "taxes" and corvées imposed by the Ottomans. Burckhardt's conversion of it into a verb is doubtless justified *frequentiae causa.*

30. Rafeq 1987: 133.

31. Rafeq 1987: 134.

32. Rafeq 1987: 131.

33. Bakhit 1982: 111. Precious details on the working of the system can be found in the estate settlement of Sulayman Jawish, the Amir al-Hajj for the Cairo pilgrimage of 1739 (Tuchscherer 1988).

34. The following is based on an illuminating timetable worked out in Barbir (1980: 152). For the actual time it took an Istanbul pilgrim to make the round-trip at the end of the eighteenth century, see Barbir (1980: 153, table 4).

35. In the sixteenth century, the first Ottoman-sponsored caravans left the city with great pomp, as we have seen, and they were met somewhere along the return journey by a "reception committee," actually a caravan with an officially designated commander and with food and water for the pilgrims (Bakhit 1982: 114). We have few other details, but this was doubtless the origin of what was, by the eighteenth century, a formal relief caravan, the *jurda* or *jarda* (or, in its Turkish spelling, *cerde*), whose chief function was to reprovision the returning Hajjis and protect them during the last and most vulnerable stage of their long journey (Rafeq 1966: 65–68; Barbir 1980: 170–174).

36. Rafeq 1966: 58–59.

37. The Persians often arrived too late for the departure of the Damascus caravan for the Hijaz. Because they preferred to wait in the city for the next year's departure rather than to chance the trip on their own, the Shi'ites were a familiar, if not always welcome, presence in Damascus, particularly in the Kharab quarter, where they tended to live together (Rafeq 1966: 60–61).

38. Rafeq 1966: 61.

39. Faroqhi 1988: 159. On the general question of the motivation of the Hajji, see Eickelman & Piscatori (1990: 6–8).

40. Barbir 1980: 134–135; Bakhit 1982: 98–99.

41. Barbir 1980: 139–140.

42. On the two groups, see Barbir (1980: 91, 95 [table 2], and 150 [the postings]). In the previous century the troop types were somewhat different, and two differently designated

units were assigned to each station: "castle guards," and a much smaller number of "special troops," who were mounted. Cf. Bakhit 1982: 98.

43. Barbir 1980: 146–149.

44. On the question of low wages and the practices that followed, see Barbir (1980: 148–150) and Burckhardt (1822: 657–658).

45. There is a list of them, together with their dates of construction, in Barbir (1980: app. 7). On the arrangements for provisioning the "castles" in the eighteenth century, see Barbir (1980: 141–145).

46. Edib 1816–1817.

47. M. Castiau, *En Syrie: Le Long du chemin des Pèlerins* (Paris, 1902), 21, cited by Grant (1937: 224).

48. In fact, the tribesmen along the pilgrims' way from Anatolia and Aleppo north of Damascus were not Arabs at all but Turkman tribes who had begun to settle the marginal areas of the steppe in the late seventeenth century and posed a threat to pilgrims and other wayfarers in that region (Barbir 1980: 168).

49. Barbir (1980: 175–176), in analyzing the twenty-four documented bedouin attacks upon the Hajj caravan between 1517 and 1757, with the number steeply mounting toward the end of the period, found that five occurred between Muzayrib and Mudawwara, ten between Mudawwara and Medina, and seven between Medina and Mecca. The sites of the others cannot be identified.

50. See Barbir (1980: 169) for the appointment and payment of the "Chief of the Arabs of Syria" in connection with the Hajj.

51. See, for example, the maneuvering and negotiating on the part of the Governor of Damascus, who led the heavily armed Syrian caravan in person in 1672. At one point, it was enough to have the military band play to convince the menacing bedouin that "this procession was not like other pilgrim processions." A little further on, at Anayza, the governor had to resort to alternating threats ("If you persist in parading on the mountain top with five or ten thousand warriors, do not speak to me of *surre*") and the mutual exchange of gifts: pedigreed horses, tiger skins, and bags of amber (Kortepeter 1979: 237, from Chelebi 1935: 583–584).

52. Rafeq 1966: 70–71.

53. There is a detailed account from contemporary sources in Rafeq (1966: 213ff).

54. Rafeq 1966: 218–219.

55. The local Istanbul aspects of this incident, which were complex and considerable, are traced in brief in Barbir (1980: 178).

56. The Cairo caravan's methods of dealing with the bedouin are described by Jomier 1953: 100ff., from Jazari [see n.57]).

57. Jomier (1953: 103): "Jazari [an official who worked in the Hajj Ministry in Cairo in the sixteenth century] considered such savings as dangerous and blames the cupidity of those who put in their own pockets the sums they should have distributed along the way. . . . Jazari was well aware that avarice was the principal cause of the hostility of the Bedouin."

58. That is, one representing each of the four major schools or "rites" of Sunni law.

59. Jomier 1953: 86.

60. Jomier 1953: 82–83. There may have been a second, somewhat more profane motive for the early departure. Jomier (1953: 85): "In the second place, ships coming from the south made port in the Hijaz a little before the pilgrimage of Dhu al-Hijja, and just as the governor of Jidda went in person each year to oversee the collection of duties a month or two before the official season of the *Hajj*, it may be that merchants had a stake in being on hand when the valuables were off-loaded."

61. During Mamluk times there is scattered evidence to suggest that every pilgrim

caravan had its own Mahmal, even ones originating in Aleppo or Karak; see Bakhit (1982: 107). It was only in Ottoman times that the portage of the Mahmal was restricted to the Cairo and Damascus caravans.

62. This was its ceremonial garb, so to speak, worn at departure and arrival. According to Burton (1893: 2:65n.3), to preserve the trappings from wear, only the bare frame of the Mahmal was borne on the road.

63. Jomier (1953: 21–26) reviews the various theories of its origin.

64. Jomier (1953: 27), citing Maqrizi (*Suluk* 1.544) under Safar 664 A.H. (=1266 C.E.): "The Sultan sent the Mahmal and covered with a robe of honor the Amir Jamal al-Din who was to lead it to the Hijaz."

65. Cited by Kortepeter (1979: 234–235).

66. The work, written in 1554, is the *al-Durar al farā' id al-munazzama fī akhbar al-Hajj* and has been studied in detail by Jomier (1953:94–99), from which the following résumé is largely derived.

67. Jomier 1953: 106.

68. Shaw (1962: 247–248) offers one reckoning.

69. Shaw (1962: 246): "If we consider only those sums which were paid to the Amir al-Hajj as part of the expenditures of the Imperial Treasury of Egypt, we find that these payments rose from 400,000 paras a year at the start of the 17th century to 942,920 paras in 1671–2, an increase of well over 200%, and to 10.9 million after 1760, making a total increase of 1060% from 1671 and 2600% from 1595!"

70. Tuchscherer 1988: 184.

71. Tuchscherer 1988: 184–185.

72. The appointment of a *qadi* was originally the Amir's to make; with the accession of the Ottomans, the naming of the "Qadi of the Mahmal," as he was called, was reserved to the Chief Justice in Istanbul. But that was by no means the end of the jurisdictional battle, as Jomier (1953: 110) indicates.

73. One source of profiteering was to sell off, at inflated prices, the caravan's own fodder in localities where there was a shortage (Jomier 1953: 113).

74. Jomier 1953: 96–97.

75. Arabic *kawwas*, literally a "bowman," later a "musketeer," and finally, under the Turks, with the spelling of *kavas* or *kavass*, a kind of gendarme or escort policeman.

76. The numerical data provided by Jazari is analyzed in Jomier (1953: 86ff).

77. Jomier 1953: 87.

78. Farahani 1990: 186–194.

79. Reigning Sharif, 1827–1828, 1852–1856, and 1880–1881. Cf. de Gaury 1951: 240–256.

80. Either Sharif Abdullah (1858–1877) or his brother Abdillah Pasha (1879–1880, 1881–1882), likely the latter.

81. The line of Meccan Sharifs, though actually Shiʿite in origin, had taken up Sunnism because most of their subjects were Sunnis. Cf. Hurgronje 1888: 63–64, 89–90; 1931: 183–184. The newly benevolent attitude remarked by Farahani likewise had a political intent: to cultivate support against Ottoman aims in Western Arabia. Cf. Abu-Manneh 1973: 4–5.

82. Rafeq 1966: 73–74.

83. Wood 1935: 167ff.

84. Veinstein 1981: 65.

85. Veinstein 1981: 65.

86. Veinstein 1981: 66.

87. Jomier 1953: 218–219; Raymond 1973–1974: 1:127. On the Damascus caravan, see Heyd (1923: 2:457) and Tresse (1937: 260).

88. Raymond 1973–1974: 1:129.

89. Tuchscherer 1988: 175.

90. Tuchscherer 1988: 181.
91. Veinstein 1981: 66.
92. Cited by Jomier 1953: 219.
93. Hogarth 1904: 80.
94. For his own reasons, Ali Bey favors the comparison of the Hajj with the Christians' Easter: later he calls the sacrifice at Mina "the Paschal sacrifice."

CHAPTER V
THROUGH EUROPEAN EYES

1. Bukhari, *The Sound, jihad* b179; Muslim, *The Sound, jihad* 55.
2. Shafi'i, *Umm* 4.100.
3. Heffening 1925: 48–49.
4. By 1910–1911, when the Persian Kazemzadeh visited the city, the following nations had consular representation in Jidda: England, Austria-Hungary, Belgium, France, Holland, Italy, Persia, and Russia (Kazemzadeh 1912: 171).
5. Burckhardt's biographer weighed the evidence and was unable to come to a conclusion (Sim 1969: 15–16).
6. Roches 1904: 191.
7. A combination passport and identity card issued in Egypt.
8. An acquaintance of Burton's in Cairo.
9. Tidrick 1981: 61.
10. Bidwell 1985: 100.
11. This is exactly opposite to the earlier usage whereby the Portuguese called the Muslim Turks *Rumis*, which in turn contradicted an even earlier usage whereby the Muslims called the Greek Christians, the former subjects of the Roman Empire, *Rumis*.
12. "Shibriyya": a kind of single, cloth-covered cot on a camel's back. "Shugduf": described by Burton (1893: 1:418) as "two solid wooden cots about four feet in length, slung along the camel's sides and covered over with cloth, in the shape of a tent." "Takht-rawan": full litters borne between two camels.
13. The column travels, according to Doughty's estimate (1888: 54) at roughly 2½ miles an hour.
14. Peters 1987: 146–169. Cf. Ochsenwald (1984: 51): "(In the nineteenth century) the title of 'Servant of the Haram' was sometimes awarded by the Amir of Mecca or by the shaykh of the Medina Haram for cash payment; the title of 'Servant of the Two Harams' was proudly borne by the sultan himself."
15. Cf. Ochsenwald (1984: 51): "Perhaps three hundred people were permanently paid by the Meccan Haram, exclusive of 50–100 teachers and 200 guides. If one added unpaid volunteers, the number of employees would, at the minimum, have been doubled. Between 400 and 600 regular staff were paid at Medina, with as many more volunteers who received only small sums as their turns came in rotation. More than 2,000 people worked at the two Harams."
16. The employment of slaves or eunuches in this mosque is of very ancient date. According to the Meccan historian al-Fasi, it was Mu'awiya ibn Abi Sufyan (Caliph, 661–680 C.E.) who first ordered slaves for service at the Ka'ba.
17. Cf. Ochsenwald (1984: 51): "The 120 eunuches in Medina in 1853 were under the command of a former slave of Sultan Mahmud II's sister. There were about 50 eunuches in the Meccan Haram throughout the nineteenth century."
18. Ochsenwald (1984: 54): "The Shaybi family held their post of keykeeper of the Ka'ba by hereditary right. . . . During the nineteenth century the Ottoman government selected the new keykeeper from among the family, although rival factions of the Shaybi

clan claimed succession, particularly in the 1870's and 1880's. . . . When the cloth covering the Ka'ba was replaced, pieces of the old were sold by the Shaybis to shops in Mecca for resale to pilgrims. The keykeeper was also given substantial presents by those admitted to the interior of the Ka'ba."

19. George Sale, the pioneer translator of the Quran into English (1734).

20. The same chamber shortly called *al-Hijrah* by Burckhardt and transcribed by Burton as *al-Hujrah*. Cf. note 23 below.

21. That is, Nasir al-Din al-Samhudi (d. 1506), the principal historian of the city whose work Burckhardt used for background.

22. This must be a slip for Hebron, where there is a great catafalque for Abraham. Ishmael was thought to be buried at Mecca, but no grave of Abraham was shown there.

23. Here Roches is certainly mistaken or misinformed. The "h" of the tomb "chamber" (*hujra*) is in Arabic an entirely different letter from the "h" of "emigration" (*hijra*).

24. That is, the eunuchs assigned here to the guardianship of the Prophet's Mosque, just as they were to the Haram in Mecca.

CHAPTER VI
STEAMSHIPS AND CHOLERA

1. Arif al-Munir 1971: 82.

2. Arif al-Munir 1971: 82–88.

3. Jacob Landau (in Arif al-Munir 1971: 28): "The merit of Arif's book is not only in being a more detailed, almost complete account of the Syrian pilgrimage route and the Bedouin tribes adjoining it. It seems to be one of the very few complete accounts of the Syrian pilgrimage itself written in modern times. In addition, it is also apparently the very last Muslim account of this pilgrimage, still using camels and donkeys for transportation and ceremoniously adhering to the accustomed pomp. . . . In other words, Arif actually wrote the epitaph of a period."

4. It is described by Doughty (1888: 2:508).

5. When the British government of India made strenuous objection, the Sultan agreed to exempt Indian Muslims from the requirement. When the British later requested that the exemption be extended to their subjects in the Straits Settlements, the Sultan refused on the grounds that he would then have to make the same concession to all of the Netherlands East Indies (Roff 1982: 150 and n.50).

6. See the breakdown of provincial expenses in the 1860s in Ochsenwald (1984: 173, table 8).

7. Ochsenwald (1984: 193–194): "The Amir [the Sharif] concluded an arrangement with the nomads whereby they received a cash payment for their runaway slaves, blood money for their losses in recent fighting and raids, and a promise that in the future refugee slaves would not be harbored in Jidda. Booty seized in caravan raids did not have to be returned. This extraordinary concession was opposed by the Vali, but he was dismissed and replaced."

8. Ochsenwald 1984: 174.

9. Beginning in 1349, by order of the Sultan Isma'il Salih, the expenses of manufacturing the *kiswa* were underwritten by a *waqf* consisting of the income of a town in Egypt. As often happened, the funds were eventually alienated. With the accession of the Ottomans, Sulayman had to reconstitute the *waqf* through the purchase of three villages. Finally, Muhammad Ali transferred the *kiswa* expenses to the state treasury (Gaudefroy-Demombynes 1954: 17).

10. Tresse 1937: 295; Landau in Arif al-Munir 1971: 49–50.

11. Literally, "an estimator," "appraiser."

12. For an estimate, see Ochsenwald (1984: 62). Cf. p. 13: "Rates were usually fixed by the Sharifs, with the result that they benefited mightily at the expense of the pilgrims. In 1887 the pilgrim going from Mecca to Medina by camel was assessed seven hundred kurush. Twenty-eight kurush were paid as tax to the Ottoman government, and the same to the head of the caravan and to the persons acting as hostages with the Bedouin tribes. Fourteen kurush were paid to the pilgrim broker and the rest to the owner of the camel. By contrast, the Mecca-Jidda-Yanbu-Medina trip by camel and steamer cost only about 300 kurush."

13. Ochsenwald 1984: 62–63.

14. Ochsenwald 1984: 192.

15. Sa'diyya is the place where pilgrims from Ta'if and the entire Yemen put on the *ihram.*

16. Kazemzadeh notes in this connection that, "despite the religious prohibition against making the pilgrimage without the means necessary to make it without (undue) privation, hundreds of poor pilgrims and dervishes accompany the caravan on foot, and many of them fall ill or die of fatigue or privation. The government of Persia, which grants full liberty in religious matters, has not wished to suppress these abuses which are contrary to religion itself" (Kazemzadeh 1912: 148n.1).

17. The guide was assigned in the pilgrim's home town when he signed his contract with the caravan leader, who was serving, in effect, as an agent for the Meccan guides.

18. Thieves who specialized in the Hajj routes.

19. Roff 1982: 151–152.

20. This latter, known as Baha'ullah, was the real founder of Bahaism, a sectarian movement initiated in 1844 by one Mirza Ali of Shiraz, who declared that he was the "Bab," or "Gate," to the Shi'ites' Hidden Imam and who later produced his own book of revelation. He was executed in 1850. Mirza Hosayn Ali lived in Acre until his death in 1892.

21. Cf. Doughty 1888: 2:64ff.

22. The Rafidi, or "Recusant," Shi'ites were those who denied the legitimacy of the three venerable Caliphs who preceded Ali at the head of the Muslim community: Abu Bakr, Umar, and Uthman.

23. Cited by Tresse 1937: 58n.2.

24. Cited by Tresse 1937: 59n.1.

25. Cf. Ochsenwald 1984: 192–193.

26. Cf. Burton 1893: 1:257–258, 265–266, 272–274.

27. Findley 1989: 509n.45.

28. Duguet (1932: 34–37), using statistics collected at the quarantine stations in the last quarter of the nineteenth century. Cf. Ochsenwald 1984: 62.

29. Ochsenwald (1984: 65): "When cholera appeared for the first time, it caused deaths not only among the poor but also among the rich and powerful. The Ottoman-Egyptian governors of Jidda and Medina and the leader of the Egyptian pilgrimage were killed by the disease. In 1832 the villagers and bedouin were severely affected. More than 10,000 people died in the Hijaz. . . . Starting in 1844 the Ottomans had sent a physician and a pharmacist to Medina at government expense, and there were some inoculators at work among the bedouin and in Mecca and Medina. . . . The Ottomans applied the quarantine rules devised by the 1851 Sanitary Conference of Paris. Casualties from cholera remained high—an estimated 10,000 died from it in Mecca alone in 1845–1846. The repetitions of cholera outbreaks in the 1850's caused the Amir [Sharif] to convoke a gathering of 32 religious leaders and notables to survey the religious practices and moral state of the population. He felt that religious purity could help end the visitations of cholera, and many pilgrims believed that charity and pure living lessened the chance of the disease."

30. Duguet 1932: 121.

31. Duguet 1932: 126–128; Long 1979: 183.

32. Long (1979: 185): "The British opposed this as interfering with the free exercise of religion and pointed to the Native Passenger Act of 1887 which (already) regulated the numbers, etc. of pilgrims per vessel. It was . . . hinted at later conferences that profits of shipping companies lay behind the British religious scruples."

33. This was the earliest of the international bodies—despite its name it was run by European consular officers in Egypt—concerned with health problems of the Hajj. Cf. Long 1979: 184.

34. Long 1979: 133. The regulations were further refined in 1884. In 1881 the Ottomans opened a quarantine station for eastern arrivals on Qamaran Island in the Bab al-Mandab (Long 1979: 171), and in 1892 an international conference recommended abandoning the Wajh quarantine and making Tur the chief station thereafter (ibid., 151).

35. Cited by Roff 1982: 146. Cf. Duguet 1932: 173.

36. Duguet 1932: 156–158.

37. Cited by Duguet 1932: 297–299.

38. Duguet 1932: 171–173.

39. Long 1979: 186–187.

40. Sultan Mahmud II instituted this agency in 1838 as a direct result of the incursions of cholera in his empire. Originally it had seven Ottoman members, of whom five were physicians, assisted by five foreign members who represented the maritime interests of the chief European powers (Germany, England, France, Italy, and Russia). Its membership fluctuated over the nineteenth century, "for reasons more often political than sanitary" (Duguet 1932: 194n.3), but as far as the public health of the Hijaz was concerned, it was the responsible body in the Ottoman Empire. Its operations ended in the First World War, and it was formally abolished by the Treaty of Lusanne in 1923. Cf. Long 1979: 184.

41. The murdered vice-consul was Dr. Abdur Razzack, earlier assigned by the British authorities to oversee the health of the Indian pilgrims, and to collect intelligence, in Mecca.

42. Cited by Duguet 1932: 183–184.

43. Cited by Duguet 1932: 215n.1.

44. Cited by Duguet 1932: 209–211.

45. Cited by Duguet 1932: 159–160.

46. Cited by Duguet 1932: 235n.1. Later, under Saudi sovereignty, as Philby assured his readers in 1931, sanitary conditions left little to be desired: "I missed the actual ceremony of the sacrificing this morning, and my personal sacrifice was offered by proxy the following day; but I may add that during those these three days at Mina I neither saw nor by other less agreeable processes became aware of the great slaughter on which others have written with so much critical emotion—nor even saw the slaughter-place now wisely removed to a reasonable distance from the main camps of the pilgrims and divided therefrom by the picturesque encampments of the human scavengers of the holy land—the Takruri colony of African residents and visitors to whom nothing comes amiss that is edible. I certainly saw a few severed sheep heads lying about where perhaps they should not have been, but otherwise there was neither stench nor offensive sight of sun-grilled putrefactions. The medical authorities have unquestionably done this part of their work exceedingly well, and their reward this year was the smallest death-rate on record for the pilgrimage up to date" (Philby 1946: 44).

47. And so, in fact, overland travel was preferable. Cf. Tresse (1937: 59): "When the international sanitary congresses subjected the pilgrims to more and more scrupulously observed quarantines and to inevitable prophylactic measures on their return from Mecca, *there occurred a renaissance in the land route. The pilgrims used the sea route to go out when it could be used without restraint. They returned by the land route when the pilgrimage was declared tainted and subjected to a maritime sanitary surveillance. The desert was the great*

cleanser, and on the first fifteen stages of the way home there died all those whom the disease had struck" (emphasis added). Later conventions did pay some minimal attention to the caravan traffic. Thus, Article 148 of the 1926 Convention provided that, "whatever the sanitary condition of the Hijaz may be, pilgrims traveling by caravan must repair to one of the quarantine stations upon their route, there to undergo according to circumstances the measures . . . for (sea-going) pilgrims who have landed" (cited by Long 1979: 187).

48. Cf. Hurgronje (1888: 218): "The entire quarantine arrangement has no real purpose except exploitation. . . . The health authorities in Constantinople have managed to convince the highest medical authorities in Europe, who are ignorant of the real conditions in the East, and who are still ignorant despite quick visits, of the working of their [the Ottomans'] system of extorting money."

49. Rihani is being somewhat coy; the best quarantine was, of course, that of his host, King Husayn, at Jidda, See Chapter VII.

50. Baldry 1978: 89.

51. Baldry 1978: 95–98.

52. Baldry 1978: 100–101. The station continued in operation until 1951.

53. Roff 1982: 153.

54. As a later report of the Saudi Ministry of Health expressed it: "Certain provisions of the 1926 Paris International Sanitary Agreement concerning the Mecca pilgrimage have always been acting as a source of irritation of the Saudi Arabian Government, who never ceased to submit their protests on many occasions to the proper authorities, requesting the deletion of those articles . . . and . . . the amendment of certain (other articles) as being incompatible with (the establishment of sanitation procedures)" (cited by Long 1979: 189).

55. Long 1979: 191.

CHAPTER VII
THE GREAT WAR AND AFTER

1. See Ochsenwald (1980: 29–30) and, on Meissner, Pönicke (1956).

2. According to Ochswenwald (1980: 32), about forty engineers were employed between 1903 and 1907; on the average, one-half were foreigners, and most of these were Germans.

3. Cf. Ochsenwald 1980: 34–36.

4. Ochsenwald 1980: 124–125.

5. Ochsenwald 1980: 122.

6. Jacob Landau in Arif al-Munir 1971: 17.

7. Jacob Landau in Arif al-Munir 1971: 16.

8. Ochsenwald 1976: 2.

9. The railway never resumed operations after the war, not because it was impossible but because Husayn's impoverished kingdom lacked the resources and the will to make the necessary repairs. In 1921 an Indian health officer who visited Medina and had an opportunity to observe the terminal there wrote what amounted to its epitaph: "The railway station at Medina is an incomplete stone building, and it appears that something grand was anticipated to be erected. It seems to be empty now as I did not see anyone there and the building is also in a neglected condition. I saw four quite big engines, three on the rails and one off the rails. It appears they are not looked after by anyone, because they are very dirty and showed signs that they had not been used for some time. They look like very powerful machines. I also saw some passenger cars and goods waggons, but they too were in a very neglected condition" (Foreign Office Papers E656/656/91, in Bidwell 1985: 3:94).

10. Fromkin 1989: 33.

11. Cf. Philby (1953: 43), who notes that in Clause V of the treaty Ibn Sa'ud undertook to keep open the pilgrim road to the Hijaz and to protect pilgrims using it.

12. Bidwell 1985: 1:13–14.

13. Bidwell 1985: 3:126.

14. Bidwell 1985: 3:127.

15. Bidwell 1985: 3:137

16. Bidwell 1985: 3:134.

17. Bidwell 1985: 3:140–141.

18. Bidwell 1985: 3:148, 154.

19. Lord Curzon's representation to the Turkish delegate at Lausanne on behalf of the Government of the Hijaz, "which has no seat at this conference," is reproduced by Bidwell (1985: 3:306).

20. Bidwell 1985: 4:46–47.

21. Bidwell 1985: 4:47–48.

22. Husayn was determined to maintain the camel monopoly in the face of other modes of transportation, and Baker (1979: 174) cites from Foreign Office Papers 686–27 the report that the king, on discovering an Indian in a motor car at Arafat personally took a crowbar to the vehicle, citing his own *hadith*, "As the Prophet had found the country, so it should remain for every good Muslim."

23. The roofing was reported in the *Qibla* of 28 May 1923, and it was generally suspected that the project was paid for in its entirety by the ex-Ottoman Sultan Wahid al-Din, who was visiting the Hijaz at the time (Bidwell 1985: 3:300). The electrification was announced by the same source in the issue of 25 June of the same year (Bidwell 1985: 3:302).

24. Bidwell 1985: 1:36–38.

25. Bidwell 1985: 3:85, 249.

26. Bidwell 1985: 3:260–262.

27. Bidwell 1985: 3:81.

28. Baker 1979: 175.

29. Rihani called on the British consul in Jidda on 3 March 1922. The latter, who thought him "a man of some culture," reported that "the alleged purpose of his tour is the collection of material for a book about Arabia with which he hopes to interest literary America" (Bidwell 1985: 3:111).

30. Bidwell 1985: 3:86.

31. Bidwell 1985: 3:250.

32. Bidwell 1985: 4:49.

33. This would be the same Thabit Pasha characterized in one report to the Foreign Office as "a Turk of the ignorant, obstructionist type, blatantly corrupt, openly xenophobe, and completely callous to human suffering" (Foreign Office Papers 689/29, cited by Baker 1979: 175).

34. Bidwell 1985: 4:53–54.

35. Bidwell 1985: 4:59.

36. Bullard appears somewhat confused here. The Mahmal *did* carry a carpet, the new covering for the Prophet's tomb in Medina, and not the *kiswa*.

37. Cf. Bullard's consular report of 29 July 1923: "The Hashimite Government announced in the *Qibla* that they had arranged to get a *kiswa* made in time. What they have really done is to bring from Medina a *kiswa* which the Turkish Government sent Sharif Haydar when he was appointed Amir of Mecca on Sharif Husayn's revolt. It reached Mecca via Yanbu, not indeed before the pilgrimage, but just in time for the Friday prayers in the pilgrimage week. This *kiswa* is said to have the cipher of the Sultan of Turkey woven on it, but as it will be illegible to most of the pilgrims, who will, moreover, be

ignorant of the hurried despatch of the *kiswa* from Medina, the king is expected to get some credit for having a substitute for the Egyptian *kiswa* made so quickly" (Bidwell 1985: 3:307).

38. Bidwell 1985: 4:61.
39. Bidwell 1985: 3:251–252.
40. Foreign Office Papers E4126/10/91 (in Bidwell 1985: 4:346–347).
41. Bidwell 1985: 4:349.
42. It was Khayzuran, al-Hadi's wife and al-Mahdi's mother, who converted what was in the eighth century still a private house into a mosque.
43. The *Umm al-Qura*, or "Mother of Towns," a title given to Mecca in the Quran, was the name of the newspaper established in Mecca by the Saudis to replace Husayn's house organ, the *Qibla*, from which it differed, according to Reader Bullard, "in that, not being written or corrected by King Husayn, it is intelligible" (Bidwell 1985: 4:235).
44. Bidwell 1985: 4:354–356.
45. Philby 1948: 76.

Works Cited

Except where specifically noted, ancient and medieval texts are cited according to their standard editions.

Abbott 1946: Nabia Abbott, *Two Queens of Baghdad: Mother and Wife of Harun al-Rashid*. Chicago: University of Chicago Press, 1946.

Abu-Manneh 1973: Butrus Abu Manneh, "Sultan Abdulhamid II and the Sharifs of Mecca (1880–1900)." *Asian and African Studies* 9 (1973), 1–21.

Ali 1954: Hashim Amir Ali, "The First Decade in Islam: A Fresh Approach to the Calendrical Study of Early Islam." *Muslim World* 44 (1954), 126–138.

Ali Bey 1816: Domingo (Ali Bey) Badia y Leyblich, *Travels of Ali Bey in Morocco, Tripoli, Cyprus, Egypt, Arabia, Syria and Turkey between the years 1803 and 1807.* 2 vols. London, 1816; rpt. London: Gregg, 1970.

Al-Rashid 1978: S. al-Rashid, "Darb Zubaydah in the Abbasid Period: Historical and Archeological Aspects." *Proceedings of the Seminar for Arabian Studies* 8 (1978), 33–45.

Anon. Hakluyt 1927: Anon., "A description of the yearely voyage or pilgrimage of the Mahumetans, Turkes and Moores to Mecca in Arabia." In Richard Hakluyt, *The Principal Navigations, Voyages, Traffiques and Discoveries of the English Nation Made by Sea or Overland to the Remote and Farthest Distant Quarters of the Earth at Any Time within the Compass of these 1600 Years,* vol. 3, pp. 167–197. London and Toronto: J. M. Dent and Sons Limited, 1927.

Ansary 1979: A. R. al-Ansary (ed.), *Sources for the History of Arabia.* Vol. I/2. Riyadh: University of Riyadh Press, 1979.

Arif al-Munir 1971: Muhammad Arif ibn al-Sayyid Ahmad al-Munir, *The Book of the Increasing and Eternal Happiness—The Hejaz Railway.* Introduction, text, and translation by Jacob M. Landau under the title *The Hejaz Railway and the Muslim Pilgrimage.* Detroit: Wayne State University, 1971.

Azraqi 1858: Abu al-Walid Muhammad al-Azraqi, *Akhbar Makka,* Edited by Ferdinand Wüstenfeld. Vol. 1 of *Die Chroniken der Stadt Mekka,* Leipzig 1858; rpt. Hildesheim: Georg Olms, 1981.

Baker 1979: Randall Baker, *King Husain and the Kingdom of the Hejaz.* New York: Oleander Press, 1979.

Bakhit 1982: Muhammad Adnan Bakhit, *The Ottoman Province of Damascus in the Sixteenth Century.* Beirut: Librairie du Liban, 1982.

Baldry 1978: John Baldry, "Foreign Interventions and Occupations of Kamaran Island." *Arabian Studies* 4 (1978), 89–111.

Barbir 1980: Karl Barbir, *Ottoman Rule in Damascus.* Princeton: Princeton University Press, 1980.

Batanuni 1911: Muhammad Labib al-Batanuni, *Al-Rihlat al-hijaziyya.* Cairo 1911.

Beck 1952: E. Beck, "Die Gestalt des Abraham am Wendepunkte der Entwicklung Muhammeds." *Le Muséon* 65 (1952), 73–84. Cited from its reprint in Rudi Paret (ed.), *Der Koran.* Darmstadt: Wissenschaftliche Buchgesellschaft, 1975.

Bell 1937: Richard Bell, "Muhammad's Pilgrimage Proclamation." *Journal of the Royal Central Asian Society* 24 (1937), 223–244.

Bidwell 1976: Robin Bidwell, *Travellers in Arabia*. London: Hamlyn, 1976.

Bidwell 1985: *British Documents on Foreign Affairs: Reports and Papers from the Foreign Office Confidential Print*. Part 2: *From the First to the Second World War*. Series B: *Turkey, Iran and the Middle East, 1918–1939*. Edited by Robin Bidwell. Frederick, Md.: University Publications of America, 1985.

Bilge 1979: M. Bilge, "Arabia in the Work of Awliya Chelebi." In Ansary 1979: 213–227.

Birkeland 1956: Harris Birkeland, *The Lord Guideth: Studies on Primitive Islam*. Oslo: H. Aschehaug, 1956.

Blunt 1881: Lady Anne Blunt, *A Pilgrimage to Nejd, the Cradle of the Arab Race*. London, 1881; rpt. London: Century Publishing Company, 1985.

Brémond 1931: Géneral Edouard Brémond, *Le Héjaz dans la Guerre Mondiale*. Paris: Payot, 1931.

Bullard 1961: Reader Bullard, *The Camels Must Go: An Autobiography*. London: Faber and Faber, 1961.

Burckhardt 1819: John Lewis Burckhardt, *Travels in Nubia*. London: John Murray, 1819.

Burckhardt 1822: John Lewis Burckhardt, *Travels in Syria and the Holy Land*. London, 1822; rpt. New York: AMS Press, 1983.

Burckhardt 1829: John Lewis Burckhardt, *Travels in Arabia*. London, 1829; rpt. New York: Frank Cass, 1968.

Burton 1893: Richard F. Burton, *A Personal Narrative of a Pilgrimage to al-Madina & Meccah* (1855). Reprint of third, memorial edition of 1893. New York: Dover, 1964.

Caetani 1905: Leone Caetani, *Annali dell'Islam*. Vol. 1. Milan: Ulrico Hoepli, 1905.

Chelebi 1897: Evliya Chelebi, *Seyahatname*. Vol. 9: *Anadolu, Suriye, Hicaz*. Istanbul, 1897.

Chelebi 1935: Mehmed Zilli ibn Dervish (ed.), *Evliya Chelebi Seyahatnamesi*. Vol. 9: *Anadolu, Suriye, Hijaz (1671–1672)*. Istanbul, 1935.

Cohen 1973: Ammon Cohen, *Palestine in the Eighteenth Century: Patterns of Government and Administration*. Jerusalem: Magnes Press, 1973.

Corancez 1810: Louis Alexandre Olivier da Corancez, *Histoire des Wahabis*. Paris, 1810.

Crone 1987: Patricia Crone, *Meccan Trade and the Rise of Islam*. Princeton: Princeton University Press, 1987.

Dagorn 1981: René Dagorn, *La Geste d'Ismael d'après l'onomastique et la tradition arabe*. Paris: Champion, 1981.

de Gaury 1951: Gerald de Gaury, *Rulers of Mecca*. New York: Harrup, 1951.

Didier 1985: Charles Didier, *Sojourn with the Grand Sharif of Makkah*. Translated by Richard Boulind, with an introductory note by Philip Ward. Cambridge and New York: Oleander Press, 1985.

Dinet & Sliman ben Ibrahim 1930: E. Dinet (El Hadj Nacir ed-Dine) and El Hadj Sliman ben Ibrahim Baâmer, *Le Pèlerinage à la Maison Sacrée d'Allah*. Paris: Librairie Hachette, 1930.

Doughty 1888: Charles Doughty, *Travels in Arabia Deserta*. Cambridge: Clarendon Press, 1888. Second American ed. in one volume. New York: Random House, [1926].

Duguet 1932: Firmin Duguet, *Le pèlerinage de la Mecque au point de vue religieuse, social et sanitaire*. Paris: Rieder, 1932.

Dussaud 1955: René Dussaud, *La pénétration des Arabes en Syrie avant l'Islam*. Paris: Paul Geuthner, 1955.

Edib 1816–1817: Mehmed Edib ibn Mehmed Dervish, *Menasik-i hacc-i sherif*, Istanbul, 1816–1817. Translated in M. Bianchi, *Itinéraire de Constantinople à la Mecque*. Paris, n.d.

Eickelman & Piscatori 1990: Dale F. Eickelman and James Piscatori (eds.), *Muslim Travellers: Pilgrimage, Migration, and the Religious Imagination*. Berkeley: University of California Press, 1990.

El Moudden 1990: Abdurrahmane El Moudden, "The Ambivalence of *Rihla*: Community Integration and Self-Definition in Moroccan Travel Accounts, 1300–1800." In Eickelman & Piscatori 1990: 68–84.

Fahd 1966: Toufic Fahd, *La divination arabe*. Leiden: E. J. Brill, 1966.

Fahd 1968: Toufic Fahd, *Le panthéon d'Arabie centrale à la veille de l'hégire*. Paris: Paul Geuthner, 1968.

Farahani 1990: *A Shiite Pilgrimage: The Journey of an Iranian Notable to the Holy Cities of Arabia through Iran, Russia, the Ottoman Empire and Egypt*. Edited, translated, and annotated from the original nineteenth-century Persian manuscript of the *Safarnameh* of Mirza Mohammad Hosayn Farahani. Austin: University of Texas Press, 1990.

Faroqhi 1988: Suraiya Faroqhi, "Ottoman Documents Concerning the Hajj during the Sixteenth and Seventeenth Centuries." In Abdeljelil Temini (ed.), *La vie sociale dans les provinces arabes à l'époque ottomane*, 3:151–163. Zaghouan (Tunisia): Centre d'Etudes et de Recherches, 1988.

Fasi 1857: Muhammad ibn Ahmad al-Fasi, *Shafaʾ al-gharam bi akhbar al-balad al-haram*. Edited by Ferdinand Wüstenfeld. In vol. 2 of *Die Chroniken der Stadt Mekka*. Leipzig, 1857; rpt. Hildesheim: Georg Olms, 1981.

Finati 1830: *Narrative of the Life and Adventures of Giovanni Finati, Native of Ferrara*. Translated and edited by William John Bankes. 2 vols. London: John Murray, 1830.

Findley 1989: Carter Vaughn Findley, "A Muslim's Pilgrim's Progress: Asci Dede Ibrahim Halil on the Hajj 1898." In C. E. Bosworth et al. (eds.), *The Islamic World from Classical to Modern Times: Essays in Honor of Bernard Lewis*, 479–512. Princeton: Darwin Press, 1989.

Firestone 1990: Reuven Firestone, *Journeys into Holy Lands: The Evolution of the Abraham-Ishmael Legends in Islamic Exegesis*. Albany: State University of New York Press, 1990.

Freeth & Winstone 1978: Zahra Freeth and H.V.F. Winstone, *Explorers of Arabia from the Renaissance to the End of the Victorian Era*. London: George Allen and Unwin, 1978.

Fromkin 1989: David Fromkin, *A Peace to End All Peace: Creating the Modern Middle East*. New York: Henry Holt, 1989.

Fück 1936: "The Originality of the Arabian Prophet" (1936). Translated in Merlin L. Swartz (ed.), *Studies on Islam*, 86–98. New York: Oxford University Press, 1981.

Gaudefroy-Demombynes 1923: Maurice Gaudefroy-Demombynes, *Le pèlerinage à la Mekke*. Paris: Paul Geuthner, 1923.

Gaudefroy-Demombynes 1954: M. Gaudefroy-Demombynes, "Le voile de la Kaʿba." *Studia Islamica* 2 (1954), 5–21.

Gellens 1990: Sam I. Gellens, "The Search for Knowledge in Medieval Muslim Societies: A Comparative Approach." In Eickelman & Piscatori 1990: 50–68.

Gil 1987: Moshe Gil, "The Medinan Opposition to the Prophet." *Jerusalem Studies in Arabic and Islam* 10 (1987), 65–96.

Ginzberg 1909: L. Ginzberg, *The Legends of the Jews*. Vol. 1. Philadelphia: Jewish Publication Society, 1909.

Goitein 1966: S. D. Goitein, *Studies in Islamic History and Institutions*. Leiden: E. J. Brill, 1966.

Goldziher 1889: Ignaz Goldziher, *Muslim Studies*. Edited by S. M. Stern and translated by C. R. Barber and S. M. Stern from *Muhammadanische Studien*, vol. 1 (1889). London: George Allen & Unwin, 1967.

Grabar 1985: Oleg Grabar, "Upon Reading al-Azraqi." *al-Muqarnas* 3 (1985), 1–7.

Graham 1983: William A. Graham, "Islam in the Mirror of Ritual." In Richard G. Hovannisian and Speros Vryonis (eds.), *Islam's Understanding of Itself*, 53–73. Malibu: Undena Publications, 1983.

Grant 1937: C. P. Grant, *The Syrian Desert*. Edinburgh: A. and C. Black, 1937.

Hawkins & King 1982: G. S. Hawkins and D. A. King, "On the Orientation of the Kaʿba." *Journal for the History of Astronomy* 13 (1982), 102–109.

Hawting 1982: G. R. Hawting, "The Origins of the Islamic Sanctuary at Mecca." In G.H.A. Juynboll, ed., *Studies on the First Century of Islam*, 25–47. Carbondale: University of Southern Illinois Press, 1982.

Hawting 1984: G. R. Hawting, "'We were not ordered with entering it but only with circumambulating it': Hadith and Fiqh on Entering the Kaʿba." *Bulletin of the School of Oriental and African Studies* 47 (1984), 228–242.

Hawting 1990: G. R. Hawting, "The 'Sacred Offices' of Mecca from Jahiliyya to Islam." *Jerusalem Studies in Arabic and Islam* 13 (1990), 62–84.

Hawting 1993: G. R. Hawting, "The *Hajj* in the Second Civil War." In Netton 1993: 31–42.

Heffening 1925: W. Heffening, *Das islamische Fremdenrecht bis zu den islamisch-fränkischen Staatsverträgen*. Hannover 1925; rpt. Osnabruck: Biblio Verlag, 1975.

Henninger 1959: J. Henninger, "Pre-Islamic Bedouin Religion" (1959). Translated in Merlin L. Swartz (ed.), *Studies on Islam*, 3–22. New York: Oxford University Press, 1981.

Heyd 1923: W. Heyd, *Histoire du commerce du Levant au Moyen-Age*. 2 vols. Translated by F. Raynaud. Augmented edition. Leipzig, 1923; rpt. Amsterdam, 1967.

Hogarth 1904: David George Hogarth, *The Penetration of Arabia: A Record of the Development of Western Knowledge Concerning the Arabian Peninsula*. New York: Frederick Stokes, 1904.

Hogarth 1917: David George Hogarth, *Handbook of Hejaz*. Reprint of *Hejaz before World War I: A Handbook* (2d ed., 1917). Cambridge and New York: Falcon-Oleander, 1978.

Hurgronje 1888: C. Snouck Hurgronje, *Mekka*. Vol. 1: *Die Stadt und ihre Herren*. The Hague: Martinus Nijhoff, 1888.

Hurgronje 1931: C. Snouck Hurgronje, *Mekka in the Nineteenth Century*. Translation by J. H. Monahan of C. Snouck Hurgronje, *Mekka*, vol. 2: *Aus dem heutigen Leben* (1889). Leiden: E. J. Brill, 1931. Photomechanical reprint, 1970.

Ibn al-Kalbi 1952: *The Book of Idols*. Translated with introduction and notes by Nabih Amin Faris. Princeton: Princeton University Press, 1952.

Ibn Battuta 1958: *The Travels of Ibn Battuta, A.D. 1325–1354*. Translated with revisions and notes by H.A.R. Gibb. Vol. 1. Cambridge: Cambridge University Press, 1958.

Ibn Hawkal 1964: Ibn Hawkal, *Configuration de la terre (Kitab Surat al-Ard)*. Translated with an introduction by J. H. Kramers and G. Wiet. 2 vols. Beirut and Paris: Committée internationale pour la traduction des chefs-d'oeuvre, 1964.

Ibn Ishaq 1955: *The Life of Muhammad*. A translation of Ishaq's *Sirat Rasul Allah*, with introduction and notes by Alfred Guillaume. Oxford: Oxford University Press, 1955.

Ibn Iyas 1955–1960: *Journal d'un bourgeois du Caire. Chronique d'Ibn Iyas*. 2 vols. Translated and annotated by Gaston Wiet. Paris: S.E.V.P.E.N., 1955–1960.

Ibn Jubayr 1949–1951: *Ibn Jobair. Voyages*. Translated and annotated by Maurice Gaudefroy-Demombynes. 2 vols. Paris: Paul Guethner, 1949–1951.

Ilgürel 1975: Sevim Ilgürel, "Menasik-i mesalik." *Tarih Enstitusu Dergisi* 6 (1975), 111–128.

Ilgürel 1976: Sevim Ilgürel, "Menasik-i mesalik." *Tarih Dergisi* 30 (1976), 55–72.

Ilgürel 1978: Sevim Ilgürel, "Menasik-i mesalik." *Tarih Dergisi* 31 (1978), 147–162.

Jomier 1953: Jacques Jomier, *Le Mahmal et la caravane egyptienne des pelerins de la Mekke*. Cairo: Institute français d'archéologie orientale, 1953.

Kazemzadeh 1912: Hossein Kazem Zadeh, *Rélation d'un pèlerinage à la Mecque en 1910–1911*. Paris: Leroux, 1912 [= *Revue du Monde Musulman* (1912), 144–227].

Keane 1881: John F. Keane, *Six Months in Meccah: An Account of the Muhammedan Pilgrimage to Meccah*. London: Tinsley Brothers, 1881.

Kister 1965: M. J. Kister, "Mecca and Tamim." *Journal of the Economic and Social History of the Orient* 8 (1965), 113–163.

Kister 1968: M. J. Kister, "Al-Tahhanuth: An Inquiry into the Meaning of a Term." *Bulletin of the School of Oriental and African Studies* 31 (1968), 223–236.

Kister 1970: M. J. Kister, "'A Bag of Meat': A Study of an Early *Hadith*." *Bulletin of the School of Oriental and African Studies* 33 (1970), 267–275.

Kister 1971a: M. J. Kister, "'Rajab is the Month of God . . . ': A Study in the Persistence of an Early Tradition." *Israel Oriental Studies* 1 (1971), 191–223.

Kister 1971b: M. J. Kister, "Maqam Ibrahim, a Stone with an Inscription." *Le Muséon* 84 (1971), 477–491.

Kister 1972: M. J. Kister, "Some Reports Concerning Mecca: From Jahiliyya to Islam." *Journal of the Economic and Social History of the Orient* 15 (1972), 61–93.

Kister 1980: M. J. Kister, "*Labbayka, Allahumma, Labbayka* . . . : On a Monotheist Aspect of a Jahiliyya Practice." *Jerusalem Studies in Arabic and Islam* 2 (1980), 33–57.

Kister 1987: M. J. Kister, "Legends in tafsir and hadith Literature: The Creation of Adam and Related Stories." In Andrew Rippin (ed.), *Approaches to the History of the Interpretation of the Qur'an*, 82–114. Oxford: Clarendon Press, 1987.

Kortepeter 1979: C. M. Kortepeter, "A Source for the History of Ottoman-Hijaz Relations: The Seyahatname of Awliya Chalaby." In Ansary 1979: 229–246.

Lammens 1924: Henri Lammens, *La Mecque à la Veille de l'Hégire*. Beyrouth: Imprimerie Catholique, 1924.

Lammens 1928: Henri Lammens, *L'Arabie occidentale avant l'Hégire*. Beyrouth: Imprimerie Catholique, 1928.

Lawrence 1935: T. E. Lawrence, *Seven Pillars of Wisdom: A Triumph*. London, 1935; rpt. Harmondsworth: Penguin, 1962.

Lazarus-Yafeh 1981: H. Lazarus-Yafeh, *Some Religious Aspects of Islam*. Leiden: E. J. Brill, 1981.

Le Strange 1905: Guy Le Strange, *The Lands of the Eastern Caliphate*. London, 1905; rpt. New York: Barnes and Noble, 1966.

Long 1979: D. Long, *The Hajj Today: A Survey of the Contemporary Pilgrimage to Mekkah*. Albany: State University Press of New York, 1979.

Lüling 1981: G. Lüling, *Die Wiederentdeckung des Propheten Muhammad. Ein Kritik am "christlichen" Abenland*. Erlangen: Verlagsbuchhandlung Hannelore Lüling, 1981.

Musil 1926: Alois Musil, *The Northern Hegaz*. New York: American Geographical Society, 1926.

Musil 1928: Alois Musil, *Northern Negd*. New York: American Geographical Society, 1928.

Nasir-i Khusraw 1986: *Naser-e Khosraw's Book of Travels (Safarnama)*. Translated with introduction and annotation by W. M. Thackston Jr. New York: Persian Heritage Foundation, 1986.

Netton 1993: Ian Richard Netton (ed.), *Golden Roads: Migration, Pilgrimage and Travel in Mediaeval and Modern Islam*. London: Curzon Press, 1993.

Netton 1993a: Ian Richard Netton, "Basic Structures and Signs of Alienation in the *Rihla* of Ibn Jubayr." In Netton 1993: 57–74.

Nevo & Koren 1990: Yehuda D. Nevo and Judith Koren, "The Origins of the Muslim Descriptions of the Jahili Meccan Sanctuary." *Journal of Near Eastern Studies* 49 (1990), 23–44.

Niebuhr 1792: Carsten Niebuhr, *Travels through Arabia, and Other Countries in the East*. 2 vols. Translated by Robert Herron from the German edition of 1772. Edinburgh, 1792.

Ochsenwald 1976: William Ochsenwald, "A Modern Waqf: The Hijaz Railway." *Arabian Studies* 3 (1976), 1–12.

Ochsenwald 1980: William Ochsenwald, *The Hijaz Railroad*. Charlottesville: University Press of Virginia, 1980.

Ochsenwald 1984: William Ochsenwald, *Religion, Society and the State in Arabia: The Hijaz under Ottoman Control, 1840–1908*. Columbus: Ohio State University Press, 1984.

Palgrave 1865: William Gifford Palgrave, *Personal Narrative of a Year's Journey Through Central and Eastern Arabia*. London, 1865; rpt. London: Gregg International, 1969.

Palgrave 1883: William Gifford Palgrave, *Personal Narrative of a Year's Journey Through Central and Eastern Arabia (1862–1863)*. London: Macmillan, 1883.

Peters 1985: F. E. Peters, *Jerusalem: The Holy City in the Eyes of Chroniclers. . . .* Princeton: Princeton University Press, 1985.

Peters 1987: F. E. Peters, *Jerusalem and Mecca: The Typology of the Holy City in the Near East*. New York: New York University Press, 1987.

Philby 1922: Harry Saint John Philby, *The Heart of Arabia*. 2 vols. London: Constable, 1922.

Philby 1946: Harry Saint John Philby, *A Pilgrim in Arabia*. London: Robert Hale, 1946.

Philby 1948: Harry Saint John Philby, *Arabian Days: An Autobiography*. London: Robert Hale, 1948.

Philby 1953: Harry Saint John Philby, *Arabian Jubilee*. New York: Day, 1953.

Pitts 1949: *The Red Sea and Adjacent Countries at the Close of the Seventeenth Century as Described by Joseph Pitts, William Daniel and Charles Jacques Poncet*, 1–49. Edited by William Foster. London: Hakluyt Society (2d ser., no. 100), 1949.

Pönicke 1956: Herbert Pönicke, "Heinrich August Meissner-Pasha und der Bau der Hedschas- und Bagdadbahn." *Die Welt als Geschichte* 16 (1956), 196–210.

Popper 1955–1957: William Popper, *Egypt and Syria under the Circassian Sultans, 1382–1486 A.D.: Systematic Notes to Ibn Taghri Birdi's Chronicle of Egypt*. 2 vols. Berkeley and Los Angeles: University of California Press, 1955–1957.

Qutb al-Din 1857: Qutb al-Din, *Kitab al-iʾlam bi aʾlam bayt allah al-haram*. Edited by Ferdinand Wüstenfeld. Vol. 3 of *Chroniken der Stadt Mekka*. Leipzig, 1857; rpt. Hildesheim: Georg Olms, 1981.

Rafeq 1966: Abdul-Karim Rafeq, *The Province of Damascus, 1723–1783*. Beirut: Khayats, 1966.

Rafeq 1987: Abdul-Karim Rafeq, "New Light on the Transportation of the Damascene Pilgrimage during the Ottoman Period." In Robert Olson (ed.), *A Festschrift in Honor of Wadie Jweideh*, 127–136. Brattleboro: Amana Books, 1987.

Raymond 1973–1974: André Raymond, *Artisans et commercants au Caire au XVIIIe siècle*. 2 vols. Damascus: Institut Français de Damas, 1973–1974.

Rifʿat Pasha 1925: Ibrahim Rifʿat Pasha, *Mirat al-Haramayn*. 2 vols. Cairo: Dar al-Kutub al-Misriyya, 1925.

Rihani 1930: Amin Rihani, *Around the Coasts of Arabia*. Translation of *Muluk al-Arab*, 2d ed. (Beirut, 1929). London: Constable, 1930.

Roches 1904: Leon Roches, *Dix ans à travers l'Islam, 1834–1844*. 3d ed. Paris: Perrin, 1904.

Roff 1982: William Roff, "Sanitation and Security: The Imperial Powers and the Nineteenth Century Hajj." *Arabian Studies* 6 (1982): 143–160.

Rubin 1982: Uri Rubin, "The Great Pilgrimage of Muhammad: Some Notes on Sura IX." *Journal of Semitic Studies* 27 (1982), 241–260.

Rubin 1984a: Uri Rubin, "The *ilaf* of Quraysh: A Study of Sura CVI." *Arabica* 31 (1984), 165–188.

Rubin 1984b: Uri Rubin, "Bara'a: A Study of Some Quranic Passages." *Jerusalem Studies in Arabic and Islam* (1984), 13–32.

Rubin 1986: Uri Rubin, "The Ka'ba, Aspects of its Ritual, Functions, and Position in pre-Islamic and Early Islamic Times." *Jerusalem Studies in Arabic and Islam* 8 (1986), 97–131.

Rubin 1990: Uri Rubin, "Hanifiyya and Ka'ba: An Inquiry into the Arabian pre-Islamic Background of the Din Ibrahim." *Jerusalem Studies in Arabic and Islam* 13 (1990), 85–112.

Rutter 1930: Eldon Rutter, *The Holy Cities of Arabia.* 2 vols., 1928. Reprinted in 1 vol. London and New York: G. P. Putnam's Sons, 1930.

Sadleir 1866: George Forster Sadleir, *Diary of a Journey Across Arabia.* Bombay, 1866. Reprinted with a preface by F. M. Edwards. Naples, New York, and Cambridge: Falcon-Oleander, 1977.

Sauvaget 1947: Jean Sauvaget, *La Mosquée Omeyyade de Medine: Etude sur les origines architecturales de la mosquée et de la basilique.* Paris: Vanoest, 1947.

Schacht 1950: Joseph Schacht, *The Origins of Muhammadan Jurisprudence.* Oxford: Clarendon Press, 1950.

Segal 1961: J. B. Segal, "The Hebrew Festivals and the Calendar." *Journal of Semitic Studies* 6 (1961), 74–94.

Shafi' 1922: Muhammad Shafi', "A Description of the Two Sanctuaries of Islam by Ibn Abd Rabbihi." In T. W. Arnold and R. A. Nicholson (eds.), *A Volume of Oriental Studies Presented to Edward G. Browne,* 416–438. Cambridge: Cambridge University Press, 1922.

Shahid 1981: Irfan Shahid, "Two Qur'anic Suras: al-Fil and Quraysh." In W. al-Qadi (ed.), *Studia Arabica et Islamica, Festschrift for Ihsan Abbas,* 429–436. Beirut: American University of Beirut, 1981.

Shaw 1962: Stanford J. Shaw, *The Financial and Administrative Organization and Development of Ottoman Egypt, 1517–1798.* Princeton: Princeton University Press, 1962.

Shaw 1968: Stanford J. Shaw, *The Budget of Ottoman Egypt 1005–1006/1598–1597.* The Hague and Paris: Mouton, 1968.

Sim 1969: Katharine Sim, *Desert Traveler: The Life of Jean Louis Burckhardt.* London: Victor Gollancz, 1969.

Storrs 1945: Ronald Storrs, *Orientations.* Definitive edition. London: Nicholson and Watson, 1945.

Tabari VI: *The History of al-Tabari.* Vol. 6: *Muhammad at Mecca.* Translated and annotated by W. Montgomery Watt and M. V. McDonald. Albany: State University of New York Press, 1988.

Tabari XXI: *The History of al-Tabari.* Vol. 21: *The Victory of the Marwanids.* Translated by Michael Fishbein. Albany: State University of New York Press, 1990.

Tabari XXIX: *The History of al-Tabari.* Vol. 29: *Al-Mansur and al-Mahdi A.D. 763–786/A.H. 146–169.* Translated by Hugh Kennedy. Albany: State University of New York Press, 1990.

Tamari 1982: S. Tamari, "Darb al-Hajj in Sinai: An Historical-Archaeological Study." *Accademia Nazionale dei Lincei: Memorie* 25 (1982), 431–525.

Tidrick 1981: Kathryn Tidrick, *Heart-beguiling Araby*. Cambridge: Cambridge University Press, 1981.

Trench 1986: Richard Trench, *Arabian Travellers*. Topsfield, Mass.: Salem House, 1986.

Tresse 1937: R. Tresse, *Le pèlerinage syrien aux villes saintes d'Islam*. Paris: Imprimerie Chaumette, 1937.

Tuchscherer 1988: Michel Tuchscherer, "Le Pèlerinage de l'Émir Sulayman Jawish al-Qazdughli, Sirdar de la Caravane de la Mekke en 1739." *Annales Islamologiques* 24 (1988), 189–206.

Varthema 1863: *The Travels of Ludovico di Varthema in Egypt, Syria, Arabia Deserta and Arabia Felix, in Persia, India and Ethiopia, A.D. 1503 to 1508*. Translated by J. W. Jones and edited by G. P. Badger. London: Hakluyt Society, 1863.

Veinstein 1981: G. Veinstein, "Les pèlerins de la Mecque à travers quelques inventaires après décès ottomans (XVII–XVIIIe siècles)." *Revue de l'Occident Musulman et de la Méditerranée* 31 (1981), 63–71.

Wallin 1850/1854: Georg August Wallin, "Narrative of a Journey from Cairo to Medina and Mecca, by Suez, Araba, Tawila, al-Jauf, Jubbe, Hail and Nejd in 1845." *Journal of the Royal Geographical Society* 24 (1854), 115–207; "Notes taken during a journey through part of Northern Arabia in 1848." Ibid. 20 (1850), 293–344. Reprinted with new prefaces as *Travels in Arabia (1845 and 1848)*. New York and London: Falcon-Oleander, 1979.

Watt 1988: W. Montgomery Watt, *Muhammad's Mecca: History in the Qur'an*. Edinburgh: Edinburgh University Press, 1988.

Wavell 1912: A.J.B. Wavell, *A Modern Pilgrim in Mecca and a Siege in Sanaa*. London: Constable, 1912.

Wellhausen 1897: Julius Wellhausen, *Reste Arabischen Heidentums*. 2d ed. Berlin: Georg Reimer, 1897.

Wellsted 1838: J. R. Wellsted, *Travels in Arabia*. 2 vols. London: John Murray, 1838. Reprinted with a new preface. Graz: Akademische Druck- und Verlagsanstalt, 1978.

Wood 1935: A. Wood, *A History of the Levant Company*. Oxford, 1935; rpt. New York: Oxford University Press, 1964.

Wright 1848: T. Wright, *Early Travels in Palestine*. London: H. G. Bohn, 1848.

Wüstenfeld 1861: Ferdinand Wüstenfeld, *Geschichte der Stadt Mekka nach den arabischen Chroniken bearbeitet*. Leipzig, 1861; rpt. Hildesheim: Georg Ohms, 1981.

Young 1993: William C. Young, "The Ka'ba, Gender, and the Rites of Pilgrimage." *International Journal of Middle East Studies* 25 (1993), 285–300.

Index